D0583296

HAND-OFF

HAND-OFF

THE FOREIGN POLICY
GEORGE W. BUSH PASSED
TO BARACK OBAMA

STEPHEN J. HADLEY
Editor

**PETER D. FEAVER,
WILLIAM C. INBODEN, AND
MEGHAN L. O'SULLIVAN**
Co-Editors

MAUREEN McGRATH
Operational and Technical Support

BROOKINGS INSTITUTION PRESS
Washington, D.C.

Published by Brookings Institution Press
1775 Massachusetts Avenue, NW
Washington, DC 20036
www.brookings.edu/bipress

Co-published by Rowman & Littlefield
An imprint of The Rowman & Littlefield Publishing Group, Inc.
4501 Forbes Boulevard, Suite 200, Lanham, Maryland 20706
www.rowman.com

86-90 Paul Street, London EC2A 4NE

Copyright © 2023 by The Brookings Institution

All rights reserved. No part of this book may be reproduced in any form or by any electronic or mechanical means, including information storage and retrieval systems, without written permission from the publisher, except by a reviewer who may quote passages in a review.

The Brookings Institution is a nonprofit organization devoted to research, education, and publication on important issues of domestic and foreign policy. Its principal purpose is to bring the highest quality independent research and analysis to bear on current and emerging policy problems.

British Library Cataloguing in Publication Information Available

Library of Congress Cataloging-in-Publication Data

ISBN 9780815739777 (cloth)
ISBN 9780815739784 (electronic)

♾™ The paper used in this publication meets the minimum requirements of American National Standard for Information Sciences—Permanence of Paper for Printed Library Materials, ANSI/NISO Z39.48-1992

To those who serve our country in its armed forces, diplomatic corps, development agencies, and intelligence services.

Note: Any and all royalties generated by sales of this book will be donated to public charities serving the needs of those communities and their families.

CONTENTS

PART 3
INTERVENTIONS AND STABILIZATION

PART 8
COMMENTARY

FOREWORD

PRESIDENT GEORGE W. BUSH

By the summer of 2008, my time as president was coming to an end. My successor was going to face a lot of challenges. There was a world wide financial crisis, which every day seemed poised to bring down the global financial system. There was the continuing fight against terrorism, including US military operations in Afghanistan and Iraq. There was also conflict between Israel and Hamas in the Gaza Strip, the Russian invasion of Georgia, and the ongoing Iranian and North Korean nuclear programs. This was all on top of America's duty to maintain the alliances and trade relationships so essential to the peace and prosperity of the world.

Given this array of challenges, I was determined to help the new president get off to a good start. So I told my cabinet and senior White House staff that the upcoming presidential transition was a top priority, even as we dealt with the worst financial and economic crisis since the Great Depression. The country needed this presidential transition to be smooth, professional, and productive. Fortunately, president-elect Barack Obama felt the same way.

The Transition Memoranda contained in this book were part of that process. They were designed to provide the incoming administration with what they needed to know about the most critical foreign policy and national security issues they would face. The memoranda told them candidly what we thought we had accomplished—where we had succeeded and where we had fallen short—and what work remained to be done.

The Transition Memoranda supported the various briefings and meetings between the incoming and outgoing national security teams. Those briefings and meetings covered some of the most pressing issues facing the country, including how to ensure that the upcoming inauguration ceremonies were not hijacked by a terrorist attack. These were perilous times.

A new president can set an administration's tone and priorities. But he or she cannot control the challenges and forces that may eventually define their presidency. I campaigned for president in 2000 largely on a domestic agenda. I wanted to strengthen our nation's economy, fix our education and health systems, and deal with longstanding problems like entitlement and immigration reform. As for foreign policy, my initial focus was close to home. My first State Dinner in the White House was for the president of our southern neighbor, Vicente Fox of Mexico. This was on September 5, 2001. Six days later—while I was in Florida to talk about education reform—came the 9/11 attacks. I became a wartime president. And my administration had to adjust its focus accordingly.

After the 9/11 attacks, my responsibility was to lead the country in its psychological and economic recovery and to make sure that such an attack could never happen again. My administration worked at this task every day, day in and day out. As I told the White House staff, we had to be on guard so that the country didn't. We had to defend a world of normalcy and safety in which people could return to life and work. So we analyzed every threat. We went on the offense, dealing with threats abroad before they could materialize at home. And we denied safe havens to those who wished to harm us again.

While keeping the country safe had to be my presidency's central focus, it could not be the only focus. There was too much else to do. I pursued a series of objectives in close, personal cooperation with world leaders such as Junichiro Koizumi of Japan, Tony Blair of the United Kingdom, John Howard of Australia, Angela Merkel of Germany, and Manmohan Singh of India. In the face of historic challenges, my administration and I worked with African leaders to confront HIV/AIDS, prevent unnecessary deaths from malaria, and end long-standing armed conflicts that had cast a shadow over the continent's future. President Alvaro Uribe of Colombia needed our help to defend his country against FARC narco-terrorists. Europe needed America's continued support in building a continent whole, free, and at peace. America's relations with China and Russia required attention. The Transition Memoranda do a good job in showing the broad range of issues with which we dealt during our eight years in office.

Another thing that any new president learns is that there is—and needs to be—a lot of continuity in American foreign policy. Almost every major international problem or global challenge ends up involving the United States. American leadership is usually needed to shape a response and make sure it is carried out. Such efforts often need to be sustained over a period of years, if not decades. Look at the post–World War II rebuilding of Germany and Japan, the Cold War struggle against Communism, the two-decades long (and still unfinished) fight against terrorism, and what will be required to deal with pandemic diseases and climate change. Meeting these kinds of challenges requires continuity across presidential administrations of different political parties, the sustained bipartisan cooperation of Congress, and the support of the America people. I wanted to encourage this as President-elect Obama prepared to take office.

As president, all the hard decisions come to your desk. No one can make them for you. You almost never have all the information you would want, and time is usually short. So you decide. Then you live with the consequences of that decision—for the country, for its people, and for those brave citizens who risk their lives protecting America at home and abroad. A president must do whatever it takes—within the law—to protect the American people. I remain at peace with the decisions I made as president.

It should come as no surprise that I may not agree with all the analysis or endorse every conclusion contained in this book. It is still too soon to draw hard and fast judgments about the performance and impact of my administration. A full history will emerge only with the passage of time and in light of future developments. But this book will be an important input to the historical record and a resource for scholars, historians, analysts, and the public who want to understand the national security, foreign, and defense policies of my administration. I thank the talented and tireless Steve Hadley for spearheading this project—and especially for his contributions as my national security adviser.

I am deeply grateful to all who served in my administration for the enormous effort, commitment, and sacrifice they made during our time in office. Let me pay special tribute to the late Colin Powell and the late Donald Rumsfeld, my secretary of state and secretary of defense, respectively, great patriots who are dearly missed by the country they served so well. The nation and I were very fortunate indeed to have had Condoleezza Rice and Robert Gates to serve as their successors. And I offer my profound thanks to my partner in service to our country, our great Vice President Dick Cheney.

Finally, I want to salute and express my boundless respect and gratitude for those who have served and are serving our country in the military, as diplomats, as intelligence officers, and in America's development agencies. They are among the nation's finest.

PREFACE

CONDOLEEZZA RICE | STEPHEN J. HADLEY

The presidency of George W. Bush was both controversial and consequential. He assumed office on January 20, 2001, at an historical inflection point. The world was transitioning from the immediate post-Cold War decade of the 1990s to the new realities of the twenty-first century. With this new century, a new set of challenges came into focus. The Bush administration was the first to face them in their full measure. Many of its responses were embraced by successor administrations to an extent not generally appreciated and became the foundation for what is—and is likely to continue to be—America's approach to these challenges. For this reason alone, the administration's responses are worthy of study and further examination.

President Bush once remarked that he had not come to office intending to be a "wartime" president. Indeed, while in office he pursued an active domestic policy agenda and addressed a wide range of foreign policy issues. Yet when asked about the Bush administration today, many people remember principally Afghanistan, Iraq, and the War on Terror. Clearly, after 9/11, the first responsibility of the American president was to defend and protect the country. But even a cursory review of the Transition Memoranda suggests that the Bush administration had broad and ambitious national security, foreign, and defense policy agendas. This despite the demands the war against terrorism imposed on America—and on its president of eight months—on that fateful day.

THE WORLD IN TRANSITION

By the time George W. Bush was inaugurated as president, the great ideological struggle of the twentieth century was over. Liberal democracy had prevailed against fascism in World War II and against communism in the Cold War. The United States had emerged as the world's preeminent power. Traditional great power competition seemed a thing of the past. The established international order—the web of norms, rules, and institutions underpinned by principles of democratic governance, rule of law, and market economics—seemed secure. The world had been liberated from the horrific great power wars of the twentieth century and was enjoying economic growth and increased global prosperity.

If it seemed almost too good to be true, it was. The attack of September 11, 2001, early in the Bush administration, focused the world's attention on terrorist groups seeking to destabilize governments, sow chaos, and impose theocratic totalitarian rule based on an extreme interpretation of Islam. What followed was a decade of terrorist attacks throughout the world. Islamist extremism represented a direct threat to international order and particularly to the prospects for a stable, and eventually free and democratic Middle East.

When Bush took office, Russia was emerging from its post-Cold War weakness under its relatively new president, Vladimir Putin. The relationship was initially cooperative, even strategically symbiotic, as the two countries found common ground in the fight against terrorism. As it became clear, however, that the Bush doctrine was not just about the war against terror but also about a democratic peace—a freedom agenda—Russia began to see US policy as threatening. This was particularly true as Putin turned more autocratic at home and more distrustful of nascent democratic movements on the territory of the former Soviet Union. Russian disaffection with these trends culminated in pressure tactics on Ukrainian leaders beginning in 2005 and eventually the invasion of Georgia in 2008. In time, Russia would become a principal challenger to the post-Cold War order in Europe, seeing it as a humiliating reminder of the loss of Soviet and ultimately Russian power on the continent and globally.

China's two-decades-long policy of economic reform and opening up had produced a spectacular run of sustained economic growth. The American-led decision to open the international system to China, encouraging its integration into the institutions and practices of the international economy, clearly accelerated that success. But liberalization of the economy began to lag, and the Chinese

Communist Party resisted appeals from its own citizens, and from the United States and other free nations, to respect human rights and reform its political system. The challenge of channeling China's rise was becoming evident. This was particularly true in the Asia-Pacific.

As both Russia and China grew in power, and the world grappled with terrorism, America's unipolar moment as the world's sole superpower began to slip away. When Bush left office, the outlines of great power competition—even conflict—were starting to emerge. Set against the backdrop of the catastrophic financial crisis of 2008, the world of January 2001 seemed a distant memory. These Transition Memoranda chronicle the efforts of the administration to meet these challenges and to construct a framework for dealing with them.

A BALANCE OF POWER THAT FAVORS FREEDOM

In his classic book *Diplomacy*, Henry Kissinger notes that throughout the twentieth century, American foreign policy largely followed the "idealist" tradition of Woodrow Wilson. Reflecting America's own founding experience, this tradition saw the nature of a regime and the principles on which it was founded as a critical and central determinant of a nation's international behavior. Consistent with this view, Wilson sought to promote a world order based on advancing American values of freedom, democracy, human rights, and a sometimes overlegalistic rule of law. One could add to this list fealty to the principle of self-determination, which led Wilson to underestimate the impact of the creation of small, weak states which became easy prey for voracious rising powers.

At the same time, American foreign policy largely rejected the "realist" tradition of continental European statecraft, which to a great extent disregarded the nature of a regime and the principles on which it was founded. What mattered to this tradition was raw power and national interests—and preserving stable power relationships among states. Indeed, promotion of democratic values was to classic realists a liability in foreign policy. This balance of power approach to international politics was viewed by its critics as un-American, morally suspect, and ultimately, unstable and prone to conflict.

Coming into office at the start of the twenty-first century, the Bush administration rejected the idea that it had to choose between these two alternatives. It sought instead an approach to international order that drew on both traditions—that was both idealist and realist at the same time. It recognized that America is at its best when it acts out of both power and principle. It believed that a balance of power is best used to empower and defend free peoples.

Bush fully appreciated the criticality of power relationships in international affairs. His administration sought to build a favorable balance of power based on the strength of America and its friends and allies. The Bush administration's 2002 National Security Strategy begins in its very first sentence with the words: "The United States possesses unprecedented—and unequaled—strength and influence in the world."[1] To ensure that this remained the case, the administration sought to bolster the foundations of American power: building up the US military (indeed, insisting that the United States would maintain a preponderance of military power), enhancing US intelligence capabilities, strengthening the economy, encouraging American innovation, shoring up alliances, and actively engaging the world diplomatically. The approach made considerable use of what some have called soft power, increasing foreign assistance massively through the President's Emergency Plan For AIDS Relief (PEPFAR) and the Millennium Challenge Corporation. To amplify American influence, the administration strengthened ties to existing friends and allies and established new relationships. It worked to enhance the diplomatic, military, and economic capability of those partners to contribute to a robust and sustainable balance of power.

But power had to have a purpose. That purpose was to assert and promote the idea that human beings should not be consigned to live in tyranny. As the 2006 National Security Strategy explained, the goal was "to help create a world of democratic, well-governed states that can meet the needs of their citizens and conduct themselves responsibly in the international system."[2] The triumph of freedom was always understood to be a very long-term goal—"the work of generations," as the 2006 NSS put it. Yet, the commitment and weight of the United States could hasten movement toward this goal through support of people across the world who craved freedom—especially since tyranny is always imposed, and never chosen.

---

1. George W. Bush, "The National Security Strategy of the United States of America," September 2002, https://georgewbush-whitehouse.archives.gov/nsc/nss/2002/.

2. George W. Bush, "The National Security Strategy of the United States of America," March 2006.

The Freedom Agenda sought to support democratic governance and market economies around the world and encourage "effective democracies" in which political and economic freedom was protected by capable institutions. Bush understood that the specific policies and institutions adopted would vary for different nations and circumstances. And he understood that the United States could not neglect other security and economic interests. But this did not preclude charting a strategic vision toward the expansion of free nations and self-government. His was, in a sense, a uniquely American realism born of the historical experiences of the twentieth century and the failures of both Wilsonian idealism and the cold-eyed calculations of the realists.

In developing his freedom strategy, Bush read history with clear eyes. He knew that the peace negotiated after World War I was more reflective of realist balance of power concepts than the idealist aspirations of President Wilson. Germany was to be punished and kept weak so that it could be balanced despite a debilitated France, a disengaged Britain, and a Russia distracted by internal strife. As such, the effort proved to be morally questionable, unstable, and ultimately produced war not peace.

As a result, the United States took a different approach after World War II. Had it thought in strict balance of power terms, it would have kept Germany and Japan weak, balanced by neighboring states, so they could never again be a threat to peace. Instead, during its occupation of those countries, America helped them to remake themselves into free, democratic states with market economies. They would be strong—not weak—and peaceful states that would partner with the United States in supporting an international order based on democratic principles. In exchange, the United States provided protection and, in the case of Europe, secured the peace through an alliance of (mostly, at the time) democratic states. NATO was thus both a military alliance to sustain the balance of power and an umbrella under which old enemies became democratic partners in peace.

Applying this approach in the twenty-first century brought a different set of challenges. America's values-based policy in the twentieth century had not extended to all of the world. In some regions, strongmen were supported as long as they were thought to be bulwarks against communism. This contradiction led those populations to see American protestations on behalf of freedom and democracy as cynical and hypocritical. Moreover, particularly in the Middle East but also in other regions, the effort to buy stability at the expense of freedom actually bought neither. Changing the direction of US policy was hard, and convincing skeptical populations that American support for freedom and democracy was real was, in some sense, even harder. Still, this became a persistent Bush administration theme in dealing with the autocrats of the Middle East, Africa, and Latin America, and caused the United States to seek partnerships with a variety of democratically elected leaders—even leftists like Lula de Silva in Brazil.

President Bush well understood that freedom and democracy could not be imposed by force. Afghanistan and Iraq were special cases. The United States had—for security reasons—deposed the governments there, and in the aftermath felt a special responsibility to help put those peoples on a pathway toward democracy. The size and scope of that effort has sometimes obscured a basic fact that Bush appreciated: people must win their own freedom, fashion governments that reflect their own culture and history, and build their own nations. At the same time, Bush believed that America could and should help. For him it was a moral issue—as he so often quoted from the Bible, "to whom much is given, much is required." But it was also a matter of American interests. He understood that there might be—day to day—tensions between American values and its interests. But he believed that in the long run there was no fundamental contradiction or conflict between the two. For as the postwar international order so amply demonstrated, a world that embraced values of freedom, democratic governance, market-based economics, and rule of law profoundly served American interests. Political scientists have demonstrated that this belief is not misplaced. Democracies generally do not fight one another, nor do they harbor terrorists, employ child soldiers, or invade their neighbors.

For these reasons, the Bush administration sought to forge this balance of power that favored freedom. The administration pressured authoritarian governments—both friend and foe—to trust their people to self-govern. It also sought to encourage civil society and promote women's empowerment, and minority and ethnic rights. These would be the pillars upholding a democratic future for their countries. And understanding that leaders who are elected do have to deliver for their people, the administration generously assisted in meeting the education, health, and economic needs of such countries. A significant part of Bush's Freedom Agenda was thus supporting those leaders who were governing wisely.

The effort to construct a balance of power that favors freedom was hard. An approach devoid of values that simply dealt with countries on the basis of power and interests would in some ways have been simpler. But President Bush thought it unworthy of a country like ours—founded on the idea that human beings deserve to live in freedom. The Transition Memoranda that follow chronicle the ups and downs—successes and failures—of this approach.

HAND-OFF

INTRODUCTION

STEPHEN J. HADLEY | MEGHAN L. O'SULLIVAN

In the summer of 2008, President George W. Bush gave his White House staff and cabinet secretaries a new high-priority task: to prepare for his successor.

Transitions from one president to another are always challenging, especially when the two presidents come from different political parties. The upcoming transition in January of 2009 would be especially challenging. The country was in the middle of the worst financial crisis since the Great Depression, was leading a global fight against terrorism, was engaged in two wars, and was dealing with a host of other challenges. Whether a Republican or a Democrat was elected in November of 2008, the new administration would immediately face as daunting a set of challenges as any had faced in a long time. And Bush wanted the best possible transition to help prepare the new team for the task ahead.

As part of this effort, the Bush National Security Council (NSC) staff prepared forty Transition Memoranda—in most cases classified, and in some cases highly classified—on the most important national security, foreign, and defense policy issues of the day. They covered a myriad of regional and functional topics, from Afghanistan to nuclear proliferation, from HIV/AIDS to how to handle China. In each case they described the situation as the Bush administration found it, the Bush administration approach, what it believed it accomplished, and what remained to be done by the Obama administration. These memoranda were not partisan talking points designed to shape the public assessment of the departing president. They were written to help the next president and his team get up to speed as quickly as possible under daunting circumstances. The memoranda

1

were to be shared only with the new president and the new president's national security team. Collectively, the memoranda represent the most well-informed, comprehensive, and contemporaneous judgment about how the Bush NSC staff saw the Bush administration's legacy at the time—and the challenges it believed the new Obama administration would face.

This book is based on thirty of these forty Transition Memoranda, newly declassified and made public here for the first time. Normally these kinds of memoranda would not be available to scholars and the general public for de-cades after the end of the administration. The texts of these memoranda are published here in full, without correcting any typos that might appear in them, and with only minimal redactions as required by government declassifying au-thorities. Shaded areas in the text of the Transition Memoranda indicate where material has been redacted for classification reasons. The memoranda provide the unvarnished record of the administration as seen at the time through the eyes of the NSC staff. Being contemporaneous means that the reader does not need to rely on the retrospective, after-the-fact memory of the author(s)—or worry that the author(s) will be "reinterpreting" the past in light of subsequent developments so as to make their work look better than it was. Instead, the reader sees the words just as President Obama and his team saw them as they entered office in January 2009.

However useful it may be simply to provide public access to these documents, this book has even larger ambitions. It adds a "Postscript" to each Transition Memorandum, prepared by the same person(s) who actually wrote the original memorandum or, in some cases, by other NSC staff members who also worked directly on the issue in the Bush administration. These Postscripts set out their reflections, now twelve years later, on the Bush administration's national security and foreign and defense policy legacy. Preparing these retrospective assessments was the occasion for many virtual reunions among the various authors and con-tributors to the book. They engaged in countless conversations seeking how best to present, with the benefit of hindsight, their unadorned views of the policies and strategies they helped fashion and execute more than a decade ago.

Here, the reader may be surprised. In many instances, these former Bush ad-ministration officials stand by their earlier efforts. But in other cases they are quick to identify flawed assumptions, failures to align resources with strate-gies, or other shortcomings in the approaches adopted and pursued.

After summarizing the Bush administration approach, the Postscripts describe what has happened since the Bush administration left office—during the Obama, Trump, and early Biden administrations. Based on these developments, the Postscripts then evaluate the Bush administration approach—what the Bush team got right and what the Bush team got wrong. In a final section, the Postscripts then draw "Lessons Learned" not only from the Bush administration but also from the record of the Obama, Trump, and early Biden administrations as well—reflecting some twenty years of American engagement on the issue during the first two decades of the twenty-first century.

Three issues covered in the book were not the subjects of Transition Memoranda prepared by the NSC staff. But they were nonetheless critical to Bush national security and foreign policy and have heightened resonance in today's world. These issues are addressed in three stand-alone essays prepared by Bush administration officials—essays that mirror the approach taken in the Transition Memoranda and Postscripts. They deal with Biodefense and Pandemic Planning, Cyber Preparedness, and Climate Change and Clean Development.

What is striking about this overall effort is how many of the big issues faced by the Bush administration—a rising China, an aggressive Russia, ongoing Iranian and North Korean nuclear programs, a resurgent Taliban in Afghanistan, a fragile but improving Iraq, continuing terrorist threats, emerging authoritarian populism, and cyber, climate, and pandemics—are literally the same big issues facing the Biden administration today. The Lessons Learned thus have continued relevance—and not only for the Biden administration, but for future presidential administrations as well, since America is likely to continue to face most of these issues in the years ahead.

We appreciate that those who have worked on an issue can never be fully objective about it. For this reason, the book includes three additional essays prepared by independent scholars evaluating the story told by the materials contained in the book: Melvyn P. Leffler's essay (entitled "An Illuminating Hand-Off") looks at the Bush record through the prism of the Freedom Agenda and evaluates it as an organizing principle of Bush foreign policy; Hal Brands' essay (entitled "Reassessing Bush's Legacy: What the Transition Memos Do (and Don't) Reveal") provides his preliminary assessment of the Bush foreign policy record—its achievements and its failures; and Martha Joynt Kumar's essay (entitled "Transferring Presidential Power in a Post-9/11 World") examines the transition from the Bush to the Obama administration—and subsequent presidential transitions—and draws Lessons Learned to guide future presidents.

For those who desire more primary sources and information about this period, we recommend a trove of additional documents—too voluminous to be reproduced in this book—made public now for the first time and available online. The Center for Presidential History of Southern Methodist University hosts a publicly accessible online archive that includes the thirty declassified Transition Memoranda contained in this book, nine others not included here, and the set of attachments that originally accompanied each of the declassified Transition Memoranda. (One of the original forty Transition Memoranda, which deals with Turkey and the PKK, will be added to the online archive should it be declassified and released.) The attachments to the declassified memoranda include unclassified and declassified presidential statements and speeches, memoranda of meetings and telephone conversations with heads of state and government, records of meetings of the National Security Council and its principals and deputies committees, key policy documents, and other relevant materials.

We hope this book and the SMU online archive will be a resource to help scholars, historians, analysts, and the broader public better understand and evaluate not only the Bush administration but also the evolution of US policy as it relates to many of the challenges that continue to confront America today. In many respects, it is the Bush administration foreign policy stripped bare, for readers to judge for themselves—without the intervention of intermediaries or commentators looking to portray the policy either more harshly or more rosily than it deserves. The book in particular is singular by its very nature: a firsthand view into national security, foreign, and defense policy issues during a presidential transition, as assessed by the outgoing team and handed over to the incoming team—and now revisited by the outgoing team.

One final note. This book was largely prepared before Russia's resumed invasion of Ukraine on February 24, 2022. That grim development does not change the basic thrust of its analysis, however, which documents at length the return of great power competition and confrontation that characterizes the present circumstance.

PART 1

The Soul of Bush Foreign Policy

INTRODUCTION

STEPHEN J. HADLEY

President Bush had an abiding faith in the human spirit. He believed that individuals living in freedom are best positioned to make the key decisions that affect their lives and the lives of their children. He sought to empower people to make those decisions free from political oppression and the tyrannies of violence, ignorance, and disease. This core conviction animated his approach to both domestic and foreign policy.

In foreign policy, he believed that societies based on freedom, democracy, human rights, and the rule of law not only represented the highest aspirations of the human spirit but were most likely to be peaceful, stable, and able to meet the needs of their people. Bush understood that ultimately people must win their own freedom and build their own societies. But he believed that America could provide important and even decisive help—and that it had a moral obligation to do so. As he often said, "to whom much is given, much is required." In this he stood squarely in the best traditions of this country and with some of the greatest of its presidents.

President Bush was also a realist. He fully appreciated the strength of the forces arrayed against his vision of freedom and free societies. He understood that to succeed, American foreign policy had to be based on both principle and power. Working with allies and friends who shared his vision, America needed to construct a balance of power that favored freedom.

CHAPTER 1

The Freedom Agenda

MICHAEL GERSON | PETER WEHNER

A president does not get to choose his or her historical moment, only the principles he or she applies to it. And the measure of those principles cannot be determined in the timeframe of a single administration, or even a single generation. History has an ebb and flow of peace and conflict, of democracy and oppression, that tests every theory we apply to it. But at least since World War II—and in some ways since its founding—America's guiding global commitment has been the nobility and utility of freedom.

This has brought celebration on memorable days such as the fall of the Berlin Wall, and required faith during darker periods of conflict, terrorist violence, and resurgent authoritarianism. But the general outlines of American policy have been broadly consistent. A core belief in the economic and political superiority of systems that honor the individual citizen's right and power to choose has led America to help create durable systems of finance, trade, and travel; aggressively promote economic development and human health in the world; build strong alliances based on shared values; and encourage human dignity and human rights as hopeful alternatives to ideologies based on power and threats.

This common inheritance of American leadership was the guiding orientation of George W. Bush's presidential administration—not perfectly, but consciously applied. And it was the substance of the transition advice offered the

Obama administration at a time when the picture of global democracy was relatively bright. Since then, places such as the broader Middle East have shown how the collapse of an old order can unleash resentments and power struggles that a new order is not yet prepared to handle. Even established democracies have not been spared instability and uncertainty—which have not bypassed our own country.

Fulfilling the hopes for a free society is a considerable task, carried out by fallible human beings. It requires the construction of effective representative institutions; the creation of durable democratic traditions; and the defense of freedom and pluralism against racism, nativism, chauvinistic nationalism, and opportunistic demagogues.

It is one thing to point out the difficulties of these tasks; it is another to despair of the values and ideals that undergird them. It is one thing to show humility in the pursuit of historically difficult goals; it is another to quail about our highest aspirations before dissidents and exiles who hope in our fortitude. It is one thing to recognize the sad hypocrisy too often found in America's own history; it is another to elevate self-flagellation or selfish transactionalism as guiding doctrines.

In the end, history shows that it is tyrannical governments—not free nations—that are inherently unstable. Oppressive regimes distrust the diffusion of choice and power—which are the sources of national prosperity and success. The hoarding of power encourages cronyism and corruption; it accumulates inefficiency and resentment. Authoritarian governments come with an inbuilt crisis—a burning fuse—because they fear and fight the very human attributes that make a nation great: creativity, enterprise, diversity, innovation, and responsibility. And nations that honor those attributes grow in wealth, strength, and moral purpose over time.

The world has learned that no advance of freedom is inevitable. Any gain can be lost. But there is a reason for the momentum of liberty across the centuries: because human beings were not designed for servitude. They were created for better things. And the human soul is restless until it rests in freedom. That was the central premise of the Bush administration's Freedom Agenda.

TRANSITION MEMORANDUM

~~TOP SECRET~~

5938
Transition

NATIONAL SECURITY COUNCIL
WASHINGTON, D.C. 20504

NSC Declassification Review [E.O. 13526]
DECLASSIFY IN PART
by William C. Carpenter 3/23/2020

November 10, 2008

MEMORANDUM FOR THE RECORD

FROM: MICHAEL G. KOZAK, DEMOCRACY, HUMAN RIGHTS AND
          INTERNATIONAL ORGANIZATIONS DIRECTORATE

SUBJECT: Freedom Agenda

This Administration's approach to advancing democracy around the globe has been based on two key concepts articulated by the President: First, that the ideals and principles of freedom on which this country was founded are universal in nature. When given an opportunity, the vast majority of people from any country in any part of the world, regardless of culture, religion, or level of education, will choose free, democratic political systems over dictatorial, authoritarian or theocratic systems. Second, supporting freedom and democracy not only reflects who we are as a people, but is essential to the long term national security of the United States. The stability of dictatorships is illusory. Over time, oppression will produce the types of frustration and despair that for some make extremism an attractive alternative.

Implementing this approach has been an uphill battle. While support for freedom has been an element in the policy of previous administrations, it has not been applied to all parts of the world nor given priority in relation to other U.S. objectives. Persuading both foreign friends and foes of democracy—and our own institutions—that we were both serious and correct has required an ongoing effort at the highest levels of government.

As we have increased our support for freedom, our opponents have also learned from our successes and fought back with campaigns to discredit those who are struggling for freedom with our assistance and to demoralize those in the public and in Congress on whose support our policy ultimately depends. As a consequence, we have seen both major progress in the advance of democracy, and setbacks during the tenure of this Administration. The former Soviet-bloc countries

~~TOP SECRET~~
Reason: 1.4(d)
Declassify on: 11/10/18

Re-Classified by: Ellen J. L. Knight
Reason: 1.4(c)
Declassify on: 11 /10/2033

of Eastern Europe have strengthened democratic institutions on their path to NATO and EU membership. The former Soviet Socialist Republics of Georgia, Ukraine, and Kyrgyzstan have seen the seating of democratically-elected governments after citizens defended their votes against fraud perpetrated by the authoritarian regimes in power. Civil society organizations have expanded activities in the Middle East, and women's rights have expanded significantly if unevenly there. Egypt held its first contested election for President, and Yemen had a credible Presidential election. Afghanistan and Iraq, following the military defeat of brutal dictatorships, held democratic elections, as did the Democratic Republic of the Congo, Sierra Leone, and Liberia following the end of conflicts in those countries. In Latin America, citizens continued to affirm their commitment to democratic processes, even when electing those with questionable democratic credentials. Freedom House reported that "the global picture suggests that 2005 was one of the most successful years for freedom since Freedom House began measuring world freedom in 1972," and that the percentage of "not free" countries was the lowest in over a decade.

We have also witnessed contractions of freedom or the manipulation of democratic processes in countries such as the Russian Federation, Venezuela, Bolivia, Ecuador, and Nicaragua. Some of the recent successes' have turned to disappointments with the imprisonment of the opposition presidential candidate in Egypt, the election favoring the terrorist organization Hamas in the Palestinian territories, and the recent military coup overturning a duly elected government in Mauritania.

This memorandum assesses the strategies, policies, programs, institutions, and resources which we have put in place to provide sustained and unambiguous U.S. support to those in other countries who are fighting for human rights and democracy. The status of our efforts to advance human rights and democracy in particular regions or individual countries are covered in memoranda concerning those regions and countries.

THE SITUATION AS WE FOUND IT:

Democracy Promotion As An Element of U.S. Foreign Policy—Always Present But Not a Consistent Priority. The promotion of democracy has since the founding of the United States been an element of U.S. foreign policy, in rhetoric and to some degree in practice. In the last century, for example, President Wilson sought to make U.S. recognition of military governments in Latin America contingent upon their commitment to hold elections in the future. President Roosevelt described our aims in World War II in terms of the "Four Freedoms." The Cold War was defined by the struggle between the "Free World" and totalitarian Soviet Communism.

In practice, however, developing free, democratic governments abroad was at best simply one of many competing objectives of our foreign policy. Many areas of the world were at various times dismissed as "not ready" for democracy. "Realism" was the dominant school of thought in which the objective of freedom had to be compromised in order to deal with immediate challenges. Dictatorships were welcomed into the camp of the Free World in order to prevent them from joining the Soviet camp, and sometimes military coups against elected governments with anti-American inclinations were welcomed. Human rights violations were not raised with the Soviets to avoid compromising progress in arms control talks. Human rights were not raised with China to avoid compromising the development of a strategic relationship to counter the Soviets.

The "Development" Approach—Good Intentions, Negative Results. The dominant approach to democracy promotion during this period was founded in development theory. President Kennedy's "Alliance for Progress" in the Western Hemisphere was a prime example of the theory that by working with stable, authoritarian governments to raise economic and educational standards and build institutions of democracy, such as an independent judiciary, the development of a functioning democracy would gradually occur. This policy did not recognize that dictatorships are rarely good incubators for democracy. While GDP rose substantially in Latin America during the 1960s and early 1970s, and other economic development goals of the Alliance for Progress were met, this did not lead to political freedom. Elected governments in Latin American countries including Brazil, Argentina, Uruguay, Panama, and Chile were replaced by military dictatorships; none transitioned from dictatorship to democracy. (Restoration of democracy in these countries did not occur until the 1980s. In general, a combination of internal pressure for civil and political freedoms, especially elections, coupled with strong U.S. support, were key to the restart of democracy.)

Empowering Democrats—Limited Application, Limited Success. The last 25 years of the 20th century saw some significant efforts to focus our support for democracy on empowering democratic dissidents and activists. President Carter made raising human rights practices and the release of political prisoners a priority, at least during the early stage of his Administration. President Reagan made support for democracy a central tenet of his Latin American policy, met with dissidents in the Soviet Union, and worked with Congress to establish institutions to support pro-freedom nongovernmental organizations (NGOs) and activists abroad. President Bush used both coercive and traditional diplomacy to secure elections in Panama, Nicaragua, and El Salvador and worked with the democratic opposition in both countries to take advantage of those elections to bring about democratic change. He led the effort to create a mechanism in the Organization of American States to defend democracy against coups and used it and sanctions to support a legitimately elected government in Haiti. President Clinton used both sanctions and force to restore the elected government in Haiti, helped mobilize the democratic opposition to oppose the Serbian dictator Milosevich in an election, and included democracy promotion as an element of his National Security Strategy.

These commendable prior efforts to make operational our support for freedom activists had significant limitations, however. In effect, they remained the exception, not the rule. We continued to rely heavily on the Kennedy-era development model, providing the bulk of our "democracy and governance" assistance to institutions of government—regardless of whether the government in question was democratically-elected or authoritarian in nature. Even in countries with authoritarian regimes unfriendly to the United States, our diplomacy was largely focused on urging reform on the authoritarians themselves. Our ties to opposition groups, NGOs, and dissidents were cautious and limited by the need not to compromise our ability to influence the government in power, which continued to be seen as the source of stability and our main channel for interaction with society. In strategically important countries like Egypt, we provided assistance to NGOs only if the government approved the specific grant and recipient. In places like Saudi Arabia, we had virtually no contact with critics of the monarchy.

Institutions to Promote Democracy—Progress and Problems. Notwithstanding the limited number of cases in which a policy of strong support for democratic actors was adopted, institutions were put in place to provide such support when desired. President Reagan along with Congress established the National Endowment for Democracy and its family of institutions to provide support to political parties, NGOs, labor unions, and free enterprise organizations. The U.S. Agency for International Development (USAID) developed a network of partners skilled in providing assistance to pro-democracy NGOs. Funding for democracy and governance was increased by successive administrations.

But serious problems existed that impeded the effectiveness of these institutions even when policy favored support for democratic actors. By 2001, a little less than $700 million was devoted to democracy and governance worldwide. But there was no reliable mechanism for determining globally the breakdown between "governance" activities (largely assistance to governments) and assistance to those struggling for democracy in un-free countries. There was no systematic means of assuring that democracy assistance was targeted at countries where support for democracy constituted a strategic priority. In countries where the Ambassador or USAID Mission Director had a clear vision and were successful in arguing for budgetary support, the programs they designed were effective; in other countries, programs were ineffective or exacerbated the underlying problems. In Egypt, for example, we provided more assistance to help the disabled vote in fraudulent elections than we did to assist the development of moderate, democratic political parties. In Nicaragua, we provided assistance to the Sandinista-controlled judiciary and election commission that were being used to intimidate their rivals and undermine the elected President.

Prior Presidents and senior officials met with some dissidents and activists from a number of countries. However, a systematic effort to reach out to activists worldwide to provide moral and political support at that level did not exist. The culture of the foreign affairs bureaucracy tended to focus on the risks of such contact—either to U.S. relations with the regime or to the activists facing potential regime retaliation. And programs to help address the unique legal, family, and medical problems of political prisoners were non-existent.

THIS ADMINISTRATION'S POLICY:

Strategy Shaped by 9/11. The President made clear his commitment to lead the cause of freedom in his first inaugural address (Tab 2). But the strategic approach to doing so was largely shaped by the Administration's response to the attacks of September 11, 2001. In effect, the decisions made by the President at that time resolved the longstanding debate between the "realist" and "idealist" schools of foreign policy—not with a victory of one over the other but with the conclusion that a policy of supporting democracy is the necessary element to achieve the objectives of both.

In the aftermath of 9/11, the President determined that the struggle with worldwide terrorism was ideological in nature and could not be won by military, law enforcement, or traditional diplomatic means alone. The dark ideology of the terrorists was attractive to a significant segment of the populations in the broader Middle East and elsewhere not because they favored the form of oppression the terrorists espoused, but because it offered the only alternative to the existing repressive regimes which robbed them of hope. The popular frustration with the status quo that the terrorists were harnessing was directed at us not because of our democratic values but because we had become identified with those repressive regimes.

The President determined that the ideological struggle could be won only if oppressed peoples were offered a positive alternative to the status quo, and that the only viable alternative was political freedom. Thus, the "ideal" policy of promoting freedom became the only "practical" policy to deal with the "reality" of terror; the long term "stability" that serves U.S. interests could be achieved only by eschewing the false stability of accommodating authoritarians. Promotion of freedom became the central element of our foreign policy and the priority policy objective of the United States.

Applying the President's Strategy Abroad. Our policy of prioritizing freedom was apparent in our war objectives in Afghanistan. Rather than install a new strongman to maintain stability and work with the United States in fighting the terrorists, we pressed for the election of a government that would bring with it the strength born of popular legitimacy. Similarly, the longstanding U.S. objective of "regime change" in Iraq was not accomplished by replacing Saddam with another strongman more friendly to the United States, but by holding popular elections.

The President's November 2003 speech on the 20th anniversary of the National Endowment for Democracy recognized that trading liberty for stability had done nothing to make us safer, and explicitly ended the "Middle East exception" to our support for democracy (Tab 4). The reaction from reformers in the region was positive as to content and somewhat skeptical as to our sincerity.

The President's second inaugural address set the bar even higher, declaring our primary foreign policy objective to be that of ending tyranny in the world and promising people throughout the world that "when you stand for your freedom, we will stand with you" (Tab 6). Secretary Rice's speech at the American University in Cairo made clear our support for those struggling for freedom rather than for the governments against which they were struggling—including explicitly governments friendly to the United States such as those in Egypt and Saudi Arabia (Tab 7).

Reforming Foreign Affairs Institutions. We reformed United States Government institutions, programs, and procedures to implement the policy priority placed on promoting freedom and supporting those struggling for freedom. The President directed U.S. diplomats and senior officials to articulate our pro-freedom polices abroad and to maintain regular contact with dissidents and democratic activists in unfree countries, and has led by example—speaking out against abuses of human rights and providing moral and political support (and not an inconsiderable degree of protection) to dissidents and activists struggling for freedom in their own countries. He has met with more than 170 activists from more than 35 countries and has held at least 30 meetings specifically at the White House with such individuals (Tab 14). He was the first President to meet with freedom activists from China, and personally arranged for continued visible moral support for them by the U.S. Embassy when they returned to China. He has not only made powerful statements concerning the human rights situation in places where relations were already strained or nonexistent (e.g., Cuba), but has stood next to traditional allies such as President Mubarak of Egypt and made clear statements of support for those struggling for freedom.

The Administration created annual awards for U.S. Ambassadors who are most effective in supporting democracy and human rights and for foreign activists or NGOs that demonstrate outstanding commitment to advancing liberty and show uncommon courage in the face of adversity.

The Administration has also put in place a $1.5 million revolving Human Rights Defenders Fund to provide immediate assistance for legal and medical costs for democracy advocates who are imprisoned or injured due to their work.

The amount of foreign assistance devoted to democracy and governance has more than doubled during this Administration, from less than $700 million in 2001 to almost $1.5 billion in 2008. Funding for the National Endowment for Democracy has more than tripled to over $100 million in 2008 from $31 million in 2001.

Because of the work done by the Department of State's new Foreign Assistance Bureau, we are now able to determine accurately the nature and scope of democracy assistance and thus are better able to determine whether it is serving our strategic objectives.

An interagency process has also been established to identify the countries where an absence of democracy or an imminent threat to democracy exists and to prioritize among those countries. The aim of this policy is to assure that our democracy resources fully fund a comprehensive, multi-year strategy in priority countries, rather than support a smattering of projects that are unlikely to be effective in bringing about change.

Driving Multilateral Support for Democracy. The Administration worked to develop multilateral efforts to promote democracy. The President proposed a United Nations (U.N.) Democracy Fund inaugurated in 2005, which for the first time explicitly committed the U.N. to promoting democratic governance. The President visited Prague specifically to allow participation in a conference of dissidents. At the Administration's initiative, the G-8 adopted its Partnership for Progress and a Common Future with the governments and peoples of the Broader Middle East and North Africa (BMENA) to strengthen freedom, democracy, and prosperity, and conducted an annual "Forum for the Future" bringing governments and civil society together to discuss reforms. The Administration launched the Middle East Partnership Initiative (MEPI) to promote democracy, education, economic growth, and women's empowerment and devoted more than $430 million in 5 years. We supported the Community of Democracies that convenes nations committed to democracy promotion and strengthening worldwide, and were successful in removing full participant status from some countries like Russia and Venezuela. We successfully persuaded the international community that the U.N. Commission on Human Rights was discredited due to its excessive focus on Israel, the presence as members of serious violators such as Cuba, Libya, Sudan, and others, and its inability to deal with serious issues such as Zimbabwe. Unfortunately the new body that replaced it was as bad or worse, and our principled disengagement from it has helped to highlight the need for real reform. Finally, the President launched the Asia-Pacific Democracy Partnership at the Sydney 2007 APEC Business Summit to address the fact that the Asia region lacks any regional organization dedicated to democracy. While, still in its formative stages, it has the participation of Japan, South Korea, Indonesia, and the Philippines as well as Canada, Australia, and the United States, and has monitored the Mongolian elections earlier this year.

WHAT HAS BEEN ACCOMPLISHED:

Successes. The policy of placing priority on democracy promotion over short-term stability reflects a long-term strategic approach the effects of which will only be fully apparent in the decades to come. Nevertheless, over the past 8 years it has produced significant results, both in the real world and in terms of developing institutions within the United States Government and internationally that are capable of carrying out this policy.

Were it not for the President's strategic determination that support for a democratic alternative to repression is the only way to win the war of ideas, it is probable that non-democratic strongmen would have been installed in Kabul and Baghdad. The opponents of our policies argue that this result would have adequately served U.S. interests at a lower cost to the United States. Few if any argue that the emergence of democratic governments in those countries would have occurred absent the U.S. effort.

Similarly, in Ukraine realism would have dictated continued reliance on the Kuchma regime rather than pressing for an open election that risked the emergence of a pro-Russian government had the Orange revolution failed. Few would argue that the Mubarak regime would have ever agreed to hold competitive Presidential elections in Egypt had it not been for U.S. pressure and support for democracy. Indeed, one can argue that the great advance of democracy in the world in 2005 as reported by Freedom House was in good measure the product of the expectations created by the President's policies. Democracy activists saw us supporting their cause; repressive regimes saw the potential for severe consequences from the United States for those who failed to move in the direction of democracy.

And Setbacks. The setbacks the advance of democracy has suffered are in part a consequence of our earlier successes. Authoritarians in the Middle East and Central Asia learned that they could shrink the space available for the development of democratic alternatives and limit the consequences to their relationships with us by threatening to reduce cooperation in the War on Terror, the Middle East Peace Process, and other policy priorities. Our own institutions have not yet sufficiently internalized the President's strategy to be able to defend it consistently in the face of such threats and to find creative ways to support democrats rather than simply accept the limitations imposed by the authoritarians. In an interesting manner, the authoritarian regimes have validated the fundamental premise of the President's approach: they deliberately seek to face us and their own societies with a choice between the repressive status quo and the rise of Muslim extremists, and to systematically eliminate pro-democratic alternatives. Thus, to extend their own hold on power they would guarantee that when change inevitably comes it will be in favor of the extremists.

Moderate, pro-democratic forces, especially in the Middle East, misinterpreted our policy as a promise to produce a democratic result rather than as a promise to support those seeking it. As a consequence, they have become prone to dismiss the initial U.S. effort as insincere. Moreover, in their efforts to defend against charges that they were U.S. puppets, many committed the cardinal error of legitimizing the authoritarians' argument that accepting assistance from foreign sources was an interference in the country's independence. More recently, they have interpreted our public focus on important issues like the peace process as abandonment of the Freedom Agenda. But all of these are questions concerning the sincerity or tactics of our policy, not the wisdom of it. Their consistent recommendations are to sincerely and vigorously implement the pro-democratic policies the President has articulated.

FUTURE CHALLENGES:

Impatience is the Enemy. The biggest danger to democracy promotion both domestically and internationally may be growing impatience and disillusionment with the policy. Opposition to the Iraq war has colored the outlook of those who might otherwise have shared our view that a democratic outcome was preferable to the imposition of a friendly dictator. Many in the foreign policy community who supported our policies in 2004–2005 when Georgia, Ukraine, Lebanon, and Kyrgyzstan had "color revolutions" have become disillusioned by the shrinking of political space and growing restrictions on civil liberties in Russia under Putin, the reversal of apparent democratic gains in Egypt, the difficulties of dealing with the fractious, weak, and sometimes corrupt and unpredictable democratic governments in the color revolution countries, the Hamas victory in the Palestinian election, the difficulties that the democratic governments of Iraq and Afghanistan have encountered, and the increased resistance of Central Asian and other autocracies to our democracy programs Those in our own foreign policy communities who have devoted considerable energy to the Middle East Peace Process, denuclearization of North Korea, nonproliferation to Iran, free trade with China, and the like are sympathetic to the argument that giving a high degree of priority to democracy is interfering with what they view as far more important and tangible goals. The combination of these concerns has resulted in a resurgence of "realist" thought that democracy promotion is not viable in many cultures, is ineffective in advancing U.S. interests, jeopardizes other U.S. interests, or costs more than the benefits it brings. A less stark but equally debilitating alternative is "gradualism" or "sequentialism" under which democracy would be achieved by building certain institutions of political or economic democracy without directly challenging the authoritarian system in place—without recognizing that real world autocrats will not allow the development of such independent institutions that will threaten their power.

An aggressive and sustained effort to make the case intellectually and politically for democracy promotion is essential. It should emphasize that the work is generational in nature (our support for pro-democracy efforts in Georgia, Ukraine, and Kyrgyzstan went on for over a decade before the color revolutions occurred), that newly democratic regimes are vulnerable until free institutions become established, and that even though newly democratic governments may be unpredictable and fractious, they still are more conducive to U.S. interests than authoritarian regimes that breed extremism and violent change.

Learning How To Succeed. A second key need is to structure our own foreign affairs bureaucracy to carry out this work. Individual Ambassadors, USAID Mission Directors, and Foreign Service Officers have contributed in major ways to supporting those struggling for freedom abroad. These successes, however, have largely been based on personal conviction and on the skills certain officers brought with them to Federal Service or learned through experimentation. The management culture of the foreign affairs agencies bureaucracies has resisted making democracy promotion a mainstream activity. For example, skills in managing contacts so that they provide protection to dissidents, in utilizing political opinion polling, and in coalition building are essential to democracy promotion, but are not addressed in department and agency training programs.

Another aspect of this management problem is that most foreign affairs personnel systems reward success in what they see as the primary mission of maintaining effective working relations with the government in power in pursuit of a wide variety of U.S. interests. Officers are rewarded for developing cooperative sources of information, influencing foreign governments' votes in the United Nations, and negotiating trade agreements. They are not normally promoted for having provoked the ire of a host government by speaking out on human rights or supporting dissidents. While the Department of State recently agreed to revise its training and promotion systems to address the problems of training and incentives, the systems are not yet in place.

Third, the bureaucratic process for obtaining concrete support for dissidents can be cumbersome, inflexible, and untimely. Programs need to be able to anticipate and respond to the actions of autocrats in a near-term process that is not a hallmark of the current bureaucratic structure.

Fourth, the inability of a fledgling democratic government to deliver services or uphold the rule of law can discredit democracy and contribute to instability. We must help embryonic democracies build strong and effective institutions and that requires a long term commitment. Our ability to do so will require maintaining congressional and public support over time. Fifth, continued efforts to multilateralize democracy promotion are essential. The institutions are in place with the U.N. Democracy Fund and the European Union, but they tend to be timid, providing only that support the repressive environment allows. We need to cultivate a new generation in democracies like India and South Africa so that they become active proponents of democracy rather than defenders of repressive regimes. The President's call for an urgent structural revision of the U.N. Human Rights Council should be pursued rather than another effort to make the current structure work.

CONCLUSION:

Building on the longstanding bipartisan tradition of support for democracy and human rights, this Administration has significantly advanced the cause of freedom, the strategy for realizing it, and the capacity of the United States, both bilaterally and multilaterally, to support those struggling for freedom worldwide. The strategies, policies, programs, and institutions designed for this purpose have been codified in National Security Policy Directive 58, which the President signed on July 17, 2008, and should provide future administrations significantly improved tools with which to pursue a longstanding U.S. objective.

Attachments

Tab 1   Chronology for the Freedom Agenda

Tab 2   President Bush's Inaugural Address (January 20, 2001)

Tab 3   President Bush's Speech at Tsinghua University (February 22, 2002)

Tab 4   President Bush's Remarks at the 20th Anniversary of the National Endowment for Democracy (November 6, 2003)

Tab 5   President Bush's Speech at the United Nations General Assembly (September 21, 2004)

Tab 6   President Bush's Second Inaugural Address (January 20, 2005)

Tab 7   Secretary Rice Remarks at the American University in Cairo (June 20, 2005)

Tab 8   Briefing Papers and Summary of Conclusions of Deputies Committee Meeting on Democracy Promotion: Global Priorities (March 28, 2006)

Tab 9   Memorandum of Conversation of Meeting with Chinese Human Rights Activists May 11, 2006)

Tab 10   President Bush Remarks in Prague, Czech Republic (June 5, 2007)

Tab 11   President Bush Remarks at APEC Business Summit (September 7, 2007)

Tab 12   President Bush Remarks at Hispanic Heritage Month Celebration (October 10, 2007)

Tab 13   National Security Presidential Directive/NSPD-58

Tab 14   List of Dissidents the President Has Met With

POSTSCRIPT

MICHAEL GERSON, PETER WEHNER

The Bush Administration Approach

President George W. Bush believed advancing democracy and institutions that sustain liberty were the only viable alternatives to repression and radicalism, were the best path to sustainable economic growth and political stability, and were consistent with America's best history and its national security interests. His administration was dedicated to creating "a balance of power that favors human freedom: conditions in which all nations and all societies can choose for themselves the rewards and challenges of political and economic liberty," in the words of the 2002 National Security Strategy.[1] He believed that the values of freedom are right and true for every person, in every society. He also believed that America should assist others in the pursuit of these goals, but that America could not do it alone—that it required alliances and multilateral institutions to assist freedom-loving nations, and that it depended on the efforts of freedom-loving peoples themselves.

President Bush knew that advancing freedom was the hard work of generations—that the path to a free society is long and not always linear or smooth—but believed it was essential work, especially after the 9/11 attacks, which showed that failed states could become lethal threats to America. In his words:

> For as long as whole regions of the world simmer in resentment and tyranny—prone to ideologies that feed hatred and excuse murder—violence will gather, and multiply in destructive power, and cross the most defended borders, and raise a mortal threat. There is only one force of history that can break the reign of hatred and resentment, and expose the pretensions of tyrants, and reward the hopes of the decent and tolerant, and that is the force of human freedom.[2]

---

1. George W. Bush, "The National Security Strategy of the United States of America," The White House, September 2002, https://georgewbush-whitehouse.archives.gov/nsc/nss/2002/.

2. George W. Bush, "Inauguration Address," The White House, January 20, 2005, https://georgewbush-whitehouse.archives.gov/news/releases/2005/01/20050120-1.html.

While acknowledging that democracy takes different forms in different cultures, President Bush was clear that successful democracies are built on certain common foundations—freedom of speech, with a vibrant free press that informs the public, ensures transparency, and prevents authoritarian backsliding; freedom of assembly, so citizens can gather and organize in free associations to press for reform, and so that a peaceful, loyal opposition can provide citizens with real choices; a free economy to unleash the creativity of its citizens and create prosperity and opportunity and economic independence from the state; an independent judiciary to guarantee rule of law and assure impartial justice for all citizens; and freedom of worship, because respect for the beliefs of others is the only way to build a society where compassion and tolerance prevail.

To put this into practice, President Bush launched an ambitious effort to reorient the policies, institutions, and resources of the US government toward promoting, in the words of the 2006 *National Security Strategy*, "effective democracies: states that are respectful of human dignity, accountable to their citizens, and responsible towards their neighbors." As the Transition Memorandum notes, the president directed US diplomats and senior officials to advocate freedom abroad and maintain regular contact with dissidents and democratic activists. He himself met with more than 170 activists from more than thirty-five countries—with at least thirty of those meetings in the White House—including meetings with freedom activists from China and those seeking a democratic Myanmar. The administration substantially increased funding for democracy promotion and governance, including creation of a Human Rights Defenders Fund to pay for legal and medical costs incurred by democracy advocates because of their work. US ambassadors began to be recognized, rewarded, and incentivized to support democracy and human rights.

The administration also developed multilateral efforts to promote democratic governance. With American sponsorship, the United Nations established a Democracy Fund, committing itself explicitly for the first time to promoting democratic governance. The administration led the G-8 nations to create the Partnership for Progress and a Common Future for the Broader Middle East and North Africa (BMENA) to strengthen freedom, democracy, and prosperity. President Bush's administration established the Middle East Partnership Initiative (MEPI) to promote democracy, education, economic growth, and women's empowerment. It also supported the Community of Democracies; sought to reform the UN Commission on Human Rights, which had been hijacked by nondemocratic human rights abusers; and launched the Asia-Pacific Democracy Partnership, the first regional organization in Asia dedicated to democracy.

Contrary to the caricature, the Bush administration did not go around the world looking to impose democracy by force of arms, "through the barrel of a gun." Where people rose up to claim their own freedom, the administration gave them diplomatic and political support—in central and Eastern Europe, as newly free populations sought to consolidate their liberty by joining the institutions of a free Europe (NATO and the EU), and in the color revolutions in Georgia, Ukraine, Tajikistan, and Lebanon, as people rebelled against authoritarianism. The administration supported those voices in the Middle East advocating freedom as the key to greater social and economic progress—seeking to support efforts by leaders like Salam Fayyad in building a democratic state for the Palestinian people, calling on even close allies like Egypt and Saudi Arabia to open up their societies and embrace the democratic aspirations of their people, and establishing BMENA as the framework for these efforts. The administration was active in Africa to resolve long-standing conflicts in places like Sierra Leone and Liberia and to support the peoples emerging from those conflicts in their efforts to establish democratic futures for their countries. Through vehicles like the Millennium Challenge Corporation and Plan Colombia, the administration provided economic, financial, and technical assistance to partner governments seeking to advance freedom, prosperity, and security for their people.

These interventions were both opportunistic and strategic—with the administration acting where it could identify and support local partners and local populations in their efforts to advance their own freedom. Where the administration did intervene militarily, most notably in Afghanistan and Iraq, it did so for national security reasons—to eliminate terrorist safe havens or national security threats. Once these threats were eliminated, the administration actively championed the efforts of these newly liberated peoples to create for themselves a democratic governance framework. The administration did so not only because it was consistent with America's long-held values but also because it was the best way to help nations with very diverse populations achieve political stability and avoid becoming safe havens for terrorists.

During the Bush administration, the world witnessed historic democratic progress. In 2005, for example, eighty-one nations improved on the democracy index while only fifty-two declined. When George W. Bush left office, 46 percent of the world's population lived in free nations.

But a decline in freedom started in 2006 and has continued every year since. All around the globe people courageously rose up on behalf of liberty and human rights. But the opponents of their efforts struck back with ferocity. By the end of the Bush presidency the forces of freedom and tyranny were engaged in a great conflict, as yet unresolved, playing out in different regions of the world. The outcome of this battle rests not only on American actions but primarily on the efforts of others to secure their own futures.

What Has Happened Since the End of the Bush Administration?

Every year since the second term of the Bush administration has seen a decline in global freedom; what Freedom House refers to as a long democratic recession, and it is deepening. The greatest retreat occurred in 2020, when forty-five nations saw declines in freedom. Some of this can be attributed to the global pandemic, with leaders using COVID-19 as an excuse to consolidate power and suppress dissent. But these trends long precede the pandemic and they will not disappear once the virus is defeated.

By 2021, the number of free countries in the world reached its lowest level since the beginning of the fifteen-year period of global democracy decline. Less than 20 percent of the world's population now lives in a free country (as defined by Freedom House), the smallest proportion since 1995. In addition, scholars warn about "democratic deconsolidation," a process in which faith in democracy and the institutions that sustain democracy erode.[3]

The reasons for the long-term decline of freedom are complex; every nation is unique, and the forces at play are complicated. But this conclusion by Freedom House is compelling: "The enemies of freedom have pushed the false narrative that democracy is in decline because it is incapable of addressing people's needs. In fact, democracy is in decline because its most prominent exemplars are not doing enough to protect it."[4]

Soon after assuming office, President Barack Obama and his secretary of state, Hillary Clinton, downplayed democracy and human rights. That changed

3. Roberto Stefan Foa and Yascha Mounk, "The Danger of Deconsolidation," *Journal of Democracy* 27, no. 3 (2016): 5–17, www.journalofdemocracy.org/wp-content/uploads/2016/07/FoaMounk-27-3.pdf.

4. Sarah Repucci and Amy Slipowitz, "Freedom in the World 2021: Democracy Under Siege," February 2022, https://freedomhouse.org/report/freedom-world/2021/democracy-under-siege.

a bit over time, but democracy promotion was never a major priority for the Obama presidency. In assessing the Obama administration's policies, Freedom House's "Freedom in the World 2013 Report" put it this way:

> Such apparent ambivalence about vigorously supporting democratic change bodes ill for the [Middle East] region, which . . . remains very much in transition and turmoil. The old order of ossified dictatorships is giving way to something else, hopefully to governments based on humane principles and free institutions. But there are many other options available. Although the future of the Middle East will be determined by the people who live there, the United States and other established democracies have some part to play . . . [5]

The report cites the uneven record of the Obama administration in supporting freedom. That record includes its failure to support the 2009 Green Revolution in Iran, in which millions of Iranians mobilized against the fraudulent presidential election. The theocratic regime in Iran was in crisis, shaken to its foundation; the Obama administration refused to take sides, even as the government brutally cracked down on those pushing for democracy. Those democratic forces pleaded with the United States not to confer legitimacy on the Iranian regime and implored the administration for support, but the Obama administration, wedded to its diplomatic outreach to Tehran and hopes to negotiate a deal on Iran's nuclear program, did little. This contributed to the failure of the democratic uprising and may have been a missed opportunity of historic proportions, in which a tyrannical regime that is a threat to the region could have been replaced by a democratic one.

Elsewhere in the Middle East—in Libya, Iraq, and Syria—the Obama administration forfeited the opportunity to advance the cause of freedom and democracy in favor of more "realistic" policies focused on securing America's interests in stability and security. In each case the administration's pursuit of these interests proved illusory.

---

5. Arch Puddington, "Freedom in the World 2013: Democratic Breakthroughs in the Balance," 2013, https://www.freedomhouse.org/sites/default/files/FIW%202013%20 Booklet.pdf.

In 2011, two years after the Iran uprising, the Obama administration authorized the US military to join the United Kingdom and France in a limited military action in Libya to protect Libyan civilians. But once it morphed into a mission to remove the Libyan despot, the failure to plan and resource the postconflict operation contributed to Libya's collapse into civil war, destabilizing North Africa. President Obama called it his "worst mistake." An opportunity to build a more free and potentially democratic Libya was lost.

Also in 2011, civil unrest that might have overturned a brutal regime in Syria was largely ignored. Narrowly defining America's interests and eschewing democracy promotion, the Obama administration minimized its involvement. What resulted was a protracted civil war that ripped Syria apart and produced over a half million dead, more than five million refugees, and nearly seven million internally displaced persons. It was at that time the largest displacement crisis since World War II: Syria's neighbors were overwhelmed and destabilized, and the massive outflow of refugees led to a nativist backlash in much of Europe.

Despite the unfolding crisis in Syria, the Obama administration decided later that same year to withdraw America's much scaled-down troop presence in Iraq. Eschewing what would have been a longer-term commitment to democracy promotion, the decision sent Iraq once again spiraling downward into sectarian violence and civil war, undermining its democracy and abridging its freedom, allowing Iran to expand its influence, and contributing to the rise of the jihadist group ISIS, which established control in large parts of Iraq and Syria.

Outside the Middle East, the Obama administration did little to champion human rights in places like China, North Korea, Burma, Belarus, Cuba, and Venezuela—despite the pleas from many dissidents in those nations for American support, and without successfully resolving any of these crises.

However lukewarm Barack Obama may have been toward the Freedom Agenda, Donald Trump was even less concerned. He rarely mentioned democracy and almost never spoke about universal human rights. He spoke about his affection for one of the most ruthless dictators in the world, North Korea's Kim Jung-Un—"we fell in love," in Trump's words—and went so far as to side with Russia's Vladimir Putin against America's intelligence agencies on Russia's 2016 election interference. President Trump reportedly told Xi Jinping that he endorsed China's genocidal campaign against Uighur Muslims in Xinjiang. He played up to authoritarians like Rodrigo Duterte, the president of the Philippines, refusing to raise concerns over human rights. The same is true with Turkish president Recep Tayyip Erdogan, who cracked down on opposition in his nation and invaded northern Syria in order to wipe out the Kurds—America's allies in fighting ISIS.

There were a few exceptions to this neglect. The Trump administration pushed for the restoration of democracy in Venezuela, supported dissidents in Cuba, and elevated the promotion of international religious freedom. Nonetheless, on balance, no other president in the postwar period has shown such indifference to the virtues of democracy or its importance to American foreign policy.

But what made President Trump uniquely damaging was the role he played in eroding democratic norms in the United States, his relentless attacks on America's institutions and on the press as the "enemy of the people" and, at the end of his term, his effort to overturn the presidential election and spread the lie that the election was rigged and his successor, Joe Biden, was illegitimate. The January 6, 2021, assault on the Capitol by supporters of President Trump has been used by dictators to discredit the United States as a champion of democracy. For example, Zimbabwean President Emmerson Dambudzo Mnangagwa said the attack on the Capitol "showed that the U.S. has no moral right to punish another nation under the guise of upholding democracy."[6] In the meantime, China and Russia have expanded their efforts to promote authoritarianism and undermine democracy around the world. With a global struggle underway, the Trump legacy hurt America's will and ability to lead the side of freedom in that contest.

How Did the Bush Administration Do?

Assessing the Bush administration's record vis-à-vis the Freedom Agenda requires disaggregation, starting with rhetoric, which was such a central part of that Agenda. George W. Bush's rhetoric was very much within the mainstream of twentieth-century presidential oratory—aspirational, confident, and prodemocratic. Democrat John F. Kennedy promised in his inauguration speech that America "shall pay any price, bear any burden, meet any hardship, support any

---

6. Zach Budryk, "Zimbabwean President: Capitol Riots Show US Has No Right Punish Other Nations 'Under the Guise of Upholding Democracy,'" *The Hill*, January 7, 2021, https://thehill.com/blogs/blog-briefing-room/news/533172-zimbabwean-president -capitol-riots-show-us-has-no-right-punish/.

friend, oppose any foe to assure the survival and the success of liberty." Republican Ronald Reagan spoke to the British Parliament about "the march of freedom and democracy which will leave Marxism-Leninism on the ash-heap of history as it has left other tyrannies which stifle the freedom and muzzle the self-expression of the people." Other presidents have struck similar tones.

After his second inaugural address, President Bush was accused by some skeptics of committing the United States to unending conflict in an effort to single-handedly end tyranny. Here is what he actually said:

> It is the policy of the United States to seek and support the growth of democratic movements and institutions in every nation and culture, with the ultimate goal of ending tyranny in our world.
>
> This is not primarily the task of arms, though we will defend ourselves and our friends by force of arms when necessary. Freedom, by its nature, must be chosen, and defended by citizens, and sustained by the rule of law and the protection of minorities. And when the soul of a nation finally speaks, the institutions that arise may reflect customs and traditions very different from our own. America will not impose our own style of government on the unwilling. Our goal instead is to help others find their own voice, attain their own freedom, and make their own way.[7]

By the end of the Bush presidency, nine of the eighteen countries in the Middle East and North Africa—the centerpiece of the Bush administration's Freedom Agenda—experienced some improvement in freedom. According to Freedom House's then director of research, Arch Puddington: "The 'Freedom in the World 2006' ratings for the Middle East represent the region's best performance in the history of the survey."[8] Yet for the most part those gains did not prove durable; the young democracies that emerged in the Middle East struggled with ongoing

7. George W. Bush, "Inauguration Address," January 20, 2005.
8. Aili Piano, Arch Puddington, and Mark Y. Rosenberg, eds., *Freedom in the World 2006: The Annual Survey of Political Rights and Civil Liberties* (Lanham, MD: Rowman and Littlefield, 2006), p. 5, https://freedomhouse.org/sites/default/files/2020-02/Freedom _in_the_World_2006_complete_book.pdf.

terrorism and religious extremism. And in some cases—like in Gaza in 2006—the winner of elections (in this case, Hamas) was a militant Islamic group that has since stifled any semblance of democratic government.

Every administration falls short of its hopes and ambitions, every administration makes errors in judgment and execution, and that includes the Bush administration. For example, Bush's administration failed to stabilize the country and provide security for the Iraqi people in the aftermath of major combat operations (this mistake was corrected in 2007, when a new counterinsurgency plan was put in place and succeeded spectacularly).

Iraq is often said to be the Bush administration's greatest failure in the context of the Freedom Agenda, discrediting the entire effort. But here a common distortion needs to be dispelled. President Bush did not decide to invade Iraq to turn it into a democracy; he ordered the invasion because Iraq was widely regarded as a grave national security threat. This assessment was based in large part on what we now know was deeply flawed intelligence, as Saddam Hussein did not have the weapons of mass destruction that the Bush administration believed he had when it went to war. But the principal motivation for the invasion was that of national security. Yet once the Saddam Hussein regime was toppled, President Bush believed the only feasible and moral option to replace it was a new government accountable to its people. The United States supported Iraq's efforts to build just that, however imperfectly. And while the substantial costs and serious mistakes of the war continue to be debated, it bears noting that Iraq today is a democracy—albeit fragile, embattled, and imperfect—and does not tyrannize its people or its neighbors as the Saddam Hussein regime did.

In 2003 President Bush also warned of the illusory stability of the brittle autocratic regimes ruling much of the broader Middle East—thus anticipating the "Arab Awakening" that sparked in Tunisia in December 2010; consumed Egypt, Syria, Libya, and other nations; and has continued to reverberate ever since. The failure of freedom and democracy to take hold in the Middle East after the Arab Awakening is arguably attributable, at least in part, to the policies pursued by successor administrations.

Each administration subsequent to that of George W. Bush made a point of contrasting its approach to the Freedom Agenda and, with some exceptions, downgraded human rights as a priority. The implicit theory was that the gains in freedom were too few, the ambitions too unrealistic, the cost too high, and that what was needed was more "realism" and less "idealism" in American foreign policy. The result, it was implied, would be a more stable world.

It hasn't turned out quite that way.

Causality is complex and often impossible to disentangle, but the inescapable fact is this: Presidents Obama and Trump both generally neglected and even disdained supporting freedom and democracy. Yet that shift in direction, which encouraged fifteen years of democratic decline, did not make the world more stable, manageable, or safe. Instead, the world is more troubled, fragile states are less stable, and America's standing in the world has eroded.

It turns out realism has its downsides, too.

What Are the Lessons Learned?

Has the history subsequent to the Bush administration discredited the concepts and the assumptions of the Freedom Agenda? Hardly. What we have learned is that democracy promotion is hard work, takes time, and presents enormous challenges. American support for freedom, democracy, and human rights does not ensure their success throughout the world. But American indifference to their advance makes it far less likely that they will spread and flourish.

Other lessons:

- *The history of democracy is that it waxes and wanes.* It is a "long, twilight struggle," in the words of President Kennedy. Even though democracy has great appeal, tribalism, sectarian differences, and ethnic hatreds have great power, too. The latter can impede and sometimes defeat the former. But because freedom faces setbacks does not mean America should abandon its defining national commitment. The war between Ukraine and Russia has reminded the world of the stakes of the struggle. It has reminded us, too, how a brave and honorable people fighting for their freedom against a brutal dictatorship still has the capacity to stir the human heart. It's not something to which the United States can be indifferent. As President Zelensky told a joint session of Congress on March 16, 2022, "Today the Ukrainian people are defending not only Ukraine. We are fighting for Europe and the world and our lives in the name of the future. That is why today the American people are helping not just Ukraine, but Europe and the world to keep the planet alive. To keep justice in history."

- *In the short run, promotion of freedom and democracy must sometimes be balanced against other interests—security, economic, and political.* But ultimately there is no need to choose between advancing America's values and its interests. A world that is increasingly illiberal is a world that is increasingly more dangerous, more inhumane, more war-torn, and more threatening to American interests.
- *Providing security is the precondition for allowing democracy to take root and thrive.* This necessary precondition is something the Bush administration struggled to establish in Iraq and Afghanistan. Security, economic well-being, and freedom and democracy must progress together. And free elections themselves do not guarantee progress on the other two—and are themselves only a necessary but insufficient condition for ensuring democracy.
- *American leadership in advancing liberty is important but not determinative.* In the final measure, every country and every people must choose and build their own free and democratic institutions and culture.

PART 2

The War on Terror

INTRODUCTION

STEPHEN J. HADLEY

The September 11, 2001 attacks remain for many people the defining event of the Bush presidency. It is impossible to recreate the mood of shock, trauma, and anger that the nation felt after al Qaeda's stunning assault—on the nation's financial center in New York City, on its military headquarters at the Pentagon, and the heroically thwarted attack on its political seat of government in the Capitol building. Almost 3,000 people representing ninety-three nations were killed and more than 6,000 injured. The question the new administration faced from nearly every quarter was "how could you have let this happen?" and, more urgently, "what are you going to do to keep it from happening again?"

The clear message was "do whatever it takes"—and waste no time in doing it, because the next attack could come at any moment. Indeed, the intelligence community issued numerous warnings that 9/11 was likely to be the first of a series of mass casualty attacks, some of which could involve weapons of mass destruction (WMD). Just seven days after 9/11, anonymous letters containing powder later confirmed to be anthrax began showing up at media companies in New York City and at government and congressional offices in Washington, DC. No one knew who was behind these anthrax attacks. They killed five people and injured seventeen.

In response to 9/11, President Bush put the nation on a war footing. America was vulnerable and blind to the full capabilities of al Qaeda and related terrorist groups. The administration initiated a wide range of programs and operations to acquire more and better intelligence from both human and technical sources, to reorganize the government and harden the country against further attacks, and to take the fight to al Qaeda and its allies abroad by launching military operations overseas.

Some of these initiatives were controversial at the time. A number were adopted in secret because if known to the terrorists, their utility would have been lost. Upon becoming public, some became a source of great controversy: interception of terrorist communications, methods of interrogation, and the rendition and treatment of prisoners. It is important to address here, however briefly, how the Bush administration understood these measures and why it adopted them.

After 9/11, the nation faced the very real prospect of more mass-casualty terrorist attacks. The administration had been severely criticized—by Congress, the media, and expert opinion—for not doing enough to prevent the first attacks ("not connecting the dots"). President Bush was determined that his administration was not going to find itself in that position again. He directed that everything be done that could be done—within the law, as it then stood—to protect the country from another attack. This required adopting measures that, while determined to be lawful by the Justice Department, might make many good and loyal Americans uncomfortable—especially after the imminent threat and acute sense of vulnerability had passed. The administration knew it might pay a political price for these programs but believed it was a price worth paying to keep the nation safe. The administration was also forced to act quickly, given the imminent threat, without the benefit of information that would later come to light or the opportunity for lengthy review.

Once the initial crisis had passed, and as the nation became better prepared to defend itself and made progress both against al Qaeda and in disrupting terrorist attacks, these measures could be—and were—relaxed. Based on successive reviews within the Bush administration, significant changes were made, including the release of more than 500 detainees from Guantanamo, the transfer of detainees previously held by the CIA to Guantanamo for prosecution, the revision of the structure of military commissions, and substantial modification of interrogation practices.

The administration briefed congressional leaders of both parties on its counterterrorism programs, consistent with legal requirements, and, in the earliest days after 9/11, even some of the most criticized measures (such as the CIA interrogation program) enjoyed a considerable degree of bipartisan support. Despite their controversial nature, many of the counterterrorism policies initiated by the Bush administration, such as the detention and prosecution of terrorist suspects under the laws of war, have been continued by subsequent administrations. Through a process of internal reviews by the executive branch under successive administrations, public discussion, court litigation, judicial decisions, congressional oversight, and often bipartisan legislation, a national consensus—or at least a majority consensus—has now emerged around a legal framework for US counterterrorism efforts. This includes general agreement on a set of what are deemed appropriate and publicly acceptable policies and practices for keeping the nation safe from terrorist attacks. The measures adopted by the Bush administration in turn evolved over time to reflect this consensus as it took shape. Indeed, most of the counterterrorism measures adopted and applied by the Bush administration were continued under both the Obama and Trump administrations and embraced as part of this hard-won consensus.

This is as it should be. President Bush instructed his administration to participate in this consensus-building process. One could argue, in retrospect, that the Bush administration should have moved earlier and more rapidly to engage and lead the effort. By the time the administration did engage, its actions were greeted with considerable skepticism and suspicion by many including, particularly, the press and civil liberties groups. Perhaps an earlier effort, conducted immediately in the shadow of the 9/11 attacks, might have produced more public political support for these measures to match the support expressed in private by leaders from both political parties. Or perhaps the consensus-building process had to be left largely to subsequent administrations once the sense of imminent crisis had waned and the nation had become better able to deal with the terrorist threat.

The only NSC Transition Memorandum related to these subjects, entitled "Detaining and Prosecuting Combatants in the War on Terror," was an unclassified memorandum prepared by the NSC legal staff discussing the legal basis for detaining al Qaeda terrorists, their due process rights, their access to the courts, and the conditions for their release. This Transition Memorandum is not included in this volume but is available on the online archive maintained by the Center for Presidential History at Southern Methodist University.

The NSC legal memorandum does not deal with the operational aspects of the interception, interrogation, and rendition programs that became so controversial. No other NSC Transition Memoranda were prepared on these programs in part because they had already received such exhaustive public discussion and review. But other departments and agencies addressed these issues as part of their transition preparations. This was particularly true of the State Department where legal adviser (and former first-term Bush NSC legal adviser) John Bellinger had assumed a key role in addressing the legal and policy aspects of these programs on behalf of Secretary of State Condoleezza Rice during the second Bush term.

By the time these controversial measures received their public scrutiny, the Bush administration had launched a government-wide effort that had transformed the way the United States sought to counter and combat global terrorism. That effort involved taking the fight to the terrorists overseas—cutting off their support, disrupting their funding sources, denying them safe haven, and targeting their leadership. It involved hardening the US homeland against terrorist attack by creating new institutions, repurposing existing ones, enhancing intelligence sharing, obtaining new legislative and legal authorities, and strengthening and expanding international partnerships. Finally, it involved countering the underlying ideology of violent extremists and promoting freedom, human dignity, and democracy as a more compelling alternative to the dark narrative of the terrorists. This overall effort is covered in the newly declassified Transition Memoranda set out in the chapters of this part 2.

CHAPTER 2

The Fight against al Qaeda

NICHOLAS RASMUSSEN

The attack on the US homeland on September 11, 2001, transformed the strategy pursued by the United States to counter and combat the threat of terrorism. Prior to 9/11, US counterterrorism efforts were largely reactive and focused on a combination of law enforcement actions against individual terrorists (such as criminal indictments) and one-time military reprisals to punish terrorist actions (often largely symbolic). After 9/11, the Bush administration pursued a globally oriented, whole-of-government offensive strategy aimed at waging war against al Qaeda (AQ) (and other linked groups) as a terrorist organization, cutting off its support, and denying it safe haven anywhere in the world, while simultaneously aiming to counter and ultimately defeat the underlying ideology of violent Islamic extremism.

This approach also applied to a more deliberate, but still comprehensive, campaign to disrupt and dismantle AQ's financial networks. The US government understood that preventing terrorist attacks and frustrating strategic ambitions required undermining and disrupting terrorist funding sources and networks. Terrorist groups need money to mount operations, establish logistics support, maintain territory or influence, and plan strategically against the United States—and this requires access to the global financial and commercial system. Cutting off access to this system and disrupting funding flows could restrict terrorists' ability to operate, govern, and extend their reach. This approach, adopted by every administration since 9/11, is intended to make it harder, costlier, and riskier for terrorist groups to raise and move money around the world. Over the last two decades, that strategy has proved remarkably effective at curtailing the freedom of action of AQ and other terror groups.

~~TOP-SECRET~~/NOFORN

7186
Transition

NSC Declassification Review [E.O. 13526]
DECLASSIFY IN PART
by William C. Carpenter 3/23/2020

THE WHITE HOUSE

WASHINGTON

January 16, 2009

MEMORANDUM FOR THE RECORD

FROM: JUAN ZARATE, COMBATING TERRORISM DIRECTORATE
          NICK RASMUSSEN, COMBATING TERRORISM DIRECTORATE
          ERIC GRANT, COMBATING TERRORISM DIRECTORATE

SUBJECT: Dismantling al-Qaida

THE SITUATION AS WE FOUND IT:

As this Administration took office, the senior al-Qaida (AQ) leadership enjoyed protection among the Taliban's fundamentalist regime in Afghanistan, having been displaced from Sudan in 1996. From its Afghan safe haven, the AQ leadership was able to recruit and train operatives, raise funds, distribute resources, and plot to conduct terrorist attacks around the world. Even though Usama Bin Ladin (UBL), Ayman Al-Zawahiri, Khalid Sheikh Mohammed (KSM), and Abu Zubaydah were all under Federal indictment and efforts were under way to detain and prosecute them, practical realities significantly limited our opportunities for success through capture, extradition, or rendition.

Following the 1998 bombings of our Embassies in Kenya and Tanzania, the United States retaliated with cruise missile strikes against AQ targets in Afghanistan and Sudan, including several known training camps. This limited military reprisal did not, however, disrupt or deter the AQ leadership from planning and conducting either the 2000 attack on the USS Cole in Yemen or the terrorist attacks of 9/11. Nor had the United Nations Security Council (UNSC) assets freeze, travel ban, and arms embargo instituted against UBL, AQ, and the Taliban pursuant to Resolution 1267 in 1999 effectively curtailed AQ's capabilities.

~~TOP-SECRET~~/NOFORN
Reason: 1.4(a) (b) (c) (d) (e) (f) (g) (h)
Declassify on: 1/16/34

Prior to 9/11, AQ senior leadership had relative freedom of action in Afghanistan despite intelligence and international law enforcement efforts to bring them to justice for their multiple offenses. The sovereignty of uncooperative regimes such as Afghanistan and Yemen—as well as sympathetic donors from the Gulf region and political supporters throughout the Muslim world—had prevented the United States from taking AQ leaders into custody and disrupting AQ's ability to function as a global network. United States intelligence had been tracking UBL and his senior associates for several years, but aggressive military and paramilitary operations to eliminate the AQ senior leadership were judged not politically viable prior to 9/11. Moreover, committed international partners were lacking in the Saudi and Pakistani Governments—whose own ranks included AQ sympathizers.

Prior to 9/11, the global threat of terrorism was viewed much differently than it is today. Combating terrorism was not the top policy priority for either the United States Government or the international community. The preface to The *9/11 Commission Report* stresses that "the institutions charged with protecting our borders, civil aviation, and national security did not understand how grave this threat could be, and did not adjust their policies, plans, and practices to deter or defeat it."

THIS ADMINISTRATION'S POLICY:

9/11 changed all dimensions of the situation that the President had inherited in 2001. Overnight, domestic and international support coalesced around the right of the United States to pursue deci-sive, offensive action to end AQ's ability to function as a global terrorist organization with central-ized leadership. Dealing with terror was no longer just a law enforcement matter. The President recognized that we were at war with a terrorist enemy and that it would require both a battle of arms and ideas to defeat the violent Islamic extremism manifested on 9/11. In waging this War on Terror (WOT), the President set forth core principles for the strategy for dealing with the terrorist threat:

- We will take the fight to the enemy abroad as a fundamental element of protecting the Home-land, so as to avoid fighting them at home;
- We will not allow threats to gather and we will preempt such national security threats;
- We believe that violence against innocent civilians is never justified no matter the credo or the cause;
- We require the world to make a choice between supporting the WOT or harboring and support-ing terrorism and terrorists; and
- We will delegitimize the idea of terrorism and counter the ideology of violent extremism with a vision of freedom, defined broadly.

This Administration's strategic vision for the WOT involved the application of all instruments of national power and influence to kill or capture the terrorists; deny them safe-haven and control of any nation; prevent them from gaining access to weapons of mass destruction (WMD); render potential terrorist targets less attractive by strengthening their security; cut off their sources of funding and other resources needed to operate and survive; and win the war of ideas. The United States-led coalition's 2001 invasion of Afghanistan and overthrow of the Taliban regime removed the AQ leadership's physical safe haven, and the subsequent WOT continues to limit their mobility and operational capacity. As summarized in the National Strategy for Combating Terrorism (revised as of September 2006), our policy to disable the senior AQ leadership and prevent its further coordination of terrorist activities has included the following efforts:

- **Incapacitate senior AQ leaders.** First and foremost, we pursued military, intelligence, and law enforcement operations to find and bring to justice both the AQ leadership and their lesser operatives. Military and paramilitary operations in the conflict zones of South Asia and the Middle East were conducted. Our efforts were aimed at capturing and interrogating AQ operatives to obtain intelligence. Our key objective with detainees was obtaining intelligence through all lawful means to prevent additional attacks, to destroy the network, and to save lives. Where possible, terror suspects were brought for prosecution in criminal and military tribunals.

- **Eliminate safe havens.** Through joint military operations with the United Kingdom and other NATO and non-NATO partners, we sought to remove AQ from Afghanistan and, subsequently, Iraq. Through diplomacy, military assistance, and law enforcement cooperation, we sought to establish independent governments in Afghanistan and Iraq that could prevent AQ from reconstituting or establishing operational bases inside their territory. In Pakistan, our policies were aimed at helping Islamabad extend its reach into the virtually ungoverned regions of the Federally Administered Tribal Areas (FATA) and the North-West Frontier Province (NWFP), where AQ had a population of potential allies. Operations were undertaken to deny AQ, the Taliban, and related militants safe haven. After 2003, when AQ took sanctuary in the South Waziristan Agency of the FATA, we sought to encourage local tribes to deny the AQ leaders refuge or work against them and restrain the domestic militant groups that often acted in concert with AQ. These efforts also included targeting terrorist leaders with lethal action.

- **Inhibit leadership communications.** Another aim of our policy towards disabling the central AQ leadership was to eliminate its ability to perform command-and-control functions as well as broadcast its ideological propaganda.

- **Enforce physical and economic isolation.** The Departments of State, Treasury, Justice (DOJ), and Homeland Security (DHS) were charged with fostering international cooperation via UNSC regimes and other bilateral measures to sever AQ's sources of funding, facilitation networks, and cover mechanisms. State's diplomatic initiatives at the United Nations (U.N.), Treasury's program for designating terrorist affiliates, the mutual legal assistance work promoted by DOJ, and DHS's aid to foreign countries for implementing international travel restrictions were all deemed integral to undermining the AQ leadership's international support network, which included financiers, couriers, charities, and others. These efforts were coordinated in part through interagency policy coordinating committees and working groups.

· **Organize political opposition.** The President's policy also aimed to internationalize the problem and build strong, foreign partnerships that prevent AQ from maintaining or establishing alliances with governments, political parties, tribal groups, or non-state actors around the world. Through bilateral and multilateral efforts with other governments and international organizations, we emphasized the global nature of the terrorist threat and the necessity of cooperative action to combat it. This included diplomatic pressure to ensure that uncooperative nations fulfilled their international legal obligations to address terrorist activities. It also meant a continued political focus on countries like Somalia, Indonesia, Egypt, Pakistan, Yemen, Saudi Arabia, and Algeria which had indigenous terrorist organizations that had affiliated with AQ. In addition, we were highly concerned about the formation of cooperative relationships between AQ and organized criminal syndicates with certain functional expertise such as document forging, illicit finance, computer hacking, human smuggling, and arms trafficking.

· **Fight the War of Ideas.** Another pillar of this Administration's policy was to reduce the AQ leadership's impact by challenging its ideology and moral authority. We have worked to counter misperceptions about U.S. goals and intentions that AQ has sought to exploit. They include illumination of the facts and AQ's own actions which undercut AQ's message. For example, although AQ cites transgressions against the Palestinians and the U.S. invasion of Iraq as primary grievances requiring violent response, AQ plotted attacks in the 1990s during times of progress in the Middle East peace process, and AQ attacked the United States prior to our toppling of Saddam Hussein. We launched a "War of Ideas" (WOI) that used public diplomacy, the media, and clandestine means to counter extremist/radical messages by publicizing credible Muslim voices that denounced violence and espoused moderate Islam. For example, broadcasts of speeches by UBL, Internet exchanges with Zawahiri, and fatwas by radical imams were all closely monitored for opportunities to respond and discredit their legitimacy within the Muslim faith. We also sought support from Islamic nations in disavowing AQ's claim to political or religious leadership of the Muslim ummah. Additionally, we have encouraged Muslim-majority nations to confront AQ's distortion of the call to jihad into murder of those they consider nonbelievers and apostates—Christians, Jews, and those of other faiths—as well as Muslims who disagree with them. Success in the WOI demands that we explain more effectively our values, ideals, policies, and actions internationally and support moderate voices willing to confront extremists and discredit radicals.

- **Establish layered defense.** This Administration's policies to disable the core senior AQ leadership responsible for managing the group's various global nodes as well as the global AQ network were intended to complement its strategy for defending the Homeland against terrorist attacks. Our offensive effort to thwart the most senior AQ leadership was the remote element of a broader plan that also included worldwide watch-listing of known terrorists so they could not travel to the United States; improving border control, immigration, and port security practices so terrorists could not enter the United States; and hardening our domestic critical infrastructures to better protect them from terrorist attacks.

WHAT HAS BEEN ACCOMPLISHED:

This Administration's strategy for eliminating the senior leadership of the AQ network, destroying its lines of support, and confronting its radical ideology achieved results, including:

- **High-value targets (HVTs).** Abu Zubaydah, KSM, successive AQ leaders who replaced them, and other AQ operatives involved with the 9/11 attacks have been captured and detained and await trial for war crimes. In addition, Abu Musab al-Zarqawi and other AQ lieutenants have been killed in military operations abroad. Even though the two most significant HVTs (UBL and Zawahiri) remain at large, their movement and communications have been severely restricted by personal security concerns. Those limitations have decreased their functional role in leading day-to-day AQ operations; however, they continue to serve as the inspirational core of AQ and oversee its strategic management. Actions taken in the FATA primarily in the second half of 2008 have resulted in significant setbacks for al-Qaida. Al-Qaida losses during the past year span the shura council, external operations, propaganda, facilitation, religious affairs, affiliates outreach, and paramilitary activities. This is testing the leadership's resilience and threatening operational capabilities rebuilt within al-Qaida's secure safehaven in 2006–2007.

- **Military operations.** Operation Enduring Freedom removed the Taliban from power in Afghanistan and deprived the AQ senior leadership of its safe haven there, although residual elements of the Taliban and AQ still conduct attacks on Coalition forces and the democratically-elected Afghan Government. AQ militants also joined other insurgents in Iraq to resist Operation Iraqi Freedom. United States military forces in 2006 killed the leader of AQ in Iraq (AQI) and dramatically reduced that organization's scope of operations by late 2007. Despite the continued presence of AQ operatives in both Afghanistan and Iraq—and strong senior leadership interest in making Iraq the central front of the war—neither country serves as an unchallenged base for AQ leadership today.

- **Financial pressure.** We have led an international campaign to combat terrorist financing that has made it harder, costlier, and riskier for AQ and other terrorist groups to raise and move money. Under the authority provided by Executive Order 13224, the USA PATRIOT Act Section 311, and United Nations Security Council (UNSC) Resolution 1267 and subsequent resolutions, we have created domestic and international mechanisms that have reduced the AQ leadership's sources of funding and capacity to operate ████████████████████ these programs have forced AQ to modify its ways of doing business, relying less on the formal financial system and more on informal value transfer systems (hawalas) and couriers. Our efforts in this case worked to address the modes that AQ and its affiliates are using to raise and move money.

- **Foreign partnerships.** Progress was made in strengthening political coalitions and maintaining international standards of accountability that will further confine the AQ leadership cadre. With varied levels of success, a broad array of counterterrorism (CT) activities have been pursued in concert with the Governments of Pakistan, Afghanistan, Iraq, Jordan, the United Arab Emirates, Saudi Arabia, and many more. After years of mixed CT efforts against AQ and associated militants, Saudi Arabia embarked on an aggressive campaign against AQ cells and activities in the Kingdom after the May 2003 attacks in Riyadh. These efforts resulted in almost total destruction of the known AQ presence in Saudi Arabia by 2007 and growing focus on attacking its international tentacles—and the crucial realization that AQ and its ideology pose a direct threat to the Kingdom. Southeast Asian nations have made great strides on the CT front, particularly in the Philippines and Indonesia. In Indonesia, for example, authorities have interdicted and brought to justice well over 100 terrorists, including those responsible for the deadly Bali bombings. UNSC Resolution 1373 imposes binding obligations on all states to suppress terrorist financing, improve border controls, enhance information sharing and law enforcement cooperation, and deny terrorists sanctuary. This diplomatic success has been reinforced by outreach and assistance programs through State, Treasury, DOD, DOJ, DHS, and the IC.

- **Counterradicalization efforts.** Progress has also been made in countering UBL's violent extremism as an ideology. Recent polls of Muslim communities around the world show that fewer individuals now support UBL or condone suicide bombings and other terrorist attacks against civilians. Although it is difficult to attribute such improvement to any specific event or policy measure, the trend is certainly positive, and reflects popular abhorrence of AQ's brutal tactics. In addition, several Islamic countries (including Jordan, Morocco, Indonesia, Malaysia, Singapore, and Saudi Arabia) have instituted domestic counterradicalization programs to refute the messages emanating from the senior AQ leadership.

FUTURE CHALLENGES:

While we have seen multiple instances of information sharing and action by partners to capture individual terrorists, disrupt plots, block financial flows, stem terrorist travel, and rehabilitate extremists, more remains to be done.

As we have expanded the coalition of nations assisting in the War on Terror (WOT), many of our foreign partners—particularly Arab or Muslim nations, and even those with long histories of combating home-grown Islamic extremists—have mixed report cards. Many have been reticent to attack AQ and its affiliates head-on until they were directly attacked or assessed that terrorists posed a direct threat to their regimes. To varying degrees, our partners and allies have made calculations to calibrate their response to the threat posed by AQ based on a mix of domestic political considerations, including not wanting to be seen as fighting America's war, fear of reprisal, and sustaining their regimes' power. Sustaining individual, and where possible multilateral, attention to the range of CT issues we confront requires sustained reinforcement at working and leadership levels, through law enforcement, intelligence, military, and diplomatic channels, as appropriate for each issue and country.

Our successors will continue to face some of the same difficulties this Administration has faced as well as new policy challenges resulting from the changing nature of AQ as an organization. Concerted attention will be required on:

- **Tribal areas in Pakistan.** UBL, Zawahiri, and other members of AQ's core leadership and operational cadre are hiding in the FATA or NWFP of Pakistan, along the border with Afghanistan, which are inhabited by Pashtun tribes. Despite multiple successes against AQ in the settled areas of Pakistan, the Government of Pakistan (GOP) has demonstrated neither the sustained will nor the capability to attack AQ effectively in the FATA, and has allowed AQ to foster strong relationships with the indigenous tribes, who view the GOP and its military as adversaries. In order to locate and apprehend the remaining HVTs, the United States military and intelligence community need to work effectively with Islamabad to combat militant insurgents and induce the local tribes to deny sanctuary to UBL and his associates. This will be a delicate political and diplomatic task given Pakistan's internal difficulties, tribal codes of honor (i.e., Pashtunwali), and the historical inclination in the region towards both fervent independence and religious conservatism. In addition, the United States Government is working to "internationalize" the problem presented by the FATA safe haven. This effort involves using existing multilateral bodies and bilateral dialogue with partner nations that have experienced terrorism stemming from the FATA directly, or recognize the need to act to counter the threat posed by the existing terrorist sanctuary in the FATA. We want to encourage these groups and nations to work together to encourage and assist Pakistan to address the FATA safe haven through concrete action.

- **Iraq and Afghanistan.** Each poses a unique situation, as we have attempted to help build CT infrastructure and institutions from the ground up. While we have seen measurable progress in the form of increasing numbers of troops and law enforcement personnel trained and deployed in CT-related disciplines, other key elements of a comprehensive CT program are more difficult to gauge, especially in the context of ongoing U.S. military and counterinsurgency operations. A key challenge will be combating AQ's attempts to regroup and return to Iraq in a more robust way. We must devote continued focus in each department and agency working with their Iraqi and Afghan counterparts to institutionalize CT tools and capabilities within an overarching commitment to rule of law and supremacy of the central government. We cannot overlook the necessity of proper engagement through all channels to overcome inherent cultural and tribal norms and tendencies that may run contrary to a functioning federal system.

- **Internet communications.** Senior AQ leaders, their subordinates, and affiliates use public websites and bulletin boards to disseminate propaganda, provide training material, recruit, raise funds, and conduct operational targeting.

- **Decentralized networks.** Today, AQ's global network is more dispersed and less centralized. Despite setbacks to its central leadership cadre in Pakistan, AQ's smaller nodes are seeking new means to recruit and organize followers, fund operations, and train their members. Decapitation of the organization will not sufficiently eliminate the threat of AQ-inspired terrorism; we must find new ways to identify and dismantle its functional cells which may begin to increase their involvement with other illicit networks.

- **Support from rogue states.** State sponsors of terrorism have ambiguous relationships with AQ that complicate and at times inhibit U.S. and international CT efforts. Syria, while fearing AQ penetration within Syria, has facilitated AQI operations in Iraq, primarily by allowing the flow of foreign fighters to continue. While detaining certain AQ members in Iran, Iranian forces also have helped promote Taliban and other insurgent attacks against U.S. interests in Iraq and Afghanistan. In 2003 and 2004, Iran detained several key AQ affiliates, including five senior AQ Management Council members as well as three of UBL's sons and their families. We believe Iran is holding these individuals as a bargaining chip against both the international community and AQ itself. Where and when possible, we need to continue to use available and appropriate public or private means to drive wedges between rogue states and AQ by fostering mistrust, aggravating inherent tensions (i.e., Sunni-Shi'a), and making each side think seriously about the possible consequences of cooperation with the other.

- **Lack of established international legal regime.** The international community is hampered by a lack of consensus on what type of legal model and rules should apply to combat the international terrorist threat. In the first instance, there remains a divide between those who view the WOT as an actual war and those who maintain that terrorism should be treated primarily as a law enforcement problem. This then creates conflicts with respect to what type of jurisprudence is applied—the laws of war, or criminal laws, or something else altogether. Despite the use of existing unilateral and multilateral regimes to address components of the problem, there are still no agreed-upon standards of proof, evidence, procedures, and sentences and how they should be applied against a loosely-connected global terrorist network.

Continued dedication to the U.N.'s 1267 and 1373 regimes—and reform when necessary—will be required to ensure that the international progress to date is not lost. In particular, the 1267 Committee and its listing/delisting procedures are currently receiving international scrutiny. Bilateral diplomatic efforts to date also have fallen short of obtaining legal cooperation from certain countries, such as Yemen, or all of the government officials among certain partners in the WOT, such as Pakistan. Maintaining or improving our political alliances to the detriment of AQ's senior leadership will be a challenge in the future.

- **Building additional strategic CT partnerships.** Building long term international strategic relationships and institutions for the WOT is critical to our success. For example, Turkey, India, Russia, and China could all serve as more aggressive and proactive partners in the WOT, including in the ideological battle against violent Islamic extremism.

All four countries have been targets of the global terrorist movement, but each remains focused intensely on the internal threats posed by extremist organizations and have yet to turn their resources, diplomatic attention, and influence appropriately to the threat of the broader global movement and the ideology that fuels it. Each also brings unique assets and influence, in particular in South and Central Asia, that we should be harnessing. At the same time, these are countries that are eager to have the United States and international community validate their internal security threats as part of the broader global terrorist threat regardless of such connections. Thus, we must continue to devote intensive diplomatic and political attention to changing the status quo and building focused and long-term CT relationships with these countries.

- **Domestic legal challenges.** We must address the lack of a comprehensive, sustained legal detention framework. We face recurring judicial challenges, including likely setbacks for both the Executive and Legislative branches. A significant challenge will be protecting against any possible acts of terror if certain detainees are released and return to the battlefield. Future Administrations will have to continue to work to develop detention, interrogation, and prosecution frameworks that receive the support of all three branches of government.

- **AQ feeding off of disillusionment.** The War of Ideas inevitably will continue in one form or another as various Islamic sects and Western voices compete for primacy before the Muslim populace. AQ has embedded its program into the larger set of Muslim community grievances and sense that "the West is at war with Islam." This approach also feeds into the demographic challenges facing several Arab and Muslim nations that have large populations of young men. Much work remains to be done on identifying and leveraging the appropriate credible voices and outlets that can effectively counter AQ's ideology of hatred and violence as well as discredit it as the vanguard of Islamic resistance to Western imperialism. The solution to this will come in the realization of hopeful futures and opportunities for the youth in Muslim communities around the world.

CONCLUSION:

Continually degrading al-Qaida's leadership and senior personnel ranks—including Bin Ladin and Zawahiri—remains a central factor to further reducing the organization's capacity to survive and threaten U.S. interests. Al-Qaida has proven a resilient enemy with a capable bench of replacements at various levels throughout the organization. To destroy the group—and in the process diminish its ability to recruit, raise money, and inspire—the United States must continue to identify and aggressively target the organization's most influential personnel and their replacements while dismantling their networks and support around the globe. We must also continue to push freedom as a hopeful alternative to extremism to further marginalize the terrorist message within Muslim societies. Continuing this approach will reduce al-Qaida's ability to conduct attacks and force it to spend its resources, energy, and time focused on survival.

Attachments
Tab 1   Chronology for Dismantling al-Qaida
Tab 2   Executive Order 13224 (September 25, 2001)
Tab 3   National Security Presidential Directive/NSPD-8 (October 24, 2001)

SEGRET WITH TOP SECRET/
TOP SECRET/   /NOFORN AND
TOP SECRET/   /ORCON/
NOFORN ATTACHMENTS

4247
Transition

THE WHITE HOUSE
WASHINGTON

January 16, 2009

MEMORANDUM FOR THE RECORD

FROM: JUAN ZARATE, COMBATING TERRORISM

           JOHN DUNCAN, COMBATING TERRORISM

SUBJECT: Combating Terrorist Financing and Using Financial
           Tools to Isolate Rogue Actors

THE SITUATION AS WE FOUND IT:

When the Administration took office, there was neither a comprehensive international or domestic campaign to combat terrorist financing nor a commitment to use targeted financial sanctions as a primary national security tool. The United States Government also lacked a strategy and the related tools to leverage our financial power and influence—especially with the private sector—to isolate rogue actors from the legitimate financial system as an integral part of our national security policy.

Though there was not a concerted campaign to attack the financial underpinnings of terrorism, there were basic elements and vehicles in place internationally and domestically focused on targeting terrorist financing and money laundering.

Internationally, the International Convention for the Suppression of the Financing of Terrorism (1999) along with United Nations Security Council Resolution (UNSCR) 1267 (1999), targeting al-Qaida (AQ) and the Taliban and related individuals, set forth the requirements for countries to criminalize terrorist financing, freeze assets, share information, issue travel bans, and impose arms bans. Anti-money laundering systems and controls—put in place in the 1980s and 1990s to address classic money laundering—were well established, and multilateral bodies like the Financial Action Task Force (FATF) defined and enforced global standards.

SEGRET WITH
TOP SECRET/
TOP SECRET/   /NOFORN AND
TOP SECRET/   /ORCON//NOFORN ATTACHMENTS
Reason: 1.4(b) (d)
Declassify on: 1/16/19

NSC Declassification Review [E.O.13526]
DECLASSIFY IN PART
by William C. Carpenter 3/23/2020
    Re-Classified by: Ellen J. L. Knight
    Reason: 1.4(d)
    Declassify on: 1/16/2034

Domestically, the United States Government had developed rudimentary tools and mechanisms to address the problem of terrorist financing. The United States had in place two Executive Orders (E.O.s) related to the Middle East Peace Process that allowed for the freezing of assets of Usama bin Laden and others who threatened the peace process, as well as an E.O. prohibiting transactions with the Taliban. Although our sanctions policy continued to rely on traditional state-based sanctions, other programs, such as in the drug trafficking arena, focused on application of targeted financial sanctions against individuals and entities. The anti-money laundering system was geared toward defending against classic drug-based money laundering in the banking sector and had not expanded to new sectors or to address methods of money movement related to terrorist financing. There were counterterrorist financing and material support criminal provisions in U.S. law, but those provisions had been used sparingly to prosecute terrorist supporters or organizations.

While focus on terrorist financing was limited or specialized, Usama bin Laden, AQ, and their allies had developed a robust global network of donors and facilitators actively raising and transferring funds. These individuals transferred funds through bank accounts, charities, fronts, and informal transfer mechanisms like hawala on behalf of AQ and their allies. In addition, rogue nations took advantage of the international financial system by using front companies, bank accounts, and illicit financing schemes to raise and move money—with little fear of scrutiny from international financial regulators or the private sector.

THIS ADMINISTRATION'S POLICY:

After 9/11, the Administration decided to use financial tools and powers to drive an international campaign to disrupt and dismantle terrorist financing networks and isolate rogue actors from the formal financial system. Our goal has been to disrupt terrorist attacks and the functioning of networks, and to force our enemies to make resources allocation choices and alter their strategic approach because of resource constraints. This policy utilized all elements of national power— including deeper and broader use of focused intelligence; law enforcement tools; administrative and targeted financial sanctions and actions; regulatory structures and laws; and international cooperation, capacity building, and standard setting.

On September 23, 2001, the President signed E.O. 13224, which expanded the authority to freeze the assets of terrorist organizations, individuals, those who support or financially facilitate their activities, or those otherwise associated. E.O. 13224, and the designations that resulted both domestically and at the UNSCR 1267 Committee, set in motion an international campaign concentrated on the use of targeted financial power and tools to isolate terrorist actors.

The Administration's policies and efforts to address terrorist financing were captured throughout the President's strategic War on Terror and anti-money laundering policy documents, including the

National Money Laundering Strategies (starting in 2003), NSPD 46/HSPD 15, the June 2006 and August 2008 National Implementation Plans for the War on Terror (NIP), and specifically in the June 2006 National Strategy to Combat Terrorist Financing (NSCTF). The NSCTF recorded our strategic approach and prioritized the finance-related counterterrorism ▒▒▒▒▒▒▒▒ tasks and activities set forth in the NIP. The strategic priorities identified in the NSCTF were:

This strategy was then converted into a more operational National Action Plan to Combat Terrorist Financing (NAPCTF). This plan is designed to coordinate, integrate, and synchronize existing and future efforts to combat terrorist financing at home and abroad.

Increasing use of PATRIOT Act Section 311 provisions set in motion the targeted financial isolation of financial entities and jurisdictions that enable terrorists, state sponsors of terrorism, sanctions evasion, money launderers, and international organized criminal actors.

WHAT HAS BEEN ACCOMPLISHED:

The Administration has achieved success in building the legal and policy framework, as well as tools necessary to prosecute an international campaign against terrorist financing and against rogue actors engaged in activity of national security concern. There now exists an established international framework to combat terrorist financing, proliferation financing, and other transnational illicit financial activity. These efforts have had real world effects, with intelligence and law enforcement services focused on collecting and sharing financial data; the private sector sensitized to their obligations to prevent illicit activity from transpiring; terrorist cells and support networks being identified and dismantled; and evidence that AQ and like-minded terrorists find it harder, costlier, and riskier to raise and move money globally.

Use of Targeted Financial Sanctions

The President's issuance of E.O. 13224 in September 2001 authorized the Secretaries of the State and Treasury to bring the Executive Branch's broad financial authorities to bear upon terrorist organizations and their support networks. Through the subsequent designation of entities as terrorist organizations and enforcement of Office of Foreign Assets Control (OFAC) sanctions, more than 460 individuals and entities have been identified publicly, resulting in freezing any related assets in the United States, blocking transactions occurring through U.S. banks, and prohibiting U.S. persons from having any financial dealings with them.

The Administration has used this tool to expose and disrupt the financial networks of several terrorist groups beyond AQ and the Taliban including, Hizballah, Hamas, Jemmah Islamiyya (JI), the Salafist Group for Preaching and Combat (GSPC)/AQ in the Islamic Magreb (AQIM), and AQ in East Africa. Our efforts have impacted their fund-raising efforts throughout the Middle East, Horn of Africa, Southeast Asia, South America's Tri-Border Area, Europe, and the United States. These actions have often been complemented by law enforcement actions, such as those taken against the Holy Land Foundation for Relief and Development, a HAMAS charity used as a financing vehicle in the United States. Before September 11, 2001, the Department of Justice had charged fewer than a dozen individuals with terrorist financing. As of December 2008, the Justice Department had charged 164 people with terrorist financing offenses.

Those purely domestic enforcement actions have driven the complementary international designations using the United Nations (U.N.) framework established in UNSCR 1267. All U.N. member states are obligated under Chapter VII to freeze the assets of individuals and entities listed under UNSCR 1267. According to an intelligence assessment issued in August 2006, countries and territories had frozen 893 AQ-linked accounts totaling $85 million and 830 Taliban and unspecified other terrorist accounts totaling $66.7 million. Our diplomatic efforts have been instrumental in passing subsequent UNSCRs, including UNSCR 1373 and UNSCR 1535, which set forth clear requirements for U.N. member states to combat terrorist financing.

In addition to their disruptive effects on terror finance networks, these enforcement mechanisms have had a deterrent impact on individuals, companies, charities, and NGOs that might otherwise have intentionally or negligently contributed funds to terrorist organizations. The fear of being "named and shamed" or having their other business operations disrupted has served as an effective deterrent to prevent additional illicit financial activity.

These actions in combination provided us with a mechanism to encourage allies—like Saudi Arabia—to address terrorist financing vulnerabilities. For example, the designations of Saudi financiers and charities, like Saudi-based Al-Haramain, served as an action-forcing event for the

Saudi Government to take serious steps to address systemic issues of concern and shut down identified sources and flows of terrorist financing. After the AQ attacks in Riyadh in May 2003, the Saudis began a campaign to dismantle AQ within the Kingdom.

Established Legislative and Regulatory Architecture

With the passage of the USA PATRIOT Act, the United States Government broadened and deepened the application of anti-money laundering regulations to new sectors vulnerable to terrorist financing while expanding financial information sharing and protections. This included expansion of "know your customer" requirements, which placed additional obligations on the private sector to engage in due diligence with respect to transactions and customers. It also gave the Secretary of the Treasury new tools to address "primary money laundering" concerns. In addition, Treasury and the IRS worked closely with the NGO community and private sector groups to increase transparency in the financial dealings of charitable organizations susceptible to abuse by terrorist organizations, including the issuance of voluntary guidelines for the nonprofit sector to address the threat from terrorists' abuse of the sector.

These new laws and regulations were enforced in a manner that underscored the importance of the regulations and the risks attendant to the private sector, especially major international banks. Stiff financial penalties and actions after 9/11 against institutions like UBS, Riggs Bank, the New York branch of Arab Bank, and AmSouth for money laundering, terrorist financing, and sanctions violations served as remediation and deterrent tools that conditioned the international financial system.

Terrorist Financing-Focused United States Government Institutions and Intelligence

The intelligence and law enforcement communities have organized themselves to focus on following the money and fully exploiting available financial data. With the emergence of the collectors began a concerted effort to focus on money flows to uncover cell activity. This was complemented by the creation of the interagency Foreign Terrorist Asset Tracking Center led by Treasury's Office of Foreign Assets Control and later the Treasury's Office of Intelligence and Analysis.

The United States Government expanded relationships with the financial community, ████████ ████████████████████████████████ to take advantage of financial data available. The signature program developed after 9/11 to uncover and track terrorist financing connections was the Treasury's Terrorist Financing Tracking Program (TFTP). Under TFTP, Treasury has issued subpoenas for terrorist-related data to the Society for Worldwide Inter-Bank Financial Telecommunication (SWIFT), a Belgian-based company with U.S. offices that operates a worldwide messaging system used to transmit financial transaction information. These subpoenas require SWIFT to provide Treasury with certain financial records for use in terrorism investigations. The information obtained through TFTP, in combination with other data, has proven invaluable in linking suspect individuals and organizations and leading to plot and cell disruptions. (The New York Times made this program public in June 2006, only later to apologize for the revelation given the program's legality and apparent effectiveness.)

The law enforcement community responded by creating several programs designed to focus enforcement attention on suspect financial activity that could be tied to terrorism.

The President and Congress created Treasury's Office of Terrorism and Financial Intelligence in 2004, to incorporate a focused intelligence function along with the policy and operational tools already available to the Treasury. That office continues to lead efforts to use our financial intelligence and powers to advance our national security interests.

International Framework and Capacity Building

Since 9/11, the campaign against terrorist financing has been international in scope given the nature of the global financial system and the location of much of the suspect financial activity of concern to the United States Government. In 2001, the Financial Action Task Force (FATF) and the Egmont Group of Financial Intelligence Units (Egmont Group) established new international standards and requirements to address the threat of terrorist financing.

The United States Government has offered and provided technical assistance and training across the globe and helped establish a G-8 Counterterrorism Action Group (CTAG) to facilitate training focused on terrorist financing further increasing the capacity of key foreign partners. In addition, the United States Government has raised the profile and increased awareness of the importance of disrupting terrorist financing through continued emphasis in bilateral and multilateral fora.

Disruption of Terrorist Finance Activity

Quantitative measures like assets and accounts frozen and terrorist financing arrests alone are not always sufficient to measure the effectiveness of our terrorist financing campaign. Anecdotal information can often provide a window into the effectiveness of our overall counter terrorist financing efforts.

Isolation of Illicit Financial Activity by Rogue Actors

The tools and framework applied in the campaign against terrorist financing have resulted in the isolation of rogue actors from the international financial system. This has been the case especially with our attempts to pressure state sponsors of terrorism to change their behavior of concern—whether it be terrorist financing/support, money laundering/financial crimes, or WMD proliferation. As a result, North Korea and Iran are struggling to reestablish banking relationships worldwide.

Beyond North Korea and Iran, this Administration has put in place new measures to isolate other rogue states and actors:

- We have used a targeted sanctions program against Sudanese Government leadership, combined with outreach to banks—such as France's PNB Paribas—to pressure the regime.
- With Burma, we have used targeted sanctions, in particular against financial facilitators for the military junta, and financial pressure against Singaporean and Thai institutions to squeeze the regime's access to the legitimate financial system.
- In Lebanon, we have designated Hizballah-related financial entities while preemptively warning key Lebanese actors of potential sanctions against those that might form a parallel government to challenge the Siniora government.

- In Belarus, we have designated Lukashenko, several officials involved in the disappearances of political opponents or in rigging elections, and commercial entities linked to them.
- In the context of the Merida Initiative with Mexico, we are expanding the use of targeted financial sanctions to expose and isolate drug cartel networks, as seen in the December 2007 Treasury actions against financial nodes of the Sinaloa cartel.

FUTURE CHALLENGES:

The following issues will be essential to expanding upon the progress that this Administration has already had in combating terrorist financing and in using our financial tools and suasion to isolate rogue actors from the legitimate financial and commercial worlds:

Alternate Mechanisms: We are facing a clever and adaptive enemy that takes precautions to cover its tracks and has learned that the use of the formal financial system presents clear vulnerabilities. Thus, the IC, regulators, and the law enforcement community will have to adapt quickly to changing circumstances and tactics—to include our enemies' use of new payment/value and transfer mechanisms, including through the Internet and cell phones.

Challenges to the Financial Sanctions Regime: The international community is now seeking additional transparency for both the listing and delisting procedures of the U.N.'s 1267 regime. There are also ongoing challenges in courts (European Court of Justice, U.K., U.S.) and in the court of diplomatic opinion to preventative targeted financial sanctions, with arguments that there are insufficient due process safeguards in place to protect the designated individuals. As we did with the passage of UNSCR 1822, the United States Government must continue to shape this debate and participate in the 1267 reform process by helping craft more efficient listing procedures as well as expeditious and better publicized delisting procedures.

Addressing Effect of Enforcement Actions: Our enforcement actions have been effective, but certain actions—like the shutdown of Islamic charities that were used by terrorists to raise and move funds—have created the perception in some quarters that our policies are anti-Islamic. As the campaign against terrorist financing continues, we will need to remain sensitive to the perceptions of our actions and take appropriate steps to explain the reason for our actions to the communities affected and create measures that limit the negative impact.

CONCLUSION:

The campaign against terrorist financing and the new paradigm using financial tools and suasion to isolate rogue actors from the international financial system were the direct result of the President's leadership, demonstrated at the outset by the issuance of E.O. 13224, which effectively served as the "first shot" in the War on Terror post-9/11. The legal and regulatory framework, the new institutions and structures, the innovative intelligence focus and discipline, the refocused international mechanisms and partnerships, and the overall strategic approach created by this Administration in this field will outlive its tenure. The President's leadership has set the stage and empowered the United States Government and international community to use a whole new set of tools and approaches for advancing our Nation's security.

Attachments

Tab 1   Chronology for Combating Terrorist Financing and Using Financial Tools to Isolate Rogue Actors

Tab 2   United Nations Security Council Resolution 1267 (October 15, 1999)

Tab 3   Executive Order 13224 on Terrorist Financing (September 24, 2001)

Tab 4   President Freezes Terrorists' Assets (September 24, 2001)

Tab 5   White House Fact Sheet on Terrorist Financing Executive Order (September 24, 2001)

Tab 6   The War on Terrorism at Home and Abroad: Financial Actions (October 2001)

Tab 7   Agendas and Related Attachments for NSC Deputies Committee Meetings on Extension of Executive Order Freezing Assets of Terrorist Groups and Associates (October 16, 2001) and on Campaign Strategy (October 24, 2001)

Tab 8   Summary of Conclusions of NSC Deputies Committee Meeting on Campaign Strategy (October 16, 2001)

Tab 9   USA PATRIOT ACT, Title III, International Money Laundering Abatement and Anti-Terrorist Financing Act of 2001 (October 24, 2001)

Tab 10   President Announces Crackdown on Terrorist Financial Network (November 7, 2001)

Tab 11   Terrorist Financial Network Fact Sheet (November 7, 2001)

Tab 12   Summary of Conclusions of NSC Deputies Committee Meeting on Terrorist Financing (December 3, 2001)

Tab 13   President Announces Progress on Financial Fight Against Terror (December 4, 2001)

Tab 14   Fact Sheet on Shutting Down the Terrorist Financial Network (December 4, 2001)

Tab 15   Summary of Conclusions of NSC Deputies Committee Meeting on Terrorist Financing (December 13, 2001)

Tab 16   President Blocks More Assets in Financial War on Terrorism (December 20, 2001)

Tab 17   Fact Sheet on Day 100 of the War on Terrorism: More Steps to Shut Down Terrorist Support Networks (December 20, 2001)

Tab 18   Agenda and Related Attachments for NSC Deputies Committee Meeting on Terrorist Financing (June 20, 2002)

Tab 19   Summary of Conclusions of NSC Deputies Committee Meeting on Terrorist Financing (June 20, 2002)

POSTSCRIPT

NICHOLAS RASMUSSEN

In the aftermath of the 9/11 attacks, it was clear that previous approaches had largely failed and that the threat posed by international terrorism was likely to be a generational one. Success would not be achieved solely by dismantling a single terrorist network, not even the one that carried out the 9/11 attacks. A key tenet of the Bush administration's approach was that the strategy needed to be a truly whole-of-government effort leveraging all elements of national power—not relying solely on law enforcement, or military, or intelligence, or public diplomacy, but a well-integrated effort involving all these tools. Throughout, the Bush administration recognized that this would require a whole new set of institutions to develop the necessary capacities and to coordinate them effectively in support of the strategy (covered in the "Institutionalizing the War on Terror" Transition Memorandum).

The Bush Administration Approach

President Bush laid out five core principles for the strategy he would pursue in dealing with the terrorist threat:

- Take the fight to the enemy abroad so we do not have to fight them here at home.
- Preempt national security threats and do not let them gather unaddressed.
- Violence against innocent civilians is never justified by any cause or creed.
- If you harbor a terrorist, you will be treated as a terrorist.
- We will counter the ideology of violent extremism with a positive vision of freedom.

President Bush's War on Terror strategic framework sought to disable and ultimately dismantle the al Qaeda (AQ) network by focusing on the key factors that had enabled the group's growth as a terrorist organization with presence and reach across the globe:

1. *AQ's strong and centralized leadership structure.* Usama Bin Ladin and a cadre of other senior leaders and operatives provided both strategic vision and operational capacity to the organization. The War on Terror strategy

sought to incapacitate this group of senior leaders through a coordinated set of military, intelligence, and law enforcement operations to take them off the battlefield. This effort neutralized Khalid Sheikh Mohammed and others involved in the 9/11 attacks; Abu Musab al-Zarqawi and other AQ leaders in Iraq; and successive generations of key AQ operational and other key leaders in various locations. The effort included attempts to capture and interrogate key AQ operatives to obtain intelligence so as to prevent additional attacks and destroy the terrorist network, thereby saving lives.

2. *AQ's safe haven in Afghanistan prior to 9/11 and in the Federally Administered Tribal Areas (FATA) of Pakistan after the group was largely displaced from Afghanistan.* Physical safe haven allowed al Qaeda to recruit and train new members, engage in operational planning, and serve as a launching pad for future terrorist attacks. Equally important, safe havens also enabled the group to advance a narrative that it was capable of remaining beyond the reach of US military power, despite the resource and technological advantages enjoyed by the United States and its allies. Accordingly, mounting military operations targeting terrorist leaders and operations was critical to ensure that there was no piece of territory where al Qaeda senior leadership could operate freely without fear of disruption by the United States, its allies, and partners. The administration also sought to help governments in Afghanistan and Pakistan (and Iraq) develop the capability of preventing their territory from being used to mount terrorist operations. Finally, the administration sought to limit the ability of AQ and other terrorist groups to conduct internal and external communications including command and control and propaganda functions.

3. *AQ's financial resources and funding sources.* Countering AQ's financing required harnessing and developing new forms of financial and economic information, tools, suasion, and diplomacy to prevent terrorists from accessing sources and channels of funding. The Bush administration significantly expanded the scope and use of new forms of targeted sanctions and proscribed conduct to target AQ and anyone providing financial support to any part of its network. The expansion of the international anti-money-laundering regime developed financial tools and intelligence specifically geared to dealing with issues of terrorism. Title III of the USA PATRIOT Act provided the baseline for the broadening and deepening of the anti-money-laundering system in the United States. These efforts were expanded multilaterally with

new regulations and international standards based on principles of financial transparency, information sharing, and due diligence.

4. *AQ's ideological appeal and rhetorical advantages over moderate Muslim voices* (covered in the "War of Ideas" Transition Memorandum).
5. *AQ's access to weapons of mass destruction (WMD-T)* (covered in the "Weapons of Mass Destruction (WMD) Terrorism" Transition Memorandum).

As noted above, under the Bush administration the US government and its international partners became very effective at using financial power and economic influence to constrain terrorist organizations. But of equal importance was enlisting the private sector to more aggressively monitor the integrity of the financial system. Private-sector actors—most importantly, banks—could often drive the isolation of rogue entities more effectively than governments—with the banks motivated to avoid any direct or indirect financial ties to terrorists principally by their own self-interest and to avoid unnecessary business and reputational risk. These measures are both defensive and offensive: in sealing the US financial system against terrorists and their supporters, banks could ensure its continued soundness and reputation; in denying these bad actors access to the most important arteries of international finance and trade, banks could cripple terrorists' ability to mount operations and move their money.

The Bush administration was also very active in enlisting international cooperation in physically, economically, and financially isolating AQ and other terrorists. It used the United Nations to give international legitimacy to those efforts (through such things as UN Security Council Resolution 1373) and built an international partnership organized around counterterrorism efforts. It sought to provide counterterrorism assistance to those countries (especially in the Middle East and Southeast Asia) that had indigenous terrorist organizations affiliated with AQ within their borders. And finally, the administration sought to help these countries disrupt terrorist operations and develop the capability of preventing terrorists from using their territory to mount operations against their neighbors.

In summary, as its institutional reforms and new capabilities came online, the Bush administration set out to incapacitate senior AQ leaders, eliminate terrorist safe havens, inhibit leadership communications, enforce physical and economic isolation, organize political opposition, and fight the war of ideas. These efforts resulted in the killing or capture of a number of high-value targets, an effective countering of radicalization, and a bevy of foreign partnerships.

In parallel with these efforts, of course, the Bush administration sought to establish a layered defense of the US homeland against terrorist attacks. It took steps including improved intelligence gathering, watch-listing against terrorists traveling to the United States, improving border controls, enhancing port security, securing domestic air travel, hardening critical domestic infrastructure, and improving the nation's ability to respond to any future terrorist attack.

What Has Happened Since the End of the Bush Administration?

Both the Obama and Trump administrations sought to carry forward and even accelerate progress aimed at dismantling al Qaeda. Indeed, with respect to the first three key elements of the Bush administration's War on Terror strategic framework—the effort to degrade and disable the senior leadership structure of al Qaeda, the effort to eliminate or dramatically shrink physical safe havens enjoyed by the organization, and the effort to disrupt its financial resources and funding sources—there is arguably more continuity than change across the administrations. Achieving these strategic objectives, however, became more challenging and complex as al Qaeda evolved and expanded its global presence via a network of franchise and affiliate groups in conflict zones across Africa, the Middle East, and Southeast Asia.

Under these two administrations, a succession of significant terrorist leaders has been removed from the battlefield. They include Usama Bin Ladin himself, and a large number of other key al Qaeda lieutenants located in the FATA. This list also includes the heads of al Qaeda affiliate organizations such as Nasir al-Wuyashi and Qasim al-Rimi (AQAP), and Ahmed Abdi Godane (al Shabaab). The United States also succeeded in eliminating successive leaders of al Qaeda in Iraq (AQI) prior to the group's transformation to ISIS (or ISIL) in 2013. ISIS leader Abu Bakr al-Baghdadi was killed by US military action in 2019.

The effort to eliminate or limit safe havens, on the other hand, has met with less success and remains a continuing challenge. In South Asia, al Qaeda still enjoys some degree of freedom in the tribal areas of Pakistan even though the group's leadership has been significantly degraded. President Biden's decision to withdraw US forces from Afghanistan and the concurrent takeover of Afghanistan by al Qaeda's longstanding ally, the Taliban, raises new concerns that transnational terrorist groups will reestablish a sanctuary there. Elsewhere, persistent conflict in Yemen, Somalia, and large portions of the Maghreb and

Sahel regions continues to offer attractive ungoverned or contested spaces that al Qaeda–affiliated organizations can exploit to their advantage.

The most significant development with respect to safe havens was the emergence of the self-declared caliphate by the Islamic State in Iraq and the Levant (ISIL) beginning in 2013, which culminated in the group's holding large swaths of eastern Syria and western Iraq for a period of years. ISIS was able to use local resources in Iraq and Syria to access banks and money; service businesses; tax shopkeepers; and smuggle oil, artifacts, and humans—all to maintain control, govern, and profit. This was a lesson for terrorist groups no longer relying on al Qaeda central leadership for funding, but instead finding ways to take advantage of local populations and resources they could control (like ports, goods, or trade routes).

Even with the physical defeat and elimination of the caliphate by US-led coalition operations by 2017, ISIL still enjoys a certain degree of sanctuary. At the same time, ISIL has also been able to capitalize upon local grievances, conflict, and unrest in parts of Africa and South Asia to create its own network of linked or affiliated extremist or terrorist organizations. While this does not match the level of territorial control ISIL enjoyed at its peak in Iraq and Syria, it does provide the organization a degree of global reach similar to that enjoyed by al Qaeda.

Beyond the persistent efforts pursued by both the Obama and Trump administrations to degrade al Qaeda and ISIL leadership, to address chronic safe-haven concerns, and to cut off funding, those administrations found themselves confronting a terrorism landscape that had changed significantly since the end of the Bush administration. The success that successive administrations enjoyed in limiting the mobility and freedom of movement of terrorists linked to al Qaeda and ISIL forced these organizations to adapt. When al Qaeda and ISIL leadership found it difficult or even impossible to organize attacks from abroad aimed at the US homeland, they turned to a strategy of mobilizing individual terrorists—wherever they could be found—who could be motivated to act against US or Western interests.

By late in the Obama administration, the clearest and most significant threat to the US homeland was posed by these Homegrown Violent Extremists or HVEs. These individuals were animated and galvanized by the terrorist ideology spread by al Qaeda and ISIL but were not formal members of those groups or even connected directly with them in any sort of command-and-control relationship. These individuals often acted alone or at most in very small groups of fellow HVEs, posing a particularly difficult challenge for law enforcement and intelligence organizations. In the absence of key indicators like formal membership in a group, prior travel to conflict zones, or direct communication with known terrorist operatives, it has become increasingly difficult for US counterterrorism authorities to identify and act against these potential terrorists before they engage in operational activity. In addition, the ability of terrorist groups themselves to network with one another, exchange information (including tactics and operational advice), and to engage in recruitment activities has been exponentially enhanced in recent years by ready access to the online environment.

The nature of the threat to the US homeland has changed fundamentally in recent years to the point where it cannot be evaluated in the same terms as that faced by the Bush administration. Threat assessments put forward by both the Trump and Biden administrations have made clear that the most significant terrorism challenge currently facing US policymakers emanates from Domestic Violent Extremists (DVEs), often drawing upon very specific forms of grievance tied to domestic political factors. The US intelligence community has labeled many of these DVEs as Racially or Ethnically Motivated Violent Extremists (RMVEs), a category that captures far-right actors, including white supremacists and other racially or ethnically motivated extremists, as well as actors on the far left. While the threat to the homeland from overseas—from international terrorist groups like al Qaeda or ISIL—has not been eliminated, in many ways it has been eclipsed in volume and intensity by the threat posed by domestic actors here in the United States. Of course, such domestic actors require a wholly different policy and strategy in response.

How Did the Bush Administration Do?

Many elements of the strategy pursued by the Bush administration proved effective. Although terrorism has not receded as a threat, the US homeland has not suffered another terrorist attack anywhere near the scale of the September 11 attacks in the two decades since. This alone would have been seen as a stunning and signal achievement in the early days of the War on Terror.

In addition, senior leaders in the AQ network and its affiliates have come under sustained pressure and many of them have been killed or captured. Military operations have prevented safe havens from being used for preparing attacks against the US homeland. Financial pressure has further strained terrorist networks and counterradicalization efforts have undermined the appeal of its ideology abroad. Finally, foreign partnerships have proven critical in preventing terrorists from getting toeholds in other countries and destabilizing their societies.

These fundamental approaches remain sound, even essential to success, particularly the focus on degrading the leadership of terrorist adversaries and eliminating their access to physical and financial safe haven. In an environment characterized by a dynamic global threat picture, it remains crucial that a persistent, offensive posture still be part of any effective counterterrorism strategy. That said, it can be argued that some elements of these approaches carried within them some internal contradictions or produced unintended consequences that created additional long-term terrorism challenges for the United States.

For example, the effort to go on the offensive and carry the fight to terrorist adversaries appears, even in hindsight, to have been the appropriate response to protect the American people and to keep them safe. At the same time, this forward-leaning, forward-deployed posture also contributed to a persistent and counterproductive narrative put forward by those same terrorist adversaries: that the United States was engaged in indiscriminate violence against peaceful Muslim populations. While that narrative was not then and is not now an accurate reflection of American policy and strategy, it continues to fuel grievances and provide powerful motivation and inspiration to many thousands of potential extremists and terrorists around the world. Successive administrations have struggled to manage this narrative challenge and will continue to do so.

The effort to eliminate completely the existence of physical safe havens for terrorists—especially in challenging environments such as Iraq and Syria, Yemen, Somalia, the Maghreb and Sahel regions of Africa, and South Asia as well—was perhaps destined to fall far short of complete success. The ability of the United States to deliver enduring and stable political and security outcomes in these parts of the world where conflict has been a feature of the landscape for decades has proven elusive, even with the sustained application of resources and political will. The enduring nature of the conflicts in Afghanistan, Somalia, and Yemen is a reminder of the limits of US power and influence in this regard.

Framing US counterterrorism efforts as a War on Terror twenty years ago was perhaps required as a means of uniting the American people around the idea of a resource-intensive, truly global campaign to defeat al Qaeda. That approach created a sense of great urgency and societal purpose at a moment in the nation's history where that was an imperative. At the same time, the War on Terror framework implicitly suggested a potential end point to the problem of terrorism, one that seems well beyond reach at present.

An alternative might be to frame US counterterrorism efforts as a persistent and enduring national security challenge to be pursued with sustained commitment, adequate resourcing, and flexible strategies and tactics. With the experience and wisdom gained from two decades of both successes and setbacks in US counterterrorism efforts, this kind of agile approach to a problem that is constantly evolving merits consideration in ways that may not have been possible in the immediate aftermath of the 9/11 tragedy.

What Are the Lessons Learned?

The clearest lessons to be learned from the experience of the post-9/11 period can be summarized as follows:

- *Continue to pursue counterterrorism as a national priority, even when threats seem more remote.* Sustained investment in the nation's counterterrorism and homeland security capacity remains a strategic imperative for the United States, even as other national security challenges emerge as equally if not more pressing. Permitting the counterterrorism enterprise built after 9/11 to atrophy or wither would invite some level of risk, because it would simply not be possible to easily rebuild that capability if it is needed once again. Efforts to rationalize, or "right-size," that counterterrorism enterprise must be pursued with this maxim in mind.
- *Continue to invest in relationships with allies, partners, and friends around the world who share our interest in effective counterterrorism work.* The network of global partnerships that is a critical element of post-9/11 counterterrorism efforts requires constant tending and reinforcement, lest it also wither and be unavailable when it is needed most.
- *Do not premise counterterrorism strategies and policies on the achievement of political and security outcomes that may well be beyond US capacity to deliver.* This point is illustrated most vividly, and most recently, with developments in Afghanistan. But the point can be made more broadly. The application of US resources and influence is likely necessary, but not sufficient, to address various regional security challenges that give rise to violent extremism and terrorism.
- *Develop an overarching strategy since individual tools cannot stand alone.* The same playbook that has been used successfully for prior campaigns

may not be the right approach for the next or a different campaign. For example, sanctions and other economic tools have been seen as either the only avenues for action to address a thorny national security issue or as silver bullets. But if these tools are to be effective, they must be used in service of an understood strategy and complemented by other tools of statecraft, power, and coercion.

- *Do not portray terrorism as a national security problem to be solved and then put to the side.* Rather, speak clearly to the American people about the enduring challenge posed by terrorism and violent extremism of various ideological flavors, thereby preparing them for what will remain a long-term effort requiring sustained investment and attention across future presidential administrations.

Contributors:
Zack Cooper
Juan Zarate

CHAPTER 3

Institutionalizing the War on Terror

MICHELE L. MALVESTI

The Bush administration pursued a long-term strategy drawing on all elements of national power to degrade and defeat al Qaeda and other terrorist enemies who threatened the United States and its interests, and its friends and allies across the globe. It recognized early on that securing the US homeland would be an enduring responsibility that necessitated a new array of transformational structures, processes, and partnerships. It therefore resolved to provide future presidents the capabilities they would need to combat terrorism and protect the homeland for decades to come.

TRANSITION MEMORANDUM

S̶E̶C̶R̶E̶T̶/NOFORN WITH
TOP SECRET████NOFORN
ATTACHMENT

THE WHITE HOUSE

WASHINGTON

January 16, 2009

MEMORANDUM FOR THE RECORD

FROM: JUAN ZARATE, COMBATING TERRORISM DIRECTORATE

             NICK RASMUSSEN, COMBATING TERRORISM DIRECTORATE

SUBJECT: Institutionalizing the War on Terror

THE SITUATION AS WE FOUND IT:

As the Administration took office, al-Qaida (AQ) posed a serious threat to U.S. interests. The group had conducted major attacks against U.S. interests overseas: in August 1998, simultaneous bombings of U.S. Embassies in Nairobi and Dar es Salaam; and in October 2000, the attack on the USS Cole during a port call in Yemen. AQ had also attacked the Homeland with the first bomb attack on the World Trade Center in February 1993. While the intelligence community assessed that the AQ senior leadership was determined to plan and carry out further strikes against U.S. targets, including potentially here in the Homeland, it was not clear what form the attacks would take or if AQ had the capability required to carry out a catastrophic attack.

The intelligence gaps and other systemic deficiencies that contributed to our vulnerability on September 11, 2001, are well documented. This paper will focus on the steps taken by the President and his Administration since September 11 to build capability and create new institutions to enable successful implementation of the President's counterterrorism (CT) strategy and on the challenges still ahead. Other Memoranda for the Record have been prepared to address additional specific War on Terror operations or policies: Attacking the AQ Network, WMD Terrorism, the War of Ideas, Combating Terrorist Financing and Intelligence Reform.

S̶E̶C̶R̶E̶T̶/NOFORN WITH
TOP SECRET████NOFORN ATTACHMENT
Reason: 1.4(a) (b) (c) (d)
Declassify on: 1/16/34

NSC Declassification Review [E.O. 13526]
DECLASSIFY IN PART
by William C. Carpenter 3/23/2020

THIS ADMINISTRATION'S POLICY:

The attacks on 9/11 made clear the need to develop a more aggressive, offensive-oriented strategy to destroy AQ. Having experienced a catastrophic attack on the Homeland, the President directed a new and different strategic paradigm for dealing with the terrorist threat. The United States will, whenever possible, act to preempt terrorist threats before they materialize. In the context of the War on Terror, this means taking an offensive approach—designed to prevent and preempt— against our terrorist enemies, their supporters, and their ideology. The President also outlined another paradigmatic shift when he stated during his September 20, 2001 address to the Joint Session of Congress and the American people that "from this day forward, any nation that continues to harbor or support terrorism will be regarded by the United States as a hostile regime." In carrying out the War on Terror, the President also indicated that "this is not just America's fight." Indeed, as the President said, this is the world's fight and "we ask every nation to join us."

The President's decision to attack AQ in the Afghan safe haven and to remove the Taliban from power demonstrated the practical application of this strategic shift.

The President's policy and strategy were articulated in more formal terms in the National Strategy to Combat Terrorism, issued in February 2003. The President's strategy outlined our strategic intent to:

- Defeat terrorist organizations;
- Deny terrorist organizations the sponsorship, support, and sanctuary they need to survive;
- Diminish the underlying conditions that lead people to embrace terrorism; and
- Defend against terrorist attacks on the United States, our interests, and our citizens.

In March 2006, the President issued NSPD-46/HSPD-15 to update the classified strategy and policy for winning the War on Terror. The document was drafted to reflect the progress that we had made since 2001, to take account of the adaptive nature of our terrorist enemy, and to acknowledge the growing realization that we were, in fact, engaged in a long war against the forces of violent Islamic extremism.

While the updated strategy did not fundamentally alter the approach set forth in the 2003 strategy, it underscored and explained with greater clarity the need to defeat violent extremism as a threat to our way of life and the requirement to create a global environment inhospitable to violent extremists and all who support them. NSPD-46 explained that our strategy has three key elements:

- Protect and defend the Homeland and U.S. interests abroad;
- Attack terrorists and their capacity to operate effectively at home and abroad; and
- Support Muslim efforts to reject violent extremism.

To enable successful implementation of the strategy, NSPD-46 also stated our intent to:

- Expand foreign partnerships and partner capacity;
- Strengthen our capacity to prevent terrorist acquisition and use of WMD; and
- Institutionalize domestically and internationally the war against terrorism.

The President's 2006 strategy therefore placed greater emphasis on the challenge of institutionalizing CT strategy to enable success in the long war against violent extremism. Departments and agencies invested in increased CT capacity immediately after 9/11. However, as we learned more about the gaps and seams in our defenses that had contributed to the success of the 9/11 attacks it was clear that we needed to develop new tools and create new institutions to address our shortcomings and position ourselves to win the long war.

WHAT HAS BEEN ACCOMPLISHED:

The President resolved to leave future Presidents with a robust set of new authorities, institutions, tools, capabilities, and relationships with which to carry out and ultimately win the War on Terror. Indeed, nearly all of the recommendations put forth by the 9/11 and WMD Commissions related to Executive Branch structures and institutions have been implemented by the Administration.

New Statutory Measures: Working with the Congress, the President and the Administration have sought to create an enduring statutory basis for the institutions and capabilities needed to win the War on Terror. The most notable pieces of legislation include:

- **USA PATRIOT Act.** On March 9, 2006, the President signed the USA Patriot Improvement and Reauthorization Act of 2005, which followed on the original USA PATRIOT Act of 2001. Both pieces of legislation enable the robust information sharing across the government that is essential to counterterrorism efforts and provide other authorities for our intelligence and law enforcement personnel.

- **Intelligence Reform and Terrorism Prevention Act (IRTPA).** On December 17, 2004, the President signed the Intelligence Reform and Terrorism Prevention Act (IRTPA), which among other things created the Office of the Director of National Intelligence (DNI) and the National Counterterrorism Center (NCTC).

- **FISA Legislation.** In July 2008, the President signed the FISA Amendments Act which provided the Intelligence Community with a durable framework for monitoring communications by terrorists outside the United States while also protecting the civil liberties of Americans at home.

- **Homeland Security Legislation.** Since 9/11, the President and Congress have worked together to pass new statutory measures on homeland security and defense initiatives that have improved our layered defenses. There are several examples. The Aviation and Transportation Security Act of 2001 established the Transportation Security Administration; the Homeland Security Act of 2002 created the Department of Homeland Security; the REAL ID Act of 2005 established Federal standards for State-issued driver's licenses and non-driver's identification cards; and the SAFE Ports Act of 2006 further improved port security requirements and enshrined into law ongoing Administration initiatives like the Container Security Initiative. These and others pieces of legislation codified important homeland defense programs and principles that will continue to allow us to screen people and goods in order to protect the Homeland.

- **Detention and Military Commissions Laws.** The President and the Congress have worked together to address the challenge of detaining and bringing to justice members of al-Qaida and affiliated terrorist organizations captured in the Global War on Terror. In December 2005, the President signed the Detainee Treatment Act, which sought to provide a sustainable structure for detaining enemy combatants in the armed conflict with al-Qaida and the Taliban. Specifically, the Detainee Treatment Act provided for administrative tribunals to evaluate the status of persons held at Guantanamo Bay, Cuba, and judicial review in federal courts thereafter. To that point, the statute provided more procedural protections than the United States or any other country had ever before given to wartime captives. In June 2008, the Supreme Court ruled in the Boumediene case that the Guantanamo detainees have the right under the U.S. Constitution to seek release (through a writ of habeas corpus) in U.S. federal court. The Supreme Court further ruled that the process afforded detainees in the Detainee Treatment Act was not an adequate substitute to federal court challenges to detention. Since the Court's ruling in June 2008, the Administration has been participating in those new proceedings in the federal district court in Washington, D.C. The initial habeas corpus cases are proving challenging. For instance, in the Boumediene case itself, the district court declined to credit an intelligence report relied upon by the Government because the record (for national security reasons) did not contain information about the underlying intelligence source. This resulted in the court ruling that the Government failed to demonstrate that the detainee was an enemy combatant.

In October 2006, the President signed the Military Commissions Act, which established detailed procedures for trying unlawful enemy combatants, such as the members of al-Qaida responsible for the 9/11 attacks, the assault on the USS Cole, and the bombings in Tanzania and Kenya. More than 20 members of al-Qaida have been charged under this new legislation. As of November 2008, there have been two military commission trials: the first trial of Salim Hamdan resulted in a conviction and a sentence of approximately 5.5 years' imprisonment, less credit for time served; the second trial of Ali Hamza al Bahlul resulted in a conviction and sentence of life imprisonment.

New Institutions and Expanded Capacity: The President and this Administration, along with Congress, have created new institutions to improve our CT performance. Resources, authority, and responsibility for critical parts of the CT and Homeland Security mission have been realigned and rationalized, providing greater focus and accountability. These new institutions include:

- **Office of the Director of National Intelligence (DNI).** While DNI's mandate extends well beyond terrorism-related intelligence, fulfillment of DNI's core mission—the collection, analysis, and dissemination of accurate, timely and objective intelligence—is critical to our CT mission.

- **National Counterterrorism Center (NCTC).** The President created the NCTC by Executive Order to serve as the primary organization in the United States Government for integrating and analyzing all intelligence pertaining to terrorism possessed or acquired by the United States Government. The NCTC fuses all terrorism information and has developed a rational, systematic process for managing terrorist identities and watchlists at the Federal level. By creating the NCTC, the President reduced the structural impediments to greater sharing of terrorism information and the production of the best possible analysis of terrorist threats. Now authorized by statute, NCTC continues to grow and develop additional capability. Progress made in terrorism information sharing across the Federal government is among our most significant achievements since 9/11.

- **Department of Homeland Security (DHS).** The merger of 22 separate government organizations into a single cabinet department represented the most fundamental restructuring of the Federal government since the Cold War. Prior to the creation of DHS, responsibility and accountability for the protection of the homeland were distributed across the Federal landscape. The President's decision to create a Homeland Security Council (HSC) and a Homeland Security Council staff, to mirror the policy making and coordination role played by the National Security Council (NSC) and NSC staff, was a critically important step to better organize the government to meet the threats that have emerged after the 9/11 attack on the Homeland. This has allowed the country to build a layered defense and push our border out to defend against terrorism in all its forms.

- **Terrorist Screening Center (TSC).** The TSC provides "one stop shopping" for every element of the Federal government charged with screening potential terrorists. TSC's database allows all government agencies to screen and run name checks against a single, comprehensive database that contains the most accurate, up-to-date information available to the United States Government. This reform of the watchlist process represents a landmark achievement and a major step forward compared to the pre 9/11 period.

- Departments and agencies have restructured internally to meet the CT challenge:

  - **The Central Intelligence Agency (CIA)** has significantly increased the size of its analytic cadre devoted to terrorism analysis, as well as the size of the National Clandestine Service, which counts operational CT work among its primary missions.

  - **The Department of Justice (DOJ)** established a National Security Division in order to create greater coordination and unity of purpose in combating terrorism between prosecutors and law enforcement agencies on the one hand, and intelligence attorneys and the Intelligence Community on the other.

  - **The Federal Bureau of Investigation (FBI)** in the period since 9/11 has redefined its primary mission to focus on the prevention of terrorist attacks, rather than on investigating terrorist attacks as a purely criminal matter. The Bureau has tripled the number of Joint Terrorism Task Forces (JTTFs), which are located in significant metropolitan areas around the United States. The FBI also engaged in a significant reorganization by creating a new National Security Branch to strengthen and integrate the Bureau's intelligence and investigative missions against the CT target. In October 2008, the Attorney General issued revised Guidelines for Domestic FBI Operations, which provide clear and uniform standards and procedures to govern the FBI's collection within the United States of national security threat information and foreign intelligence, as well as its conduct of national security investigations, among other things.

  - **The Department of Defense (DOD)** created homeland security-related policy offices in the Office of the Secretary of Defense to meet its expanding homeland security responsibilities and established Northern Command, for the first time tasking a combatant command to focus solely on defending the Homeland and improving coordination of DOD support to civil authorities.

  - Treasury established the **Office of Terrorism and Financial Intelligence (TFI)** to focus United States Government resources and tools to disrupt and dismantle the flow of terrorist financing and other illicit financial activity. This has created a new capacity in the United States Government to use our financial levers creatively with partners and the private sector to isolate rogue and illicit actors in the international financial system.

In addition to adding capacity and capability across the Federal government, the Administration also has sought to develop new and more effective patterns of cooperation among United States Government agencies and with foreign partners. As we looked back on what happened on 9/11, it was clear that, beyond the intelligence issues, there were also concerns about our ability as a government to integrate and coordinate action among all of the elements of national power—military, diplomatic, intelligence, law enforcement, economic, and homeland security.

Enhanced Interagency Planning. To address those concerns, the NSC and HSC, working with the NCTC, have undertaken an effort to change the way we develop and execute our counterterrorism strategies and plans, to ensure proper interagency coordination, integration, and synchronization of counterterrorism activities across the government. Under the terms of the IRTPA, NCTC was given specific responsibility for conducting strategic operational planning for counterterrorism activities, integrating all elements of national power.

Using the updated 2006 strategy as a point of departure, departments and agencies worked together under the auspices of NCTC to create the National Implementation Plan (NIP) to serve as the strategic planning blueprint for protecting the Homeland and winning the War on Terror. The aim of the NIP was to identify all of the tasks and activities that need to be accomplished to protect the Homeland and attack the enemy and its ideology, assign each of them to a lead agency or department, and then require the lead agency or department to target their programs and actions as necessary to accomplish our CT strategic objectives.

In August 2008, Principals approved the current National Implementation Plan, NIP 2008. This updated and streamlined planning document will set the counterterrorism policy agenda and guide United States Government efforts into the next Administration. Work on this approach to interagency planning continues, in conjunction with ongoing efforts to fully coordinate, integrate, and synchronize our CT activities.

In addition to building a comprehensive plan to win the War on Terror, the Administration also created smaller, more focused interagency action plans aimed at addressing particularly difficult or urgent aspects of the terrorism challenge and ensuring appropriate focus by departments and agencies. These plans included:

- The National Strategy to Combat Terrorist Travel (February 2006);
- The National Action Plan to Combat Foreign Fighters (June 2006);
-

- The National Action Plan to Combat Terrorist Financing (March 2007).

To ensure that the National Implementation Plan is being implemented in the context of specific regional terrorism problems, the Administration has developed Regional Guidance and Prioritization strategies for key regions of concern (Eastern Mediterranean, Europe, North Africa, Horn of Africa, South Asia, Central Asia, SE Asia and the Trans-Sahara) as well as tailored action plans dealing with country-specific terrorism challenges in places like

In each case, the application of these new interagency planning processes has helped ensure that all elements of national power were engaged in the effort to counter a particular tactic or capability employed by our terrorist enemies or to address a particular terrorism challenge in a key region.

During periods of heightened threat concern, particularly involving the Homeland, the Administration has turned to a senior level Interagency Task Force (ITF) mechanism to develop and oversee implementation of specific measures aimed at developing more intelligence on the particular threat streams of greatest concern and disrupting those plots. The ITF work is another example of the organizational and planning evolution underway in the CT community.

Expanded Foreign Partnerships. Beyond the work done internally to increase interagency coordination and integration, the Administration has both expanded existing foreign partnerships and created relationships with new counterterrorism partners to leverage our own efforts. Long-standing security cooperation with traditional partners such as the United Kingdom, France, Germany, Israel, Saudi Arabia, Thailand, and the Philippines has expanded even more deeply into the counterterrorism area, including real-time sharing of information, coordination of operations, and even in some cases joint activities and investigations.

With other states, such as Yemen, Libya, and Malaysia, the Administration has developed and nurtured cooperation on critical counterterrorism issues, even as other parts of the bilateral relationship remain underdeveloped or even troubled. The essential bottom line of our efforts has been the creation of a worldwide network of CT partnerships that can be drawn upon to address both imminent terrorism threats and more systemic issues that contribute to the spread of violent extremist ideology.

We are also seeing patterns of cooperation emerging in key regions in which regional powers are taking greater responsibility for addressing terrorism concerns within their regions, which makes U.S. involvement at the forefront of such efforts less essential. Australia and Singapore have played leadership roles in addressing terrorism in Southeast Asia, while Ethiopia and Kenya have done the same in East Africa. And we are increasingly looking to Saudi Arabia and the United Arab Emirates to lead the way in regional counterterrorism efforts on the Arabian peninsula.

We have also developed a variety of mechanisms to improve regional attention and approaches to CT. These have taken a variety of forms around the world, including the Trans-Sahel Counter Terrorism Partnership, East Africa CT initiative, trilateral security talks with Australia and Japan, and the 3-plus-1 (Argentina, Brazil, and Paraguay) discussions in the Triborder area. This is then amplified by the State Department-led Regional Strategic Initiatives (RSI) intended to bring collective United States Government focus to problematic CT issues of regional concern. The RSI process is an important part of the effort to develop and implement regional CT strategies tailored to the specific threat picture and particular partner arrangements we have in regions around the world.

Multilateral Efforts to Combat Terror. Another accomplishment in the Administration's efforts to institutionalize the War on Terror has been the steps taken to energize multilateral institutions to address terrorism issues. The Administration has, with tangible results, pushed both United Nations (U.N.) member states and the U.N. bureaucracy to make the U.N. relevant and effective in the effort to combat terrorism. UNSCR 1267 and successor resolutions require member states to impose asset freezes, travel bans, and other sanctions on groups or individuals associated with bin Laden, AQ, or the Taliban. Shortly after 9/11, the UNSC also issued UNSCR 1373, which obliges member states to take a number of measures to prevent and criminalize terrorist-related actions, and created a U.N. Counterterrorism Committee to monitor and report on state compliance.

Beginning in 2002, successive G-8, APEC, and NATO Summit documents also have reflected agreement to take concrete action to combat terrorism, particularly in the terrorist financing area. These multilateral, diplomatic efforts complement the operational counterterrorism work underway with partner nations, and they ensure that terrorism issues remain on the agenda of important multilateral institutions.

FUTURE CHALLENGES:

More work needs to be done to institutionalize new United States Government capabilities to fight the War on Terror and in the international/multilateral realm. One key area of focus should be to make sure that the array of new laws and tools developed since 9/11 not be permitted to expire or otherwise be rolled back. The July 2008 FISA Amendments Act, which provides important authorities for monitoring communications by terrorists outside the United States, expires in 2012. Important authorities in the USA PATRIOT Act and subsequent reauthorizations expire at the end of 2009. It is essential that the U.S. government preserve, refine, and protect our CT tools.

Other areas of priority focus should include:

Updating the Legal Paradigm. As we work with international partners to identify, track, and apprehend known or suspected terrorists and otherwise prevent terrorist attacks, it is essential that we develop an enduring legal framework to govern these efforts. The question of how to address the threat posed by terrorist groups and individual terrorists, who often operate outside the reach of traditional legal tools, must be addressed on a multilateral basis. Any such framework should be developed in concert with key partner countries to lend legitimacy to the effort and avoid the impression that the United States is seeking to divine its own rules to deal with international terrorism and the AQ threat. Part of this effort will involve reexamining traditional notions of sovereignty, given the real and immediate threat posed by terrorists utilizing sovereign territory as a safe haven from which to plan and train for terrorist attacks. By establishing an enduring legal paradigm, our CT mission would be put on a more broadly accepted and sustainable foundation.

Creating a Widely Accepted Definition of Terrorism. A key companion piece to the effort to create an enduring, broadly accepted legal paradigm governing counterterrorism activities would be an effort to reach a consensus definition of terrorism within the international community. Widespread acceptance of a consensus definition would greatly facilitate multilateral action to disrupt and constrain terrorist-related activity and would allow us to move beyond traditional, and often stale and outmoded, debates about who exactly is a terrorist and what constitutes terrorist activity. We have made progress in this area since 9/11 with countries and international organizations adopting principles and positions that establish more clearly those acts that are considered to be terrorism and therefore unjustifiable under any circumstance. At this year's United Nations General Assembly, the President used his remarks to highlight and sharpen this emerging consensus, which will bolster efforts to discredit terrorists and the ideology of violent extremism.

Enhancing Interagency Integration. The progress that we have made in the creation of new interagency structures and institutions should not obscure the fact that we still have much to do to ensure that our CT efforts are properly integrated, coordinated, and synchronized. The kind of interagency strategic operational planning for CT that is underway at NCTC is an important first step in addressing shortfalls identified by the 9/11 Commission and others, but we are not yet at the point where we have achieved the necessary level of integration and synchronization of activities among all of the various departments and agencies with an operational role in the War on Terror.

Continuing Growth in CT Expertise, Collection, and Analytical Capability. The new institutions that we have created (NCTC, DNI, and others) have all made impressive strides in their early years, but require continued investment in human capital. Much of our CT work force, particularly the cadre of intelligence analysts tracking threats and producing finished intelligence analysis, is young and relatively inexperienced. Time will address the shortfall in experience among analysts, but we must continue recruit the best and brightest minds to work on the CT challenge within our intelligence, law enforcement, diplomatic, and military institutions. The investment we have made in HUMINT collection through increases in the numbers of case officers, as well as innovative and aggressive recruitment programs, must also be sustained over time if we are to gather the necessary intelligence to allow us to dismantle terrorist organizations.

Creating Additional New Institutions. As we have dealt with the challenge of combating violent Islamic extremism and prosecuting the War of Ideas, we have repeatedly bumped up against the question of whether existing institutions and authorities are sufficient to allow us to use all elements of national power and enlist private sector actors. We have worked to create pockets of expertise and assigned responsibility for countering Islamic radicalization within existing departments and agencies, but it is not clear that we are yet properly organized to address the long-term dimensions of violent Islamic radicalization in Muslim communities at home and abroad. A new construct to leverage private and public tools to counter the emerging radicalization in certain communities may be warranted.

Attachments

POSTSCRIPT

The Bush Administration Approach

The challenge of terrorism required the Bush administration to work with Congress to establish the following new institutions and authorities, as outlined in the Transition Memorandum.

- The Office of the Director of National Intelligence (DNI) was created to better coordinate the intelligence community's counterterrorism efforts into a more unified and effective whole.
- The National Counterterrorism Center (NCTC) became the primary US government organization for analyzing, sharing, and integrating all terrorism-related intelligence and developing and assessing the effectiveness of strategic operational planning efforts designed to achieve counterterrorism objectives.
- The Department of Homeland Security (DHS) consolidated under one authority the vital security missions of twenty-two previously separate federal entities to better help prevent and, as necessary, respond to terrorist attacks within US borders.
- The Terrorist Screening Center (TSC) combined and centralized terrorist watch lists and served as a one-stop shop in support of all federal screenings of potential terrorists.

Supporting the creation of these institutions were statutory measures that included the USA PATRIOT Act in 2001 and its reauthorization in 2006, and the Intelligence Reform and Terrorism Prevention Act (IRTPA), which President Bush signed into law in 2004. Beyond the 2002 Homeland Security Act that created DHS, the president and Congress also worked together to pass other legislative initiatives related to homeland security, including the Aviation and Transportation Security Act of 2001, which established the Transportation Security Administration (TSA); the REAL ID Act of 2005; and the SAFE Ports Act of 2006.

Existing departments and agencies also restructured internally, reprioritized their efforts, or did both in order to further strengthen the federal government's architecture for combating terrorism.

— The Department of Justice (DOJ) established its National Security Division, and the Federal Bureau of Investigation (FBI) redefined its primary mission from the criminal investigation of terrorist attacks to the prevention of terrorist acts. It created a new National Security Branch and tripled the number of its Joint Terrorism Task Forces (JTTFs), which facilitated information collection and sharing and operational collaboration on investigations.

— The Department of Defense established a new combatant command—US Northern Command—focused solely on defense of the homeland.

— The Department of the Treasury established the Office of Terrorism and Financial Intelligence (TFI) to disrupt the flow of terrorist and other illicit financing activities.

In order to strengthen coordination among these new organizations, offices, and mission sets, the administration also enhanced its interagency planning structures and processes through the creation of a Homeland Security Council (HSC) and an HSC staff.

A final key element in the Bush administration's efforts to institutionalize the War on Terror was strengthening and expanding international partnerships and partnership capacity. This included broadening cooperation with traditional US security partners to include a focus on counterterrorism while also nurturing counterterrorism collaboration with countries where the United States had an uneven or, in some cases, a challenging bilateral relationship.

The administration forged regional initiatives to combat terror, and many of the United States' most important successes in combating terrorism would be made possible through effective regional partnerships. These included the East Africa Counter Terrorism Initiative, the Trans-Sahel Counter Terrorism Partnership, and the 3-plus-1 (Argentina, Paraguay, and Brazil) discussion in the Tri-border area.

The administration also energized multilateral efforts that contributed to the United Nations passing UNSCR 1267 and UNSCR 1373. These resolutions sanctioned individuals and groups linked to al Qaeda or the Taliban, and placed obligations on member states to enact measures to help prevent terrorist-related activities, respectively. The administration's efforts led to consecutive NATO Summit, G-8, and APEC agreements to take concrete steps to defeat terrorism.

The Bush administration recognized that continued success would depend on a global coalition maintaining an unrelenting, united front against imminent terrorist threats and the spread of violent extremist ideology.

What Has Happened Since the End of the Bush Administration?

As anticipated, these efforts laid the foundation on which successor administrations built and pursued their own War on Terror initiatives. Both the Obama and Trump administrations continued to invest in and develop the key counterterrorism and homeland security institutions created during the Bush administration. Beyond these structural components, however, there are at least three other notable areas of continuity across the Bush, Obama, Trump, and Biden administrations that demonstrate how the nation has institutionalized its efforts to combat terrorism over the long term.

First is the continuation of robust interagency collaboration in the form of information sharing and the operational integration of authorities, expertise, and capabilities across all instruments of national power, including through various joint task forces and fusion centers. This is a result, in part, of institutional commitment and the interagency planning structures and processes that were put in place during the Bush administration. The Obama administration in 2009 ultimately integrated the Homeland Security Council staff with the long-established National Security Council (NSC) staff—a structural departure from the Bush administration's approach. This progression, however, reflected a maturation of staff processes rather than any dramatic organizational departure.

A second area of continuity is the persistent, powerful reliance on international partnerships to combat terrorism, even as the precise nature of those partnerships have changed over time in response to new and evolving threats. For example, in 2014, the United States helped establish a broad international coalition to defeat the Islamic State of Iraq and Syria (ISIS), ultimately diminishing the group's territory to a mere fraction of what it once controlled. Although the Trump administration did not embrace multilateral and coalition approaches to counterterrorism in the way the Bush and Obama administrations did, it continued to invest in the counterterrorism capacity and security capabilities of foreign partners. The Biden administration has also recommitted to revitalizing the nation's partnerships and alliances and reaffirmed the importance of working with partners to address terrorism and violent extremism.

A final noteworthy area of continuity has been the recognition across administrations that securing the US homeland is a responsibility built on a foundation of partnerships that extends beyond federal, state, local, and tribal governments to include efforts by communities, individual citizens, and the private sector. The result of this post-9/11 mindset shift has been to inculcate a broader culture of preparedness and resilience that is essential to America's security, enabling the country to better respond to and recover from terrorist attacks and other natural and man-made disasters. Beyond structures, processes, and institutions, the resilience of the American people may be one of the more enduring features of the efforts to institutionalize the War on Terror.

On balance, there has been more continuity than change over the past two decades of institutionalizing America's ability to protect and defend itself from terrorist attacks, but differences have manifested themselves across presidential administrations. Take, for example, the application of the nation's formidable direct action capabilities in combating terrorism. The Obama administration's approach to utilizing these assets to preemptively attack terrorist targets was a clear extension of policies pursued by the Bush administration. At the same time, President Obama also introduced a greater degree of structure and transparency to such decisions. Structure took the form of a Presidential Policy Guidance (PPG) document setting forth with specificity the standards being applied to such decisions. The effort to provide greater transparency included carefully crafted public explanations of both the policy process and the precise standards required for using these potentially lethal tools, as well as aggregate reporting on civilian casualties resulting from US actions.

How Did the Bush Administration Do?

The Bush administration appropriately anticipated that protecting and defending the US homeland from the scourge of terrorism would be a generational fight requiring a transformative approach to national security. Utilizing new structures and processes, the administration was able to develop and execute a National Strategy to Combat Terrorism in 2003 and an updated version in 2006; a National Strategy to Combat Terrorist Travel in 2006; and National Action Plans to Combat Foreign Fighters and Terrorist Financing (in 2006 and 2007, respectively). Various classified interagency counterterrorism (CT) strategies, policies, and plans also were developed, approved, and implemented through these integrative planning efforts. These included NSPD-46/HSPD-15 and its National Implementation Plan, which served as a strategic blueprint for the War on Terror.

While assessing effectiveness and performance can be fraught with pitfalls, the array of new systems, structures, and processes put in place after 9/11 has helped to achieve two durable outcomes: remedying systemic failures that rendered the country susceptible to the 9/11 attacks, and preventing another catastrophic international terrorist attack on US soil now for over twenty years. Given the threatening environment the Bush administration faced at the time, few would have predicted this record of success in the darkest hours following September 11, 2001, or that it would extend over three presidential administrations and into a fourth.

The Transition Memorandum forecast several key challenges and areas of focus that future administrations would need to prioritize in order to further institutionalize the ability of the United States to combat terrorism. Some—such as enhancing and further synchronizing the integration of our interagency activities, in addition to strengthening our intelligence collection, analytic capabilities, and broader counterterrorism expertise—have remained persistent challenges for all administrations. In recent years, these challenges have become even more formidable due, in part, to the Trump administration's systematic undermining of faith and confidence in US law enforcement and intelligence institutions and organizations. Other challenges identified at the time of the presidential transition in January 2009—such as achieving international consensus on a widely accepted definition of terrorism and associated legal paradigm that would further support multilateral action on a broader scale—may be less of a priority today while remaining a bridge too far. Notwithstanding, there has been significant progress in maintaining international standards of accountability, with countries and international organizations adopting and promulgating best practices in combating terrorism.

There are, however, two key areas where the Bush administration may not have fully anticipated the need for new institutional frameworks, given the terrorist landscape the country would face twenty years later. The first concerns the legal paradigm, where the Bush administration did not account for the full range of *domestic terrorism* issues as part of the enduring legal framework. As it surveys the terrorist threat landscape in early 2021, the Federal Bureau of Investigation (FBI) has elevated domestic terrorism, including far-right extremist organizations, as a national threat priority.[1] Early in the Biden administration, lawmakers on Capitol Hill reintroduced the Domestic Terrorism Prevention Act in order to strengthen the ability of law enforcement to investigate, prevent, and respond to acts of domestic terrorism—whether from the political right or the political left. There is a clear resolve to address this evolving threat while building on the structures and processes established in the wake of 9/11.

A second area still requiring an institutional framework concerns the relationship between the federal government and the private sector. As the Bush administration designed and matured its homeland security architecture, it created both formal and informal structures and pathways for engagement with key elements of the private sector—particularly the private entities that own and operate the majority of the nation's critical infrastructure. While they have helped produce important successes, these structures and pathways have not proven to be as robust when it comes to collaboration between government and the technology sector. No administration has managed to establish a sustainable framework for engagement between the federal government and the technology companies that provide the digital platforms on which a significant volume of terrorism-related activity has occurred. Engagement remains episodic and ad hoc rather than strategic and systematic.

What Are the Lessons Learned?

As future presidential administrations work to address existing areas of vulnerability and further strengthen both our counterterrorism regime and the resilience of the American people, they should consider three lessons from the Bush administration's efforts to institutionalize the War on Terror.

- *First, adapting and elevating the performance of structures, processes, and partnerships to meet emerging threats requires presidential leadership, but it also should draw on a reservoir of broad stakeholder support that must be re-energized over time.* Future administrations will need to guard against potential complacency, continue to resource sufficiently the homeland security and counterterrorism enterprise, and maintain a flexible and adaptive approach. Faced with competing national security priorities in a resource-constrained

---

1. See, for example, congressional testimony by FBI Director Christopher Wray, Hearing Before the Committee on Homeland Security, House of Representatives, October 3, 2019.

environment, this will require concerted efforts to secure and maintain the kind of broad political consensus required (including in the Congress) to sustain resolve and commitment over the long term.

- *Second, the public, the Congress, and the courts are all part of the institutionalization process and must be engaged accordingly.* As was the case after 9/11, future national security crises may require the adoption of new measures to defend the country with which the American people may be uncomfortable both at the time and certainly after the crisis has passed. For this reason, any future administration facing such a challenge should engage the public, Congress, and the courts in a process of developing a national consensus on the policies and legal frameworks to be applied to any such measures.
- *Third, 9/11 taught the nation that it can never again wait for failure before addressing gaps in the nation's security posture.* Over the last two decades, successive administrations have been anticipatory in creating transformational structures to protect and defend the country against terrorism. Future administrations must apply the experience and knowledge the nation has gained in dealing with the terrorism threat since 9/11 to other priority national security challenges, especially those that will require collaboration with international partners, the technology sector, and a society-wide approach. This will enable the United States to institutionalize the best practices, institutions, and processes required to establish the right foundation for success against the full range of twenty-first century threats the country will confront now and in the future.

Contributors:
Zack Cooper
Juan Zarate

CHAPTER 4

The War of Ideas

FARAH PANDITH

From the outset, the Bush administration recognized that the terrorist network that attacked the United States on 9/11 was animated by a vicious ideology; and that the attacks themselves were intended as a dramatic symbolic act that the terrorists hoped would make their ideology more attractive to observers all around the world, especially within Muslim communities. As a consequence, the Bush administration understood that its response would require marshalling all elements of US national power, to include new efforts and soft power innovations to engage in an ideological war—a war of ideas—as well as a war of arms. The administration put in motion a wide array of initiatives in support of this effort, but at the end of its tenure, it also recognized that much work remained to be done. Perhaps no aspect of the global War on Terror was more important and more challenging than this war of ideas. More than twenty years on, with the end of the American effort in Afghanistan and the rise of homegrown terrorist movements, the effort to combat the appeal of violent extremism remains as fraught as ever.

TRANSITION MEMORANDUM

~~SECRET~~ WITH
SECRET/NOFORN
ATTACHMENTS

6877
Transition

THE WHITE HOUSE

WASHINGTON

NSC Declassification Review [E.O. 13526]
DECLASSIFY IN PART
by William C. Carpenter 3/23/2020

January 15, 2009

MEMORANDUM FOR THE RECORD

FROM: JUAN ZARATE, COMBATING TERRORISM DIRECTORATE

SUBJECT: WAR OF IDEAS

THE SITUATION AS WE FOUND IT:

At the start of the Administration, the United States was cognizant of the terrorist threat from al-Qaida, but the Government and the American people did not yet recognize the ideological dimensions of this conflict.

With the events of September 11, 2001, these perceptions changed overnight. The President recognized that we were facing an historic ideological struggle against a violent Islamic extremist movement manipulating one of the great world religions to justify its terror and propagate intolerance and indiscriminate violence. The enemy used its ideology to radicalize individuals and recruit them to commit terrorist acts, with the objective of destabilizing governments and leading to the establishment of a totalitarian empire based on an extremist interpretation of Islamic religious law and history.

Facing this extremist ideological threat, the President recognized that the Government's capability for fighting it was insufficient. The mechanisms we had used during the Cold War to wage the ideological battle against communism had largely been dismantled—with bipartisan support in the 1990s after the Berlin Wall fell. For example, the United States Information Agency (USIA) was merged out of existence, the number of public diplomacy officers fell, Radio Free Europe was cut back, and funding for ideological engagement dried up. There was no focused "war of ideas" strategy and no infrastructure to implement one, especially in the age of new

~~SECRET~~ WITH
SECRET/NOFORN ATTACHMENTS
Reason: 1.4(b)(d)
Declassify on: 1/15/19

Re-Classified by: Ellen J. L. Knight
Reason: 1.4(d)
Declassify on: 1/15/2034

media and in a religiously-charged context. United States Government programs were focused primarily on traditional nation-state public diplomacy policy and activities, as well as international education and cultural exchange programs.

The President recognized the challenge of combating the dark ideology of al-Qaida, which pretends to defend the interests of all Muslims, argues that the "West is at war with Islam," and indoctrinates believers with the notion that they must take up arms against non-believers in order to be true Muslims. The President also recognized that this was an enemy that understood the value of winning hearts and minds by manipulating the media and exploiting centers of radicalization, the despair of Muslim youth, and the power of the Internet to spread its message.

THIS ADMINISTRATION'S POLICY:

The President concluded that the long-term solution to winning the War on Terror is the advancement of freedom and human dignity through effective democracy. He also concluded that the United States Government and our allies had to undermine the ideological underpinnings of violent Islamic extremism and garner the support of nonviolent Muslims around the world. Fighting this war of ideas would require both traditional public diplomacy tools such as education and cultural exchanges, as well as a new effort to win the battle of ideas through ideological engagement. Success also required a concerted focus to promote nonviolent ideologies, encourage moderate, anti-extremist voices, and discredit and denigrate the enemy's ideology.

The President codified his comprehensive approach to winning the War on Terror in NSPD-46/ HSPD-15 and in the National Strategy to Combat Terrorism. This strategy was used as the basis for a strategic plan for waging this war, the "Countering Violent Islamic Extremism" (CVIE) component of the National Implementation Plan (NIP). This was the first attempt to set forth a comprehensive plan for the United States Government to wage the War of Ideas. The plan noted the following:

> Key to winning the ideological contest for Muslim minds is the ability to offer a vision of a better future. CVIE provides processes that will help: identify and address some of the issues terrorists exploit; diminish some of the conditions they exploit; encourage political and economic freedom and opportunity in Muslim countries; and boost development of stronger judicial and educational systems in countries where extremism is a problem. Success in reshaping this environment to make it inhospitable to violent extremism will be one of the critical indicators of success in the War on Terror.
>
> -National Implementation Plan, Counter
> Violent Islamic Extremism (June 2006)

In the original plan, the President defined the specific objectives of the War of Ideas:

(1) Undermine the idea that the West is at war with Islam.
(2) Delegitimize terror as an acceptable tactic to achieve political goals.
(3) Isolate and discredit terrorist leaders, facilitators, and organizations; hamper their ability to disseminate their message.
(4) Actively engage Muslim communities; foster debate within Islam, and amplify moderate Muslim voices.
(5) Promote democratization and good governance as a path to a positive future in just, secure, and pluralistic societies.
(6) Build U.S. and foreign government capacity to enhance our collective effectiveness in winning the War on Terror.

These objectives were supplemented with subobjectives and specific tasks for departments and agencies, as well as department and agency supporting plans to ensure the effective implementation of this plan. In 2008, the objectives for this component plan were framed in the revised National Implementation Plan for the War on Terror as end states to be achieved:

(1) Muslims, their religious leaders, and the governments of nations with Muslim populations believe that terrorism is illegitimate, carries high costs, and is not an acceptable tactic to achieve political, economic, or social goals;
(2) Violent extremist leaders, facilitators, and organizations are isolated and their narrative that "the West is at war with Islam" is undermined and discredited; and
(3) Muslims and governments of Muslim populations have favorable attitudes toward and publicly support equitable pluralistic societies, rule of law, good governance, and respect for human rights.

The Administration has engaged in a range of activities including classic public diplomacy and denigration of the enemy's message and leadership to effectuate this strategy. The following have been some core United States Government activities:

· Destroy the credibility of al-Qaida and violent extremists and recraft the "West at war with Islam" paradigm by empowering local communities to stand up and challenge violence. This has required new, devoted analysis

to attack the extremists' messages and empower Muslims who are committed to promoting and expanding tolerance, understanding, and dialogue. Specific efforts have highlighted the indiscriminate brutality of terrorist groups in Iraq, Afghanistan, Pakistan, Indonesia, and the Philippines for publics in those countries.

- Encourage the growth of a global grassroots countermovement that challenges the ideology of violent extremism and its adherents. This has required finding new ways to leverage existing private sector mechanisms and activists—in the Homeland and abroad,

- Coordinate a national domestic effort to encourage Muslim Americans to become overt allies in the War of Ideas, including an intensified United States Government effort (local and Federal) to empower the American Muslim community through partnership and support for joint projects. This has occurred through numerous outreach programs and mechanisms created by agencies like DHS, Treasury, and the FBI, as well as enlistment in programs like the State Department's Citizen Ambassador program. The President set forth a framework for preventing violent Islamic extremist radicalization in the United States, memorialized in the October 2007 National Homeland Security Strategy. That Strategy set forth four core areas of activity:
  (1) Engage key communities as partners in the WOT;
  (2) Identify and counter the sources of radicalization;
  (3) Enhance Federal, State, local, and Tribal government capacities to address radicalization; and
  (4) Continue to advance our understanding of radicalization.

WHAT HAS BEEN ACCOMPLISHED:

As this Administration prepares to leave office, a strategy, United States Government platforms, and a new way of doing business—including with the private sector—are in place, ready for use by the next administration.

To date, the Administration has promoted our core values, defended the image of America, and attacked the image and illegitimacy of the enemy and its message. The following examples demonstrate how the United States Government has attempted to achieve these goals:

- The State Department expanded U.S. international broadcasting into 60 languages and increase the audience to 175 million adults, a 75 percent increase since 2002. Of the 75 million new listeners, approximately half are Arabic speakers. Regional media hubs in London, Brussels, and Dubai were established to strategically book more American spokespeople particularly on Arab television.

- Recognizing that higher education is one of America's most sought-after assets, State worked to ensure continued opportunities for foreign students despite new visa requirements mandated after 9/11: 600,000 international students came to study in the United States in the 2007–08 academic year, a record number. United States Government-sponsored educational exchange programs increased from 27,000 participants in 2004 to more than 40,000 in 2007.

- State also increased its information programs, sending 800 experts in science and public policy abroad each year, holding dozens of videoconferences to talk about America and its policies, and developing multilingual websites such as America.gov.

- In 2006, the President designated the Under Secretary of State for Public Diplomacy to lead the interagency—primarily State, USAID, Defense, and the Intelligence Community—in the War of Ideas and established a Policy Coordinating Committee for Strategic Communications.

- Departments and agencies have developed new tactics, techniques and procedures to enhance strategic communication, audience and cultural understanding, and metrics. This has included more funding and dedicated units at the State Department, CIA, NCTC, DOD, and the Combatant Commands to execute this mission.

- In 2007, State established the Counterterrorism Communications Center (CTCC) as an inter-agency coordination mechanism for ensuring all U.S. public diplomacy efforts have common talking points and themes for use in information campaigns.

- The National Counterterrorism Center (NCTC), under its strategic operational planning mission, is coordinating short-term campaigns involving tools available to the diplomatic, military, and intelligence communities to exploit near-term opportunities to counter violent extremism.

- In 2007, Deputies approved the Near-Term Anti-Al-Qaida Communication Action Plan (ACAP) to provide field elements with a unified set of objectives, while leaving implementation open to local circumstances and resources.

- The President placed a copy of the Quran in the White House Library in 2005 to show respect for Islam, and appointed a Special Envoy to the Organization of the Islamic Conference (OIC) in 2008 to improve dialogue and engagement with Muslim communities globally.

- In 2008, State broadened the Counterterrorism Communications Center and transformed it into the Global Strategic Engagement Center (GSEC) to serve as the day-to-day hub of activity for the War of Ideas, utilizing a subject-matter advisory group to provide interagency guidance on topics and issues related to the War of Ideas.

- In order to create an alternative charity option for Americans wishing to donate to good causes in the Muslim world but unable or afraid to because of terrorist-finance tainted charities, in 2008 USAID partnered with a nonprofit organization, American Charities for Palestine (ACP). Through this partnership, ACP will donate funding it receives through charitable donations to USAID for implementation of projects jointly agreed upon by ACP and USAID to enhance the health and education sectors in the Palestinian Territories.

- "Traditional" public diplomacy programs like English language teaching programs have imparted skills for upward mobility, but also powerful ideas associated with our democracy. The Access Micro-scholarship Program has taught English to 30,000 teenagers in after-school programs over the past 4 years.

- The Defense Department has developed a range of products and capabilities in the field designed to deliver our common themes in key regions quickly and effectively, including websites established by the Combatant Commands and the use of multiple Military Information Support Teams (MIST) located in embassies around the world to amplify hearts and minds efforts.

We have seen measurable effects of these efforts, including the increasing rejection of al-Qaida's ideology and brutality.

- The United States Government, in partnership with the Government of Iraq, has achieved a significant Sunni Arab rejection of the al-Qaida movement in Iraq.

- According to multiple private and United States Government international polls and surveys, there has been a significant decline in international and Muslim support for al-Qaida, its violent tactics, and Usama bin Laden.

- According to multiple private and United States Government international polls and surveys, there is a significant rise in international awareness of the problem of terrorism and a desire to solve the issue.

- ▓▓▓▓▓▓▓▓▓▓▓▓▓▓▓▓▓▓▓▓▓▓▓▓▓▓▓▓▓▓▓▓▓▓▓▓▓▓ support for suicide bombing has declined in Afghanistan, Bangladesh, Egypt, Indonesia, Jordan, Kenya, Lebanon, Macedonia, Pakistan, the Philippines, and Turkey.

- There has been an increase in the number of moderate voices and religious leaders who seek to counter the ideology of terrorism, including ex-extremists organizing to confront former colleagues and violent groups.

- Young people are using social networking sites to build antiterrorism networks. In Colombia, a group of young people used Facebook to build a movement of 12 million people around the world to hold street demonstrations against the FARC in February 2008. The demonstrations are credited with accelerating desertions from the FARC.

- We have broadened consensus in the international community that terrorism is unlawful and unjustified.

  - In 2006, U.N. Member States passed the U.N. Global Counterterrorism Strategy, the first time that all members have agreed to a common strategic approach to fight terrorism. The strategy sends a clear message that terrorism is unacceptable in all its forms and manifestations.

  - The Organization of the Islamic Conference, an association of 57 Muslim nations, revised its Charter in 2008 to pledge "to cooperate in combating terrorism in all its forms and manifestations" and in September 2008 released a statement condemning suicide bombings.

  - In 2008, the G-8 declared in its "Toyako Principles" that all terrorist acts are criminal and must be universally condemned.

  - In September 2008, the U.N. Secretary General held a conference to highlight victims of terror, where he stated that terrorism can never be justified.

  - The President summarized this growing international consensus in his speech at UNGA: "No cause can justify the deliberate taking of innocent human life—and the international community is nearing universal agreement on this truth... The vast majority of nations in this assembly now agree that tactics like suicide bombing, hostage-taking and hijacking are never legitimate."

FUTURE CHALLENGES:

While much effort had been invested in the War of Ideas, the threat posed by the violent ideology of al-Qaida and similar organizations is still present and capable of resurgence and growth. Violent Islamic extremism is a long-term problem, and much remains to be done, especially by Muslim leaders and in Muslim communities. There are a number of areas where the United States Government faces challenges and opportunities that build off current efforts:

Undermining the Notion of the "West being at war with Islam." Though challenges remain in promoting and defending the values of the United States and undercutting and undermining the ideology and image of the enemy, the greatest challenge in the War of Ideas is persuading Muslim communities around the world that the United States is not at war with Islam and does not seek as a matter of policy or practice to attack or suppress Muslims. Polls from Muslim communities around the world reflect high percentages believe this to be true. Al-Qaida's success in the ideological battle has been to hitch its agenda and propaganda under the broader argument that the West is at war with Islam and that all ills and grievances can be understood and attributed to this perceived reality. The United States Government will need to continue to communicate and demonstrate real world values and respect for Islam, Muslim communities, and the integration of Muslim Americans, as well as the positive impact and hope of freedom and effective democracy in Muslim majority countries. This should happen while we continue to counter the terrorists' narrative—with images and locally relevant mechanisms—and label and explain al-Qaida as a foreign entity that itself is at war with Muslims. As opposed to being defenders of Islam, al-Qaida must be seen as murderers of Muslims, and the accepted paradigm that Islam is under assault by the West must be overturned.

Enhancing Government-wide Coordination and Resources. The Administration has established processes and mechanisms to coordinate our broad War of Ideas efforts, but those structures are relatively new and will need to be buttressed and enhanced, especially as we seek to use and coordinate all elements of national power to effect the War of Ideas. Since the end of the Cold War, resource decisions, legislative changes, and advances in technology and globalization have combined to limit the effectiveness of the United States Government to accomplish strategic communication efforts. Although the State Department's Under Secretary for Public Diplomacy has the interagency lead on advancing the War of Ideas, he has not had the resources or organizational reach to carry out this broad mandate. He relies upon the mechanisms of the White House and the policy coordinating process to create consensus with interagency partners who hold the resources necessary to accomplish key elements of the mission. More must be done to strengthen the Under Secretary's tools for leadership in this area. The resources devoted to this dimension of the War on Terror remain inadequate compared to the much larger figures and resources applied to other dimensions of the war where a return on the investment is more readily apparent. This requires not just applying more resources within the United States Government, but finding a way to leverage foreign partner capacity and private sector resources to amplify and effectuate the United States Government's goals.

Coordination with the Private Sector. To be completely effective in the War of Ideas, it is critical to continue to partner with the private sector and individuals, including through third-party vehicles and credible voices:

- **Third-Party Vehicles.** For War of Ideas efforts to be sustainable and carry forward into future generations, the United States Government may want to encourage "third-party vehicles." Having multiple private organizations engaged in this effort would help the United States Government by mutually reinforcing government-led activities in the War of Ideas—especially building awareness, developing new and expanded networks, providing funding, and amplifying the ability of those opposed to violent extremism to sustain a global countermessaging effort.

- **Credible Voices.** The United States Government must also continue to engage partners to identify, amplify, support, and network credible voices and key communicators who can challenge al-Qaida's narrative and counter violent ideologies. These voices can also, as appropriate, amplify messages that counter terrorism and extremist ideologies.

- **Advisory Board.** Outside expertise, whether in the foundation/philanthropic world, business, technology, marketing, or other fields, could be harnessed to guide United States Government efforts and help focus resources on strategic goals. In early 2008, the National Security Advisor convened a series of meetings with leading private sector figures in the fields of internet-based media, philanthropic foundations, financial services, Islamic studies, and marketing to discuss War of Ideas challenges facing the government. State is building on the success of that effort by developing an Advisory Board on Strategic Engagement, comprised of 10 non-governmental members from the private sectors. Such an Advisory Board will help institutionalize this dialogue and ensure fresh ideas, perspectives, and review of efforts are regularly injected into government activities.

CONCLUSION:

The events of September 11, 2001, necessitated a dramatic rethinking of the way we were organized to fight our enemy in a battle of arms and ideas. Traditional nation-state public diplomacy activities and international education and cultural exchange programs were no longer sufficient to meet these new challenges. Advances in technology and globalization increased the difficulty of drowning out the negative messages of extremism.

We have made progress in how we are structured and organized to win the War of Ideas, and we have made progress in undermining the voices of violent Islamic extremism. But more innovation and improvements are still needed. The structure established to fight the war of ideas during the Cold War is frequently cited as a model, but it took several years and some false starts by the Truman and Eisenhower administrations to create an effective war of ideas operation in the early Cold War years. This administration faced and the next administration will face similar organizational challenges. Simply restoring the structures created and used in the Cold War is not the answer.

The President's commitment to combating the underlying ideology that supports extremism and violence with a vision based on the hope and opportunity of freedom, and our efforts to help, empower, and engage with Muslim communities around the world, form an important platform and lasting legacy to America's long-term efforts to win the War on Terror.

Attachments

Tab 1   Chronology for the War of Ideas
Tab 2   Remarks by the President at Islamic Center of Washington, D.C. (September 17, 2001)
Tab 3   Agenda for Deputies Committee Meeting on Campaign Strategy and the Report on the Strategic Information Campaign (October 26, 2001)
Tab 4   Remarks by the President at Iftaar (November 19, 2001)

POSTSCRIPT

FARAH PANDITH

President Bush recognized that al Qaeda's power was not only in its capacity for violence but also in its ability to manipulate one of the world's great religions—both to justify that violence and to attract and motivate recruits to commit it. Thus, it was essential that America stand up an entirely new kind of effort to undermine the ideological underpinnings of violent Islamic extremism while simultaneously building connections and support from Muslim communities worldwide. The president's long-term solution to winning the War on Terror was the advancement of freedom and human dignity through effective democracy. Toward that end, the effort had to include advancing political freedom and economic opportunity in Muslim communities, and boosting the development of stronger judicial, educational, and health systems in countries challenged by extremism. America needed to engage in a new kind of war in order to make communities resilient to violent extremist ideology.

The Bush Administration Approach
With no focused strategy or infrastructure already in place to wage the ideological war, especially in the age of new media and in a religiously charged context, President Bush recognized that winning the war of ideas would require a comprehensive plan.

The plan had defined objectives:

- Undermine the idea that the West was at war with Islam.
- Delegitimize terror as an acceptable tactic to achieve political goals.
- Isolate and discredit terrorist leaders and disrupt and counter their message.
- Actively engage Muslim communities and empower anti-extremist Muslim voices.
- Promote democratization, good governance, and tolerance as paths to a positive future.
- Build US, foreign government, and grassroots capabilities to win the War on Terror.

The President codified his comprehensive approach in NSPD-46/HSPD-15 and in the National Strategy to Combat Terrorism (2006). This strategy was the basis for the "Countering Violent Islamic Extremism" (CVIE) component of the original National Implementation Plan and its subsequent 2008 revision: success in reshaping the environment to make it inhospitable to violent extremism. The 2007 National Homeland Security Strategy sought to make American Muslims allies and supporters of local and federal efforts to protect communities from the effort of violent extremists to recruit and radicalize. Other administration efforts included:

- The State Department expanding US international broadcasting into sixty languages and adding seventy-five million new listeners (with half being Arabic speakers).
- The President in 2006 designating the Under Secretary of State for Public Diplomacy to lead the interagency effort in the war of ideas, and establishing an NSC/HSC Policy Coordinating Committee for Strategic Communications.
- The State Department in 2007 establishing the Counterterrorism Communications Center (CTCC) (which in 2008 became the Global Strategic Engagement Center [GSEC]) as an interagency mechanism for day-to-day coordination of the war of ideas.
- The President in 2008 appointing a Special Envoy to the Organization of the Islamic Conference (OIC), an association of fifty-seven Muslim-majority nations, to improve global engagement with Muslim communities.

By 2009, the Bush administration's approach to the war of ideas had a comprehensive strategy, multiple lines of effort, new US government platforms, and an unprecedented way of doing business—including with the private sector. The administration was promoting its core values and defending the image of America while attacking the image and illegitimacy of the enemy. And it was achieving results. For example:

- Multiple opinion polls showed significant declines in international and Muslim support for al Qaeda, its violent tactics (including suicide bombings), and Osama bin Laden.
- Religious leaders, former extremists, and other Muslims were increasingly speaking out against terrorist ideology.
- The Organization of the Islamic Conference (OIC) in 2008 pledged cooperation in combating terrorism in all its forms and condemned suicide bombings.

What Has Happened Since the End of the Bush Administration?

Twenty years after the September 11, 2001 attacks, violent extremism today is more complex, agile, endowed, and multidimensional than ever before. Efforts to address the ideological elements of the threat are labeled "CVE" (Countering Violent Extremism), a term that evolved from "CVIE," which reflected specific attention to an extremist movement that manipulated Islamic religious law and history. The evolution of terms was necessary to include additional motivational inspirations that have emerged since 9/11, such as some new forms of hate and extremist ideology. Thus, CVE is equivalent to the ideological war effort previously known as the war of ideas.

Successive administrations mostly continued along the lines laid out by President Bush, although with somewhat different emphases, language, and priorities. President Obama's immediate priority was to focus on the elements of the extremist ideology that promoted the myth that America was at war with Islam. To do this, the administration engaged with Muslims around "mutual interest and mutual respect" rather than security, and developed a broad set of initiatives and programs to build relationships with Muslims and amplify moderate Muslim voices. Globally, however, CVE undertakings abroad were more consistent with the approach taken in the Bush administration: building local approaches and networks rejecting extremist ideology, delegitimizing violence, increasing credible voices, and isolating and discrediting terrorist leaders, facilitators, and organizations.

The Obama administration also enhanced government-wide coordination, responsibility, and resources, and sparked a larger, global CVE movement including the ability to build third-party vehicles for partnering with private parties. CVE work in the US homeland was framed as violence prevention and community resilience. The ideology of violent extremists of all kinds was the focus, explicitly broadening the framing of the threat. While the language and framing during the Obama administration was not explicitly about the War on Terror, the domestic approach was similar to the Bush administration's focus, in the words of the Transition Memorandum, on "engaging key communities as partners," "identifying and countering sources of radicalization," "enhancing Federal, State, local and tribal government capabilities on radicalization," and "advancing understanding of radicalization." The Obama administration's CVE effort was clear on the ideological connection between the domestic and the international, as well as the growing impact of the internet. Its efforts culminated in a 2015 White House CVE Summit and new federal grant moneys focused at the local level in 2016.

President Trump's CVE effort shared some of the tactics used by the Bush and Obama administrations. However, there were immediate changes in funding streams for the federal grant program and staffing levels. The Trump administration's National Security Strategy for Counterterrorism in 2018 acknowledged the need to build a preventative architecture, but it was defined around "America first" objectives and the danger of "radical Islamist ideology." The key goal for CVE in the Trump administration was to ensure extremist ideologies did not undermine the "American way of life." While acknowledging at the very start of the administration the importance of defeating the ideology of violent extremists, there was little that was new in terms of approach, initiatives, or global cooperation. Importantly, there was no effort to undermine the idea that the West was at war with Islam.

The Trump administration's CVE approach was primarily focused on countering the recruitment and radicalization capabilities of groups like ISIS and al Qaeda. Despite these defined objectives, CVE in the Trump administration lacked resources—financial and personnel—and leadership. By 2018, violent far-right and white supremacist violence and movements were rising in the US homeland as well as a mainstreaming of conspiracy theories of groups like QAnon. There were no CVE enhancements by the administration to meet these developments, or efforts to incorporate the recruitment and radicalization of white supremacist groups into CVE. By 2020, President Trump's Global Engagement Center was focusing on countermessaging propaganda from state adversaries.

The Biden administration immediately placed a new focus on domestic terrorism due to the January 6, 2021 attack on the Capitol, and data that showed dramatic and dangerous changes in the ideological threat landscape from white supremacists. In June 2021 it released America's first-ever National Strategy for Countering Domestic Terrorism, which includes enhanced efforts to prevent radicalization and to intervene when individuals radicalize to violence. The administration has continued (and expanded) the community-based approach and has increased funding for prevention programs.

The field of CVE is now a vast industry that encompasses dozens of governments, universities, multinational organizations, researchers, practitioners, analysts, and policymakers. There are new global CVE multinational, best-practice sharing, and organizing platforms like Hedayah, the Global Counterterrorism Forum, and the Global Community Engagement and Resilience Fund. Dozens of new CVE organizations now exist in America and elsewhere.

Yet, the US government CVE effort has been plagued with misinterpretation and politics, hindering the potential of all elements of society to build resilience at home and abroad. Other nations have faced a similar level of pushback on CVE. Years of rewording, redefining, and reviewing the scope of this soft power effort have harmed progress. It has become a lightning rod for some American minority communities, while overseas it has taken on a similar profile. There is CVE fatigue from those on the front lines, while at the same time they struggle for funding resources.

Over the last twenty years, technological developments, alongside a growing skill set of extremists in recruiting followers, have created a complex ideological battlefield. Moreover, the mushrooming of various violent extremist ideologies has been profound, and previously unimagined when CVE work began. Not just ideologies that use the religion of Islam, but religious ideologies manipulating Christianity and other faiths have emerged. Moreover, the ideological terrain is infested not just with members of a particular group, but today national actors are also involved in the dissemination of ideologies and conspiracy theories online. Furthermore, America is witnessing a resurgence in the homeland of violent far-right, white supremacist, and other forms of neo-Nazism as well as leftist ideologies.

How Did the Bush Administration Do?

The purpose of embarking on the war of ideas was to starve the enemy of ideological oxygen so that it could no longer use ideology to radicalize individuals and recruit them to commit terrorist acts. Some twenty years after 9/11, America still has not "won" the ideological battle originally outlined against al Qaeda. Their ideology still has agency and recruiting prowess, and its continued presence has spawned other types of bad actors—including the so-called Islamic State—who manipulate Islam to propagate us-versus-them narratives and to justify violence. Nevertheless, the premise of the strategy has retained its intellectual integrity: undermining the ideology is vital. There is consensus that it is impossible to defeat terrorists if they can still recruit and radicalize. For this reason, it is essential that America (and others) focus on the ideological war.

Significantly, the premise that if the leader of a terrorist organization like al Qaeda or ISIS is removed it will result in an eventual diminishing of the ideological appeal has not withstood reality. Ideological appeal has staying power aided by the enormous digital footprint of social media platforms. Images, memes, symbols, and merchandise have created a subculture with ideological lifestyle brands, and adherents are far more open and professionalized today. This information ecosystem allows ideology to flow, and it is the gateway for far more radicalization to take place. Whether the growth in new ideological threats seems plausible (e.g., QAnon) or not, the ideological war has been expanded well beyond its original focus on al Qaeda. The United States government is lagging in this effort, despite a continued CVE effort by both the Obama and Trump administrations.

In spite of this sobering assessment, and now (again) an ascendant Taliban and a resilient al Qaeda, it is clear that the Bush administration effort to build capabilities for countering extremist ideology was important.

1. *The Bush administration's assessment of the unique challenge posed by this enemy was correct.* Al Qaeda was embarking on a long-term war effort that required winning the emotional and intellectual sympathies of Muslims worldwide. Without the Bush administration's initial understanding of the vast, historical shift represented by this type of enemy, the US strategy to defeat al Qaeda would have been entirely different—and America would have missed a fundamental element of twenty-first-century terrorism: the power of ideas to mobilize a global movement.

2. *The assessment of the limits to extant US capabilities was also accurate.* America did not have a 24/7 strategic communications machine or tools beyond traditional public diplomacy. There were few avenues for engagement with Muslims beyond bilateral relationships with Muslim-majority states, and America did not have the cultural intelligence to understand what was happening within Muslim communities. The decision to stand up an entirely new ideological war infrastructure today seems obvious. At the time, it was a bold initiative with mixed support.

3. *President Bush's conclusion that America had to work on all elements of the ecosystem experienced by Muslims was significant but also complicated.* By nesting the ideological effort within a broader framework of advancing a better vision for Muslims, the administration thus concluded that if individuals had the prospect of a better life, they were less likely to be exploited by al Qaeda. The administration rightly assessed that working on education, rule of law, economic conditions, political concerns, and freedom were fundamental needs in Muslim communities, but this did not mean that without these things individuals were more vulnerable to violent extremist ideology. The issue of identity and belonging is at the core of what is

now known about vulnerability to radicalization. Nevertheless, the broader conclusion that offering Muslims alternative visions for their own future could help build resilience against extremism had value and still proves to be essential to influencing the system underlying extremism.

4. *The objective to delegitimize the underpinnings of extremist ideology and the justification for violence through third parties was prescient.* Mobilizing credible entities from allies and partners—influential religious leaders, the United Nations, the Organization of Islamic Cooperation (OIC)—helped to generate a common cause around the principle that extremist violence was never justified.

5. *The objectives and methodology of the war of ideas are some of the stronger elements of the Bush administration's effort.* The Bush administration's methodologies provided a blueprint for the CVE work of future administrations, and included innovation around how to do the work that was needed both at home and abroad. Despite limited connections to American Muslim communities before the September 11, 2001 attacks, the Bush administration responded forthrightly, working around unpopular military engagements in Iraq and Afghanistan to become convener, facilitator, and intellectual partner with Muslim civil society, grassroots groups, and many different types of local actors. This formed the bedrock of how America defines successful CVE programs today.

At the same time, several limitations in the Bush administration approach are clearer now than they were at the time.

1. *The approach failed to anticipate the growth of a dangerous white supremacist threat to the homeland.* This is not surprising, to the extent that it resulted from events and policies occurring after the Bush administration had left office.

2. *Though the administration did focus on Muslims living as minorities and recognized that extremist ideology could impact them, the Bush administration did not assess the potential danger of radicalization to be as great as it turned out to be—and did not anticipate how Muslims growing up after 9/11 would experience what they considered to be an anti-Muslim backlash.* The assessment was made that American Muslims were more immune to radicalization due to their history and lived experience. This

was a mistake in hindsight. Connecting the dots on identity navigation and exploration online could have significantly helped America to understand the core of the system underlying extremism.

3. *CVE efforts were inadequately funded.* The CVE effort has suffered dramatically due to the fact that much greater resources were applied to other dimensions of the War on Terror where a return on investment was more readily apparent. A more balanced funding allocation would have dramatically influenced what happened in the years afterward. Making the case for a robust effort with state-of-the-art communications, powerful granting structures, and larger, more coordinated efforts through DHS and the State Department, was a missed opportunity.

4. *The administration was wrong to assume that, even though Muslim-majority nations had rejected al Qaeda's ideology, they had bought into the larger effort to oppose extremism more generally and to give respect and support to non-extremist Muslim voices.* In particular, the Bush administration did not demand enough from Saudi Arabia in stopping the spread of Wahhabi ideology, one of the most important planks in the global system underlying extremism.

5. *The administration underestimated the impact of technology, and the responsibility borne by American technological companies for the spread of extremism.* New terrorist groups exploited these technologies to overtake al Qaeda as the primary adversary in the war of ideas.

What Are the Lessons Learned?

Based on now twenty years of experience in dealing with the challenge of extremist ideology, the following lessons seem to have emerged:

- *Organization matters.* America cannot get ahead of this enemy if the effort is ad hoc and uncoordinated. Standing up the correct infrastructure and putting a leader in charge with both authority and responsibility is essential. Loose definitions of CVE, of what constituted a CVE program, and of how CVE success would be measured greatly disabled progress. Regional strategies did not connect to one another and there was little information sharing.
- *The whole of government needs to be involved in order to disassemble the system underlying extremism.* The ideological effort does not have borders. There is no domestic versus international. The ideological war impacts edu-

cation, mental wellness, identity navigation, prison recruitment, veterans, and more. There needs to be a long-term strategy to protect youth from dark ideologies that is integrated and built around all elements of society.

- *Technology companies, especially social media platforms, must be engaged differently.* Their role is vital, and the US government must advance a determined approach through various means both to hold them accountable for the spread of hate and violent extremism and to provide clear guidelines as to what this accountability requires of them.

- *Preparedness for navigating the ideological landscape means very different kinds of analysis.* The US government must reconfigure its strategy to reflect a more precise understanding of the cultural components of identity navigation as it applies to Generation Z, Generation Alpha, and whatever comes after that. American policymakers have so far not been equipped for this analysis, representing a generation that understood extremist ideology in very different terms from those experiencing it.

- *The US government needs to be more proactive in partnerships.* Assuming that philanthropy would come to the table on its own was the wrong calculation. The American government cannot fight this war alone as it does a traditional conflict; it needs to build broad and deep alliances and partnerships with the private sector in general and the philanthropic community in particular.

- *NGOs are doing the bulk of the work, yet they remain small and have serious issues around safety of their personnel.* Since the US government is dependent on these local partners, it must find a better way to protect them from bad actors who can find them and render them unsafe.

- *Local, state, and federal efforts are essential.* The success of CVE is entirely dependent on community-led and supported efforts. Making communities safe from ideological predators requires the resources to make a long-term human infrastructure investment.

- *The US government must widen the lens.* It must get buy-in from the American public that fighting hate and violent extremism in all its forms is a priority. The American government cannot win this ideological war alone; it takes everyone.

Contributors:
Zack Cooper
Juan Zarate

PART 3

Interventions and Stabilization

INTRODUCTION

STEPHEN J. HADLEY

The Bush administration's military interventions in Afghanistan and Iraq have been at the center of public debate and discussion now for almost twenty years. After removing regimes in both countries judged to be national security threats, the United States over multiple administrations, and along with friends and allies, sought to stabilize and reconstruct what were shattered, fragile, conflict-plagued societies. It did this by helping the people of both countries, after suffering under brutal tyrannies, to build states based on freedom, democracy, rule of law, and respect for human rights. The effort reflected not only America's founding principles but was, in the view of the Bush administration, the best way to create inclusive, stable governments that would hold together and be able to prevent their countries from becoming safe havens for terrorists.

The efforts in Afghanistan and Iraq were part of a broader initiative by the Bush administration to support the people of the region in their attempt to transform the Middle East. The Middle East had missed the democratic governance and market-based economic reforms that had transformed Europe and much of Asia into stable, secure, and prosperous societies. For much of the twentieth century, American policy in the Middle East had accepted tyranny as the price of regional stability. It turned out to be a bad bargain. It helped create instead an unstable region plagued by economic stagnation, political despair, and now terrorist extremism. The Bush administration tried to work with those in the region desiring a different future and to midwife a transition to a more democratic and more stable Middle East. This represented in many ways the high watermark of America's historical engagement in the region.

Underpinning this Middle East "Freedom Agenda" was an insertion of military, economic, and diplomatic power by the United States, NATO, and a coalition of friends and allies to create in the region a "balance of power that favors freedom." Military bases in Afghanistan, Iraq, Qatar, Bahrain, and the UAE were critical elements. This "balance of power" platform was the foundation for combating terrorism, deterring and containing rogue states (like Syria and Iran), and helping the people of the region to build freer, more democratic, more prosperous, and more stable nations resistant to terrorist extremism.

As described in the Transition Memoranda, this effort involved:

— Combating terrorism and countering Islamic extremism.
— Stabilizing and helping to reconstruct Afghanistan and Iraq.
— Encouraging and pressuring both allies and adversaries to give their people more political freedom and democratic governance.
— Trying to broker a peace between the Israelis and the Palestinians as part of a broader peace between Israel and the Arab states.
— Helping the Palestinian people to build a secure, peaceful, and prosperous democratic state that could live side-by-side with Israel in peace and security.
— Freeing Lebanon from Syrian occupation so that the people of Lebanon could take control of their own future.
— Seeking to eliminate Iran's nuclear program and to curb its disruptive activity in the region through negotiation backed by diplomatic, economic, and military pressure.

This effort to transform the Middle East would require incremental, pragmatic steps working with the partners we had—not the ones we were encouraging them to become. Success would be hard to come by. To help the Middle East achieve democratic stability and market-oriented prosperity would require years if not decades of sustained effort. The work would have to be done primarily by the people of the region themselves but with the help of the United States and the rest of the international community. It would be an effort comparable to what was done after World War II in Asia (in Japan and South Korea) and in Europe (in Germany and in the creation of the European Union).

As of the end of the Bush administration, this effort was at best a work in progress. That said, the enormous exertions by the people of the region and the investments made by the United States, NATO, friends and allies, and international institutions have had an impact. The vision of a different Middle East has been embraced by millions of its citizens, particularly by women, youth, and minorities. They have had a taste of greater freedom of expression, the right to vote in elections that mattered, the chance to take more responsibility for their own futures, and the hope and opportunity for a better life. And many do not want to give them up.

This vision of a different Middle East sparked a responsive chord in the uprisings of the Arab Spring in 2011. Despite the disillusionment that followed, this vision continues to inspire people to press for greater freedom, respect for human dignity and human rights, less corrupt and more accountable and more inclusive governance, greater security, and economic opportunity. This vision was reflected in the actions of the people of Sudan as they rose up and overthrew the authoritarian regime of Omar al-Bashir in 2019. This vision was reflected in the actions of the people of Algeria whose public protests in that same year led to the ouster of longtime dictator Abdelaziz Bouteflika. And this vision was reflected in the actions of the people of Iraq, Lebanon, and Jordan whose protests in 2018 and 2019 led to new prime ministers in all three countries.

The Abraham Accords between Israel and the UAE, Bahrain, Sudan, and Morocco, respectively, were a remarkable accomplishment which reached fruition during the Trump administration. They purport to offer a framework for advancing peace, security, and prosperity in the Middle East. They promise every person "a life of dignity and hope, no matter their race, faith or ethnicity." They commit the parties to "respect for human dignity and freedom, including religious freedom." Perhaps they can become a framework for moving over time toward this vision of a different and transformed Middle East.

Although not the reason for the interventions, the Bush administration hoped that Afghanistan and Iraq would help catalyze this transformation. In both Afghanistan and Iraq, the US-led coalitions quickly toppled the existing regimes. Stabilizing and securing the countries proved more difficult. Helping the people build legitimate, effective, democratic governments that could meet their needs and prevent terrorist safe havens proved more difficult still.

Seeking democratic governance was consistent with the vision of the Freedom Agenda and a "democratic peace" in the Middle East. But it also reflected the practical judgment that in countries with linguistic, religious, and ethnic differences, only a democratic framework would allow these various groups to live together in unity and peace.

The US effort in Iraq was burdened from the start by the prewar intelligence failure wrongly concluding that Saddam Hussein still maintained the large stocks of weapons of mass destruction that he had amassed in the mid-1990s. It was burdened further by the failure of the Bush administration from 2003 to 2006 to stabilize Iraq and to bring peace to its people. This squandered the leverage generated by the quick toppling of the regimes first in Afghanistan and then in Iraq—leverage needed to manage the challenges represented by Iran, Syria, and North Korea in particular. President Bush's courageous 2007 decision to "surge" and change strategy brought the defeat of al Qaeda in Iraq and relative peace to the country. But it came late.

Some 2,500 American military remain in Iraq at the time of this writing. This presence reflects not only America's continuing security interest in what happens in Iraq but also the considerable progress that the Iraqi people have made over the last almost twenty years. Iraq is a work in progress, still fragile but less conflict-ridden, an emerging democratic state that has conducted six elections and multiple peaceful transfers of power and has resumed its important place in the region. With its considerable physical infrastructure, substantial economic resources, and high level of human capital, Iraq has the potential over time to become an imperfect but stable democratic state able to provide security, prosperity, and peace to its people. It could offer hope that the transformation of the Middle East is possible.

America withdrew its military forces from Afghanistan in the summer of 2021. By mid-August, the Taliban had taken control. Time will tell whether the over twenty-year investment made by America, the coalition, and the international community was in vain. Will the Taliban be able to govern a country that is now so different from the one they ruled in the 1990s? Will they succeed in imposing their theocratic tyranny on its people? Or will they have to make concessions to those Afghans who have gotten used to some measure of freedom, democracy, human rights, and the rule of law over the last two decades? One should not bet against the women, young people, and other Afghans who have had a taste of freedom and do not want to lose it.

Afghanistan and Iraq were not the only Bush administration efforts to encourage stability and democratic governance in fragile states racked by violence, whether terrorist, sectarian, or religious. Although not involving the kind of interventions the United States made in those two countries, these other efforts nonetheless reflected a significant commitment of American diplomatic, economic, and security assistance resources. Not all succeeded. But a number did. Plan Colombia is one success story, told in chapter 8 of this part 3. Lebanon is another, as chapter 9 describes, although very much a work in progress at the end of the Bush administration. The Europe and Western Balkans Transition Memoranda in chapter 16 of part 5 describe successful peace operations in Kosovo, Macedonia, and southern Serbia. Bush administration efforts helped resolve violent conflicts in six African countries (Liberia, Sierra Leone, Burundi, Angola, Sudan North-South, and the Democratic Republic of the Congo), as described in chapter 25 in part 6.

There are lessons here. Peacemaking, stabilization, and reconstruction efforts in fragile states wracked by violence are extremely challenging. But they can succeed with careful planning, sound strategies, adequate resources appropriate to the task, and sustained and patient engagement. Most importantly, they require strong, committed, and capable local partners. Where these partners own the strategy, provide effective governance, and lead their people, the chances of success go up. Where there is a safe haven next door in which terrorists, narcotraffickers, and violent armed groups can find shelter and support, the chances go down. Success also requires civilian capabilities for peacemaking, stabilization, and reconstruction that are often in short supply both in the United States and in the international community more generally. Without investment of these kinds of resources, the risk of a return to violence is high.

CHAPTER 5

Afghanistan

PAUL D. MILLER | DOUGLAS LUTE | MEGHAN L. O'SULLIVAN

The US focus on Afghanistan from 2001 to 2021 was evidence of the dramatic reorientation of American foreign policy in the wake of the 9/11 attacks. For twenty years, the United States, alongside its coalition allies and Afghan partners, sought both to ensure that Afghanistan did not reemerge as a sanctuary for terrorism and to build institutions of the Afghan state. There were multiple chapters to US engagement in Afghanistan spanning four presidential administrations, espousing different goals with varying levels of military and civilian commitment. The transition from President Bush to President Obama was one of several periods in which Washington was reassessing its strategy toward Afghanistan, given the persistent challenges and the shortcomings of US strategy as evaluated by policymakers.

TRANSITION MEMORANDUM

~~TOP SECRET~~

4192

NATIONAL SECURITY COUNCIL

Transition

WASHINGTON, D.C. 20504

January 16, 2009

MEMORANDUM FOR THE RECORD

FROM: PAUL D. MILLER, DIRECTORATE OF IRAQ AND AFGHANISTAN

SUBJECT: Afghanistan

THE SITUATION IN 2006:

In 2006, Afghanistan faced a sharp rise in violence and corruption, a dangerous convergence of the insurgency and the drug trade, and a persistent lag in effective governance. The United States and the international community began to reexamine their approach to the security, governance, and economic development in the country, which had been relatively successful since 2001. The U.N.-brokered 2001 Bonn Agreement succeeded in producing a transitional government, a new Constitution, a presidential election in 2004, and legislative elections in Afghanistan in 2005. The Afghan economy grew quickly from its low base after 2001 as a result of a rapid expansion in the construction, telecommunications, and banking sectors. A new, multiethnic Afghan National Army began to take shape, and government institutions slowly began to resume operations after a quarter century of continuous conflict. A variety of opinion polls showed that Afghans were confident that their government would follow through on its promises to provide better security, more accountable government, jobs, and basic services. By 2006, however, the Taliban enjoyed safe haven in Pakistan, and insurgent violence was worsening in Afghanistan. The economy had grown quickly, but many Afghans believed that economic development and reconstruction efforts did not benefit them. Governance remained weak, and government institutions were riddled with corruption. The drug trade was growing unchecked and feeding the insurgency.

THIS ADMINISTRATION'S POLICY:

In late 2006, the Administration undertook a review of U.S. policy and strategy for Afghanistan. The review reiterated that our goal is for Afghanistan to be a reliable, stable ally in the War on Terror;

~~TOP SECRET~~
Reason: 1.4(d)
Declassify on: 1/16/19

NSC Declassification Review [EO 13526]
DECLASSIFY IN FULL
by William C. Carpenter on 3/23/2020

moderate, democratic, with a thriving private sector economy; capable of effectively governing its territory and borders; and respectful of the rights of its citizens.

The 2006 review recommended three steps to advance our goals and respond to the situation that had emerged by 2006:

1. Follow through on post-conflict stabilization and development.

2. Increase Afghanistan's resilience against the insurgency:
    - Increase the effectiveness of President Karzai's leadership
    - Resolve the crisis of weak and bad governance, especially in the provinces
    - Ensure the International Security Assistance Force (ISAF) has the capacity and resources to prosecute effective counterinsurgency operations
    - Accelerate the development of the Afghan National Security Forces
    - Reinforce security efforts with counter-insurgency infrastructure building and economic development
    - Reverse the increase in narcotics cultivation and suppress narcotics trafficking.

3. Induce a strategic shift in Pakistan-Afghanistan relations. It will not be possible to end the insurgency without addressing the problem of sanctuary in both countries. Pakistan has not yet ended the cross-border insurgent threat.

In the fall of 2007, the Administration assessed progress implementing our strategy and reconfirmed our focus on improving security, strengthening governance, and facilitating economic growth.

From September through November 2008, the Administration conducted a second strategy review for Afghanistan and Pakistan. The results of that review are summarized starting on page 6.

WHAT HAS BEEN ACCOMPLISHED:

1. Follow through on post-conflict stabilization and development.

    - Our efforts: Following the U.S.'s leadership, the international community agreed to empower the United Nations Special Representative of the Secretary General for Afghanistan as the senior civilian for coordinating international reconstruction and governance efforts. The U.N. Security Council unanimously passed a resolution (UNSCR 1806) in March 2008 to this effect. With U.S. support, the Afghan Government completed and submitted the Afghanistan National Development Strategy (ANDS), the government's five-year plan for security, governance, economic growth and poverty reduction. The plan was approved by the World Bank and International Monetary Fund (IMF) in May 2008 as part of an IMF requirement for

Afghanistan and was endorsed by the international community in June at a donors' conference in Paris. The donors' conference itself was a major milestone, securing over $21 billion in pledges for Afghanistan. Building on the success of the April 2008 NATO Summit in Bucharest (see page 4), we worked closely with the French to encourage them to host the conference, which brought the total pledges for Afghanistan since 2001 to $57 billion. The United States more than doubled its overall assistance to Afghanistan since the 2006 strategic review from $12.7 billion through FY06 to a total of $31.9 billion through FY09. Effect: The international community substantially increased its commitment to Afghanistan's economic and social development and reconstruction. Donors endorsed the ANDS as a tool to coordinate efforts and also agreed to measures to increase aid effectiveness. The Afghan economy continued to grow and inflation remained manageable, although the government fell short of its revenue targets for the year ending March 2008. Afghanistan is in the process of qualifying for debt-relief under the IMF's Heavily Indebted Poor Country (HIPC) program.

2. Increase Afghanistan's resilience against the insurgency.

- Increase the effectiveness of President Karzai's leadership. Our efforts: We inaugurated a periodic SVTC between the President and President Karzai as a means of shaping President Karzai's policy agenda and providing regular discussions on Afghanistan's progress. We helped empower the United Nations Assistance Mission in Afghanistan (UNAMA) to give Karzai another source of international support and encouraged Karzai into a leading role at the Bucharest NATO Summit and Paris donors conference. Effect: Karzai has responded positively to the regular high-level engagement. He has demonstrated greater energy and stability; we intend to focus continued engagement on increasing his decisiveness and resolve.

- Resolve the crisis of weak and bad governance. Our efforts: Funding for governance increased from $822 million from FY02-06 to a total of $1.9 billion through FY09. USAID's Capacity Development Program started in 2007 and spent almost $220 million building the Ministries of Agriculture, Education, Communications, Finance, Reconstruction and Rural Development, Energy and Water, Health, Labor, and others. We increased our engagement with senior Afghan officials to cultivate a broader set of ties and mentor new leadership. In July 2008, we began a review of our governance assistance strategy and are planning a "governance surge." We encouraged the Afghan Government to remove the administration of local government function from the largely corrupt Interior Ministry and place it under the Palace in the Afghan Independent Directorate for Local Governance (IDLG). We have supported IDLG programs to introduce merit-based selection of local officials and strengthen ties between the central government and provincial governance. Effect: The establishment of the IDLG has resulted in appointments of several qualified governors in place of corrupt and/ or ineffective ones and mobilized international attention on the need to further strengthen governance, particularly at the sub-national level. Recent IDLG initiatives have strengthened public perception of government leadership. Most U.S. governance programs will require a longer-term investment to show an effect in Afghanistan. Afghanistan's severe human capital shortage limits improvement in institutional capacity in the short term.

- Ensure ISAF has capacity and resources. Our efforts: The President and the Secretary of State championed the idea of a "Comprehensive Approach" among NATO allies to push NATO members to adopt counterinsurgency methods in Afghanistan; NATO adopted the Comprehensive Approach at its November 2006 summit in Riga. We pressed Allies to fill the Combined Joint Statement of Requirements and led the way with increased U.S. troop deployments, including adding a second U.S. combat brigade in Regional Command East in early 2007 and 2,000 Marines to Regional Command South in early 2008. At the Bucharest Summit in April 2008, we helped craft NATO's first Strategic Vision Statement for Afghanistan and pushed forward the first Comprehensive Strategic Political-Military Plan (CSPMP). Through the Vision Statement, Allies affirmed their long-term commitment to success in Afghanistan and identified clear short and medium-term goals to improve International Security Assistance Forces (ISAF) operational effectiveness and civil-military coordination. In October 2008, in response to our initiative, the Senate confirmed General McKiernan, the Commander of ISAF, in the newly-created position of Commander of U.S. forces in Afghanistan, enabling him to increase coordination between ISAF and Operation Enduring Freedom (OEF). Effect: The U.S. and NATO Allies and partners deployed an additional 10,708 troops to ISAF since the end of 2006, an increase of about a third. ISAF has grown from a disparate force of uncoordinated national elements with little tie-in to civilian reconstruction efforts into a larger, more cohesive force committed to pursuing a comprehensive approach of kinetic and non-kinetic lines of action. Denmark dropped its caveats and Italy relaxed its geographic restrictions. The U.S. model in Regional Command East proved relatively successful in 2007, where violence rose more slowly than in Regional Command South. The streamlined command structure brought improved coherence to the ISAF and OEF missions.

- Accelerate development of Afghan National Security Forces. Our efforts: Funding for the ANSF increased from $5.6 billion in FY02-FY06 to a total of $17.7 billion through FY09, an increase of $12.1 billion since our 2006 Strategic Review. We deployed 1,100 Marines to accelerate ANSF training in 2008. We trained and equipped commando units within the Afghanistan National Army (ANA) and improved quality and lethality of equipment we supplied to the ANA in order to improve its counterinsurgency capacity. We supported the Afghans' request to increase the targeted end-state for the ANSF to 216,000. Effect: The ANA more than doubled in size from 30,800 at the end of 2006 to an estimated 78,133 by the end of 2008, and is increasingly taking the lead in military operations. Eighteen ANA battalions have reached capability milestone 1—the ability to independently plan, execute, and sustain operations at the battalion level with no operational coalition support for organic functions—up from zero at the end of 2006. The Afghan Uniformed Police (AUP) increased from 50,700 at the end of 2006 to an estimated 75,925 by the end of 2008, and through the Focused District Development program it is improving in competence and gaining the trust of the people. Twenty-one AUP units have reached capability milestone one, up from zero at the end of 2006. Both forces are increasingly able to hold ground in the aftermath of international military clearing operations.

- Reinforce security efforts with counter-insurgency infrastructure and economic development. Our efforts: Funding for infrastructure including roads, power, schools, drinking water and irrigation, hospitals, and other efforts increased from $3.2 billion in FY02–06 to a total of $6.1 billion through FY09, an increase of $2.9 billion since our 2006 strategic review. Effect: Since 2006, the United States has built about 230 kilometers of paved roads that serve over 2.5 million Afghans. Highway One (the "ring road") is 75 percent complete. The Afghan-Tajik bridge, a major infrastructure project, opened in August 2007. Due to the improved road network Afghans have greater access to markets for their products, helping the economy grow 11.5 percent in 2007–8 and a projected 7.5 percent in 2008–9. At the same time, security forces are more mobile and can protect larger areas of the country. USAID executed a contract for a 100MW diesel power-plant in Kabul in 2007, which began producing electricity in December 2008. The refurbishment of Kajaki dam accelerated in the last few years and is expected to nearly double generation capacity to Kandahar and crucial southern provinces. With our investments in improving both availability and access to basic health care, fewer women are dying in child-birth, and infant and child mortality have been dramatically reduced. About 6 million Afghans are in school, including 1.5 million girls. The construction sector has shown strong growth, and there are now 6.5 million mobile-phone subscribers in Afghanistan, compared to almost none in 2001.

- Counternarcotics. Our efforts: Funding for counternarcotics increased from $1.4 billion in FY02–FY06 to a total of $3 billion through FY09, an increase of $1.6 billion since our 2006 strategic review. We refined the comprehensive Counternarcotics Strategy in 2007. Effect: The number of poppy-free provinces increased from 6 (of 34) in 2006 to 18 in 2008, and overall poppy cultivation fell 22 percent from 2007 to 2008. The Afghans have functional eradication forces which eradicated 15,300 hectares in 2006, 19,000 hectares in 2007, and about 5,000 hectares in 2008.

3. Induce a strategic shift in Afghan-Pakistani relations.

- Our efforts: The President brokered an agreement between Presidents Karzai and Musharraf in 2006 that inaugurated the cross-border bilateral peace *jirga* process. We are helping to build Border Coordination Centers to improve border security and foster operational cooperation among the security forces of Afghanistan and Pakistan. As part of our efforts to improve trade, we are working with the Congress to pass legislation creating Reconstruction Opportunity Zones (ROZ) that will stimulate legitimate economic activity in Afghanistan and parts of Pakistan near the border with Afghanistan. Under General McKiernan's leadership we reinvigorated the U.S.-Afghanistan–Pakistan Tripartite Military Commission. We have encouraged a strong and cooperative relationship between Presidents Karzai and Zardari. Effect: The first cross-border *jirga* was held in August 2007; a subset of the *jirga* met in Islamabad in October 2008. Tribal elders reached agreement on economic, security, and cultural issues and condemned terrorism and the drug trade. The next meeting should focus on implementation of the agreements. Progress slowed in 2007–8 because of Pakistan's political instability. In March 2008, Senator Cantwell (with Senators Hatch, Bond, Lieberman, and Hagel) introduced the Administration's proposed bill establishing an Reconstruction Opportunity Zone (ROZ) program. A House version was introduced by Representative Van Hollen. The new Congress is expected to consider the legislation in the new year. The legislation is expected to create jobs in Afghanistan and in Pakistan; to foster non-drug trade investments and business opportunities; and provide incentives for the two countries to cooperate on customs and trade. Karzai and Zardari have met on several occasions and improved the tenor of bilateral discussions on a range of issues.

FUTURE CHALLENGES:

Despite progress in all areas, challenges remain. The drug trade provides the Taliban with between $53 and $80 million per year. Violence has risen more than five fold over the last five years. The quality of governance has declined because of rampant corruption. Afghan public support for the Afghan Government and international military forces has steadily dropped over the last few years. Borders remain porous. The Taliban continue to enjoy safe haven in Pakistan.

In September and October 2008, the President directed an interagency review to assess the current situation in the Afghanistan–Pakistan theater and likely trends into 2009 and to form recommendations. (See Tab 4, "Strategic Review: Afghanistan–Pakistan" for details.) The review resulted in the following ten recommendations:

For Both Afghanistan and Pakistan:

1. Operationalize U.S. objectives. We should adopt an integrated, mid-term (3–5 years) operational objective for Afghanistan and Pakistan along these lines:

Defeat the insurgency in Afghanistan by improving security in order to enable democratic governance and development, with our most urgent goal being successful 2009 elections. Disrupt the safe haven in the frontier regions of Pakistan while assisting Pakistani efforts to deny safe haven over time. Stabilize Pakistan through a sustained partnership that enables improved security, democratic governance, and economic growth. In short, our mid-term strategy should be "secure Afghanistan, disrupt the safe haven, stabilize Pakistan."

For Afghanistan:

2. Put counter-insurgency first. We should organize U.S. efforts around counter-insurgency, aligning all other efforts in support.

3. Address both the center and the periphery. Our capacity building efforts must be targeted and effective at both the central government and the local, district, and community levels.

4. Generate unity of civilian effort in east and south. We should re-establish the role of the U.S. Embassy as the overall leader of the international civilian assistance effort, with priority to the east and south.

5. Empower the Afghan Government, then hold them accountable. Every program, engagement, and operation should have an Afghan lead. Properly enabled, the government must show measurable progress.

For Pakistan:

6. Expand disruption of the safe haven. Efforts to disrupt al-Qaida and the Taliban in the frontier regions are essential to attaining our objectives in Afghanistan and Pakistan. We must expand joint efforts beyond the Federally Administered Tribal Areas and North West Frontier Provinces to Quetta to disrupt the Taliban's senior shura.

7. Align ends, ways and means. We must increase and focus our assistance programs, both military and civilian, to support the vital U.S. interests in Pakistan's stability.

8. Build a long-term partnership. The single most important strategic shift we can make in Pakistan is to invest in a bilateral partnership that over time convinces the Pakistani people, the government, and the military that we intend to stick with them.

For the Region:

9. Promote Afghan-Pakistan cooperation. As part of our midterm approach to both Afghanistan and Pakistan, we need to expand links between the two. Most fundamental is to press Pakistan to change its policy that supports militant groups that threaten Afghanistan.

10. Work the other actors. India, Iran, the Central Asian states, Saudi Arabia, China, and Russia all have key strategic interests in Afghanistan and Pakistan. All these countries share key objectives with us; political instability, terrorism, and narcotics threaten all their societies.

The results of the strategic review will be passed to the incoming administration for consideration.

Attachments

Tab 1	Chronology for Afghanistan
Tab 2	2006 Strategic Review
Tab 3	2008 Afghanistan-Pakistan Strategy Review (slides)
Tab 4	2008 Afghanistan-Pakistan Strategy Review (paper)
Tab 5	Summary of Discussion of National Security Council Meeting on Afghanistan (December 10, 2008)
Tab 6	Memorandum of Telephone Conversation with President Karzai of Afghanistan (November 8, 2008)

POSTSCRIPT

PAUL D. MILLER, DOUGLAS LUTE, MEGHAN L. O'SULLIVAN

Afghanistan went from being a low priority in American foreign policy to one of the highest in the span of a few short days following 9/11. Once intelligence established al Qaeda's responsibility for the tragedies of that day and the presence of that organization in Afghanistan, the Bush administration demanded that the Taliban—which had control over Afghanistan at the time—hand over the leadership of al Qaeda. When the Taliban refused, the United States used military force to remove the Taliban from leadership, pushing remnants of the organization into Pakistan. This military operation was initially done with a very small military footprint and in partnership with Afghan forces on the ground long opposed to the Taliban. In the months and years that followed, the United States was joined by multiple partners including NATO both to fight the insurgency that emerged as the Taliban reconstituted and to help Afghans build a different political, economic, and security future.

US policy toward Afghanistan was at a crossroads—another crossroads—at the time of the transition from President Bush to President Obama. The United States had already been in Afghanistan for more than seven years, and its strategy toward the country had changed dramatically in the years after 9/11.

The Bush Administration Approach

The Bush administration was uncompromising in its pursuit of al Qaeda. It initially rejected any compromise that would have left the Taliban a political role and focused somewhat narrowly on counterterrorism and the Bonn Process for defining a future for Afghanistan. The administration explicitly rejected the idea of deploying large-scale military or civilian resources into Afghanistan, wary of appearing like an occupying force and distorting the economy. In addition, even before March 2003, Afghanistan had to compete with Iraq for attention and resources. Yet as noted in the Transition Memorandum, these first several years up to 2006 were considered to be "relatively successful." That judgment is partly true, recognizing the adoption of a new constitution, successful elections in 2004 and 2005, the UN's efforts to demilitarize warlords' militias, the growing Afghan economy, and indices of human development that started to track upward for the first time in decades. However, this positive assessment was perhaps too glib, given the enduring challenges, including endemic state weakness, the emerging Taliban insurgency including Pakistani support, and the drug trade.

The deteriorating situation on the ground led to a strategic review in 2006, and the Bush administration shifted toward a counterinsurgency approach. The administration concluded that the extremely fragile Afghan state demanded more robust attention and support if it were to withstand pressures from the growing insurgency. The United States rededicated itself to the goal of an Afghanistan that, in the words of the Transition Memorandum, was "a reliable, stable ally in the War on Terror; moderate, democratic, with a thriving private sector; capable of effectively governing its territory and borders; and respectful of the rights of its citizens," and increased its efforts across the board.

In particular, in the following years, the Bush administration further internationalized the effort in Afghanistan. The United Nations, the World Bank, and other international development banks increased their involvement in Afghanistan. The United Nations Special Representative of the Secretary General for Afghanistan became the senior coordinator for all international reconstruction and governance efforts, while donor countries around the world significantly upped their pledges to support Afghanistan's development. The United States expanded its effort to establish and support Provincial Reconstruction Teams (PRTs)—bodies that included both military and civilian personnel partnered with coalition security forces and operating in Afghanistan's many provinces. The mission of these PRTs was to extend the reach of both the Afghan government and coalition forces through development and other governance programs well beyond Kabul. Whereas in late 2003, only three partner countries—New Zealand, Britain, and Germany—were leading PRTs in Afghanistan, by 2009, that number had risen to sixteen.

Militarily, the United States also increased its footprint (as did its coalition partners) and accelerated development of the Afghan National Security Forces. In 2007 and 2008, the Bush administration roughly doubled the number of US troops in Afghanistan, from 20,000 to about 40,000. It helped NATO broaden its involvement in Afghanistan; the alliance expanded its command structure, gradually adopted more counterinsurgency efforts, and some countries dropped restrictive national caveats that constrained their military role. Finally, in the years following the review, the administration, acknowledging the central role of Pakistan, tried to bring Afghanistan's neighbor "on side" with its efforts, offering Pakistan a strategic relationship that transcended counterterrorism cooperation.

Particularly in terms of human development, the results were significant. Life expectancy, immunization rates, and access to sanitation, clean water, and telecommunications all rose; and maternal mortality declined thanks to more widely available healthcare. More than six million Afghans were in school by 2009, including more than 1.5 million girls. In many parts of the country, women joined the workforce and were able to move about freely. The total value of all imports tripled, and exports rose fivefold. The government's revenue as a percentage of GDP rose from less than 1 percent to over 10 percent, indicating its slowly growing institutional capacity.

Yet, despite more resources and an approach geared at building the capacity of the Afghan state and combating the negative influence from Pakistan, the overall security situation continued to deteriorate. As noted in the Transition Memorandum, violence increased dramatically, and the quality of governance declined due to corruption. The Bush administration concluded that the still-deteriorating situation warranted yet another strategic review in late 2008. This review concluded that by virtually every meaningful metric, the situation was still getting worse, not better. The results of the 2008 review reiterated the imperative of counterinsurgency and the goal of "defeat[ing] the insurgency." It emphasized the need for greater coordination, accountability, regional sensitivity, and a long-term perspective in Afghanistan, as well as the critical role of Pakistan. The 2008 strategy review was the Bush administration's effort to candidly assess the strengths and weaknesses of the 2006–2008 policy, and to give the Obama administration a running start on developing its own policy.

What Has Happened Since the End of the Bush Administration?

President Barack Obama initially embraced the Bush administration's approach before repudiating it and pursuing a different course. Obama came into office having promised to prioritize US efforts on Afghanistan and Pakistan over Iraq and to win the Afghan war. Shortly after taking office, Obama convened his own strategy review, supported by the newly created Special Representative for Afghanistan and Pakistan and the National Security Council staff, most of which he had asked to stay on from the Bush administration. The results of this review were prefigured by the 2008 Bush review; the new president ordered 21,000 additional US troops to Afghanistan and defined the goal clearly as "to disrupt, dismantle, and defeat al Qaeda in Pakistan and Afghanistan, and to prevent their return to either country in the future." His policy explicitly committed the

United States to "promoting a more capable, accountable, and effective government in Afghanistan" that required "executing and resourcing an integrated civilian-military counter-insurgency strategy in Afghanistan."[1] He quadrupled the number of US diplomats and aid workers in the country and increased civilian assistance by $2 billion from 2009 to 2010. He explicitly linked his administration's efforts in Afghanistan and Pakistan to Bush's own, acknowledging the interdependencies.

But following a series of developments in 2009, President Obama convened yet another strategy review in late 2009. Violence dramatically spiked, the August 2009 Afghan presidential election was marred by fraud, Obama administration officials publicly sparred with President Karzai, and International Security Assistance Force (ISAF) Commander General Stanley McChrystal delivered a withering critique of the war and an unanticipated request for tens of thousands more troops in his August 2009 commander's assessment. The assessment leaked to the press, helping fuel a public perception that the Obama administration's new policy was failing even though it had not had time to be implemented fully.

The result was a third NSC strategy review in less than a year. President Obama's new policy, announced in December 2009, moved decidedly away from a fully resourced counterinsurgency or state-building strategy. Instead, it aimed at degrading the Taliban, training Afghan security forces to operate with decreasing international support, and pared back ambitions for building the Afghan state. Obama ordered a temporary surge of troops to try to degrade the Taliban and enable the development of Afghan capacity, but simultaneously announced a timeline to begin their withdrawal—an approach that critics insisted would be counterproductive. He subsequently announced a series of further withdrawals throughout the remainder of his presidency as Afghan forces were fielded.

The war reached its greatest intensity in 2010 and 2011, when 140,000 deployed US and coalition troops came closest to implementing a partial counterinsurgency campaign. The US-led coalition made important progress: Afghan security forces grew in number and capability, and the Taliban suffered significant military setbacks. Al Qaeda had little presence in Afghanistan and a 2011 raid into

---

1. "Remarks by the President," March 27, 2009, https://obamawhitehouse.archives.gov /the-press-office/remarks-president-a-new-strategy-afghanistan-and-pakistan; "White House White Paper," March 27, 2009, https://foreignpolicy.com/2009/03/27/white -house-white-paper-on-u-s-policy-to-afghanistan-and-pakistan/.

Pakistan brought bin Laden to justice. But tactical military gains were not sufficient to add up to strategic success as progress on Afghan governance lagged, the partnership with the Karzai government became unreliable, and Pakistan refused to deny the Taliban safe haven. Despite attempts to explore diplomatic openings with the Taliban, overall progress—military, political, diplomatic—was not sufficient to force the Taliban to the negotiating table.

US funding for civilian reconstruction fell every year after 2010 and, following the administration's timetable, US troops began to withdraw after 2011. At the end of 2014 responsibility for security passed to the Afghan government, and the NATO ISAF changed its mission to train, advise, and assist Afghan forces. President Obama announced his intent to complete the withdrawal of all US troops by the end of 2016 but reversed course after the Taliban resurged and briefly seized Kunduz—Afghanistan's fifth-largest city—in late 2015. The Taliban continued to gain ground as US forces withdrew. About 9,800 US troops remained in Afghanistan at the end of the Obama administration.

President Donald Trump inherited a war that he had campaigned against and promised to end. Like Presidents Bush and Obama, he had both an early policy and a later one. In August 2017, following the input of National Security Advisor H. R. McMaster and Defense Secretary James Mattis, Trump repudiated talk of withdrawal, vowed to win the war, pledged a modest increase in troop numbers, and promised to loosen the rules of military engagement. He also foreswore nation building, like Obama after 2009, and did not invest in civilian reconstruction and stabilization. It was not a return to the earlier, limited counterinsurgency strategy, but a beefed-up version of the earlier counterterrorism strategy, with additional focus on training Afghan security forces.

One year later Trump appointed Zalmay Khalilzad as Special Representative for Afghanistan Reconciliation to begin peace talks with the Taliban. It was not the first attempt at talks with the Taliban, but the Trump administration departed from earlier efforts in several ways. Like Obama's diplomatic efforts, but unlike Bush's, the talks took place without any preconditions on the Taliban—the Taliban were not required to denounce al Qaeda, accept a ceasefire, or recognize the new Afghan constitution. The talks were the first officially acknowledged bilateral talks between the US government and the Taliban (at least since the 1996 attempt by the Clinton administration to facilitate a gas pipeline through Afghanistan), and thus were the first to give the post-2001 Taliban legitimacy as an actor on the international stage.

Although widely criticized for circumventing the Afghan government, the talks resulted in an agreement between the United States and the Taliban, signed in February of 2020. Although not all parts of the agreement were made public, its essential elements involved the eventual full withdrawal of US troops in exchange for the Taliban bringing down violence, promising to restrain al Qaeda (a promise for which there were no enforcement or verification mechanisms), and engaging in talks with the Afghan government toward a ceasefire and political settlement (talks that had never occurred previously, despite numerous past efforts to foster them). While the Taliban did cease attacks on coalition forces, violence against Afghan forces and civilians increased and the Taliban continued its relationship with al Qaeda. Talks between the Afghan government and the Taliban got off to a slow start and then were suspended. Yet despite the Taliban failing to meet its obligations under the agreement, the Trump administration proceeded with the US drawdown, leaving only 3,000 or so US forces in Afghanistan by the time of the transition from Trump to Biden.

In April 2021, after its own internal review, the Biden administration decided to continue with the complete drawdown of American forces, albeit on a slightly modified timeline. After the drawdown was substantially complete, and with speed that surprised many, the Taliban successfully swept through Afghanistan's provinces, negotiating surrender agreements with many Afghan forces, allowing it to take control of towns, rural areas, and even major cities often without resistance. A quick collapse of the Afghan government gave way to a full Taliban takeover of Afghanistan. The Taliban entered Kabul on August 15, 2021, roughly two weeks before the Biden administration had intended to complete its full withdrawal of American forces. Afghan military and civilian institutions proved unable to sustain themselves in the face of the rapid withdrawal of support from the United States and the international community. By August 31, the United States and its NATO partners had withdrawn all their forces from Afghanistan and shuttered their embassies.

How Did the Bush Administration Do?

Initially, from 2001–2006, the Bush administration pursued a more limited, counterterrorism-centric approach while espousing ambitious state-building goals at the same time. The smaller footprint approach—adopted in part to prevent an occupation narrative from taking root and the economy from being distorted by inflation and corruption—was inadequate to build a state of the type envisioned in the Bush administration's end-state goal.[2] But it also proved insufficient to keep the Taliban at bay—especially given the underlying conditions in Afghanistan and the uneven cooperation Pakistan was offering to the Bush administration. While the Taliban never threatened the United States outside Afghanistan, the Bush administration perceived the Taliban as a threat to the United States, given the Taliban's close relationship with terrorist organizations. Despite the evident achievements of this period, the Taliban gained strength more quickly than the Afghan government gained capacity, forcing the United States to reevaluate whether it could achieve either its counterterrorism objectives or its more ambitious state-building goals with its limited engagement. Whether it could have advanced its narrow interests related to al Qaeda and other internationally focused terrorist groups, while being indifferent to the fate of the Afghan state, was never tested.

The Bush administration later shifted to a limited counterinsurgency approach, as it realized the shortcomings of its earlier strategy. It devoted more resources to Afghanistan in its final years—as did the Obama Administration early on—but still struggled to make headway. There is some weight to the argument that this counterinsurgency approach, while tried, was still underresourced and not given sufficient time to succeed, as the Obama administration announced its intent to withdraw troops as early as December 2009 and in 2011 agreed to begin transitioning Afghan forces to take charge of security. There is also something to the argument that it was difficult for Afghanistan to receive the necessary resources and attention, given the demands of the war in Iraq, the financial crisis in the developed world, and other competing priorities on the international landscape. And while many of the Afghans working with the coalition were notably steadfast and courageous, some proved corrupt and opportunistic. Collectively, these factors significantly constrained what might have been achievable in Afghanistan.

Pakistan also proved to be an enduring obstacle to a successful strategy in Afghanistan that neither the Bush administration nor the administrations that followed were able to overcome. Even as al Qaeda relocated to Pakistan, the Pakistani Taliban emerged and Pakistan continued to leverage terrorist proxies

---

2. As noted above, the goal was "a reliable, stable ally in the War on Terror; moderate, democratic, with a thriving private sector; capable of effectively governing its territory and borders; and respectful of the rights of its citizens."

against India, risking conflict between nuclear powers. US policymakers were unable to shift the strategic calculations of Pakistan to make it a true ally in American pursuits in Afghanistan and against terrorists. The United States had comparatively far less ability to influence events in Pakistan than in Afghanistan—yet many experts would argue that it was in Pakistan where vital American interests lay and that the ultimate outcome of the war in Afghanistan was to be determined. The United States became trapped in a situation in which the most significant leverage points were beyond its reach.

Some observers now question whether the United States ever had the ability and know-how to rebuild the Afghan state. Nation building on the scale required by Afghanistan—a country with little physical infrastructure or human capital and no modern institutions—would have been unprecedented among peace-building operations since World War II. The United States may simply have lacked the knowledge and expertise to accomplish it. The Biden administration, in explaining its decision to withdraw all US forces from Afghanistan, seemed to espouse this view.

Others counter that the United States and international community simply lacked the will and strategic patience to succeed. They had built considerable expertise in peace building during the previous decade. Particularly in the later Bush years, the United States sought to address gaps in expertise and capabilities by bringing in the United Nations, its European allies, and others to help with state building. These observers emphasize not a lack of US competencies but will; they argue that the United States ultimately balked at the level and intensity of resources, effort, and time that would have been required. Whether the United States lacked the know-how or the political will—or both—to help Afghans transform their country into a moderate, stable, democratic country, the collective efforts of the United States and its partners were insufficient to bring about success in the time period that American administrations were willing to devote to it.

It is this lack of American capacity or will to build the Afghan state that contributed to what is commonly perceived as the overmilitarization of US policy in Afghanistan. US policymakers were aware of the importance of social, cultural, economic, and political dimensions of their engagement in Afghanistan. But the historical underinvestment in US civilian capabilities meant that policymakers frequently—if reluctantly—turned to the American military by default to take on missions for which they were not prepared. This not only put undue strain on the US military, but it extended the perception of the militarization of state building in Afghanistan and contributed to unanticipated and counterproductive results.

What Are the Lessons Learned?

The US experience in Afghanistan, under the Bush administration and after, is sobering despite the enormous commitment and expertise that US and coalition military and civilians brought to the effort. The most fundamental lessons are the following:

- *Especially at the outset, embracing ambitious goals was viewed as less of a choice than a necessity.* To many, the goals espoused by the United States in Afghanistan were overly ambitious, divorced from the extreme poverty of the country, its supposed lack of foundations for democracy, and the hostile countries surrounding it. Others acknowledge the large gap between aspirations and on-the-ground realities, but point out that the United States was compelled by 9/11 to take on a challenge of this proportion. It did not do so naïvely or with the expectations that the United States could deliver a different future to Afghans without great difficulty. Rather, the Bush administration took on this challenge reluctantly, realizing that a failure to bring a more secure, effective state to Afghanistan ran the risk of a repetition of the events of 9/11 which had resulted, in its view, from a failure to mount such an effort after the Soviets had been expelled from Afghanistan.
- *Yet the United States repeatedly failed to align ambitious goals with the resources needed to achieve them.* Regardless of whether one believes that the goals were too ambitious, or were simply what the situation required, the fact remains that rarely, if ever, were the resources accorded to Afghanistan commensurate with the goals espoused. Throughout the twenty years that the United States remained involved militarily in Afghanistan, America alternatively espoused ambitious goals of nation building and more modest ones related only to counterterrorism—yet arguably never closed the gap between goals and the resources devoted to achieving them. The years of 2001–2005— while the Taliban was regrouping in Pakistan—were the most promising because the coalition faced the most favorable operational environment. Yet, those years were marked by the most ambitious goals, but modest resourcing. Some argue that this mismatch—which they attribute in large part to the re-

source demands of Iraq—contributed to America's strategic failure in Afghanistan. Yet there was concern at the time—whether justified or not—that greater resources would have overwhelmed the weak Afghan economy and, in Afghan eyes, converted American liberators into foreign occupiers. Subsequent administrations continued to grapple with the challenge of aligning resources with goals, a challenge made progressively more difficult by the deteriorating security situation.

- *The continual focus on transition undermined the strategic coherence of US policy.* Afghanistan is known by most Americans as the country's longest war. However, the desire and goal of transitioning to Afghan control and departing Afghanistan was omnipresent throughout most of the twenty years that the United States was involved in Afghanistan. From December 2009, nearly every speech made by a US president on Afghanistan focused on leaving the country, except for Donald Trump's August 2017 speech. While the United States was inevitably going to leave Afghanistan once its interests dictated it, the constant emphasis on the temporary nature of America's commitment created a political and psychological dynamic that worked against efforts to create enduring institutions, battle corruption, and strengthen the Afghan state vis-à-vis its neighbors.

- *Domestic rhetoric about "forever wars" constrained policymaker options.* Reference to America's "forever wars" became commonplace by both Republican and Democratic lawmakers and politicians wanting to end US involvement in Iraq and Afghanistan after decades-long commitments. This language obscured the fact that over the many years the United States was involved in both countries, its military presence, mission, and commitment had shifted and shrunk dramatically. In the case of Afghanistan, by 2021, the United States had only about 3,000 troops there—just 2 percent of the number of US troops in Afghanistan a decade earlier. Moreover, those 3,000 troops were largely limited to supporting Afghan forces (which were the ones on the front line), whereas the 140,000 coalition troops deployed to Afghanistan during the 2009 surge of forces were engaged in direct combat. The "forever war" moniker, however, obscured this changed reality and drove the policy conversation toward ending the war and away from consideration of whether the existing minimal commitment might have been commensurate with America's greatly diminished, but still existent, national interests in Afghanistan.

- *Policymakers overestimated the ability of the United States to produce an outcome.* In Iraq, a period of adequate resourcing and alignment of goals and resources during the "Surge" produced an interval of clearly positive momentum. The same cannot be said for Afghanistan. Perhaps the time given for a reasonably resourced counterinsurgency strategy was insufficient, and the strategy was certainly undermined by President Obama's withdrawal timetables. However, it is also possible that the scope and scale of the mission undertaken was simply beyond the capabilities of the United States, the coalition, and the international community at the level of resourcing they were willing to devote to it. Even if ambitious goals were achievable in theory, the US strategy did not consider the practical limitations of the US government and particularly its civilian departments and agencies—their lack of the organization, capabilities, and preparation required for executing two simultaneous and protracted stabilization and reconstruction operations, one in Iraq and one in Afghanistan. A more effective strategic conversation might have identified such limitations and made commensurate adjustments. None of the four administrations that wrestled with this problem gets high marks on this score. Priorities between the two theaters were set more in response to political than strategic considerations.

- *Policymakers underestimated the impact of variables beyond US control.* A parallel lesson to overestimating American, coalition, and international capabilities is underestimating the importance of factors that remained outside their control. Be it Pakistan, the region more broadly, the growing crisis with Iran, the deteriorating relationship between Washington and Beijing and Moscow, the global financial crisis, the poor quality of some Afghan leaders, or the COVID crisis, many factors that were ultimately beyond the control of the United States and its coalition and international partners have been significant in determining developments and outcomes in Afghanistan.

CHAPTER 6

Pakistan

MARK WEBBER

If asked to identify the most challenging foreign policy issues facing the incoming Obama administration in January 2009, senior Bush administration officials leaving the White House would likely have included Pakistan in the top three. Pakistan posed daunting challenges for the new team, including the aftermath of the November 2008 terrorist attacks in Mumbai, India, by Pakistan-based extremists, Pakistan's refusal to accept the existential threat posed by such terrorist groups to its own national security, the threat of these terrorists to the United States and its allies and partners, the steady flow of Pakistan-based insurgents into Afghanistan and India, a vulnerable nuclear arsenal, a struggling new civilian government, and a collapsing Pakistani economy. Yet in 2022 it is unlikely Pakistan would be included in a similar list of top US national security priorities—even though many of these challenges have endured.

There are good reasons why Pakistan does not feature as prominently in US foreign policy discussions today as it did in 2009. The death of Osama bin Laden and degradation of the al Qaeda network, the absence of a major terrorist attack stemming from Pakistan over the past decade, the withdrawal of US forces from Afghanistan, and the broader foreign policy paradigm shift away from counterterrorism to "great power" competition have pushed Pakistan down the priorities list. But there are also more troubling reasons why Pakistan is no longer at the forefront of US foreign policy—most notably, the return of a historical tendency for both the United States and Pakistan to view their relationship as a function of events in other nations (e.g., Afghanistan, India, China) rather than on its own terms.

The inability to solidify a partnership that recognizes the intrinsic value of their bilateral cooperation has hindered the United States' work with Pakistan. This has resulted in the United States fluctuating between "getting tough" on Pakistan and then repairing relations to facilitate negotiations with third parties or to advance other objectives. In turn, this approach has fueled the perception that the United States continues to be the "on-again-off-again" partner Bush administration officials lamented in the Transition Memorandum. At the same time, Pakistan has not made cooperation easy. For two decades, US efforts to improve the relationship and address mutual national security priorities have been met with resistance, obfuscation, double-dealing, and little reciprocation from successive Pakistani governments.

TRANSITION MEMORANDUM

~~TOP SECRET~~

7749

NATIONAL SECURITY COUNCIL

WASHINGTON, D.C. 20504

Transition

NSC Declassification Review [E.O. 13526]
DECLASSIFY IN PART
by William C. Carpenter 3/23/2020

January 16, 2009

MEMORANDUM FOR THE RECORD

FROM: MARK WEBBER, SOUTH AND CENTRAL ASIAN AFFAIRS
             JORGAN ANDREWS, SOUTH AND CENTRAL ASIAN AFFAIRS
             ANISH GOEL, SOUTH AND CENTRAL ASIAN AFFAIRS
             PATRICIA MAHONEY, SOUTH AND CENTRAL ASIAN AFFAIRS

SUBJECT: Pakistan

THE SITUATION AS WE FOUND IT:

Actions by Pakistani governments throughout the late 1980s and 1990s had triggered successive statutory U.S. sanctions on Pakistan, most recently imposed in response to nuclear testing in 1998 and a military coup in 1999. In addition, during the 1990s, Pakistan supported the Taliban regime in Afghanistan, hosting al-Qaida training and operational facilities. These actions stymied more productive bilateral relations with the United States. Pakistan was importing only $540 million of United States goods, and United States development assistance, crucial to building the people-to-people links that underpin robust relations, was virtually nil. Our on-again-off-again pattern of suspending aid as individual Pakistani actions triggered specific statutory sanctions failed to convey a clear and consistent message as to our primary objectives with Pakistan, including establishing a long-lasting bilateral partnership and helping Pakistan to become a strong, stable, and prosperous state. Instead, our actions had created a flawed impression of the United States as a capricious, opportunistic, fair-weather friend. As President Musharraf described it to the President in a September 15, 2001 telephone conversation,

In addition, Pakistani tensions with India had brought the two nuclear-armed rivals to the brink of conflict in the spring of 1999. Pakistan's efforts to ensure its national security through questionable

~~TOP SECRET~~
Reason: 1.4(b) (d)
Declassify on: 1/16/19

Re-Classified by: Ellen J. L. Knight
Reason: 1.4(b), (c), and (d)
Declassify on: 1/16/2034

means—whether by recognizing and backing the Taliban; enabling cross-border militants, such as Lashkar-e-Tayyiba (LT), to attack and pressure India; or creating a nuclear arsenal without appropriate safeguards—significantly undermined the safety and stability of the entire world.

Pakistan's history as an intermittent democracy also colored relations. In 1999 General Musharraf declared an extended state of emergency, suspended the constitution, disbanded Parliament, and deposed the elected   leadership. The sense of relief that initially greeted this coup among the general population demonstrated the depth of disillusionment many Pakistanis felt toward the two major political parties, which had alternated in leading ineffective and corrupt governments throughout the 1990s.

THIS ADMINISTRATION'S POLICY:

Prior to September 11, 2001, this Administration recognized the geopolitical importance of improving relations with our former ally. By mid-2001, the Administration had begun a formal review of sanctions on both India and Pakistan, and in June 2001, a National Security Council Deputies Committee meeting identified key objectives related to Pakistan, including:

- Gaining its support for eliminating al-Qaida,
- Reducing regional tensions that could lead to nuclear war, and
- Preventing third-party proliferation.

In an August 4, 2001 letter to President Musharraf, the President stressed the "significant threat to American lives from terrorists headquartered in Afghanistan" and urged Pakistan to "use its considerable influence to stop the Taliban from harboring terrorists … and engage actively against al-Qaida." The President also emphasized the link between an improved economic outlook for Pakistan and a return to democracy, and welcomed President Musharraf's commitment to hold elections and restore civilian rule in 2002.

The horrific events of September 11 highlighted the urgency of engaging Pakistan. Following a phone call between Secretary Powell and President Musharraf on September 13, 2001, the President spoke with Musharraf on September 15, 2001. During that call, Musharraf pledged to join us in the War on Terror. However, securing Pakistan's full cooperation against terrorism would also require Pakistan to: (1) overcome fears about India's regional power and ambitions; (2) conclude that extremist groups, tolerated and nurtured by Pakistan's Inter-Services Intelligence (ISI), posed a threat to the region and Pakistan itself; and (3) strengthen nonproliferation efforts and eliminate the network headed by Pakistani scientist A.Q. Khan.

To be successful, U.S. engagement would have to overcome the Pakistani leadership's suspicion of eventual abandonment upon achievement of our immediate goals. To develop this level of trust, our engagement would have to be broad-based and multifaceted, rather than focused primarily on short-term counterterrorism objectives. The United States would need to revitalize our friendship with the Pakistani people and dispel misperceptions that the War on Terror was a war on Islam.

Finally, our engagement with Pakistan was designed to lead it back toward a democratic path. Recognizing that extended emergency rule, the absence of basic freedoms, and disenfranchisement help fuel extremism and instability, the United States worked to push Pakistan toward democracy. In the long run, a democratic Pakistan would be a more effective partner and reliable ally.

Accordingly, the Administration's policy sought to:

- Promote Pakistan's peaceful transition to democracy;
- Secure Pakistan's cooperation in the War on Terror and improve its counterterrorism capabilities, including through military assistance programs;
- Encourage improved Indo-Pak relations and Pakistan's development as a responsible regional actor;
- Improve the safety and security of Pakistan's nuclear program, including equipment and technology, through enhanced nonproliferation measures; and
- Assist in Pakistan's economic development.

WHAT HAS BEEN ACCOMPLISHED:

Beginning with the lifting of sanctions in September 2001, the Administration fostered the development of an increase in political, military, and economic support to Pakistan, helping to transform it from a proliferation pariah to a Major Non-NATO ally in 2004. By 2006, Pakistan had become the third largest recipient of U.S. economic support funds, behind Israel and Egypt. Two-way trade doubled from approximately $2.8 billion in 2001 to approximately $5.6 billion by the end of 2007. And the quick and comprehensive disaster relief response by the United States in the wake of the devastating 2005 earthquake led to a surge in popularity for the United States among Pakistanis, albeit for a short time. During a historic visit to Islamabad in 2006, the President established with President Musharraf the U.S.-Pakistan Strategic Partnership.

Despite such breakthroughs, the results of U.S. efforts to achieve our policy goals have been mixed, due in part to political and economic instability and Pakistan's reluctance to embrace the strategic shift necessary to address the growing threat of terrorism inside its borders.

Democratic Transition. Beginning in 2001, the Administration, led by the President's personal engagement, particularly in 2006 and 2007, maintained steady pressure on Musharraf to restore civilian government, hold credible democratic elections, and resign as Chief of Army Staff. The United States provided assistance to encourage this effort, including in the areas of election administration, judicial reform, and independent media. Musharraf's desire to control the pace of democratization, however, proved counterproductive, especially once he perceived that his two greatest achievements—a freer press and a more independent judiciary—were turning against him.

In March 2007, Musharraf tried to force Chief Justice of the Supreme Court Iftikhar Chaudhry to resign his position. When he refused, Musharraf dismissed him, spurring large demonstrations through the country that lasted well into the summer of 2007.

After being reelected President by the existing parliament in October 2007, and fearing that the judiciary and political opposition were undermining him, Musharraf declared a state of emergency (SOE) in November 2007, despite U.S. efforts to convince him that such a move was unnecessary and counterproductive. As part of the SOE, which was approved by the National Assembly, Musharraf suspended Pakistan's constitution, dismissed 60 judges and half of the Supreme Court, and arrested 8,000–9,000 people, many of whom were members of the political opposition.

The President, recognizing the implications of Musharraf's actions, took steps to convince Musharraf to resolve the volatile situation through a number of immediate and necessary events, including: setting a firm date for the national elections; resigning as Chief of Army Staff; lifting the SOE; and ensuring that the elections proceeded as scheduled and were free and fair.

The sustained engagement of the President and broader U.S. influence paid off when Musharraf stepped down as Chief of Army Staff in November 2007, and when he lifted the SOE in December 2007. Subsequently, in February 2008, Pakistan held parliamentary elections, after postponing the original date due to the assassination of the highly popular Benazir Bhutto on December 27, 2007. The elections were widely regarded as reflective of the will of the people. Extremist Islamic parties were routed, and a coalition civilian government, led by the Bhutto's Pakistan People's Party Parliamentarians (PPPP) was installed under the leadership of Prime Minister Yousaf Raza Gillani.

Ultimately, Musharraf's heavy-handed actions against the judiciary and imposition of the state of emergency proved to be too politically unpopular to sustain his presidency. In August 2008, faced with little support from the people or the military and almost certain impeachment by the new parliament, President Musharraf resigned. Asif Ali Zardari, Bhutto's widower, was subsequently elected President in September 2008.

The reestablishment of an elected civilian government and credible elections that ushered moderate, secular opposition parties back to power opened a new chapter in Pakistan's democratic history and a strategic opportunity for the United States.

Cooperation in the War on Terror. With approximately 1,400 members of its security forces killed since September 11 and hundreds of Pakistani civilians targeted by terrorists, Pakistan has suffered more casualties than any of our Operation Enduring Freedom (OEF) allies. Pakistan's assistance, including through information sharing, logistical and base support, and coordinated military operations, initially led to the capture of several hundred terrorist suspects – including senior Al Qaida and Taliban leaders – primarily in the country's settled areas rather than the largely autonomous Federally Administered Tribal Areas (FATA). However, Pakistan's efforts began to flag, and al-Qaida and Taliban leadership remain largely safe from Pakistan's counterterrorism efforts. U.S. efforts have focused on:

- Implementing a robust campaign plan to disrupt the terrorist safehaven in Pakistan;
- Supporting Pakistan's security, development, and governance plan in the border regions;
- Building Pakistani counterterrorism capabilities and capacity;
- Reimbursing Pakistan for its support of coalition efforts in Afghanistan;
- Improving the public messaging campaign to encourage Pakistanis to recognize the terrorist threat to Pakistan; and
- Encouraging a strategic shift away from a focus on fighting a war with India toward eliminating militant groups in Pakistan, including Kashmiri extremists, which represent the greatest threat to Pakistani national security interests.

Counter-terror Campaign Plan: By 2007, the threat to the United States, our allies, and Pakistan itself from extremist groups planning, training, and conducting attacks from the border regions had significantly increased. Pakistani peace accords signed with the tribal leaders in the FATA in 2006 had failed to reduce cross-border violence in Afghanistan and eliminate the international terrorist safe haven. The GOP's offensive efforts against al-Qaida and its affilitates in the FATA proved to be inadequate.

In response, the Administration undertook an effort to develop a counterterrorism campaign plan that would address the threat posed by al-Qaida, the Taliban, and associated groups to the Homeland and our troops in Afghanistan. In particular, the campaign plan focused on removing senior leaders and key operatives, destroying known terrorist facilities, and disrupting ongoing plotting, training, communications, and travel of the militants in the border regions. The campaign has had success disrupting the safehaven and systematically dismantling senior AQ leadership. AQ losses during 2008 span the shura council, external operations, propaganda, facilitation, religious affairs, affiliates outreach, and paramilitary activities. These effects are testing the leadership's resilience and threatening operational capabilities rebuilt within AQ's secure safehaven in 2006–2007.

FATA Security Development Policy: In parallel, the United States continued to work with the Pakistani Government on implementing the longer term economic, political, and security strategy in the FATA. Responding to President Musharraf's original request to support Pakistan's strategy to improve security, strengthen governance, and boost economic development in the Federally Administered Tribal Areas (FATA), the Administration committed to and began implementing a Security Development

Plan in 2006 that included funds to train and equip the paramilitary Frontier Corps, increase Pakistani special operations capabilities, and improve communication among Afghan, ISAF, and Pakistani forces. By September 2008, we began to see positive developments from these commitments as the Pakistani Army started carrying out sustained military operations in terrorist strongholds in the Afghan-Pakistani border regions.

Pakistan also instituted more robust cooperation with the United States on counterterrorism and counterinsurgency, including opening the first Border Coordination Center with U.S., Pakistani, and Afghan troops; implementing U.S. training for Pakistani security forces; seeking to expand intelligence information sharing; and considering other joint operational capabilities, including a Joint Cooperation Center.

Coalition Support Funds and Foreign Military Financing: Pakistan's logistical supply line and air support to OEF has proven crucial to maintaining operations. Beginning in Fiscal Year 2002, the Administration began reimbursing Pakistan, via the Coalition Support Funds (CSF) program, for costs sustained in supporting OEF. By the end of 2007, we had provided Pakistan more than $5.3 billion in reimbursements – approximately $1 billion per year. Recently, the central supply links to Afghanistan have increasingly been targets of militants, highlighting both the fragility and importance of Pakistan to allied efforts in Afghanistan.

Assistance to improve the Pakistani Army's abilities and capacity to counter terrorism is critical to building ties with the Pakistani military and support for the war on terror. Each year from 2005–2009, the United States has provided $300 million in Foreign Military Financing (FMF) funds to help build Pakistan's conventional military and counterterrorism capabilities. The Administration also has expanded its International Military Education and Training (IMET) program to restore the personal and professional linkages lost during successive waves of sanctions.

In 2005, following almost two decades of frustration from Pakistan over intermittent sales of F-16 fighter aircraft, the President recognized the value of committing to sell Pakistan a new generation of F-16s. The decision, first discussed between the President and President Musharraf in New York in September 2004, was announced on March 25, 2005. The overall package, worth $3.1 billion, included new planes, associated munitions, and 46 mid-life updates (MLUs) for Pakistan's existing fleet. (The number of new planes was reduced from 36 following the 2005 earthquake in Kashmir.)

Strategic Communications: With the assassination of Bhutto and the rise in suicide attacks within Pakistan, the Administration also stepped up its efforts to urge the new Pakistani Government to take ownership over the struggle against violent extremism that posed a direct threat to Pakistan itself. After a series of lethal attacks nationwide during the summer of 2008, the bombing of the Islamabad Marriott hotel in September 2008 was the most glaring example of the insurgency turning inward on Pakistan. In 2008, Pakistan had begun to build support for the War on Terror exemplified by the statements of President Zardari and Prime Minister Gillani, who in his July 2008 meeting with the President ▓▓▓▓▓▓▓▓▓▓▓▓▓▓▓▓▓▓▓▓▓▓▓▓▓▓▓▓▓▓ While this is an encouraging sign from the GOP leadership and has been reflected in more aggressive Pakistani military operations and more tolerance of the U.S. campaign plan, it has not translated into substantial Pakistani public support for more robust CT actions.

Laskhar-e-Tayyiba and Kashmir: The late-November 2008 terrorist attacks in Mumbai highlighted the increase in prominence of traditional Kashmir-based militant groups in international terrorism. The United States took steps to protect our national security interests and diffuse tensions between India and Pakistan, including:

- Urging the Indian government to act with restraint;
- Assisting India with the investigation of the attacks;
- Pressuring Pakistan to take immediate and demonstrable action against LT and associated groups; and
- Encouraging Indo-Pakistani cooperation in the investigation and working together to counter terrorism in the region.

As a result, Pakistan has taken promising steps, but success will be measured by the long-term effort to shut down terrorist networks and the willingness of Indian and Pakistan to cooperate.

Strategic Shift: Pakistan continued to focus its military capacity and capability on India. While the Mumbai attacks remind us of the potential for armed conflict between these two nuclear powers, the success in the war on terror will depend on Pakistan making a strategic shift to focus on the terrorist threat. The President recognized that this must including reforming the Pakistani ISI, ▓▓▓▓▓▓▓▓▓▓▓▓▓

Pakistan as a Responsible Regional Actor.

Afghanistan: After 9/11, Pakistan joined the United States in its fight against the Taliban, but Afghan-Pakistani relations have been strained. While Pakistan renounced the Taliban, it continued to provide safe haven for senior Shura members in Quetta and Peshawar. Afghanistan has accused Pakistan of destabilizing the fragile democracy, although both President Musharraf and Afghan President Karzai were prone to criticizing the other in public. In an effort to diffuse tensions, the President hosted a trilateral dinner at the White House in 2006, during which Pakistan agreed to a cross-border jirga (meeting of government, tribal, and religious leaders) with Afghanistan to provide a forum for regular dialogue on security and economic issues. With United States encouragement, the two countries have sought to improve relations with each other, with President Karzai attending the September 2008 inauguration of President Zardari, and expand cross-border military cooperation.

India: The Administration also has quietly encouraged confidence-building measures under the Composite Dialogue with India, begun in 2004. Pressed by the President, President Musharraf clamped down on cross-border extremists in Jammu and Kashmir, resulting in a dramatic decrease in incursions. However, Pakistan's alleged involvement in the July 2008 bombing of the Indian Embassy in Kabul set back Pakistani relations with both India and Afghanistan.

In the wake of the Mumbai attacks, our strategy of encouraging cooperation from Pakistan and patience from India is intended to forge a new sense of responsibility and accountability in the region regarding the fight against terrorism. To date, both sides have responded with restraint and a focus on eliminating terrorist safe havens.

Improved Nuclear Safety and Nonproliferation.

In 2007, the United States agreed to   build a dialogue with Pakistan regarding responsible nuclear deterrence policy. Pakistan participates in the Secure Freight Initiative and the Global Initiative to Combat Nuclear Terrorism.

Economic Development and Assistance. The Administration moved quickly after lifting sanctions in 2001 to restore United States economic assistance to Pakistan, beginning with:

- Direct budgetary support;
- Debt rescheduling;
- Reestablishment of Overseas Private Investment Corporation (OPIC) and Export-Import (EXIM) programs; and
- Increased Generalized System of Preferences (GSP) benefits.

To demonstrate our long-term support, the United States has provided $300 million annually from 2005–2009 in Economic Support Funds. The breadth of current U.S. programs is aimed at improving the lives and livelihoods of average Pakistanis and includes:

- Education: 400,000 children educated in U.S.-supported schools and 45,000 teachers trained, providing a viable alternative to madrassa education;

- Health: TB detection, polio vaccination, maternal, and child health;
- Governance: election assistance, local leader, and party training; and
- Economic growth: 350,000 microfinance loans and competitiveness training.

United States assistance after the 2005 earthquake, including military disaster relief operations, boosted the public image of the United States and secured substantial if short-lived goodwill. In addition, we agreed to work with Pakistan to increase its economic and investment climate through the establishment of direct commercial flights, negotiations on a bilateral investment treaty, and renewed trade and investment framework agreement discussions.

FATA Assistance and Reconstruction. Opportunity Zones (ROZs): Recognizing the urgent need to offer economic opportunities in the border regions, the President in 2006 committed to provide $750 million over 5 years in economic development to support President Musharraf's strategy to stabilize the FATA. An important piece of this plan is the Reconstruction Opportunity Zones (ROZ) initiative, unveiled by the President during his 2006 visit to Islamabad, to allow duty-free access to specific goods manufactured in Afghanistan and parts of Pakistan, including the FATA. Bipartisan legislation supporting this initiative was introduced in both houses of Congress.

Food Aid: In July 2008, the Administration continued to expand its assistance and commitment to the Pakistani people, most notably with $115.5 million in food security assistance to help Pakistan cope with skyrocketing food and agricultural prices.

Economic/Financial Crisis: Nonetheless, 2008 proved to be a difficult year for the Pakistani economy. The United States recognized the looming economic crisis and encouraged Pakistan to undertake aggressive reforms that could potentially prevent a collapse. Despite some politically unpopular cuts in subsidies and other relief measures, by October 2008 there were growing signs of concern:

- Pakistan's foreign currency reserves had dropped to crisis levels (less than $4 billion);
- The account deficit on the year grew by 74 percent;
- Foreign direct investment had fallen by 10 percent; and
- High inflation (approx. 30 percent) and a plummeting currency had driven up the cost of food and fuel, increasing the potential for domestic strife.

In large part based on United States insistence, Pakistan agreed to an International Monetary Fund program to shore up its flagging economic situation. The program provides Pakistan $7.6 billion over two years and requires Pakistan to take concrete steps to increase confidence in its economic and investment climate. The program will likely stave off an immediate economic collapse, but success will require effective Pakistani implementation and international donor support. The U.S. has led the effort to encourage a donors' conference in January 2009.

FUTURE CHALLENGES:

<u>Eliminating safe havens and terrorism in Pakistan:</u> Pakistan's current counterterrorism capabilities and political will remain insufficient to eliminate terrorist safe havens and end terrorist activities. While the U.S. Counterterrorism Campaign Plan and Security Development Plan have been tactically effective, implementing a comprehensive, well-funded, long-term counterinsurgency strategy will be required to address Pakistan's lack of military capability. Without the support of the Pakistani civilian and military leadership, this will not be possible.

<u>Building Pakistan's counterterror and counterinsurgency capacity:</u> Military assistance should focus on U.S. counterterrorism priorities and help improve Pakistani counterterrorism capabilities. International Military Education and Training (IMET) programs should be significantly increased to build ties with the generation of military officers denied training during sanctions, and other military aid should continue to be directed toward programs that will boost counterterrorism capabilities.

<u>Afghan-Pak Border Region Development:</u> Concurrently, the United States needs to hold the Pakistanis to their commitment to use our support effectively in transforming the FATA. As the GOP seeks to extend its writ over the FATA, the United States continues to explore ways to mobilize other nations to help us assist the GOP in addressing the FATA safe haven—through the Friends of Democratic Pakistan effort—and the multilateral threat that originates there. Increasing economic assistance for the border regions will be an integral part of our success.

<u>Economic Recovery:</u> Throughout 2008, Pakistan's economic situation deteriorated to near crisis levels. The implementation of a program with the IMF has improved the situation, but the economy remains in precarious situation. The United States needs to continue steps to avoid a potential collapse, including urging continued structural reforms, international support, and improving investment climate.

<u>Strategic Messaging:</u> Eliminating violent extremism in Pakistan will depend on the new government's ability to achieve public consensus that the war on terror is their war and that terrorist safe havens pose a threat to Pakistan as well as the West. Proving our long-term friendship is essential to helping Pakistan recognize this reality. We also should strive to improve the Pakistani people's understanding of our goals and policies. Despite our robust assistance, popular opinion of the United States in Pakistan remains low, with support at less than 10 percent throughout 2008.

<u>Regional Relations:</u> We must continue to advance the Composite Dialogue and other fora for cooperation with India, particularly in the wake of the Mumbai attacks, to encourage greater cooperation in all aspects. Providing U.S. assistance for confidence-building measures in the back-channel dialogue is a significant opportunity for improving Indo-Pakistani relations. In

addition, we must continue to encourage Pakistan to cooperate with the legitimate government in Afghanistan, build cross-border cooperation, and expand tripartite engagement.

Pakistani Democracy: Pakistan's fragile coalition government will need substantial support in tackling tough, imminent challenges like the burgeoning terrorist threat, a crumbling economy, and crippling power shortages—and in proving that democracy can deliver on its promises. The U.S. will need to continue to encourage a truly independent and apolitical judiciary and full civic freedoms—press, religion, speech. The Pakistani military will need to adapt to its new role as subordinate to the civilian leadership, as a new balance of power between the Prime Minister, President, and Army is established. Finally, Pakistan's existing democratic political parties must be reformed; the existing internal party structures discredit the democratic process and undermine political stability. United States support will be crucial to helping Pakistan successfully complete this important transition.

A Bilateral Long-term Relationship: The U.S. will need to increase funding for Pakistan, particularly security assistance, economic development, and strategic messaging. U.S. assistance must be commensurate with the strategic priority that Pakistan represents. Overall success in Pakistan depends on convincing the people and leadership of Pakistan that the United States be involved in the future. The most effective way of achieving that is to build a broad-based, long-term relationship, backed by adequate funding.

Attachments

Tab 1   Pakistan Chronology
Tab 2   Message For President Musharraf (August 4, 2001)
Tab 3   Telcon with President of Pakistan (September 15, 2001)
Tab 4   Memcon with President Musharraf of Pakistan (June 24, 2003)
Tab 5   Designation of the Islamic Republic of Pakistan as a Major Non-NATO Ally (April 16, 2004)
Tab 6   Joint Statement Between the United States of America and the Islamic Republic of
          Pakistan (September 22, 2004)
Tab 7   Memcon with President Musharraf of Pakistan (December 4, 2004)
Tab 8   Telcon with President of Pakistan (November 17, 2005)
Tab 9   Memcon with President Pervez Musharraf of Pakistan (March 4, 2006)
Tab 10   Joint Statement on United States-Pakistan Strategic Partnership (March 4, 2006)
Tab 11   Summary of Conclusions for Deputies Committee Meeting on Pakistan-Afghanistan
          (August 22, 2006)
Tab 12   Memcon with Pervez Musharraf President of Pakistan (September 22, 2006)
Tab 13   Greeting, Statement, and Working Dinner with the President of Pakistan and the
          President of Afghanistan (September 27, 2006)

POSTSCRIPT

MARK WEBBER

The Bush Administration Approach

US policy on Pakistan during the Bush administration was shaped by the necessary response to the 9/11 attacks. As has been well documented elsewhere and discussed in the Transition Memorandum, Bush administration officials, including the president himself, clearly laid out what was required of Pakistan in the early days of the War on Terror. In the following years, the Bush administration tried to strike the right balance between support for Pakistan as a strategic partner and pressure on Pakistan to address US national security policy priorities. Finding this Goldilocks approach to Pakistan has been the challenge of every administration since.

Bush administration engagement with and support of Pakistan was both broad and deep. It included sanctions relief, debt rescheduling, direct budgetary support, trade benefits, various forms of development assistance (including in the tribal areas in support of Pakistan's counterinsurgency effort there), weapons sales and military assistance (including to improve Pakistan's counterterrorism capability), help to ensure the safety and security of Pakistan's nuclear weapons, support for Pakistan's democratic transition and institution building, and initial but declining counterterrorism cooperation. At the same time, the Bush administration acted unilaterally to disrupt terrorist activity in Pakistan that threatened America's effort in Afghanistan.

Ultimately, the Bush administration was unable to achieve the strategic shift it sought from Pakistan, but not because of unrealistic expectations or an inability to recognize the various actors working against US interests. As clearly laid out in the Transition Memorandum, Bush administration officials understood well the challenges—including the role Pakistani intelligence forces played in undermining US counterterrorism objectives—and the limited toolbox that was available to address these challenges. Identifying the problem was not the issue; finding effective solutions was.

Pakistan's lack of will to undertake necessary counterterrorist operations compounded its inability to conduct those operations and govern the Pashtun border regions. The Bush administration approach was to build Pakistani capacity and thereby bolster both its will and capability to eliminate extremism, but with reasonable expectations of what could be achieved and how fast progress could be made.

Most importantly, the Bush administration recognized that achieving counterterrorism success in the border regions was dependent on success elsewhere in Pakistan. Helping Pakistan to achieve a united, secure, democratic, and economically stable nation was the best—and perhaps only—way to achieve the strategic shift necessary to accomplish mutual security objectives.

What Has Happened Since the End of the Bush Administration?

In January 2009, the Obama administration was focused on incentivizing Pakistan to support a new US strategy in Afghanistan, which would help the United States achieve a quick victory and exit from the country. The infiltration of foreign fighters from Pakistan had been a growing problem for US and coalition forces as attacks continued to increase. The United States could not achieve its objectives in Afghanistan without addressing the threat posed by the Pakistani border regions. Accordingly, the new Obama administration ramped up operations targeting Pakistan-based insurgents, which had begun in earnest during the last year of the Bush administration, while continuing the focus on building Pakistani capacity to conduct counterterrorism operations.

The Obama administration's strategy sought to induce the same Pakistani strategic shift described in the Transition Memorandum—that is, prioritizing the threat of extremist groups in the north over the perceived threat of India in the south—while at the same time cutting off support for the insurgency inside Afghanistan. Nonmilitary aid to Pakistan increased, including humanitarian assistance in response to natural disasters. In addition, the Obama administration established a strategic dialogue in March 2010 to move away from the less-structured approach to direct engagement with senior Pakistani leadership in order to encourage coordinated decision making with the military and civilian government leaders—as well as to signal a long-term commitment to Pakistan.

The increase in US counterterrorism and counterinsurgency efforts was successful in further degrading the operational capacity of al Qaeda but could not eliminate the extremist forces in the Pakistani border regions, which were hindering progress in Afghanistan. Pakistani forces similarly increased efforts to target insurgent groups considered to be risks to internal security. However, Pakistan has refused to change its fundamental national security posture, stem cross-border attacks into Afghanistan, or eradicate the extremist safe havens within its own borders. Moreover, Pakistan's actions to shut down the terrorist networks responsible for the November 2008 Mumbai attacks were inadequate and only taken reluctantly.

The most significant achievement of the Obama administration in Pakistan was also the most traumatic to long-term relations. The successful operation to eliminate Osama bin Laden was a historic turning point for ongoing counterterrorism efforts, but it also exacerbated growing tensions and reinforced the lack of trust between the two partners. Pakistan's inability (or unwillingness) to bring bin Laden to justice and the US recognition that the operation would need to be conducted without Pakistan's help or knowledge were clear indicators that the countries had drifted dangerously far apart. By the end of 2011, US-Pakistan relations reached a low point when Pakistani troops fired on coalition forces during a counterterrorism operation near the Afghanistan-Pakistan border. Ten years later, the relationship had not appreciably improved.

After 2011, Pakistan underwent a series of civilian government transitions. These transitions projected a veneer of democratic reform, but ultimately disappointed hopes that democracy promotion efforts had achieved the much-needed stability and accountability of elected Pakistani officials. Both President Zardari, who entered office in 2008, and Nawaz Sharif, who promised to rectify the Zadari government's failures when taking over in 2013, eventually left under clouds of rampant corruption and systematic abuse of power. The flip-flop between the established Pakistani political parties that relied, in large part, on regional divisions and personal patronage for support, gave rise to populist forces in 2018. Former prime minister Imram Khan entered office lambasting long-standing domestic corruption and capitalizing on widespread anti-American sentiment. Nevertheless, his removal from office after an April 2022 no-confidence vote in parliament marked another premature exist for a Pakistani head of government. Throughout these transitions, the military has remained a major source of power within the Pakistani system. Time will tell whether the newest prime minster, Shehbaz Sharif, can bridge the divide between the two pillars of Pakistani authority—one political, one military—that remain largely bifurcated and asymmetrically powerful, further hindering the progress of civil-military reform.

In 2017, the Trump administration picked up the reins with a new promise to put pressure on Pakistan, linking the continuation of US aid to progress on counterterrorism, which led to the cessation of security assistance in 2018. The renewed pressure did little to encourage meaningful cooperation, and later that year, the Trump administration shifted course again to enlist the Pakistani government in the Afghanistan peace process. Negotiations with the Taliban had begun in earnest during the Obama administration but made little progress. As successive administrations looked to wind up US involvement in Afghanistan, a negotiated settlement with the Taliban became more and more critical to long-term stability and the US exit plan. In February 2020, the Trump administration concluded an agreement between the Taliban and the United States, pledging a conditional withdrawal of all US troops in 2021. After reviewing this commitment upon entering office, the Biden administration decided to continue drawing down US forces, despite the significant increase in violence, and concluded the withdrawal in the summer of 2021. Pakistan's role in the future of the region becomes even more important in the wake of the American withdrawal from Afghanistan, although the nature of that role remains uncertain.

As Pakistan struggles to deal with these security and political challenges, its economic outlook is also bleak. Prior to the COVID-19 pandemic that ushered in negative growth in 2020, Pakistan was already facing macroeconomic trends that required a new international assistance package in 2019. And despite two decades of US aid and reimbursement payments that reached its peak in 2011, Pakistan has failed to achieve sustained economic growth. Pakistan's inability to wean itself from international support has created an environment ripe for other foreign competitors to take advantage of its economic needs. Pakistan is now the central focus of China's Belt and Road Initiative, intended to expand China's regional sphere of influence, with billions of dollars for new infrastructure projects flowing into the China-Pakistan economic corridor.

How Did the Bush Administration Do?

The Bush administration effort to seek a close relationship with both the military and civilian components of the Pakistani government and to focus on building security capacity and reinforcing democratic institutions had mixed results. While it helped to prevent a regional war with India after the Mumbai attacks, forestall economic collapse, and maintain pressure on extremist groups, it did not achieve the ultimate goal of inducing a strategic shift in Pakistani behavior that was—and still is—needed. The administration has been criticized for having unrealistic expectations of what could be achieved, and some observers have claimed that the administration was unaware of the forces inside Pakistan working against US interests. The Transition Memorandum makes clear that this was not the case. And after rebranding a new "Af-Pak" strategy, the Obama administration largely carried on and intensified most of the initiatives already underway.

The Bush administration's focus on Pakistani defense capacity was essential for any long-term success. Senior US officials sought to expand security cooperation efforts through regular interactions with senior Pakistani officials. The focus was to try to ensure that Pakistan had the necessary equipment and capabilities to conduct counterterrorism operations. These capacity-building efforts were adversely affected by the on-again, off-again tendency in US engagement with Pakistan. For example, Pakistan's failure aggressively to pursue counterterrorism operations caused the United States to deny some defense exports in an attempt to hold Pakistan accountable for its failure, which had a disruptive effect on the relationship.

In retrospect, Pakistan's support for the Taliban in Afghanistan and for extremist groups in the border regions largely offset the benefit of Pakistan's help in eliminating al Qaeda. What was seen early on as American willingness to tolerate Pakistan's support for the Taliban and for non–al Qaeda terrorist groups resulted in decreased US leverage over time, which has meant continued resistance to legitimate governance and security efforts in the border region to this day.

The Bush administration's approach to democratization in Pakistan was tempered by the need for Pakistan's support in Afghanistan. In the wake of the September 11 attacks, President Musharraf played a critical role in supporting the US response. Over time he proved to be a necessary actor but inadequate partner in addressing US counterterrorism concerns. The Bush administration was right to encourage President Musharraf to step down as army chief of staff and permit credible elections, which was an important turning point for civil-military relations in Pakistan. However, in retrospect, the Bush administration was also right to be concerned that Pakistan's weak democratic institutions would not be sufficient to prevent a series of political collapses that have undermined Pakistan's stability and bilateral relations.

The Bush administration did succeed in preventing a regional war in response to the Mumbai attacks. The personal involvement of President Bush in defusing tension showed the value US engagement can have in resolving regional issues. But regarding long-standing bilateral disputes between India and Pakistan, including Jammu and Kashmir, the Bush administration took a hands-off approach to facilitating dialogue. Later administrations' more active efforts to broker a resolution to these disputes only frustrated relations with both New Delhi and Islamabad.

Regarding economic reform, the Bush administration struggled to assist Pakistan in implementing effective initiatives that would have meaningful long-term benefits. Expanding coalition support funds and the strong emphasis on aid to support counterterrorism efforts had the unintended consequence of reinforcing Pakistan's dependence on US assistance. The Pakistan military and government eventually came to expect and take for granted the US assistance, thereby undermining its ability to incentivize reform. It is telling that the final sentence in the Transition Memorandum stresses that the most likely path to success in Pakistan is to "build a broad-based, long-term relationship, *backed by adequate funding*" (emphasis added). The strategy was always predicated on US aid, which has diminished over time. The challenge is how to provide such assistance in a way that is effective and encourages reform but does not create dependence.

What Are Lessons Learned?

Relations with Pakistan will remain tumultuous, no matter the US strategy. Divisions between the Pakistani civilian and military leadership, continued reliance on extremist organizations to support perceived security interests, rampant corruption, economic decline, and a deeply unpopular public perception of the United States are the most notable forces working against a robust and productive bilateral relationship. The United States must remain committed to long-term cooperation with Pakistan. The persistence of ungoverned spaces in South Asia that enables extremist organizations to operate unfettered will continue to pose an unacceptable risk to US and regional security interests. Sustained US involvement is essential. Several lessons are relevant to policymakers charged with the ongoing, but still unrealized goal of inducing a strategic shift in Pakistani behavior.

- *Do not subordinate the bilateral relationship to other foreign policy priorities.* As the United States ends its military presence in Afghanistan and shifts its focus to competition with China and Russia, there is a risk that Pakistan will again be neglected or, more likely, be "re-hyphenated" and subordinated to some other foreign policy priority (whether it is US relations with India, China, or something else). Historically, this has proven to be short-sighted. Pakistan's willingness to embrace a strategic shift, eliminate extremist safe havens, and conduct effective operations against terrorists that threaten itself and its neighbors is dependent on economic growth, political stability, and security throughout Pakistan. These should be the focus of the US approach to Pakistan.

- *Do not prioritize relations with the military over the civilian government.* The United States must work with both the civil and the military leaders to accomplish its objectives; it is not one or the other. This will require sustained institutional engagement that continues from one US administration to the next. Elements of both the civilian and military establishments can be expected to work against US interests. Like many aspects of Pakistan, it is important not to view institutions, including the Pakistani intelligence services, as unified in approach. Institutionalizing the dialogue with a variety of decision makers is the only way to overcome this challenge.

- *The United States must remain a reliable defense partner.* Without adequate counterterrorism capacity, Pakistan will never be able to accomplish the security objectives that the two countries share. If the United States remains an on-again, off-again partner, it should not be surprised that Pakistan looks to other partners—including potential US adversaries—to fulfill its defense needs. At the same time, while the United States and Pakistan will not see eye-to-eye on all issues, the United States cannot tolerate a strategic partner that is willing to work directly against US interests. Defense cooperation, in particular, must be made conditional upon the pursuit of common objectives, including eliminating extremists that also pose an existential threat to Pakistan as a nation-state.

- *Economic growth and stability in Pakistan are essential to its long-term viability.* Pakistan has the promise of creating a vibrant, free-market economy. The United States should do everything it can to assist in this regard, including supporting economic reforms and the opening of new markets. The United States need not try to compete with other nations, such as China, that have invested disproportionately in Pakistani infrastructure development. Continued US aid will be necessary but will not of itself provide a path to self-sufficiency. Assistance from other sources will be required.

- *Increased regional economic engagement may be the best path to resolution of security concerns.* The United States should encourage increased cross-border trade between Pakistan and India. Indeed, regional economic integration is in the interest of all South and Central Asian states. Particularly following the US departure from Afghanistan, the imperative to execute a plan to encourage regional economic integration and cooperation is greater than ever.

- *Do not judge the success of the bilateral relationship based on the popularity of the United States among Pakistanis.* It is unlikely that most Pakistani citizens will view the United States in a positive light for the foreseeable future. This should not be viewed as indicative of a failed US foreign policy. Rather, the United States should be focused on strengthening legitimate Pakistani institutions so as to instill in the Pakistani people a greater confidence in their own government as effective, legitimate, and transparent. Cultural exchanges, disaster relief, and health and public welfare programs should continue to be important components of US policy in Pakistan but for their humanitarian value and longer-term impact rather than in pursuit of some short-term success in winning over hearts and minds.

- *The future of Pakistan ultimately remains with the leaders of the country and their ability to meet the wide array of serious challenges facing it.* Pakistani leaders must recognize that eliminating security threats, establishing good relations with strong and independent governments in neighboring states, and promoting economic reforms provide the greatest opportunity for Pakistan's growth and prosperity. As the Transition Memorandum made clear in 2009, US objectives in Pakistan will only be accomplished when the Pakistani government, military, and population embrace these challenges as their own.

Contributors:
Ashley Tellis
Anish Goel

CHAPTER 7

Iraq

MEGHAN L. O'SULLIVAN

Iraq haunted the Bush administration for its entire tenure, much as it had troubled the previous two administrations. The decision in 2003 to definitively deal with the threat posed by Saddam Hussein was one of the most fateful decisions made by President Bush. But as the transition approached in the fall of 2008, the Bush administration could take a measure of satisfaction in the results it had achieved. A change in strategy and a significant increase of military, economic, and political resources into Iraq in early 2007 (the Surge) had reversed a badly deteriorating situation and at least temporarily stabilized the country. The road had been a long one, with advances and setbacks that the administration had not anticipated. Although success was far from certain, the Surge had created a dramatic improvement in security that offered real opportunities for progress and the ultimate stabilization and reconstruction of Iraq.

TRANSITION MEMORANDUM

~~CONFIDENTIAL~~ WITH
SECRET ATTACHMENT

NATIONAL SECURITY COUNCIL
WASHINGTON, D.C. 20504

6480
Transition

January 16, 2009

MEMORANDUM FOR THE RECORD

FROM: BRETT MCGURK, IRAQ DIRECTORATE

SUBJECT: Iraq

STRATEGIC IMPORTANCE OF IRAQ TO U.S. NATIONAL SECURITY: U.S. policy in Iraq is guided by three fundamental principles:

- **First, that success in Iraq remains critical to U.S. national security and to success in the War on Terror.** We define success as a unified, democratic, federal Iraq, at peace with its neighbors, that can govern itself, defend itself, sustain itself, and be an ally in the War on Terror. That success would greatly improve U.S. national security and advance broader U.S. goals for the Middle East by promoting stability and the empowerment of moderates over extremist actors.

- **Second, failure in Iraq would have serious consequences for the United States, the region, and our allies.** That failure—defined as leaving behind an Iraq that cannot govern, sustain or defend itself—would strengthen al-Qaida and other extremist groups within and beyond Iraq, including militant groups backed by Iran; create conditions for mass killings and sectarian cleansing inside Iraq; and leave a potentially failed state in the heart of the greater Middle East.

- **Third, there is no magic formula solution in Iraq.** All policy options in Iraq involve trade-offs between various risks under conditions that are constantly changing. An overall approach, therefore, that remains agile, flexible, pragmatic, and tied to evolving conditions on the ground is the best route to durable success.

NSC Declassification Review [E.O. 13526]
DECLASSIFY IN PART
by William C. Carpenter 3/23/2020

~~CONFIDENTIAL~~ WITH
SECRET ATTACHMENT
Reason: 1.4 (a) (c) (d)
Declassify on: 1/16/19

Re-Classified by: Ellen J. L. Knight
Reason: 1.4(c) and (d)
Declassify on: 1/16/2034

The months following the February 22, 2006, bombing of the Askariya Shrine in Samarra witnessed a significant deterioration of security conditions in Iraq. As of mid-2006, Iraq was facing three distinct but increasingly inter-related security challenges: a broad-based Sunni insurgency; a growing terrorist threat from al-Qaida; and increasing sectarian violence—the latter fueled by mass casualty al-Qaida in Iraq (AQI) attacks on Shi'a civilians and retributive attacks by Shi'a extremists (led by the Jaysh al-Mahdi (JAM)) on Sunni civilians. By the early fall of 2006, violence in every category reached record levels, and AQI and JAM were on a trajectory to become the dominant movements among Sunni and the Shi'a, respectively, controlling territory and the population.

Iraqi Security Forces which had been reorganized, re-equipped, and retrained were not ready to handle this deteriorating situation on their own, and pushing them too fast risked breaking units and the force (including the Army) as a whole. Moreover, in areas facing sectarian violence, including Baghdad, Iraqi National Police often contributed to the problem, both in fact and in perception as being an arm of Shi'a parties. Despite tactical adjustments in the summer of 2006, including two Baghdad Security Plans, Iraqi army and police were unable to "hold" areas cleared by Coalition forces, and there were not enough Coalition forces to "hold" territory themselves. In sum, Iraq faced a significant and worsening security problem, and the security assets available to the Iraqi Government and the United States were proven insufficient to effectively contain the violence.

The formation of a national unity government in June 2006 was the culmination of three years of effort to bring Sunni Arabs inside the political process and provided new opportunities for political reconciliation. But levels of violence made meaningful political and economic gains impossible. Violence escalated through the fall reaching all time highs in October. Hundreds of thousands of Iraqis had been displaced from their homes, and the conditions on the ground had begun to parallel historical preconditions for mass civilian killings and civil war.

THIS ADMINISTRATION'S POLICY:

While the Administration's long-term goal remained unchanged, by late 2006 it was clear that maintaining course would not achieve this goal and would result instead in serious risks to U.S. interests in the greater Middle East. Key assumptions upon which our previous strategy had been based were no longer valid, most notably (1) that a Sunni-based insurgency presented our primary security challenge and (2) that political and economic gains could drive security gains. Instead, immediate action was required to change the trajectory of violence and deterioration and reset the conditions for longer-term stability.

Beginning in the summer of 2006 and formalized in November, the National Security Council undertook a comprehensive strategic review to assess all available policy options. This process brought together senior NSC, State, Defense, Treasury, and intelligence officials to assess the risks of different courses of action and present the President with a full set of options. On January 10, 2007, the President addressed the Nation and announced the New Way Forward, commonly known as the surge.

The strategic review process focused on identifying the inherent problems in Iraq and then identifying solutions. The immediate problem was security, and it demanded urgent security solutions. The new strategy altered course in five significant ways:

1. **Focus on Population Security.** The primary Multi-National Forces-Iraq (MNF-I) mission shifted from "transition" to supporting the Iraqi Government in providing population security in key strategic areas. To accomplish this mission, the President authorized the deployment of five additional U.S. combat brigades to Iraq, with the first surge brigade arriving in February 2007 and the last arriving in June 2007. The Iraqis in turn pledged at least three additional brigades to the fight in Baghdad and to ensure deployment of brigades in adequate strength to accomplish the "hold" phase of operations. This change in doctrine—from a primary focus on transition to a primary focus on population security to enable transition over time—contributed by September 2007 to both improving security conditions and improving ISF competence and capacity.

2. **Accelerate the transition.** The new population security mission did not take pressure off Iraqis to take charge of their future. To the contrary, the new mission was designed to allow them to do just that, and the new strategy demanded reciprocal obligations from the Iraqi Government. In a series of one-on-one videoconferences before the new strategy was launched, Prime Minister Maliki pledged to the President that he would apply the law even-handedly and would not restrict our operations—a pledge he immediately began to honor. Further, to strengthen the capacity of Iraqi forces and mitigate the risks of transition, we conducted a top-to-bottom review of ISF readiness, supported an Iraqi decision to increase the size of the Iraqi Army, revamped our own Foreign Military Sales (FMS) program to streamline the flow of resources to our Iraqi partners, enhanced small groups of trainers and force enablers (known as Military Transition Teams (MITTs)) with Iraqi units, and partnered each Iraqi unit with an MNF-I counterpart.

3. **Decentralize and Integrate civilian-military efforts.** The strategy review highlighted the increasingly decentralized power structure of Iraq and recommended a civilian and military force posture that would allow U.S. policy to guide decentralization toward our long-term objectives. The new strategy thus shifted our efforts to more flexible and decentralized engagement. For example, it doubled the number of Provincial Reconstruction Teams (PRTs) and partnered Brigade Combat Teams with an embedded PRT (ePRT) component. PRT leaders were given additional authorities and resources to push decision-making to the lowest possible level and support moderate actors in their areas of responsibility. New PRTs were

established in critical strategic areas, such as Najaf and Karbala, where the U.S. presence had receded entirely in 2006. State, together with other civilian agencies, committed additional personnel to the PRT mission and codified responsibilities with the military, removing barriers to cooperation. Funding for the Commander's Emergency Response Program (CERP) also increased, a force-multiplier that together with civilian Quick Response Funds allowed brigade commanders and PRT leaders to jointly improve conditions in key local areas across Iraq.

4. **Empower Anti-AQI groups (from the bottom up).** Beginning in the latter part of 2006, Sunni tribal groups across Iraq began turning against AQI, cooperating with Coalition and Iraq forces, and forming groups later called the Sons of Iraq (SOI) to expel AQI from their areas. The strategy review concluded that for these movements to succeed (taking note that similar movements had failed in 2005) a robust and visible U.S. force presence was necessary to turn the balance of power against AQI and in favor of the SOI. The new strategy was designed to do this, particularly with the deployment of 4,000 additional Marines and the tripling of PRT personnel in Anbar Province. The shift in strategy helped to fully empower non-governmental leaders—sheikhs, SOI, and religious leaders—in areas where the GOI was weak, as long as they demonstrated an ability to provide security and turn the population against AQI and other extremist groups. At its peak in mid-2008, 104,000 Iraqis had volunteered to support these local security initiatives, and AQI's ability to move freely and recruit had been greatly diminished. Prime Minister Maliki in October 2008 directed the GOI to incorporate SOI into Iraqi Security Forces and civilian employment and to takeover the SOI payroll, an effort that General Odierno is watching carefully, and thus far remains on track.

5. **Emphasize Regional Dynamics.** The new strategy sought to substitute what had been a vicious cycle of destabilization in Iraq and unhelpful regional conduct with a virtuous cycle of security gains in Iraq and an institutionalized regional architecture to help ensure that those gains would be durable and lasting. The new strategy thus focused on the following diplomatic tracks:

   · **Institutionalize the U.N.-Backed Neighbors Process.** These U.N.-sponsored conferences serve as a contact group among all of Iraq's neighbors, the Permanent Five members of the U.N. Security Council, the G-8, and the Arab League. Under the new strategy, the Neighbors group held quarterly ministerial meetings, with Iraq increasing its leadership role at each conference.

   · **Reestablish Iraq's Role as a Key Arab (and Gulf) State.** With the Neighbors Process as a platform, Iraq was slowly welcomed into the Gulf Cooperation Council as an observer, together with Jordan and Egypt (the GCC+3). The GCC+3 is now an essential vehicle for addressing affairs common to the Gulf, including the threat all members feel from Iran.

- **Establish a Regional Security Architecture.** The Gulf Security Dialogue (GSD) remains the blueprint for a regional security architecture, with Iraq as an essential component. These engagements had been bilateral (United States to partner state), but under the leadership of Secretary Gates, there is the potential to formalize them into a multilateral security forum, focused on common threats.

- **Institutionalize Regional Economic Engagement.** The International Compact with Iraq (ICI) launched in May 2007, with Iraq and the U.N. in the lead and participation by over 60 nations, the World Bank, and IMF. The ICI focuses on policy objectives in sound governance, economic and social development, and aims through incentives to modernize and reintegrate Iraq's economy into the global marketplace.

- **Confront Iranian Aggression Inside Iraq.** The new strategy formally authorized a carrot and stick approach to Iranian meddling in Iraq—authorizing U.S. military operations against known Quds Force operatives inside Iraq, while also authorizing U.S. diplomats in Baghdad to meet their Iranian counterparts to discuss issues pertaining to Iraq. United States and Iraqi military operations have sent a clear message to Tehran that the United States and the Iraqi Government will not tolerate Iran's provision of lethal aid and training to Iraqi extremist groups. The talks, however, have not advanced, due to Iran's repeated demand to expand the focus beyond Iraq (to include, for example, the nuclear file) and their continued denial of their direct support for extremist actors. The Embassy and MNF-I are presently carrying out a joint approach to confronting and containing Iran's lethal activities inside Iraq, an approach that is increasingly aided by the Government of Iraq and a Shi'a population that has begun to turn against Iran, at least in its role as a purveyor of support to illegal armed groups.

- **Counter Syria and Stem Foreign Fighter Flow.** The United States launched a comprehensive interagency and multilateral effort to stem the flow of foreign fighters through Syria and into Iraq. This program has had an impact, through a combination of financial, military, and diplomatic steps. There is some evidence that Syria has taken steps to clamp down on the flow of foreign fighters, but it has not gone far enough. Syria continues to believe that allowing extremist facilitators to move fighters to Iraq helps defend itself against extremists who might otherwise target the Asad regime. While diplomatic relations between Syria and Iraq have improved, Prime Minister Maliki supports a tough approach to foreign fighter facilitators.

- **Improve Iraqi-Turkish Relations and Manage the PKK.** We have worked with the Governments of Iraq and Turkey and the Kurdish Regional Government to mediate border issues and manage Turkish cross-border attacks on Kurdish Workers Party (PKK) targets.

Turkey in the process has become a critical ally of U.S. long-term objectives in Iraq, taking tangible steps in recent months to assist with negotiations of the U.S.-Iraq Security Agreement and meeting at high levels for the first time with President Barzani and other key leaders of the Kurdistan Regional Government (KRG).

Normalize the U.S.-Iraq Relationship. The new strategy finally sought to set conditions to normalize an enduring bilateral relationship. On August 26, 2007, Iraq's five principal leaders formally requested a long-term relationship with the United States to follow the U.N. Security Council Resolution that since 2003 had governed the U.S. military presence in Iraq. The President responded favorably to this request, and on November 26, 2007, he and Prime Minister Maliki jointly signed the "Declaration of Principles for Friendship and Cooperation" which outlined a vision of security, economic and political cooperation and served as the table of contents for future negotiations. Negotiations on a Security Agreement (often called a Status of Forces Agreement) and a Strategic Framework Agreement began shortly thereafter. The negotiations were aimed at one purpose: to set the conditions for a new phase of U.S. engagement in Iraq including a more limited U.S. security role over time and development of long-term relations in all areas of our relationship, including security, education, science, culture, and economics. These agreements were ratified by the Iraqi parliament in November 2008 and now establish the contours for U.S. bilateral relations with Iraq.

WHAT HAS BEEN ACCOMPLISHED:

The new strategy has succeeded in improving the security environment, decreasing the standing and influence of extremist groups, and setting the conditions for longer-term political and economic progress. The most dramatic difference can be seen in security:

AQI is Degraded But Remains a Threat. AQI now has reduced capabilities, and their network is under severe pressure. While they are still capable of high profile attacks, AQI attacks now average 20–25 per month, a fraction of the average 80 per month at their height in the fall of 2007. A combination of popular revolt against AQI and nightly U.S. and Iraqi special operations against leadership targets continues to degrade the network and weaken its ability to reconstitute. AQI will continue, however, to seek to regain strength and is looking to the key electoral events in 2009 as opportunities to exploit.

JAM is Fractured and Less Dependent on its Militant Wing. In 2006, JAM had grown into a non-state force with power (similar to an early Hizballah in Lebanon) to take on and defeat the official state security apparatus. That is no longer the case. A mix of military and political initiatives has greatly degraded the capacity and appeal of JAM as a militia force, and JAM itself is looking for non-violent means of transformation and survival. Muqtada al-Sadr's flight to Iran shortly after the surge also removed JAM's figurehead leader from the scene, leaving the movement increasingly disparate and weakened by internal division and dissent. And Maliki's security operations in the

Spring and Summer of 2008 (in Basra, Sadr City, and Amarah) significantly reduced JAM'S safe havens. Extremist splinter elements of JAM (including Iranian-backed "Special Groups"), however, still constitute a threat to U.S. and Iraqi forces and to stability in Iraq. Like AQI, they will seek to exploit the 2009 elections to regain status and prominence.

Sectarian Violence is Negligible. Sectarian violence is now negligible, often with no weekly recorded incidents, down from a high of 950–1050 attacks per month in late 2006. As the chart below demonstrates, attack levels overall now parallel levels seen in early 2004, with many weeks recording the lowest levels of violence since statistics were first tracked in mid-2003.

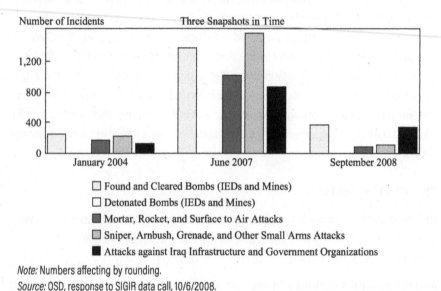

Number of Incidents — Three Snapshots in Time

☐ Found and Cleared Bombs (IEDs and Mines)
☐ Detonated Bombs (IEDs and Mines)
■ Mortar, Rocket, and Surface to Air Attacks
☐ Sniper, Ambush, Grenade, and Other Small Arms Attacks
■ Attacks against Iraq Infrastructure and Government Organizations

Note: Numbers affecting by rounding.
Source: OSD, response to SIGIR data call, 10/6/2008.

The drawdown of surge forces that began in December 2007 has not negatively impacted security, demonstrating that the conditions are being set for further reductions in U.S. force levels with Iraqi forces increasingly able (and eager) to take the lead.

ISF Capacity Continues to Rise. Iraqi Security Forces continue to grow in quantity and quality and are increasingly able to handle the security environment on their own. Both the Army and the Police have matured across the board since 2006, particularly in discipline, command and control, and deployability. Iraqi operations in Basra in March and April 2008, followed by operations in Sadr City, Maysan, and Diyala, demonstrated a new level of capacity and confidence. All U.S. operations are now conducted in full coordination with Iraqi forces, consistent with the Security Agreement now in effect.

A Strengthening Bilateral Relationship is in Place. As noted above, the U.S. relationship with Iraq is now governed by two international agreements: a Strategic Framework Agreement (SFA) and a Security Agreement (SA). The SFA sets the foundation for our bilateral relationship. The Security Agreement provides our troops with the protections and authorities they need to sustain positive security trends for the next 3 years. The Security Agreement also sets the dates of June 2009 for U.S. combat forces to relocate out of cities and towns and December 31, 2011 for the withdrawal of all U.S. forces from Iraq. Iraqi leaders, including the Prime Minister and the Presidency Council, have told us that they will seek a follow-on arrangement for training and logistical (and probably some special operations) forces beyond 2011. Unlike the politically-charged negotiations of these two agreements, however, follow-on arrangements can be negotiated after the U.S. presence has been reduced and in a less charged environment.

Top Down Politics are Maturing. The Iraqi political system is slowly maturing after 30 years of dictatorship, but remains dominated at times by mutual fear and suspicion among the main Sunni, Shi'a, and Kurdish blocs. The Council of Representatives (COR) passed important legislation at critical points during 2008, including laws to govern local elections, reform of de-Ba' athification, amnesty, the budget, and the SFA and SA. The COR is also coming into its own as an independent branch of government. But the COR still seeks to do its business by "consensus," giving extremist actors substantial weight even where a moderate cross-sectarian majority exists. The Executive Council (consisting of the Prime Minister and the Presidency Council) is the essential institution to overcoming sectarian gridlock, though it too has yet to develop an institutional identity beyond its individual actors. National elections in December 2009 will be a watershed event and a true test of the development of the Iraqi political system. If run properly, elections can go a long way to reorienting national politics away from sectarian identity and toward issues-based agendas.

Bottom up Politics are Taking Prominence. Grassroots politics are emerging throughout Iraq in the wake of security gains, and January's provincial elections have the potential to reset the provincial political landscape, rebalance leadership in mixed provinces, and pave the way for national elections in late 2009. But groups that have taken prominence where national governance is weak—such as the SOI and tribal leaders—remain fractured and disorganized, potentially allowing established political parties to retain influence. The showing of these new players in local elections may be less than they expect, creating a tense period in the months after election results are announced. As for the established provincial council structures, the GOI has improved its disbursement of capital investment funds, though execution remains weak. PRTs are now focused intensely on institution- and capacity-building at the provincial and local levels, enabling provinces to improve performance in budget development and execution, reconciliation efforts, and public outreach.

Economic Development on the Mend. Increased security proved to have a direct effect on economic growth in Iraq. Real GDP growth faltered in late 2006 and through 2007 due to security challenges but recovered strongly in 2008 and is expected to continue strongly in 2009. Budget allocations and expenditures are also increasing. In 2008, the GOI paid nearly 80 percent of their security costs, and GOI appropriations now exceed U.S. funding for reconstruction and security. United States and Iraqi reconstruction projects yielded sustained increases in essential services, such as electricity generation. Regional economic integration has been facilitated through the ICI and the IMF Stand-By Arrangement, which allowed Paris Club debt forgiveness. Iraq is also working on its WTO accession with United States Government assistance, and consistent with the SFA. The Iraqi budget overall remains nearly wholly dependent on oil revenues, but the government has shown prudence thus far in advance pricing projections and recently reset its budget based on a $50 per barrel projection.

Regional Engagement is Solidifying. Regional engagement has increased since the government began taking on Shi'a militants in spring-summer 2008. Iraq is now a member of the GCC+3 and in the latter half of 2008, saw regional states finally establishing diplomatic missions in Baghdad. Iraqi capacity and a stabilizing security environment should continue to foster these positive diplomatic trends.[1] In addition to increasing Arab engagement, the actively negative influence of Iran and Syria appears to have decreased in late 2008. Iran continues to seek a weak Iraq free of U.S. forces and actively fought the passage of the U.S.-Iraq SFA and Security Agreement, but Iranian-backed militants have been less active since Iraqi operations targeting JAM militants. Foreign fighter flow from Syria is also down from more than 80 a month in early 2007 to approximately 20 per month at the end of 2008.

FUTURE CHALLENGES:

We identify five primary challenges that may focus U.S. engagement through at least December 2010.

1. **Ensuring Successful Elections (and post-Elections).** This will be a year of elections in Iraq: provincial elections in January 2009, municipal elections in July, and national elections in December. Each election carries significant strategic risk—and opportunity. Local elections, as noted above, can rebalance power in mixed provinces and empower a new generation of "grass roots" leaders. They may also, however, lead to dashed hopes for some groups and open a window for AQI and Special Groups to exacerbate periods of uncertainty. National elections in late 2009, followed by government formation, and a non-violent transition of

---

1. The key to Arab engagement has been an Iraqi state standing up and becoming an undeniable influence in the region—with increasing security competence and economic opportunities. Conferences, such as the Neighbors Process, have proven effective when coupled with signs of Iraqi capacity and growth; they have not proven effective as the leading edge of increased engagement. Saudi Arabia has begun making steps toward Baghdad at lower levels, but it is likely to be the last Arab state to fully embrace a Shi'a-dominated government in Baghdad. Egypt, Jordan, the UAE, Bahrain, and even Kuwait, however, have begun to lead the way through strengthening bilateral ties.

power, will be the critical test for Iraq in the near-term. As we saw in 2006, the period of government formation (which may take a period of months after election day) will be fraught with high stakes bargaining and uncertainties that extremists will seek to exploit.[2]

2. **Defeating al-Qaida and Special Groups While Drawing Down.** It will remain a challenge to keep pressure on and ultimately defeat AQI and Special Group cells while U.S. combat power decreases under the Security Agreement. As of January 2009, AQI and Special Groups are damaged but still capable of high profile attacks that exacerbate ethno-sectarian fault lines and hamper political reconciliation in Baghdad. While U.S. Special Forces continue to strike AQI and SGs, population security has proven to be the essential element to ridding an area of militant cells, a task that will increasingly fall to the ISF, with U.S. forces in an overwatch posture.

3. **Implementing the Bilateral Agreements.** While implementation of these agreements is on track, 2009 will witness constant balancing of Iraqi desire to demonstrate full sovereignty against the continued flexibility U.S. forces need to operate effectively. Tension will be inherent and natural and should be worked out in most instances through joint committee structures now in place in Baghdad. The tension can be mitigated on the security side by concerted and visible implementation of the SFA, which covers the breadth of the U.S.-Iraq relationship. The Iraqis have high hopes for development of non-security ties and the SFA is likely to take a front seat in terms of both focus and expectations. Overall, deferring to Iraqi sovereignty concerns where the level of risk is acceptable has proven effective in weakening the sails of extremist groups. Key Shi'a leaders viewed the SA as critical to driving a wedge between irreconcilable Shi'a extremists and those that can be brought into the political process, and implementation will help these leaders reduce the number of extremists that need to be fought. Successful SFA and SA implementation can also set the foundation for Iraq's long-term stability with the United States as an ally across many fields of a multi-faceted relationship.

4. **Managing Iraqi Development of a National Vision.** For nearly 5 years, Iraqis have intensely debated the allocation of power between central, regional, and provincial governments. At its heart, this federalism debate gets to the future of the Iraqi state and the distribution of resources and responsibilities among Iraq's key political and sectarian groups. Issues such as the creation of a national energy strategy, a comprehensive hydrocarbons law,

---

2. The new administration should expect calls for a change of government in Baghdad—calls that are repeated approximately every 4 months. The leaders of this movement, mainly the Kurdish Alliance, the IIP, and ISCI, have been unable to organize a vote of no confidence with a new prime minister and cabinet ready to take its place. The uncertainty that would be generated is not in the U.S. strategic interest, and we have thus counseled against such a move, emphasizing the focus on programs and institutions, as opposed to personalities, and to the upcoming elections as the vehicle for change.

resolving disputed internal boundaries, implementation of provincial powers, constitutional review, and the role of regional security forces will remain critical in the coming years and may periodically boil into mild political crises in Baghdad. The U.S. role in these debates is increasingly and appropriately diminishing, though our engagement (together with the U.N.) has proven welcomed and essential at key moments to break deadlocks. This will likely remain the case through 2009 and 2010.

5. **Integrating the Sons of Iraq.** The SOI thus far are being successfully integrated and/or paid by the Iraqi Government, but we will need to monitor closely the development of these integration programs. The integration of the SOI into the structures of the new Iraq is the vital, final step in ending the Sunni insurgency which took hold of Iraq from 2004 through early 2007, and the United States will likely wish to maintain pressure on the Iraqi Government to follow through on its commitments to these groups which were key to reversing the security situation.

CONCLUSION:

The surge strategy reset negative trends and set the conditions for longer-term stability. **The coming 18 months, however, may be the most strategically significant period in Iraq since the fall of Saddam Hussein.** AQI is down but not out and a series of elections will define Iraq's future. If elections go well and a new government takes power through a peaceful transition, the constitutional system now in place is likely to endure, and extremist groups will have lost their ability to seriously challenge the viability of the Iraqi state. But until that can happen, these groups will continue to seek opportunities to gain the upper hand against Iraqi forces and with the Iraqi people. This process will play out against the backdrop of the new bilateral framework that charts the path to a responsible drawdown of U.S. forces and the development of strong bilateral ties in non-security spheres. These ties can further integrate Iraq into the global economy and gradually tilt Iraq toward America's sphere of influence and away from the negative influence of Iran and its sponsored militant groups. But what was true during the strategy review of 2006 remains so: there is no magic formula in Iraq. While our policy is now on a more stable and sustainable course, we should expect shocks to the system that will require a flexible and pragmatic approach at least through government formation in the first quarter of 2010.

Attachments

Tab 1   Chronology for Iraq since 2006
Tab 2   Formalizing the Ongoing Iraq Review (November 12, 2006)
Tab 3   PowerPoint presentation: Highlights of the Iraq Strategy Review" (January 2007)
Tab 4   President's Address to the Nation—The New Way Forward in Iraq (January 10, 2007)

POSTSCRIPT

MEGHAN L. O'SULLIVAN

Iraq had been both a threat and an irritant to the United States and the international community since the end of the Gulf War in 1991. For the next 12 years, across three different US presidential administrations, the United States led diplomatic efforts that resulted in sixteen UN Security Council Resolutions seeking to force Saddam Hussein to account for and destroy his weapons of mass destruction (WMD) and to cease threatening his neighbors, supporting terrorists, and oppressing his own people. The diplomatic effort was backed up by various sets of economic sanctions, multiple inspection regimes, no-fly zones over the northern and southern parts of the country, military strikes on Iraq by the Clinton administration, and even a US congressional resolution making regime change American declared policy.

A seventeenth resolution, UNSCR 1441, passed unanimously by the Security Council in November 2002, threatened "serious consequences" if Saddam continued to defy the United Nations. After Russian President Putin, German Chancellor Schroeder, and French President Chirac broke with the United States over Iraq in February of 2003, Saddam thought that President Bush would not invade without an eighteenth Security Council resolution which Putin and Chirac would block. This miscalculation was fateful for Saddam.

For President Bush, military action in 2003 did not constitute a "war of choice," but rather an option of last resort. The urgency of resolving the Iraq situation increased dramatically after 9/11 for two reasons. First, intelligence that was tragically later proven wrong suggested that Saddam Hussein still had weapons of mass destruction and was getting close to having a nuclear weapon. Second, the tolerance of President Bush and his team for lingering security threats to the United States greatly diminished after the terrorist attacks of September 11. From President Bush's perspective, the military invasion of Iraq in March 2003 came only after all diplomatic avenues had been exhausted and where the alternative was to let Saddam Hussein defy the international community, the United Nations, and the United States without consequences—and to allow Saddam to continue to threaten the United States and the region.

The Bush Administration Approach

The military operations that followed the March 2003 invasion quickly achieved their initial objectives, but the transition to stable governance and security proved elusive. An unanticipated collapse of order and Iraqi institutions prevented the United States from being able to transition sovereignty to Iraqi political leaders rapidly, as had been done in Afghanistan. Instead, the US-UK coalition reluctantly took on the responsibilities of an occupying power under the auspices of UNSC Resolution 1483 in May 2003 and established the Coalition Provisional Authority (CPA). After months of growing unrest in Iraq and disagreements in Washington over the nature and purpose of the open-ended occupation, in November 2003, the United States and its coalition partners committed to a date-certain transfer of power in June 2004. The CPA devoted its limited remaining time in power to laying the foundation for a sovereign Iraqi government to take over and govern the fractious and traumatized society.

The CPA's achievements during this time were notable, including the completion, in conjunction with the Iraqi Governing Council, of the Transitional Administrative Law—effectively an interim constitution that laid out the organs of government and how power would be divided among competing groups pending an elected government and a permanent constitution. The CPA could also point to significant strides in stabilizing the collapsing economy and, through work done primarily in Washington, the renegotiation of Iraq's enormous sovereign debt. Yet Iraq during this time was increasingly beset by a growing Sunni insurgency protesting the rising influence of Shi'a and Kurdish communities and strengthened by some CPA decisions that effectively dismantled parts of the Iraqi state.

For much of 2004 and 2005, the United States, the coalition, and their Iraqi partners could point to political progress in the form of legitimate elections, a peaceful transfer of power, and the writing and approval by referendum of an Iraqi constitution. Yet these significant political milestones happened against the backdrop of a rapidly deteriorating security situation further complicated by interference by Iraq's neighbors, particularly Iran but also Syria, and the emergence of Zarqawi's al Qaeda in Iraq (AQI). The situation deteriorated to the point of widespread sectarian violence and increasing chaos in the aftermath of attacks against Shi'a holy places in Samarra in February 2006.

In the months that followed, President Bush directed a searching policy review. The failure to prevent Iraq's descent into chaos came at an enormous cost in American and coalition lives and treasure, in widespread death and horrific suffering among the Iraqi people, in opening the door to AQI and to expanded Iranian influence, and in squandering US credibility that was sorely needed to deal with Iran and Syria. And after all that, the war looked to many as if it had been lost.

The president's review led to the Surge, a strategic reorientation that involved not only more troops, but different approaches to their positioning and mode of employment and a renewed American commitment to the long-term success of the new government in Iraq. The decision by President Bush to add more military and civilian resources to Iraq at the time when nearly all members of Congress and the foreign policy establishment were counseling the opposite was bold and unexpected. But in the several months that followed the full contingent of American Surge troops arriving in Iraq, the security situation began to turn around in a dramatic way. The American shift in strategy and evident recommitment to Iraq worked in tandem with other positive developments, including the marginalization of Moqtada al-Sadr—a powerful, violent Shi'a political force—and the rise of the Sunni Awakening and the Sons of Iraq (SOI)—a largely tribal effort to fight AQI alongside coalition forces who shared the same objectives.

By the time of the transition from President Bush to President Obama, conditions in Iraq had improved substantially from their nadir in 2006. Violence had declined by some 90 percent. AQI had been crippled, Iranian-backed Shi'a "special groups" had retreated to the sidelines, and Iranian influence in Iraq had been largely contained. Transition to Iraqi security control with US and coalition forces in "overwatch" was far advanced. The United States and Iraq had negotiated and signed a Status of Forces Agreement providing a new framework for the continuation of a reduced number of American forces on Iraqi soil for the next three years and had finalized a Strategic Framework Agreement to help the bilateral relationship flourish across multiple nonmilitary dimensions.

These improvements in security created conditions for real progress in development, governance, and political reconciliation. Countries in the region, while in most cases still not welcoming Iraq's political transition, had curbed their interference. Iraqi politics appeared to be broadening beyond the sectarian and ethnic identities that had dominated since Saddam's fall. The United States was bringing down its force levels and transitioning responsibilities to Iraqi forces, without resulting upticks in violence. Although fragile, the scene appeared set for Iraq to continue along these tentative but unquestionably positive trajectories.

Clear challenges remained, however. As noted in the Transition Memorandum, the eighteen months following the presidential transition in the United States—roughly January 2009 to June 2010—was a critical period, with five key areas to Iraq's subsequent success or failure: ensuring successful elections and the postelection period; defeating al Qaeda and special groups while drawing down US forces; implementing the bilateral agreements between the United States and Iraq in security and nonsecurity realms; managing the development of a national Iraqi vision; and integrating the Sons of Iraq, the military forces that had worked with the coalition outside formal Iraqi security structures to defeat AQI.

What Has Happened Since the End of the Bush Administration?

President Obama inherited a stable, if fragile, situation in Iraq and a well-defined relationship between the United States and Iraq. Rather than seeking to meet his campaign promises to end the war in Iraq and rushing to exit, he proceeded carefully in the initial years, building on what the previous administration had left in place.

Provincial council elections, held only weeks after the transition from President Bush to President Obama, demonstrated a strong shift in Iraqi political sentiment away from parties touting sectarian ideologies. National elections followed in March of 2010. For the first time in Iraq's post-Saddam history, politicians and parties sought to present themselves as nationalists, running on platforms that appealed across sectarian and ethnic lines. Iraqi voters rewarded these more nationalist parties, giving the multisectarian party "Iraqiya" a plurality of votes, but leaving no party or leader in a clear position to form a government.

Despite these promising results, a long, postelection effort to forge a new Iraqi government ended up reseeding the landscape with sectarianism. Many Iraqis expected the United States to support the election results favoring Iraqiya, but instead the Obama administration and Iran—separately—supported a continuation of then-Prime Minister Nouri al-Maliki in office. A painful negotiation ensued to patch together something resembling a government of national unity. Rather than strengthening Iraq's fragile democracy, the national elections of 2010 ended up undermining it, further empowering Maliki and enhancing Iran's influence over the country's politics.

From this point forward, Iraq's prospects began to dim. In Washington, a growing preoccupation with Afghanistan and focus on US economic recovery had moved Iraq to the back burner. Communication between President Obama and the Iraqi prime minister grew more infrequent. Sectarian reconciliation and national unity began to dissipate under Iranian influence and Prime Minister Maliki's increasingly centralized and sectarian approach. Maliki sought to seed the Iraqi military with his political allies and was reluctant to integrate the Sons of Iraq into Iraq security structures.

The security situation held steady during this period, creating a false sense of stability in the run-up to the 2011 debate over whether US forces would be asked to stay beyond the withdrawal date specified in the 2008 Security Agreement. The death of Zarqawi in 2006, the Anbar Awakening, and appearance of the Sons of Iraq, combined with the Surge and an increasingly effective Iraqi Security Forces (ISF), had punished AQI severely. Though not destroyed, its remnants were now focused on survival and could mount no more than occasional attacks. Similarly, Iranian-backed special groups had retreated from center stage when confronted by much stronger Surge forces and a maturing and increasingly professional ISF.

The Transition Memorandum further clarifies one of the most important lingering controversies about post-2008 Iraq policy: whether President Obama *chose* to leave Iraq at the end of 2011 or whether that choice was *imposed upon* him by Bush-era commitments. During the 2012 presidential campaign, the Obama team touted the decision as an example of Obama campaign promises made and kept; in subsequent years, the messaging shifted to recast the move as decided by Bush. Yet, as the Transition Memorandum notes, when the Security Agreement was first negotiated in 2008, both the American and Iraqi sides indicated that before its expiration at the end of 2011 they would seek "a follow-on arrangement for training and logistical (and probably some special operations forces) beyond 2011" to allow for a longer-term American commitment.

The environment, however, had changed significantly by the time this issue became ripe for consideration in 2011. In the United States, the Obama administration had maintained remarkable continuity with its predecessor administration in keeping to the agreements negotiated at the end of the Bush administration, and even embarked on negotiations to extend the US deployment. But the Obama administration had little interest in maintaining the US presence in Iraq. Iraqi Prime Minister Maliki was enjoying the greater autonomy he had as US forces began to recede. Given its own ambivalence about a continued US military role, the Obama administration imposed several conditions for maintaining US forces in Iraq, including requiring that the Iraqi parliament approve any new security agreement and grant US forces full immunity. Unwilling or unable to take major political risks to extend the stay of US forces, Maliki refused these conditions, resulting in the full departure of US forces by the end of December 2011. Ironically, the Obama administration later deemed these conditions unnecessary when it returned American troops to Iraq in 2014.

The withdrawal of all US troops proved to be premature. It accelerated the previously mentioned negative trends both in Iraqi politics and security. Maliki escalated his efforts to centralize and consolidate his control and to marginalize Sunni politicians and other actors. Fearing an armed Sunni force paid for by the government, Maliki moved quickly to suppress the Sons of Iraq, which had proven critical to the defeat of AQI. Despite commitments made to the US-led coalition, integration of the Sons of Iraq into the ISF did not occur on any significant scale. In many cases, Sons of Iraq members were detained or actively targeted both by government forces and by terrorist organizations. By 2013, Prime Minister Maliki and the Iraqi security services had moved to active suppression of the Sunni community, contributing to the rise of the Islamic State or ISIS.

By mid-2014, the United States had militarily returned to Iraq, responding to desperate Iraqi pleas to help the government in Baghdad defend itself against ISIS, which had gained control of more than a third of the country. For the next several years, during both the Obama and Trump administrations, the United States and the US-led Global Coalition to Defeat ISIS supported Iraqi, Syrian, and other forces as they battled fighters from the Islamic State. It was not until December 2017 that Iraqi Prime Minister Abadi declared ISIS defeated in Iraq, after a great cost of lost lives, treasure, infrastructure, and other institutions. Large Iranian and Iranian-sponsored paramilitary units also played an important role in the defeat of the Islamic state, and their existence has created a major vulnerability for the Iraqi state.

Several factors contributed to the dramatic rise of ISIS in Iraq. The first was the sectarian politics of Prime Minister Maliki and his growing centralization of power, and exclusion and persecution of the Sunnis. The second was US policy toward Syria. Not wanting to engage in more wars in the Middle East, the Obama administration chose modest responses to the emerging civil war unfolding next door to Iraq in Syria and the growth of ISIS there. More vigorous action there might have stemmed the growth of ISIS in Syria and prevented its subsequent reinfection of Iraq. ISIS leadership saw Iraq and Syria as an open battlespace supporting their aspirations; ISIS was able to return to Iraq after incubating and growing in strength in Syria. The final factor contributing to the rise of ISIS in Iraq was the withdrawal of US forces, which precipitated a diminished US involvement in the security, intelligence, political, and diplomatic arenas at a time when the Iraqi state was clearly still in need of buttressing across all domains.

Driving ISIS out of Iraq was a major achievement for Iraqis, but it did not usher in a period of stability. The Kurdish Regional Government (KRG) sought to translate the near-state status it had acquired in the fight against ISIS into actual statehood. Baghdad reacted with force to a provocative Kurdish independence referendum in September of 2017, seeking the return of territory and resources incrementally claimed by the Kurds over the preceding years and bringing the country to the brink of civil war. Although eventually defused, the competing visions different groups have for Iraq remain a source of contention.

The Trump administration maintained a modest military presence in Iraq, even once the threat from ISIS subsided, often framing its interests in Iraq primarily in terms of its desire to contain Iran. In July 2021, the Biden administration welcomed Iraqi Prime Minister Mustafa Al-Kadhimi to Washington, announcing a mutual decision to withdraw all *combat* US forces from Iraq by the end of 2021. This announcement strengthened Kadhimi's standing in Iraq, given the growth in strength of Iranian-influenced militia and other Iraqis resentful of the continued presence of American forces. But in an artful twist of semantics, the United States now plans to maintain forces in Iraq in a supportive role to Iraqi forces, which is the mission of the overwhelming majority of its very limited (2,500) troop contingent as of the summer of 2021.

Iraq has weathered a near-constant cascade of internal and external crises and challenges since the Bush administration left office in January 2009. Although security is much improved, ISIS remains a persistent threat. The predominantly Shi'a paramilitary forces that claim some of the credit for defeating ISIS have neither been disbanded nor successfully integrated into Iraqi forces, creating major problems of credibility and stability for the Iraqi government and a significant source of Iranian influence over Iraqi internal affairs. The unprecedented drop in global demand for oil in the wake of the COVID pandemic plunged Iraq into financial crisis, while the Ukraine crisis and the instability of oil markets is now reviving its export flows. Notwithstanding, the prospect of a global energy transition weighs heavily on Iraq given its near total dependence on oil revenues and limited plans for diversification.

Iraq has witnessed three prime ministers since Prime Minister Maliki was pressured to step aside as a condition of US assistance against ISIS in 2014. Each has struggled with the weakness of the state, the intervention of outside actors, rampant corruption, and—in the case of the last two—widespread protests by Iraqi youth wanting more promising futures. None have yet been able to make the extensive and widespread reforms that Iraq needs if it is to stabilize and avert state collapse.

Although Iraq can be classified as a failing state, it also has the markings of a resilient state. Despite the incredible challenges it has faced over the years, it has not tipped into collapse. Its democracy is young, dysfunctional, and highly imperfect, but at the same time, it is also constitutional, pluralistic, and reasonably representative. Its leaders, however, must find a way to make the system deliver for the growing numbers of Iraqis who have known little stability or prosperity throughout their entire lives.

How Did the Bush Administration Do?

An evaluation of the Bush administration approach toward Iraq may best begin with the major shift in strategy represented by the Surge and announced by President Bush in January 2007. In many respects, the new approach was the result of a strategic review that identified and acknowledged many, if not most, of the shortcomings of the 2003–2006 strategy. The most significant deficiencies included a mistaken belief that, in the circumstances as they existed then, political progress would drive security improvements; a tendency to underresource the military component; a strategy that sought too aggressive a timeline to transition full responsibility to Iraqi institutions; and a failure to take on Iranian influence more directly.

The Surge strategy addressed these and other weaknesses in the prior US approach and produced the dramatic results mentioned earlier. As acknowledged previously, the Surge alone is not responsible for the significant improvements in Iraq at that time. But the shift in US strategy did reinforce and buttress positive developments already happening in Iraq; they were very much connected. For instance, President Bush used his personal relationship with Prime Minister Maliki and the leverage that additional military and civilian resources gave him to convince Maliki to hold Shi'a militia accountable (and not just Sunni violators of the law). Moreover, the Surge was developed with the explicit objective of reinforcing the small number of US forces already working with Iraqi tribes in fighting AQI.

The results of this strategic shift and the situation in Iraq at the time of the transition to the Obama administration indicated that, after costly mistakes made in earlier years, the Bush administration had found a strategy that could and did produce meaningful results in both the security and political realms. A legitimate question remains, however, in light of the downturn in Iraq's trajectory that followed during the Obama administration: whether the Surge provided only temporary improvement in the situation while US forces remained, or whether it in fact offered a new beginning to Iraqis.

The purpose of the Surge was to help stabilize Iraq's security situation in order to enable Iraqis to resolve their disputes through political means. One cannot claim for certain whether the positive momentum in Iraq at the end of the Bush administration could have been sustained either under different subsequent administrations or had different policies been enacted. Nevertheless, two major policy decisions by the Obama administration viewed in hindsight seem to have been fateful: the 2010 decision to support Maliki's continuation in power despite election results to the contrary, and the 2011 decision not to renew or extend the Security Agreement and to withdraw all US troops from Iraq. Had the United States opted for a different approach in both instances, Iraq may have consolidated the fragile gains of earlier years, rather than dissipated them. This is not to say that a different government in Baghdad and a continued US military presence in Iraq could have entirely prevented the emergence of ISIS, particularly if American policy toward Syria had remained the same. But there would have been far less Sunni disaffection for ISIS to exploit and the threats it posed could have been identified and addressed sooner, limiting the damage to Iraq's institutions, body-politic, and infrastructure that ensued.

What Are the Lessons Learned?

The lessons learned from American engagement in Iraq are extensive and worthy of careful study. This postscript can do scant justice to the effort. But some of the most critical lessons for policymakers are readily apparent:

- *Iraq still matters.* Its geostrategic position in the Gulf, its potential as an Arab counterweight to Iranian expansion, its large energy reserves, and its population and landmass will always make Iraq an important player in regional politics and security. A collapsed or failed Iraqi state, with scores of nonstate armed groups, or an Iraq drawn fully into Iran's orbit, would represent a major threat to regional stability and US interests. Iraq's success or failure will also have a direct bearing on US credibility in the region and a reflection of its ability and willingness to live up to its commitments. Finally, the fate of Iraq's democracy is of interest to many governments and peoples in the region, who either fear or welcome its success.

- *The Middle East—of which Iraq remains a lynchpin—should continue to be a priority for the United States.* In reality, however reluctant American policymakers are to lavish time and resources on the Middle East, the future of the region is interwoven with US interests. Some of those interests are enduring, be it the security of Israel and our Arab allies, the need to tamp down terrorist threats, or the imperative of pushing back on Iranian aggression and aspirations to become a regional hegemon. Moreover, even though the energy landscape is shifting and the world is intensifying its efforts to move away from fossil fuels on account of climate change, the Middle East will remain an important player on the energy landscape. Not only are some Middle Eastern countries seeking to position themselves as renewable energy or hydrogen powerhouses, but they are likely to remain influential oil producers—even as many other, more costly sources of oil curtail production. Finally, the Middle East will become a theater in which great power rivalry between the United States and China plays out, rather than a region that will become less relevant due to this competition.

- *America is neither all-powerful nor impotent.* For challenges like those posed by postconflict Iraq, the United States, no matter how powerful and no matter how many resources it has at its disposal, cannot secure a specific outcome on its own. While the United States shares much blame and credit, Iraqis themselves bear much of the responsibility for where the country is today. At the same time, US policymakers must not swing too far in the other direction. America's experience in Iraq demonstrates that it is neither all-powerful nor powerless; it has the ability to help countries make dramatic changes. But it should not underestimate the significant time, resources, and energy that doing so requires—and the overwhelming importance of a committed, capable local partner.

- *The US record on stabilization and reconstruction is a sobering one.* Some of the early errors made in Iraq are part of a pattern seen in other efforts to rebuild postconflict nations, underscoring the difficulty of the task particularly in countries as large and as complex as Iraq. Only after several years in Iraq and the reassessment that resulted in the Surge did America's efforts begin to produce what might have been sustained and lasting results. The failings in prior years included difficulty defining a clear, commonly agreed, and realistic objective and end state; relying on planning assumptions that turned out to be wrong; a reluctance or inability to match resources to goals at the outset; competing visions and varying levels of commitment and capability among US departments and agencies; an inability to forge a common program with the region and the international community; and difficulty maintaining the reservoir of US popular support that is so essential for long, grinding campaigns. Given that such problems also dogged US efforts in Vietnam, Afghanistan, Somalia, Bosnia, Kosovo, and Haiti, the lesson is clear: significant efforts to rebuild countries should only be undertaken when truly vital US interests are at stake. The Bush administration believed this standard was met in the case of Iraq, but success required subsequent administrations to have a similar commitment to see the project through to a successful conclusion.

- *Democracy is both essential to success and far more difficult to build and sustain than anticipated.* The Bush administration is often accused of trying to impose democracy on Iraq through the barrel of a gun. In reality, the critical emphasis placed on helping Iraqis build democratic institutions came more out of post-Saddam experience in Iraq than prewar rationales for the US invasion. Saddam Hussein was deposed because the Bush administration believed he represented a national security threat to the United States and its friends and allies. After Saddam fled Baghdad, and security virtually collapsed in the country, the United States and its coalition partners faced a stark choice. They could have sought to replace Saddam with some Western-friendly autocrat who would foreswear pursuit of WMD, support for terrorists, or invasion of Iraq's neighbors while maintaining power through the extreme repression that most outsiders underappreciate was pervasive in Iraq under Saddam. Alternatively, they could help Iraqis—who in huge numbers wanted more accountable leadership regardless of their view of Saddam's ouster—build a democratic political system as the only way a traumatized nation could peacefully manage the competition for power and resources among Sunni, Shi'a, Kurds, and the many other groups within Iraq. The Bush administration adopted the second approach. It better aligned both with American values and with American interests. It offered the best chance for achieving a stable, sustainable Iraq that did not threaten those interests. Yet the challenge was real. No society is incapable of democracy. But the various layers of institutions, norms, and practices required for a sustainable democracy take considerable time to construct and remain perilously fragile long after they are initially established.

- *The now common phrase "endless wars" fails to distinguish sustainable foreign commitments from unsustainable ones.* In the past eighteen years, the United States troop commitment to Iraq has varied hugely, from 166,000 at the height of the Surge, to a few hundred after the 2011 withdrawal, to several thousand in 2021. Similarly, the mission of these troops and the role they have played in Iraq's recent past has ranged from being the primary providers of Iraq's security to largely training and supporting Iraqi troops. It is true that the American people cannot indefinitely sustain the level of commitment required at the most intense periods of this engagement, and that few Iraqis would want such a pervasive US presence to be open-ended. But it does not necessarily follow that a full withdrawal of all US forces in the name of ending "an endless war" is the better option. In fact, America's engagement in Iraq has demonstrated that a much more modest commitment of troops, with a true partnership with a host government, can be both sustainable over a long period of time and extremely helpful to the country in question. Iraq in 2022 offers such a model—an alternative to the "endless wars"—which does not require an overwhelming military commitment, but instead a modest one in a supporting role, which enables other kinds of nonmilitary US engagement. Ending these more modest commitments, especially for political reasons, in some cases is more likely to harm US interests than advance them if local institutions on the ground are not sufficiently robust—and building such institutions, as we now know, can take years.

- *The United States needs to better fund civilian capabilities to prevent the "overmilitarization" of foreign policy.* The common criticism that the Bush administration "militarized" Iraq policy is valid in the sense that it did rely too heavily on the military and military tools to execute its strategies. But this reliance was not a reflection of a particular preference or ideology, but of a practical constraint. The administration appreciated that many necessary missions in Iraq—be it governance, anticorruption, economic development, social reconciliation, or rehabilitation—would be more appropriately undertaken by civilians. Yet the civilian capabilities of the US government were woefully lacking due to insufficient investment in them. The "militarization" of US efforts in Iraq was the direct consequence of a longstanding (and continued) American tendency to fund military expenses and starve civilian ones.

Contributor:
Richard Hooker

CHAPTER 8

Colombia

THOMAS SHANNON | DANIEL W. FISK

As the twentieth century drew to a close, the bilateral relationship between the United States and Colombia lay in tatters while the security situation in Colombia had deteriorated. During the presidency of Ernesto Samper, allegations that Colombian drug cartel money had funded Samper's presidential campaign, and US concerns that cartels exercised extensive influence within the Samper government, had badly damaged the bilateral relationship. US cooperation on security and development had shrunk dramatically, and the United States had limited access to or influence over the government. The involvement of Colombia's principal insurgent group, the Rebel Armed Forces of Colombia (FARC), in the production and distribution of cocaine provided a lucrative source of funding to the armed insurgency and linked the FARC and the drug cartels in their fight against the Colombian state.

The election of Andres Pastrana as Samper's successor in 1998 opened space for the United States to reengage with the Colombian government. However, an unsuccessful peace process led by the United Nations, the escalating violence of the civil conflict, the weakness of the state, and the ineffectiveness of Colombia's armed forces and security agencies in containing and controlling the FARC and other insurgent forces in the countryside, threatened the integrity of the state, the well-being of Colombian society, and fundamental interests of the United States.

In 1999, Colombian President Pastrana and the Clinton administration, working with the US Congress, fashioned Plan Colombia to significantly expand counterdrug cooperation and modernize Colombia's national security institutions. However, by 2001 it had become apparent that US assistance was too narrowly focused, and that the counterdrug assistance would not address the larger security threat posed by armed insurgents and paramilitary groups. Continuing violence throughout Colombia, growing levels of coca leaf cultivation, and a stalled economy had caused a domestic crisis of confidence, and support for the Pastrana government had plummeted.

TRANSITION MEMORANDUM

~~CONFIDENTIAL~~ WITH
SECRET ATTACHMENT

NATIONAL SECURITY COUNCIL
WASHINGTON, D.C. 20504

2844
Transition

November 10, 2008

MEMORANDUM FOR THE RECORD

FROM: ROBERT A. KING, WESTERN HEMISPHERE AFFAIRS
             DIRECTORATE

SUBJECT: Colombia

THE SITUATION AS WE FOUND IT:

By the late 1990s, Colombia was on the verge of becoming a failed state—and possibly a narco-state—as leftist and paramilitary terrorist groups had taken control of much of the countryside, violence spiraled out of control, and the economy was in a free fall. The situation became so dire that two-thirds of Colombians believed that armed guerrillas could gain full control of their country.

The threat from the illegal armed groups and the deterioration of state control and the resulting surge in violence precipitated a social and economic crisis. At their high point in 1990–2001, the two main leftist terrorist groups, the Revolutionary Armed Forces of Colombia (FARC) and National Liberation Army (ELN) had some 20,000 members and a presence in 60 percent of the country's municipalities. The Colombian National Police, the only central government presence in many parts of the country, had been driven out of nearly 200 of Colombia's 1,100 municipalities. To address the failure of the Colombian Government to challenge the presence and momentum of the FARC and ELN, private armies and paramilitary movements emerged. Violence permeated the country, with some 3,200 kidnappings alone in 1999 and a murder rate of 62.2 per 100,000 people in the last half of the 1990s. The economy was in recession, and unemployment rose to 18 percent and poverty to 57.5 percent. As a result of the violence and hopeless economic prospects, some 1.8 million Colombians were displaced, and many fled the country.

~~CONFIDENTIAL~~ WITH
SECRET ATTACHMENT
Reason: 1.4(b) (d)
Declassify on: 11/10/18

NSC Declassification Review [EO 13526]
DECLASSIFY IN FULL
by William C. Carpenter on 3/23/2020

The FARC and the paramilitaries financed their operations through a symbiotic relationship with the drug trade that earned them millions of dollars. With little government control of the countryside, by 1999 there were an estimated 122,000 hectares of coca being cultivated and cocaine production reached 520 metric tons. Colombia hit its low point when the FARC, having been granted a large demilitarized zone by President Pastrana as a venue for conducting peace talks, used the zone instead to rest, train its forces, grow coca, hold kidnapped Colombians, and plan operations.

As Colombia was hitting rock bottom, President Pastrana announced in September 1999 "Plan Colombia," an ambitious, 5-year program intended to significantly expand counterdrug activities, modernize the military, strengthen the economy, reform the political and judicial systems, and end the 40-year insurgency. The plan was developed in close collaboration with the United States Government and received strong bipartisan congressional support.

Plan Colombia helped crystallize the need for a comprehensive strategy, but by January 2001 it had fallen short as a political and operational roadmap for change. Pastrana's inconsistent leadership, bureaucratic infighting within the Colombian Government, inadequate military and law enforcement institutional capacity, and delays in international and domestic funding hindered implementation of the plan. For example, Pastrana's commitment to make an aggressive counterdrug push into southern Colombia—to reduce drug production and deprive the insurgents and paramilitaries of income—contradicted his deeper personal commitment to continue the peace talks with the FARC, which controlled much of that region.

In 2001, the violence continued: Colombian military and police forces suffered frequent defeat at the hands of the FARC, while the paramilitaries continued to operate unimpeded, and sometimes in direct collaboration with the military. As a result, coca production remained elevated, with an estimated 169,000 hectares of coca under cultivation. Colombia produced 90 percent of the cocaine entering the United States. The economy experienced meager growth in 2000–2001, pushing unemployment to around 20 percent, and slow growth left the Pastrana government with few resources to implement Plan Colombia, address enduring social inequities, and strengthen the security forces. Public confidence in Pastrana's administration and its ability to provide even basic services and protection had plummeted, and by the time he left office in July 2002 Pastrana's approval rating was 21 percent.

THIS ADMINISTRATION'S POLICY:

Upon coming to office in 2001, the Bush Administration expanded U.S. assistance to Colombia to combat illegal drugs and support Colombian efforts to achieve peace, justice, and economic prosperity. The Administration targeted monies under the Andean Counter-Drug Initiative (ACI) and reduced limitations on civilian contractors during aerial eradication missions. Plan Colombia remained the cornerstone of U.S. assistance to Colombia, but there was a recognition that without a more aggressive effort to provide security and combat narco-terrorism, Plan Colombia would not achieve its objectives. This new focus was given impetus with the 2002 election of President Alvaro Uribe in Colombia and his determination to include counterterrorist goals.

- The Administration redesignated the ELN and FARC as foreign terrorist organizations (FTO) in 2001; it also designated the largest paramilitary alliance, the United Self-Defense Forces of Colombia (AUC), as an FTO in 2001.

- In August 2002, the Bush Administration received congressional approval to broaden the authorities of Plan Colombia to allow U.S. funds to be used to support Colombian efforts against the narco-terrorist FARC, ELN, and AUC.

- To increase the tools available to U.S. policymakers, the FARC and AUC were designated in 2003 Significant Foreign Narcotics Traffickers under the Foreign Narcotics Kingpin Designation Act. This designation denied the FARC and AUC access to the U.S. financial system by freezing their assets in U.S. jurisdictions, and banned U.S. entities from doing business with them.

In October 2002, the President issued National Security Presidential Directive 18, which articulated United States policy to help the Colombian Government strengthen its democratic institutions and respect for human rights and the rule of law, and reduce the threat of narcotics trafficking and terrorism. The President directed the United States to assist the Colombian Government regain control of its national territory, establish the rule of law, and improve its ability to defeat the FARC, ELN, and AUC, other illegal armed groups, and narcotics trafficking organizations.

The United States Government has provided more than $5 billion in economic and security assistance under Plan Colombia since 2001. Colombia provided an estimated $6.7 billion during the period 2000–2005. U.S. security assistance combats drug trafficking and terrorism through training, equipment, and technical assistance. It supports Colombian military aviation, which is essential for all programs—civilian or military—outside Colombia's major cities. U.S. economic aid focuses on alternative development, assisting displaced and other vulnerable communities, and promoting human rights and democratic institutions and the reintegration of demobilized fighters.

With the expiration of Plan Colombia in 2005 and the continued need for U.S. assistance, the United States Government encouraged Colombia to develop a follow-on strategy. The United States continued its assistance, but began a transition to greater Colombian financial responsibility and operational control, leading, in January 2007, to the Colombian Government presenting its Plan

Colombia "consolidation strategy" (2007–2013) to consolidate state control throughout Colombia, protect the population, eliminate the illegal drug trade, maintain a deterrent capability against external threats, and ensure the transparent and efficient management of resources. Colombia pledged greater investment in a wider range of programs than in the original Plan Colombia, emphasizing the building of social cohesion, strengthening local governance, protecting human rights, and helping displaced people, Afro-Colombians, and indigenous communities. It also aims to reintegrate more than 45,000 demobilized ex-fighters and deserters into Colombian society and to promote Colombia's licit exports.

Separate from Plan Colombia, a second, smaller but still key policy tool for helping Colombia has been trade preferences under the Andean Trade Preference Act (ATPA) and then expanded in 2002 in the Andean Trade Preference and Drug Eradication Act. The Bush Administration has pushed to lock in the benefits of our bilateral trade relationship with the U.S.-Colombia Free Trade Agreement (FTA), which was signed in November 2006 and, once approved by the Congress, will make permanent the access to the U.S. market that Colombia enjoys under ATPA. Equally important is the incentive for long-term investment in Colombia that the FTA will generate, assisting with the policy goal to further stimulate economic opportunities for Colombians in the licit/legal economy. The FTA also sends a political signal to the region that the United States stands by its allies.

WHAT HAS BEEN ACCOMPLISHED:

Determined leadership by President Uribe, assisted by substantial bipartisan support from the United States, has resulted in significant accomplishments. Colombia has made significant progress in addressing long-standing problems by strengthening state authority over most of the country and improving the everyday security situation for most Colombians. The improved security situation, in turn, has made possible noteworthy improvements in economic conditions, human rights, and society. The noticeable accomplishments include:

- **Reducing the Terrorist Ranks.** Over 32,000 paramilitary members—most of them from the rightist United Self-Defense Forces of Colombia (AUC)—have been demobilized, and the government has acted aggressively to investigate and prosecute paramilitary crimes. The government has the upper hand against the FARC; more than 10,000 guerilla members have turned themselves in or been captured, and the rest are under sustained assault by the military, including the killing of two FARC Secretariat members in March 2008—the first combat deaths of the FARC's political leadership in that organization's 44-year history. Those deaths, as well as that of Supreme Commander Marulanda in March, prompted a surge of defections and raise prospects that FARC's defeat is only a matter of time.

- **Restoring Legitimate State Authority.** The improved security situation has allowed the government to establish for the first time its presence in all 1099 municipalities and deliver services that have significantly improved social and economic conditions. Enrollment in public schools has increased to 92 percent.

- **Reducing Violent Crimes.** Since President Uribe took office in 2002, homicides have dropped have dropped by 40 percent, kidnappings by almost 83 percent, and terrorist attacks by 76 percent. Implementation of the new accusatory criminal justice system has reduced the time needed to resolve criminal cases by over 75 percent and boosted conviction rates to 60 percent, up from 3 percent under the old system. The Unites States Government assistance has been critical to the successful implementation of the new system.

- **Fostering Economic Growth.** Colombia's economy is thriving (it grew by 7.5 percent in 2007, the highest since 1978), pushing unemployment to its lowest level in a decade. Poverty has declined by 21 percent since 2002. Increased job opportunities have reduced the allure of the FARC and the drug trade as a way of life for Colombians.

- **Reducing Drug Trafficking.** The Colombian Government has made significant strides in its battle against narcotics trafficking, but has fallen short of the original goal of Plan Colombia of a 50 percent reduction in coca cultivation over 6 years. Cocaine production has fallen by a third, coca cultivation has declined by 7 percent, and drug seizures have more than doubled. Alternative development programs have benefited over 135,000 families and supported 158,000 hectares of licit crops.

Before Plan Colombia, the public sensed that drug traffickers and guerrillas had the upper hand, and that drug-related corruption had permeated public life. However, since 2000 polls show a marked improvement in public confidence in the government, military, and police. Plan Colombia also has gone a long way in improving the image of the United States in Colombia. Polling consistently shows that since 2000 the public has been pro-United States and wants the United States to remain Colombia's key ally.

FUTURE CHALLENGES:

Colombia has made significant gains since 1999 in addressing the problems that almost led to state failure a decade ago. Nonetheless, more work remains to be done to consolidate the gains. Without sustained U.S. assistance, progress could be reversed. The Colombian Government is seeking funding from the United States and European countries for its consolidation strategy, even as it takes on a growing responsibility for funding the program. The Colombians will continue to need U.S. security assistance to combat drug trafficking and terrorism, including training, material aid, and technical assistance to security forces and other institutions.

Moreover, implementation of the U.S.-Colombia FTA is one of the most effective ways of bolstering Colombia's fight against violence because it will reduce investor uncertainty and spur economic growth, which will provide the government with resources for more social services. It also reduces poverty and creates alternative opportunities for Colombians, depriving the guerrillas and drug traffickers of new recruits to their cause.

Assisting Colombia to consolidate its gains will continue to be in the U.S. national interest. Among the challenges that Colombia will need to address in the coming years with his consolidation strategy are:

- **Consolidating state authority over the entire country.** Although mayors and the police are now located in all of Colombia's municipalities, greater government expenditures are needed on security, judicial, and civil presence, including teachers, health and social services.

- **Improving the rule of law.** The Colombian Government will need to hire and train more judges, public defenders, and investigators to make justice more accessible and transparent. On January 1, 2008, Colombia initiated the final phase of a 4-year, phased implementation of its new Criminal Procedure Code, which introduces an accusatory criminal justice system, but additional resources will be needed to ensure its success, including changing the mindset and culture of justice sector officials trained in the inquisitorial tradition. U.S. assistance remains critical to ensure this change is implemented effectively and thoroughly.

- **Following through on paramilitary demobilization.** Paramilitary demobilization has put strain on the state, which has been unable to fully implement the Justice and Peace Law that governs the investigation and prosecution of past paramilitary abuses, compensates victims, and investigates and prosecutes links between the paramilitaries and political and military figures. Colombia also needs to incorporate former paramilitaries into society to prevent their turn toward organized criminal activities, including narco-related activities.

- **Keeping the pressure on illegal armed groups to demobilize.** Although the Colombian Government has significantly weakened the FARC and ELN, the two sides are no closer to a political settlement that would result in the demobilization of the narco-terrorist groups. The FARC, in particular, will not consent to peace talks and will try to wait out the Uribe government to try to get a better deal from a future government.

Attachments
Tab 1   Chronology for Colombia
Tab 2   Summary of Conclusions of Principals Committee Meeting on Colombia (February 26, 2002)

POSTSCRIPT

THOMAS SHANNON, DANIEL W. FISK

While the development of Plan Colombia during the Clinton administration was a signal and important step, and laid the groundwork for what came next, it was not sufficient for success. Deep concerns about the continuing influence of cartels within the government, the rise of paramilitary forces in the Colombian country-side, and congressional concerns about human rights violations by the Colombian armed forces and national police limited how the United States could engage with Colombian authorities. Conceived of primarily as a counterdrug effort, Plan Colombia was unable in its early incarnation to address the alliances that had formed between drug cartels and insurgents or to grasp the symbiotic relationship that eventually fused cartels and insurgents into narco-terrorists. Given the bitter aftertaste that still lingered in Congress from US involvement in Central America, and the harsh partisan battles this had engendered, efforts to fashion a bipartisan approach to Colombia initially limited the type, kind, and manner of assistance to Colombia's government.

The Bush Administration Approach

It fell to the Bush administration to help Congress understand the challenge in Colombia in a new light and to expand US operational support while never losing sight of a central element of Plan Colombia: This was Colombia's fight. The United States would be a supportive partner but would not substitute American troops for Colombian troops and would measure its success or failure on the ability of Colombians to protect their own state and society from the ravages of narco-terrorists.

The Bush administration's response was, first, to use existing tools to expand counterdrug and economic assistance. However, it then sought to transform Plan Colombia into a more comprehensive effort to reassert Colombian state authority throughout Colombia's national territory. This required an expansion of legal authorities to permit US assistance to support Colombian military efforts against the major insurgent and paramilitary groups. Accompanying this expansion of authorities, the Bush administration also designated these groups as Foreign Terrorist Organizations and as Significant Foreign Narcotics Traffickers. President Bush then issued National Security Presidential Directive 18, expanding the purpose of

US policy to include strengthening Colombia's democratic institutions and promoting respect for human rights and the rule of law. This linkage of security and political assistance underscored the transformational nature of the partnership in which the United States and Colombia had entered.

US policy, however, required the commitment of the Colombian people and capable leadership. The election of Alvaro Uribe as Colombia's president in 2002 provided that leadership and was a clear indication that the Colombian people were determined to fight the armed groups threatening to overwhelm their society.

It is impossible to overstate the role that President Uribe played in forging the successful partnership with the United States. The relationship between Uribe and President Bush was one of immediate understanding and common purpose, and played a central role in driving cooperation between the two governments. It was shaped in the shadow of September 11 and the larger War on Terror. Although the terrorism afflicting Colombia had no jihadist or Islamist roots, nor connection to al Qaeda, Uribe was adept at linking Colombia's fight for survival to those of America's partners in the Middle East and elsewhere. His purpose was to make clear to President Bush and Congress that, given the right kind of assistance, he could prevail. In the process, Uribe developed the concept of "democratic security," which asserted that a state could respond to an existential threat without sacrificing its democratic government or aspirations.

By the end of the Bush administration, significant progress had been made in strengthening state authority, improving security, and spurring economic progress throughout most of the country. The government finally had the upper hand against the FARC, having killed key leaders and captured or accepted the surrender of over 10,000 guerilla fighters. Over 32,000 rightist paramilitary members had been demobilized. Homicides, kidnappings, and terrorist attacks were down dramatically. The economy was growing, unemployment was declining, and poverty rates reducing. The government was present in all 1,099 municipalities and providing improved services to the population.

What Has Happened Since the End of the Bush Administration?

The Obama administration largely embraced Plan Colombia upon assuming office in 2009. While continuing funding for counterdrug and counterterrorism operations, the administration began increasingly to shift the balance of funding to expanding state capacity and presence in Colombia's interior and conflict zones. Building on the successful 2006 trade negotiations of the Bush administration, the Obama administration worked to win US congressional ratification of the United States-Colombia Trade Promotion Agreement in 2011.

In 2012, the Colombian government began peace negotiations with the FARC under President Juan Manuel Santos (elected in 2010), holding initial conversations along the Colombia-Venezuela frontier, then moving to Oslo, and finally to Havana, Cuba, for the duration of the talks. The Obama administration offered its support. As the talks progressed, Secretary of State John Kerry appointed former Assistant Secretary of State Bernard Aronson as Special Envoy to the Colombian Peace Process. In February 2016, the Obama administration announced "Paz Colombia" or "Peace Colombia," a $450 million aid program designed to promote implementation of the peace accords and create a new framework for the next phase in the United States-Colombia bilateral relationship. A final agreement between the Santos government and the FARC was reached in August 2016.

The agreement generated significant political controversy in Colombia. Former President Uribe was a vocal opponent of the deal, arguing that it gave a political lifeline to a failed insurgent group that had largely alienated the Colombian people. The Santos administration argued that the deal demobilized a still large and dangerous armed group, broke the relationship between the insurgency and drug cartels, incorporated the FARC into Colombian politics, reintegrated FARC fighters into Colombian society, and laid out a political framework for Colombian democracy that would keep Colombians from using violence to resolve political problems in the future. A hotly argued referendum was put to a vote in October of 2016, with the peace accords rejected by a slim margin, 50.2 percent to 49.2 percent. The Santos administration returned the peace accords to the negotiators for refinement, and then presented the agreement to the Colombian Congress, where it was approved by both houses on November 29–30, 2016.

During the Trump administration, US interest in Colombia largely returned to counterdrug cooperation. President Trump was alarmed by the growth in coca leaf cultivation and cocaine production in Colombia, as were members of the US Congress. US security and development assistance was pegged to Colombia's willingness to return to the initial purpose of Plan Colombia: fighting the illicit production of cocaine. The election of President Ivan Duque in 2018, a protégé of former President Uribe, led to a more traditional focus in the bilateral relationship, with an emphasis on counternarcotics cooperation, trade, regional diplomacy (especially with respect to Venezuela and its increasingly chaotic situation), and migration. The Trump administration, in an effort to promote Colombia within South America, offered its support to Colombian accession to the Organization of Economic Cooperation and Development (OECD), an organization that only Chile, as a South American country, had been able to join.

How Did the Bush Administration Do?

Successful US foreign policy usually depends on the partners America chooses. There is no doubt that the Bush administration chose wisely in Colombia, and was fortunate to have Alvaro Uribe as Colombia's president. This partnership allowed President Bush to foster broad support for his Colombia policy, incorporating not only the national security institutions of the executive branch, but also of Congress. That the accomplishments in Colombia were understood as the product of bipartisan cooperation in Washington allowed them to endure across changes of presidential administrations and laid the groundwork for the Obama administration's work in support of the Colombian peace process.

It is commonplace today to assess Plan Colombia, and what followed, as a singular success. Not only did the United States help a country save itself from collapse, it did so at a moment when Colombia found itself alone in South America. Colombia's isolation in the region demoralized the Colombian people and the institutions of the Colombian state. The US commitment to Colombia rejuvenated Colombian society and institutions and made clear that Colombians would have a partner in their battle. The success of Plan Colombia, and especially the Bush administration effort to transform the US relationship with Colombia, has created a South American partner and ally of great vitality, purpose, and importance.

Colombia still faces many challenges that are a consequence of nearly six decades of internal conflict. Coca leaf and cocaine production are still significant and have become the battleground of armed criminal groups vying for control of this lucrative drug trade. The return of large swaths of Colombian territory to state control, and to participation in Colombian life, has shifted Colombian politics and challenged political parties and elites that had previously enjoyed unfettered influence in Colombian life. The violence that had defined Colombia during so many years is not easily ended, and killing of human rights, indigenous, and political activists still plagues parts of Colombia. But none of these problems threaten the Colombian state. They can be addressed by Colombians and within the institutions and structures that define Colombian democracy. At the same time, there is no doubt that progress in Colombia has been slowed and made more difficult by the safe haven that its neighbor Venezuela is providing to terrorist and insurgent groups using its territory to destabilize Colombia.

What Are the Lessons Learned?

Plan Colombia, originally conceived of as a counterdrug strategy, became a counterterrorism and state-building strategy. While Colombia's ongoing production of cocaine for the US market calls into question whether Plan Colombia achieved its initial purpose, there can be no doubt that it succeeded in its larger purpose of saving Colombia from failure and collapse.

- *Counterinsurgency and state building can succeed.* The lesson many people are drawing from the American experience in Libya, Syria, but especially in Afghanistan and Iraq, is that "nation building" is a fool's errand doomed to failure and that counterinsurgency efforts cannot produce enduring stability and security. Colombia is the counter example. There, a strategy of counterinsurgency paired with domestic institution building and external political, security, and economic support did succeed in bringing stability, security, and economic progress to a state and a people beset by a long-standing, violent insurgency and terrorism.
- *Countries and their peoples need to fight and win their own freedom.* But despite all of America's power and capability, at the end of the day, the struggle against insurgency and terrorism had to be Colombia's fight. Plan Colombia and its successor efforts were successful because they enhanced and supported the Colombian government and its people but never sought to provide a substitute for them. In the end, success or failure would largely have to turn on their efforts.
- *A critical element to success is a capable and committed local partner.* Success will depend heavily on a local government and political leadership able to take the lead and rally the population. In the case of Colombia, Uribe headed a government with the capacity and the tenacity to carry the fight to its enemies, the Colombian people were prepared to support and follow strong domestic leadership, and both were prepared to work with a determined but respectful ally in both the fight against terror and insurgency and in significant state-building efforts.
- *Success is much more difficult with a terrorist and insurgent safe haven next door.* One of the great tragedies is how Venezuela has set back progress in

Colombia, destabilized its security, and imposed additional burdens on its state-building efforts. Terrorists and insurgent groups operating out of Venezuela threaten Colombian security. Refugees fleeing Venezuela by the hundreds of thousands impose a burden on the Colombian economy that it can ill afford. The resulting political demonstrations in Colombia threaten to destabilize the government. As the American experience in Vietnam and Afghanistan and now Colombia shows, the presence of a neighboring safe haven is a red flag for any counterinsurgency and state-building effort. The effort may still have to be made, but the safe haven problem is one for which no clear strategy has emerged.

CHAPTER 9

Lebanon

MICHAEL SINGH

US policy toward Lebanon since its independence in the 1940s has been characterized by sporadic, intensive engagement followed by long periods of relative inattention. Despite its position as a regional banking center and favored hub for international business and tourism until civil war broke out in the 1970s, Lebanon in the twentieth century was neither an economic nor military power and was not a key player in the region's geopolitics, leaving it at the fringes of US policy for the most part. US troops intervened in Lebanon at the direction of President Eisenhower in the 1950s in order to stave off a feared Nasserite insurrection, and again in the 1980s as part of the Multinational Force deployed in response to the violence racking the country. With those troops' departure following the bombing of the US Marine barracks in 1983—and the horrific death of 241 Marines just months after a bombing at the US Embassy killed seventeen Americans—Lebanon was relegated to the sidelines of US policy in the Middle East once again. Syrian occupation of the country in 1991 marked the end of the civil war but also the end of Lebanese sovereignty and freedom.

During the presidency of George W. Bush, Lebanon became significant to American strategy in the Middle East. In Lebanon, US concerns—given priority and urgency by the 9/11 terrorist attacks—about the Iraqi and Iranian regimes and about the region's deficit of freedom converged, resulting in a new level of

US engagement that was unprecedented and sustained throughout the administration. The international outrage and domestic demonstrations generated by the assassination of Lebanese Prime Minister Rafiq Hariri in 2005, along with US, French, and regional support, helped the people of Lebanon to achieve what previously seemed unthinkable—the ouster of the decades-long Syrian occupation and the return of Lebanese sovereignty. The gains achieved in this "Cedar Revolution" were, however, already at risk in 2009, and US attention to Lebanon faded thereafter.

TRANSITION MEMORANDUM

SECRET

5254
Transition

NATIONAL SECURITY COUNCIL
WASHINGTON, D.C. 20504

January 16, 2009

MEMORANDUM FOR THE RECORD

FROM: MEAGHEN MCDERMOTT, NEAR EAST NORTH AFRICA
           JENNIFER GAVITO, NEAR EAST NORTH AFRICA

SUBJECT: Lebanon

THE SITUATION AS WE FOUND IT:

On January 20, 2001, Lebanon was occupied by Syria, and the Lebanese people enjoyed neither sovereignty nor democracy. Syria had occupied Lebanon since the conclusion of the Lebanese civil war in 1991. Syria's military and intelligence apparatus had consolidated its hold through a series of treaties, protocols, and "high councils" governing bilateral relations. Hizballah, a creation of the Iranian Islamic Revolutionary Guard Corps (IRGC) and the only Lebanese militia not to disarm following the civil war, continued to wage terror attacks against Israel while at the same time expanding its influence over southern Lebanon via intimidation and extensive patronage.

THIS ADMINISTRATION'S POLICY:

Our overarching goal has been to neutralize Hizballah's threat to the United States and strengthen Lebanon's democracy, while denying Syria and Iran influence within Lebanon.

Between 2001 and 2004 the Administration's policy focused on Lebanon in a post 9/11 regional context. Hizballah, an international terrorist organization supported by Syria and Iran, undermined the authority of Lebanon's central government by operating as a state within a state. We sought to diminish Hizballah's activities and influence, while implementing economic and democratic reform

NSC Declassification Review [EO 13526]
Declassify in Part
by NSC Access on 2/24/2021
Re-Classified by: Corey Nightengale Sr.
Reason: 1.4(d)
Declassify on: 1/16/2034

SECRET
Reason: 1.4(a)(b)(d)
Declassify on: 1/16/19

aimed at strengthening Lebanon's legitimate institutions. President Bush consulted with French President Chirac on the need to strengthen democracy in the broader Middle East and in particular in Lebanon. In June of 2004, President Bush traveled to France, where he and his French counterpart agreed to advance a U.N. resolution aimed at ending Syrian interference in Lebanon.

As cooperation grew between Paris and Washington to secure Lebanon's independence, National Security Advisor Hadley and Secretary of State Rice met often with French National Security Adviser Gourdault-Montagne to synchronize American and French actions and advance the Administration's policy. Working together, and with European and Arab partners, we galvanized opposition to Syria's interference in Lebanon, and the international community responded by passing U.N. Security Council Resolution 1559 on September 2, 2004. That resolution, coauthored by the United States and France, called for Syria to withdraw from Lebanon, a free and fair electoral process, and the disarmament of all militias (including Hizballah).

Syria's hold on Lebanon became even clearer when, in 2004, Lebanese President Emile Lahoud's mandate was extended 3 years by a Syrian-orchestrated amendment to the Lebanese constitution. Growing international support for Lebanon's sovereignty encouraged Lebanese political figures to speak out more openly and candidly against Syria's role. The February 2005 assassination of former Prime Minister Rafiq Hariri, an increasingly outspoken critic of Syrian interference in Lebanon, deepened the President's resolve to champion Lebanon's independence. Presidents Bush and Chirac met again on February 21 and agreed that a formal inquiry should be made into Hariri's murder and the international community should increase pressure on Syria to withdraw from Lebanon. International pressure to withdraw intensified and Lebanese public sentiment turned against Syria, evidenced by mass demonstrations in Beirut that were labeled "the Cedar Revolution." Throughout February and March thousands of Lebanese protestors rallied calling for an end of Syrian occupation and blaming Syria and the pro-Syrian president Emile Lahoud for the murder. President Bush reaffirmed his support for full implementation of UNSCR 1559. Syria responded to the pressure by eventually withdrawing its troops and ending its 29-year overt military presence in Lebanon on April 26, 2005.

In June 2005, the anti-Syrian "March 14" Coalition headed by Rafiq Hariri's son Saad won parliamentary elections and brought Prime Minister Fouad Siniora's government to power. Almost immediately, the opposition coalition, which included Hizballah and other Syrian proxies in Lebanon, sought to paralyze the government. For example, opposition Shi'a ministers withdrew from the government for months, making Sunni Prime Minister Siniora vulnerable to criticism that his government was making decisions without Shi'a input. A continuing string of politically motivated assassinations, all of them targeting foes of Syria, kept Lebanon unsettled and was widely attributed to Syria's intelligence services. President Bush sought to maintain the international community's commitment to Lebanon by issuing a number of statements condemning the assassinations.

The political situation further deteriorated as a result of the July 2006 war between Israel and Hizballah, which undermined the Siniora government and may have boosted Hizballah's popularity. Throughout the war, the President consulted with British Prime Minister Blair, German Chancellor Merkel, and U.N. Secretary-General Annan. He sought agreement from world leaders on the importance of a meaningful cease-fire that would leave Hizballah permanently weakened and prevent state sponsors of terrorism like Syria and Iran from resupplying the group. Secretary of State Rice traveled between Israel and Lebanon trying to broker a cease-fire while NSA Hadley coordinated with Israeli officials including Yoram Turbowicz, Chief of Staff to the Prime Minister, to identify the terms of a cease-fire. In late July and early August, State Department and NSC senior officials worked with the French on drafting UNSC Resolution 1701, the document that ultimately brought a cessation of hostilities between Hizballah and Israel. The passing of UNSCR 1701 on August 11 resulted in a cessation of hostilities between Hizballah and Israel and a strengthening of UNIFIL's 1978 mandate in southern Lebanon, and called on it to assist the Government of Lebanon in extending its authority over southern Lebanon, securing its borders, and stemming the flow of illicit arms.

The opposition's efforts to hamstring the government culminated in November 2006 when opposition cabinet members (including all of the Shi'a ministers) resigned again, and Parliament Speaker Nabih Berri shuttered Parliament pending the resolution of the ongoing political stale-mate. Hizballah and opposition supporters in December erected a "tent city" near the Prime Minister's office in an attempt to force out the Siniora cabinet. This stalemate paralyzed attempts to elect a new president following the end of Lahoud's term in November 2007, and promoted political brinkmanship between Lebanese factions.

The already tense situation erupted in May 2008 when Hizballah for the first time turned its weapons on its fellow citizens to protest a series of decisions taken by the Lebanese Government that Hizballah perceived as threatening to its existence. The Arab League eventually brokered a deal, referred to as the "Doha Agreement," to end the violence and break 18 months of political deadlock. The Doha Agreement provided a mechanism for the immediate election of Lebanese President Michel Sleiman and kicked off an intense political competition between the March 14 Coalition and the Hizballah-led opposition as each prepares for the National Assembly election, scheduled for June 7, 2009.

In pursuit of our goals to support Lebanese sovereignty and democracy, oppose Syrian and Iranian influence, and disarm the various militias, including Hizballah, we have pursued the following policies.

Support for the Siniora Government: The government of Fouad Siniora, representing the Hariri-led "March 14" Coalition, has been under steady attack by Syrian proxies in Lebanon, Hizballah, and other members of the opposition from the beginning. Additionally, "March 14's" parliamentary majority has dwindled due to assassinations and occasional defections. The "March 14" Coalition hopes to maintain its majority over the Hizballah-allied opposition in parliamentary elections scheduled for June 7. The election outcome is uncertain, but it is clear that the Christian vote will be a key factor. We have used tools such as security and economic assistance, financial stabilization, public diplomacy, and engagement of Arab and European partners to strengthen Siniora and counter attempts by the Lebanese opposition, including Hizballah, to bring down Siniora's government. President Bush has consistently reaffirmed U.S. support for Lebanon in front of European and Arab allies.

Support for Lebanon's Security Services: To achieve our goal of a democratic and sovereign Lebanon, we have worked to strengthen the Lebanese Armed Forces (LAF) and Internal Security Forces (ISF) as the best defense against internal armed groups, including Hizballah, political violence, and foreign interference. Both the previous and current Commander of U.S. Central Command have traveled to Lebanon to advance our close cooperation with the Lebanese Government.

Implementation of UNSCR Resolutions: Several U.N. Security Council Resolutions support our objectives in Lebanon, including UNSCR 1559 (calling for Syrian withdrawal from Lebanon and the disarmament of militias, including Hizballah), UNSCR 1701 (passed in the aftermath of the 2006 Israel-Lebanon War, which calls upon the Government of Lebanon to secure its borders and imposes a legally binding obligation on all states to prevent weapons smuggling into Lebanon), and UNSCR 1832 (which renews the UNIFIL mandate in southern Lebanon). We have worked with the international community and Lebanese parties to push for their immediate and unconditional implementation. In particular, we have repeatedly warned that we expect it to be the explicit policy of the new Lebanese Government and its president to implement these resolutions.

Isolation of Syria: On numerous occasions U.S. officials have demonstrated a willingness to engage Syria, but Damascus has failed to cease its interference in Lebanon, facilitation of foreign fighters traveling into Iraq, support for terrorism, and domestic repression. In May 2003, Secretary of State Colin Powell met with Syrian President Assad in Damascus. Later that year, Department of State Assistant Secretary for Near Eastern Affairs Bill Burns met with Assad, Burns returned to Damascus in September 2004, noting that Syrian behavior had not changed. In July 2005, Deputy Secretary of State Richard Armitage met Assad in Damascus. In each of these efforts, the United States told the Syrians that we would judge their intentions based on deeds, not words, but that bilateral relations could improve quickly if Syrian actions changed. In each case, the Syrian Government promised to take action against the flow of foreign fighters into Iraq, to end interference in Lebanon, to expel Palestinian terrorist leaders from Damascus, and to end Syrian state sponsorship of terrorism. The Syrian Government has not followed through on any of these promises, and as a result, it has been our policy to isolate the Syrian regime politically and economically in an effort to change its behavior.

NSA Hadley and Secretary Rice also consulted frequently with European counterparts who planned visits to Damascus to coordinate messages and ensure transparency in U.S. and European strategies. We have urged European and Arab countries to enact sanctions, designate regime members and supporters, and cease high-level engagement with Damascus. We engaged the Egyptians, Saudis, and Jordanians in a series of frank conversations about Syria's leadership. Saudi Arabia, in particular, has been a steadfast ally in our policy to isolate Syria.

WHAT HAS BEEN ACCOMPLISHED:

Democratic Elections: Lebanon held its first postwar parliamentary elections, largely free of Syrian interference, in the aftermath of the 2005 Hariri assassination.

Removal of Syrian Military: The withdrawal of Syrian troops from Lebanon in April 2005 ended nearly 3 decades of occupation. Although Syria has retained undesirable influence over the Lebanese political system and its economy, the withdrawal of its troops is significant in that it was the first large-scale attempt of the Lebanese population to assert Lebanon's sovereignty and was ultimately accomplished through broad international pressure.

Special Tribunal for Lebanon: On May 30, 2007, the U.N. Security Council adopted Resolution 1757, establishing a Special Tribunal for Lebanon (STL) to bring to justice those responsible for the assassinations of Rafiq Hariri and others. The establishment of the STL was accomplished despite efforts to block it by Lebanon's pro-Syrian politicians, including then-President Emile Lahoud and Speaker of the Parliament Nabih Berri, who refused to open Parliament's doors, depriving the majority of its right to approve the STL. At Prime Minister Siniora's urging, the U.N. Security Council bypassed the Lebanese political deadlock and established the Tribunal through a resolution that invoked Chapter VII, justifying that the resolution has the support of the Lebanese majority.

The provisions of the U.N.-Lebanese agreement to establish the STL entered into effect on June 10, 2007, and by February 2008 international contributions sufficient to fund the STL's first year had been collected, leading the U.N. Secretary-General to declare the STL "irreversible." Nearly $55 million in voluntary contributions have been collected to fund STL start-up costs and year one operations, but per the U.N.-Lebanese agreement that established the STL, Ban must secure enough contributions or pledges to cover years two and three before STL operations can be declared operational. Additional financial support from Saudi Arabia, the United Arab Emirates, and Kuwait will be important.

The U.N.'s Independent International Investigation Commission (UNIIIC) continues to build its cases for possible prosecution by the STL in the near future. UNIIIC head Daniel Bellemare issued his final report in December 2008 and per his request, the UNSC authorized a 2-month extension of UNIIIC's mandate until February 28, 2009, to ensure a smooth transition of Bellemare's investigation from

Beirut to prosecution in The Hague. The United Nations has announced the Special Tribunal will start on March 1, 2009.

Strengthening of Lebanese Security Services: Since September 2006, the United States has committed $400 million in security assistance to the LAF and ISF, including Humvees, rifles, ammunition, and communications equipment. This represents an enormous increase over the $500,000 in assistance we provided in 2001 and 2002. We have also conducted joint exercises, initiated a multiyear Comprehensive Training Program, and enhanced our intelligence sharing. Much of this support was provided on an emergency basis during and after the LAF's hard-fought victory over the Fatah al-Islam terrorist group in the Nahr al-Bared refugee camp in summer 2007. Lebanon's Palestinian refugee camps have long been hotbeds for terrorism, and the 3-month battle was the first successful attempt by the Lebanese army, which previously had a policy of noninterference, to exercise control over the camps. U.S. security assistance gave the LAF a critical edge in its unprecedented campaign, but the operation's ultimate success stemmed from the LAF's determination and public support. Even Hizballah, which proclaimed LAF entry into the camp was a redline, was forced to backpedal when it became clear that public opinion favored the government. The victory also represented an important step toward reestablishing the LAF as sole guarantor of security in Lebanon.

Territorial Control: The LAF has made some strides in extending its control over parts of Lebanon previously beyond its reach. Lebanese troops have been deployed to Hizballah-dominated south Lebanon for the first time in decades, as well as alongside international naval forces in the UNIFIL Maritime Task Force. In coordination with UNIFIL, the LAF has investigated rocket launch sites and begun joint counterrocket operations. There has been some displacement of armed Hizballah presence from south Lebanon but much remains to be done. The LAF has taken limited control of Lebanon's border with Syria through additional deployments, creation of border checkpoints, and the closure of unmonitored military access roads used by well-connected Syrians and their allies, but the LAF (like UNIFIL) continues to avoid the confrontations with Hizballah that strict enforcement could bring.

Economic Reform: Despite the lack of a functioning parliament needed to approve many economic measures, the Siniora government has been successful in keeping economic reform moving forward. In 2006, the United States supported negotiation of an emergency post-conflict arrangement, which was the first formal arrangement between Lebanon and the International Monetary Fund (IMF). Quantitative targets resulting from that arrangement were met and most monitored actions were completed ahead of schedule. Lebanon received pledges of $7.6 billion in support at a third Donors Conference for Lebanon (Paris III) in January 2007. In July 2007, we signed with Lebanon a Memorandum of Understanding for $250 million in budget support. As of March 2008, Lebanon had met the benchmarks to qualify for $125 million of the $250 million pledge.

FUTURE CHALLENGES:

Lebanese Legislative Election: Lebanese politicians from the March 14 Coalition and the Hizballah-led opposition expect the legislative election, scheduled for June 7, to be close and the outcome to be decisive for the country's future. Security officials have expressed conflicting views over whether the government can provide adequate security before and during voting because of the new, shorter election period (one day instead of four consecutive Sundays). A March 14 victory would continue the generally pro-West and moderate orientation the country has followed since Syria withdrew its troops in 2005. However, the opposition would continue to influence policy decisions even with a Coalition win. An opposition majority in the National Assembly would provide Hizballah with political cover for undermining Lebanon's compliances with UNSCR 1559, 1701, and 1757. An opposition government and Assembly probably would not overhaul Lebanon's political system but would work to keep Lebanon hostile to Israel.

End Syrian Interference in Lebanon: Despite its 2005 military withdrawal from Lebanon, Syria continues to exercise considerable influence over Lebanese decision-makers, particularly those in the opposition, through bribery, blackmail, financial ties, and an alliance with Iran and Hizballah. Many in Lebanon today are wary of the continued presence of agents of Syria's intelligence services, as well as Syria's sustained alliance with Hizballah. We are working   to consolidate Arab opposition to Syria's role in destabilizing Lebanon. Major Sunni Arab nations—such as Jordan, Egypt, and Saudi Arabia—are increasingly seeing the Lebanese political crisis as a Syrian—and Iranian-led effort to establish Shi'a control in Lebanon. Now we must get them to act on this conclusion. While we have recommended against European engagement of Syria, we are urging them to press the Assad regime to take concrete steps to normalize relations with Lebanon, to demarcate the border, and to improve its human rights record before reaping the benefits of international engagement. We have publicly acknowledged Israel's indirect talks with Syria by stating our general support for any initiative that brings greater stability to the region, while emphasizing that any agreement should be comprehensive and address Syria's support for terrorist groups, its undue involvement in Lebanon, its proliferation activities, and its support for foreign fighters.

Disarm Hizballah and Secure Lebanon's Borders: Hizballah continues to rearm, with assistance from Iran and Syria, following its summer 2006 war with Israel. Despite the LAF's victory in Nahr al-Bared, it is not a military counterweight to Hizballah and is unable to take full control away from Hizballah of southern Lebanon and parts of the Bekaa Valley. In fact, since the conclusion of the 2006 war, Hizballah has been building an infrastructure beyond the traditional boundaries of its stronghold in southern Lebanon and the Bekaa. Its weapons and equipment generally arrive from

Iran and Syria through the porous Lebanon-Syria border in violation of UNSCR 1701 and other resolutions. The United States and the Europeans have sought to help Lebanon secure that border, but the Siniora-led government has been reluctant to provoke Syria or Hizballah by requesting, or even allowing, meaningful projects to that end.

End to Political Violence: A wave of political violence and assassinations began in Lebanon in September 2004 when a car bomb exploded wounding Marwan Hamadeh, a cabinet member and confidant of Walid Jumblatt. In addition to Rafiq Hariri, political party leaders, cabinet ministers, members of Parliament, journalists, military officials, and ordinary citizens have been the targets of a campaign of violence attributed primarily to Syrian interest in further destabilizing Lebanon. Although violence has abated in the last year, these tactics have been a mainstay of Lebanese political life throughout its history. Permanently blunting this pattern will require progress toward the disarming of Hizballah, establishment of secure borders, creation of a political system that looks beyond religious confessions, and independence from Syrian and Iranian preferences.

Terrorism: Despite the LAF's victory over Fatah al-Islam in the Nahr al-Bared camp, Lebanon continues to be a breeding ground for terrorists of various organizations. Hizballah continues to operate as a "state within a state," with military and international terrorist capabilities, a domestic political infrastructure, and as a social service provider to Shi'a supporters in southern Lebanon, southern Beirut, and the Bekaa. In addition, Sunni extremists and al-Qaida affiliates increasingly are establishing a foothold in the country, primarily in the various Palestinian refugee camps, to recruit, arm, train, raise funds, and plot attacks in the region.

Economic Reform: Government management of debt and the economy remain weak. Improvement in Lebanon's tenuous economic situation, especially reduction of its massive debt, is unlikely until after the legislative elections, scheduled for spring of 2009. Once political conditions support a renewed push toward economic reform, priorities should include: revision of the tax codes; privatization of telecommunications and other government-owned entities; energy sector reform; and negotiation of a follow-on program with the IMF. Lebanese officials and some economists are concerned that the global financial crisis could start to affect Lebanon in the next few months.

Attachments
Tab 1   Chronology for Lebanon
Tab 2   Memorandum of Telephone Conversation with President Chirac
               of France (May 25, 2004)
Tab 3   Memorandum of Conversation with President Chirac of France
               (June 5, 2004)

POSTSCRIPT

MICHAEL SINGH

When the Bush administration entered office in 2001, Syria still occupied Lebanon, and Hezbollah had grown considerably in stature since its emergence in the 1980s. American policy toward Lebanon during the 1990s had largely been subordinated to the Israeli-Syrian peace process and maintaining calm along the Israeli-Lebanese border, rather than focusing on the problems within Lebanon itself. Shortly after the Bush administration took office, however, these priorities changed following the 9/11 terrorist attacks.

The Bush Administration Approach

The attacks of 9/11 changed the United States' perspective on both Syria and Lebanon. While Syria was not included along with Iraq, Iran, and North Korea in the so-called Axis of Evil in President Bush's 2002 State of the Union address, it was regarded by the administration as a state sponsor of terrorism. Damascus was, at that time, a regional hub for terrorist groups—Hezbollah, Hamas, Palestinian Islamic Jihad, and PFLP included—where they could coordinate with one another and with sympathetic states like Iran. In addition, Syria's occupation of Lebanon was carried out in coordination with Hezbollah and its patrons—and Syria's close partners—in Tehran. And if Syria was part of the problem so dreadfully illuminated on 9/11, the Bush administration saw support for Lebanon, and in particular the aspirations of its people to be free of both Syrian occupation and Iranian malign influence, as part of the answer to addressing the problem of extremism in the region—part, that is, of what President Bush would term the Freedom Agenda.

Initially, the Bush administration sought to sway Damascus through engagement, sending envoys to push Syrian President Bashar al-Assad to end his support for terrorism and purchases of oil from Saddam Hussein's Iraq, and to pursue domestic political and economic reforms. When it became clear that this support for terrorism was not only continuing but expanding as Syria became a key facilitator and transit point for foreign fighters bound for a liberated Iraq, Washington shifted its focus. It undertook efforts aimed at isolating Assad, exerting pressure on Syria's presence and Iran's influence in Lebanon, and supporting Lebanese actors who were pro sovereignty and seeking to build the resiliency of Lebanese national institutions to Iranian and Syrian subversion over the long term. This approach preceded but was catalyzed by the assassination of Lebanese Prime Minister Rafiq Hariri in February 2005, an act that was intended to stifle Lebanese independence but in fact sparked the "Cedar Revolution" that hastened Syria's ouster.

In support of this policy, the Bush administration used the full range of tools at the United States' disposal. In the diplomatic realm, Washington—benefiting from an entrepreneurial and engaged ambassador in Beirut, Jeff Feltman—coordinated closely with the pro sovereignty March 14 alliance in Lebanon, supporting its stand against Damascus and Tehran through statements, visits by March 14 figures to the White House, and other actions. These steps arguably bolstered the March 14 alliance domestically and helped to align international actors in the region and in Europe behind the American approach.

The administration coordinated particularly closely with France, which had continued to enjoy influence within the country and took a particular interest in Lebanon in the decades following the expiration of its UN mandate for Lebanon. Washington and Paris did not always see eye-to-eye on Lebanon policy, but both supported Rafiq Hariri and both saw value in finding common ground in a region where US-French relations had been severely strained over the Iraq War. In cooperation with Paris, the Bush administration was highly active in the UN Security Council, where it led the drafting and adoption of fifteen UN Security Council resolutions affecting Lebanon, including Resolution 1559 calling for the full and immediate withdrawal of Syrian forces, and Resolution 1595 establishing an independent international investigation into the Hariri assassination. The latter led to the creation of the Special Tribunal for Lebanon.

In the economic sphere, the Bush administration significantly ramped up US economic aid to Lebanon, which had largely dried up during the late 1980s and the 1990s, more than doubling annual assistance to $36 million in 2002 and further increasing it to over $50 million by 2008. Just as importantly, President Bush signed into law the Syria Accountability and Lebanese Sovereignty Restoration Act, the first of numerous actions to target financially those Syrians, Lebanese, and others who were complicit in Syria's occupation of Lebanon or Hezbollah's and Iran's malign activities in the country.

In the security realm, the Bush administration in 2006 resumed the provision of Foreign Military Financing (FMF) to the Lebanese Armed Forces (LAF) and provided other forms of assistance to Lebanon's Internal Security Forces (ISF). This aid could not realistically enable the LAF or ISF to confront Hezbollah, even if they had wished to do so, and was not intended by Washington for that purpose. It proved crucial, however, in tackling threats such as terrorism, as demonstrated during the LAF's conflict in 2007 with the Fath al-Islam terrorist group in the Nahr al-Bared refugee camp.

The political situation in Lebanon was a particular challenge. The March 14 alliance won the June 2005 elections held in the wake of the Syrian withdrawal. But Hezbollah and other Syrian proxies immediately sought to paralyze the government of Prime Minister Fouad Siniora—with considerable success. The July 2006 war between Israel and Hezbollah, fought largely on Lebanese territory, further undermined the Siniora government. Secretary of State Rice, with State and NSC support, brokered first a ceasefire and then UNSC Resolution 1701, which ended hostilities and sought to help the Lebanese government extend its authority over Hezbollah-controlled southern Lebanon, secure the country's borders, and stem the flow of illicit arms to Hezbollah and other terrorist groups. These efforts had only limited success. Despite a good showing by the March 14 coalition in 2009 parliamentary elections, Lebanon faced mounting political gridlock—fueled in large part by Hezbollah's growing political clout following its May 2008 takeover of Beirut and by the subsequent Qatari-brokered Doha Agreement—by the time President Bush left office.

What Has Happened Since the End of the Bush Administration?

On the surface, US policy toward Lebanon has changed little in the years since its general direction was set by the Bush administration. The United States has continued to express support for what remains of the March 14 coalition and the international inquiry into the Hariri assassination; it has continued to provide economic and security assistance to Lebanon, amounting to more than $4 billion since 2010; and it has continued to apply pressure to Hezbollah, primarily through sanctions. However, broader US policy toward the Middle East has fluctuated significantly since the end of the Bush administration in 2009, and Lebanon has declined as a US regional priority even as it has continued to descend into political and economic dysfunction and crisis.

When President Obama assumed office in 2009, he did so as a critic not only of the Iraq War, which was a major issue in the 2008 presidential campaign, but of the Bush administration's approach to the Middle East writ large. While some of its institutional elements like the State Department's Middle East Partnership Initiative (MEPI) office survived, the Freedom Agenda was largely put aside. For the

Obama administration, democracy promotion had come to be associated with military intervention and viewed as ineffective. Likewise, the Obama administration eschewed President Bush's efforts to isolate the Syrian and Iranian regimes, instead adopting what it called a "strategy of engagement."

In an early articulation of the Obama administration's approach, Obama's Assistant Secretary of State for Near Eastern Affairs said that the administration sought "a sustained, principled dialogue with Syria to advance the interests of the United States and our allies." He further asserted, "We believe that Syria and the United States share some common interests, including a comprehensive peace in the region, and that Syria can potentially play a constructive role in realizing our common goals, provided Syria addresses a number of key concerns."[1] US officials resumed their visits to Damascus, and—as the Assistant Secretary of State's remarks suggested and Special Envoy for Middle East Peace George Mitchell's meetings with President Assad reinforced—the pursuit of Israeli-Syrian peace once again climbed Washington's regional agenda.

The Obama administration's engagement with Assad was cut short by the lack of progress on the peace process, and then cut off entirely by the Syrian civil war, which broke out in 2011. The Obama administration initially called for Assad's removal from power but then was unwilling to act to bring about that outcome. By contrast, Russia and Iran increased their presence in the country in support of the Assad regime. As Syria descended into greater violence and humanitarian disaster, it posed increasing challenges for Lebanon, especially in the form of a significant influx of Syrian refugees.

Unlike its dealings with Syria, the Obama administration's engagement with Iran persisted and ultimately culminated in a series of nuclear agreements from 2013 to 2015 under which Washington lifted many of the financial sanctions that had pinched the Iranian regime's finances. While the administration continued to target Hezbollah and Iran's Islamic Revolutionary Guard Corps (IRGC) with sanctions, the effect of American engagement initially with Syria and on a sustained basis with Iran on the nuclear file reverberated in Lebanon, where US partners—like those throughout the region—believed an American realignment

---

1. Regional Overview of the Middle East: Hearing before the Subcommittee on the Middle East and South Asia of the House Foreign Affairs Committee, 111th Cong. D1245 (2009) (Testimony of Jeffrey D. Feltman, Assistant Secretary, Bureau of Near Eastern Affairs, Department of State).

was underway and sought to ease tensions with both countries and their proxies.

The Trump administration's approach to Lebanon was also strongly affected by its Iran policy, albeit in a very different way from the Obama administration. President Trump withdrew from the 2015 nuclear accord, reimposed the previously suspended sanctions on Iran, and further expanded those sanctions as part of what it termed a policy of "maximum pressure" on the Iranian regime. These sanctions targeted not only Iran proper, but also Iranian proxies like Hezbollah, which also suffered due to the constriction in the Iranian regime's finances. Nevertheless, Hezbollah by that point was firmly entrenched in power in Lebanon, and together with its allies won a majority of the seats in Lebanon's parliament for the first time in 2018. Washington's employment of financial pressure on the group was not part of any larger strategy for bolstering pro sovereignty forces within Lebanon or promoting necessary economic and political reforms.

How Did the Bush Administration Do?

The Bush administration's approach to Lebanon produced notable successes, particularly in the aftermath of the 2005 Cedar Revolution sparked by the assassination of Prime Minister Rafiq Hariri. The use of multilateral diplomacy—including pressure from international bodies such as the United Nations and the withdrawal of European and regional support for Assad partly at the insistence of the United States—contributed to the ouster of Syrian forces from the country. Bush administration policy also contributed to the establishment of an international tribunal to hold accountable Hariri's killers and their backers—ultimately delivering the conviction of a Hezbollah operative—and to the electoral success of the March 14 coalition.

Hezbollah's arms—provided along with significant financial aid by Iran to ensure its proxy could continue to threaten Israel and dominate Lebanon—proved an obstinate problem, and one that prevented Lebanon's legitimate security institutions from exercising their prerogatives and the state from truly achieving sovereignty. The 2006 Israel-Hezbollah war resulted in a military defeat for Hezbollah but elevated the terrorist group's popularity in the region. UN Security Council Resolution 1701 expanded the United Nations Force in Lebanon (UNIFIL), called for Hezbollah's disarmament, and barred the export of arms to nonstate actors in Lebanon, but was weakly enforced, in large part due to Hezbollah's predominance on the ground in Lebanon.

In 2008, Hezbollah turned its weapons against its Lebanese rivals, effectively taking over western Beirut and other areas of Lebanon in which the March 14 grouping enjoyed influence, as the US-supported LAF looked on. While the 2008 crisis was ultimately resolved by the Doha Agreement, in retrospect, the agreement cemented the Hezbollah-led opposition's position in government and contributed to the political gridlock that would plague Lebanon in the years afterward. While many Lebanese have shown great courage in standing up to Hezbollah—frequently paying with their lives—no other force or institution in Lebanon, even with international support, has so far proven able to overcome the group's military might, willingness to resort to force, political lock on Lebanon's Shia community, and considerable external backing from Iran.

Hezbollah's predominant influence also has contributed to a broader problem that has bedeviled US efforts in Lebanon—the failure of the country's entrenched political elites to enact needed political and economic reforms. Corruption, state capture, and political paralysis have prevented a meaningful response to Lebanon's deep-seated economic and governance problems, which in recent years have contributed to increasingly dramatic economic hardship and political unrest, especially in the aftermath of the devastating August 2020 explosion in the port of Beirut. Successive American administrations have arguably been too ready to accept Lebanon's dysfunctional political status quo and insufficiently attentive to the critical importance of reform to Lebanon's economic and social stability.

What Are the Lessons Learned?

- *Keep up the pressure on Hezbollah and Iran.* Iran's provision of arms and funding to Hezbollah not only undermines Lebanon's sovereignty, but it threatens the stability of the region. While pressure on Hezbollah is no silver bullet and cannot be the sole focus of US policy in Lebanon, it will remain an important part of any successful approach. The United States should continue to exert financial pressure on the group and seek to block its import of arms, recruit international partners to do the same, and seek to support Lebanese Shia who oppose Hezbollah. In addition, the United States should not limit its pressure to Hezbollah but should seek ways to impose a cost on Iran for actions that undermine Lebanese sovereignty and contribute to insecurity in the Levant, lest Tehran be led to believe that it can operate through proxies with impunity.

- *Press for political and economic reform.* Lebanon's current woes—rampant inflation and shortages, the limited availability of fuel and electricity, the collapse of its currency and banking system, among other problems—result from years of political gridlock, corruption, and failure to enact needed political and economic reforms. US and international economic aid should be tied to Lebanon's political leadership seriously tackling these problems, which now pose an existential threat to the country's stability and prosperity.
- *Avoid viewing Lebanon through the lens of other regional issues.* US policy in Lebanon has enjoyed its greatest success when Washington has wielded its policy tools in concert to promote Lebanon's sovereignty and prosperity, with the understanding that Lebanon's success would contribute to the broader stability and security of the region. Viewing Lebanon as ancillary to other regional priorities—the Middle East Peace Process or Iran, for example—has, on the other hand, failed to pay dividends for US interests.

Contributor:
David Schenker

CHAPTER 10

Stabilization and Reconstruction Operations

RICHARD HOOKER

As the transition of administrations approached in late 2008, the US government and its coalition partners were deeply committed to stabilization and reconstruction operations in both Iraq and Afghanistan, despite an initial Bush administration bias against nation building and some reluctance to maintain any enduring military presence in either country. This original reluctance had given way to the reality that each country needed state structures and a civil society with at least a minimal capacity to function without massive external assistance if security threats to the United States were to be controlled. Relatively quickly, it became clear that a swift handover to newly constituted host-nation governments was simply not feasible given ongoing threats and the paucity of state capacity. The previous regimes had been effectively dismantled, but it would take time, effort, and investment to replace them with new institutions and infrastructure. Grudgingly at first, US leaders and their coalition counterparts became convinced that state building would become an essential component of any successful strategy in both countries.

TRANSITION MEMORANDUM

CONFIDENTIAL

6273
Transition

NATIONAL SECURITY COUNCIL
WASHINGTON, D.C. 20504

January 16, 2009

MEMORANDUM FOR THE RECORD

FROM: CHRISTOPHER BROUGHTON
            RELIEF, STABILIZATION AND DEVELOPMENT

SUBJECT: Reconstruction and Stabilization Operations

THE SITUATION AS WE FOUND IT:

The September 11, 2001 attacks on the United States, conceived in and emanating from Afghani-stan, demonstrated that threats to America's vital national security interests could emerge from failed states and states emerging from conflict. Such states pose a threat to U.S. national security because of their potential to foment regional instability, trigger humanitarian crises, and provide safe havens for terrorists and international criminal networks.

From 1990 to 2001, the United States was involved in 15 operations to stabilize failed and post-conflict countries. The United States deployed personnel and committed financial resources to respond to conflicts in Bosnia, Cambodia, Colombia, El Salvador, Georgia, Guatemala, Haiti, Kosovo, Liberia, Mozambique, Nicaragua, Rwanda, Somalia, Sierra Leone, and Timor-Leste.

Although the frequency, duration, and importance of such operations are increasing, United States Government doctrine for reconstruction and stabilization operations (i.e. nation building) remained nascent. The emerging doctrine recognized the utility of civil-military cooperation and joint action with coalition partners. The doctrine also recognized that operations should include not only military and peacekeeping elements, but also political, economic, and security assistance components to secure the peace. While Presidential Decision Directives 25 (1995) and 56 (1997) provided policy guidance for multilateral peace operations and complex contingency operations, the directives' guidelines were never fully implemented, and interagency roles and responsibilities remained in dispute.

CONFIDENTIAL
Reason: 1.4(d)
Declassify on: 1/16/19

NSC Declassification Review [EO 13526]
Declassify in Full
by NSC Access on 2/24/2021

Overseas deployments revealed that the U.S. Agency for International Development (USAID) and the State Department, the principal civilian agencies responsible for these operations, were not sufficiently organized, trained, or equipped to mount a rapid and effective government-wide response to conflicts. USAID and the State Department did not have the funding, staff, or institutional capacity necessary to rapidly deploy large teams of trained and equipped personnel. USAID and the State Department also lacked the doctrine, planning capability, and interagency experience required for successful crisis deployments. Coordination between civilian agencies and the military was ad hoc. There was no systematic effort to integrate and coordinate the operations of all United States Government agencies.

While the military is organized, funded, trained, and equipped to respond rapidly to security crises, it was not in a position to assume the civilian functions required in post-combat stability operations. Civil affairs and policing experts were in short supply, and stability operations were not a principal focus of the Department of Defense. Military planning for post-combat operations was undertaken without significant input from civilian agencies.

THIS ADMINISTRATION'S POLICY:

Early during the wars in Afghanistan and Iraq, the Administration realized that success on the battlefield would be short-lived without robust, parallel, and coordinated reconstruction and stabilization operations. This Administration has conducted reconstruction and stabilization operations on the largest scale and fastest pace since the Marshall Plan. Approximately $80 billion has been spent in Afghanistan and Iraq to establish democratic, capable governments, strong economies, and viable military and police forces that hold a legitimate monopoly over the use of force. These operations require the effort of the entire United States Government because of their size, complexity, and range of action.

In order to guide the formulation and execution of policy, this Administration has strengthened doctrine for reconstruction and stabilization operations. Three circumstances compel the United States to undertake such operations: regime change caused by U.S. military action, failed states which threaten U.S. national security interests, and prevention of conflict and instability in order to avoid the use of military force.

First, as a responsible world power, the United States is obligated to respond to the aftermath of conflicts in which U.S. and/or coalition military forces have instigated a regime change, such as in Afghanistan and Iraq. The objective of such a response is not to replace one dictator with another, but to help build and foster free and democratic societies that are responsive to the needs of their people. In such cases, reconstruction and stabilization operations consist of the restoration and maintenance of civil order, functioning democratic government, and economic systems of production and trade. These stability operations often need to be reinforced with other components of full spectrum military operations, both offensive and defensive, in order to secure the peace and achieve desired reconstruction and governance end-states.

Second, the United States may need to act in failed states which threaten U.S. national security interests. In these operations, the objective of the United States is to extend and strengthen the rule of the existing government to ungoverned or contested spaces (e.g. the Federally Administered Tribal Areas in Pakistan). In such cases, full spectrum operations are still employable, though the balance of effort is focused on non-kinetic activities.

Third, the United States may also conduct reconstruction and stabilization operations to prevent conflict or instability in states with internal institutional weaknesses and susceptibility to terrorist basing, organized crime, internal rebellion, humanitarian disasters, and/or narcotics production and trafficking. In such cases, it is in the interests of the United States to strengthen weak institutions and build indigenous capability to take corrective action. The intent of these operations is to defuse threats that would later necessitate the use of military force.

Across all three cases, the Administration's doctrine has been executed through a wide variety of tools to address the manifold requirements of each operation. Such tools include military assistance and, when necessary, use of force; intelligence and counterintelligence activities and covert action; political and governance reform; economic assistance; public diplomacy; and information operations. The balance between military and civilian elements, and between offensive, defensive, and stability operations will depend on the specific case, and may change over time as circumstances require.

The Administration's policy has also focused on better integrating and balancing the United States Government's hard and soft power assets. Since 2001, the Administration has increased funding for development and diplomacy by over 50 percent and requested 1,400 new positions within the Department of State and USAID. The Administration also took steps to expand the institutional capacity of civilian departments and agencies to successfully conduct reconstruction and stabilization operations. An independent office was established to recruit, train and deploy an expeditionary civilian corps, which would act in concert with the military. The Administration also pursued and obtained new legal authorities and budget resources to build military capacity to conduct stability operations. Simultaneously, the Administration has strengthened the capability of partner states to conduct stability operations, provide for their own security, and support peace in their regions.

WHAT HAS BEEN ACCOMPLISHED:

This Administration has conducted major reconstruction and stabilization operations in Afghanistan and Iraq, created a Coordinator for and Presidential Directive on reconstruction and stabilization operations, encouraged civil-military cooperation and capability, and worked with other countries and multilateral institutions to improve reconstruction and stabilization operations.

Afghanistan and Iraq. As to Afghanistan, the Administration started in December 2001 to work with the international community to create a new democratic government and constitution for Afghanistan, while commencing efforts to rebuild the country's destroyed economy and resume basic public services. In June 2003, President Bush approved the Accelerating Success Initiative for Afghanistan, which recognized the importance of increasing the level of civilian effort to support military operations. This initiative, followed by the President's Strategic Review of Afghanistan policy in 2006, led to a significant increase in the economic and political lines of operation to complement the ongoing military campaign. For additional information on this topic, see the Presidential Memorandum on Afghanistan.

As to Iraq, in April 2003, the Administration established the Coalition Provisional Authority as the transitional government of Iraq, and assigned to it authority over the executive, legislative, and judicial branches of government. Once a new, sovereign Iraqi Government was formed in July 2004, the Administration created the Iraq Reconstruction Management Office to manage the largest U.S. assistance program since World War II, dedicated to supporting the new government of Iraq. In January 2007, President Bush announced the New Way Forward for Iraq, which included a rapid increase of civilian staff to complement the military surge. For additional information on this topic, see the Presidential Memorandum on Iraq.

Provincial reconstruction teams have played an important role in the reconstruction and stabilization of Afghanistan and Iraq by providing a platform for civil-military unity of effort. Since the first Provincial Reconstruction Team (PRT) was formed in Afghanistan in February 2003, PRTs have subsequently been established throughout Afghanistan and Iraq. In 2005, civilian-led provincial teams were expanded in Iraq to intensify capacity and institution-building efforts.

Coordinator for Reconstruction and Stabilization. The Administration has taken steps to build a permanent institutional capacity within the United States Government to manage and conduct reconstruction and stabilization operations effectively. Pursuant to an April 2004 Principals Committee decision, the Department of State established the Office of the Coordinator for Reconstruction and Stabilization (S/CRS) to coordinate and oversee civilian post-conflict and crisis-response activities. Prior to the establishment of S/CRS, there was no single office of the United States Government with this responsibility.

S/CRS has been staffed by civilian, military, and intelligence experts with the skills, experience, and training necessary to conduct reconstruction and stabilization operations worldwide. S/CRS officers have drawn on their practical experiences in the Balkans, Sudan, Afghanistan, and Iraq to guide the establishment and operations of the office.

In a speech in May 2005, President Bush remarked that "one of the lessons we learned from our experience in Iraq is that, while military personnel can be rapidly deployed anywhere in the world, the same is not true of United States Government civilians." The President announced that the Office of Reconstruction and Stabilization would create a new Active Response Corps of government employees which would deploy as "civilian 'first responders.'" President Bush also noted that the office would expand the use of civilian volunteers from outside the government.

S/CRS began its work by developing common operating principles and guidance for United States Government agencies involved in reconstruction and stabilization operations. In May 2005, S/CRS published "Post-Conflict Essential Tasks," a comprehensive framework for action in post-conflict reconstruction and. stabilization operations. In December 2005, S/CRS published the "U.S. Government Planning Framework for Reconstruction, Stabilization and Conflict Transformation," which provides the United States Government with its first government-wide planning framework for civilian agencies and serves as an effective complement to military planning processes. Both documents provide an approved concept of operations for interagency unity of effort in Washington, at regional combatant commands, and in individual countries.

S/CRS has applied these planning and operating principles to specific foreign policy priorities. S/CRS has led contingency planning for an eventual political transition in Cuba, interagency planning for the Sudan Comprehensive Peace Agreement, and supported planning for Kosovo's independence. S/CRS officers have advised provincial reconstruction teams in Afghanistan and are routinely involved in military exercises and planning, particularly for post-combat stability operations.

NSPD-44. In order to establish a lasting United States Government capability to conduct reconstruction and stabilization operations, the President also issued National Security Presidential Directive/NSPD-44 in December 2005. The directive assigned the Department of State the responsibility for organizing and leading reconstruction and stabilization operations, which it does through S/CRS. NSPD-44 directed other Executive departments and agencies to coordinate with and assist S/CRS, and the Secretaries of State and Defense in particular to fully coordinate military operations with reconstruction and stabilization activities, where appropriate. The Departments of the Treasury, Defense, Justice, Agriculture, Commerce, Health and Human Services, and Homeland Security, along with USAID, have all taken steps to implement NSPD-44. NSPD-44 has established a nascent United States Government capability to conduct reconstruction and stabilization operations.

Implementation by the Department of Defense. As NSPD-44 was being developed, the Department of Defense (DOD) took parallel steps to improve its capability to plan and conduct reconstruction and stabilization operations in conjunction with civilian agencies. In November 2005, DOD issued Directive 3000.05, which established stability operations as a core U.S. military mission that the Department would be prepared to conduct and support. DOD has strengthened both stability operations doctrine and the capability to conduct stability operations in partnership with civilians.

DOD has improved its foreign language and cultural knowledge base, nonlethal capabilities, and ability to train and equip foreign security forces. DOD has also rebalanced its force structure to increase the availability of units that are in high demand during stability operations (e.g., civil affairs units, engineers, military police). The Administration pursued and received new legislative authorities, such as section 1207 of the National Defense Authorization Act, which have facilitated the conduct of stability operations worldwide. DOD has used these authorities to provide funding for security and stabilization projects that are developed in partnership with the Department of State. The projects serve national security objectives by preventing the need for direct U.S. military engagement or by reinforcing ongoing military operations.

DOD guidance and planning processes emphasize security cooperation and stability operations as top priorities for military planning and budgeting. For example, DOD consults with the State Department when developing "Guidance for Employment of the Force," the strategic planning document that provides guidance for Combatant Commands. "Guidance for Employment of the Force" also directs specific Combatant Commands to plan for certain contingencies with other departments and agencies.

There has been civilian-military integration at the tactical, operational, and strategic levels. Secretary of Defense Gates underscored the importance of soft power as a complement to hard power in several speeches, including a September 2008 address at the National Defense University, where he stated, "over the long term, we cannot kill or capture our way to victory. Where possible, kinetic operations should be subordinate to measures to promote better governance, economic programs to spur development, and efforts to address the grievances among the discontented from which terrorists recruit."

Resources and Support. President Bush has worked to provide departments and agencies the resources and capabilities required for effective reconstruction and stabilization operations. In the 2006 National Security Strategy, President Bush noted that "peace and stability will only last if follow-on efforts to restore order and rebuild are successful," and that those efforts would rely on all agencies of the government working in concert with the military. In the 2007 State of the Union Address, President Bush called for the establishment of a Civilian Reserve Corps to ease the burden on the armed forces by allowing civilians with critically-needed skills to be hired for missions abroad. President Bush advanced this message in two additional public speeches, an appearance with Secretary of Defense Gates and the Joint Chiefs of Staff in August 2007, and at a speech at the groundbreaking of the United States Institute of Peace in June 2008.

These efforts have helped produce a growing expeditionary capability for S/CRS. As of October 2008, 10 United States Government members of the active component of the Civilian Response Corps are available for deployment within 48 hours in emergency situations. An additional 100 United States Government employees will be hired with $75 million from the FY 2008 supplemental appropriation. The United States Government standby component of the Civilian Response Corps, which is available for deployment within 30 days, currently stands at 492 members. No members of the Civilian Reserve Corps, which is comprised of non-government civilians, have been hired yet since needed funding is still pending. S/CRS will have the staff, resources, and organizational capacity to deploy rapidly in response to the next reconstruction and stabilization crisis and coordinate an effective government-wide response. In a large-scale operation, S/CRS could assume a coordinating function similar to role the Iraq Reconstruction Management Office played in Iraq.

Complementary Efforts. The structures put in place to implement NSPD-44 have served as a model for similar efforts by the United Nations (U.N.) and other countries. S/CRS has become a resource that has allowed the United States to lead internationally in this area. S/CRS assisted with the development of the U.N. Peacebuilding Commission, which seeks to perform a function similar to S/CRS within the U.N. system, and the United States has obtained G-8 member commitments to cooperate in reconstruction and stabilization activities as a complement to peacekeeping operations.

FUTURE CHALLENGES:

The national security threat posed by failed and post-conflict states will remain a challenge for the United States for the foreseeable future. The next administration may want to consider a number of legislative and procedural initiatives to continue to develop these emerging institutions and planning processes:

- Further recruitment and training of the Civilian Reserve Corps;
- Definition of peacetime roles and responsibilities of the U.S. military in supporting civilian-led reconstruction and stabilization operations; and
- Development of standard operating procedures for the deployment of United States Government civilian assets in internationally-led reconstruction and stabilization missions.

Attachments

POSTSCRIPT

RICHARD HOOKER

The Bush administration pushed hard for success in Iraq and Afghanistan. As the Transition Memorandum documents, the administration identified early on a lack of adequate US capacity for stabilization and reconstruction operations as a limiting factor. It undertook steps to build such capacity, gradually recognizing that the task would require sustained effort extending into future US administrations. The Bush administration efforts to institutionalize capacity for stabilization and reconstruction operations had mixed success. But they were largely not pursued by the subsequent Obama and Trump administrations, which increasingly abandoned the stabilization and reconstruction mission in favor of narrowing US objectives to counterterrorism, reducing the American role more generally, and bringing US troops home. The role of stabilization and reconstruction under the Biden administration is unclear. Nevertheless, its early decisions on Afghanistan suggest stabilization and reconstruction operations will not be a significant priority for the administration.

The Bush Administration Approach

Bush administration stabilization and reconstruction efforts were built on the organizations and processes used in more than a dozen overseas operations conducted between 1990 and 2001. A series of new institutions were established, including the Department of State Coordinator for Stabilization and Reconstruction (S/CRS), the Civilian Reserve Corps, and Provincial Reconstruction Teams (PRTs) in both Iraq and Afghanistan to coordinate and execute efforts in the field. NSPD-44, published in December 2005, provided policy guidance designating the Department of State as lead agency for stabilization and reconstruction and establishing a supporting interagency Policy Coordination Committee. In the same year, the Department of Defense designated stabilization as a core mission and published supporting doctrine and guidance. Regular interagency meetings, from the working group level through the Deputies and Principals Committees, were conducted to refine policy guidance, monitor implementation, and address issues and friction points as they emerged.

The size of the stabilization and reconstruction effort was striking. A total of $80 billion was spent on reconstruction in Iraq and $143 billion in Afghanistan. Every major agency, including the Departments of Commerce, Agriculture, and the Department of Justice, in addition to State, Defense, and Treasury, was involved. On the ground, civilian experts from State, USAID, and Agriculture collaborated with military counterparts down to the brigade level in an effort to harmonize military operations with stabilization and reconstruction operations. The military Surge in Iraq, and later in Afghanization, was accompanied by a civilian "surge" to reinforce the development and governance lines of effort.

What Has Happened Since the End of the Bush Administration?

The Obama administration took office with a clear intent to withdraw the US troop presence in Iraq and later Afghanistan. Significant initiatives related to reconstruction and stabilization operations, such as the Civilian Reserve Corps, were not championed and failed to gain traction. S/CRS was subsumed under a new Bureau for Conflict and Stabilization Operations which largely shed the reconstruction mission to focus on conflict prevention and "security sector reform." While congressional funding for both theaters continued at significant levels, program execution on the ground suffered due to corruption, organizational rivalries, and the sheer number of national, international, and nongovernmental organizations involved. The rise of ISIS, competing crises in places like Syria, the Donbas, and Sudan, and domestic challenges related to the 2008 economic recession, all crowded the policy agenda and hindered any push to strengthen and expand reconstruction and stabilization operations capacity. As conditions in Iraq deteriorated and progress in Afghanistan faltered, institutional focus and support for reconstruction and stabilization operations there and elsewhere declined.

These trends continued under President Trump, as all forms of foreign assistance came under greater scrutiny. With a far more transactional approach to foreign policy and an aversion for globalization, the Trump administration eliminated stabilization funding earmarked for areas recovered from ISIS and sponsored a Stabilization Assistance Review in 2018 that deemphasized large-scale reconstruction activities. In the waning days of the administration, the State Department published a *United States Strategy to Prevent Conflict and Promote Stability*, intended to implement the 2020 Global Fragility Act, which directed the president to develop a ten-year strategy to contribute to the stabilization of conflict-affected areas, address global fragility, and strengthen the capacity of the United States to be an effective leader of international efforts to prevent extremism and violent conflict.

These are ambitious goals in view of a lack of success, despite enormous effort and sacrifice, in Iraq and Afghanistan and, for that matter, in Vietnam as well. It is, in any event, uncertain whether the vision of the Global Fragility Act will be pursued under the Biden administration, given the priority it has given to the challenge presented by China and the return of great power competition and an ideological struggle between authoritarian state capitalism and free market democracy.

How Did the Bush Administration Do?

Extraordinary efforts were made in conflict zones during the Bush administration to achieve and refine civil-military coordination; establish new organizations and structures; secure funding; enable democratic governance; and repair and upgrade infrastructure such as roads, schools, hospitals, industrial plant, the power grid, and the energy sector. Notwithstanding many obstacles and significant host-nation corruption and lack of capacity, significant progress was achieved.

However, a number of factors hampered both the Bush administration's efforts to stabilize and reconstruct Iraq and Afghanistan, as well as efforts to create new organizational infrastructure for stabilization and reconstruction operations that could be needed in the future. For starters, differences in departmental perspectives emerged quickly and powerfully, with the State Department arguing in favor of a larger troop presence to ensure security and set conditions for stable transition, and the Pentagon arguing that progress on governance and economic development was the key to improving the security situation. These tensions adversely affected stabilization and reconstruction efforts throughout the Bush administration and would never be fully resolved, at least until the Surge in Iraq announced in January 2007.

Despite the intensity and duration of the stabilization and reconstruction effort, results were mixed. On the positive side, in both Iraq and Afghanistan, rapid progress was achieved in setting up governance structures led by Iraqis and Afghans selected through democratic elections with participation from most major ethnic groups. Provincial and district governments as well as central government ministries were established, along with legal systems and financial agencies. US and coalition PRTs connected with local governments to plan and execute development projects directly at the point of need. In just a few short years, access to primary health care and to secondary education improved significantly. Transportation networks and power grids in particular received special emphasis. These gains were achieved despite terrorist and insurgent violence that constantly challenged the coalition. Major spikes in violence occurred in Iraq in 2006 and in Afghanistan in 2008 that required large troop increases and took many months to contain.

Inter- and intra-agency conflict over roles and missions was perhaps the most powerful obstacle inhibiting successful stabilization and reconstruction. Agency cultures, disagreements over authorities, perceived challenges to institutional "equities," distorted funding in favor of the Department of Defense (vice State and USAID), and bureaucratic resistance all combined to limit or inhibit successful policy execution. Bureaucratic disputes between USAID and the State Department colored all stabilization and reconstruction operations throughout, while tensions between the State Department and the Department of Defense permeated both campaigns. Understandably, the Department of Defense saw its role in armed conflict as paramount, despite presidential guidance designating the State Department as lead agency for stabilization and reconstruction operations. On the ground, neither military theater commanders nor diplomatic chiefs of mission were fully in charge; both were forced to cooperate in uneasy alliance. Where personalities allowed, as with General Petraeus and Ambassador Crocker in Iraq (and later Afghanistan), effective coordination could and did occur. Where they did not, competing chains of command often collided or worked at cross-purposes.

A significant example of interagency discord was the shifting priority accorded to the security, development, and governance lines of operation. The failure to identify security as the paramount concern early on contributed to faulty efforts in the economic and political arenas in Iraq and Afghanistan. Originally, security and political and economic development proceeded in tandem with equal priority, reinforcing one another and balancing the interests of the various actors involved in Washington. However, when the security situation deteriorated, there was no initial consensus that the security effort needed more resources and political capital. When the security line of effort received clear priority later on and sufficient security gains were achieved, local economies could revive and government capacity improve, although both were still severely limited by local partner capacity.

There are other examples. PRTs were staffed with both civilian and military experts who were often pulled in different directions by unit commanders, who had short time horizons, and USAID and State Department officials in Baghdad and Kabul who were more concerned with long-term sustainability. Different funding streams invited competition over how best to commit financial resources. Even inside departments, bureaucratic struggles could frustrate optimal performance.

The formation of S/CRS was a major step forward in building capacity for stabilization and reconstruction operations but was never fully embraced by the more powerful and long-established State Department regional bureaus. Inside the Pentagon, interservice rivalry continued to flourish; one study conducted in 2008 found that in Kandahar alone, ten separate chains of command attempted to manage ten different functions.

Support from Congress is essential to mission success in stabilization and reconstruction efforts. In many ways—above all, in providing massive funding for Operations Iraqi Freedom and Enduring Freedom (for Afghanistan)—Congress played a positive and essential role. Still, wary of long-term commitments, legislators sometimes hedged their bets. For example, the Bush administration's push to establish a Civilian Response Corps of on-call experts, able to deploy into contested areas to conduct stability operations, was authorized by Congress. Nevertheless, envisioned to have 250 active members, supported by 2,000 "standby" experts and another 2,000 in reserve, the initiative was starved of funds from its inception. Although small numbers of full-time members were onboarded under S/CRS, the standby and reserve components were stillborn. Today, although some nascent structures survive, the intent to build a stronger institutional capacity for stabilization and reconstruction remains aspirational at best.

The UN and other international and nongovernmental organizations have traditionally played major roles in stabilization and reconstruction in conflict areas, and they were seen initially as the best hope for transitioning US forces out relatively quickly. These hopes foundered on a persistently intractable security environment (the chief of the UN Mission in Iraq, Sérgio Vieira de Mello, was killed along with twenty other UN employees in a terrorist attack in 2003). No formal mechanism existed to coordinate stabilization and reconstruction activities with international and nongovernmental organizations, a challenge that also extended to coalition partners. Ad hoc arrangements proved to be less than ideal. With thirty-four partner countries in Iraq and sixty in Afghanistan, each responding first to national direction and only then to coalition priorities, effective "enterprise-wide" coordination was never truly possible. While the contributions of coalition partners and international organizations were of course highly significant, lasting progress was elusive despite large funding commitments.

Fewer obstacles caused more harm to effective and sustained stabilization and reconstruction than corruption and poor program oversight, a function not only of the massive amounts of funding flooding Iraq and Afghanistan, but also the multiplicity of actors and organizations and the understandable inability of standard oversight mechanisms to track and monitor fiscal execution in a combat zone. Numerous congressional studies, as well as reporting from the Special Inspectors General for Iraq and Afghanistan Reconstruction, highlighted this problem.

Despite serious and prolonged efforts to address them, the presence of fraud, waste, and abuse, and deep-rooted corruption among Afghan ministries hindered stabilization and reconstruction operations, resulting in the loss of billions in taxpayer dollars and in some cases indirectly financing insurgent operations. As most stabilization and reconstruction funding was executed through the Department of Defense (about 80 percent), the Pentagon shouldered most of the responsibility, but no agency escaped criticism. In addition, the focus generally was too much on funding inputs, with too little attention to outputs—to results on the ground. Stabilization and reconstruction undoubtedly brought tangible benefits to the local population. Overall, however, the administration's ambitious goals for stabilization and reconstruction in both Iraq and Afghanistan were not fully realized, and the Bush administration proved unable to institutionalize capacity for these operations sufficiently within the US government before it left office.

What Are the Lessons Learned?

Some of the reluctance to support efforts to institutionalize capabilities for stabilization and reconstruction operations in the US government stemmed from a widespread desire within Congress and beyond to never again take on large-scale efforts such as Iraq and Afghanistan. But even beyond the potential need for reconstruction and stabilization capacity in the event of future currently unforeseen US military interventions, the United States may need such capability to prevent fragile states from falling into conflict or for reconstructing and stabilizing postconflict states even where the United States has not intervened. The effort to develop such capability that is effective, durable, and civilian-based therefore needs to continue, despite the increasing focus on China and the challenges it presents. The lessons below should be considered by policymakers undertaking stabilization and reconstruction efforts or seeking to right-size the US capabilities in this area.

- *Need a durable, whole-of-government approach.* Efforts to overcome interagency and interservice rivalries and to resolve such disputes are essential to success in stabilization and reconstruction operations. To be successful, any future stabilization and reconstruction effort must embrace a whole-of-government approach. Here the need for *durable* processes and institutions to enable long-term success after military forces depart is paramount.

- *Anticipate and consider downstream effects of policy shifts.* Reconstruction and stabilization efforts will inevitably be subject to shifting policy environments, given the likelihood that they will span more than one administration. These policy shifts can stem from the political desire to create separation from previous administration policy, the rotation of senior leaders, domestic politics, and changed political priorities. Though inescapable in a democracy, policy changes can greatly impact stabilization and reconstruction efforts over time. Major examples include the shift from early exit policies in Iraq and Afghanistan to longer-term campaigns focused on state building; the decision by President Obama to wind down in Iraq and later to focus on al Qaeda, not the Taliban, as the main effort in Afghanistan; the abrupt replacement of four-star commanders in Afghanistan in 2009 and 2010; and the decision to set a "date certain" for beginning the withdrawal of Surge troops there. However well founded, these decisions impacted reconstruction and stabilization programs and efforts significantly, highlighting that policy shifts create downstream effects that may or may not be anticipated.

- *Plan from the desired end state and work backward from there.* The inherent challenges in developing and executing whole-of-government stabilization and reconstruction operations over a long period of time (which is generally the timeframe required for success) should give policymakers pause before engaging in such efforts. If US decisionmakers believe that interventions which will demand extensive stabilization and reconstruction efforts are required, they should, as General John Allen has suggested, begin their planning with the outcome they wish to achieve (what the military calls Phase IV planning) and work backward. If US decisionmakers have doubts about whether the nation has the necessary capacity to succeed in the stabilization and reconstruction effort, then they should take this into account in deciding whether and how to enter the conflict or initiate the intervention.

Contributors:
Douglas Lute
Meghan L. O'Sullivan

PART 4

The Proliferation Problem

INTRODUCTION

STEPHEN J. HADLEY

The material in part 2 has described in some detail the dramatic and far-reaching steps taken by the Bush administration to transform the architecture and capabilities of the United States and the international community to deal with the threat of terrorism. The result was a dramatic reduction in the terrorist threat. The wave of mass casualty attacks predicted by the US intelligence community in the wake of 9/11 simply did not materialize.

The proliferation of weapons of mass destruction (WMD) was another major threat the administration was determined to counter—particularly nuclear weapons and the ballistic missiles that could be used to deliver them. The administration's response to this challenge was every bit as ambitious and comprehensive as its response to the threat of terrorism. The Bush administration transformed the approach and capabilities of the United States, its friends and allies, and indeed most of the international community for countering and disrupting the spread of these fearsome weapons—and especially the spread of nuclear weapons, particularly to terrorist groups. Causality is difficult to assess. But there have been no new nuclear weapon states since the Bush administration, and at this point no terrorist group is known to have demonstrated access to nuclear weapons or to enough weapons-grade nuclear material to make such a weapon.

This positive judgment is tempered by the failure of now four US administrations to persuade North Korea to give up its nuclear weapons and Iran to abandon its pursuit of them—and the ballistic missiles that could be used to deliver them. The Bush administration worked with allies and partners, using a combination of carrots and sticks, to try to persuade the leaders of both countries to make a "strategic shift." If they pursued nuclear weapons, ballistic missiles, and other nefarious efforts, they would face international isolation, diplomatic pressure, economic sanctions, and potentially military force. But if they would abandon these efforts, they would receive diplomatic recognition, security assurances, economic assistance, and a full embrace by the international community. This latter promise had a Freedom Agenda character. It would help convince these countries to open their economies, better serve their people, and move toward freer and more democratic governance.

But the key point here is that the effort to convince countries to make such a strategic shift would have had no chance of success if it had not been credible. And credibility depended on being backed by a "balance of power that favored freedom" that could deliver on both the threats and the promises.

As the Transition Memorandum in chapter 12 shows, such an effort worked in the case of Libya. The Bush administration sought to make this success a prototype for how other nations could surrender their WMD programs and be embraced by the international community. But after some apparent initial success, neither North Korea nor Iran ultimately chose to pursue this path.

The Bush administration had been seized early on with the problem of the proliferation of ballistic missiles. Early in his presidency, President Bush withdrew from the Anti-Ballistic Missile Treaty so that the United States could develop and deploy limited defenses against the ballistic missiles that countries like North Korea and Iran might use to deliver nuclear weapons. This turned out to be a prudent move, given the failure of the Bush administration and its three successor administrations to persuade these two countries to forswear nuclear weapons.

The chapters of this part 4 tell this proliferation story.

CHAPTER 11

Meeting the Challenge

MICHAEL ALLEN

After 9/11, terrorism became the most urgent national security challenge faced by the Bush administration. The administration took a number of steps to increase dramatically the nation's capability and capacity to disrupt and prevent terrorist attacks: new legal authorities, new institutions, restructuring of existing organizations, enhanced interagency processes for planning and coordinating government-wide operations, and expanded international partnerships and increased partnership capacity. The result of this strengthened national and international architecture was a dramatic reduction in terrorist threats to the US homeland.

Of equal urgency was the need to combat the spread of weapons of mass destruction (WMD) and particularly to terrorist groups. Experts predicted that it was likely that terrorists would succeed in their aspirations for an "American Hiroshima." The death and destruction the world witnessed on 9/11 from nineteen al Qaeda terrorists armed only with box cutters would pale in comparison with what terrorists could do if they got their hands on nuclear, biological, chemical, or radiological weapons—and the ballistic missiles and other means to deliver them.

President Bush was well aware of the risk, declaring nuclear terrorism as the single most serious threat to the national security of the United States. In parallel with its effort against terrorism, therefore, the administration undertook a similar effort to increase the capability and capacity of the nation, its friends and allies, and the broader international community, to check the spread of these weapons and particularly to keep them away from terrorists. Because of these efforts, the same experts that warned of a nuclear event on American soil instead note that US counterterrorism and counterproliferation actions have significantly diminished both the means and the opportunities for such an event.

TRANSITION MEMORANDA

TOP SECRET   5054

NATIONAL SECURITY COUNCIL   Transition

WASHINGTON, D.C. 20504

January 16, 2009   NSC Declassification Review [EO 13526]
DECLASSIFY IN FULL
by William C. Carpenter on 3/23/2020

MEMORANDUM FOR THE RECORD

FROM: MICHAEL ALLEN, COUNTERPROLIFERATION STRATEGY
            RENEE PAN, COUNTERPROLIFERATION STRATEGY
            CHARLES LUTES, COUNTERPROLIFERATION STRATEGY
            JOYCE CONNERY, COUNTERPROLIFERATION STRATEGY
            JAMIE FLY, COUNTERPROLIFERATION STRATEGY

SUBJECT: Counterproliferation Policy

METHODOLOGY:

This memorandum provides a summary of over one dozen significant counterproliferation policy initiatives that this Administration has pursued. Chronologies of three initiatives, seven National Security Presidential Directives (NSPDs), and other key background documents on the initiatives are attached. While other transition memoranda embed references to background documents in a single issue chronology, the multiplicity of distinct regional and functional initiatives addressed in this memorandum does not facilitate a single counterproliferation issue chronology. Rather, references to the attachments are embedded throughout the body of this memorandum.

THE SITUATION AS WE FOUND IT:

As this Administration took office, states hostile to the United States shared a common desire to acquire Weapons of Mass Destruction (WMD) and their means of delivery, such as ballistic missiles, which would enable them to threaten the United States and our allies. To counter these threats, the United States relied on arms control regimes that established international nonproliferation standards, such as the 1972 Anti-Ballistic Missile (ABM) Treaty (the "Cornerstone of Strategic

TOP SECRET

Reason: 1.4 (a) (b) (d)

Declassify on: 11/17/23

Stability"), the Nuclear Nonproliferation Treaty (NPT), the Biological Weapons Convention (BWC), the Chemical Weapons Convention (CWC), and the multilateral export control regimes.

It became increasingly clear, however, that multilateral agreements alone could not ensure the security of the United States and that rogue states were willing to take substantial risks, ignore their international obligations, and exploit export control loopholes in their pursuit of WMD and missiles. These developments, coupled with the lack of a capability to defend our populace or deploy defenses against WMD delivered by ballistic missiles, created the prospect that the United States could be susceptible to coercion or blackmail by the world's most dangerous regimes. In May 2001 remarks at the National Defense University, the President described the situation as:

> More nations have nuclear weapons and still more have nuclear aspirations. Many have chemical and biological weapons.... Most troubling of all, the list of these countries includes some of the world's least responsible states. Unlike the Cold War, today's most urgent threat stems not from thousands of ballistic missiles in Soviet hands, but from a small number of missiles in the hands of these states, states for whom terror and blackmail are a way of life. They seek weapons of mass destruction to intimidate their neighbors, and to keep the United States and other responsible nations from helping allies and friends in strategic parts of the world (see Tab 2).

September 11, 2001 introduced a new element into the proliferation equation—the specter of a terrorist armed with WMD. A catastrophic terrorist attack against U.S. targets abroad, or on the Homeland itself, was no longer unimaginable. Moreover, because the very states proliferating WMD and their means of delivery were often also state sponsors of terrorism, we could no longer assume that the world's most dangerous weapons were beyond the reach and capability of al-Qaida or associated terrorist groups.

This situation was rendered even more threatening by inadequate global controls and monitoring of special nuclear material, biological agents, WMD components, WMD scientists, and sensitive facilities. Rogue states and terrorists were determined to develop or acquire WMD capabilities at a time when the tools and materials needed to achieve that goal were more readily available than ever before.

As this Administration surveyed the post-Cold War, post-9/11 landscape, we recognized that the problem of WMD proliferation required a more comprehensive, global approach that incorporated novel ideas for denying rogue states and terrorists access to catastrophic capabilities.

THIS ADMINISTRATION'S POLICY:

From the outset of the Administration, the President made clear his commitment to develop the counterproliferation capabilities needed to deter and defend against WMD threats. He established a new paradigm on the premise that the greatest threat to the United States did not come from "other big powers in the world, but from terrorists who strike without warning or rogue states who seek weapons of mass destruction" (see Tab 3). This new paradigm combined active nonproliferation, counterproliferation, and defenses. At its heart were new concepts of deterrence relying on both offensive and defensive forces. An adversary could be deterred by threatening retaliation with offensive forces and by denying the adversary its military objectives with our defensive forces. But fielding defenses required moving beyond the constraints of the ABM Treaty, which prohibited the United States from pursuing technology to defend ourselves. Accordingly, the President announced in December 2001 that the United States would withdraw from the ABM Treaty.

This Administration's operationalization of a ballistic missile defense system coupled with our willingness to use force signaled that those who illicitly pursue WMD and their delivery systems must carefully consider the risks inherent in their actions. Rather than these weapons contributing to their security, they would have the opposite effect, since the United States was resolved to use all available means to defend our national security.

Meeting new challenges required changes in thinking and strategy since "doctrines designed to contain empires, deter aggressive states, and defeat massed armies" could not fully protect the United States. The President developed and issued a new National Strategy to Combat WMD. The Strategy, which is articulated in NSPD-17 and a December 2002 unclassified version of the directive, established three pillars in a comprehensive approach to counter the threat posed by WMD (see Tabs 4–5). First, the strategy placed new emphasis on counterproliferation efforts that included proactive interdiction to halt the movement of WMD-related materials, technology, and expertise from supplier states, through intermediaries, to hostile states and terrorist organizations. Second, the strategy highlighted the importance of active multilateral and bilateral nonproliferation diplomatic efforts to dissuade supplier states from cooperating with rogue regimes and terrorists and to compel these regimes to end their WMD and missile programs. Finally, the strategy addressed the need for increased capability to defend against the use of WMD through both active and passive measures, and increased preparedness to minimize the consequences of WMD use against our population—to deter adversaries by persuading them that they cannot achieve their objectives by using WMD.

Today, the United States is exercising global leadership in opposing the development of WMD by rogue states and terrorists; interdicting WMD, their delivery systems, and related material/technologies; and defending against the potential use of WMD/ballistic missiles (see Tab 6).

WHAT HAS BEEN ACCOMPLISHED:

Libya. Through the efforts of the United States and our partners, we convinced Libya to voluntarily abandon its WMD programs, thus setting an example for other states that continue to pursue illicit WMD and missile programs. (See separate Presidential Memorandum on Libya.)

North Korea. Upon taking office, the President recognized that North Korean issues could not be addressed bilaterally, but required multilateral diplomacy incorporating a mix of inducements and sanctions as needed. By engaging North Korea in a multilateral framework that included regional players wielding leverage with Pyongyang—Russia, South Korea, Japan, and especially China—a significant breakthrough was achieved when the North committed, in the September 19, 2005 Joint Statement, to abandon all nuclear programs. In turn, the other five parties stated their willingness to provide the North with economic cooperation and energy assistance based on the principle of "action-for-action." When North Korea pulled out of the talks in 2006 and conducted long-range ballistic missile and nuclear tests, the United States and its partners responded by leading successful efforts to obtain international support for a Chapter VII U.N. Security Council Resolution (UNSCR). UNSCR 1718 required all U.N. members states to: prevent WMD-related material transfers to or from the North; freeze the financial assets of designated persons or entities; take steps to prevent the travel of designated persons; prevent the transfer of specified luxury goods to the North; and prohibit the sale of certain conventional weapons to North Korea. Soon thereafter, North Korea returned to the talks; in 2007 it began disabling its plutonium production facilities at Yongbyon, and in 2008 it provided a declaration of its plutonium production capabilities, and included a confidential minute addressing its uranium enrichment and proliferation activities. In late 2008, the United States and North Korea agreed to a set of verification measures that will serve as the basis for a Six-Party verification protocol to be applied to this declaration package and future denuclearization efforts. These measures include sampling, visits to declared and undeclared sites, interviews with personnel, and document reviews. In addition to verification, the next phase of the Six-Party process will need to include the removal of all nuclear material and weapons. (See separate Presidential Memorandum on North Korea.)

Iran. The President recognized that the most effective way to persuade Iran to renounce its nuclear weapons ambitions was to have partners at America's side. The United States was instrumental in garnering international support to adopt UNSCRs 1737, 1747, and 1803 to address the threat posed by Iran's WMD and missile programs. We have supported the International Atomic Energy Agency's (IAEA's) investigation of Iran's illicit nuclear activities. We have also joined our partners in the P-5 plus Germany to make it clear to Tehran that Iran must verifiably suspend enrichment, but that if it does so we are prepared to negotiate a resolution of the nuclear issue on the basis of an offer of diplomatic, economic, and security benefits to Iran that has been tabled by the P-5 plus Germany. We also have made clear to Iran and the international community that we rule out no option in our effort to stop Iran from obtaining nuclear weapons. We are pursuing a campaign of coordinated diplomatic, economic, intelligence, and other actions to set back or destroy the Iranian nuclear program and put pressure on Iran to make a strategic decision to abandon its nuclear ambitions and other destructive policies. (See separate Presidential Memorandum on Iran.)

Syria. Syria's illicit construction of a nuclear reactor highlights the importance of a robust counterproliferation strategy. Israeli action eliminated this threat at least in the near term. We are supporting the IAEA's investigation of Syria's undeclared nuclear activities. We are also highlighting this challenge to the NPT and IAEA safeguards regimes in our bilateral and multilateral diplomacy.

Iraq. Despite the failure of the Iraq Survey Group to discover WMD stockpiles, it was clear that, prior to 2003, Saddam Hussein preserved the capability and maintained the intention to reconstitute his WMD programs when sanctions were lifted (see Tab 7). With the removal of his regime and the establishment of a democratic Iraq, this threat has been eliminated. Additionally, 550 MT of proliferation-attractive yellow cake was packaged, removed from theater, and sold to a commercial entity in Canada.

A.Q. Khan. Working with our partners across the globe as well as the IAEA, we disrupted and dismantled the Khan network and ended years of proliferation activity by Khan's black market network of financiers, middlemen, and other enablers. This effort enabled us to confront Libya about its covert nuclear program and provided valuable insight into the Iranian and North Korean programs. We were also able to use the Khan experience to press key transshipment points, such as the United Arab Emirates, that had been exploited for years by the network and other proliferators to implement national export controls and take a more aggressive posture in countering proliferation. (See separate Presidential Memorandum on the A.Q. Khan proliferation network.)

Proliferation Security Initiative (PSI). The President launched PSI in 2003 as a multinational response to the growing challenge posed by the proliferation of weapons of mass destruction (WMD), their delivery systems, and related materials. It uses legal, diplomatic, economic, law enforcement, customs, military, and intelligence tools to build international cooperation to stop or interdict proliferation activity. PSI has become the new model for active international collaboration. More than 90 nations are now partners in this effort (see Tabs 8–12).

Missile Defense. The deployment of missile defenses has been the cornerstone of our efforts to transform our deterrence and defense policies to meet the new threats we face. Building upon decades of research, we now have the ability to protect our citizens at home, friends and allies, and our deployed military forces from some types of missile-delivered WMD. We continue to work with partners in NATO and with Russia to establish a global missile defense system that protects the United States, our friends and allies, and potential partners from emerging missile threats. (See separate Presidential Memorandum on missile defense.)

UNSCR 1540. The United Nations Security Council adopted UNSCR 1540, which obligates states to refrain from supporting by any means non-state actors that are developing, acquiring, manufacturing, possessing, transporting, transferring, or using nuclear, chemical, or biological weapons or their delivery systems; it further imposes binding obligations to control those weapons and their delivery systems by establishing appropriate controls over related materials. UNSCR 1673 reinforced the obligations of 1540 to include controls on proliferation financing.

Nuclear Nonproliferation. The United States has worked to strengthen the Nuclear Nonproliferation Treaty and worked to make the Additional Protocol the new standard for nuclear safeguards. In 2004, the President proposed that the Nuclear Suppliers Group (NSG) should "refuse to sell enrichment and reprocessing equipment and technologies to any state that does not already possess full-scale functioning enrichment and reprocessing plants." The NSG rejected an outright ban, but through the G-8 the United States was able to secure a series of 1-year moratoria allowing time for the NSG to explore a strict criteria-based approach. The United States has now tabled amendments to the NSG Guidelines allowing transfers only when very strict criteria are met, and is pursuing adoption of the amended Guidelines at the NSG (see Tab 13).

G-8 Global Partnership. Responding to proposals made by the President, in 2002 the G-8 leaders launched the Global Partnership Against the Spread of Weapons and Materials of Mass Destruction, committing $20 billion over 10 years to address nonproliferation, disarmament, counterterrorism, and nuclear safety issues through cooperative projects in such areas as destruction of chemical weapons; the security and disposition of nuclear and fissile materials; and rechanneling employment of former weapons scientists to peaceful endeavors. In 2008, the G-8 Global Partnership is expanding its assistance efforts beyond Russia and the Former Soviet Union (FSU) to address global threats (see Tab 14).

Global Threat Reduction Initiative (GTRI). Under GTRI, we are partnering with other nations, including many former Soviet republics, to better secure nuclear materials. We have helped convert 52 nuclear reactors in 31 countries from highly-enriched uranium to low-enriched uranium. We also have secured more than 600 vulnerable sites around the world that together contain enough material to make about 9,000 radiological or "dirty" bombs.

Bratislava Initiative. At Bratislava, the United States and Russia agreed to accelerate and expand bilateral nuclear security cooperation in five areas: emergency response; best practices; security culture; conversion of Russia-origin research reactors in third countries; and Russian nuclear security. This initiative provided upgrades at over 120 Russian nuclear material and warhead sites and ensures that Russia will continue these security measures beyond 2012 (see Tab 15).

Declaration on Nuclear Energy and Nonproliferation. On July 3, 2007, the United States and Russia issued a declaration on joint actions to strengthen the nuclear nonproliferation regime and to promote the expansion of nuclear energy worldwide (see Tab 16). The goal of the declaration is to work together and with other nations to develop mutually beneficial approaches for economical and reliable access to nuclear energy designed to permit developing nations to gain the benefits of nuclear energy while creating a viable alternative to their acquisition of sensitive fuel cycle technologies.

Global Nuclear Energy Partnership (GNEP). In 2006, GNEP was created to develop the next generation of civil nuclear capability that will be safe and secure, improve the environment, and reduce the risk of nuclear proliferation. The effort now has 21 partner nations aimed at accelerating the development and deployment of advanced fast-reactor fuel-cycle technologies and recycling that do not involve separating plutonium (which then might be acquired by terrorists or rogue states). Such advanced technologies would substantially reduce nuclear waste, simplify its disposition, and draw down existing inventories of civilian spent fuel in a safe, secure, and proliferation-resistant manner.

Proliferation Finance. We have championed international efforts to combat WMD finance, greatly curtailing the ability of proliferators to profit from or often even carry out their activities. In 2005, the President issued Executive Order 13382 authorizing the Departments of the Treasury and State to financially target proliferators and their support networks in the same way in which terrorists are targeted financially. We also have worked with partners through groups such as the Financial Action Task Force to highlight the threat posed to the international financial system by proliferators such as Iran, North Korea, and Syria (see Tab 17).

Reforming Export Controls. Through the issuance of NSPD-55 and NSPD-56, this Administration has enhanced controls over highly sensitive goods and technologies to prevent them from reaching those who aim to do us harm, while streamlining the export control process to allow for a more effective continuation of the legitimate trade in controlled goods. The Global War on Terror also exposed the inadequacies of our export control system to get needed items to coalition forces arrayed to combat terrorists and terrorism around the world. The defense trade cooperation treaties signed by this Administration with the United Kingdom and Australia greatly contributed to strengthening and deepening the defense relationships with two of our staunchest allies (see Tabs 18–22). This Administration also has increased bilateral efforts to strengthen foreign export control systems to prevent sensitive goods and technologies from reaching illicit end-users, and we continue efforts to strengthen multilateral control regimes to address current concerns.

Container Security Initiative and Megaports. Ninety percent of the world's trade occurs via container cargo shipped in and out of seaports. After 9/11, two programs were established to help secure shipping lanes. Starting in 2002, the Container Security Initiative, run by the Department of Homeland Security, deploys teams of customs officers to target all containers that pose a potential threat. Complementing this program, the Department of Energy's Megaports program deploys radiation detection equipment in high-volume international seaports and trains local personnel to check for nuclear or other radioactive materials.

Global Initiative to Combat Nuclear Terrorism. The United States and Russia launched the initiative in 2006 to help build international capacity to prevent, defend against, and respond to nuclear terrorism. There are currently 72 partner nations that are working cooperatively to advance the Global Initiative through workshops, technical exchanges, field exercises, and other concrete cooperative efforts (see Tab 23).

Declaratory Policy. In December 2007, the President approved a new declaratory policy that will reinforce efforts to deter terrorist acquisition or use of WMD. That policy reads as follows:

> "For many years, it has been the policy of the United States that we reserve the right to respond with overwhelming force to the use of WMD against the United States, our people, our forces, and our friends and allies. Additionally, the United States will hold any state, terrorist group, or other non-state actor fully accountable for supporting or enabling terrorist efforts to obtain or use WMD, whether by facilitating, financing, or providing expertise or safe haven for such efforts." (Tabs 24–25)

FUTURE CHALLENGES:

Our challenge continues to be to reinforce the global norm against proliferation of WMD and their delivery systems. Building on the three pillars of our National Strategy to Combat WMD, this means using all the means of American power to confront rogue states and terrorists who desire to acquire WMD, continuing to improve our nonproliferation efforts with the countries of the former Soviet Union and other countries that forgo their deadly ambitions, and continuing to improve our defenses against WMD and ballistic missiles. This will involve:

- Confronting rogue states such as Iran and Syria about their illicit WMD programs and, if necessary, pursuing consideration of the Syrian nuclear issue by the U.N. Security Council;
- Working with partners from the Six-Party Talks to ensure that the progress in verifiably denuclearizing North Korea continues;
- Ensuring the continued vigor of PSI and promoting the global norm that responsible nations subscribe to and advance the principles that nuclear materials and sensitive technology must be

both secure and nontransferable, and that "global community" action (e.g., interdictions, export controls) is required;

- Establishing a global missile defense system to protect against emerging threats from rogue states such as Iran;
- Encouraging partners to establish increased measures to combat proliferation finance;
- Implementing means to assure reliable access to nuclear energy while preventing the spread of dangerous nuclear fuel cycle technologies (enrichment and reprocessing);
- Fully developing the Global Initiative to Combat Nuclear Terrorism to leverage the world's existing capabilities against WMD terrorism;
- Extending G-8 nonproliferation assistance efforts beyond 2012;
- Working to develop new nuclear safeguards technologies to ensure the security of materials;
- Taking steps to reinvigorate our aging nuclear expertise and supporting infrastructure to ensure we have the capability needed to support forensic and attribution activities;
- Continuing efforts to adjust our domestic export control system to ensure the right mix of controls and the ability to maintain our defense industrial base, increase bilateral efforts to strengthen foreign export control systems, and continue to take steps in international fora to enhance multilateral control regimes to prevent sensitive goods and technologies from reaching proscribed destinations; and
- Posturing ourselves to respond swiftly and effectively in the event or immediate threat of a WMD attack if our counterproliferation and nonproliferation prove unsuccessful.

Attachments

Tab 1   Chronology for Major Counterproliferation Initiatives
Tab 2   Remarks by the President to Students and Faculty at National Defense University (May 1, 2001)
Tab 3   Remarks: President Discusses National Missile Defense (December 13, 2001)
Tab 4   NSPD-17: National Strategy to Combat Weapons of Mass Destruction
Tab 5   December 2002 Unclassified National Strategy to Combat Weapons of Mass Destruction
Tab 6   Remarks by the President on Weapons of Mass Destruction Proliferation (February 11, 2004)
Tab 7   NSPD-21: Support for Inspections in Iraq
Tab 8   Chronology: Proliferation Security Initiative (PSI)
Tab 9   PSI Statement of Interdiction Principles
Tab 10   Remarks by National Security Advisor Stephen J. Hadley at the Proliferation Security Initiative Senior Level Meeting (May 28, 2008)
Tab 11   NSPD-20: Counterproliferation Interdiction

THE WHITE HOUSE

WASHINGTON

NSC Declassification Review [E.O. 13526]
DECLASSIFY IN PART
by William C. Carpenter 3/23/2020

November 10, 2008

MEMORANDUM FOR THE RECORD

FROM: JUAN ZARATE, COMBATING TERRORISM DIRECTORATE
MICHAEL ALLEN, COUNTERPROLIFERATION STRATEGY
DIRECTORATE

SUBJECT: Weapons of Mass Destruction (WMD) Terrorism

THE SITUATION AS WE FOUND IT:

September 11, 2001, provided graphic evidence of what terrorists were willing to do to inflict damage on the United States and our interests. A catastrophic attack against U.S. targets, or on the Homeland itself, was clearly a realistic possibility. Moreover, we had to assume—with some confidence—that a catastrophic attack involving WMD was within the reach and capability of al-Qaida or associated terrorist groups.

In the period since September 11, 2001, we have learned much about al-Qaida's quest to acquire WMD capabilities, including the effort already well underway in the late 1990s. Taliban rule in Afghanistan afforded al-Qaida leaders the luxury of a safe haven from which to pursue ambitious nuclear, chemical, and biological development efforts. On the nuclear side, al-Qaida aimed to acquire improvised nuclear devices (INDs) or perhaps radiological dispersal devices (RDDs). On the chemical side, detainee reporting indicated that al-Qaida was experimenting with a number of potentially lethal chemical agents. Furthermore, on the biological side, the group attempted to develop a capability to produce quantities of anthrax for use in attacks against the West.

Al-Qaida's clear intent to acquire and use WMD was itself a major threat to U.S. interests and evidence that terrorists were willing to employ new methods to create catastrophic effects. The potential for catastrophic terrorism was rendered even more threatening by the increased willingness of rogue states with ties to terrorist groups to engage in proliferation of WMD and

Re-Classified by: Ellen J. L. Knight
Reason: 1.4(c), (d), and (g)
Declassify on: 11/10/2033

associated materials, creating the potential for greater access to those weapons and materials by transnational terrorist groups like al-Qaida. That situation was exacerbated by inadequate global controls and monitoring of special nuclear material, chemical and biological agents, WMD components, WMD scientists, and sensitive facilities. In short, the world's most dangerous terrorists were determined to develop or acquire WMD capabilities at a time when the tools and materials needed to achieve that goal were more available to them than ever before.

THIS ADMINISTRATION'S POLICY:

Our policy and strategy to address the challenge of WMD terrorism had to leverage and build on the collective knowledge and capability of three communities: the counterproliferation (CP) community, which focuses on nation state efforts to acquire or proliferate WMD; the counterterrorism (CT) community, which focuses on the capabilities and intentions of individual terrorists, terrorist groups, and the networks that support them; and the homeland security community, which focuses on preventing, protecting, and responding to direct threats to the United States. It was essential that we reorient these three communities to address the emerging WMD terrorism threat in a coordinated way and that we address any gaps, seams, and overlaps in their combined efforts.

To address the WMD terrorism challenge, our strategy aims to create a comprehensive, robust, and layered defense against the threat, with a particular focus on nuclear terrorism. In order to accomplish that objective, our strategy has six pillars:

- We must develop the intelligence necessary to determine terrorists' intentions, capabilities, and plans for developing or acquiring WMD. However, developing intelligence is essential to our ability to disrupt terrorists' efforts to develop, acquire, or use WMD.
- We must deny terrorists access to WMD-related materials, expertise, and other enabling technologies—a challenge made more difficult as knowledge, technology, and material from state programs leak into the broader community.
- We must detect and disrupt terrorists' movement of WMD-related materials, weapons, and personnel, particularly into the Homeland.
- We must increase our capability to prevent and respond to a terrorist-related WMD attack, with an emphasis on robust response and recovery plans that would deny al-Qaida their ultimate aim—to disrupt or destroy our way of life.
- We must develop the tools we need to determine precisely the nature and source of a terrorist-employed WMD device.
- We must deter terrorists from employing WMD.

The degree of deterrence that can be achieved in the WMD terrorism arena is a matter of some debate, but our policy aims to affect the calculus of both potential terrorists and those who would support or facilitate—knowingly or unknowingly—their efforts to acquire WMD or carry out a WMD attack. This includes not only denying terrorists their objectives, but also attacking the theological and moral legitimacy claimed by those who would engage in WMD terrorism—and deterring the various actors who may form part of the WMD supply chain.

In December 2007, the President approved a new declaratory policy that will reinforce efforts to deter terrorist acquisition or use of WMD:

"For many years, it has been the policy of the United States that we reserve the right to respond with overwhelming force to the use of WMD against the United States, our people, our forces, and our friends and allies. Additionally, the United States will hold any state, terrorist group, or other non-state actor fully accountable for supporting or enabling terrorist efforts to obtain or use WMD, whether by facilitating, financing, or providing expertise or safe haven for such efforts."

WHAT HAS BEEN ACCOMPLISHED:

The Administration has undertaken a broad-based effort to build both new institutions and capabilities to carry out our WMD terrorism policy and strategy and build a broad, layered defense against WMD terrorism. This "defense in depth" strategy has matured significantly since September 11, 2001, and we continue to deepen the layers of this strategy both at home and abroad.

Among these new institutions and capabilities are:

- **DNI's WMD Terrorism Steering Group.** Under the auspices of the Director of National Intelligence (DNI), we are aiming to develop the clearest possible intelligence picture of terrorist capabilities and intentions, including with respect to WMD. This includes the DNI's WMD Terrorism Steering Group, created in October 2007 to harness all capabilities of the Intelligence Community (IC) to enhance analysis and collection.
- **National Counterterrorism Center (NCTC).** NCTC collocates the intelligence community's full range of capabilities to gather and analyze terrorist threat information, including information regarding WMD terrorism. NCTC has taken up the task of leading the WMD Terrorism Task Force focusing on ensuring implementation of our WMD strategy, with an emphasis on near- and mid-term actions related to the nuclear terrorism threat.
- **National Conterproliferation Center (NCPC).** NCPC provides strategic direction to intelligence community efforts to fight the entire range of proliferation challenges, to include terrorists seeking WMD.

- **Domestic Nuclear Detection Office (DNDO).** Created within the Department of Homeland Security, DNDO works to improve our capability to detect and respond to unauthorized importation, transport, or storage of nuclear or radiological material.
- **National Technical Nuclear Forensics Center (NTNFC).** NTNFC resides within the DNDO and focuses on improving our Nation's technical forensics capabilities supporting the attribution of nuclear materials and devices.
- **Department of State Office of WMD Terrorism.** This office helps partner nations assess the risks they face from WMD, provides technical assistance, and works with foreign governments to ensure continuous improvement in our collective capabilities to reduce the risk from WMD terrorism.
- **FBI's WMD Directorate.** Within its National Security Branch, the FBI created the WMD Directorate in 2006 to consolidate WMD and counterproliferation initiatives within the FBI.

We have also developed and advanced a number of diplomatic initiatives aimed at implementing our WMD terrorism strategy and reducing the risk of WMD terrorism. These include:

- **Proliferation Security Initiative (PSI).** PSI was launched by the President in 2003 to stem the flow of illicit materials used for WMD programs. More than 90 nations are now partners in this effort to coordinate individual national capabilities to detect and interdict illicit materials.
- **United Nations Security Council Resolution (UNSCR) 1540.** In 2004, the United States cosponsored and helped secure approval of UNSCR 1540, which requires states to enact and enforce effective export controls for dangerous weapons and materials, and prosecute those who transfer WMD or sensitive technologies to terrorists.
- **Global Initiative to Combat Nuclear Terrorism.** The United States and Russia launched the initiative in 2006 to help build international capacity to prevent, defend against, and respond to nuclear terrorism. There are currently 72 partner nations that are working cooperatively to advance the Global Initiative through workshops, technical exchanges, and other concrete cooperative efforts.
- **Global Threat Reduction Initiative (GTRI).** Under GTRI, we are partnering with other nations—including many former Soviet republics—to better secure nuclear materials. We have helped convert 52 nuclear reactors in 31 countries from highly-enriched uranium to low-enriched uranium, equivalent to roughly ____ nuclear bombs worth of HEU. We have also secured more than 600 vulnerable sites around the world that together contain enough material to make about 9,000 radiological or "dirty" bombs.
- **Bratislava Initiative.** At Bratislava, the United States and Russia agreed to accelerate and expand bilateral nuclear security cooperation in five areas: emergency response; best practices;

security culture; conversion of Russia-origin research reactors in third countries; and Russian nuclear security. This initiative provided Upgrades at more than 120 Russian nuclear material and warhead storage sites that are to be completed in 2008 and ensures that Russia will continue these security measures beyond 2012.

We have also taken concrete, practical steps to bolster security at home and abroad to protect against smuggled radioactive materials, nuclear devices, and dangerous biological pathogens. These include:

- **Radiation detection reporting protocols** for timely United States Government notification, technical adjudication, and resolution of alarms generated by all United States Government detection systems.
- An expanded **Second Line of Defense** program, which deploys radiation detection equipment at locations overseas.
- Creation of the **Container Security Initiative (CSI)** and other programs to detect the movement of dangerous materials in foreign countries. CSI has been expanded to 58 foreign ports, with U.S. inspectors working with foreign partners to screen cargo before it is loaded on a ship destined for the United States. This covers 86 percent of all United States-bound maritime cargo.
- Creation of the **Megaports Initiative** to provide key ports around the world with radiation detection equipment and to train local law enforcement to detect, deter, and interdict illicit trafficking in nuclear and radioactive materials.
- Implementation of **screening procedures for nuclear devices and material at Ports-of-Entry** (POEs) on the United States border. Presently, Customs and Border Protection (CBP) operates ▮▮▮▮▮ radiation portal monitors at U.S. POEs, including ▮▮▮▮ radiation portal monitors at seaports. CBP also utilizes ▮▮▮▮ large-scale non-intrusive inspection devices to examine cargo.
- Implementation of a plan to equip all CBP inspectors, Coast Guard boarding personnel, and Border Patrol agents with **portable radiation detectors.**
- **Investments through the National Institutes of Health** in research and development for medical countermeasures to chemical, biological, radiological, and nuclear active agents. The Department of Health and Human Services has also created a transparent and predictable architecture through Project BioShield to support and promote the integrated development and acquisition of medical countermeasures.
- Deployment by the Department of Homeland Security of the first-ever **bioaerosol monitoring system (BioWatch)** to more than 30 major metropolitan areas to provide early warning of a biological weapon attack and enable quick and accurate response.

- Use of **targeted financial sanctions under E.O. 12938** signed by the President on June 29, 2005, to identify and block the property of WMD proliferators and their supporters.

We also have embarked on major efforts to improve our response and recovery capability in the event of a WMD attack, to include:

- Greater emphasis on **nuclear and radiological preparedness** within our National Exercise Program in order to improve our capabilities and response.
- Greater capability—including new and expanding capability within the FBI—for the **Render Safe mission** of neutralizing or disabling a nuclear device.
- Development of a **National Response Framework** to serve as the comprehensive structure for the management of the response to a domestic WMD incident.
- Development of **Nuclear Protective Action Guides** to support decision-making to protect the public when responding to or recovering from a radiological dispersal device or improvised nuclear device incident.
- Certification by DOD of 53 National Guard Weapons of Mass Destruction **Civil Support Teams** (WMD-CST) stationed in each State, territory, and the District of Columbia to provide critical communications links and consequence management support to local, State, and Federal agencies.
- Creation of Joint National Guard CBRNE **Enhanced Response Force Packages** (CERFPs) located in each FEMA region, as well as Alaska and Hawaii (12 CERFPs total) to provide search and rescue, decontamination, and field medical care.
- **Establishment of a WMD attribution process** to clarify roles, responsibilities, and authorities of the United States Government departments and agencies regarding the attribution of a WMD attack or attempted attack to its source.

FUTURE CHALLENGES:

The most effective current measure we could take to address the challenge of WMD Terrorism would be to eliminate the safe haven that the al-Qaida senior leadership currently enjoys in the Federally Administered Tribal Areas (FATA) of Pakistan. The reemergence of a safe haven in the FATA potentially allows the group to pursue its WMD ambitions in a more focused way. Absent a change in that situation, we are left playing "defense" against this threat.

Beyond that strategic concern, and despite the wide range of activities and efforts already underway, there is more that we must do to strengthen our efforts to create a layered defense against WMD terrorism. First, we must accelerate implementation of ODNI and NCTC initiatives to refine our focus on and responsiveness to WMD terrorism threat trends and issues. We must make sure our best analytical minds and full range of collection resources are aimed at this critical problem set. We also need to take steps to reinvigorate our aging nuclear expertise and supporting infrastructure to ensure we have an enduring capability needed to support nuclear intelligence, technical forensics, and attribution activities.

Beyond that, we must continue working with partner nations in cooperative engagement programs to thicken the layers of defense and increase the likelihood that weapons or material will be detected and interdicted far from U.S. borders. We must aggressively disseminate, reinforce, and if necessary act on the President's declaratory policy to bolster our deterrent posture.

In an October 28, 2008, speech at the Carnegie Endowment for International Peace, Secretary Gates provided further public explication of the President's declaratory policy, echoing and amplifying themes articulated in speeches delivered earlier in 2008 by National Security Advisor Hadley at Stanford University and again at a Proliferation Security Initiative (PSI) conference. We must also attempt to influence the debate within the Muslim world by reinforcing the idea (as reflected by key Muslim leaders, scholars, and religious figures) that the use of WMD is against the tenets of Islam.

We must also posture ourselves to respond as swiftly and effectively as possible in the event of a WMD attack. We must continue to strengthen all aspects of our response capability, to include foreign consequence management, attribution, and the time critical detection and deployment of medical countermeasures in response to a biological attack. We must also continue to improve protective action guidelines to protect our citizens and those engaged in critical life-saving activities, specifically from the effects of a nuclear detonation.

Finally, we must also take further steps to coordinate our efforts to implement the WMD terrorism strategy across the counterproliferation and counterterrorism communities. The lack of a single senior official in the NSC/HSC structure whose sole focus is on WMD terrorism issues has been identified as a potential weakness in our organizational efforts. To address this concern we are moving ahead with a proposal to create a new Deputy Assistant to the President for WMD Terrorism within the White House. This individual, reporting to both the Assistant to the President for National Security Affairs and Assistant to the President for Homeland Security and Counterterrorism, would be responsible for overseeing and coordinating the work of all of the departments and agencies engaged in implementation of our WMD terrorism strategy. By assigning this responsibility to one person, we will resolve concerns about the CP/CT divide, thereby ensuring unity of effort against this priority national security challenge.

In short, we need to deepen the application and effectiveness of the WMD terrorism strategy domestically and internationally, while continuing to pressure and disrupt terrorist networks, to prevent terrorist organizations from acquiring, developing, or using WMD.

Attachments

POSTSCRIPT

MICHAEL ALLEN

The Bush Administration Approach

Of the countries pursuing WMD capabilities, the Bush administration was most concerned about Iran, Iraq, North Korea, Syria, and Libya. The first three were particularly worrisome because each was pursuing its own WMD while also supporting terrorist groups, making these states a potential avenue by which terrorist groups might obtain such weapons.

The Bush administration addressed these WMD programs in a larger policy framework involving three lines of effort: (1) counterproliferation efforts to proactively interdict the movement of WMD materials, expertise, and technologies to WMD-seeking states and terrorist groups; (2) nonproliferation efforts to convince WMD-seeking states to give up their quest and to dissuade WMD-supplier states from dealing both with those states and with terrorist groups; and (3) defensive measures—both active and passive—to deter and protect against any potential use of WMD, while at the same time preparing to deal with the consequences of any such use. These areas of focus were elaborated in the first ever National Strategy to Combat Weapons of Mass Destruction.

The Bush administration had to enhance America's own capacities and capabilities against WMD proliferation by creating new institutions and processes, restructuring and repurposing existing organizations, and enhancing interagency planning and coordination. Among other things, the administration:

— Enhanced US export controls over WMD-sensitive goods and technologies.
— Established domestic authorities (Executive Order 13882) and mechanisms to target and cut off the flow of funds and financing to WMD proliferators and their support networks.
— Instituted a Container Security Initiative and a Megaports program to monitor cargo container traffic into the United States for potential threats including especially nuclear or other radioactive materials.
— Improved intelligence support by such steps as creating the National Counterproliferation Center (NCPC), the Domestic Nuclear Detection Office (DNDO), the FBI's WMD Directorate, and the State Department's Office of

WMD Terrorism, as well as by making dramatic improvements in intelligence, law enforcement, and other information sharing.

— Developed the National Response Framework for managing the response to a domestic WMD incident, certified a National Guard WMD Destruction Civil Support Team for every state, and deployed BioWatch monitoring systems to more than 30 cities to warn of any biological weapons attack.

President Bush wanted a policy framework that included valued partnerships and alliances but also recognized the need to work outside traditional approaches, including with potential adversaries. This approach yielded new, dynamic, and durable international partnerships, building global commitment and capacity to combat WMD proliferation. The most significant were the following:

— UN Security Council Resolution 1540 obligated all UN member states to refrain from supporting nonstate actors seeking WMD and to establish appropriate export controls enforced by criminal sanctions (with follow-on Resolution 1673 requiring controls to cut off WMD proliferators from the global financial system).
— The Proliferation Security Initiative (PSI) under which over ninety nations agreed to coordinate their legal, diplomatic, economic, law enforcement, customs, military, and intelligence tools to detect and interdict the flow of illicit WMD materials.
— US collaboration with a number of key partners that halted the ongoing illicit nuclear proliferation networks led by A. Q. Khan and by North Korea, respectively.
— The Global Initiative to Combat Nuclear Terrorism under which over seventy countries partnered to prevent, defend against, and respond to nuclear terrorism.

The effort was comprehensive in scope and global in reach. What is particularly striking is how actively engaged China and especially Russia were in these efforts. In addition to the Global Initiative to Combat Nuclear Terrorism, Russia partnered with the United States in several other initiatives including:

— At Bratislava, Slovakia, the two nations agreed to increased bilateral nuclear security cooperation that ultimately provided security upgrades at more than 120 Russian nuclear material and warhead storage sites.

- Under the Global Threat Reduction Initiative (GTRI), cooperation with Russia and many former Soviet republics helped convert fifty-two nuclear reactors in thirty-one countries from highly enriched uranium (HEU) (which represents a significant proliferation risk) to low enriched uranium (LEU) and helped secure over 600 vulnerable sites where nuclear materials were present.
- In their Declaration on Nuclear Energy and Nonproliferation, the two nations agreed to help developing countries gain the benefits of nuclear energy without the need for uranium enrichment and plutonium reprocessing facilities, and their attendant proliferation risk.

In seeking to protect the United States from the threat of WMD, President Bush endorsed a new concept of deterrence. It recognized that an adversary state could be deterred from using WMD not only by threatening military retaliation to any such use (the long-standing, traditional approach) but also by using defensive military systems to deny an adversary the military objectives that it might seek by such use. Unable to achieve its objectives, and risking retaliation if it used WMD, an adversary state might be persuaded that pursuing WMD was just not worth the effort. Indeed, given US willingness to use military force to thwart such efforts (as demonstrated by its invasion of Iraq and military strikes against terrorists), rather than potentially enhancing security, efforts to develop or acquire WMD might actually put an adversary state's security at risk. The Bush administration was also clear that there would be economic and diplomatic benefits leading to normalized diplomatic relations for any adversary state willing to make a strategic decision transparently and verifiably to give up its pursuit of WMD.

With respect to terrorist groups seeking WMD, the deterrence problem was much harder. Given their reliance on theological justification, they were susceptible to an ideological challenge disputing the theological and moral legitimacy of any WMD use. Terrorists might also be denied achievement of their objectives in such use. But deterrence by threat of retaliation was harder, since such groups were better able to hide their hand in any WMD use (the attribution problem) and were less threatened by retaliation (having as a general matter no fixed territory to defend). To shore up deterrence against terrorist acquisition and use of WMD, the Bush administration targeted those who might facilitate, finance, or provide expertise or safe haven to terrorist WMD-seeking efforts. In a new deterrence message, the Bush administration stated publicly and clearly that the United States would hold any state, terrorist group, or other nonstate actor fully accountable for supporting or enabling terrorist efforts to obtain or use WMD.

What Has Happened Since the End of the Bush Administration?

Both President Obama and President Trump carried forward most of President Bush's WMD proliferation initiatives. President Obama started his term with a major address in Prague laying out goals for worldwide disarmament and a push for frameworks to secure nuclear materials and detect illicit efforts to acquire them. Accordingly, the Obama administration further pursued the Bush administration Global Threat Reduction Initiative (GTRI) to close or convert highly enriched uranium (HEU) reactors worldwide and to dispose of spent HEU fuel and materials. Building on the Prague speech, President Obama convened the Nuclear Security Summit, which provided a new multilateral forum for targeting HEU reduction, nuclear facility security, and combating nuclear terrorism.

The Obama administration continued and expanded participation in the Proliferation Security Initiative (PSI) and helped define and grow the Global Partnership Against the Spread of Weapons of Mass Destruction, launched by the Bush administration at the G-8 in 2002. Originally focused mainly on Russian nonproliferation projects, the group extended the original mandate of ten years and further expanded participation. Building on prior proposals to curb the spread of enrichment and reprocessing technology, the Obama administration successfully led the Nuclear Suppliers Group (NSG) to establish a system that would allow the sale of relevant nuclear equipment and technology only to countries that met demanding criteria.

One area that has seen evolution is WMD border security controls. Under President Bush's Megaports Initiative, the Department of Energy provided partners with the tools to enhance radiation detection for container ships destined for the United States. In parallel, under the Container Security Initiative (CSI), the Department of Homeland Security sought to secure shipping supply chains to the United States. According to a 2012 GAO report, the Obama administration cut the Megaports program by 85 percent, arguing that there were no clear metrics for success and that it was duplicative of other efforts. The administration turned instead to mobile detection capabilities targeting fewer ports. The Container Security Initiative, by contrast, has continued to expand, and as of 2019 some fifty-eight operational CSI ports prescreened over 80 percent of all container cargo bound for the United States. In 2020 Congress asked the GAO how the United States could achieve the 100 percent mandate for screening called for in the Safe Ports Act.

The record on efforts to halt WMD proliferation in countries of concern is mixed. The success of the so-called Libya model that had resulted in Muammar Qaddafi committing to give up Libya's WMD was clouded by subsequent developments. In return for Qaddafi's commitment, President Bush and UK Prime Minister Tony Blair agreed to facilitate Libya's shedding of its pariah status and rejoining the community of nations. But then European governments and the Obama administration decided to intervene militarily in Libya's first civil war. Qaddafi's subsequent death in a ditch sent a cautionary message to Iran and North Korea that the West could not be trusted—and that giving up WMD does not produce the peace and security promised in return.

The collection and destruction of Libya's remaining WMD became more challenging as the country destabilized and arms proliferated to nonstate and terrorist groups. As this second Libyan civil war grew worse, the Libyan Government of National Accord requested in July 2016 that the Organization for the Prohibition of Chemical Weapons (OPCW) assist in the removal of the final Libyan caches of WMD materials and weapons—ending a chapter started by President Bush thirteen years prior.

In Syria, President Obama's declaration in 2012 that the use of chemical weapons by the Assad regime would cross a US red line and cause a military response was muddied when President Obama hesitated and ultimately abandoned the option of military force in response to such use. Instead, President Obama acceded to a Russian offer to facilitate access, inspection, and destruction of Syria's chemical weapons stockpiles. Further use of chemical weapons by Syria during the Trump administration showed that Assad had not lived up to the Russian deal.

Making matters more complicated, ISIS emerged in the war-torn areas of Syria and northern Iraq as a new, ruthless terrorist threat that concocted and used chemical weapons. Despite the OPCW's involvement, the Assad regime continued chemical attacks on major cities. To shield President Assad, Russia vetoed efforts to continue the OPCW-UN mandate. The Trump administration, which had warned that the Assad regime would "pay a heavy price" for further attacks, conducted retaliatory air strikes, alongside France and the UK, against Syrian chemical weapon facilities. The OPCW continues to investigate Syrian chemical attacks but is hampered by limited access to sites and information.

Efforts to stop Iran's pursuit of WMD (particularly nuclear weapons) have cast a long shadow over US national security policy over the past three administrations. The Bush administration's diplomatic efforts were in partnership initially with the so-called EU-3 (the UK, France, and Germany) and later with China and Russia as well (the "P-5 plus 1"). Combining active diplomacy with a coordinated effort to sanction Iran and deny it access to financial and material resources for its WMD and missile programs, an agreement was reached during the Bush administration under which Iran would freeze and then give up uranium enrichment and plutonium reprocessing (the two routes to a nuclear weapon) in exchange for sanctions relief and economic assistance. But Iran backed out of the deal.

The Obama administration rallied other nations and dramatically increased sanctions on Iran while mounting a new diplomatic effort. This two-track approach produced in July 2015 the Joint Comprehensive Plan of Action (JCPOA) establishing time-limited restrictions on Iran's various nuclear programs in return for the full removal of nuclear-related sanctions. When President Trump took office in January 2017, one of his early actions was to withdraw the United States from the JCPOA and reimpose many of the sanctions lifted in the previous administration. Over time Iran moved out from under key restraints of the JCPOA.

Elected in part as an Obama critic, President Trump entered the White House with an "America First" agenda, and initiated efforts to withdraw from several multilateral agreements (including the Paris Climate Accord, the Intermediate Nuclear Forces [INF] Treaty, the Open Skies Treaty, as well as the JCPOA) and even questioned long-standing US alliances like NATO. These actions yielded some reforms (such as increased contributions to alliance activities) but cast a shadow on traditional partnerships and ended several Obama-initiated multilateral efforts such as the Nuclear Security Summit.

After initially threatening a military confrontation with North Korea over its nuclear weapon and ballistic missile programs, President Trump turned to a one-on-one diplomatic approach to the North Korean leader seeking a strategic shift away from these programs and toward diplomatic and economic openness. This represented a bold step and a significant departure from the approach of his predecessors but was ultimately unavailing.

Domestically, President Trump expanded the Bush administration's E.O. 13324, making it easier for the State and Treasury Departments to designate terrorists seeking or proliferating WMD, and for Treasury to act when financial firms cooperate with terrorists and other bad actors. President Trump's 2018 National Strategy for Countering WMD Terrorism (WMD-T) reflected many of the Bush administration initiatives in its lines of effort to include: denying access, defeating plots, globalizing the counterproliferation fight, and enhancing the national defense against WMD-T.

Russia and China, often partners on WMD proliferation efforts under the Bush administration, have increasingly become proliferation problems and targets of these efforts. One more recent area of concern relates to the use of chemical weapons-grade poisons traced back to Russia. After the poisoning of a former Russian spy living in the UK, the Trump administration backed UK-led condemnation of Russia. President Trump also condemned Russia's support of continuing Syrian chemical weapon attacks on the Syrian population.

Additionally, there is increasing concern about China sending WMD technology and materials to countries seeking WMD weapons and delivery systems. Indeed, unclassified intelligence reports presented to Congress stated that China has been a "key supplier" of technology, notably by certain companies having important nuclear and missile capabilities.[1]

How Did the Bush Administration Do?

The Bush administration deserves credit for building up a counterproliferation regime designed to keep WMD out of the hands of rogue states and terrorists. Its policy framework and initiatives remain central to current efforts against WMD proliferation, are fully integrated into present-day policies, and underpin ongoing counterproliferation actions. The range of global partnerships, new tools, and legal authorities (to include tools to limit illicit financing, the lifeblood of proliferators, rogue states, and terrorist operations) have had a profound impact on how countries understand the proliferation trade, how they are organized to prevent it, and how they can partner to stop it. These partnerships have remained functioning and effective even when relationships between the United States and some of these countries have frayed over other foreign policy issues. President Bush's focus on

1. Shirley A. Kan, "China and Proliferation of Weapons of Mass Destruction and Missiles: Policy Issues," Congressional Research Service Report, January 5, 2015, https://sgp.fas .org/crs/nuke/RL31555.pdf.

counterproliferation helped promote the global norm that the proliferation of WMD should be as anathema as piracy or slavery.

Of course there have been setbacks. While the Bush administration made some progress in addressing the proliferation threats presented by Iran and North Korea, each of these countries continues to pose a significant proliferation challenge. Notably, however, there has not been the cascade or proliferation tsunami of new nuclear weapons states in Asia and the Middle East predicted by some experts. Very likely, North Korea had at least one nuclear weapon when the Bush administration entered office. But while the North Korea nuclear program is now far more advanced, no additional states have attained nuclear weapons and there have been no terrorism attacks using them. This is a singular achievement for which the Bush administration deserves its share of the credit.

The Bush administration routinely engaged the Chinese government seeking to prevent it from sending WMD technology and materials to countries like Iran, North Korea, and Syria, but this could have been elevated as a more central concern. Sanctions by the Bush administration against certain Chinese companies, including state-owned enterprises, were not enough to persuade China to halt these efforts. The Bush administration sought to convince China to use its broader engagement with North Korea and Iran to pressure them to halt their nuclear programs. While some progress was made, both the Bush and Obama administrations were unable to get the Chinese to exert the kind of decisive pressure that they believed China possessed.

As to Russia, even as it became a more challenging partner, cooperation on WMD proliferation continued. It is likely to remain an important area of strategic engagement with Russia now that the Biden administration has codified with Russia an extension of the New START Treaty and has initiated discussions on strategic stability.

Innovative arrangements like PSI and the Global Initiative to Combat Nuclear Terrorism, and global norms like those in UNSCR 1540, will continue to be important instruments in preserving nonproliferation norms and counterproliferation practices in the face of challenges by a risen China and a disruptive Russia to the rules-based global order. Unless the United States and its allies and friends remain united, however, the closer ties between China and Russia—and their mutual interest in using their relationships with Iran and North Korea for their own ends—will make it more difficult to maintain today's WMD proliferation architecture.

What Are the Lessons Learned?

- *To build lasting impact, use unilateral action by the United States to create a broad international effort.* President Bush's initiatives, such as the Global Threat Reduction Initiative, the G-8 Global Partnership, and PSI, each continued to grow, adapt, and expand during successive US administrations. Such global partnerships become essential spaces for international collaboration, joint programming, institutional capacity building, and collective response as well as for discussion and sharing of knowledge related to current WMD threats and trends.

- *Avoid initiative churn.* Shifting priorities between presidential administrations is an unavoidable reality but one that can undermine US counterproliferation efforts. The desire of a new administration to start fresh or refocus existing programs can disrupt the overall effort, undermine organizational morale, and leave partner countries confused and even hesitant to join US efforts. Such changes in direction may also suggest that the United States does not know what it is doing, which does not inspire confidence. The end of the Megaports initiative under the Obama administration is an example.

- *Stay engaged.* As national security attention turns toward great power competition and coping with dramatic technological change, there is a risk that the focus, effort, institutions, and processes developed to address WMD proliferation will be allowed to atrophy. While continuing to recruit and retain the leading WMD proliferation experts of today, the United States must also be educating and training the next generation. They must not only have the right technical skills but also have an appreciation for the policy frameworks and global partnerships that are critical parts of the counterproliferation architecture.

- *Develop more effective deterrence.* The lack of a more robust coordinated response to Russian and Syrian usage of chemical WMD suggests a potential unraveling of deterrence, at least in discrete cases. The sanctions imposed after such use clearly have not restored effective deterrence. How to do so is a current challenge for the United States and its WMD proliferation partners.

- *Set realistic goals.* In hindsight, Bush administration-led targets of 100 percent scanning of all incoming cargo under the SAFE Ports Act or the complete prohibition of enrichment and reprocessing (ENR) exports by the Nuclear Suppliers Group (NSG) proved unachievable. The former project continues to struggle with technological challenges and significant costs, while the latter was endorsed by the NSG under the Obama administration only as a recommendation to producers. Bold statements have their place in motivating and inspiring action. But success is often built incrementally, setting step-by-step goals for making progress over time.

- *Reinvigorate WMD partnerships.* A growing divide between democratic and authoritarian states and an increase in great power competition is creating cracks in long-standing cooperation on WMD proliferation. Future US administrations must continue to evolve and adapt the WMD proliferation frameworks, initiatives, and partnerships in the face of these challenges to preserve as much cooperation as possible among states that are now at odds over other issues.

Contributor:
Patti McNerney

CHAPTER 12

Turning Libya/Thwarting A. Q. Khan

WILLIAM TOBEY

While the Bush administration knew it faced nuclear proliferation problems in Iran, North Korea, and Iraq, dismantling Libya's weapons programs, as well as Abdul Qadeer Khan's proliferation network, were far from top of mind as it entered office in 2001. Nor should they have been, because Khan's work to spread uranium enrichment technology to Iran, Libya, North Korea, and elsewhere, as well as American intelligence efforts to track and stop him, were among America's most closely held secrets.

The 2000 Republican platform discussed nuclear proliferation at length, citing Iran, Iraq, and North Korea as transgressors, but omitting Libya. The platform's primary policy countering proliferation was missile defense.[1] A word search of the 2001 Inaugural Address reveals that its only mention of "proliferation" referred to prisons.[2] Moreover, since the Reagan administration, Libya had languished as a pariah, despite Clinton administration efforts to resolve the Lockerbie bombing issue.

---

1. "2000 Republican Party Platform," Republican Party Platforms, The American Presidency Project, updated July 31, 2000, https://www.presidency.ucsb.edu/documents/2000-republican-party-platform.
2. "President George W. Bush's Inaugural Address," The White House, updated January 20, 2001, https://georgewbush-whitehouse.archives.gov/news/inaugural-address.html.

All that changed between September 11, 2001 and December 19, 2003. The horror of the 9/11 attacks focused President Bush and his senior advisers on the danger of a convergence between dictators supporting terrorism and the proliferation of nuclear weapons. Violent autocrats long abounded, but by fall 2002, a nuclear proliferation tsunami also seemed to loom. In August 2002, a dissident Iranian group disclosed clandestine uranium enrichment and heavy water production facilities at Natanz and Arak in Iran.[3] Throughout summer 2002, reports of an illicit DPRK uranium enrichment program grew in number and detail, leading to a secret diplomatic mission to Pyongyang in October where, after being confronted by American diplomats, the North Koreans admitted to such a program.[4] Also in October 2002, a National Intelligence Estimate—*now known to have been deeply flawed*—judged that, "[I]f left unchecked, [Baghdad] probably will have a nuclear weapon during this decade. (See INR alternative view at the end of these Key Judgments.)"[5] Meanwhile, American intelligence watched A. Q. Khan making hundreds of millions of dollars marketing nuclear weapons technology to despots.

In the end, a combination of Bush administration diplomatic, military, intelligence, and sanctions policies—some successful and some not, some enlightened and some misguided—averted a nuclear proliferation cascade. The number of states with nuclear weapons today remains the same as it was three decades ago. The Transition Memoranda in this and later chapters recount what happened, what was accomplished, and what remained to be done in January 2009.

3. "Chronology of Iran's Nuclear Program," *New York Times*, August 8, 2005, https://www.nytimes.com/2005/08/08/international/chronology-of-irans-nuclear-program.html on December 20, 2020.

4. "U.S. 'Ready to Talk' with N. Korea," CNN, January 13, 2003, https://www.cnn.com/2003/WORLD/asiapcf/east/01/12/nkorea.nuclear/index.html.

5. "Key Judgments: Iraq's Continuing Programs for Weapons of Mass Destruction," National Intelligence Estimate, Central Intelligence Agency, October 2002, https://nsarchive2.gwu.edu/NSAEBB/NSAEBB129/nie.pdf.

TRANSITION MEMORANDUM

~~TOP SECRET~~ WITH

TOP SECRET

/FGI/NODIS/

NOFORN ATTACHMENTS

NATIONAL SECURITY COUNCIL
WASHINGTON, D.C. 20504
WASHINGTON, D.C. 20504

30135
Transition

NSC Declassification Review [E.O. 13526]
DECLASSIFY IN PART
by William C. Carpenter 3/23/2020

January 14, 2009

MEMORANDUM FOR THE RECORD

FROM: RENEE PAN, COUNTERPROLIFERATION STRATEGY
             JAMIE FLY, COUNTERPROLIFERATION STRATEGY

SUBJECT: U.S. Efforts to Turn Libya and Dismantle the A.Q.
             Khan Nuclear Proliferation Network

THE SITUATION AS WE FOUND IT:

Before this Administration took office,

When this Administration took office in January 2001,

~~TOP SECRET~~
Reason: 1.4 (b) (d)
Declassify on: 1/14/24

At the outset of this Administration, the President made clear his determination to employ all available tools—intelligence, diplomacy, sanctions, interdiction, and if necessary, military force—to counter the growing threat from WMD proliferation. (A comprehensive discussion of the U.S. counterproliferation strategy can be found in the transition memo on Counterproliferation Policy.) It was within this broader counterproliferation framework that the President directed the Administration's policy on the A.Q. Khan network and Libya's WMD programs.

The Administration's approach relied on close partnerships between the U.S. policy and intelligence communities as well as

Working with the U.K. significantly increased the resources available for our efforts. The President and Prime Minister Blair committed to dismantling the Khan network "root and branch."

In March 2003, Libya approached   with an offer of talks with the U.K. and U.S. to "clear the air" on Libya's WMD program. Initial contact was approved by the President, coordinated by a restricted NSC-led process,

In September 2003, we learned that a shipment of Khan network-origin centrifuge parts would be shipped aboard the *BBC China* from Malaysia to Libya's nuclear program. In coordination with security liaison partners in Germany and Italy, and in the spirit of the then four-and-a-half month old Proliferation Security Initiative, the United States and U.K. redirected the *BBC China* to Taranto, Italy for inspection of the cargo. The shipping containers aboard the vessel were confirmed to contain thousands of centrifuge parts manufactured in Malaysia by the Khan network.

Confronted by evidence of a clandestine nuclear program, Libya consented to two on-site visits by U.S.-U.K. technical teams. Policy-level engagement with Libya in London commenced when Libya admitted to having WMD programs and committed to verifiably eliminate those programs. The United States and U.K. required a clear, public Libyan statement on possession and elimination at the outset before we would take positive steps to improve relations and remove barriers to Libya's reintegration into the international community. During these policy discussions, Prime Minister

Blair was in direct contact with Qadhafi, the President maintained regular with Prime Minister Blair, and the President also conveyed a personal message to Qadhafi These contacts proved useful in pressing for a strategic decision by Libya at the highest level to publicly give up its WMD programs.

The December 19, 2003, announcements by Qadhafi, Libyan Foreign Minister Shalgham, Prime Minister Blair, and the President cemented this arrangement. Libya disclosed to the United States and U.K. significant information about its nuclear and chemical weapons programs as well as information on its biological and ballistic missile-related activities. Libya also committed to accept international inspections and monitoring to verify the information it provided to the United States and U.K.

Libya's pledge to give up its WMD and Missile Technology Control Regime (MTCR)-class ballistic missile programs was a significant step forward for the Administration's nonproliferation efforts. The United States used the promise of improved relations with the United States and its allies as leverage with Libya to ensure that Libya made good on its assurances in a staged process where Libya's dismantlement actions were met action-for-action with a lifting of existing restrictions and improvement in relations. Libya's decision thus highlighted the benefits available to states that verifiably abandon their WMD programs in contrast to the isolation they face if they decide to continue their pursuit of WMD. As the President stated on December 19, 2003, "Leaders who abandon the pursuit of chemical, biological, and nuclear weapons, and the means to deliver them, will find an open path to better relations with the United States and other free nations."

The inevitable public exposure of the A.Q. Khan network that accompanied the December 19 announcements on Libya gave momentum to   efforts with other countries to take down the A.Q. Khan network. A takedown strategy that engaged diplomatic   and law enforcement counterparts in countries where the network operated— including Turkey, Pakistan, UAE, South Africa, and Malaysia—was implemented to investigate, prosecute, and punish individuals and companies involved   Working with the International Atomic Energy Agency (IAEA), the United States also launched a multilateral effort to strengthen the international safeguards regime and to plug export control loopholes to ensure that the network was not reconstituted and that other proliferators would not follow the route of A.Q. Khan.

WHAT HAS BEEN ACCOMPLISHED:

- **Discovered full extent of Libya's WMD and missile programs.** Libya's WMD and missile programs were more advanced than we believed. Tripoli possessed a nuclear weapons program, as well as specialized equipment and materials for P2 centrifuge rotor production, and was working on obtaining a domestic production capability for uranium hexafluoride (UF6). Tripoli had also acquired nuclear weapons design documents from the Khan network. Libya possessed a chemical weapons (CW) stockpile of roughly 25 tons of sulfur mustard, aerial bombs for the mustard agent, and small amounts of nerve agent. In addition, Libya had many Missile Technology Control Regime (MTCR) Category I missile items, including five SCUD C missiles and associated transporter-erector launchers (TELs) and related equipment as well as more than 400 SCUD B missiles and related equipment. After several visits to Libya and discussions with Libyan officials and experts, ▮▮▮▮▮▮▮▮▮▮▮▮▮▮▮▮▮▮▮▮▮▮▮ Libya did not possess a biological weapons program.

- **Compelled Libya to verifiably dismantle its WMD and MTCR-class missile programs.** Specifically, Libya has:
  - Turned all nuclear weapons design documents (received from the A.Q. Khan network), centrifuge components, and containers of UF6 over to the United States;
  - Removed more than 15 kilograms of fresh high enriched uranium reactor fuel to Russia;
  - Permitted the United States, U.K., IAEA, the Organization for the Prohibition of Chemical Weapons (OPCW), and other relevant international organizations, to verify the elimination of its WMD/missile programs;
  - Declared all nuclear activities to the IAEA and acceded to the Additional Protocol;
    - Eliminated its MTCR-Category I SCUD C missiles, associated TELs, and related missile equipment;
  - Acceded to the Chemical Weapons Convention (CWC);
  - Terminated its CW program and completed destruction of more than 3,500 unfilled chemical bombs and CW production equipment;
  - Agreed to deadlines for destruction of remaining CW stockpile; and
  - Pledged bilaterally to the United States that it will end all military trade with Iran, North Korea, and Syria.

- **Improved the U.S.-Libyan bilateral relationship.** Libya's willingness to dismantle its WMD programs set the stage for additional improvements in the U.S.-Libyan bilateral relationship. This included the reestablishment in 2004 of a U.S. diplomatic presence in Tripoli for the first time since 1979 as well as rescission of Libya's designation as a state sponsor of terrorism and revocation of Executive Order sanctions against Libya. Moreover, Libya has agreed to compensate U.S. citizen victims of Libyan terrorism under a claims settlement agreement signed in 2008. Despite this rapprochement in U.S.-Libya relations, the United States has made clear to Libya that future progress in the U.S.-Libyan relationship will depend on progress made in other areas such as human rights.

- **Mobilized governments to take enforcement actions against A.Q. Khan associates and ensure that the network is not reconstituted.**
  - Pakistan investigated A.Q. Khan and placed him under virtual house arrest from 2004–2008. In July 2008, a Pakistani court ordered an end to Khan's confinement. Khan can now travel within Pakistan, meet with friends and family, receive treatment from any doctor of his choice, and conduct research on topics cleared by the Pakistan Science Foundation. As of July 2008, Khan was not allowed to speak to the press, and the GOP will continue to monitor his activities. The U.S. Ambassador in Islamabad has stressed repeatedly to Pakistan's current political leadership the need to maintain restrictions on Khan.
  - South Africa reached plea agreements with Gerhard Wisser and Daniel Geiges, both centrifuge technology manufacturers for the network. The SAG is still pursuing prosecution against Gotthard Lerch, another gas centrifuge supplier.
  - Germany is also prosecuting Gotthard Lerch. His trial began in June 2008; a verdict is not expected until 2009.
  - Malaysia detained B.S.A. Tahir, principal middleman and Khan network financier, from 2004–2008 under Malaysia's Internal Security Act. Tahir was released in 2008 on "suspended detention" status and subsequently placed under restrictions by Malaysian authorities. Current restrictions include continued monitoring, a ban on international travel, and a prohibition on meeting with the media.

- **Discovered A.Q. Khan network support to Iranian and North Korean nuclear programs.** In addition to supporting Libya's covert nuclear weapons program, Khan also provided support to Iran and North Korea's nuclear programs. Iran purchased first-generation centrifuge designs and components in the early 1990s from Khan's network; by the late 1990s, the network had supplied Iran with parts for hundreds of centrifuges. In addition, Khan visited North Korea multiple times. In his confession, he claimed that he provided North Korea with P-1 and P-2 centrifuges along with drawings, sketches, technical data, depleted UF6, and technical assistance.

- **Strengthened the IAEA's ability to pursue its safeguards mandate.** The IAEA has gained access to Khan network associates and cooperation from governments where the network operated. The IAEA thus received critical information that allowed it to move forward on the Libyan, Iranian, and North Korean nuclear files.

FUTURE CHALLENGES:

Ensure that Libya fulfills its commitments. While Libya has met many of its December 2003 commitments, it still has several important tasks to complete. Libya needs to:

- Eliminate its remaining CW agent and precursor stocks by the OPCW-established deadlines of December 31, 2010 (for the mustard agent) and December 31, 2011 (for remaining CW agents and chemical precursors). To this end, Libya recently contracted with an Italian firm to design and build a CW destruction facility.
- Eliminate its remaining MTCR-class missiles by September 2009 (when a replacement for these missiles is obtained). Libya still possesses more than 400 MTCR Category I SCUD B missiles and related equipment. Libya maintains that it has been unable to find a replacement system compliant with MTCR standards. The United States is working with Libya to find a missile system that does not exceed MTCR standards that can replace the SCUD Bs.

The United States and U.K. will need to continue to engage Libya on these issues to ensure that it fulfills its 2003 commitments in their entirety.

Prevent emergence of future A.Q. Khans.

In order to dissuade others from following the route of A.Q. Khan and to make such proliferation activity more difficult and costly, the United States needs to continue to keep pressure on foreign governments to:

- prosecute and penalize key Khan network members;
- close export control loopholes that allowed such a network to operate on their soil; and
- pass laws imposing stiff penalties for proliferation-related offenses.

The United States should also continue to work with key partners to:

- encourage continued cooperation with the IAEA's investigation of the Khan network and the network's relationship with Iran, North Korea, and possibly other customers; and
- work to ensure that the free trade zones around the world do not become safe havens for proliferation trade.

Hold A.Q. Khan network associates accountable. A sanctions package that would consider sanctions on more than 40 Khan network-related companies and individuals was delayed, inter alia, due to complicated issues arising from highly classified intelligence downgrades.[1] The

---

1. The information on which the sanctions package is based is derived from highly classified sources. Completion of the package was delayed due to the need to ensure the information disclosed in the sanctions package met the legal standard of the Nuclear Nonproliferation Prevention Act (NPPA) of 1994, the Export Import Bank Act, Executive Order 12938,

package is now in the final stages of completion. The United States should expeditiously impose sanctions against the Khan network to publicly expose those involved, help buttress the pending legal cases in other countries, propel others to take similar actions, and ensure that network elements do not reengage in proliferation.

Seek answers on DPRK and Iran. We should also leverage the GOP's desire to close the Khan chapter to gain answers from the GOP and from Khan himself to critical outstanding questions related to the DPRK and Iran nuclear files, consistent with the June 2008 Deputies-approved strategy. Toward this end, we should continue to find opportunities to engage senior GOP officials on these questions.

Attachments

Tab 1   Chronology for Libya
Tab 2   Chronology for A.Q. Khan Network
Tab 3   Restricted Handling Chronology for A.Q. Khan Network
Tab 4   Presidential Message to Qadhafi, November 22, 2003
Tab 5   Memorandum of Conversation of the President's Conversation with Tony Blair, December 10, 2003
Tab 6   U.K. Evaluation of Second Technical Visit, December 14, 2003
Tab 7   Libyan Foreign Minister Statement, December 19, 2003
Tab 8   Qadhafi Statement, December 19, 2003
Tab 9   Prime Minister Blair Statement, December 19, 2003
Tab 10   President Bush Statement, December 19, 2003
Tab 11   White House Fact Sheet, December 19, 2003
Tab 12
Tab 13   Diplomatic Strategy for Rolling Up A.Q. Khan Network, February 18, 2004
Tab 14   President's NDU Speech, February 13, 2004
Tab 15   White House Fact Sheet, February 13, 2004
Tab 16   President's SVTC with Tony Blair, February 17, 2004
Tab 17   President's Letter to Turkish Prime Minister, April 7, 2004
Tab 18   U.S. Briefing to Nuclear Suppliers Group, May 2004
Tab 19   U.S. Briefing to Nuclear Suppliers Group, October 2004
Tab 20   Deputies-approved Next Steps on A.Q. Khan, June 2008

---

as amended, and Executive Order 13382, while protecting sources and methods and ongoing operational equities. Furthermore, information bolstering the legal cases continued to become available as other countries concluded their own investigations.

POSTSCRIPT

WILLIAM TOBEY

Despite his crushing workload months after the 9/11 attacks, in late November 2001, CIA Director George Tenet boarded a plane at Andrews Air Force Base[6] and flew 14,000 miles round trip for a one-hour meeting. What matter could be so urgent and so important for him to spend more than a day cooped up in an airplane for a one-hour meeting? Tenet and Rolf Mowatt-Larssen, who was charged with finding and stopping al Qaeda's WMD efforts, were off to meet Pakistani President Pervez Musharraf in Islamabad.

When Tenet gave Mowatt-Larssen his assignment the previous month, he told him, "Three weeks before 9/11, we received information from a close liaison partner that a Pakistani nuclear scientist was working with Bin Laden. The same scientist offered his services to other 'Arab states.' God knows what he told al-Qaeda. In the last few days, we confirmed that there were several Pakistani scientists in discussion[s] with al-Qaeda about WMD. We don't know how far along they got."[7] In Islamabad, Tenet opened by telling Musharraf that a "consortium of Pakistani scientists and military officers had met with senior members of the Taliban and al-Qaeda to discuss supplying the terrorist group with chemical, biological, and nuclear weapons and expertise. The [consortium] offered weapons of mass destruction to the Taliban and al-Qaeda. Osama Bin Laden himself was involved in the negotiations."[8]

Musharraf resisted, saying, "Men in caves cannot do this." He further argued that nuclear weapons did not fit al Qaeda's *modus operandi*, which relied on simpler methods. Tenet and Mowatt-Larssen persisted, citing specific connections between al Qaeda and Pakistani scientists, and raising the issue of Pakistani nuclear security.[9] At Tenet's prompting, Mowatt-Larssen acknowledged Musharraf's point, but countered:

Al-Qaeda's interest in nukes surprised us too. We first heard about it before 9/11. We learned that Osama Bin Laden and Ayman Zawahiri met with

---

6. Renamed Joint Base Andrews on October 1, 2009.

7. Rolf Mowatt-Larssen, *A State of Mind: Faith and the CIA* (self-pub., 2020), 222.

8. Mowatt-Larssen, *A State of Mind*, 226.

9. Mowatt-Larssen, *A State of Mind*, 226–27.

Bashiruddin Mahmud in Afghanistan. Mahmud was the head of your plutonium [production] reactor, right? A year before 9/11, Mahmud and Bin Laden were sitting around the campfire in Kandahar, having dinner. Bin Laden asked Mahmud for advice on how al-Qaeda could get their hands on nuclear weapons. Mahmud replied that it would be too hard, too expensive for al-Qaeda to pursue nuclear weapons. Bin Laden wasn't satisfied with that answer. He asked your man, 'What if I already have the material?'[10]

Again, Musharraf deflected, "I have spoken with my top nuclear man, Dr. Abdul Qadeer Khan, on this matter. Dr. Khan assured me that there is nothing to these contacts between extremists and our scientists. He dismisses Dr. Mahmoud as being a crackpot."[11] As the meeting ended, Mowatt-Larssen told Musharraf, "It would be a good time to physically inventory all of your nuclear material. Don't count lots. Eyeball every weapon. Every gram. You can't be too thorough to make sure everything is accounted for."[12]

Two years later, in a New York City hotel suite, Tenet told Musharraf that his "top nuclear man," A. Q. Khan, had for years peddled Pakistani nuclear weapons technology and materials to Iran, Libya, North Korea, and others. Tenet almost gloated, "Khan has stolen your nuclear weapons secrets. We know this because we stole them from him."[13] Of course, Tenet had known all this when he met Musharraf in Islamabad but could not reveal it until the United States and its allies were ready to roll up the Khan network.

The Bush Administration Approach

The removal of uranium enrichment centrifuges, a uranium conversion facility, uranium hexafluoride, nuclear weapon design documents—in 2004—and 20 kg of highly enriched uranium research reactor fuel—in 2004 and 2006—gutted Libya's nuclear weapons program. In the nuclear realm, the disarmament was complete.

---

10. Mowatt-Larssen, *A State of Mind*, 227.

11. Musharraf's answer, despite no prior explanation of the purpose of Tenet's mission, even to US embassy officials, may have unconsciously revealed that the Pakistani president was already concerned about nuclear security problems. Mowatt-Larssen believes this is a possibility.

12. Mowatt-Larssen, *A State of Mind*, 229.

13. "Tenet showed nuclear blueprints to Musharraf," Dawn (website) May 1, 2007, https://www.dawn.com/news/244904.

Efforts to eliminate Libya's chemical weapons proved more difficult. The Libyans were less candid about this program, initially declaring only 750 unfilled chemical munitions, but eventually destroying *over 3,000* such weapons.[14] Moreover, disposing of chemical weapons agent is costly and difficult. Thus, at the uprising in 2011, according to declarations, 11.3 tons of mustard agent and 845 tons of precursors remained in Libya, awaiting destruction, about half the original stocks.[15] Worse, Libya's National Transitional Council and the Organization for the Prohibition of Chemical Weapons (OPCW) disclosed that the Qaddafi government retained hundreds of undeclared chemical artillery shells[16] and the sulfur mustard agent to fill them, purchased from Iran over many years—a clear violation of both understandings with the United States and the United Kingdom and the Chemical Weapons Convention.[17] Operations in 2016 and 2017 undertaken by twelve countries, including the United States, and the OPCW, destroyed all remaining Libyan chemical agents and precursors.[18]

In 2003 and 2004, US and British experts found no evidence of an active Libyan biological weapons program, and none has since come to light. The 2004 disarmament efforts eliminated Libya's most capable ballistic missiles, SCUD-Cs. A follow-on agreement allowed Libya to retain 417 SCUD-Bs until replacement defensive weapons could be obtained or the missiles were converted to a lower range/payload capability. In any event, neither outcome was achieved before Qaddafi fell.[19] His forces fired at least three such missiles against the rebels. It remains to be seen what will become of the balance of the missiles.[20]

---

14. William Tobey, "A Message from Tripoli, Part 3, How Libya Gave Up its WMD," The Bulletin of the Atomic Scientists (website), December 5, 2014, https://thebulletin.org/2014/12/a-message-from-tripoli-part-3-how-libya-gave-up-its-wmd/.

15. Nathan E. Busch and Joseph F. Pilat, "Disarming Libya? A Reassessment after the Arab Spring," *International Affairs* 89, no. 2 (March 2013): 461–62, https://www-jstor-org.ezp-prod1.hul.harvard.edu/stable/pdf/23473546.pdf?refreqid=excelsior%3A21f59b19a2ec0cd4d9fedb924b4b1486.

16. Libya declared only aerial bombs, not artillery shells, as munitions it possessed.

17. Busch and Pilat, "Disarming Libya?," 461–62.

18. "Libya and the OPCW," OPCW (website), undated document, https://www.opcw.org/media-centre/featured-topics/libya-and-opcw.

19. Busch and Pilat, "Disarming Libya?," 459.

20. "Libya—Missile," Nuclear Threat Initiative (website), January 2015, https://www.nti.org/learn/countries/libya/delivery-systems/.

Of more lasting consequence will be the lessons drawn from Qaddafi's decision to give up his WMD programs and the subsequent damage done by the US and European military intervention resulting in Qaddafi's overthrow. While academics may debate the precise role that the Iraq War played in Qaddafi's calculus, to policymakers, the linkage was inescapable. Qaddafi had long been looking for a way to get out of the pariah box, and the US commitment to forcible counterproliferation so vividly on display in the Iraq invasion gave his quest renewed urgency. Yet what President Bush had in mind was not serial invasions to enforce WMD disarmament, but rather a new muscular approach to diplomacy.

When President Bush first discussed the possibility of eliminating the Libyan nuclear and chemical weapons programs with UK Prime Minister Tony Blair at Camp David in March 2003, they both saw the opportunity for a new model of WMD disarmament, even as the Iraq war unfolded. Diplomacy and mutual interest, not military force, would be the key to the model. They would demand evidence of a "strategic decision" by Libya to renounce such weapons. They would expect candor and compliance, not grudging half measures. They would offer to welcome Libya back into the community of nations once the disarmament was complete. In short, they sought to establish a nonproliferation model that was the opposite of the American experiences with Iraq (military intervention) and North Korea (protracted and ultimately unsuccessful negotiations).[21]

For a time, it worked. Libya divested its nuclear, chemical, and longer-range missile programs. It compensated the victims of the Pan Am 103 and UTA 772 bombings. The United States and Libya reestablished diplomatic relations in 2004, and the United States removed Libya from its list of state sponsors of terror. Washington lifted sanctions, and Western aid and investment began to flow, although not in amounts that satisfied Tripoli. Libya's return to the community of nations was confirmed by its election to the United Nations Security Council in October 2007—unimaginable even five years earlier.

What Has Happened Since the End of the Bush Administration?

Libya   In 2011, the Arab Spring swept North Africa. In Libya, protests grew into rebellion, which escalated into civil war. By autumn, France, the United Kingdom,

---

21. Tobey, "A Message from Tripoli, Part 2," https://thebulletin.org/2014/12/a-message -from-tripoli-part-2-how-libya-gave-up-its-wmd/.

and the United States launched cruise missile and air strikes to prevent a massacre of civilians at Benghazi by government forces. NATO's intervention also tipped the military balance. After missile strikes halted his escape convoy from the 2011 Battle of Sirte, rebel forces eventually pulled Qaddafi from a drainpipe and killed him.

The impact on global nonproliferation efforts was no less dramatic. North Korea's official news agency opined in 2016: "The Saddam Hussein regime in Iraq and the Qaddafi regime in Libya could not escape the fate of destruction after being deprived of their foundations for nuclear development and giving up nuclear programs of their own accord."[22] Leaders in North Korea, Iran, and perhaps elsewhere must have wondered why should they forego nuclear weapons given Qaddafi's fate. Robert Joseph, who negotiated the disarmament deal with Libya, observed that the Obama administration "made the decision to intervene without a day-after plan or any sense of what nonproliferation message that would send."[23]

Confirming Joseph's charge requires proving a negative, that nonproliferation issues were not considered during deliberations on military intervention in Libya—a tough task, but there are clues. Former Secretary of State Hillary Clinton, who supported the action, devotes eight pages of her memoir to discussions on whether or not to intervene in Libya, citing pros and cons, but makes no mention of nonproliferation issues.[24] More tellingly, former Secretary of Defense Robert Gates, who led the opposition to intervention within the Obama administration, and who devoted five pages of a recent book to the Libya decision, said he argued at the time, "Qaddafi had given up his nuclear program and posed no threat to US interests." If he extended his argument to the deleterious effects on *future* nonproliferation efforts of deposing a dictator who had chosen to disarm, he made no mention of them, nor did he cite them as one of two "strategic mistakes" made in the Libya intervention.[25] In an earlier memoir, Gates said he

22. Uri Friedman, "The Word that Derailed the Trump-Kim Summit," *The Atlantic*, May 24, 2018, https://www.theatlantic.com/international/archive/2018/05/libya-trump-kim/561158/.

23. Peter Baker, "Libya as a Model For Disarmament? North Korea May See It Very Differently," *New York Times*, April 29, 2018, https://www.nytimes.com/2018/04/29/us/politics/bolton-libya-north-korea-trump.html.

24. Hillary Rodham Clinton, *Hard Choices* (New York: Simon and Schuster, 2014), 298–306.

25. Robert M. Gates, *Exercise of Power: American Failures, Successes, and a New Path Forward in the Post-Cold War World* (New York: Alfred A. Knopf, 2020), 297–302.

made three arguments against using force against Qaddafi; none involved non-proliferation issues.[26]

Michael Lewis spent six months shadowing President Obama during the period of the Libya decision. He reported the key Situation Room meeting on Libya in detail but made no reference to nonproliferation considerations.[27] President Obama only reluctantly authorized the use of force in Libya and recounts his deliberations over nine pages in his memoir but makes no mention of nonproliferation concerns.[28] A former Obama administration NSC official, when asked whether the nonproliferation office was consulted during the Libya deliberations, responded, "Oh, God no! You know the regional people."[29] All decisions taken in the Oval Office are hard ones—otherwise they would be made at lower levels. All involve tradeoffs, risks, and uncertainties.[30] The decision to intervene in Libya is defensible. What is inexplicable and indefensible is the absence of *even a discussion* of its nonproliferation ramifications.

If the Obama administration damaged the "Libya model" of WMD disarmament, the Trump administration destroyed it. In the days before the 2018 Singapore Summit between US President Donald Trump and North Korea's Kim Jong-un, then-National Security Adviser John Bolton cited the Libya model as his approach to the North Korea problem, meaning that he was looking for evidence of "a strategic decision" by the North to abandon nuclear weapons—not the example of a dictator dead in a ditch.[31] Nonetheless, North Korean negotiator Kim Kye Gwan erupted, "It is absolutely absurd to dare compare [North Korea], a nuclear weapon state, to Libya which had been at the initial stage of nuclear development.

---

26. Robert M. Gates, *Duty: Memoirs of a Secretary at War* (New York: Alfred A. Knopf, 2014), 511.

27. Michael Lewis, "Obama's Way," *Vanity Fair*, September 11, 2012, https://www.vanityfair.com/news/2012/10/michael-lewis-profile-barack-obama.

28. Barack Obama, *A Promised Land* (New York: Crown, 2020), 653–62.

29. Telephone interview with the author, January 13, 2021.

30. President Obama himself explained to Lewis: "Nothing comes to my desk that is perfectly solvable. Otherwise, someone else would have solved it. So you wind up dealing with probabilities. Any given decision you make you'll wind up with a 30 to 40 percent chance that it isn't going to work. You have to own that and feel comfortable with the way you made the decision. You can't be paralyzed by the fact that it might not work out."

31. "John Bolton on Push to Rid North Korea of Nuclear Weapons," Fox News Sunday transcript, April 29, 2918, https://www.foxnews.com/transcript/john-bolton-on-push-to-rid-north-korea-of-nuclear-weapons.

The world knows too well that our country is neither Libya nor Iraq which have met miserable fates."[32]

President Trump then made matters worse by accepting the DPRK's interpretation of the "Libya model" over his own National Security Adviser's and by offering North Korea "protections" to smooth things over.[33] He went on to say: "We went in and decimated [Qaddafi]. And we did the same thing with Iraq. That model would take place if we don't make a deal, most likely. But if we make a deal, I think Kim Jong-un is going to be very, very happy."[34] Then-Vice President Mike Pence also put his foot in it, saying, "This will only end like the Libya model ended if Kim Jong-un doesn't make a deal."[35] Thus, the Trump administration managed to turn the Libya model, which was intended to involve a strategic decision to divest of WMD because of self-interest, into a threat of regime change—and to underline with a figurative Sharpie, the lesson that dictators who brandish nuclear weapons are safer than those who renounce them.

Khan   While the Transition Memorandum expressed confidence in the "takedown strategy" employed against the Khan network, it also recommended the Obama administration "keep pressure on foreign governments to prosecute and penalize key Khan network members." This did not happen. By 2011, one analyst concluded that: "Prosecuting those involved in this proliferation network, however, has proved difficult. Today none of the people associated with the Khan network remain in prison."[36] Indeed, Khan himself, who had been subject to on-and-off house arrest for about five years, was fully exonerated two weeks into the Obama administration by Pakistan's highest court.[37] Khan and his ring of nuclear proliferators in Europe, Africa, and Asia trafficked weapons technology that could kill millions, but served less jail time than might be expected from a

---

32. Friedman, "The Word that Derailed the Trump-Kim Summit."

33. Friedman, "The Word that Derailed the Trump-Kim Summit."

34. Friedman, "The Word that Derailed the Trump-Kim Summit."

35. Friedman, "The Word that Derailed the Trump-Kim Summit."

36. Eben Harrell, "Nuclear Proliferation: The Crime with No Punishment," *Time*, September 16, 2011, http://content.time.com/time/world/article/0,8599,2092585,00.html.

37. Saeed Shah, "Pakistan Releases 'Father' of Nuclear Bomb from House Arrest," *The Guardian*, February 6, 2009, https://www.theguardian.com/world/2009/feb/06/nuclear-pakistan-khan.

US armed robbery conviction.[38] This result is both unjust and a nonproliferation policy failure.

How Did the Bush Administration Do?

Although oddly omitted from the Libya Transition Memorandum, the institutional innovations designed by the Bush administration to prevent the recurrence of illicit proliferation networks fared far better than the subsequent efforts to punish the perpetrators.[39] For example, United Nations Security Council Resolution 1540, which requires all nations to enact and enforce effective export controls, secure proliferation sensitive materials, and criminalize proliferation by nonstate actors, was initially controversial. By 2011, however, that had changed: "Since its adoption in 2004, international perceptions of Resolution 1540 have shifted from controversy over its legitimacy to general acceptance of its role in preventing the spread of weapons of mass destruction to non-state actors."[40]

Similarly, the Proliferation Security Initiative, the Global Initiative to Combat Nuclear Terrorism, and new techniques for imposing financial sanctions— all innovations in response to the Khan network—remained useful tools under both the Obama and Trump administrations. As to Libya, the Bush administration succeeded in its tactical objectives of peacefully dismantling Libya's WMD programs. And it tentatively established a new model for countering WMD proliferation—a strategic decision to disarm in return for diplomatic and economic benefits—that substituted diplomacy for military action. But because of actions by subsequent administrations, this new, more compelling model for disarmament was ultimately discredited.

What Are the Lessons Learned?

- *Successful policy requires acknowledging and building on the accomplishments of predecessor administrations.* At their best, presidential campaigns are built on a belief that America can do better. That is constructive. The natural and unfortunate obverse of this tenet is a tendency to ignore or to denigrate the

---

38. About ten years.

39. These innovations were mentioned briefly in a separate Transition Memorandum.

40. Cole J. Harvey, "Two Steps Forward, One Step Back: Slow, But Steady Progress Implementing UNSCR 1540," Nuclear Threat Initiative (NTI), July 20, 2011, https://www.nti.org/analysis/articles/unscr-1540/.

accomplishments of prior administrations. The takedown of the Khan proliferation network and the dismantlement of Libya's illicit weapons programs
were signal accomplishments. Moreover, they once offered *a model for more
successful nonproliferation efforts*—avoiding both war and endless wrangling
without true disarmament. Sadly, it is now generally accepted common
knowledge that dictators with nuclear weapons are safer than those without
them—just the opposite of what Saif Qaddafi concluded in 2003.[41]

- *Failure to consider proliferation impacts risks sacrificing proliferation objectives to the law of unintended consequences.* To be sure, the choices facing
President Obama were hard. Nonproliferation goals often compete with other
important national security interests. Preventing the slaughter of civilians is
a manifestly worthy objective. The decision to intervene militarily in Libya,
however, led to a strategic defeat in the campaign to halt or reverse the
spread of nuclear weapons.

---

41. Tobey, "A Message from Tripoli, Part 5," https://thebulletin.org/2014/12/a-message
-from-tripoli-part-5-how-libya-gave-up-its-wmd/.

CHAPTER 13

Iran

MICHAEL SINGH

Iran has been a vexing national security challenge for successive US administrations since the country's 1979 revolution saw the American-allied shah overthrown and replaced by a theocratic regime hostile to Washington and its regional partners. Throughout the 1980s and 1990s, the chief threat posed by the Iranian regime was terrorism; indeed, prior to 9/11, Iranian proxies were responsible for more American terrorism-related deaths than any other forces. The Reagan, George H. W. Bush, and Clinton administrations dealt with Tehran using a variety of tools—sanctions, military force, and diplomatic engagement, which, while occasionally promising, rarely yielded meaningful results.

During the George W. Bush administration, Iran became a growing national security focus for a different reason—its expanding nuclear program, which was judged by the US intelligence community to be directed at developing nuclear weapons. Preventing nuclear proliferation had long been a top priority of US national security policy. Iran presented a particularly alarming challenge, given that as it pursued its nuclear ambitions it was simultaneously expanding and enhancing its ballistic missile capability, continuing to support terrorism, training and equipping nonstate proxy forces, and proliferating dangerous and destabilizing conventional weapons such as precision-guided missiles and improvised explosive devices, all aimed at undermining governments in the region and oppressing the Iranian people.

TRANSITION MEMORANDUM

~~TOP - SECRET~~   6091

NATIONAL SECURITY COUNCIL   REDO

WASHINGTON, D.C. 20504   Transition

NSC Declassification Review [E.O. 13526]
DECLASSIFY IN PART   January 16, 2009
by William C. Carpenter 3/23/2020

MEMORANDUM FOR THE RECORD

FROM: KELLY MAGSAMEN, NEAR EAST AND NORTH AFRICA
             DIRECTORATE

SUBJECT: Our Approach to Iran

THE SITUATION AS WE FOUND IT:

The Situation in Iran. In 2000, Iran's reformist President and his supporters in the legislature were faltering and failing to meet their promises on reform. The vast majority of the Iranian people had voted in favor of President Khatami's platform for greater internal economic reform and development, political and social freedoms, and the rule of law. But Khatami did not deliver: unemployment and inflation were near 30 percent. Iran had become the world's leader in "brain drain," with one of every four Iranian university degree holders living outside the country.

As the Iranian people began to realize that President Khatami was not reforming as quickly as they would like, student movements and opposition newspapers grew restless. In response, after a brief loosening, the regime shut down much of the independent and pro-reform media. Supreme leader Khamenei and other hardliners were consistently able to checkmate the reformists. Many Iranians abandoned hope that "reformists" could produce economic progress and democratic change under the present system.

President Khatami pursued a slightly increased degree of openness with the international community, but he also sustained the regime's attempts to build nuclear weapons and to support extremists and terrorists in the region. By 2001, Tehran continued to arm Palestinian terrorist groups as well as Hizballah, which gained power both politically and militarily as Israel withdrew from southern Lebanon in May 2000.

~~TOP SECRET~~
Reason: 1.4(c) (d)
Declassify on: 1/16/19

Re-Classified by: Ellen J. L. Knight
Reason: 1.4(b), (c), and (d)
Declassify on: 1/16/2034

Relations with the United States. From 1993-1997, the Clinton Administration expressed willingness to engage in government-to-government dialogue with Iran, without preconditions. Following the election of President Khatami, from December 1997 - March 2000 the United States pursued high-level talks with the Iranian Government. The Iranian regime rejected all these overtures. The United States' overtures included, in August 1999, a letter from President Clinton to President Khatami inviting dialogue. The Iranian regime refused the offer, and the Supreme Leader Ali Khamenei publicly denounced the United States. While higher-level talks never came to fruition, the "Six Plus Two" group on Afghanistan continued at lower levels.

The Department of State observed the following about United States-Iran interaction in the 1990s:

- The United States made virtually all the overtures.
- The United States consistently stated its readiness to engage in bilateral talks without preconditions.
- Iran responded to U.S. overtures by demanding "confidence-building measures" or "a change in Washington's behavior." Iran considered United States policies "hostile," and indicative of a lack of "readiness" for United States-Iran dialogue. When the United States reached out to meet Iran's preconditions, Iran increased its demands.

THIS ADMINISTRATION'S POLICY:

The Iranian regime presents a significant strategic and ideological challenge to the United States. The regime oppresses the people of Iran, undermines stability by providing lethal assistance to militant groups in Iraq and Afghanistan, supports terrorism globally, backs Hamas actions to frustrate Israeli/Palestinian peace efforts, uses extremists and terrorists to threaten and intimidate the region's emerging democracies and moderate governments, openly threatens Israel, and finally seeks weapons of mass destruction and their means of delivery including technologies and capabilities that will one day allow it to develop a nuclear weapon—which exacerbates all these threats. Tehran aims to extend its dominance throughout the region and spread its radical ideology throughout the world, including vulnerable parts of Africa and Latin America. Iran uses all the tools of its own national power—ranging from economic blackmail to lethal assistance—to subvert the international system, foment instability, and develop alternative power centers that cater to its goals.

The regime also has significant vulnerabilities, mostly due to ▮▮▮▮▮▮▮▮▮ and its increased isolation from the international system. A profound Iranian contradiction augments these vulnerabilities: Iran rejects the same international system in which it so desperately wants to achieve status. Fundamentally the United States seeks to sharpen the choice for Iran. The regime could either suspend its nuclear enrichment activities and achieve direct talks with the United States, or face continued and widened isolation on all fronts. We have always made clear that we do not oppose

Iran's right to pursue civilian nuclear energy for peaceful purposes, but Iran needs to answer the questions posed by the International Atomic Energy Agency (IAEA), comply with United Nations Security Council resolutions (UNSCRs), and restore international confidence in its intentions. On this basis, the purpose of our policy is to change the regime's behavior. We made consistently clear that our pressure was aimed at the regime, not the people. As Secretary Rice noted publicly several times, America maintains no permanent enemies and harbors no permanent hatreds.

OUR APPROACH TO IRAN:

On January 29, 2002, President Bush delivered his State of the Union Address, in which he referred to Iran as part of an "axis of evil," thus setting the course for a new approach to Iran that confronted publicly Iran's continued support for terrorism and pursuit of nuclear weapons as well as its poor record on human rights. While the regime's leaders claimed to be upset by President Bush's characterization,

The Nuclear Narrative. In August 2002, the National Council of Resistance of Iran (NCRI) publicly disclosed the existence of Iran's covert uranium enrichment site at Natanz and its covert heavy water reactor at Arak. The IAEA immediately requested to inspect the facilities, but Iran refused IAEA access until February 2003 (shortly before the United States began major combat operations in Iraq in March 2003).

In June 2003, the IAEA declared that Iran had failed to meet its obligations under its Nuclear Non-Proliferation Treaty-mandated Safeguards Agreement and in September 2003 called on Iran to provide accelerated cooperation and full transparency and to suspend all further uranium enrichment activities and any reprocessing activities.

To relieve growing international pressure over its nuclear program, Iran made a series of back-and-forth agreements with our European partners between 2003 and 2005 to suspend its declared nuclear activities (all eventually violated by Iran). In the October 2003 Tehran Agreement, Iran committed to cooperating fully with the IAEA and to suspending voluntarily all uranium enrichment and reprocessing activities—but did not act on its agreement. It was sometime during 2003, around the build-up to the Iraq war and the quick removal of Saddam Hussein from power, that we believe Iran decided to halt, or perhaps to suspend, its nuclear weaponization efforts, while continuing both to enlarge its uranium enrichment and reprocessing capability and to develop delivery systems.

In February 2004, Iran agreed to a narrower definition of suspension, but still little progress was made on actual suspension. Only a few months later in September 2004, the IAEA noted Iran had resumed its enrichment activities. Despite Iranian intransigence, European efforts continued to convince Iran to suspend. In November 2004, the EU-3 (France, Germany, and the United Kingdom) and Iran signed the Paris Agreement which states that Iran has decided to continue and extend its suspension to include all enrichment-related and reprocessing activities, while negotiations proceed on a mutually acceptable agreement on long-term arrangements. To support the efforts of our European partners, in March 2005 we offered to drop our objection to Iran's application to the World Trade Organization and to consider licensing spare parts for Iranian civilian aircraft.

Meanwhile, in the backdrop of these international efforts to engage Iran, the reformists' position in Iran weakened and in June 2005, the reform movement suffered its final blow. Mahmoud Ahmadinejad, former Mayor of Tehran and hardliner, was elected President of Iran. In August 2005, Iran declared to the IAEA its intent to resume activities at Esfahan uranium conversion facility. That same month, the EU-3 offered Iran a detailed and far-ranging proposal of incentives in exchange for suspension. Iran immediately rejected the proposal. Over the next year, Iran systematically reduced its cooperation with the IAEA, and in January 2006, Iran restarted its enrichment activity. In February 2006, the IAEA referred the Iran case to the United Nations Security Council (UNSC).

Russia over this period had become more supportive of a tougher position on Iran's nuclear efforts. In early 2005, Russia conditioned its cooperation on the Bushehr nuclear power plant on Iranian acceptance of a fuel supply contract in which Russia would supply nuclear fuel to Bushehr in exchange for an Iranian agreement to return all spent nuclear fuel—which, if reprocessed, could be used to create a nuclear weapon—to Russia. In November 2005, then-Russian President Putin proposed—and President Bush supported—an international uranium enrichment consortium on Russian soil with Iranian management, but not scientific participation. Iran rejected the proposal.

- **The First Offer and the Period of Sanctions.** In June 2006, the United States joined the P5+1 (U.K., France, China, Russia, and Germany) in offering Iran negotiations over a package of incentives (including technical cooperation on nuclear power generation) in return for the regime suspending its uranium enrichment and reprocessing activities. Secretary Rice further stated that she would be willing, in the context of such discussions, to meet with her Iranian counterpart for discussions on any topics the Iranians wished to raise, as soon as Iran fully and verifiably suspended its enrichment and reprocessing activities. Iran rejected the offer. As a result, the P5+1 pursued sanctions against Iran, starting with UNSCR 1696 (July 2006). Iran responded by calling for unconditional negotiations. In September 2006, the United States agreed to postpone consideration of further sanctions to allow time for EU High Representative Javier Solana and Iran's nuclear negotiator Ali Larijani to discuss the nuclear issue. The talks were unsuccessful, and in December 2006, the UNSC passed UNSCR 1737, deciding Iran must suspend all enrichment-related and reprocessing activities and work on the heavy water research reactor, banning sales of goods and services related to the nuclear and missile programs, freezing assets of specified entities and individuals, and requiring notification of travel of those individuals. Iran continued to expand its enrichment activities and began to install centrifuges in a production-scale facility at Natanz. In March 2007, the UNSC adopted UNSCR 1747, reaffirming that Iran must suspend all enrichment-related and reprocessing activities, banning sales of certain armaments to and from Iran, and expanding the list of sanctioned entities including Bank Sepah. Iranian enrichment activities continued during this entire period, and by April 2007, Iran had achieved industrial-scale enrichment at Natanz.

- **The Second Offer and Current Situation.** In June 2008, the P5+1 offered a "refreshed" incentives package to Iran to convince it to suspend enrichment in exchange for suspension of sanctions. This package outlined in more detail the benefits, including economic and energy cooperation, that Iran would receive if it complied with its international obligations. In order to persuade Iran to accept the proposal, Javier Solana, on behalf of the P5 + 1, again suggested an interim step of "freeze-for-freeze" wherein further sanctions would be suspended for a period of 6 weeks as long as Iran froze all new nuclear activity during that period. In July 2008, we took the additional step of sending Under Secretary of State Burns to participate in the P5 + 1 talks with Iran in Geneva, Switzerland. This was meant to convey the seriousness of our offer to the Iranians and to solidify P5 + 1 unity. The P5 + 1 gave Iran 2 weeks to respond to the offer. On August 5, 2008, the Iranians finally provided yet another unclear response, playing for more time. The P5 + 1 immediately agreed to discuss elements of a fourth UNSCR.

The discussions on a fourth resolution stalled, however, after the Russian invasion of Georgia in August 2008. Many countries—especially Iran—expected international unity to erode. Despite the Russian and Chinese unwillingness to support additional sanctions, at the September 2008 U.N. General Assembly meetings, the Security Council convened and passed UNSCR 1835, which calls upon Iran to suspend its nuclear enrichment activities immediately and to comply with the three previous U.N. sanctions resolutions.

While no agreement has been reached to impose any additional sanctions on Iran (China and Russia remain opposed), the P5 + 1 continues to consult and coordinate on approaches. In addition to the P5 + 1 track, the United States is working closely with other like-minded countries on coordinated national measures to pressure Iran in the financial, insurance, and energy areas. Unilateral U.S. actions, such as designations of Iranian entities involved in the proliferation of weapons of mass destruction and their means of delivery under Executive Order 13382, have also been effective in pressuring Iran. The Treasury Department has raised international awareness of the risks of doing business with Iran, and the arguments of reputational risk and moral suasion are gaining traction with international banks and businesses.

Iran Continues to Support Terrorism. Iran has established itself as the primary sponsor, trainer, and financier of extremist forces in the Middle East. The Iranian regime utilizes the skills and discipline of the IRGC-Qods Force to support terrorist activity throughout the region, including by working directly with Hamas, Hizballah, Palestinian Islamic Jihad, the Popular Front for the Liberation of Palestine-General Command (PFLP-GC), and militants in Iraq and Afghanistan to threaten the region's emerging democracies and moderate governments. The Government of Iran uses Bank Saderat to channel funds to terrorist organizations, transferring $50 million from the Central Bank of Iran for the benefit of Hizballah fronts in Lebanon from 2001 to 2006. Iran's terrorist training camps churn out thousands of trained militants each year, especially Lebanese and Palestinian, who threaten stability in the entire Middle East region. Although the Iranian regime has focused mainly on providing support to Shi'a militants around the region, ▮▮▮▮▮▮▮▮▮ ▮▮▮▮▮▮▮▮▮▮ the IRGC-QF and the Ministry of Intelligence and Security also maintain ties to Sunni terrorists and extremist groups in nearly every region of the world.

Iran's relationship with al-Qaida is uneven at best. Whereas Iran has engaged in outright support for terrorist groups operating against Israel, its dealings with al-Qaida have been characterized by periods of activity against the organization limited by a desire not to antagonize the group to the point of attacking Iranian interests. Since 2003-2004, Iran's detention of five members of al-Qaida's senior management council (and several other individuals including three of Usama bin Laden's sons) has dominated Iran's relationship with al-Qaida. While Iran has used these detainees—who are currently under some form of house arrest—as leverage and protection against al-Qaida's advancement of an anti-Iran agenda, al-Qaida has sought through multiple channels to obtain the release of its detained members—a goal that remains one of the organization's top priorities.

Despite the security risks, al-Qaida operatives continue to use Iranian territory as a transit hub, especially for individuals traveling between Iraq and the Persian Gulf and the Afghanistan-Pakistan theater. Iran has demonstrated a willingness on occasion to crack down on this activity and has captured multiple al-Qaida members in the past year.

Our approach to this tricky relationship has focused on "triangulating" between the two natural enemies and seeking to ensure above all that they do not become partners of convenience against the United States. Al-Qaida has expected a military confrontation between the United States and Iran and had hoped to benefit from it by increasing its own pressure on Iran. The organization has increased its plotting against Iran as well as its anti-Iran rhetoric; in April 2008, Ayman al-Zawahiri publicly criticized Iran's "expansionist" policy in the Arab world.

Our decisions on how to address this dynamic have centered on three key elements. First, we want to keep Iran from releasing the al-Qaida detainees it has in custody, having failed in efforts to convince Iran to transfer these detainees to the United States or their countries of origin. We have periodically called for Iran to make a public accounting of what it has done with the detainees as a means of keeping a spotlight on this issue and deterring Iran from releasing them. Second, we have sought to minimize al-Qaida's ability to use Iran as a viable sanctuary and facilitation hub—a task that has been difficult given our limited ability to influence events on the ground in Iran. Third, we have looked to maintain a healthy tension between the two sides such that any antagonism is viewed as keeping them from aligning, even on minor points.

Our counterterrorism strategy on Iran has focused on raising international awareness of Iranian support for terrorism and increasing diplomatic pressure on Tehran ("name and shame"), while isolating the regime and constraining its ability to sponsor terrorism ("isolate and constrain"). Through public diplomacy, targeted designations under Executive Order (E.O.) 13224, financial sanctions to restrict Iran's ability to fund terrorism, and periodic action to disrupt Qods Force (QF) officers and Iranian surrogates in Iraq and Afghanistan, the United States has raised the profile of Iran's terrorism apparatus and increased the cost of Tehran's dealings with terrorists. We have also sought to limit Iran's primary proxy, Hizballah, by providing $410 million in military assistance to the Government of Lebanon since 2005 and seeking to strengthen the Lebanese state and its political and military institutions. Key U.S. actions to curb Iranian support for terrorism:

- Iran has been designated by the Secretary of State as a State Sponsor of Terrorism since January 1984, resulting in restrictions on U.S. foreign assistance; a ban on defense exports and sales; certain controls over exports of dual use items; and miscellaneous financial and other restrictions.
- In October 2007, the United States designated the Islamic Revolutionary Guard Corps (IRGC) and the Ministry of Defense and Armed Forces Logistics (MODAFL) under E.O. 13882 for proliferation-related activities. In addition, Iran's state-owned Banks Melli and Mellat were also designated under this E.O.
- The United States designated the IRGC-Qods Force under E.O. 13224 in October 2007 for providing material support to the Taliban and other terrorist organizations and Bank Saderat as a terrorist financier.

Countering Iranian Malign Influence in Iraq and Afghanistan. Iran has pursued its own multi-track policy in Iraq and Afghanistan, with its strategic intent focused on securing its broader regional influence while ending Western military presence in each country. The regime has sent humanitarian assistance, expanded trade, and established a robust diplomatic and intelligence presence across both its borders. But the regime has also trained, funded, and supplied weapons to violent extremist groups such as Shi'a "special groups" in Iraq and warlords and the Taliban in Afghanistan. The only discernible difference in Iran's approaches to Iraq and Afghanistan has been the emphasis on lethal support, which has been greater in Iraq. In Afghanistan, Iran strikes an uncomfortable balance; it does not want the Taliban to reclaim power in Kabul but also aims to use them to bleed the United States. Iran has also funded and supported political groups in Kabul to undermine President Karzai's influence. However, in the cases of both Iraq and Afghanistan, Iran has proven that it can calibrate its lethal support as necessary to achieve its goals.

Our policy has been to urge both the Iraqis and Afghans to pressure Iran to cease its lethal support to elements in those countries. At times, we also have spoken out publicly against Iran's destabilization of its neighbors and have taken appropriate action inside Iraq and Afghanistan to disrupt Iran's malign activities. For example, in Iraq we have responded by capturing weapons caches and the extremists who seek to use them; arresting members of the IRGC-QF who facilitate these attacks; and even engaging Iran in three rounds of trilateral talks with the Government of Iraq to demand better security cooperation and seek avenues for building cooperation on mutual interests. These talks were largely unproductive, as the Iranians denied all evidence we presented on their lethal activities in Iraq, and instead blamed the U.S. and Coalition presence as the cause of instability. In May 2008, we began implementing our "Countering Iranian Influence" strategy and are currently in the processing of evaluating progress on this strategy. In Iraq, Iran has continuously, although so far unsuccessfully, attempted to undermine the democratic Iraqi political system and its links to the West through diplomatic pressure, bribes, and threats.

In Afghanistan, the International Security Assistance Force (ISAF) has worked to interdict the flow of weapons across the border.   Iran as of September 2008 continues to supply the Taliban with weapons shipments (small arms, IEDs, mortars, and limited MANPADS).

We are careful to acknowledge that Iran's efforts in Afghanistan have not been all bad (in some cases, such as counternarcotics, they have been largely cooperative). In the case of reconstruction in Afghanistan's western provinces, local Afghans are benefiting from Iranian investment in roads, clinics, and development in general, but their strategic intentions remain murky, and the trendlines are enough to elicit caution.

FUTURE CHALLENGES:

The Iranian regime believes its strategy of confrontation, delay, and resistance is working and appears more confident in its path. We believe Iran, and to some degree our more reluctant allies, are counting on an extended period of American inaction and deliberation with the incoming Administration. At the same time, Iran steadily continues to enrich uranium with increasing skill and at an increasing pace. While Iran's nuclear timeline will inevitably drive our sense of urgency and the patterns of our engagement going forward, the Iran challenge is broader than the nuclear issue, and the stakes are high.

The steps we have taken, while they have raised the pressure on Tehran on many fronts, have not yet prompted a strategic shift in Iranian behavior. It is uncertain whether this is because international pressure is not yet sufficient, or because the regime sees precisely the conduct we view as most dangerous as essential to its survival.

As we enter 2009, the Iranian economy is increasingly feeling the burden of international sanctions and falling oil prices, but it is uncertain whether the economic pain will be fast and deep enough to produce the desired effect on Iranian decision-making in the limited time we have to roll back Iran's nuclear progress.

To Talk or Not to Talk. The decision over whether and how to engage Iran has confronted every President since 1979. In fact the United States has been talking to Iran directly and indirectly in many ways for many years, but so far with disappointing results. As the United States views engagement, including direct talks, as a means rather than an end while the Iranian regime seeks such U.S. engagement as a way to legitimize itself, we will need to evaluate suggestions for further engagement to determine what benefits if any—above all what changes in Iranian conduct with respect to terrorism and nuclear activities—such actions would produce, and at what cost. The next Administration's approach to Iran will most likely need to confront the following issues of substance and process:

- Whether the P5 + 1, with all its natural constraints and fissures, is the most useful multilateral mechanism for demonstrating international unity on Iran. Perhaps a broadened coalition of like-minded states would be more useful.
- Whether to establish a real consular presence in Tehran, with American diplomats in residence, in order to increase people-to-people contacts.
- How to adequately address the Iranian "safe haven" and lethal assistance/training of militants.
- How to prevent Iran from leveraging stronger relationships in vulnerable regions in Latin America and Africa.
- How to convince Gulf countries to act publicly, implement financial measures of their own, and use their wealth as leverage. We have made some progress here, but more action especially from Saudi Arabia and the United Arab Emirates is needed.
- How to balance U.S. attention to the nuclear issue with all of the other competing issues like human rights and support to terrorism.
-

- Afghanistan: If the United States increases its military footprint in Afghanistan, we will need to be prepared for a potential increase in the flow of Iranian lethal support/training to extremists.

- Syria: Despite new interest in undermining the Iranian-Syrian relationship, indications are that Iran and Syria continue to collaborate on sensitive military and intelligence projects including direct support to Hizballah as well as development of missiles.

Attachments

Tab 1   Chronology for Our Approach to Iran
Tab 2   Executive Order 13224 (September 23, 2001)

POSTSCRIPT

MICHAEL SINGH

By the time of the transition from the Bush administration to the Obama administration in January 2009, Iran had become one of the most difficult issues in American foreign policy. But while the Bush administration inherited a crumbling containment regime in Iraq, with respect to Iran it was bequeathed what it regarded as a fruitless campaign of engagement with the reform-minded but disempowered President Mohammad Khatami. Viewing Iran as the foremost state sponsor of terrorism, the Bush administration saw little value in continuing that effort—and indeed little prospect that the path to better US-Iran relations lay in talks with regime officials of any stripe. But the need for a new Iran policy seemed less than urgent.

The Bush Administration Approach

Even after the public revelation of Iran's clandestine nuclear activities in 2002, the threat posed by Iran appeared to be a manageable one. In 2003, Iran suspended its nuclear weapons activities and reached a diplomatic accord with key European states to limit its nuclear activities. After Tehran abrogated this accord, the United States proceeded to support and encourage the EU-3 (UK, France, and Germany) to negotiate a permanent suspension of Iran's enrichment and reprocessing efforts. While the Bush administration did not directly join the talks, it believed that US military threats—arguably the key factor in Iran's 2003 decision to scale back its pursuit of nuclear weapons—and the withholding of the US engagement that Tehran apparently desired, added to our allies' leverage in the negotiations. When an EU-3 agreement with Iran was reached in 2004, President Bush believed that the Iran nuclear threat had been defused through a combination of European diplomacy and American military deterrence. "The Europeans had done their part," he wrote in his memoir, "and we had done ours."[1]

Apart from these efforts to curb Iranian nuclear pursuits, the United States remained focused on Iran's regional behavior. It ramped up its rhetoric by labeling Iran part of the "axis of evil." Although controversial, it reflected the admin-

---

1. George W. Bush, *Decision Points* (New York: Crown, 2010), 415.

istration's view that Iran, together with Iraq and North Korea, embodied an acute threat: a state sponsor of terrorism that was also pursuing weapons of mass destruction, and which might in turn provide those weapons to its terrorist proxies. The administration confronted Iran on the ground, engaging in military skirmishes with Iranian forces amid the fighting in Iraq. At the same time, however, it also conducted outreach to Iran—for example, sending envoys to discuss regional issues with Iranian diplomats and providing assistance to Iran in the wake of the devastating Bam earthquake in 2003.

In 2005, US policy toward Iran under the Bush administration gained greater urgency. The reformist government of President Khatami gave way to that of the bombastic hard-liner Mahmoud Ahmadinejad, who ran on a platform of overturning the 2004 nuclear accord and prosecuting those who negotiated it as traitors. Once in office, he restarted and expanded Iran's nuclear program. His anointing by Iran's Supreme Leader signaled a shift in Iranian politics away from any negotiated agreement limiting its program, at least for a time. Compounding the threat, Iranian forces and proxies stepped up their military campaign against US forces and partners in the region.

The Bush administration responded with a policy that would ultimately prove enduring in various manifestations: a combination of more active and US-led diplomacy in concert with the newly formed "P5 + 1" grouping of the United States, UK, France, Germany, China, and Russia, and economic pressure through multilateral and unilateral sanctions. The administration oversaw the drafting and often-unanimous adoption of four UN Security Council resolutions—drawing support not just from Europe but from Moscow and Beijing—which imposed international sanctions on Iran and provided a foundation for additional national sanctions by US partners—while offering Iran a diplomatic off-ramp from confrontation if it would suspend nuclear enrichment and reprocessing. The United States also emphasized the threat of military action against Iran, while nevertheless rebuffing pressure from some allies to use force to eliminate Iran's nuclear program due to the unattractiveness of available military options. At the same time, President Bush and Secretary of State Rice were always careful to distinguish between Iran's regime and its people, offering support for Iran's courageous but heavily persecuted civil rights activists while continuing to prioritize people-to-people exchanges.

What Has Happened Since the End of the Bush Administration?

As is evident from the Transition Memorandum, Iran's behavior—in the nuclear domain, in the support for terrorism, and in its mistreatment of its own citizens—had only worsened by the time President Bush was handing the reins to President Obama. Increasingly, the US focus was on the nuclear file, given what was by 2009 an escalating nuclear crisis. President Barack Obama largely continued the Bush administration's "diplomacy-plus-pressure" approach to Iran. The P5 + 1 gave Iran the choice of either halting illicit nuclear activities related to uranium enrichment and plutonium reprocessing and renewing nuclear negotiations *or* facing additional UN sanctions. Completing the strategy was the American threat of military force, always said to be "on the table," should Iran defy international demands via nuclear breakout.

While the contours of this policy resembled that of the Bush administration, the Obama approach to Iran differed in two key respects. First, the Obama administration emphasized direct US engagement with Iran. The Bush administration had engaged diplomatically with Iran on regional issues such as Afghanistan and Iraq. In 2006 Secretary of State Condoleezza Rice offered to join P5 + 1 talks if Tehran suspended its enrichment and reprocessing activities as demanded by the United Nations. President Obama and some US allies in Europe and elsewhere felt that the US conditions on engagement with Iran were partly to blame for the lack of diplomatic progress—even though they had been relaxed in August 2008 when the Bush administration sent then-Under Secretary of State Bill Burns to a P5 + 1 meeting with Iran.

Second, the Obama administration pursued what it termed a "reset" with Russia. Following Russia's invasion of Georgia in 2008, the Bush administration worked with allies to put relations with Moscow in a "deep freeze" to emphasize the strategic costs of Russia's action and deter future adventurism. The impact was felt not just in Europe, but on overall great-power cooperation and UN Security Council diplomacy on a host of issues, including Iran. The Obama administration's subsequent reversal of the US isolation of Russia opened the door to resumed cooperation but undercut the deterrence message the Bush administration had sought to send.

The Obama administration's initial efforts yielded a powerful new UN Security Council sanctions resolution, but no end to Iranian defiance; its nuclear activities continued to expand inexorably, as did its military intervention in Iraq, Syria, and elsewhere. Meanwhile, American intervention in the Middle

East grew amid uprisings in Libya, Syria, and elsewhere as did, paradoxically, US fatigue with its regional commitments, already salient during the 2008 presidential campaign.

Eager to prevent the escalating nuclear crisis with Iran from erupting into a new conflict even as it was seeking to wind down existing ones, the Obama administration made a sharp break from preexisting US strategy in 2012. It decided to negotiate bilaterally with Iran and agreed to accept ongoing uranium enrichment by Iran as part of any eventual deal, a position that the Bush administration had not previously explicitly rejected or embraced but had reserved as a potential deal closer if needed—not as a deal opener.

The result was a controversial one. The changes ultimately yielded another nuclear agreement. But the accord created friction with US allies in the Middle East and to some extent beyond, and left Iran in possession of a potential nuclear weapons capability that would grow over time. Indeed, the deal—called the Joint Comprehensive Plan of Action or JCPOA—represented a significant shift in US policy toward Iran. Previous to the JCPOA, US policymakers had assumed that any sustainable nuclear accord with Tehran would likely have to follow a broader strategic shift by Iran. This had been the case with Libya where Qaddafi's relinquishment of nuclear weapons-related activities was coupled with a broader strategic realignment. The JCPOA turned that logic on its head; it hoped that the Iranian nuclear deal would prompt a broader moderation in Iran's behavior—or at least make it easier to address other aspects of its activities. When this turned out not to be the case, the Obama administration lacked a strategy to address these other troubling aspects of Iran's behavior. Indeed, many believed that the Obama administration was even willing to give Iran a pass on other issues in order to secure and preserve the JCPOA.

The Trump administration's approach to Iran represented yet another shift in US policy. In part because there was little congressional support for the JCPOA and the agreement had been implemented through executive actions, the Trump administration was able to withdraw from the JCPOA in May 2018 and institute a policy of heavy, largely unilateral economic sanctions. Although seemingly an abrupt rupture in US policy, this shift was not as dramatic as often portrayed. Although the Trump and Obama administrations' policies differed in many ways—and their rhetoric toward Iran differed more starkly still—both sought to transform the US-Iran relationship through a combination of diplomacy and pressure, and both aimed to address the threats from Iran while decreasing the US commitment to the Middle East more broadly. In the long-running debate over whether fundamental change in Iran was ultimately dependent on internal Iranian dynamics or could be brought about through the use of American policy tools, both President Obama and President Trump took the latter position.

How Did the Bush Administration Do?

The Bush administration fell on the other side of that debate. It agreed that political change in Iran—not necessarily regime change, but a change profound enough to usher in a strategic shift in Tehran's policies—was necessary to achieve a sustainable end to US-Iran hostilities and Iran's pursuit of activities threatening to US interests. But it also viewed that political change as being one that remained largely in the hands of the Iranian people, and not a change that the United States could impose or orchestrate from outside.

Nevertheless, President Bush did not view the United States as powerless to affect events and decisions in Iran. The Bush administration viewed supporting human rights and democracy activists in Iran both as morally imperative and as sensible policy. In addition, the administration believed that regime officials should be presented with incentives and disincentives, and that this—rather than seeking to empower a particular individual or faction within the regime—was the key to pushing Iranian policy in the right direction.

To this end, the policy the Bush administration settled on was for the United States and its international partners to present Iranian leaders with a strategic choice—continue pursuing their destabilizing policies and prolong their international isolation; or drop those destabilizing policies and reap the benefits of economic and diplomatic engagement with the world. The aim of the policy was not just a deal, nuclear or otherwise; rather, it was a strategic shift by Iran, which in turn could either result in an agreement or render one unnecessary. It is for this reason that the Bush administration chose not to focus on the nuclear file to the near exclusion of other issues, and why it was skeptical that reaching a limited nuclear deal would induce broader changes in Iranian behavior in other domains.

The Bush administration's approach had upsides and downsides. It did produce a broad international coalition of states, spanning the globe, working in concert to exert diplomatic, economic, and military pressure on Iran—a coalition that included the (sometimes grudging) participation of Russia and China. To facilitate this pressure, the Bush administration pioneered new forms of sanctions—first wielded against North Korea—that proved more powerful than any which had been enacted previously. However, while Iran could not ignore this pressure, neither did it force Iran to capitulate or induce the sort of strategic shift the administration sought. Instead, Iran proceeded to significantly expand its nuclear activities, limited only by the deterrent effect of US military capabilities.

The Bush administration also believed that Iran's nuclear and regional policies, while posing different degrees of threat to the United States and its vital interests, were ultimately linked. Both were elements of an Iranian security strategy that aimed to destabilize neighbors in order to prevent their becoming threats to Iran and to advance Iran's bid for regional hegemony; to develop forms of power—asymmetric capabilities, ballistic missiles, and perhaps nuclear weapons—to compensate for Iran's conventional weakness and to intimidate its neighbors; and otherwise project Iranian power and influence throughout the region. This did not imply that no Iranian threat could be addressed if all of them were not addressed. But it did mean recognizing that until Iran's strategy changed, it would retain an underlying motivation to cultivate proxies and preserve its nuclear options, regardless of how diplomacy, sanctions, or military deterrents sought to curtail Tehran's freedom of action.

This linkage also meant, however, that negotiating with Iran on the nuclear front—and extending the prospect of sanctions relief—was complicated by the imperative to confront Iranian regional policies, on which Washington and its P5 + 1 partners did not always share the same priorities. And the Bush administration underestimated the extent to which the toppling of regimes in Afghanistan and especially in Iraq would provide Iran with opportunities to pursue its regional strategy with greater abandon, burrowing its proxies into the fabric of both states just as it had done in Lebanon earlier. If the Bush administration's careful coalition building on the nuclear front hemmed Iran in, the international disunity and regional tumult that followed the initial US success in Iraq and Afghanistan produced the opposite.

What Are the Lessons Learned?

As future administrations devise their approaches to Iran, yet another shift in US policy is inevitable. Yet the threats that Iran poses to US interests remain much as they were when President Bush entered office, although their severity has intensified. Iran's nuclear pursuits, missile and conventional arms proliferation, regional destabilization, and sponsorship of terrorism remain pressing challenges to the United States, the region, and the international community.

In tackling these threats, future presidents can benefit from the lessons learned by their predecessors. Chief among these lessons are:

- *The United States has had its greatest success when combining diplomacy and pressure, and when that pressure is presented in multiple forms—including economic sanctions, international isolation, military threat, and support for human rights.* Managing the challenge of Iran means first and foremost limiting the further development of its nuclear and missile threat, using the full complement of US policy tools, while maintaining and enhancing deterrence by building our partners' capabilities, enhancing cooperation among them, and maintaining (even if in reduced form) key US capabilities in the region. While the United States will have little influence over who makes policy decisions in Iran, it can make clear that challenging US and allied interests will be costly, whereas refraining from doing so will yield benefits. This will hopefully strengthen the hand of those in Tehran advocating the sort of strategic shift for which Iran's neighbors and much of the world hopes. And while supporting human and civil rights in isolation is no more a silver bullet than diplomacy or sanctions, it too can contribute to a shift in Iran and must have a place in any successful US strategy. Supporting Iran's people is not only a moral imperative, but a strategic one—for only a fundamental shift in the orientation of Iran, one brought about by its own people and not outsiders, will address the many challenges Iran currently poses.
- *To be sustainable, any diplomatic accords with Iran—whether partial or more thoroughgoing—must have bipartisan support from Congress and support from the American people as well.* Relying on executive action and single-party support doomed both the Obama and Trump administration policies to impermanence and produced swings in policy that have undermined American leverage and credibility. For any agreement or policy to succeed, an administration must eschew shortcuts and build bipartisan support. And any approach to the nuclear issue must be connected to a clearly articulated and adequately resourced strategy that addresses the other threats posed by Iran.

- *It is important not to mistake a nuclear accommodation for a strategic shift, or to neglect the links between Iran's nuclear ambitions and its broader security strategy.* Debate in Washington often focuses on whether nuclear issues, regional issues, or both should be included in US-Iran negotiations. In reality, however, these threats are inextricably connected. Iran is unlikely either to give up its nuclear ambitions or its regional policies in isolation. Nor is any US concession such as sanctions relief sustainable over the long term if Iran is determined to continue mounting a serious challenge to US interests, whatever form that challenge may take. While this does not necessarily argue for a comprehensive diplomatic settlement or against limited deals, it does suggest that the problems Iran poses may have to be managed rather than solved unless and until Iran makes a strategic shift in its approach to its security.

CHAPTER 14

North Korea

VICTOR CHA | MICHAEL ALLEN | J. D. CROUCH | MICHAEL GREEN | PAUL HAENLE

President Bush inherited a North Korea denuclearization policy that he concluded was not adequately serving US national security interests. While the Clinton administration's Agreed Framework had stopped long-term planning and construction on future nuclear projects in North Korea (i.e., the fifty megawatt and 200 megawatt reactor plans), and had frozen extant plutonium production capabilities at the five megawatt reactor in Yongbyon, North Korea had still not committed to permanently dismantling its nuclear program. The regime was receiving up-front energy shipments for a freeze that was entirely reversible. President Bush also wanted to address other elements of the threat from North Korea including conventional forces, ballistic and cruise missiles, proliferation, and human rights. He believed that the North Korea problem should not belong solely to the United States and that it required a regional solution that leveraged coalitional pressure and resources.

TRANSITION MEMORANDUM

~~SECRET~~   5436
NATIONAL SECURITY COUNCIL   Transition
WASHINGTON, D.C. 20504

NSC Declassification Review [E.O. 13526]
DECLASSIFY IN PART   January 14, 2009
by William C. Carpenter 3/23/2020

MEMORANDUM FOR THE RECORD

FROM: DENNIS WILDER, EAST ASIAN AFFAIRS
             MICHAEL ALLEN, COUNTERPROLIFERATION

SUBJECT: North Korea and Six-Party Talks

THE SITUATION AS WE FOUND IT:

Prior to 2001, the centerpiece of U.S.-North Korea policy was the Agreed Framework, a 1994 bilateral agreement between the United States and the North. Under the terms of the agreement, North Korea (the Democratic People's Republic of Korea, or DPRK) promised to freeze its reactors and related facilities in exchange for U.S.-provided heavy fuel oil and to eventually dismantle those facilities once the United States completed construction of Light Water Reactors (LWRs). Both sides also committed to work together for peace and security on a nuclear-free Korean Peninsula and to move toward full normalization of political and economic relations.

Upon taking office, the President concluded that the Agreed Framework was not adequately serving our interests:

- The agreement provided North Korea with large energy benefits up front in the hope (but by no means the certainty) that the North would eventually agree to do more than just freeze its plutonium production capability.
- The agreement dealt with the plutonium production program in isolation from other issues—without a clear, long-range plan for generating meaningful change in other North Korean policies.
- The agreement did not address the massive North Korean buildup of forces on the Demilitarized Zone (DMZ), the North's nuclear-related high explosives testing program, its long-range ballistic

~~SECRET~~   Re-Classified by: Ellen J. L Knight
Reason: 1.4 (b) (d)   Reason: 1.4(c) and (d)
Declassify on: 1/14/19   Declassify on: 1/14/2034

missile development program, North Korean proliferation activities, and the regime's brutal and inhumane treatment of its people.

The President was concerned that the American approach to North Korea was too bilateral and:

- Put the United States at a clear disadvantage with a North Korean leader (Kim Jong-Il) who was skilled at holding the world hostage through fits of anger designed to get his way.
- Took advantage of the United States as an open society. Kim had the ability to mobilize international public opinion to try to get us to yield to his demands, as other nations feared what he might do and pressed the United States to make concessions.
- Allowed China and the other regional powers to avoid direct responsibility for the North Korean problem because the United States had shouldered the negotiations burden.

THE ADMINISTRATION'S POLICY:

The President began his Administration by making clear that it would not be business as usual with North Korea and that a new approach was required. The President told South Korean President Kim Dae-Jung during a March 7, 2001 Oval Office meeting that the United States could not reward a regime that mistreated its people and could not keep to the terms of its agreements.

The President assessed that a long-range strategic plan for transformation of North Korea was required. It would necessarily begin with   making sure that it was not able to threaten its immediate neighbors, not able to proliferate dangerous weapons of mass destruction (WMD) technologies, and not capable of threatening the United States. This imperative became even more salient in the aftermath of the 9/11 tragedy.

we could then turn our attention to helping the North Korean people by providing economic and energy assistance and other forms of aid that would eventually open up the North Korean society. These "carrots" would appear to help the regime survive, but would actually undermine the regime's hold on power by exposing average North Koreans to far greater influence from outsiders. This opening would almost certainly lead to either the demise of Kim Jong-Il's regime or its transformation into a less hostile one in a manner perhaps similar to the Chinese economic reforms of the 1980s.

- Negotiations were to be predicated on the fundamental importance of obtaining effectively verifiable written agreements on a range of issues: first and foremost, the denuclearization of North Korea, then North Korea's proliferation of missiles and missile-related technology; its chemical and biological weapons programs; its harboring of terrorists; and its treatment of its people.

- The President made clear that we would not be driven into negotiations with the North by threats and provocations; we would not reward bad behavior; and we would ensure that any agreements we pursued must be verified.

The President also assessed that North Korean intransigence meant that we would need to mobilize all the resources available to press it to alter its behavior. First, diplomacy with North Korea would need to be pushed out of the bilateral context and into a multilateral context where everyone who had influence with the North—Japan, South Korea, China, and Russia—would be mobilized to use their leverage with Pyongyang. The President understood that active Chinese cooperation would be particularly important because of China's unique geographic, historical, and economic ties to the North.

Another set of resources that the President felt had been underutilized was the international community's ability to target North Korea's international financial vulnerabilities and to disrupt North Korea's WMD proliferation activities. He encouraged the   Treasury Department to analyze Kim Jong-Il's international financial networks and work with foreign governments to disrupt North Korea's banking activities. A prominent success in this regard was the 2005 USA PATRIOT Act Section 311 action against Banco Delta Asia in Macau, which had acted as a major front for many illicit activities of the North Korean regime. This not only put Kim Jong-Il on notice of our ability to disrupt his illicit operation, but it also led other reputable, international banking institutions to severely restrict the North's banking opportunities. The President's creation of the Proliferation Security Initiative (PSI) in May 2003 was also a major tool   by creating a multilateral mechanism for interdicting WMD and missile-related exports from North Korea and other proliferators.

Finally, the President's decision to build a viable capability to shoot down North Korean ballistic missiles launched at the United States or its allies was a key element in taking away Kim's ability to blackmail the world. The President, in his first and succeeding defense budgets, secured neces-sary funding from Congress to build interceptor sites in Alaska and California. He also worked with Prime Minister Koizumi to persuade the Japanese to agree to joint missile defense cooperation and to station long-range missile defense radars in Japan.

WHAT HAS BEEN ACCOMPLISHED:

During the first year-and-a-half of the Administration, North Korea rebuffed U.S. attempts to engage on the President's new approach and instead preferred extended squabbling at working levels over the details of U.S. obligations regarding the Light Water Reactors in the Agreed Framework. The President used this period to build his personal rapport with key world leaders and lay the groundwork for the multilateral approach that would eventually become the Six-Party Talks. He held summits with President Jiang of China, President Kim of South Korea, President Putin of Russia, and Prime Minister Koizumi of Japan. He also articulated to the American people his concerns about the dangers of allowing North Korea to continue down its nuclear weapons path, most notably in his 2002 State of the Union address. There he warned that North Korea, Iran, and Iraq posed serious dangers and declared that the United States would "prevent regimes that sponsor terror from threatening America or our friends and allies with weapons of mass destruction."

Establishing the Six-Party Framework

Assistant Secretary of State James Kelly led a U.S. delegation to North Korea in October 2002 to meet with First Vice Foreign Minister Kang Sok Ju. Kang acknowledged that North Korea had been pursuing uranium enrichment, denounced what he termed "hostile" U.S. policies, and stated that the Agreed Framework and other agreements had been nullified.

North Korea's admission that it had violated its commitments enabled the President to begin galvanizing others to be part of a multilateral approach. Just after the Kelly visit to North Korea, the President met with Chinese President Jiang Zemin at the President's ranch in Crawford, Texas. The President told President Jiang that the North Korean pursuit of nuclear weapons was a regional problem requiring a regional solution. President Jiang wanted this to remain an American-North Korean problem, but did agree, for the first time, that denuclearization of the Korean Peninsula was a common goal of the United States and China. The President labeled this the "Crawford Consensus" and used it as the basis for drawing China deeper into the process.

In December 2002, North Korea played another card in brinkmanship politics by removing the International Atomic Energy Agency (IAEA) seals from the facilities at Yongbyon and expelling the IAEA inspectors. On January 10, 2003, North Korea formally withdrew from the Nuclear Nonproliferation Treaty (NPT). That same day, the President called President Jiang to suggest that it was time for the United States, China, Japan, South Korea, and Russia to bind together with a "common purpose" of denuclearizing the Peninsula.

He warned President Jiang in successive phone calls and letters that, should the North continue down this road, a nuclear arms race might begin in Northeast Asia, with Japan and even South Korea pursuing nuclear weapons. The President also made clear in a letter to President Jiang on February 20, 2003, that "the United States reserved the right to exercise a full range of responses, including multilateral sanctions, interdiction of North Korean arms trade, and increased military presence in the region and other steps."

President Jiang was apparently convinced that China had to take greater responsibility to avoid a conflict on the Korean Peninsula, and by late April North Korea agreed, under Chinese pressure, to a trilateral meeting in Beijing between U.S., North Korean, and Chinese negotiators. Over the summer, the United States pressed for inclusion of Japan, Russia, and South Korea in these talks and on August 27, 2003, the First Round of the Six-Party Talks convened in Beijing.

The September 19, 2005 Agreement and "Action for Action"

This first meeting offered the United States its first real opportunity to advocate a new concept of negotiations based on pay-for-performance or, as it came to be known, "action-for-action." Under this approach, the five parties would only fulfill commitments in parallel with North Korea fulfilling its commitments on denuclearization. In this way, rather than first providing benefits to the North in the hope it would carry out its commitments, the five parties would receive North Korean commitments up front, and as the North carried them out, benefits would be provided.

After many months of fits and starts with the North, on September 19, 2005, a major breakthrough occurred with the signing of a Six-Party Joint Statement. In that agreement, North Korea committed to abandon all nuclear weapons and existing nuclear programs and return at an early date to the NPT and to IAEA safeguards. In turn, the other five parties stated their willingness to provide the North economic cooperation and energy assistance under the principle of "commitment-for-commitment, action-for-action."

North Korea Seeks to Split the Six Parties

In the fall and winter of 2005, North Korea—surprised by the effectiveness of U.S. financial sanctions against Banco Delta Asia—sought to push back by staging a boycott of the Six-Party Talks until the freeze on its funds was lifted. The President used this opportunity to put new pressure on China to punish the North for its intransigence. During a White House summit with Hu Jintao on April 20, 2006, the President took an unusual step of rearranging the seating so that he could sit directly adjacent to the Chinese President at lunch and have an extremely candid discussion on North Korea. The President expressed his desire for a peace treaty on the peninsula, but explained to President Hu that only China possessed the ability to convince the North of U.S. sincerity. President Hu immediately sent his foreign policy czar, Tang Jiaxuan, to deliver this message to Kim Jong-Il on April 27, 2006. In addition,   China—for the first time—began to enact some financial sanctions of its own against North Korean banking.

Kim Jong-Il reacted in anger to the joint pressure from China and the United States and began trying to split the five parties by preparing for missile tests. The President called President Hu to warn of the impending tests, and China urged the North to stop. The United States also consulted closely with our South Korean and Japanese allies to demonstrate unity in the face of the North Korean provocations. On July 4, 2006, Kim Jong-Il tested several short-, medium-, and long-range ballistic missiles, to include the Taepo Dong-2 capable of reaching the United States. The North's relationship with China deteriorated from this point onward because the North had broken long-standing promises to inform China in advance of its actions and had acted against China's explicit wishes. China, for the first time, voted in favor of a U.N. Security Council Resolution (UNSCR 1695) to demand that North Korea suspend all activities related to its ballistic missile program and establish a moratorium on missile launchers. Japan and Australia adopted sanctions against entities tied to the North Korean WMD programs.

The North tried to further defy the international community on October 3, 2006, by announcing publicly that it had the right to test a nuclear weapon. The President once again used Kim's reckless behavior to galvanize international action. He told President Hu that China had a responsibility to act, and the Chinese attempted to talk the North out of the test. The United States also led an initiative in the United Nations Security Council to get a Presidential statement warning against the test. Hoping it could again break international unity, North Korea tested a nuclear weapon on October 9, 2006. Immediately after the test the President told President Hu that the North had once again defied China and asked President Hu what he was going to do about it. President Hu acted quickly to place sanctions on the North. He again sent Tang Jiaxuan to Pyongyang to tell the North that, if tensions escalated and the United States used limited force against the North, China would not intervene. He also threatened to cut off all aid. Meanwhile, China agreed to a Chapter VII resolution, UNSCR 1718, that was quickly adopted, obligating member states to prevent the transfer to and export from the DPRK of nuclear and ballistic missile equipment. It also banned the import of luxury goods to North Korea and provided member states the authority to freeze funds of entities associated with the DPRK's ballistic missile and nuclear related programs. Recognizing that its attempts to split the international community had failed and facing increasing international isolation, the North returned to the Six-Party Talks in December 2006.

Implementing the September 17, 2005 Agreement

With the North's return, the Six-Parties set out to begin achieving the goal of the September 19, 2005, Joint Statement to verifiably eliminate all of North Korea's nuclear weapons and programs. On February 13, 2007, as a first step in implementing this agreement, the Six Parties concluded the "Initial Actions Agreement for the Implementation of the Joint Statement." In that agreement, the DPRK agreed to shut down and seal the Yongbyon nuclear facility, and to allow IAEA personnel to monitor and verify those actions. In turn, the other parties agreed to provide emergency energy assistance to North Korea with an initial shipment of 50,000 tons of heavy fuel oil (HFO). The other parties also committed to a phase-in of energy and economic assistance and normalization of relations with the North as the North moved down the path to abandoning all nuclear weapons and nuclear programs and returning at an early date to the Treaty on Non-Proliferation of Nuclear Weapons (NPT) and to IAEA safeguards. The Six Parties established working groups on Denuclear-ization of the Korean Peninsula, Normalization of U.S.-DPRK Relations, Normalization of Japan-DPRK Relations, Economy and Energy Cooperation, and Northeast Asia Peace and Security Mechanism.

On September 6, 2007, the Israeli Air Force bombed a covert plutonium reactor being built by Syria with North Korean assistance. The revelation of this clandestine cooperation offered the United States a new opportunity to stress to China and other international partners the dangers of North Korea's nuclear proliferation and helped lead to the second major breakthrough of the Six-Party Talks with the signing of the October 3, 2007, Agreement on "Second-Phase Actions for Implementa-tion of the Joint Statement." North Korea agreed to disable all existing nuclear facilities subject to abandonment under the September 2005 Joint Statement and to provide a complete and correct declaration of all its nuclear programs. They also reaffirmed their commitment not to transfer nuclear materials, technology, or know-how. The other parties in turn agreed to provide North Korea with economic, energy, and humanitarian assistance up to the equivalent of one million tons of HFO. The United States reaffirmed its intent to remove the designation of North Korea as a state sponsor of terrorism and terminate the application of the Trading with the Enemy Act (TWEA), dependent upon the North's fulfillment of its commitments regarding the declaration and disablement.

Since November 2007, U.S. experts have been on the ground in Yongbyon overseeing the disable-ment of the three core facilities of the North's nuclear weapons program: the 5-MW(e) reactor; the fuel fabrication facility; and the reprocessing facility. Many of the agreed disablement tasks at these three facilities have been completed, including the removal of key equipment at the reprocessing plant necessary for the separation of plutonium from spent fuel rods, and the disablement and removal of major pieces of equipment at the fuel fabrication plant. The North has discharged more than half of the spent fuel in the 5-MW(e) reactor.

North Korea's Declaration of Its Nuclear Program

North Korea missed the December 31, 2007 deadline to submit its declaration, but the President continued to work with the Chinese and our other partners to convince the North to submit not only a declaration of its plutonium programs, but also an acknowledgment that North Korea had a uranium enrichment program and had proliferated nuclear technology to Syria.

- President Bush, on February 16, 2008, sent President Hu a letter warning the Chinese leader that the Six-Party process was at an impasse and that China must use its influence to get North Korea to move forward.

- Later in February 2008, the President sent Secretary of State Rice to Beijing to reinforce the message with President Hu. On February 26, 2008, she told President Hu that North Korea's nuclear proliferation to Syria—one of the world's leading sponsors of terrorism—made it extremely difficult to meet the North Korean demand that it be taken off the terrorism list. Thus, we required a North Korean admission of its proliferation actions to move forward.

In May 2008, the North provided the United States with nearly 19,000 pages of operating records from the 5-MW(e) reactor and the reprocessing facility at Yongbyon. This was an important step in the process of beginning to verify North Korea's claims about its nuclear programs. At the same time, particles of highly enriched uranium (HEU) and yttrium (which can be used in producing HEU metal) were found on the 19,000 pages of documents. These particles were consistent with particles found on an aluminum sample provided by North Korea in October 2007 from a Russian shipment of aluminum tubes. Analysis of these particles by the Intelligence Community raised doubts about North Korea's claim that it was not engaged in uranium enrichment activities.

On June 26, 2008, North Korea formally submitted a declaration of its nuclear programs to China and, the next day, destroyed the 5MW(e) reactor cooling tower at Yongbyon in front of international media. The North declared its plutonium production program without mentioning its uranium enrichment, proliferation, and weapons-related activities.

As to weapons-related activities, the Six Parties had agreed that nuclear weapons would not be addressed until the next phase of the talks.

North Korea's Removal from the Terrorism List

On the same day that the North turned in its declaration, the President issued a proclamation lifting the provisions of TWEA with respect to North Korea. The President also notified Congress of his intent to rescind North Korea's designation as a State Sponsor of Terrorism after 45 days dependent upon North Korean cooperation on establishing verification principles, a verification protocol, and a Monitoring Mechanism for tracking Six-Party obligations, as well as commencement of verification activities. North Korea stalled for some time over verification, but finally agreed to a verification memorandum and clarifications that allowed Secretary Rice on October 11, 2008, to delist North Korea.

Removing North Korea from the State Sponsors of Terrorism List was a difficult decision. On the one hand, we had increasing evidence of the existence of highly enriched uranium in North Korea, which raised more questions about the regime's efforts to develop a uranium enrichment program. Additionally, there were concerns about delisting the North so soon after learning about North Korean assistance in Syria's developing a nuclear reactor, a leading state sponsor of terrorism. On the other hand, removal was consistent with the letter of the law since the North had provided assurances that it would not support acts of international terrorism in the future and the intelligence community had no evidence of North Korean support for international terrorism during the preceding 6 months. Moreover, it was clear to the President that we were learning more about HEU only as a result of activity and access obtained through our Six-Party diplomacy. In addition, the United States possessed other effective tools to hold the North to account if it balked at compliance with its obligations. Therefore, the President decided to approve the removal of the State Sponsor of Terrorism designation to keep the Six-Party process going, but to use the verification mechanism to get to the bottom of the HEU story.

FUTURE CHALLENGES:

The next Administration may face a period of extreme uncertainty in dealing with North Korea if the hemorrhagic stroke that left Kim Jong-Il partially paralyzed in mid-August of 2008 has impaired his cognitive abilities or leads to a succession struggle. Medical professionals note that world leaders who suffer major strokes or other major illness often become more rigid and inflexible in their decision-making. Even if Kim Jong-Il is deposed, we believe the same issues that brought Kim Jong-Il to the Six-Party table—primarily the inexorable decline in the North Korean economy—will face the new leaders. They may have even greater reason to negotiate because they may lack the legitimacy afforded to the offspring of the founder of North Korea, but they may also be fearful of straying from the regime's most conservative positions.

In the near term, the key challenge for the Six-Party Talks is to ensure the North continues on the path of disablement and makes progress in completing its obligations under the October 3, 2007, Second Phase Actions agreement. The Six Parties will need to reach an agreement on the verification protocol if U.S. policymakers are going to be able to assure the American people that North Korea is fulfilling its pledge to abandon all of its nuclear programs, as well as its pledges that it is not proliferating, and to return to the NPT under IAEA safeguards. The goal of the verification effort will be to make cheating as hard as possible, to enhance the ability to detect violations, to get to the bottom of DPRK enriched uranium and proliferation activities, and to enable U.S. policymakers to respond in a timely manner if violations are detected.

Once a Six-Party verification protocol is in place, future U.S. policymakers will need to turn to the next and final phase of denuclearization. During this abandonment phase, the North must be convinced to dismantle all facilities related to its nuclear program, declare and abandon its nuclear weapons, and give up all of its nuclear materials.

U.S. policymakers also will continue to face the issue of the deplorable conditions of the North Korean people. The President has often expressed his concern for the North Korean people and has continued to press the North Korean regime to improve their lives. In August 2005, the President appointed a Special Envoy on Human Rights in North Korea to increase awareness and promote efforts to improve the human rights of the North Korean people. The Administration also has helped to resettle North Korean refugees fleeing repression and misery and has helped facilitate talks between Japan and North Korea concerning the Japanese abductees. The President has been consistent in reminding the international community of the importance of North Korean human rights issues, including through meetings in the Oval Office with North Korean refugees and dissidents.

As it ponders its future, if North Korea makes the right choices, it will be in a better position to repair its relationship with the international community. If North Korea again chooses confrontation, future U.S. policymakers will need to mobilize the partners in the Six-Party Talks to respond accordingly. The President remains convinced that multilateral diplomacy through the Six-Party framework is the best way to peacefully resolve the nuclear issue with North Korea. Our progress shows that tough multilateral diplomacy can yield promising results, yet the diplomatic process is not an end in itself. Our ultimate goal remains clear: a stable and peaceful denuclearized Korean Peninsula, where people are free from oppression, hunger, and disease.

Attachments

Tab 1	Chronology of North Korea and Six-Party Talks
Tab 2	Memorandum of Telephone Conversation with President Kim Dae-jung (January 24, 2001)
Tab 3	Memorandum of Conversation with President Kim Dae-jung of South Korea (March 7, 2001)
Tab 4	Statement by the President Announcing North Korea Policy (June 2001)
Tab 5	Public Articulation of the "Bold Message" (July 2002)
Tab 6	Memorandum of Conversation with President Jiang Zemin in Crawford (October 2002)
Tab 7	Joint Remarks with President Jiang Zemin in Crawford (October 2002)
Tab 8	Joint United States-Japan-Korea Trilateral Statement (October 26, 2002)
Tab 9	Memorandum of Telephone Conversation with President Jiang Zemin (January 10, 2003)
Tab 10	Memorandum of Telephone Conversation with President Jiang Zemin (February 7, 2003)
Tab 11	Letter to President Jiang Zemin (February 20, 2003)
Tab 12	Joint Statement Between the United States and Korea (May 14, 2003)

POSTSCRIPT

VICTOR CHA, MICHAEL ALLEN, J. D. CROUCH,
MICHAEL GREEN, PAUL HAENLE

President Bush put in place a new approach to the problem of North Korea. After eight years, the administration made some progress on denuclearization and created a multilateral security forum in Northeast Asia to address the issue but fell short of its goal of complete and verifiable disarmament, handing off to its successor a North Korean nuclear problem every bit as challenging as the one it inherited. In the dozen years since, both the Obama and the Trump administrations have struggled with the issue just as much as the Bush administration did with finding a formula for lasting success.

The Bush Administration Approach

The Bush administration's policy toward North Korea was guided by four core principles. First, the goal of any diplomacy would be the complete, verifiable, and irreversible dismantlement (CVID) of all nuclear weapons and existing nuclear programs in North Korea. Second, the president would seek a peaceful diplomatic resolution of the nuclear issue that would have the support of the UN Security Council. Third, the United States would invite participation from all the regional stakeholders to share responsibility for solving the problem. Fourth, the president would oppose Chinese free riding and challenge Beijing to address the issue in concert with the United States, and with a much greater sense of urgency than it had to date. Ultimately, the president wanted the North Korean leader to make the strategic decision to disarm and to join the international community.

President Bush had no illusions about the difficulty of achieving denuclearization. The previous administration's efforts had achieved a freeze on North Korea's plutonium reactor that held as long as the United States, along with allies, were locked into compensating the regime with oil shipments. President Bush wanted agreements with North Korea that the regime could not easily back out of and that permanently stopped elements of its program. The president was also skeptical of whether the North Korean leader was willing to trade his weapons program for political recognition and international economic assistance which would unleash liberalization forces that would help the people of North Korea while threatening the dictatorship. Nevertheless, the unimpeded growth of the weapons program was an unacceptable reality that necessitated the president's investment in denuclearization diplomacy, as difficult as the objective seemed.

Rather than pursue negotiations in the US-DPRK bilateral context used by the previous administration, the Bush administration opted for and created a multilateral approach—the first of its kind in Northeast Asia. The innovation of the Six-Party Talks—involving the United States, Japan, China, Russia, and the two Koreas—was more than form. It was designed to achieve two goals. First, the Six-Party format would align the common interests and negotiating strategies of the five countries that wanted denuclearization of North Korea such that the regime could not look to exploit gaps among them. Second, the new format would put more pressure on China, as the host, to take responsibility for persuading its junior partner to give up its weapons. The administration "multilateralized" the problem further by bringing it to the United Nations. With China and Russia as integral members of the denuclearization negotiations, they understood first-hand the difficulties of North Korean brinksmanship. The result was the achievement of the first-ever unanimous UN Security Council sanctions resolutions on North Korea in the aftermath of its weapons demonstrations.

On the core goal of denuclearization, the Bush administration made several gains. It reached an agreement in September 2005 (the Six-Party Joint Statement) in which North Korea agreed to abandon all nuclear weapons and related programs. With subsequent agreements in 2007, the administration achieved the reintroduction of international inspectors into North Korea, which not only helped to implement the 2005 Joint Statement denuclearization commitments but also revealed new information about its secretive programs. It secured a verifiable freeze on plutonium bomb-making production activities; disablement of three key facilities used to make fissile material for nuclear weapons; and demolition of the iconic cooling tower, all at the Yongbyon nuclear site. In addition, the administration obtained 19,000 pages of operating records for the main nuclear reactor providing novel insights into the history of bomb-making activities, and samples of aluminum tubes that were believed to be related to a second secret uranium-based bomb program. While these gains are notable, they were far from comprehensive or conclusive. North Korea continued to develop its ballistic missile capabilities; moreover, it crossed the nuclear weapons threshold by testing its first device in October 2006.

What Has Happened Since the End of the Bush Administration?

The Obama administration sought denuclearization negotiations like its predecessor and focused on China as a key interlocutor and facilitator. In the end, however, North Korea's walking back of all the Bush-era agreements, its incessant drive to improve its weapons capability, and its breach of a 2012 agreement left the Obama administration with a policy focused almost exclusively on sanctions.

Several weeks after President Obama took office in 2009, North Korea launched a three-stage rocket over Japan, followed by its second nuclear test. The administration sought UN sanctions in response, leading North Korea to announce that it would no longer be bound by the Bush-era Six-Party agreement. Pyongyang conducted further provocations the following year (notably, sinking of the South Korean Cheonan naval vessel and conducting an artillery shelling of a South Korean island), and in November 2010, it admitted publicly to the existence of a secret uranium-based nuclear program in violation of previous agreements.

The most sustained period of negotiations for President Obama was an eight-month stretch starting in July 2011. A bilateral agreement was reached on February 29, 2012 (hence, the "Leap Day" agreement) in which North Korea agreed to resume suspension of operations at Yongbyon and refrain from missile and nuclear testing in return for food assistance (240,000 metric tons). An April 2012 launch of a three-stage rocket by North Korea, which Pyongyang denied was a violation of the new agreement, led to the demise of this short-lived accord. In addition, in a clear statement of its intentions in mid-2012, North Korea revised its constitution, declaring itself as a nuclear weapons state.

The default policy for President Obama thereafter was one of "strategic patience," putting sanctions on the regime with the hope that this would compel North Korea to return to the negotiating table. North Korea instead used the time to accelerate its weapons testing and development, completing the unraveling of the Bush-era denuclearization agreements. By the time President Obama left office, the situation had degenerated to the point that the outgoing president felt obliged to highlight the problem to his successor.

The Trump administration's North Korea policy careened wildly from threats of war to leader-to-leader summit diplomacy. President Trump and Kim Jong-un nearly took the peninsula to war in 2017. The two leaders then shifted abruptly to summit diplomacy in 2018–19. Neither approach precipitated denuclearization on the Korean peninsula.

Three weeks after President Trump's inauguration, North Korea tested a solid-fueled medium-range submarine-launched ballistic missile (SLBM) using new cold launch compressed gas canisters, demonstrating dramatic advances in a survivable nuclear weapons capability. It tested a bevy of ballistic missiles in March through November, including three intercontinental ballistic missiles (ICBMs) (Hwasong-14 and 15 or KN-20, KN-22) on lofted trajectories that indicated a range that could reach deep into the continental United States. In September, it conducted its sixth nuclear test, a claimed hydrogen bomb with an explosive yield in excess of 100 kilotons of TNT. All told, in the last year of Obama and the first year of Trump, North Korea launched forty-two ballistic missiles and conducted three nuclear weapons tests, which demonstrated vast improvements in weapons capability including miniaturization, solid fuel, mobile launch, higher-yield nuclear bombs, and ICBMs capable of striking all of the continental United States.

President Trump's policy review recommended a strategy of maximum pressure on North Korea, and like Presidents Bush and Obama, Trump used DPRK provocations to enlist others in tougher sanctions, including the sanctioning of North Korean individuals and companies, secondary sanctions against third parties, and general trade sanctions (i.e., UNSCR 2375 and UNSCR 2397). These measures, however, were overshadowed by President Trump's personal threats to the North Korean leader, the reciprocation of which raised the specter of inadvertent conflict on the Korean peninsula in the first eighteen months of the presidency. The August 2017 missile launches induced Trump's threat to rain "fire and fury [on North Korea] like the world has never seen."[1] Not to be outdone, North Korea responded by detailing a plan to launch four IRBMs targeting US bases in Guam (August 9). President Trump tweeted two days later that military measures were "locked and loaded." Kim Jong-un followed three days later reiterating his Guam "strike plans"; releasing a picture of a thermonuclear weapon small enough to fit atop an ICBM; and then conducting an actual thermonuclear test on September 3. In an address before the United Nations on September 19, Trump derided the North Korean leader as "Rocket Man [who] is on a suicide mission for himself and

---

1. "Remarks by President Trump Before a Briefing on the Opioid Crisis," The White House, August 8, 2017, https://trumpwhitehouse.archives.gov/briefings-statements /remarks-president-trump-briefing-opioid-crisis/.

for his regime."[2] The North Korean leadership responded two days later calling Trump "mentally deranged" and vowing that Trump's UN speech would make a North Korean missile attack against the US mainland "inevitable." The United States skirted the North Korean coastline with B-1B strategic bombers two days later and relisted North Korea as a state sponsor of terrorism (November). Trump tweeted "North Korea won't be around much longer."

This extraordinary public standoff between the leaders departed from the posture of the Bush and Obama administrations, which adopted hardline policies toward North Korea but were always measured in their public statements, stressing the need for peaceful diplomacy. The casual references to war by Trump and Kim precipitated a dangerous spiral of escalation. The president's reported desire to tweet out calls for the evacuation of US dependents from South Korea and his reported consideration of military options ranging from limited "bloody nose" strikes to more expansive offensive operations could arguably have sparked a conflict given the hair-trigger military signals and warning systems on both sides of the DMZ.

In an abrupt swing to diplomacy, advances in inter-Korean relations facilitated Trump's first summit meeting with Kim Jong-un in Singapore in June 2018. This meeting produced a four-paragraph joint document in which the two leaders agreed to improve political relations, work toward a future Korean peace regime, work toward complete denuclearization of the Korean peninsula, and return POW/MIA remains from the Korean War. President Trump agreed to halt US-ROK military exercises, and North Korea stopped their torrent pace of missile testing, but no timeline or concrete steps to implement the North Korean leader's denuclearization commitment akin to the work plans established in the Six-Party talks ever emerged in follow-up meetings.

President Trump met Kim again in Hanoi (February 2019) in an effort to elicit a strategic decision to disarm, but the effort failed because the two leaders could not even agree on the conditions for reestablishing a freeze at Yongbyon, let alone more expansive disarmament. Despite numerous private letters between Kim and Trump, there were no tangible denuclearization steps. Moreover, North

---

2. Donald E. Trump, "Remarks by President Trump to the 72nd Session of the United Nations General Assembly" (speech, New York, NY, September 19, 2017), https://trumpwhitehouse.archives.gov/briefings-statements/remarks-president-trump-72nd-session-united-nations-general-assembly/.

Korea rescinded its halt to testing. From May 2019 until Trump's term ended, North Korea finished as it had started—duplicating the number of missile tests done in 2017 (more than twenty). Trump dismissed the 2019 tests as unimportant because they were not ICBM or nuclear tests, thereby effectively decoupling US security from the allies.

An unintended consequence of President Trump's personal diplomacy with Kim was an improvement of relations between North Korea and China. While President Bush worked hard to separate China from its communist ally by emphasizing mutual interests with Jiang Zemin and Hu Jintao in dealing with North Korea, Trump's summits with Kim caused China to abandon its arm's-length treatment of the uncooperative North Korean leader in order to avoid being cut out of any US-North Korea deals. Xi Jinping would agree to four summits with Kim in the aftermath of Trump's March 2018 summit announcement, thereby reducing daylight between the two rather than expanding it.

How Did the Bush Administration Do?

The approaches of the Obama and Trump administrations provide useful context in evaluating how the Bush administration handled North Korea. The weapons programs have grown considerably both in quantity and quality since the Six-Party talks agreements, the responsibility for which belongs mostly on the North Koreans. Arguably, no amount of US diplomacy short of maximalist concessions (e.g., full sanctions removal, generous economic assistance, troop withdrawals, regime security guarantees) could have moderated this ambition. But even that is not clear.

The Six-Party agreements made modest progress on denuclearization, more than subsequent efforts by Presidents Obama and Trump. The Six-Party agreements produced a clearly documented definition of denuclearization agreed to by North Korea ("the abandonment of all nuclear weapons and existing nuclear programs"); a verifiable freeze on reactor operations; disablement of critical components; and dismantlement of the cooling tower. However, these accomplishments were short-lived and far from the complete verifiable denuclearization objective set by the administration for itself. North Korea eventually undid all that had been accomplished, it crossed the nuclear threshold, and it continued to develop its weapons programs. Other threats from North Korea remain unresolved.

The Bush administration created new compellence tools to deal with the proliferation threat from North Korea. The maximum-pressure campaigns pursued by the Obama and Trump administrations—targeting proliferation financing by North Korean individuals, companies, and third parties—owe their origins to Bush-era Treasury Department and law enforcement actions that used tools like the USA Patriot Act to target North Korean money in Chinese banks. Another new tool was the 2003 Proliferation Security Initiative (PSI), which eventually grew to include 107 countries as an effective counterproliferation tool with several interceptions of North Korean weapons of mass destruction (WMD) trade. Subsequent administrations would also build on the ballistic missile defense interceptor and X-band radar capabilities that were stood up during the Bush administration, including President Obama's emplacement of a THAAD battery in South Korea.

The Bush administration created new multilateral diplomacy to North Korea in two respects. The first involved creating the Six-Party format, which was hailed as the first regional security institution involving the powers of Northeast Asia. Having all of the governments in one room together preempted North Korean efforts to drive wedges between the parties and limited China's freedom of action in protecting its North Korean ally. It allowed the United States to play Russia and China against each other somewhat, and it allowed the United States to stay closely coordinated with Japan on the abductions issue and with South Korea's engagement initiatives with North Korea. More broadly, it provided an Asia-based regional forum that promoted cooperation with Australia, India, and other countries, and offered a credible message of unanimity among North Korea's neighbors. Demonstrating a US commitment to Six-Party diplomacy also helped the United States take responsible defensive measures to protect itself and its allies against the North Korean threat even as it negotiated with it.

The second element of multilateralism involved the successful US effort to obtain unanimous UN Security Council resolutions sanctioning North Korean behavior. Gaining positive votes from China and Russia in the Security Council was integral to a strategy that presented Pyongyang with a united international front seeking to compel a strategic decision to disarm. Subsequent administrations would build on this multilateral diplomacy, seeking multiple UNSCRs, but would fail to adopt the Six-Party format.

President Bush put special focus on human rights abuses in North Korea. His administration saw a number of landmark measures including signing into law the North Korean Human Rights Act, appointing a Special Envoy for human rights, establishing a North Korean refugee resettlement program in the United States, and inviting North Korean refugees into the Oval Office. These were all firsts in US foreign policy on the Korean peninsula. Previous and subsequent administrations went as far as renewing applicable legislation but did not press the issue further for fear of complicating the nuclear diplomacy. President Bush, by contrast, believed that a strategic decision by North Korea to disarm and join the international community could only be manifested and sustained in the context of a liberalization of society evidenced by greater respect for human rights. This policy position received bipartisan support from Congress.

The danger of a military conflict emerged in 2017 with the North Korean leader and President Trump openly and heatedly trading threats about instigating nuclear war. President Bush's 2002 inclusion of North Korea in the "Axis of Evil" also raised concerns about impending conflict. However, his subsequent emphasis on peaceful diplomacy helped to minimize risk and miscalculation, even while backed by force and tough sanctions; gained the widespread support of governments in the region; and helped to isolate the regime.

Furthermore, although not always yielding results, the constant diplomatic effort to keep North Korea engaged at the table helped to avert destabilizing outbursts by the regime. Historical data show that periods without dialogue are highly correlated with accelerated testing and provocations by North Korea. For example, as already noted, during the last year of Obama's and the first year of Trump's terms of office, there was no diplomatic outreach and North Korea responded with forty-two missile and three nuclear tests, a far larger number than we saw during any two-year period of the Six-Party talks.

With the benefit of hindsight, one can have a better sense of areas and ways in which Bush Administration policy might have been more effective. An argument could be made that the United States had too intense a focus on the North Korean nuclear problem. Given the growth of North Korea's WMD programs over the fifteen years after the 2005 Six-Party agreement, one could credibly argue that no amount of diplomacy could have measurably altered North Korean intentions. Rather than seeking to contain or "quarantine" the program, the Bush administration set a very high bar of eliminating the program (CVID). This effectively made the United States the *demandeur*, constantly pursuing North Korea and seeking its cooperation, forfeiting the chance to degrade North Korea's nuclear capability even if it could not be eliminated.

The Bush administration's strategy may have had misplaced expectations of China as a partner in dealing with North Korea. At the time, it was a novel pivot from a purely bilateral negotiation to one that prevented China from laying the problem solely at America's door while backchanneling food, energy, and trade to North Korea that undercut the effect of economic sanctions. President Bush's efforts to bring China in as a core stakeholder were evident not just in making China the host of the Six-Party talks but also in the president's personal efforts with Jiang Zemin and Hu Jintao to find common purpose in a nuclear-free Korea. The Obama administration placed a similar emphasis on China's role in the diplomacy.

With hindsight, however, this emphasis on obtaining Chinese cooperation on North Korea may have overestimated both US capacity to bring China along as well as Beijing's ability to influence Pyongyang. The argument was that it was in China's own interest to achieve denuclearization of the Korean Peninsula and not something China was being asked to do as a favor to the United States. But Beijing may not have perceived the North Korean threat—i.e., the threat to regional security, the threat of proliferation to third countries, and the threat to the nonproliferation regime—in the same way as Washington. China had counterbalancing reasons—including not precipitating the collapse of the North Korean regime—for not pressing the regime too hard, which effectively reduced its leverage on North Korea. And North Korea had its own reasons for not wanting to appear to be giving in to Chinese pressure.

President Bush's disgust with the North Korean leader's human rights abuses caused him to rule out any direct communication with Kim or the sort of summitry that President Trump would undertake over a decade later. The absence of direct, high-level contact, however, made it difficult to decipher the state of play in North Korea in 2008 when Kim Jong-il suffered a debilitating stroke. Of course, one cannot just assume the counterfactual proposition that leader-to-leader exchange would have led to a different outcome. Trump's personal ties with Kim Jong-un did not create any greater transparency from the opaque regime when the leader went missing in 2020 and, in the end, produced no progress on denuclearization. Nevertheless, one cannot escape the logic that seeking to convince a one-man dictatorship to make a strategic shift to disarm and join the international community requires some manner of leader-to-leader dialogue, for only the president could be in a position to make that case credibly and effectively.

While any administration lays out clear and consistent negotiating parameters, it must eventually decide whether to risk larger equities to maintain forward momentum. Some have argued that the administration's decision to remove North Korea from the State Sponsor of Terrorism List and the Trading with the

Enemy Act was ill-advised diplomatic overreach, especially after revelations of North Korean proliferation of a nuclear reactor to Syria. The delisting actions also happened despite an incomplete nuclear declaration provided by North Korea as part of the Six-Party agreements. In addition, damage was done to relations with Japan, which considered the unresolved issue of North Korean abductions of Japanese nationals as a terrorist act. Yet, the president was willing to take the diplomatic risks associated with these measures to send a credible signal of US intent to move the process forward with a distrustful adversary and not to present the Obama administration with a crisis in US-North Korean relations in its opening days in office.

What Are the Lessons Learned?

The Bush administration's experience with North Korea, as well as what has transpired over the past two administrations, suggests several lessons for dealing with this perennial national security problem.

- *Maintain denuclearization goals but be realistic.* The goal of US policy must be a strategic shift by North Korea: to agree to complete, verifiable, and irreversible denuclearization and join the community of nations; however, policymakers should be under no illusions that this will be achieved in the near term.
- *Reduce risk through dialogue.* In the interim, the United States and partners should seek steps to reduce risk, increase stability, and constrain and contain North Korea's nuclear and missile programs and nefarious activities—all while retaining the ultimate goal of full denuclearization.
- *Retain strong alliances.* Whether North Korea's strategic shift is attained or not, the United States should retain strong alliances, and close bilateral and trilateral policy coordination with South Korea and Japan. At no time should North Korea policy weaken our alliances, nor should it dictate our alliance policies.
- *Enhance defense and deterrence.* A core element of this alliance strengthening is to shore up defense and deterrence capabilities, including military exercising for readiness, missile defense, and other joint capabilities to both deter and pressure North Korea and China.
- *Work multilaterally.* The United States must be vigorous in working with UN member states to disrupt North Korean nuclear, missile, and other

programs, including the transfer of such technologies to actors threatening to the United States and its allies.

- *Work with, but do not rely on China.* While the United States should invite China's cooperation (such as in sanctioning North Korea or fostering diplomacy), it should be wary of allowing Beijing's cooperation on this issue to distract from, or influence inordinately, our recognition of the challenges posed by China to vital American interests and those of our Allies. China simply does not see the same degree of threat from a nuclear North Korea and has not evidenced a willingness to use its full leverage to achieve denuclearization.

- *Raise human rights.* US policy should raise the issue of human rights abuses not just because it is a US responsibility to speak out for those who cannot, but because human rights cannot be separated from any negotiated settlement. Economic assistance from the private sector or international financial institutions cannot flow to North Korea in return for disarmament if human rights abuses remain unaddressed.

- *Don't rush into summits.* The United States should be wary of high-level summitry and should only consider it if there is solid evidence that the regime really is prepared to make a strategic shift.

CHAPTER 15

Missile Defense

WILLIAM TOBEY

President George W. Bush entered office determined to transform strategic relations with Russia to reflect post–Cold War realities, and to meet emerging threats posed by ballistic missile programs in North Korea and Iran. The former would make defenses against ballistic missiles politically feasible, and those missile defenses would help to accomplish the latter.

During the 2000 campaign, in a key speech to the National Press Club on May 23, then-Governor Bush argued: "When it comes to nuclear weapons, the world has changed faster than US policy. The emerging security threats to the United States, its friends and allies, and even to Russia, now come from rogue states, terrorist groups and other adversaries seeking weapons of mass destruction and the means to deliver them."[1] He continued: "It is time to leave the Cold War behind and to [de]fend against the new threats of the 21st century. America must build effective missile defenses based on the best available options at the earliest possible date."[2]

---

1. George W. Bush, "Bush Outlines Defense and International Relations Plans," Rush Transcript, CNN, May 23, 2000, http://edition.cnn.com/TRANSCRIPTS/0005/23/se.01 .html.
2. Bush, "Bush Outlines Defense and International Relations Plans."

Bush saw the imperatives of changing the relationship with Russia and employing defenses against emerging adversaries as elements of a novel and consistent strategic vision. In his view, the new strategic relationship with Russia offered an opportunity to address long-standing Soviet and later Russian concerns about US missile defenses. Bush explained: "[T]here are positive, practical ways to demonstrate to Russia that we are no longer enemies. Russia and our allies in the world need to understand our intentions: America's development of missile defenses is a search for security, not a search for advantage."[3]

In Governor Bush's view, Cold War deterrence calculations were a barrier both to better, more realistic relations with Russia, and to deployment of effective defenses against the threat posed by North Korea, Iran, and perhaps others. To emphasize this idea, he offered to transform radically the basis of the American deterrence calculations.[4] In the same National Press Club speech, President Bush said, "America should rethink the requirements of nuclear—for nuclear deterrence and a new security environment. The premises of Cold War nuclear targeting should no longer dictate the size of our arsenal."[5]

---

3. Bush, "Bush Outlines Defense and International Relations Plans."

4. The dysfunction of Cold War nuclear planning was recounted by Fred Kaplan in a February 4, 2020 interview with the Bulletin of the Atomic Scientists, in which he references the efforts of Franklin Miller, who later served as Special Assistant to the President and Senior Director for Defense Policy and Arms Control in the George W. Bush administration:

> [D]uring the George H. W. Bush administration, when the US and the Soviets were negotiating an arms reduction treaty, Miller asked one of his people out at SAC [Strategic Air Command] headquarters near Omaha, "If we reduced the number of nuclear weapons to such and such an amount, would you still be able to accomplish your mission?" And the officer said, "Well that's not the kind of question that we deal with. We take the weapons that we have and we assign them to the targets that we've listed." There was a SAC commander named General John Chain in the '80s who once said at a congressional hearing, "I need 10,000 weapons because I have 10,000 targets." People who heard that thought that he was either joking or just wasn't very bright, but no, that was the mechanics of how this was done. It was completely out of control. It was a broken apparatus that just followed a completely circular logic where policy didn't really even enter into things.

> Due to Miller's and others' efforts, the George H. W. Bush administration greatly improved nuclear planning and reduced the American nuclear arsenal by roughly half. The Clinton administration did not implement new reductions. The new Bush administration clearly thought more could be accomplished.

5. Bush, "Bush Outlines Defense and International Relations Plans."

Perhaps too subtly or tentatively to be understood or believed in Moscow, *he was offering no longer to size the US nuclear arsenal based on Russia's*—any more than the United States deployed forces based on the size of British or French nuclear deterrents. He also promised to "[P]ursue the lowest possible number [of nuclear weapons] consistent with our national security," and that "[i]t should be possible to reduce the number of American nuclear weapons significantly further than what has been already agreed to under START II without compromising our security in any way."[6]

The National Press Club speech was neither bellicose unilateralism nor American triumphalism, but perhaps it did not translate well into Russian. As the Transition Memorandum will recount, its optimistic, even radical, vision of a transformed strategic relationship with Russia went unrealized. But despite this failure, the United States was nonetheless able to deploy national ballistic missile defenses against limited strikes.

---

6. Bush, "Bush Outlines Defense and International Relations Plans."

TRANSITION MEMORANDUM

~~TOP SECRET~~

6928

NATIONAL SECURITY COUNCIL
WASHINGTON, D.C. 20504

Transition

NSC Declassification Review [E.O. 13526]
DECLASSIFY IN PART
by William C. Carpenter 3/23/2020

January 16, 2009

MEMORANDUM FOR THE RECORD

FROM: JAMIE FLY, COUNTERPROLIFERATION STRATEGY

SUBJECT: Missile Defense

THE SITUATION AS WE FOUND IT:

When this Administration entered office in 2001, the United States had limited ability to protect America and its allies from the threat posed by weapons of mass destruction delivered by long-range ballistic missiles. Constrained by the 1972 Anti-Ballistic Missile (ABM) Treaty, and with a lack of international support for the concept of missile defense, the United States had few options against ballistic missiles being developed by North Korea and Iran which could be used to threaten American forces abroad, U.S. allies, and the U.S. homeland. The only available tool was traditional Cold War-era deterrence which relied on the threat of retaliation to deter attack. As President Bush noted in his May 1, 2001 speech at National Defense University, "To maintain peace, to protect our own citizens and our own allies and friends, we must seek security based on more than the grim premise that we can destroy those who seek to destroy us." The threat had changed significantly, but we had not adapted to respond to it.

While little progress was being made on missile defense, the roster of states possessing ballistic missile technology had grown. In 1972, only eight states possessed such technology. By the beginning of this Administration, ballistic missile technology had proliferated to more than 20 states, including to state sponsors of terrorism. Despite the proliferation of ballistic missile technology during the 1990s, missile defense was not a priority and underfunding hampered the Department of Defense's missile defense efforts. There was at least rhetorical Congressional support for the concept of missile defense, evidenced in the National Missile Defense Act of 1999's call for "the United States to deploy as soon as it is technologically possible an effective National

~~TOP SECRET~~
Reason: 1.4(b)(d)
Declassify on: 1/16/19

Re-Classified by: Ellen J. L Knight
Reason: 1.4(b) and (d)
Declassify on: 1/16/2034

Missile Defense system capable of defending the territory of the United States against limited ballistic missile attack." But there was an inadequate commitment to appropriating the funds required to make this goal a reality.

THIS ADMINISTRATION'S POLICY:

During his campaign for President in 2000, then Governor George W. Bush made clear that missile defense would be a priority for his Administration. At the National Press Club on May 23, 2000, he stated that "It is time to leave the Cold War behind and to fend against the new threats of the 21st Century America must build effective missile defenses based on the best available options at the earliest possible date. Our missile defense must be designed to protect all 50 states and our friends and allies and deployed forces overseas from missile attacks by rogue nations or accidental launches." He noted the need to move beyond Cold War-era concepts of deterrence to a new paradigm in which the United States would rely on defenses as well as offenses. To this end, he expressed a willingness to work with Russia to draw down strategic forces. He stated that "It is possible to build a missile defense and diffuse confrontation with Russia. America should do both." He also previewed what later became the Bush Administration's strategy for engaging Russia on strategic issues, saying, "we should invite the Russian Government to accept the new vision that I have outlined, and act on it. But the United States should be prepared to lead by example because it is in our best interests and the best interests of the world."

Once in office, President Bush initiated a detailed review of U.S. participation in the ABM Treaty, which he announced in a May 1, 2001 speech at the National Defense University. He noted the importance of cooperation with Russia "to develop a new foundation for world peace and security" that leaves "behind the constraints of an ABM Treaty that perpetuates a relationship based on distrust and mutual vulnerability." He announced that the United States would conduct a series of consultations with friends and allies to develop a new framework to replace the ABM Treaty. Delegations led by Deputy Secretary of State Richard Armitage, Deputy Secretary of Defense Paul Wolfowitz, and Deputy National Security Advisor Steve Hadley conferred with officials in Moscow, London, Paris, Rome, Warsaw, The Hague, Copenhagen, Istanbul, New Delhi, Beijing, and Seoul.

The following month, at his first meeting with Russian President Putin in Ljubljana, Slovenia, President Bush outlined his concerns about the ABM Treaty, saying, "The ABM Treaty codified our relationship as enemies. A reliance on blowing each other up is not stability." At this meeting, the two leaders agreed that Russian and U.S. experts should meet to discuss a common threat assessment as well as other missile defense issues. President Bush met President Putin again on July 22, 2001 on the margins of the G-8 Summit in Genoa, Italy, where they issued a joint statement reaffirming their plan to "begin intensive consultations on the interrelated subjects of offensive and defensive systems." Subsequently, in September 2001 in Moscow, a senior U.S. delegation presented Russian counterparts with a comprehensive proposal outlining how the United States and Russia could cooperate on missile defense.

In a meeting on October 21, 2001 in Shanghai, China, Presidents Bush and Putin agreed on the need for the United States and Russia to cooperate to combat the threats posed by terrorism and rogue states. President Bush proposed a new relationship that would include new agreements on offenses and defenses. He presented Putin with a choice about how to move beyond the ABM Treaty. He noted that "I want an agreement, and not [to] go alone. But I could go alone, and not make it a big deal. Still, I don't want to make a decision about this until we create an agreement." He also informed Putin that U.S. action on defenses would be coupled with action on reducing levels of offensive weapons. Putin responded They both agreed to continue to work toward an agreement on missile defense.

At meetings the following month in Washington, D.C. and Crawford, Texas, the two Presidents outlined major reductions in the U.S. and Russian strategic arsenals that went considerably beyond the 1991 START Treaty. Despite the conventional wisdom that deploying defenses would be destabilizing and would prevent reductions in the level of offensive forces, President Bush showed that it was possible to develop defenses against the threat posed by ballistic missiles while simultaneously making progress with Russia on reductions to strategic offensive nuclear forces.

President Bush announced the U.S. intention to withdraw from the ABM Treaty on December 13, 2001, and the withdrawal took effect on June 13, 2002. As a result of President Bush's work with President Putin, Putin kept the promise he made to President Bush at their October 21, 2001 meeting in Shanghai, and responded to the U.S. announcement by noting that while Russia disagreed with the U.S. action, the U.S. withdrawal was not a threat to Russia's security. Despite the concerns raised by commentators and foreign leaders who argued that the consequences of a U.S. withdrawal would be disastrous, the fallout turned out to be modest. The United States was now able to pursue a research, development, testing, and evaluation program necessary to develop effective missile defense systems.

At a summit in Moscow on May 24, 2002, President Bush and President Putin signed the Moscow Treaty on Strategic Offensive Reductions under which the United States and Russia committed to reduce their strategic nuclear warheads to a level of 1,700–2,200 by December 31, 2012. They also released a Joint Declaration that stated that "the United States and Russia have agreed to implement a number of steps aimed at strengthening confidence and increasing transparency in the area of missile defense, including the exchange of information on missile defense programs and tests in this area, reciprocal visits to observe missile defense tests, and observation aimed at familiarization with missile defense systems." In September 2002, the U.S.-Russia Missile Defense

Working Group was established as a U.S.-Russian forum to explore the areas of cooperation outlined in the Moscow Summit Declaration.

As efforts continued to implement the decision of Presidents Bush and Putin to explore U.S.-Russian cooperation on missile defense, the Bush Administration turned to revitalizing the U.S. missile defense effort given the freedom now possible because of the U.S. withdrawal from the ABM Treaty. The September 2002 National Security Strategy stated that "The gravest danger our Nation faces lies at the crossroads of radicalism and technology. Our enemies have openly declared that they are seeking weapons of mass destruction, and evidence indicates that they are doing so with determination. The United States will not allow these efforts to succeed. We will build defenses against ballistic missiles and other means of delivery."

To advance U.S. efforts to build these defenses, President Bush signed National Security Presidential Directive (NSPD) 23 "National Policy on Ballistic Missile Defense" on December 16, 2002, laying the groundwork for missile defense during the rest of his Presidency. NSPD-23 outlined steps the Administration would take to address what President Bush described as the "unprecedented threats" facing the United States. President Bush directed the Department of Defense to deploy an initial missile defense capability in 2004 through an "evolutionary approach" that would begin with a set of capabilities that would be modified as new technologies were developed. The missile defense system would include ground-based and sea-based interceptors, including Patriot Advanced Capability-3 (PAC-3) units, and sensors on land, at sea, and in space. NSPD-23 also noted that future improvements to the system should include deployment of the Terminal High Altitude Area Defense (THAAD) (to defend within a regional area of operations), Airborne Laser systems, and development of boost-phase and mid-course interceptors that destroy the threatening missile in the early and middle stages of flight. NSPD-23 also stressed the importance of internationalization of missile defense, stating that it was "essential" that the United States cooperate with allies on missile defense, including within alliances such as NATO, but also "with new friends like Russia." The policy also underscored the importance of eliminating obstacles to effective industrial cooperation on missile defense with partners.

The missile defense system envisioned by NSPD-23 and operationalized by the Department of Defense in 2004 provided protection against limited threats from rogue states, focused initially on North Korea. President Bush's adoption in NSPD-23 of an evolutionary program that was as international as possible allowed for efforts to expand the system to better protect the U.S. homeland against threats emanating from the Middle East through establishment of a missile defense radar in the Czech Republic and interceptors in Poland.

This Administration's policy, has been to overturn the previous arms control-centric paradigm which relied on negotiated constraints and limitations to prevent proliferation and threats to peace. The

ABM Treaty, which limited the deployment of defenses, was seen as the "cornerstone of strategic stability" because it was thought that only by limiting defenses could reductions in the levels of offensive nuclear forces be achieved. In its place, President Bush forged a new relationship with Russia that moved beyond this Cold War-era framework and established new concepts of deterrence that rely on both offensive and defensive forces. In addition, President Bush recognized that the attacks of September 11, 2001 created new imperatives for U.S. national security to deal with the threat posed by the potential acquisition of weapons of mass destruction by terrorists and rogue states. As a result of his efforts with Russia during the first year of the Administration, President Bush was able to announce his intention, in NSPD-23, "to develop and deploy, at the earliest possible date, ballistic missile defenses drawing on the best technologies available."

WHAT HAS BEEN ACCOMPLISHED:

Overcame Cold War Constraints. On December 13, 2001, President Bush announced his intention to withdraw from the ABM Treaty, stating that, "Defending the American people is my highest priority as Commander in Chief, and I cannot and will not allow the United States to remain in a treaty that prevents us from developing effective defenses." This announcement, coupled with his significant personal diplomacy during 2001 with Russian President Putin, allowed the United States to forge a new framework for cooperation with Russia on missile defense and a concurrent reduction in U.S. and Russian strategic offensive forces. It also did away with several byproducts of the Treaty such as the outmoded distinction between theater and national defenses (with the treaty only limiting the latter). Withdrawal freed the United States from the ABM Treaty's constraints, thus laying the groundwork for President Bush's operationalization of missile defense and ongoing efforts to develop the system.

Operationalized Missile Defense. Released from ABM treaty constraints, missile defense development accelerated. In January 2002, Secretary Rumsfeld established the Missile Defense Agency (MDA), building on the existing Ballistic Missile Defense Organization. The Administration also received increased funding for missile defense. Since 2001, the MDA has conducted 36 successful "hit to kill" tests out of 45 attempts spread across the ship-based Aegis Ballistic Missile Defense, the ground-based Midcourse Defense, and the THAAD programs in which threatening missiles were destroyed upon impact with the interceptors. Since 2007, 12 intercepts out of 13 attempts have been successful. These tests have confirmed the missile defense system's effectiveness against short-, medium-, and long-range threats.

In December 2002, President Bush directed the Secretary of Defense "to proceed with fielding an initial set of missile defense capabilities" by 2004 and indicated our intention to seek agreement from the United Kingdom and Denmark to upgrade early-warning radars in their countries. The

United Kingdom agreed to the upgrades in February 2003, Denmark in August 2004. These upgrades allowed the Department of Defense to take the first step of the evolutionary approach to effective missile defense directed in NSPD-23, establishing an initial capability to defend against limited rogue state attacks or accidental launches by the end of 2004. By the time of North Korea's ballistic missile tests in 2006, the U.S. system was operational and capable of engaging missiles directed at the United States. MDA has since increased U.S. missile defense capacity further, developing missile defenses against ballistic missiles of all ranges and the capability to intercept missiles in all stages of flight. Long-range ballistic missiles threaten the U.S. homeland. Deployed U.S. forces and U.S. allies face a growing threat from short- and medium-range ballistic missiles. To defeat these disparate threats, President Bush sought a layered defense that includes Airborne Laser and Kinetic Energy Interceptors for defense against missiles in the early stages of flight, or boost phase; Aegis sea-based, Ground-Based Midcourse Defense, and multiple kill vehicle programs for defense against missiles in the middle of flight, or mid-course; and THAAD and PAC-3 for defense against missiles in their final, or terminal, phase of flight.

To defend against the threat posed to the U.S. homeland by intermediate-range and intercontinental ballistic missiles, MDA employs Ground-Based Interceptors (GBIs), which consist of large solid fuel ballistic missiles that carry a kill vehicle to the incoming missile's predicted location in space in order to destroy the missile in its midcourse phase of flight. The United States now has 26 deployed ground-based interceptors (22 at Fort Greeley in Alaska and 4 at Vandenberg Air Force Base in California). Ground-Based Midcourse Defense fire control centers are based in Colorado and Alaska.

For defense of areas within a regional theater of military operations, MDA is developing the THAAD system. THAAD will be rapidly deployable and transportable via airlift worldwide within hours. It will enable the United States to defend allies and forces deployed abroad from short- and medium-range missiles.

The PAC-3 system is used to defend smaller areas from the threat posed by short- and medium-range missiles. PAC-3s are currently deployed with the U.S. Army to protect U.S. forces abroad as well as U.S. allies.

MDA has also made great strides with sea-based missile defense. Under the Aegis Ballistic Missile Defense system, the United States has been able to deploy three Aegis Cruisers and 15 Destroyers with the ability to intercept short-to-medium-range ballistic missiles with the Standard Missile 3. The system was successfully used to destroy an errant satellite in February 2008.

All of these systems operate in conjunction with a network of early warning satellites, land and sea-based radars, and an integrated command, control, battle management and communication infrastructure. Some of these radars are forward deployable, allowing the United States to quickly deploy radars to regional hotspots. One such radar is currently deployed to Israel and is being integrated with Israel's Arrow missile defense system to improve Israel's ability to counter threats from Iran. Another, a sea-based X-band radar, provides flexibility for support to MDA's testing as well as quick deployment in times of crisis to positions from which it can cover any part of the globe.

As our adversaries work to develop countermeasures to foil our missile defense system, President Bush has requested funds for extensive research and development efforts to enhance our ability to overcome such countermeasures.

While more work needs to be done, these capabilities now enable the United States to defend the U.S. homeland against ballistic missile attacks from North Korea and Iran and serve as a solid foundation for future enhancement of the system.

Committed to Protecting our Allies. The United States also worked closely with allies in Asia, such as Japan, to develop defenses against short- and medium-range threats from North Korea and made progress toward expansion of the system to defend U.S. allies in Europe and the Middle East from the threat posed by rogue states, such as Iran. To this end, in 2008, after more than 18 months of negotiations begun in January 2007 at the direction President Bush, the Administration concluded Ballistic Missile Defense Agreements to establish a missile defense radar site in the Czech Republic and a ground-based interceptor site in Poland. The Administration also concluded Strategic Declarations with the Czech Republic and Poland. These declarations record and demonstrate the U.S. commitment to our bilateral relationships with both countries and establish a framework for future cooperation. At several stages of the process, President Bush, Vice President Cheney, and Secretary Rice intervened with the leaders of both countries to help conclude these historic agreements, paving the way for the extension of our missile defense system to our closest allies. The United States has also sought to develop defenses for deployed NATO forces. Building on NATO's 1999 Strategic Concept, Allies launched work to develop Theater Missile Defense (TMD) capabilities to protect NATO's deployed forces in May 2001, and awarded the first test contract for TMD in September 2006. NATO also began TMD cooperation under the NATO-Russia Council framework, with four NATO-Russia TMD exercises occurring from March 2004 to January 2008.

Internationalized Missile Defense. The policy outlined by President Bush in NSPD-23 stressed the importance of an internationalized concept of missile defense that included protection of U.S. allies as a key aim. With President Bush's extensive consultations with allies and Russia about his decision to withdraw from the ABM Treaty and the more recent bilateral agreements with the Czech Republic and Poland, the Administration has made progress in the effort to explain our benign intentions and to correct misperceptions that U.S. missile defense initiatives were directed against Russia. Prior to 2001, some allies were skeptical about the necessity of missile defense and unaware or unconvinced of the threat from rogue states. During President Bush's first NATO summit in 2001, many of our closest allies expressed skepticism of and even opposition to U.S.

missile defense plans. Today, many allies now want to join the international missile defense effort. The United States has concluded agreements with the United Kingdom, Denmark, Italy, Japan, and Australia. Other missile defense cooperation occurs with France, Israel, Ukraine, Spain, Germany, and the Netherlands, among other nations. As President Bush noted in his October 23, 2007 speech at the National Defense University, "missile defense has gone from an American innovation to a truly international effort to help defend free nations against the true threats of the 21st Century."

Gained NATO Endorsement. This internationalization of missile defense has been especially apparent in NATO. After a prolonged ~~diplomatic~~ effort by the United States and key NATO allies, including personal diplomacy by President Bush, NATO recognized the threat posed to allies by the proliferation of ballistic missiles at the 2006 NATO Summit in Riga and agreed at the April 2008 NATO Summit in Bucharest to seek greater missile defense cooperation with Russia and to develop options for a NATO-wide missile defense system linked to the U.S. system. The Heads of State and Government recognized "the substantial contribution to the protection of Allies from long range ballistic missiles to be provided by the planned deployment of European based United States missile defense assets." This declaration of a shared threat represented a dramatic change from the transatlantic debates of the 1990s. As French President Sarkozy noted in March 2008, "It is indeed Europe's security that is at stake."

Pursued Cooperation with Russia. President Bush also worked to cooperate with Russia on a regional missile defense architecture. From his early conversations in 2001 with President Putin, to his meetings with President Putin at Kennebunkport in July 2007 and at Sochi in April 2008, President Bush outlined specific proposals for U.S.-Russian cooperation on missile defense. President Bush's efforts to engage Russia on missile defense also had the added benefit of assuaging some European concerns about U.S. intentions.

On the margins of the G-8 Summit in June 2007 in Heiligendamm, President Putin offered to share data from a Russian-leased, Azerbaijani-owned early warning radar at Qabala. Subsequently, during his meeting with President Bush at Kennebunkport, Maine, on July 2, 2007, Putin also offered data from a radar site under construction in Southern Russia at Armavir. President Putin argued that by using data from the Russian sites in combination with Aegis-capable U.S. naval assets, the United States would not need the proposed U.S. sites in Central Europe. At the press conference following the meeting, President Putin expressed his willingness to continue a dialogue on this issue and noted the potential for "an entirely new level of cooperation between Russia and the United States" that could "lead to a gradual development of strategic partnership in the area of security."

Seizing the opportunity to build a broader regional missile defense architecture from "the ground up," the United States built a cooperative proposal integrating these two sites as well as the two U.S. sites in Europe. Administration officials, including President Bush and Secretaries Rice and Gates, conducted discussions with their Russian counterparts putting forward various concrete proposals. These included transparency and confidence-building measures to alleviate Russian concerns that the planned sites in the Czech Republic and Poland were targeted at Russia, and proposals aimed at reaching agreement with Russia in principle on a broader architecture. These exchanges included unprecedented presentations of U.S. classified intelligence to Russia about Iran's missile programs.

The problem faced by these proposals was that Russia conditioned its participation on the U.S. dropping altogether its sites in Poland and the Czech Republic. At Sochi in April 2008, President Bush and President Putin agreed on a "U.S.-Russia Strategic Framework Declaration." Among other things, the Declaration stated that: "Both sides expressed their interest in creating a system for responding to potential missile threats in which Russia and the United States and Europe will participate as equal partners. The Russian side notes that it does not agree with the decision to establish sites in Poland and the Czech Republic and reiterated its proposed alternative. Yet, it appreciates the measures that the U.S. has proposed and declared that if agreed and implemented such measures will be important and useful in assuaging Russian concerns. We agreed to intensify our dialogue after Sochi in issues concerning MD cooperation both bilaterally and multilaterally."

However, despite additional meetings between senior U.S. and Russian delegations, the United States and Russia were unable to agree on the specifics of missile defense cooperation or on specific actions that would fully assuage Russian concerns. On November 5, 2008, National Security Advisor Hadley sent a letter to his Russian counterpart, Sergey Prikhodko, conveying a proposal for a post-START treaty as well as a detailed briefing on the Transparency and Confidence Building Measures the United States was willing to implement at the missile defense sites in the Czech Republic and Poland. On the same day, during his annual State of the Nation address to the Duma, President Medvedev announced Russian plans to deploy Iskander missiles to Kaliningrad "to neutralize, if need be, the [U.S.] missile defense system" and stated that "electronic counter-measures will be carried out against the new elements of the U.S. missile defense facilities." Medvedev later clarified that Russia would not take action until "America makes the first step" and operationalizes the sites.

FUTURE CHALLENGES:

Since the threat posed by ballistic missiles continues to grow, continued U.S. action and leadership on this issue will be necessary. States such as North Korea and Iran continue to develop their ballistic missile systems and export ballistic missile technology to others.

European Missile Defense. The Administration established an operational missile defense system to protect the United States against missile threats from North Korea and Iran. Much work, however, remains to be done to expand the current missile defense system to combat future threats from Iran. The construction of European based assets in the Czech Republic and Poland will contribute to this future system. But construction cannot proceed until the bilateral agreements with the Czech Republic and Poland are ratified, an outcome which, in the case of the Czech Republic, remains uncertain. Full support from the new Administration and full funding by the Congress will be necessary if the sites are to be operational early in the next decade. Russia's effort to entice us out of the two European sites in exchange for dropping its missile deployments to Kaliningrad will also have to be resisted. Iran's August 2008 attempt to place a satellite into orbit highlights the continued threat posed by Iran's development of ballistic missile technology. In time, Iran may possess long-range ballistic missiles capable of striking the United States.

Iran can strike U.S. forces and allies in the region with the short- and medium-range ballistic missiles it already possesses. The United States will need to explore partnerships with allies in the region such as Turkey, Jordan, and Israel to develop effective defenses against this threat. In April 2009, NATO leaders gathering at the NATO Summit in Strasbourg-Kehl will review options prepared by technical committees for a comprehensive missile defense system. The system would cover all of the allies, including those in southeastern Europe such as Romania, Bulgaria, and Turkey, that are within the range of Iran's current missile inventory but will not be covered by the U.S. system in Poland and the Czech Republic. Continued U.S. leadership will be required to ensure technical work remains on track and that any future NATO system is integrated with the U.S. system and effectively provides coverage of all allied populations and territory. Cost will also be a factor in negotiations as Allies such as France and Germany have so far rejected any NATO common funding for such a system.

Relations with Russia. Despite extensive efforts to accommodate Russian concerns on missile defense, Russia has reacted harshly to our missile defense agreements with the Czech Republic and Poland. As already noted, at Sochi in April 2008, President Bush obtained President Putin's agreement that transparency and confidence-building measures, once agreed, will be "useful in assuaging Russian concerns." However, Russia's August 2008 invasion of Georgia made missile defense cooperation with Russia more difficult. Nonetheless, finding a way to cooperate with Russia on missile defense remains in the U.S. interest. As the U.S.-Russia Strategic Framework concluded at Sochi states, the United States and Russia "must move beyond strategic principles, which focused on the prospect of mutual annihilation, and focus on the very real dangers that confront both our nations." The United States may want to explore additional areas of missile defense cooperation, such as in Asia, where the U.S. system is already established and may be perceived by Russia to be less threatening.

Evolving Threats. Finally, as the U.S. missile defense system becomes more established, rogue states will continue to develop their ballistic missile systems and attempt to design missiles that can evade U.S. defenses. Strategies to manage the risks associated with improvements in ballistic missile technology should consider continued investment in missile defense and in innovative programs such as the airborne laser, kinetic energy interceptors, and the multiple kill vehicle.

Attachments

POSTSCRIPT

WILLIAM TOBEY

In 1997, Richard Pipes asked, "Is Russia still an enemy?" He answered, "It is not and ought not to be."[7] This was the premise of the Bush administration's Russia policy and the context for its approach to missile defense. Today, both Moscow[8] and Washington[9] regard each other as adversaries, if not enemies. Missile defense policy both affected and was affected by the broader US-Russia relationship. Thus, it is central to the story of how the United States and Russia went from tentative friendship in the 1990s to open hostility today.

The Bush Administration Approach

Initially it appeared that the 2001 US decision to withdraw from the ABM Treaty would not cause a rift in US-Russian relations. Saying that he had "concluded that the ABM Treaty hinders our governments' ways to protect our people from future terrorist or rogue state missile attacks," President Bush referred to Russian President Vladimir Putin as "my friend," and placed his decision in the context of "a new much more hopeful and constructive relationship" with Moscow. He also said that President Putin and he had agreed that "my decision to withdraw from the treaty will not, in any way, undermine our new relationship or Russian security."[10]

---

7. Richard W. Pipes, "Is Russia Still an Enemy?," *Foreign Affairs* 76, no. 5 (September–October 1997): 78. (Pipes' longer answer, that "it might become one, if those who guide its destiny, exploiting the political inexperience and deep-seated prejudices of its people, once again aspire to a glory to which they are not yet entitled save by the immensity of their territory, meaningless in itself, vast mineral resources that they cannot exploit on their own, and a huge nuclear arsenal that they cannot use" shows admirable prescience.)

8. Andrew Osborn and Alexander Marrow, "Russia Calls US an Adversary, Warns its Warships to Avoid Crimea," Reuters, April 13, 2021, https://www.reuters.com/world/europe/russia-warns-us-warships-steer-clear-crimea-for-their-own-good-2021-04-13/.

9. Robert D. Blackwill and Phillip H. Gordon, "Containing Russia Again: an Adversary Attacked the United States—It's Time to Respond," Council on Foreign Relations, January 19, 2018, https://www.cfr.org/article/containing-russia-again-adversary-attacked-united-states-its-time-respond.

10. "U.S. Withdrawal from the ABM Treaty: President Bush's Remarks and Diplomatic Notes," Arms Control Today (website), December 14, 2001, https://www.armscontrol.org/act/2002-01/us-withdrawal-abm-treaty-president-bush's-remarks-us-diplomatic-notes.

Putin appeared to affirm this view. He called the decision a "mistake," but averred mildly, "[a]s is well known, Russia and the United States, unlike other nuclear powers, have for a long time possessed effective means to overcome missile defenses. Therefore, I fully believe that the decision taken by the president of the United States does not pose a threat to the national security of the Russian Federation." Thus, while he did not endorse a new strategic relationship, he also did not claim that US deployment of missile defenses would damage the old one.

Moreover, less than six months later, the United States and Russia signed the Moscow Treaty, further limiting the two countries' strategic nuclear arsenals. The US approach to the negotiations matched President Bush's vision of a new strategic relationship. Washington in effect told Moscow: "We intend to take the US strategic warhead count down to the range of 1,700 to 2,200. If you would like to join us, we can codify it in a treaty, but the United States is headed there in any event."[11] No nuclear arms control treaty has been negotiated so quickly, before or since. Had Moscow believed that US withdrawal from the ABM Treaty presented a strategic threat, it hardly would have been likely to sign a new limitation on offensive arms.

In addition, as outlined in the Transition Memorandum, the Bush administration made multiple efforts spanning its full eight years in office to engage Russia in missile defense cooperation. This was yet another effort to reassure Putin that Russia's strategic interests would not be threatened by US pursuit of ballistic missile defenses, and to avoid disrupting ongoing efforts to establish a new post–Cold War relationship with Russia. For example, right after withdrawing from the ABM Treaty, at the May 24, 2002 Moscow Summit, the two leaders agreed to exchange missile defense program information, conduct reciprocal visits to observe missile defense tests, and take steps to improve familiarization with each side's capabilities—all aimed at reassurance against strategic surprise. Despite these efforts by the Bush administration, Putin's initial benign view of US withdrawal from the ABM Treaty and missile defense deployments did not hold.

For more than half a century, world leaders have gathered annually at what is now known as the Munich Security Conference, held in one of Bavaria's oldest and grandest hotels, the Bayerischer Hof. Vladimir Putin attended his first Munich conference in 2007. Warning that his speech might be "unduly polemical," he was exactly that. Stunning the mostly European audience with his ferocity,

---

11. Interview of Robert Joseph, June 8, 2021.

Putin railed against US policies across the board, including "plans to extend certain elements of the missile-defense system to Europe," asking the Europeans whether this would lead to "an inevitable arms race." He also raised the concern that Russia's nuclear forces would be "completely neutralized."[12] Angela Stent summarized the larger significance of the speech:

> [I]n retrospect it marked the beginning of a new phase in Russia's relations with the West—and particularly with the United States. Putin felt emboldened to deliver a strong message. Russia was no longer willing to accept an agenda set by the United States. Instead of showing respect, so the Kremlin felt, the United States had taken a series of steps inimical to Russia's interests, including expanding NATO, invading Iraq, supporting color revolutions in Russia's backyard—and constantly criticizing Russia for its democratic deficits. Russia had had enough.[13]

Ostensibly, Putin had just a year remaining in office, and the Bush administration chose to downplay the significance of the speech. Defense Secretary Robert Gates responded succinctly the next day, "One Cold War was quite enough." As a former CIA Soviet analyst, Gates, however, returned to Washington shaken, and reported to President Bush that he believed "[T]he relationship with Russia had been badly mismanaged after Bush 41 left office . . ." and that Washington had underestimated Moscow's "deep and long-term resentment and bitterness."[14]

Washington premised its policy on a new strategic relationship, while Moscow was aggrieved and determined to maintain the relevance of its one remaining claim to superpower status—the world's largest nuclear ICBM force. In the meantime, as the Transition Memorandum summarized, plans for expanded Ground-based Interceptor (GBI) and radar deployments in the United States,

12. Vladimir Putin, "Speech and the Following Discussion at the Munich Conference on Security Policy," February 10, 2007, http://en.kremlin.ru/events/president/transcripts /24034.

13. Angela Stent, *Putin's World: Russia Against the West and With the Rest* (New York: Twelve, 2019), 294–95.

14. Robert M. Gates, *Duty: Memoirs of a Secretary at War* (New York: Alfred A. Knopf, 2014), 156–57.

Poland, and the Czech Republic advanced. In addition to concerns about the effect on Russian offensive forces, Moscow also resented the permanent stationing of US troops in Eastern Europe. While they would not have offensive capability against Russia, the Kremlin worried that they might precede later and larger deployments on its borders—again confounding missile defense with issues in the broader security relationship.

What Has Happened Since the End of the Bush Administration?

In the spring of 2009, the Pentagon began to reassess missile defense options for Europe. New analysis revealed that an improved version of the Navy's Standard Missile-3 (SM-3) interceptor appeared to have several advantages over the GBI. Late in the Bush administration, to reduce risks to people on the ground, the Navy used the system to bring down a failing satellite with an amazingly accurate shot. While still in development, the new version of the SM-3 had also been tested successfully eight times against increasingly longer-range targets. If early assessments were correct, the improved SM-3 could be deployed faster, in greater numbers, and with less cost than the larger, older GBI system. It could also be reloaded relatively rapidly and might even be more reliable than GBI. Moreover, space-based sensors could outperform the radar intended for the Czech Republic. Secretary Gates, retained by President Obama, recommended altering course from the third GBI site in Poland (the others being at Fort Greely, Alaska and Vandenberg Air Force base in California) that he had earlier proposed, and moving forward with SM-3, also known as "Aegis Ashore."[15]

Unfortunately, word of the new plans leaked before there could be coordinated consultations and an announcement. Worse still, it appeared that the United States had reneged on its agreement with Poland on the seventieth anniversary of the World War II Nazi-Soviet invasion. *Wired* magazine headlined its story on the matter, "Dear Poland, Happy Soviet Invasion Day. Love, Uncle Sam."[16] Nonetheless, plans for Aegis Ashore went forward, with an interceptor deployment envisioned in Romania (initial operating capability was achieved in 2016), and a later one on Poland (initial operating capability planned for 2022).

---

15. Gates, *Duty*, 401–02.

16. Nathan Hodge, "Dear Poland, Happy Soviet Invasion Day. Love, Uncle Sam," Wired (website), September 17, 2009, https://www.wired.com/2009/09/dear-poland-happy -soviet-invasion-day-love-uncle-sam/.

In March 2012, at the Seoul Nuclear Security Summit, President Obama was caught unawares by a hot microphone with Russian President Dmitri Medvedev in a discussion about missile defense:

> PRESIDENT OBAMA: On all these issues, but particularly missile defense, this, this can be solved but it's important for him [Putin] to give me space.
> PRESIDENT MEDVEDEV: Yeah, I understand. I understand your message about space. Space for you . . .
> PRESIDENT OBAMA: This is my last election. After my election I have more flexibility.
> PRESIDENT MEDVEDEV: I understand. I will transmit this information to Vladimir.[17]

This is a remarkable conversation on two counts. First, it reveals what later became obvious, that Putin remained the real power in Moscow, with Russia's president pledging to carry a message to its prime minister. Second, the president of the United States is offering future concessions to Russia on a national security issue in return for the "space" he needs to get reelected.

As late as the fall of 2012, President Obama still seemed to share hope for a new strategic relationship with Russia, despite the sea change manifested by Putin at the 2007 Munich Security Conference. During a presidential campaign debate, President Obama mocked his opponent, Mitt Romney, for calling Russia "our number one geopolitical foe." He jibed, "[T]he 1980s are now calling to ask for their foreign policy back." But the hoped-for new relationship for the twenty-first century was not to be. Russia's annexation of Crimea and aggression in Eastern Ukraine beginning in 2014, interventions in Western elections in 2016, assassination attempts with chemical weapons in 2018 and 2020, and ongoing crackdowns on all political opposition soured any chance of a different strategic relationship, however tenuous. Russia's February 24, 2022 further invasion of Ukraine obliterated any hope of a new strategic relationship.

---

17. Jake Tapper, "President Obama Asks Medvedev for 'Space' on Missile Defense—'After My Election, I Have More Flexibility,'" ABC News, March 26, 2012, https://abcnews .go.com/blogs/politics/2012/03/president-obama-asks-medvedev-for-space-on-missile -defense-after-my-election-i-have-more-flexibility.

Despite President Trump's personal commitment to better relations with Russia, the US continued to progress on missile defenses. The number of deployed GBIs in the United States rose from thirty to forty-four. More significantly, the SM-3 system successfully intercepted an ICBM-class test target in November 2020.[18] Unless changed, the United States plans about 100 Aegis-equipped ships, each with almost 100 launchers. While the Navy routinely deploys such vessels with sea-launched cruise missiles, antiship missiles, and other air defense missiles—limiting capacity for SM-3 interceptors—this, nonetheless, represents an important latent anti-ICBM capability. Five Aegis-class ships could cover a footprint the size of the continental United States—albeit with a thin layer of defenses. Russia and probably China likely have "penetration aids" that would defeat or at least degrade missile defenses through spoofing or decoys (as noted by Putin in 2001), but SM-3 interceptors will be an important capability against North Korea and perhaps Iran.

How Did the Bush Administration Do?

Missile defenses are both a practical matter—how can the United States remain invulnerable to attacks by rogue states such as Iran and North Korea—and an issue of high diplomacy with Russia—must we remain in a relationship of mutual vulnerability? Three American presidents in a row—Bush, Obama, and Trump—sought to improve relations with Russia. Each failed.

At his 1985 Geneva Summit with Mikhail Gorbachev, Ronald Reagan espoused the view that "nations do not mistrust each other because they are armed; they are armed because they mistrust each other."[19] Missile defenses were both complicated by and complicated US-Russian relations. Paradoxically, the nadir in relations afforded the United States greater flexibility in missile defense deployments and contributed to a bipartisan consensus backing them.

US missile defense capabilities are greater today than ever before. While the United States remains vulnerable to strikes by Russia or China, North Korea (or in the future Iran) could not be certain that its missiles would penetrate US defenses.

---

18. "US Successfully Conducts an SM-3 Block IIA Test Against an Intercontinental Ballistic Missile Target," Department of Defense Press Release, November 17, 2020, https://www.defense.gov/Newsroom/Releases/Release/Article/2417334/us-successfully-conducts-sm-3-block-iia-intercept-test-against-an-intercontinen/.

19. "Transcript of Reagan's Speech to UN General Assembly," *New York Times*, September 23, 1986, https://www.nytimes.com/1986/09/23/world/transcript-of-reagan-s-speech-to-the-un-general-assembly.html.

Moreover, the Aegis system affords the United States the ability to grow these capabilities rapidly. Most important, there is a strong bipartisan consensus behind deployment of effective ballistic missile defenses. In this regard, the recommendations and aspirations of the Transition Memorandum on operationalizing and deploying missile defenses were largely fulfilled.

It must be recognized, however, that the Bush administration and its successors failed to realize the transformed strategic relationship with Russia envisioned by President Bush in May 2001, when he said:

> I want to complete the work of changing our relationship from one based on a nuclear balance of terror, to one based on common responsibilities and common interests. We may have areas of difference with Russia, but we are not and must not be strategic adversaries. Russia and America both face new threats to security. Together, we can address today's threats and pursue today's opportunities. We can explore technologies that have the potential to make us all safer.[20]

What Are the Lessons Learned?

- *Strategic breakthroughs between competing powers require a common framework or shared perception of the problem.* The history of ballistic missile defense under the George W. Bush and subsequent US administrations illustrates the problem when two critical foreign policy strategic objectives collide. The United States wanted to be free of the ABM Treaty and able to deploy missile defenses against limited third-country threats while still transforming US-Russian relations from Cold War adversaries to post–Cold War partners. The Bush administration saw these as complementary ideas, but Moscow came to see them as contradictory.

- *Fundamentally competing strategic objectives are unlikely to be reconciled.* The Bush administration had a strategy for finessing this problem: try to achieve ABM Treaty withdrawal on terms acceptable to President Putin; try to reassure Putin that US missile defense efforts were not directed against Russia; as further reassurance, try to enlist Russia in missile defense cooperation against common third-country threats; and pursue dra-

---

20. George W. Bush, "President Bush Speech on Missile Defense, May 1, 2001," https://fas .org/nuke/control/abmt/news/010501bush.html.

matic reductions in strategic nuclear forces to levels that were affordable for Russia and preserved its status of nuclear parity with the United States. In the end, however, the Bush administration got half a loaf—freedom from the ABM Treaty and the ability to deploy defenses, but not the new strategic relationship it sought with Russia.

- *Arms control reflects underlying political and geopolitical realities much more than it drives them.* One might have hoped that progress on arms control would have contributed to progress in transforming US-Russian relations. And it might have, to some degree. But any progress in that arena was overwhelmed by the impact of other developments: the return of Russian economic stability and growth due to the increasing price of oil (and other natural resources) together with the adoption of sounder fiscal policies; Russia's real sense of grievance at how the Cold War ended and its enduring aspiration to be treated as a great power; the US invasion of Iraq, granting independence to Kosovo, and the Western overthrow of Gaddafi—all over Russian objections; the expansion of NATO toward Russia's western border; and Western support for color revolutions that Russia saw as producing anti-Russian regimes on its border and as a dress rehearsal for destabilizing Russia itself. It was these political and geopolitical factors that derailed the transformation of US-Russian relations. And they would have even if the United States had stayed within the ABM Treaty and abandoned its missile defense efforts.

- *Sometimes you take half a loaf.* In light of this reality, and with a transformed relationship with Russia not in the cards, the Bush and Obama administrations were right to get out of the ABM Treaty and develop and deploy the capability to defend America's military forces, its friends and allies, and its homeland from ballistic missile attack by rogue states and terrorist groups. To sacrifice missile defense on the altar of a vain hope for improved US-Russian relations would have been a strategic mistake.

PART 5

Great Power Competition

INTRODUCTION

STEPHEN J. HADLEY

There is rightly much talk today about a "revanchist Russia" and an "aggressive, hegemonic China." But that is not the China or the Russia that President Bush faced at the outset of his administration. The end of the Cold War and the collapse of the Soviet empire in 1989–1991 seemed to mark a major inflection point in world history—the "end of history" to some. Under American leadership, so-called Western values of freedom, democracy, human rights, and rule of law had prevailed first over fascism in World War II and then over communism in the Cold War. Those values seemed to be on their way to universal acceptance as the organizing principles for modern and successful states. The international order established by the United States and its allies at the end of World War II based on those values seemed unchallenged and secure. And for one of those rare moments in history, great power competition seemed to have almost vanished as a central factor in world affairs.

This largely continued to be the case through the decade of the 1990s. Both Russia and China signaled an intent to pursue political and economic reform. The incipient democratic and free market experiment in Russia largely soured. But Russia remained too weak to challenge the international order even if it had wanted to. Political reform efforts in China stalled although its dramatic economic rise continued. But China was more intent on joining the international order than challenging it. Neither Russia nor China seemed to want a direct confrontation with the United States.

The Bush administration had essentially the same strategy for dealing with each country. It sought to bring them into the established international order. By helping them to understand its benefits, the administration sought to win their support for that order and the principles on which it was based. The administration was under no illusions that either China or Russia would become "Jeffersonian democracies" modeled on the US political system. And the success of Bush administration strategy did not depend on such an outcome. But the administration did hope that by incorporating them into the international order, developing a constructive, cooperative, and productive bilateral relationship with each of them, and with American encouragement, the two nations might over time move toward democracy, market-based economies, and greater respect for the rights of their people. Perhaps more realistically, the Bush administration believed that such an approach, working with friends and allies in Europe and Asia, would moderate and help deter any Chinese or Russian behavior that might threaten the international order or the fundamental interests of the United States and its friends and allies.

This strategy elicited considerable cooperation from both Russia and China on key issues during the Bush administration (as described in the Transition Memoranda).

Russia cooperated on disrupting international terrorism (including by facilitating US operations in Afghanistan), countering the proliferation of weapons of mass destruction (including by joining in both sanctioning and negotiating with Iran and North Korea), preventing nuclear terrorism, reducing the strategic nuclear arsenals of both countries, and deepening government-to-government cooperation on a whole host of issues of common interest. This cooperation came to an abrupt halt, however, so far as the Bush administration was concerned, when Russia invaded Georgia in August of 2008.

Similarly, China joined the United States and its friends and allies in cooperating on nuclear negotiations with Iran and North Korea, on nonproliferation and counterproliferation efforts more generally, on counterterrorism initiatives, antipiracy operations off the Horn of Africa, conflict resolution and peacekeeping operations in Africa, clean energy and climate, pandemics and disease control, and stabilization of the global financial system in the wake of the 2008 financial crisis. This cooperation continued throughout the Bush administration.

At the same time, the Bush administration sought to hedge its bets by strengthening ties to friends and allies. These efforts, well described in the Transition Memoranda, were supported by America's own active presence politically, diplomatically, economically, and militarily in both Europe and the Asia-Pacific. Collectively, these efforts would build a "balance of power that favored freedom" in both regions. Such a balance of power was essential to undergird and give strength to the administration's approach to both China and Russia.

With respect to Russia, the Bush administration supported strengthening NATO, increasing European integration through the European Union (EU), further expanding NATO by including the states of Central and Eastern Europe and the Baltic states, and encouraging the EU to do the same. In this way, the administration sought to encourage a growing, united, and secure Europe as a strategic objective in its own right. But it also served both as an incentive for positive Russian behavior and as a potential hedge against a negative evolution both within Russia and in Russian policy and actions.

Initially, President Putin, perhaps because of his sense of Russian weakness, was willing to work with the United States on key national security and foreign policy issues. But over the course of the Bush administration, Russia became more and more disaffected with US policy and the US-led international order. This disaffection was driven in no small part by Putin's perception that the so-called color revolutions in Georgia in 2003, Ukraine in 2004, and Kyrgyzstan in 2005 were American-backed efforts to encircle Russia with pro-Western, anti-Russian regimes—and ultimately to destabilize Russia itself.

Putin also argued that America ignored the principles and constraints of the international order when it suited America's purposes—usually to Russia's disadvantage. Increasingly Putin saw Russia's interests in terms of autocracy at home and domination of former Soviet states abroad. He, as well as many Russians, came to see the international order as a threat to Russian sovereignty and contrary to deep-seated Russian political traditions.

President Bush supported giving both Ukraine and Georgia a path to NATO membership (a Membership Action Plan) as a way of solidifying their efforts at democratic reform. He believed that a free and liberalizing Ukraine and Georgia in NATO posed no security threat to Russia. Although Russia initially offered little objection to NATO enlargement, under President Putin it has become the leading example of how the United States and NATO have refused to take Russia's "legitimate security interests" into account. But as his statements surrounding

Russia's invasion of Ukraine have made clear, objection to NATO enlargement is a smoke screen for Putin's real goal: to bring Ukraine under a Russian sphere of influence and ultimately into confederation with Russia and Belarus to form the core of a reconstituted Russian empire. And this may not be the limit of Putin's ambitions. In light of these developments, NATO enlargement looks increasingly like a wise and right policy.

In the case of China, America sought to strengthen its regional alliances and relationships with Japan, South Korea, and Australia; bolster relationships with Taiwan and with the nations of Southeast Asia; and maintain a strong US military, economic, and diplomatic presence in the region. Working with friends and allies, the administration sought to create a regional security and economic architecture that was of value in itself but would, again, both encourage positive Chinese behavior and also potentially hedge against a more aggressive and hegemonic China.

China during the Bush administration was still following Deng Xiaoping's dictum of "hiding its strength and biding its time." It was focused heavily on its internal economic development through "reform and opening up." It believed that for this effort to succeed, it needed a benign international environment. As a result, China pursued a fairly measured and moderate foreign policy. It did not formally challenge the international order but sought to integrate into it, seeking to play a bigger role in its key institutions: the G-20, the WTO, the IMF and World Bank, and the United Nations. Perhaps the high water mark was its cooperation and statesmanlike response to the global financial crisis in 2008.

At the same time, however, China's rapidly growing economy was translating into an expanded military and increased diplomatic and economic clout. A younger generation of Chinese was beginning to question the policy of "hide and bide" and to argue for a more assertive Chinese role in the world. This new generation focused less on China's further integration into the international system and more on the idea that it was time for the international system to make accommodations to China's rising power and different political and economic system.

Despite its efforts, by the end of the Bush administration the relationship with Russia had become adversarial at best and the future problems with China were beginning to emerge. These trends accelerated during subsequent administrations. A revanchist if declining Russia and a rising, assertive China pursued more avowedly anti-American policies. Putin's Russia pursued increasingly more ambitious efforts to roll back post–Cold War arrangements in Europe (including by making war on Ukraine), to challenge American interests beyond Europe (in places like Syria), and to interfere in Western democratic elections. As Xi Jinping consolidated control in China, Beijing began positioning itself as a challenger to American power, exerting greater economic and political influence globally, using its growing military to intimidate Taiwan and other Asian neighbors, and seeking to reshape international organizations and norms to protect and advance Chinese interests. Both nations sought increasingly to achieve strategic advantage through joint action against the United States on an expanding circle of issues.

As relations with both China and Russia have deteriorated, the Bush administration's steps to strengthen ties with friends and allies have taken on even greater significance. They have been a major underpinning of efforts by successor administrations to deal with the negative evolution in the attitude and behavior of both countries, receiving even more prominence under the Biden administration.

Perhaps its most strategic contribution in this regard was the Bush administration's efforts to transform the relationship between India and the United States. It started with "Next Steps in Strategic Partnership," which began initial cooperation between the two countries in the fields of nuclear power, space operations, missile defense, high-technology trade, and defense cooperation. This led to the agreement on civil nuclear cooperation, which captured the imagination of the people of both countries.

The specific areas of cooperation were important in themselves. But the strategy was to use this cooperation for a higher purpose. The goal was to transform the US/India relationship; change the expectations of both countries as to what that relationship could become; break down decades of suspicion, grievance, and even hostility between the two countries; and create a true strategic partnership. The force behind this initiative was President Bush's belief that while the whole world was focused on China's rise, India was also emerging as a global player. And because the two countries shared democratic values, Bush believed that India was a natural partner for the United States in advancing these values and meeting shared challenges.

In particular, the transformation of India-US relations has gained even greater significance in the more than a decade since the Bush administration left office. Over time it has helped to move India away from its dependence on Russia and increased its diplomatic freedom of action. With China's more aggressive behavior, India has become more willing to join publicly with the United States and like-minded friends and allies. This shift was evidenced most recently in the revitalization of the "Quad." Made up of India, the United States, Japan, and Australia, the Quad was initiated in 2007 by President Bush in response to the Asian tsunami. It has now been given new life under the Trump and Biden administrations in the face of the China challenge.

Clearly the Bush administration and subsequent administrations did not achieve all they had hoped for in terms of constructive, positive relationships with China and Russia. This raises the question of whether there is something that America knows now about Russia and China that it could have or should have known and factored into US policies—and whether over the last twenty years this might have produced a better result. The chapters on China and Russia that follow seek to provide at least a partial answer to this question.

CHAPTER 16

Europe

DAMON WILSON | JUDY ANSLEY | DANIEL FRIED

The Bush administration—building on the work of the two preceding administrations—sought to enlarge a Europe whole, free, and at peace, and to work with a united Europe as the principal US partner to advance freedom in the world and to address global problems. President Bush outlined this strategy in his June 2001 Warsaw speech: "We plan and build the house of freedom— whose doors are open to all of Europe's peoples and whose windows look out to global challenges beyond."[1]

The terrorist attacks of September 11, 2001, and the wider War on Terror, complicated this vision. The invasion of Saddam Hussein's Iraq initially divided the United States from key European allies, especially France and Germany, and inflamed European publics. In the second term, the Bush administration mounted a sustained and successful effort to heal these divisions, with many European nations joining military missions in both Afghanistan and Iraq and playing key diplomatic roles in both conflicts. But the administration's Freedom Agenda was complicated, and to a degree compromised, by association with the

---

1. "Remarks by the President in Address to Faculty and Students of Warsaw University," The White House, June 15, 2001, https://georgewbush-whitehouse.archives.gov/news /releases/2001/06/20010615-1.html.

Iraq War and some aspects of the War on Terror, particularly in relation to the treatment of detainees. Some key European leaders inclined to work with the United States were politically hurt.

Despite these challenges, the Bush administration largely succeeded in its effort to advance freedom in Europe. It used NATO enlargement as the main instrument because the United States, as a member of NATO, could help lead that process. In parallel, the administration encouraged the European Union (EU) to expand to include the countries of Central and Eastern Europe and the Balkans. The administration also galvanized transatlantic support for democracy and reform in Georgia and Ukraine following their respective color revolutions. And it pushed the EU to advance the accession process for Turkey, which, in at least the early years of the Justice and Development Party ("AK Party") and Recep Tayyip Erdogan's rule, appeared to be on a convergence course with Europe.

The Bush administration pursued this effort in parallel with outreach to Russia, also building on the approach of the two preceding administrations. After some initial success, especially after September 11, 2001, President Putin began to move in an authoritarian direction that has become a hallmark of his rule. He also made clear he would not accept the transatlantic integration of countries that he regarded in Moscow's sphere of influence, particularly Georgia and Ukraine, countries that Russia subsequently invaded in 2008 and 2014, respectively. He pivoted from strategic cooperation with the United States and the transatlantic community to undermining Western goals.

TRANSITION MEMORANDA

S̶E̶C̶R̶E̶T̶-WITH
TOP SECRET
ATTACHMENT

THE WHITE HOUSE

WASHINGTON

30232
Transition

NSC Declassification Review [E.0.13526]
DECLASSIFY IN PART
by William C. Carpenter 3/23/2020

January 9, 2009

MEMORANDUM FOR THE RECORD

FROM: JUDY ANSLEY, DEPUTY NATIONAL SECURITY ADVISOR

                DAMON WILSON, EUROPEAN AFFAIRS DIRECTORATE

                ADAM STERLING, EUROPEAN AFFAIRS DIRECTORATE

SUBJECT: Europe Whole, Free and at Peace

THE SITUATION AS WE FOUND IT:

Nearly a decade after the end of the Cold War, debates were continuing in Europe's established democracies over the rightful place of Europe's new democracies within European and transatlantic institutions. The Czech Republic, Hungary, and Poland had joined NATO in 1997, but Allies differed on whether or when membership would be right for nine other Central and East European countries in NATO's Membership Action Plan (Albania, Bulgaria, Estonia, Latvia, Lithuania, Macedonia, Romania, Slovakia, and Slovenia). Similarly, while the European Union (EU) had begun accession negotiations with ten Central and East European countries (Bulgaria, the Czech Republic, Estonia, Hungary, Latvia, Lithuania, Poland, Romania, Slovakia, and Slovenia), its member states lacked a common vision for enlargement, with many doubting that at least some of the candidates from what was still called "the East" belonged in the EU.

A future integrated into the institutions of Europe was even less clear for the countries of the Western Balkans. Despite a number of positive developments in 2000, such as the overthrow of the Milosevic regime in Serbia, doubts remained about whether the people of the Balkans could or would put their devastating decade of ethnic conflict behind them. Doubts also pervaded the European vision for promoting freedom and democracy in the countries on Europe's eastern frontier (Ukraine, Moldova, Belarus, Azerbaijan, Armenia, and Georgia) and drawing them closer to Europe. Many

S̶E̶C̶R̶E̶T̶ WITH
TOP SECRET ▓▓▓▓▓ ATTACHMENT
Reason: 1.4(b) (d)
Declassify: 1/9/19

Re-Classified by: Ellen J. L. Knight
Reason: 1.4(c) and (d)
Declassify on: 1/9/2034

Europeans did not foresee a future in which these countries would be fully integrated into Europe, or even potentially free of the Russian orbit. The persistence of frozen conflicts over Nagorno-Karabakh (Azerbaijan and Armenia), Abkhazia and South Ossetia (Georgia), and Transnistria (Moldova), combined with backsliding on reforms in Ukraine and a Soviet-style dictatorship in Belarus, rendered these countries particularly daunting targets for European integration. Turkey remained a special case. While the EU formally recognized Turkey in 1999 as an EU membership candidate on equal footing with other candidates, leading EU members continued to question whether it belonged in the EU.

U.S.-European relations in the 1990s, as in preceding decades, focused on problems in Europe, notably in dealing with the changes on the continent in the aftermath of the end of the Cold War and the Balkans wars. NATO's only active military operations were on the continent, in Bosnia and Kosovo. The United States and Europe cooperated ad hoc on international challenges such as Middle East peace, but no global agenda or clearly articulated set of common values guided the partnership.

THIS ADMINISTRATION'S POLICY:

From the outset, the Bush Administration has sought to promote the goal of a "Europe whole, free and at peace"—in other words, a unified and democratic Europe free of the dividing lines of its Cold War past. In the centerpiece address of President Bush's first official trip to Europe, delivered on June 15, 2001, to faculty and students at Warsaw University, President Bush set forth a vision in which, "All of Europe's new democracies, from the Baltic to the Black Sea and all that lie between, should have the same chance for security and freedom—and the same chance to join the institutions of Europe—as Europe's old democracies have." He called for "an open Europe," undivided by "false lines," in which "every European nation that struggles toward democracy and free markets and a strong civic culture must be welcomed into Europe's home." He underscored this vision of an undivided Europe by referring to Warsaw as "the center of Europe," calling for an end to distinctions between "East and West."

The President's Warsaw speech traced "the true source of European unity" to Europe's common values. He said that these values—respect for the dignity of the individual and for social, political, and economic freedoms—also bind together Europe and the United States as they derive from our common history and "pervade our history and our partnership in a unique way." More than just a source of U.S.-European unity, he said, these values call for a U.S.-European partnership to confront challenges worldwide in a manner that advances these same values.

To achieve the goals set forth in President Bush's June 2001 Warsaw speech, the Administration pursued the following major policy objectives for Europe:

- Promoting European freedom, reform, and unity through support of open-door membership policies in both NATO and the EU.
- Supporting the development of stable, democratic states in the Western Balkans, including Kosovo, with viable prospects for full integration into Europe.
- Backing closer Turkish integration into Europe by championing its candidacy for EU membership.
- Advancing freedom, democracy, reform, and prospects for European integration in the countries on Europe's eastern frontier.
- Working with Europe as partners to confront global challenges, guided by a common strategic vision based on shared values.

Our strategy for pursuing these objectives included:

- **Focusing on the process of NATO and EU expansion** as the primary engine for reform and democratic consolidation in Europe's emerging democracies. Administration policy called not only for an open door to membership for all European democracies seeking membership in the Euro-Atlantic institutions, but also for active support for candidate countries to meet membership criteria. We also encouraged the EU to develop more effective mechanisms to engage European democracies not yet on an EU membership track. With U.S. support, the EU developed a comprehensive European Neighborhood Policy, increasingly backed it up with resources, and assumed a greater presence on the ground in places like Moldova and Belarus by opening Commission offices.

- **Creating a sense of inevitability about the ultimate expansion of NATO and EU** to all the democracies of Central and Eastern Europe and the Western Balkans. President Bush set this theme in his June 2001 Warsaw speech when he said about NATO enlargement, "the question of 'when' may still be up for debate within NATO; the question of 'whether' should not be." This statement paved the way for NATO's "big bang" decision in 2002 to invite seven candidates into the Alliance, and gave momentum to continued enlargement. The President maintained this public line concerning Georgia and Ukraine, laying the groundwork for the 2007 Bucharest Summit decision that these nations will become NATO Allies.

- **Using dedicated U.S. assistance programs** under the Support for Eastern European Democracy (SEED) Act and the Freedom Support Act (FSA), as well as military assistance programs, to support reforms in Europe's new democracies. Over the course of the Administration, we have spent $3.76 billion in SEED and $4.46 billion in FSA, targeting our assistance to help the countries of Central and Eastern Europe to complete the transition they began with the end of Communism.

- **Demonstrating U.S. backing for leaders willing to make tough choices** for reform in Europe's new democracies. The President's private diplomacy and public statements underscored that the United States would put its full support behind those prepared to advance free-market and democratic reforms. Similarly, we made it clear that we would not orchestrate revolutions, but would stand with a people demanding their say about their own future and government—whether in Ukraine, or Georgia (successfully), or Belarus.

- **Pursuing an ambitious schedule of diplomacy** with the leaders of Europe's new democracies, including frequent White House meetings and Presidential visits to all the new NATO allies and membership candidates such as Georgia and Ukraine. Most Presidential trips to Europe included a stop in a new democracy in Europe, a pattern noticed within Europe and which reinforced our objective to treat our newest allies as credible partners, not clients.

- **Enlisting Europe's new democracies as partners drawing from their own post-Communist transitions** to assist the development of nascent democracies in Europe's East and to support democratic forces in authoritarian states such as Belarus and Cuba.

- **Shining a constant light on Belarus,** Europe's last dictatorship. The President's engagement, including in White House meetings with democratic activists from Belarus, helped elevate the lack of freedom in Belarus from an inconvenience to many of our European partners, to a leading topic of policy coordination.

- **Emphasizing shared values as the core of the new global focus of U.S.-European relations.** The President emphasized this theme in his major addresses on the U.S.-European partnership, notably his June 2001 Warsaw address, in which he declared that "The unity of values and aspiration (between Europe and the United States) calls us to new tasks. Those who have benefited and prospered most from the commitment to freedom and openness have an obligation to help others that are seeking their way along that path."

- **Underscoring to Europe's new democracies that they did not have to choose between the United States and the European Union.** The President told Central and Eastern European leaders and audiences, particularly at the height of tensions with France and Germany over Iraq, that friendship with the United States did not imply any cost to their relationship with the European Union. The President made clear that Central and Eastern European democracies could be good NATO Allies and loyal members of the EU, and that the United States fully supported their countries' accession to the European Union.

- **Stressing that the advance of democracy was not a threat to Russia.** Although Moscow continued to see the advance of democracy into the states of the former Soviet Union as a challenge to its authority, the President's message that democracies posed no threat but constituted good neighbors helped limit confrontation with Russia in Europe's East. The

Administration's approach also reassured Western European Allies that our support for new democracies was not aimed at Russia.

WHAT HAS BEEN ACCOMPLISHED:

NATO/EU Enlargement into Central and Eastern Europe. Less than a year-and-a-half after President Bush's Warsaw speech, NATO at its November 2002 Prague Summit extended member-ship invitations to seven candidates (Bulgaria, Estonia, Latvia, Lithuania, Romania, Slovakia, and Slovenia). This meant that at the time the seven countries formally became members of NATO in March 2004, all of Moscow's former Warsaw Pact allies, plus the three Baltic states, were members of the Alliance. The reform momentum generated by NATO expansion in 1997 and 2004 contributed to a more rapid and ambitious expansion of the EU than many would have predicted, with ten countries (the Czech Republic, Estonia, Hungary, Latvia, Lithuania, Poland, Slovakia, and Slovenia, as well as Cyprus and Malta) admitted to the EU in May 2004. Romania and Bulgaria subsequently joined the EU in January 2007.

European Perspective for the Western Balkans. Doubts about whether the countries of the Western Balkans could aspire to full integration within Europe were put to rest by 2003. In May 2003, Secretary Powell and the foreign ministers of Albania, Croatia, and Macedonia signed in Albania the "Adriatic Charter," in which the three countries pledged their adherence to NATO values and the United States pledged its support to help the countries implement reforms necessary for NATO membership. The Presidents of the "Adriatic Three" had proposed the idea of this Charter to President Bush at the 2002 NATO Prague Summit, drawing their inspiration from the U.S.-Baltic Charter of 1998 that had helped pave the way for NATO membership for the Baltic states. One month after the signing of the Adriatic Charter, EU leaders gathered at Thessaloniki with the leaders of Albania, Croatia, Macedonia, Bosnia and Herzegovina, and Serbia and Montenegro, affirmed their "unequivocal support to the European perspective of the Western Balkan countries" and approved "The Thessaloniki Agenda for the Western Balkans: Moving Towards European Integration."

NATO invited Albania and Croatia to join the Alliance at its 2008 Bucharest Summit, pending ratification of their accession protocols in NATO capitals. Leaders agreed that NATO would extend a membership invitation to Macedonia once its name dispute with Greece is resolved. On the EU front, Croatia was close to completing its EU accession negotiations by late 2008 and hoped to join the EU in 2010. Two other key events in 2008 helped move the countries of the region away from the legacy of the Balkans wars of the 1990s and toward a greater focus on their European future: the peaceful establishment of an independent Kosovo (despite continuing Serbian, Russian, and other international objections) and the signing by a recently elected, pro-European Serbian Government of a Stabilization and Association Agreement with the EU.

A Maturing Turkey Close to the United States, Moving Closer to the EU. The United States and Turkey enjoy strong ties and close cooperation despite significant challenges faced in our bilateral relationship and Turkey's periodic domestic political turmoil. Our alliance faced serious strains in the wake of the 2003 decision by the Turkish parliament not to allow U.S. forces to transit Turkish territory in the run-up to Operation Iraqi Freedom. Through more coordinated U.S. diplomacy, the United States overcame this challenge as we focused U.S.-Turkish cooperation on advancing joint goals. In 2004, the Administration worked closely with Ankara to help forge a deal on Cyprus which Turkey and the Turkish Cypriots supported, although the deal, "the Annan plan," was later rejected by the Greek Cypriots. The United States also enlisted Turkey in reinforcing U.S. and European efforts to press the Iranian Government to accept the "P5" proposal to suspend its uranium enrichment in exchange for generous incentives. Turkey delivered clear and direct messages to Tehran about the choice Iran faced.

The watershed in U.S.-Turkish cooperation came in November 2007, when President Bush met with Turkish Prime Minister Erdogan. During the meeting, which occurred on the heels of devastating attacks by the Kurdistan Workers' Party (PKK) in Turkey that killed 50 people, the President committed to provide   assistance to Turkey against PKK targets in northern Iraq, and publicly affirmed that the PKK is a terrorist organization and an enemy of the United States, Turkey, and Iraq. Since then,   cooperation against the PKK has created an environment for Turkey to broaden its efforts with its Kurdish population and its cooperation with the Iraqi Government and the Kurdish Regional Government. This collaborative effort has created opportunities for U.S.-Turkish cooperation on Iraq, most notably Turkish leaders' efforts to encourage Iraqi Sunnis to support the U.S.-Iraqi Strategic Framework Agreement and Status of Forces Agreement.

Over the last several years, Turkey also has taken great strides in its domestic reform efforts, which have strengthened Turkey's economy and improved the lives of its citizens (including measures to increase the rights of its Kurdish minority). The growth of civil society has also been an important factor in strengthening Turkey's democracy. The Administration has been supportive of Turkey's EU aspirations, which benefit Turkey and the EU, and welcomed the EU's decision in December 2004 to open accession talks with Ankara (formal accession negotiations began in October 2005). President Bush has reaffirmed U.S. support for Turkey's EU aspirations in his meetings with Turkish leaders and the leaders of EU member states, and has also publicly underscored that support, including during the 2008 U.S.-EU Summit. We have pressed Turkey to continue to pursue reforms to advance its EU candidacy, and have encouraged the EU in Brussels and EU Member States to continue their engagement with Turkey. While the historical secular-religious struggle continues within Turkey, the outcome of the Constitutional Court case in July 2008 (to fine, but not close, Turkey's ruling Justice and Development Party), was a welcomed outcome in preserving Turkey's EU accession path as well as reaffirming Turkey's democratic foundations and respect for the will of the voters.

Color Revolutions in Georgia and Ukraine. Popular uprisings against rigged presidential elections in Georgia and Ukraine led to the establishment of democratically resilient, if tempestuous, governments that provide a model of democratic reform in the former Soviet space and a tangible prospect for European unity extending to Europe's eastern reaches. In Georgia's "Rose Revolution," protesters succeeded in forcing the resignation of President Eduard Shevardnadze in November 2003 after his party won parliamentary elections that international and domestic observers concluded were grossly fraudulent. The Western-oriented and pro-reform Mikheil Saakashvili was elected President in a new election in January 2004 that was judged democratically legitimate. Similar protests in Ukraine followed presidential elections in November 2004 that were also blatantly fraudulent. Ukraine's "Orange Revolution" triggered a new election in January 2005 won by another Western-oriented reformer, Viktor Yushchenko.

Under their new governments, both Georgia and Ukraine have embarked on comprehensive, if uneven, democratic and free-market reform programs. NATO initiated an Intensified Dialogue about potential NATO membership with Ukraine in 2005 and with Georgia in 2006. Ahead of NATO's Bucharest Summit in April 2008, both Georgia and Ukraine requested an advance to the next step in NATO's membership process, a Membership Action Plan (MAP). Allies failed to reach a consensus on MAP for the two countries at Bucharest, although the Summit communiqué affirmed that both countries "will become members of NATO."

Presidents Saakashvili and Yushchenko remained in power in late 2008, both still strongly adhering to a Western orientation for their countries, but facing increasing internal and external challenges. Since the NATO Summit in Bucharest, Russia has intensified its efforts to place obstacles in the way of the Western trajectory of both countries, notably with challenges to their territorial integrity. Russia's August 2008 invasion of Georgia and subsequent recognition of the independence of Abkhazia and South Ossetia have, in particular, exacerbated the nervousness of some European Allies about drawing Georgia closer to NATO and Europe. The United States responded to the invasion by approving a $1 billion assistance package for reconstruction and for returning Georgia as quickly as possible to a course of dynamic economic growth and reform. Russian rhetorical challenges to Ukraine's sovereignty over its Crimea region, coupled with the October 2008 dissolution of the second "Orange Coalition" government in Ukraine, has similarly reinforced doubts in Europe about Ukraine's readiness for further integration with NATO and Europe, and confirmed skepticism about Yushchenko's ability to deliver on his vision for his country.

Moldova's European Path. A December 2002 White House meeting between President Bush and President Voronin of Moldova contributed to a shift in Moldova's orientation away from Moscow and toward Europe. Voronin began to look to the West for help in resolving the frozen conflict with Russia over Moldova's separatist Transnistria region and to advance at home economic liberalization and anti-corruption measures. In February 2005, Moldova signed an Action Plan with the EU that set forth a roadmap of democratic and free market reforms to guide Moldova toward greater Euro-Atlantic integration. The EU in turn took a more active role in Moldova by deploying the EU Border Assistance Mission (EUBAM) to the border between Transnistria and Ukraine. Despite modest progress on reforms, Moldova remains Europe's poorest country (other than Kosovo) and heavily dependent on remittances from its citizens working abroad. As part of Voronin's effort to secure Russian support to resolve Transnistria, Moldova has indicated that it might be willing to commit to neutrality and eschew pursuit of NATO membership, even as it seeks membership in the EU.

A Common Front Against Europe's Last Dictatorship in Belarus. President Bush has drawn attention to repression in Belarus, including by references to it in speeches such as his 2007 State of the Union and U.N. General Assembly addresses, and by welcoming democratic and civic activists from Belarus on several occasions to the White House. Following the fraudulent presidential election in Belarus in 2006, the Administration, in coordination with the EU, imposed visa restrictions and an asset freeze on President Lukashenka and other senior officials of the Belarusian regime deemed responsible for electoral fraud and abuse. In November 2007, the Bush Administration extended the asset freeze to the Belarusian state-owned petrochemical conglomerate, Belneftekhim, which alone accounted for approximately 25 percent of all exports from Belarus. These punitive measures, combined with close, continuing U.S. coordination with EU officials in Brussels and officials in a number of European governments, have helped to amplify pressure on the Belarusian regime and led to the release of all political prisoners in Belarus by August 2008.

As the Administration and the EU had long insisted on the unconditional release of all political prisoners as a minimum condition for improving relations with Belarus, the Administration reacted to the release of the last political prisoners by granting temporary licenses for business transactions to some Belneftikhim subsidiaries. The EU temporarily lifted travel restrictions on President Lukashenka and most other regime officials on the EU visa ban list. In the wake of Russia's invasion of Georgia, we began to discuss with the EU how to leverage Lukashenka's concerns about his dependency on Moscow to entice him to take further steps to come closer to the West. While the EU continues to pursue a greater level of engagement with Minsk, the momentum toward improved relations diminished as a result of badly flawed parliamentary elections on September 28.

A United Transatlantic Community Confronting Global Challenges. U.S.-European cooperation during President Bush's first term was impeded by differences over Iraq and a French-inspired vision (under former French President Chirac) of Europe as a "counterweight" to U.S. global influence. Chirac was supported by Chancellor Schroeder, and the two of them often enlisted President Putin. Changes in leadership in both Germany and France, growing Russian distancing from common European values, and a cooling of European concerns on Iraq have greatly reduced the appeal of Chirac's "counterweight" idea. To strengthen and broaden the U.S.-European partnership, President Bush took the first foreign trip of his second term to Brussels (where he met with both NATO and EU leaders), Mainz, Germany, and Bratislava, Slovakia in February 2005. The trip set the tone for deepened and globally focused cooperation with Europe during the second term. This new level of cooperation and focus outside Europe has included significant improvements in joint counterterrorism efforts, a strong common front with the EU-3 (France, Germany, and the U.K.) in confronting Iran over its nuclear program, and a strengthened European commitment to a secure and prosperous future for Afghanistan.

FUTURE CHALLENGES:

Despite progress over the past 8 years in realizing the vision of a Europe whole, free and at peace, notably with respect to the full European integration of ten formerly Communist countries of Central and Eastern Europe, gaps in the vision remain to be filled. The transatlantic consensus that the countries of the Western Balkans have a future in NATO and the EU must be brought to fruition, and remaining issues related to Kosovo and Serbia must be cleaned up. A European consensus recognizing Turkey's inevitable future in the EU must still be forged. The nascent trajectory of Georgia and Ukraine toward European integration must overcome countervailing pressure from Russia and become irreversible. Moldova will need help in becoming a viable candidate for greater European integration, both in terms of its political and economic development, and in resolving the frozen conflict over its Transnistria region. The frozen conflicts in the Caucasus must also be resolved. Finally, Europe's last dictatorship must come to an end in Belarus. Priorities for the coming years should include:

Balkans. The EU will need continued coaxing to play its necessary leadership role in the Balkans, notably through an accelerated EU integration process to stabilize the region. For NATO integration of the region to continue moving forward, there will need to be resolution of the Macedonia name issue eventually enabling Macedonia's membership, approval of MAP for Bosnia and Montenegro as early as 2009 if they continue to implement needed reforms, and closer NATO cooperation with Serbia and Kosovo. Gaining Serbia's tacit acceptance of the independence of Kosovo will be essential for Kosovo's ultimate success, and help create the conditions in which Serbia will pursue NATO membership.

Turkey. Continued engagement with both Turkey and the EU is needed to encourage forward movement in Turkey's EU bid. Turkey's role as an energy link between the Caspian region and Western Europe can deepen Turkey's ties with and importance to the rest of the continent. In addition, further reform by the Turkish Government, to include reopening Greek Orthodox Halki Seminary and repealing Article 301 (recently amended, Article 301 makes it a crime to "insult" the Turkish state), will benefit Turkey's minorities and assist Turkey's western integration. A Cyprus settlement is also critical to Turkey's EU accession goals. In addition, underlying tensions in the relationship between NATO and the European Security and Defense Policy (ESDP), exacerbated by Turkish-Cypriot spats, need to be resolved.

Georgia/Ukraine. Making Georgia and Ukraine's European trajectory irreversible will require a concerted and unified U.S.-European front against Russian efforts to hold back Georgia and Ukraine. For Georgia this will mean, in particular, continuing efforts to secure substantial levels of U.S. and international assistance to overcome the effects of the Russian invasion. It will also require continuing support for reforms in both Georgia and Ukraine. Given the doubts among some European leaders about the readiness of Georgia and Ukraine for closer integration with Europe, including through NATO MAP, the United States will have to use the privileged relationship it enjoys with the Governments of Georgia and Ukraine to nurture more mature and effective leadership in both countries.

Prospects for the European integration of Georgia and Ukraine will remain constrained, including with respect to MAP, as long as their sovereignty and territorial integrity remain under challenge by Russia. A long-term strategy to help Georgia reassert sovereignty over Abkhazia and South Ossetia is essential for countering Russia's assertion of a right to intervene in neighboring countries to protect its "privileged interests." The strategy must, however,

Efforts to reinforce Ukrainian sovereignty could include a strategy for strengthening Crimea's ties to the rest of Ukraine, the development of transparent and commercially based natural gas supply arrangements with Russia, and greater diversification of Ukraine's energy supplies.

Frozen Conflicts. Russia's actions in Abkhazia and South Ossetia reinforce the importance of resolving the other frozen conflicts of Nagorno-Karabakh and Transnistria, which continue to obstruct the European integration of the countries in Europe's East. Strong diplomatic efforts in coordination with Europe, notably through the Organization for Security and Cooperation in Europe (OSCE), would be necessary if we are to jump-start movement toward resolution of these conflicts. This would likely require the establishment of an international peacekeeping force in Transnistria to replace the current Russian "peacekeeping" mission, and a stronger U.S. and EU role helping Armenia and Azerbaijan overcome their mutual suspicions over Nagorno-Karabakh.

Belarus. Advancing freedom in Belarus will require continuing both pressure on the regime and support for civil society and democratic activists. While some unilateral U.S. sanctions, such as an asset freeze on the Belneftikhim petrochemical conglomerate, have had a significant impact on the regime's access to resources, the sort of sustained pressure that can moderate regime behavior would require a unified U.S. and European front. The European temptation, to "engage" the regime before it has taken any meaningful steps to reform is, however, a constant threat to this unified front. The United States will need to continue to work closely with our European partners to prevent the Belarusian regime from concluding that it can evade international accountability. Near-term support for civil society and democratic activists could focus on expanding democratic space inside Belarus through increased access to unfiltered information and increased participation in the political system.

Attachments

Tab 1   Chronology on Europe Whole, Free and at Peace
Tab 2   Joint Press Conference with President Bush and President Aznar (June 12, 2001)
Tab 3   Remarks by the President in Address to Faculty and Students of Warsaw University (June 15, 2001)
Tab 4   President Bush Welcomes Romania to NATO (November 23, 2002)
Tab 5   Memorandum of Conversation between the President and President Mikheil Saakashvili of Georgia (February 25, 2004)
Tab 6   Letter to President Kuchma of Ukraine (March 24, 2004)
Tab 7   Memorandum to the President on Enlisting European Support to Help Meet 21st Century Challenges (November 3, 2004)
Tab 8   Press Statements on Ukraine's Elections (November 2004)
Tab 9   Scope Memorandum to the President on Trip to Belgium, Germany, and the Slovak Republic (February 20–24, 2005)
Tab 10   President Discusses American and European Alliance in Belgium (February 21, 2005)
Tab 11   Briefing Memorandum to the President for His Greeting with the Champions of Freedom and His Remarks to Citizens of Slovakia (February 24, 2005)
Tab 12   Memorandum of Conversation, Joint Statement, and Remarks from the Meeting between the President and President Yushchenko of Ukraine (April 4, 2005)
Tab 13   President Addresses and Thanks Citizens in Tbilisi, Georgia (May 10, 2005)
Tab 14   Discussion Papers and Summary of Conclusions from the NSC Deputies Committee Meeting on Belarus (October 4, 2005)
Tab 15   Summary of Conclusions, Discussion Papers, and Follow-Up Papers from the NSC Principals Committee Meeting on Ukraine (March 10, 2006)
Tab 16   President Bush Discusses NATO Alliance During Visit to Latvia (November 28, 2006)

TOP SECRET

THE WHITE HOUSE
WASHINGTON

November 17, 2008

MEMORANDUM FOR THE RECORD

FROM: JUDY ANSLEY, EUROPEAN AFFAIRS DIRECTORATE
        DAMON WILSON, EUROPEAN AFFAIRS DIRECTORATE
        BERTRAM BRAUN, EUROPEAN AFFAIRS DIRECTORATE
        KATHERINE HELGERSON, EUROPEAN AFFAIRS DIRECTORATE

SUBJECT: Western Balkans

THE SITUATION AS WE FOUND IT:

During the 1990s, the Western Balkans lurched from crisis to crisis as the former Yugoslavia broke apart. Ethnic conflict, boundary disputes, rampant crime and corruption fueled violence and widespread ethnic cleansing. Approximately 100,000 people were killed in the Bosnia war and another 10,000 were killed in Kosovo. While some individuals made large profits from this chaos, most of the region's people became increasingly impoverished.

In the second half of the 1990s, the United States became the leading international force in the Balkans. In 1995, the United States brokered the Dayton Peace Agreement, ending the war in Bosnia. In 1999, the United States led the North Atlantic Treaty Organization (NATO) campaign to bomb Yugoslavia and drive Yugoslav forces out of Kosovo. By 2000, the United States was deeply involved in the Balkans, both in terms of resources (e.g., troops, aid) and involvement in the complex politics of the various countries.

The year 2000 saw a number of positive developments. With the end of the conflict in Kosovo, for the first time in a decade there was real peace in the Western Balkans and, by the end of 2000, all governments in the region were on a democratic path. Key developments in 2000 included:
- the peaceful overthrow of the Milosevic regime in Serbia by a coalition of democratic parties;
- the stabilization of Kosovo under the United Nations (U.N.) administration after a period of chaos following the end of the NATO bombing campaign;

TOP SECRET
Reason: 1.4 (b) (d)
Declassify on: 11/17/18

NSC Declassification Review [EO 13526]
DECLASSIFY IN FULL
by William C. Carpenter on 3/23/2020

- the victory of the opposition in Croatia, after almost 10 years of rule by President Tudjman's nationalist party; and
- the election of a less nationalistic leadership in Bosnia.

These positive developments, however, masked continued deep divisions and instability within the region, including:
- secessionist intentions by the Montenegrin Government;
- an ethnic Albanian insurgency in Southern Serbia;
- the overwhelming desire for independence among Kosovo Albanians;
- unclear and incompetent governance of Kosovo by the U.N.;
- the beginnings of an ethnic Albanian insurgency in Macedonia;
- Albania's slow recovery from a period of state collapse and lawlessness; and
- deep ethnic divisions in Bosnia, and a bloated, dysfunctional public sector still under international oversight.

Throughout the region, disputed borders, organized crime, weak economies, massive unemployment and the lack of any formal link to the European Union (EU) integration process and NATO were impeding the development of modern, democratic institutions.

THIS ADMINISTRATION'S POLICY:

Upon coming into office in January 2001, the Bush administration's goal for the Balkans was to extend "Europe whole, free and at peace" to include and permanently stabilize the Balkans. Our strategy for achieving this goal was to:
- use the attraction of integration of the Balkan nations into transatlantic institutions (both NATO and the EU) to encourage needed political and economic reform;
- work through international administrations giving way to local institutions as these institutions mature;
- encourage cooperation among the states in the Balkans;
- encourage greater EU responsibility since the future of these nations lay within the EU; and
- support the process and make clear there was no need to choose between the U.S. and the EU.

This goal and strategy resulted in a policy focused on three priorities for the Balkan region:
- supporting democratic governments;
- encouraging greater European leadership, including promoting EU and NATO integration; and
- reducing U.S. military involvement without undermining stability.

U.S. handling of the ethnic Albanian insurgencies in southern Serbia and Macedonia are illustrative of the application of this strategy. In the **Presevo Valley** of southern Serbia, the Administration worked closely with the Serbian Government, local ethnic Albanians, the EU and NATO to find a peaceful solution to the ethnic Albanian insurgency that erupted in 2000. The insurgency, led by the ethnic Albanian Liberation Army of Presevo, Medvedja, and Bujanovac (UCPMB), was sparked by local Albanians' discontent with political and economic inequalities and radicals' desire to join the majority-ethnic-Albanian area to Kosovo. U.S. and EU officials quickly engaged diplomatically with the then-newly-elected democratic Serbian Government and with the rebels to stress that the United States and EU supported a peaceful resolution of the conflict within existing borders, and to work out a political agreement that provided for increased ethnic Albanian involvement in local institutions, new municipal elections, and the establishment of the Coordination Body to enable Belgrade to assess local needs and fund projects. NATO's Kosovo Force (KFOR) also helped by stepping up patrols within Kosovo to deny rebels the ability to stage attacks across the border. NATO's agreement to allow Serbian security forces to return to the ground safety zone—the five-kilometer strip of land along the Kosovo border that they were required to avoid under the 1999 Kumanovo Agreement, which allowed KFOR to deploy to Kosovo—also allowed Serbia to prevent the reemergence of a lawless zone that could allow radicals to reignite the insurgency.

This successful international effort had several key components: 1) sending a clear message to ethnic Albanian leaders in southern Serbia and Kosovo that the United States supported a negotiated solution to the conflict and strongly opposed any efforts to join the area to Kosovo; 2) restoring security through good cooperation between Serbian authorities and NATO in patrolling the border area between Serbia and Kosovo in which insurgents were especially active; 3) working with the EU, Serbian authorities, and local ethnic Albanians to address the Albanians' legitimate grievances through the establishment of a political framework including a multiethnic police force, greater inclusion in local government, and new local elections; 4) a generous program of U.S. and EU financial assistance to alleviate the poverty that fueled local Albanians' sense of grievance; and 5) working with Serbia to establish the Serbian Government's Coordination Center, which provided ongoing Serbian Government support to interethnic reconciliation in the area through infrastructure and economic projects. The United States worked closely with European allies to make clear to both sides that they faced a choice between peacefully settling their differences to move toward the peace and prosperity of eventual EU and NATO integration, and living in an impoverished and violent region cut off from western institutions.

The Administration successfully adopted a similar policy to deal with the ethnic Albanian insurgency that began in **Macedonia** in 2001. The insurgency, led by the National Liberation Army (NLA) ethnic Albanian radical group, began in February 2001 with a series of incidents near the Kosovo-Macedonian border. It escalated in March 2001 after Macedonian authorities cracked down on rebel areas with excessive force and quickly resulted in over 20,000 persons being displaced. NATO played a key role in bringing an end to the crisis by increasing KFOR patrols near the border in Kosovo; engaging with both sides to urge restraint; and brokering a ceasefire between the NLA and the Macedonian Government in July 2001. High-level U.S., NATO, and EU diplomatic involvement— including calls between the President and Macedonian President Trajkovski and the use of U.S., NATO, and EU special envoys—also helped persuade both sides to show restraint and work out a political solution that would address ethnic Albanian grievances while respecting the rule of law and keeping Macedonia intact.

The United States, NATO, and the EU made clear that we opposed the use of violence to pursue interethnic grievances and supported the eventual integration into the EU and NATO of a Macedonia that met democratic standards, including respect for minority rights. The United States worked with the EU, NATO, the Macedonian Government, and ethnic Albanian leaders to negotiate the Ohrid Framework Agreement, which provides robust guarantees of ethnic Albanian rights including participation in the army, police, and other public institutions; municipal redistricting and decentralization; and expanded official use of the Albanian language. The United States supported NATO in its successful efforts to broker a ceasefire and subsequently disarm insurgents and field the Amber Fox peacekeeping mission. The Administration subsequently supported the handover of security responsibility to EU Operation Concordia and the OSCE's work on community policing and rule of law, and assisted Macedonia's economic recovery by contributing $116 million of a total of over $500 million at an international donors' conference in 2002.

Several lessons emerged from the successful efforts to defuse these ethnic Albanian insurgencies in southern Serbia and Macedonia:

- Early and active diplomatic engagement with all parties, both local and international, is key to success. United States engagement with the EU and NATO to jointly press for negotiated solutions and to offer the incentive of eventual NATO and EU accession, and active engagement with all parties to the conflicts, were important in both cases.

- Active U.S. engagement was vital in bringing an end to the insurgencies, since ethnic Albanian leaders tend to trust the United States more than European governments.

- International involvement in guaranteeing security—which, in the Macedonian case, included a NATO peacekeeping mission and subsequent EU police mission—is necessary to create an environment for good-faith negotiations. The NATO role in providing security to end both insurgencies was critical to preventing the fighting from escalating and eventually bringing it to an end.

- A credible political framework for addressing the grievances that sparked an insurgency is necessary for a durable peace. In both cases, the achievement of political solutions to ethnic

Albanian grievances—including guarantees of equitable ethnic Albanian inclusion in governing and security institutions—was key to ending the insurgencies. International follow-up was also critical to ensuring that the governments followed through on promises to implement minority rights measures, many of which were difficult or controversial with their own constituencies.

- Economic measures are also needed for a durable solution. Each conflict was fueled, in part, by inequitable allocation of economic opportunities. Donor assistance by the United States and EU helped pay for programs to address these inequalities (for instance, training for new multiethnic police forces) as well as to repair damaged infrastructure and fuel economic development in ways that fostered interethnic reconciliation.

- Well-timed turnover of responsibility to local authorities also is important for a durable solution. Once the two insurgencies had been defused, handing over primary responsibility for implementation of the new political frameworks to local leaders allowed them to take greater ownership of the issues and avoid long-term dependence on the international community, as well as allowing international organizations and governments to devote attention and resources to other issues.

In **Bosnia,** the Administration supported robust intervention by the international High Representative to improve the functioning of the Bosnian state, while at the same time gradually phasing out NATO's Stabilization Force (SFOR) peacekeeping mission. The last U.S. peacekeepers left Bosnia at the end of 2004, handing over responsibility to the EU mission in Bosnia (EUFOR). In 2005, the United States initiated a constitutional reform process in Bosnia; however, the Bosnian parties were unable to agree on a compromise. The Administration has continued to support the basic Dayton formula of "one country, two entities and three peoples."

In **Serbia,** the Administration tried to balance support for the new democratic government in Belgrade with U.S. insistence that all those indicted by the International Criminal Tribunal for the former Yugoslavia (ICTY) be arrested and turned over for trial as quickly as possible. Serbia's political and economic reforms since 2000 were surprisingly successful, given the severe damage inflicted on government institutions, the economy, and the rule of law during the Milosevic era. However, issues left over from the 1990s, especially the arrest of war criminals and Kosovo's independence, have proven to be major stumbling blocks in Serbia's political development. Many Serbs continue to distrust the intentions of the United States and the West. Therefore, support for nationalist, anti-western political parties has remained strong. Nonetheless, President Tadic won a decisive victory in May 2008 elections on the basis of his promise to move Serbia toward Europe.

The Administration's policy on **Kosovo** evolved over the course of its eight years in office. Initially, the United States fully endorsed the international policy of "standards before status," in which the Provisional Institutions of Self-Government (PISG) in Kosovo were required to meet specified standards of democratic governance and minority rights before the international community would start a process to decide Kosovo's final status. "Standards before status" was intended to reassure Serbs in Belgrade and Kosovo that the international community would not cede full governing authority to Kosovo institutions unless and until those institutions could demonstrate that Serbs would be safe and have a viable future in Kosovo. Progress was slow and ethnic Albanian frustration continued to grow, however, since the Kosovo Albanian public feared that making the required concessions to Serbs—including large-scale return of displaced persons and administrative decentralization—without any guarantee that Kosovo would become independent would strengthen Belgrade's hold on Kosovo and jeopardize Kosovo's chances of statehood.

The anti-Serb riots in March 2004 made it clear that the status quo was untenable and that Kosovo's future stability and democratic development—especially with regard to minority rights—would require clarity on Kosovo's future status. In October 2005, the United States engineered the creation of a U.N.-led process to resolve the status of Kosovo. The United States made clear from the outset to both Belgrade and Pristina that the end result of this process would be independence for Kosovo. The U.N. Secretary-General's Special Envoy, former Finnish President Martti Ahtisaari, was charged with working with Pristina and Belgrade to craft a solution to Kosovo's status. Ahtisaari presented his recommendation (the "Ahtisaari plan") for an independent Kosovo with strong guarantees of minority rights and a continued international supervisory role for an interim period to the U.N. Security Council (UNSC) in April 2007. This plan for "supervised independence," as it came to be known among international diplomats working the issue, would make Kosovo an independent state, but leave an international presence with some authorities in place for a several-year transitional period. By setting the clear goal of Kosovo's independence, the Ahtisaari plan alleviated many of the Kosovo Albanians' concerns that granting broader rights to Serbs would harm Kosovo's chances of independence. Kosovo authorities endorsed the plan, which included provisions for significantly stronger guarantees of minority (i.e. Serb) rights than they had previously accepted.

The United States and European allies had hoped to gain UNSC endorsement for the Ahtisaari plan, but Russia's threat to veto any plan that Serbia did not accept, prevented such an endorsement. This led to a further, 120-day round of negotiations led by a "Troika" of U.S., EU, and Russian negotiators. This round of negotiations confirmed that there was no possibility of a negotiated solution both sides would accept, and left the United States and Europe with a choice between pushing for international recognition of Kosovo's independence without a UNSC resolution—which would go against Russian and Serbian wishes but would provide for significant international leverage to induce the Kosovo authorities to accept a continued international supervisory presence and strong guarantees of the minority rights set forth in the Ahtisaari plan—or allowing the issue to fester, stalling progress on minority rights and Kosovo's economic and democratic development and risking a return to violence. Faced with this choice, the United States took the lead, with our key European partners, in pushing for rapid international recognition of Kosovo and the termination of the U.N.'s mandate to administer Kosovo.

The United States has been a leading force for NATO integration and, less directly, EU integration. Through intensive involvement in each of the countries, the U.S. has pushed forward political, military, and economic reforms. Between 2001 and 2008, the U.S. provided over $3.8 billion in direct assistance to the countries of the Western Balkans.

WHAT HAS BEEN ACCOMPLISHED:

After the wars of the 1990s, the past 8 years have been a time of relative peace and stability in the Western Balkans. During this time, the region has become more democratic, more prosperous, and more integrated with the EU and NATO. Notable accomplishments include:

- **Peace in Macedonia and Southern Serbia.** Deft diplomacy by the U.S., the EU, and NATO prevented the ethnic insurgencies in Southern Serbia and Macedonia from developing into full-scale wars. The U.S.-backed Ohrid Accords which ended the violence in Macedonia stand out as a model among Balkan peace agreements. The steady implementation of Ohrid has allowed Macedonia to develop as a modern, multiethnic democracy, and a model for the region.

- **U.S. Troops Reductions.** In January 2001, there were 3,500 U.S. troops deployed in NATO's SFOR mission in Bosnia and almost 8,000 U.S. troops deployed in NATO's KFOR mission in Kosovo and Macedonia. Today, the SFOR mission has been phased out and residual peacekeeping duties are being carried out by the EU, without U.S. involvement. In Kosovo, the overall KFOR troop strength has been reduced from 42,750 in 2001 to 16,000 today, of which only 1,500 are U.S. troops. This reduction of some 10,000 U.S. troops has taken place without any increase in violence or instability in the Balkans.

- **War Criminals Brought to Justice.** In January 2001, out of a total of 69 persons indicted for war crimes by the ICTY, 26 (38 percent) were at large. Today, out of a total of 161 persons indicted by the ICTY, only 3 are still at large. Of the two most-wanted indictees, Radovan Karadzic now faces justice in The Hague, while Ratko Mladic is among the remaining fugitives. In addition to trials at the ICTY, dramatic progress has been made in local prosecution of war crimes. Croatia, Bosnia, and Serbia today each have functioning war crimes courts that have proven they can objectively and professionally try war crimes cases. Convictions in public trials by local courts with local judges have had a strong impact on changing local attitudes about what happened in the 1990s.

- **EU Integration.** The main driver of reform in the Balkans has been the desire by people in all the countries in the region to achieve the security and prosperity enjoyed by the countries of the EU. The United States has been a strong advocate of EU enlargement into the Balkans. In 2003,

EU leaders met in Thessaloniki and pledged that all Balkan countries would become members of the EU. Slovenia became an EU member in 2004—the first of the nations of the former Yugoslavia to join the EU. Today, Croatia is in the final stages of EU accession negotiations and hopes to join in 2010, Macedonia has been granted EU candidate status and hopes to begin the formal accession negotiations this year or next. Albania, Montenegro, Serbia, and Bosnia have all signed Stabilization and Association Agreements (SAAs) with the EU, which, once ratified by EU members, will lead to EU candidate status. All Balkan countries aspire to EU membership, and are making progress at varying rates toward that goal. The process of EU integration will help Balkan countries resolve most of their remaining problems.

- **NATO Integration.** The United States has also been a strong advocate of NATO integration for the Western Balkans. Slovenia joined NATO in March 2004. At the April 2008 NATO Summit in Bucharest, Croatia and Albania were invited to join the Alliance and are now awaiting ratification by NATO members. At the Summit, Greece blocked Macedonia's invitation over the issue of Macedonia's name; however, NATO allies agreed that Macedonia had met the criteria for NATO membership and would be invited to join the Alliance as soon as Macedonia resolves the name dispute with Greece. Montenegro, Bosnia, and Serbia joined NATO's Partnership for Peace (PfP) program in 2007, and Montenegro and Bosnia entered into NATO's "Intensified Dialogue" (ID) program at the Bucharest Summit. NATO made clear at Bucharest that an ID program is available to Serbia when it is prepared to accept it. Montenegro and Bosnia are likely to apply for NATO membership by requesting Membership Action Plans (MAP) within the next 2 years.

- **Montenegro Independence.** The desire of the Montenegrin elite for the Republic's independence posed two significant challenges: 1) ensuring Serbia's acquiescence; and 2) ensuring domestic stability, since the population was deeply divided on the question of independence. The Administration took a neutral stance on the desirability of Montenegrin independence, while supporting Montenegro's right to hold an independence referendum. The United States encouraged the EU to take the lead in mediating criteria for the independence referendum. By negotiating a referendum formula under which both pro-independence and anti-independence forces thought they could win, the EU was able to ensure that both sides accepted the outcome of the process. The result was a peaceful and non-disputed secession by Montenegro.

- **Kosovo Independence.** Kosovo's independence has proven more complicated, but was also accomplished relatively peacefully. After U.N.-sponsored negotiations with Serbia failed, Kosovo (with strong U.S. support) declared independence unilaterally on February 17, 2008. The United States and most of Europe quickly recognized Kosovo, but many other countries and most international organizations did not, leaving Kosovo in legal limbo. Serbia, deeply dissatisfied with both Kosovo independence and the way it came about, remains (with Russian support) intent on maintaining its claim to Kosovo and its control over the Serbs who live in Kosovo, especially in the Serb-majority north. The Kosovo Serbs for the most part prefer rule from Belgrade to rule from Pristina. Even with independence, Kosovo will remain the poorest country in Europe for years to come.

Progress continues on many fronts, however. The newly independent Kosovo Government quickly endorsed the Ahtisaari plan and passed the legislation on democratic institutions and minority rights that the plan requires. The EU Rule of Law Mission (EULEX) is deploying to Kosovo to train and mentor Kosovo legal and police institutions and to replace UNMIK as the main international supervisory authority, and KFOR will remain in place to maintain a safe and secure environment until conditions on the ground allow it to gradually phase out. The goal of the United States, European allies, and the Kosovo Government is to stand up a Kosovo state with authority over all of Kosovo; implementation of Ahtisaari-guaranteed local self-government in Serb areas, but no partition of Kosovo; and reconciliation and constructive neighborly relations between Kosovo and Serbia.

- **Economic and Democratic Development.** The period from 2001 to 2008 saw strong economic growth throughout the Western Balkans, as countries rebounded from war or, in the case of Albania, from internal chaos. Growing political stability and economic reforms led to an increase in foreign investment, especially in Serbia and Croatia. In parallel, democratic institutions became stronger. With the exception of Montenegro, each of the countries has had a peaceful change in government, with the opposition coming to power democratically. Human rights in all the countries have improved dramatically. State institutions have become stronger and better able to deal with organized crime, although problems remain.

These successes have all depended to a significant degree on several key principles:

- The prospect of membership in the EU and NATO is a powerful motivator for countries that aspire to the prosperity and security enjoyed by western countries and that see themselves as "part of Europe." This incentive has helped foster most of the progress the Balkan countries have made in recent years on issues ranging from economic reform to quelling insurgencies to arresting war crimes indictees.

- Fostering greater European ownership of European issues is important, especially as the Balkan states aspire to join the EU, but the U.S. role remains relevant. The most successful solutions of regional problems involved active cooperation between the United States and EU officials.

- Engaging early to address problems is important—as demonstrated in the insurgencies in southern Serbia and Macedonia—but handing over authority to local officials as soon as they are ready to assume it empowers them to find solutions and avoids long-term dependency.

- Fostering cooperation among Balkan states can both improve regional relations and hasten all the countries' progress toward shared goals such as EU and NATO accession.

FUTURE CHALLENGES:

Despite the progress of the past 8 years, there is much left to do. The Western Balkans are still poor, democratic institutions are still fragile, and there are a number of unresolved disputes. Above all, it is essential to maintain the Balkans' new-found stability, which is crucial for continued economic growth and democratic development. The United States will have to continue to work closely with the EU and with individual European countries to ensure that the region remains on a positive track. Priorities include:

- **Accelerating EU Integration.** EU members are understandably nervous about taking in new members, especially ones with such troubled pasts. Nevertheless, success in the Balkans depends on rapid EU integration. The stabilizing influence of the EU integration process increases as the countries get closer to membership. The United States will have to maintain positive pressure on the EU to play its necessary leadership role in the Balkans. The United States will also have to work with the EU to keep pressure on the countries of the Western Balkans to complete the reforms required for EU membership.

- **Accelerating NATO Integration.** EU integration goes hand-in-hand with NATO integration. The Macedonian name dispute with Greece needs to be resolved as quickly as possible to allow Macedonia to join NATO, and to avoid any backsliding that an uncertain future can lead to in Macedonia. If Bosnia and Montenegro continue to implement reforms, the U.S. should consider backing them for MAP status in 2009, and NATO relations with Serbia and Kosovo should be upgraded as fast as possible. In addition, the positive regional relations fostered by the Adriatic Charter (a group the U.S. initiated in 2003 to help Albania, Croatia, and Macedonia cooperate to advance their NATO integration aspirations) and the South East Europe Defense Ministerial (a larger group of countries in the region dedicated to improving cooperation on a variety of defense issues) should be continued and expanded.

- **A Democratic Serbia Firmly on a Pro-Western Path.** Serbia is the keystone of the Western Balkans; its stability is essential for the region's stability. Politically, Serbia remains deeply divided between the wealthier, better educated, and younger Serbs who embrace an EU future and the poorer, less educated and older Serbs for whom the post-Milosevic transition has been difficult and national grievances still resonate. In order for Serbia to irreversibly commit to liberal democracy and the EU path, the second group must see more benefits from reform and EU integration. This will require the EU to reach out more effectively and for the Serbian Government to ensure economic benefits reach the poorer segments of the population. Also, the West must allow Serbia to regain its dignity and sense of pride in being part of modern Europe. Insisting on collective guilt for Milosevic's actions will lead to a collective rejection of the West.

- **Kosovo Becomes a Viable State.** Despite Kosovo's declaration of independence in February 2008, the status of Kosovo has not yet been fully implemented. Kosovo will not be a fully functional country until Serbia accepts its independence and Kosovo gains more widespread international recognition. Kosovo is also surrounded on two sides by Serbia and will have to find a way to resolve a series of bilateral issues in order to succeed economically and to create institutions capable of governing throughout its territory. A particularly difficult bilateral issue is the situation of Kosovo's Serbs, who are reluctant to participate in Kosovo institutions due to pressure from Belgrade and skepticism that ethnic Albanian-dominated institutions will serve their interests. Resolving these issues will require dialogue between Pristina and Belgrade. Although unlikely in 2008, it is in the U.S. interest that this dialogue start as quickly as possible. As Serbia moves closer to EU membership and the anger over "losing" Kosovo recedes, solutions that may not be possible today will arise. The sooner the status of Kosovo is fully accepted, the better for both Kosovo and Serbia. Because of the special respect the U.S. enjoys in Kosovo, we have a special responsibility to continue to counsel tolerance, maturity and non-violence as the Kosovars encounter inevitable frustrations in their development.

- **Implementation of the Ahtisaari Plan.** Western recognition of Kosovo's independence was contingent on Kosovo's genuine and full implementation of the Ahtisaari plan, especially decentralization, the heart of the plan. This will require Kosovo quickly creating five new Serb-majority municipalities and allowing these municipalities considerable autonomy in governance, as well as giving Kosovo Serbs the reassurance of mutually agreed, transparent, and well-defined ties to Belgrade. By helping ethnic Serbs and other minorities feel secure in Kosovo, the Kosovo Government will gain credibility and avoid potentially divisive governance problems. The Kosovo Assembly and Government have committed to implement the Ahtisaari plan and have passed relevant legislation, but continued international engagement will be necessary to ensure that they fully implement the plan. Such engagement will be particularly needed to successfully implement decentralization, since decentralization will require the active cooperation of Pristina authorities and Kosovo Serbs, and the acquiescence of Belgrade authorities to the Kosovo Serbs' participation.

- **Kosovo's Economic Development.** Kosovo's long-term success depends primarily on its ability to create a viable economy for its rapidly growing population. Despite problems, all the other countries of the Balkans have economies that are sustainable and growing. This unfortunately is not yet true of Kosovo. Working with the international community, the Government of Kosovo needs to rapidly establish the basis for economic growth: education; sound institutions; modern infrastructure; and investment. The July 2008 EU-sponsored donors conference helped finance Kosovo's development plan. The EU should also open its labor market to young Kosovars as a safety valve to relieve social discontent.

- **Organized Crime, Islamic Extremism and Corruption.** Throughout the Balkans, weak states have been unable stop the spread of organized crime and extremism. Heroin from Afghanistan, weapons smuggling, and prostitution fill the coffers of criminal gangs and the pockets of politicians. Poverty and war-time grievances have led to a rise in Islamic extremism, which is often mixed with ethnic nationalism, especially in Bosnia, Serbia, Kosovo and Macedonia. To combat these threats, countries will need to create strong modern states, with effective police and courts, that can cooperate within the region and internationally. The impact of moderate, successful, indigenous Muslim populations becoming part of the EU can help advance other U.S. policy objectives and mitigate extremist influences within Europe's Muslim immigrant populations.

Attachments

Tab 1   Chronology for the Western Balkans

Tab 2   Joint Press Availability with Prime Minister of Albania, Dr. Sali Berisha (June 10, 2007)

Tab 3   Remarks: by President Bush and Prime Minister Sanader of Croatia in Zagreb, Croatia (April 5, 2008)

Tab 4   Remarks by the President to the American Troops in Kosovo (July 24, 2001)

Tab 5   NSC Discussion Paper and Summary of Discussion of NSC Meeting on Kosovo (March 23, 2007)

Tab 6   Summary of Conclusions of the Principals Committee Meeting on Kosovo (June 19, 2007)

Tab 7   NSC Discussion Paper and Summary of Discussion of the NSC Meeting on Kosovo (November 30, 2007)

Tab 8   Text of a Letter from the President to the President of Kosovo (February 18, 2008)

Tab 9   Summary of Conclusions of the Principals Committee Meeting on Kosovo (April 8, 2008)

Tab 10   Memorandum of Conversation with President Trajkovski of Macedonia (May 2, 2001)

Tab 11   Memorandum of Telephone Conversation with President Trajkovski of Macedonia (August 14, 2001)

Tab 12   NSC Discussion Paper, PFP Membership Options for Serbia Discussion Paper, and Summary of Conclusions of the Principals Committee Meeting on the Balkans (November 7, 2006)

Tab 13   Memorandum to the President on Key Elements for Success in the Balkans (January 31, 2008)

POSTSCRIPT

DAMON WILSON, JUDY ANSLEY, DANIEL FRIED

Developments in Europe during the Bush and subsequent administrations can best be understood and analyzed through four distinct lines of effort: growing the core of Europe by extending its central institutions—NATO and the EU—to new members; advancing freedom in nations to Europe's east; encouraging Turkey's reform efforts; and cooperating on meeting global challenges.

The Bush Administration Approach and Subsequent Developments

Growing Core Europe   The Bush administration's efforts to advance freedom in Europe were most successful with Central Europe and the Baltics. NATO admitted seven new countries: Estonia, Latvia, Lithuania, Slovakia, Slovenia, Romania, and Bulgaria. All of them, plus Poland, Hungary, and Czechia, which had acceded to NATO during the Clinton administration, also joined the EU. The administration laid the basis for NATO admission of Albania, Croatia, and North Macedonia and led the effort for Kosovo's independence, becoming the first nation to recognize Kosovo as an independent nation and opening the way for over 100 countries to do the same.

President Obama entered office embraced by European publics, partly in reaction to the Iraq War. His administration worked to narrow differences with key EU nations on issues such as the Middle East and climate. The Obama administration viewed further enlargement skeptically, however, given the economic challenges of the Great Recession, the uneven reforms of aspiring nations, and higher geopolitical risks given Putin's pushback. The integration process slowed in the Western Balkans (and halted in Europe's east). The administration's focus on improved relations with Russia, deference to European capitals on European issues, and a policy focus on Asia and the Middle East combined to diminish attention to a Europe whole, free, and at peace. But progress continued, nonetheless. Albania and Croatia joined the NATO alliance in April 2009 and Croatia joined the EU in 2013.

At the outset, the Obama administration tried to "reset" relations with Moscow. This produced the New START agreement, signed in 2010, to limit further deployed strategic nuclear warheads and launchers. However, Putin's government accelerated its repression of dissent at home and increased efforts to reverse the post–Cold War gains toward a Europe whole, free, and at peace. After Russia's 2014 invasion of Ukraine, the Obama administration reversed course, leading an effort to impose sanctions on Russia and deploying US with other NATO combat forces to the Baltic States and Poland.

The Trump administration placed its "America First" approach over transatlantic relations. President Trump was skeptical about NATO's mutual defense commitment, championed Brexit, and viewed the EU more as an economic competitor than a values-based partner. The administration disparaged EU institutions, and took a jaundiced approach to transatlantic trade, imposing tariffs on imports from allies. The administration deepened ties with specific European nations such as the UK, Poland, and Hungary, despite charges of democratic backsliding against the latter two. Continuing the efforts of every US president since Truman, Trump pushed European allies to increase their defense spending, with some success.

Despite President Trump's rhetorical disparagement of NATO, his administration continued the process of enlargement, supporting Montenegro's accession in 2017. However, President Trump sent mixed signals by publicly questioning the value of small allies and the contributions of others, notably Germany. The administration nonetheless agreed to allow Bosnia-Herzegovina to begin its MAP (Membership Action Plan) in 2018. And US diplomacy helped Athens and Skopje conclude the historic Prespa Agreement in 2018, paving the way for North Macedonia to join NATO in 2020. Furthermore, the Trump administration improved relations with Serbia and made progress toward normalizing Serbia-Kosovo relations.

In conclusion, there was a lot of continuity and success, over three very different administrations, in growing the core of Europe.

Advancing Freedom in Europe's East   The Bush and subsequent administrations enjoyed less success with advancing freedom in a wider Europe. Georgia and Ukraine, with their respective 2003 and 2004 Rose and Orange Revolutions, seemed poised to follow the free market, democratic transformations pioneered by Central Europe and the Baltics. With transatlantic support, both countries made significant (though uneven) advances in their reforms at home but had less success in advancing their NATO and EU aspirations. Despite efforts by the Bush administration and other allied nations at the April 2008 NATO Summit in Bucharest, Romania, NATO leaders decided not to offer Georgia and Ukraine a Membership Action Plan (MAP). Opposition by several key allies (particularly Germany and France) stymied this effort. Leaders instead agreed that both nations would become NATO members in the future. In response, however, Russian president Vladimir Putin, speaking at the summit, questioned Ukraine's sovereignty and made a territorial claim to Crimea.

This ambivalence in NATO support likely encouraged Russia to invade Georgia four months later in August 2008. The rapid and robust US response, along with staunch Georgian resistance, helped halt the advance of Russian forces. European-led diplomatic efforts helped secure Russian withdrawal from Georgian territory, although Russia maintained its prewar presence in Abkhazia and South Ossetia. America's $1 billion assistance package helped Georgia avert financial collapse and rebuild. And the Bush administration concluded a strategic partnership charter with Georgia (as well as Ukraine), while imposing sanctions on the occupied territories of Abkhazia and South Ossetia.

The Obama administration continued US support for EU outreach to Europe's east. But Russia vehemently opposed this outreach and pressured Armenia and Ukraine to abandon their negotiations with the EU. Moscow's bullying prompted Ukraine's Euromaidan Revolution of Dignity in 2013 in which Ukrainians demanded a European future. After the Kremlin supported Ukrainian president Yanukovych in staging a violent crackdown, protestors drove him from office. In the spring of 2014 Russia responded by annexing Crimea and invading Ukraine's Donbas region. Ukrainian forces, with Western political support (and US-European sanctions on Russia), halted the advance of Russian-backed forces, although Crimea and parts of the Donbas remain under Russian control and are a source of ongoing conflict.

The Obama administration responded to Russia's invasion by increasing US and NATO military presence in Central and Eastern Europe, helping to reassure allies and deter further Russian aggression. This reversed the post–Cold War US military drawdown in Europe. However, wary of provoking Russia, the Obama White House turned down requests by Ukraine and Georgia for lethal weapons.

Despite President Trump's personal embrace of Putin, his administration continued supporting the efforts of nations in Europe's east to resist Russian aggression, including by providing lethal weapons to Ukraine and Georgia. Unfortunately, President Trump undercut this aid by pressuring President Zelensky to target Democratic presidential candidate Joe Biden.

While much of the focus during this period was on Georgia and Ukraine, a separate drama was playing out in Belarus. The Bush administration had played the long game there, forging a common US-EU front to support the democratic opposition to the Lukashenka dictatorship and increase pressure on the regime, including with sanctions and the Belarus Democracy Act. Obama administration policy continued along these lines. The Trump administration attempted outreach to Lukashenka with some success, including the release of political prisoners in exchange for upgraded relations. But in the wake of fraudulent elections in Belarus in 2020 and widespread protests, the Trump and later Biden administrations worked closely with the EU to support democratic forces and increase sanctions on the Lukashenka regime.

Encouraging Turkey's Reforms   The Bush administration reached out early to Turkish leader Erdogan and his initially reform-minded team, recognizing the potential benefits if the Islamist AK Party lived up to its initial promise as a pro-democracy, pro-free market party worthy of EU membership. After miscalculating Turkey's position on the liberation of Iraq, the administration subsequently forged a common approach with Ankara to the PKK terrorist threat, including in northern Iraq. The administration attempted to advance a peace deal on Cyprus, working with Turkey to that end. It also supported Turkey's EU aspirations, pushing the EU and skeptical member states (like France and Germany) to be receptive. However, the EU accession process with Turkey stalled due to EU member state reluctance. Erdogan increasingly turned in an authoritarian and anti-Western direction, thus deepening EU reluctance. This frustrated the administration's strategy of supporting Turkey's free market, democratic transformation by its integration with Europe.

The Obama administration initially invested heavily in relations with Turkey, for the same reasons that motivated the Bush administration. Several factors bedeviled this outreach, including the outbreak of civil war in Syria in 2011, the subsequent metastasizing of the Islamic State in Iraq and Syria in 2014, and differences over negotiations with Iran. Washington and Ankara clashed over US support for Kurdish forces in Syria and failed to coordinate on the campaign against the Islamic State or on supporting Syrian opposition forces. A failed coup by members of the Turkish military in 2016 complicated relations as the Turkish leadership falsely suspected US involvement (given the alleged coup leader Fetullah Gülen's presence in the United States). President Erdogan's continued authoritarianism and widespread post-coup crackdown further tarnished his image in the West.

The Trump administration pursued an ambivalent approach to Turkey. President Trump formed a close personal relationship with President Erdogan, but bilateral relations remained tense. Following a successful campaign against ISIS in 2019, President Trump's desire to withdraw from Syria led the United States to concede control of much of northern Syria to Turkey. Facing a widespread backlash, Trump reluctantly reversed course and agreed to leave some US troops in Syria. The rift with Turkey widened as Ankara courted Moscow, culminating in the purchase of Russian S-400 missiles. This prompted significant NATO and US pushback, including expelling Turkey from the F-35 program and the imposition of US sanctions. From Bush onward, there was a worthy, but ultimately failed, attempt to tie Turkey more closely with the institutions of Europe.

Cooperating on Global Challenges Differences on the Kyoto climate agreement, arms control, elements of the War on Terror (such as treatment of detainees), and the Iraq War admittedly strained transatlantic cooperation during the first Bush term, especially with respect to common efforts outside Europe. President Bush's outreach to Europeans at the start of his second term (including support for "a strong Europe as a strong partner of the United States"), combined with new leaders in Germany and France, helped repair these divisions and much improved transatlantic relations. The Bush administration decided to begin cooperation on Iran with France, Germany, and the UK, an understanding President Bush himself reached with outgoing French President Chirac, symbolically healing the earlier rift. The Europeans also worked with the United States to help stabilize politics inside Iraq.

The Obama administration built on this progress to expand partnership with Europe on global challenges. Coordinated transatlantic diplomacy produced an agreement with Iran to temporarily freeze parts of its nuclear program. The United States helped finalize the Paris Accord on climate change. Some NATO allies played important roles in the anti-ISIS campaign. The United States supported France and the United Kingdom in the NATO military intervention in Libya in 2011.

Transatlantic discord widened under President Trump. The United States withdrew from the Iran nuclear deal and the Paris climate accords. The United States and Europe clashed over trade issues at the World Trade Organization and frequently differed at the United Nations, the World Health Organization, and other multilateral fora.

In conclusion, new issues emerged to challenge transatlantic relations. These included the need to establish new norms to deal with the consequences of new technologies, including privacy concerns, disinformation, and cyber aggression—the latter particularly from Russia and China, which became apparent toward the end of the Obama administration. The nature of the problems facing the United States and Europe—and thus the areas of potential cooperation—have thus both broadened and changed.

How Did the Bush Administration Do?
Growing the Transatlantic Community, Europe, and Integrating the Balkans

Successive rounds of NATO and EU enlargement brought formerly communist nations into a free, undivided Europe and catalyzed their prosperity. Bush administration policies cemented the place of Europe's new democracies within European and transatlantic institutions. This achievement was sweeping and, perhaps as a result, is often taken for granted.

The Bush administration and subsequent administrations did not, however, anticipate the rise of populism in Europe, including authoritarian politics and the emergence of corrupt governance in some countries. The Trump administration was conflicted about these trends, with President Trump and some of his close aides supporting authoritarian populism.

The Bush administration adapted Cold War institutions to post–Cold War environments. After 9/11, this meant urging NATO to become capable of expeditionary operations outside Europe and to recognize that threats to its members could originate from anywhere. The trade-off, however, was neglect of more classic and hybrid security challenges in Europe as Putin's aggression deepened.

The Bush administration (and its successors) had mixed success in its efforts to stabilize the Western Balkan nations and secure a better future for their people. The once-violent region remains peaceful, but with inconsistent reforms, too frequent corruption, and weak rule of law. The lengthened time horizon for potential EU enlargement weakened incentives to tackle these tough issues. Serbia remains ambivalent about whether it seeks a future with Europe or Russia. The Bush administration angered Serbia by supporting Kosovo independence. But the alternative—seeking to maintain and improve UN administration of a dependent Kosovo—would likely have failed, while alienating Kosovars and diminishing stability. While Serbia remains recalcitrant, over 100 nations recognize Kosovo's independence, Belgrade and Pristina are engaged in a diplomatic process, and the prospect of renewed conflict is remote. On a separate issue, though the Bush administration failed to resolve the name dispute between Athens and Skopje, its support for Skopje set the stage for the Prespa Agreement that reconciled Greece and North Macedonia.

Advancing Freedom in Europe's East   The Bush administration's efforts to support freedom in Ukraine and Georgia met Putin's violent resistance. President Bush correctly observed in 2008 that the post-1989 window of opportunity for such efforts might be closing, and that subsequent presidents might not have either the chance or the will to expand the ranks of freedom.

Many critics have argued that US support for the Freedom Agenda in Europe—including NATO enlargement and support for the color revolutions—alienated Putin and caused his anti-Western and anti-democratic turn. This argument fails on many grounds. President Putin's initial authoritarian moves, such as destroying independent television, began before the color revolutions and before the November 2002 Prague NATO Summit where membership offers were extended to seven nations, including the Baltic States. Putin decided independently of NATO's enlargement that what he considered Russia's "chaos" of the 1990s could be remedied by control from the top which, as it turns out, meant replacing Russia's flawed and oligarch-dominated democracy under Yeltsin with Putin's kleptocratic authoritarianism buttressed by assassination and repression.

NATO's enlargement took place alongside sustained outreach to Russia. Bush's positive initial meeting with Putin in June 2001 followed Bush's forward-looking speech on NATO enlargement. That meeting ushered in a period of constructive US-Russia relations that lasted past the Prague Summit when allied leaders invited the Baltic States to join NATO.

Strains started growing later, especially after the color revolutions in Georgia and Ukraine. The United States did not instigate the color revolutions, despite what Putin might think. But it welcomed their results, including the replacement of ineffective, corrupt, or undemocratic leaders by those who at least promised better forms of leadership and, to some degree, delivered. It is hard to imagine any American president doing otherwise.

Some critics have suggested that using the EU rather than NATO as the leading instrument for advancing the Freedom Agenda in Europe might have been less provocative to Putin. However, the origin of Ukraine's 2013 revolution was Putin's pressure on President Yanukovych not to sign an Association (not membership) Agreement with the EU. President Putin objected to "his" sphere of influence being integrated with the West, whether through the EU or NATO. Putin's price for good relations with the West was and remains acquiescence in a Kremlin sphere of domination over former Soviet republics—an arrangement that is neither right nor stable because it requires the subjugated peoples to accept Kremlin-style corruption and repression.

Critics have a better case, however, when they argue that the United States erred by pushing so hard for a MAP for Ukraine and Georgia in 2008 despite staunch German and French objections. In the end, the failure was more the need for earlier, effective diplomacy with key allies to forge consensus rather than the support for the two new democracies. The Bush administration made a long bet that failed, and the price was an alliance divided. This likely encouraged Putin to invade Georgia just four months later.

Encouraging Turkey's Reforms　The Bush administration efforts to support a more democratic, European-oriented Turkey may have failed, but it was right to try. The fact that the Obama administration also failed in this objective, despite not carrying the baggage of the Iraq War and War on Terror, suggests that the problem was not in the US effort, but in misjudging Erdogan's intentions. Indeed, many of his more liberal advisers and senior AK Party leaders also misjudged him and broke with him as his authoritarian turn became clear.

Cooperating on Global Challenges　After a complicated start, the Bush administration in its second term began partnering with Europe effectively on global challenges as it embraced "a strong Europe, because we need a strong partner in the hard work of advancing freedom and peace in the world."[2] The Bush administration joined European governments in Iran diplomacy and successfully encouraged the EU to begin focusing on China, anticipating the emergence of China as a major challenge globally and in Europe. These efforts started closing a strategic disconnect with Europe, a welcome process continued by the Obama administration.

---

2. "Bush's Speech in Brussels," *New York Times*, February 21, 2005, https://www.nytimes.com/2005/02/21/international/europe/bushs-speech-in-brussels.html.

What Are the Lessons Learned?

The experiences of the Bush, Obama, and Trump administrations in Europe suggest the following:

- *Even great successes are vulnerable.* With NATO and EU enlargement, Europe whole, free, and at peace seemed at hand. But the democratic breakthroughs in Central Europe in and after 1989 are beset by challenges from populism, corruption, and even authoritarianism. These worrying trends are matched by similar ones throughout Europe and even to a degree in the United States. Democracy itself seems on the defensive in ways not matched since the 1930s. Authoritarian rulers in Moscow and Beijing believe that their time has come. To halt and reverse these trends, the democracies must consider and correct the mistakes—starting from within—that have led to this situation.

- *Setbacks are reversable.* By the end of the Bush administration, the Western democracies had generally regarded Belarus and Moldova as lost causes in the drive for free market, democratic transformation. Yet Belarusian society erupted in sustained protests against the falsified results of its 2020 elections. A mass, pro-democracy movement grew and has maintained itself despite repression. Ukrainian society keeps rising up to demand better, more democratic governance than that country's political class has delivered. In Moldova, a liberal, pro-Western leader won election as president against a Moscow-backed rival and subsequent elections ushered in the most reform-minded parliament since its independence. Liberal political leaders have emerged and won elections in Slovakia, Czechia, and Estonia. The challenges and setbacks to democracy are real. But experience also shows that, in the end, societies do not accept corruption and autocracy. Freedom seems resilient.

- *Europe whole, free, and at peace is more stable than a divided Europe.* For all its flaws and failures, the US goal of a united, democratic Europe seems more viable than the principal alternative of a sphere of influence under Russian domination. Every US administration from 1989 has reached out to Russia. Each attempt has achieved something. But US-Russia relations have kept running into the problem of Moscow's demand for control over its neighbors. Such a model is inherently unstable because so long as Moscow remains autocratic and economically backward, its dominance is inconsistent with the interests and aspirations of the people it subjugates. This was a lesson of the Cold War and worth keeping in mind. The United States should not be tempted by such deals (such as Moscow's help with China in exchange for Russian domination of Ukraine).

- *Continuity in US foreign policy is greater than it seems—and that is a good thing.* The degree of continuity from the George H. W. Bush through the Obama administrations is striking. All operated within a framework that saw US interests and values as advancing together. All sought to achieve an undivided, democratic Europe allied with the United States. President Trump personally seemed indifferent or against that approach, but his administration continued this policy in many ways and President Biden has embraced it. US leadership based on these values remains key.

CHAPTER 17

Russia

THOMAS GRAHAM

Upon entering office, the George W. Bush administration set out to build a "qualitatively different" relationship with Russia that moved beyond Cold War rivalry to cooperation in meeting the urgent challenges of the twenty-first century. Initial efforts were focused on shared interests, including global and regional security challenges; counterproliferation; nuclear security; counterterrorism; and expansion of political-military, economic, scientific, and societal ties. This effort at strategic cooperation led to extensive interactions and relationships between the two countries across a broad set of issues.

At the same time, the Bush administration attempted to hedge its bets should its efforts to build a more constructive relationship fail and should it instead be faced with a more adversarial Russia. The Bush administration engaged Russia on policies on which the two nations differed—like Kosovo, NATO enlargement, missile defense, the evolution of newly independent states in the former Soviet space, Russia's war on Chechnya, and Russian President Vladimir Putin's increasingly authoritarian rule. The goals were to advance American interests, reach mutual understanding where possible, and responsibly manage differences where not.

As part of this effort, President Bush cultivated good personal ties with Putin. In frequent meetings, he sought frank discussion that would enable their two countries to broaden their cooperation and constructively address each side's concerns.

To advance this vision and overcome bureaucratic inertia, the two leaders created a checklist, a set of mutually agreed priority tasks that were assigned to heads of specific agencies in both countries, who then reported on progress to the two presidents at regular intervals. The two leaders also launched the Strategic Dialogue Group, a White House-Kremlin channel for discussing sensitive issues and developing a strategic framework for the US-Russia relationship.

In their meetings, President Bush sought to persuade President Putin of his historic opportunity to bring Russia permanently into the family of democratic societies and free-market economies. In a November 13, 2001 Joint Statement, the presidents committed their two countries to a "new relationship . . . founded on a commitment to the values of democracy, the free market, and the rule of law."[1] To encourage a democratic evolution within Russia, President Bush and his senior officials met with Russian business leaders, independent journalists, and human rights advocates; and increased people-to-people exchanges. But despite some initial progress, Russia over time became increasingly authoritarian in its politics and statist in its economy.

These trends continued under subsequent US administrations. The transformed, sustainable, and constructive relationship with Russia sought by the Bush administration did not come to pass. Did this reflect Putin's authoritarianism, Russia's underlying political and social culture, or a failure by several US administrations to understand contemporary Russia—and to build a partnership more sensitive to Russian concerns while not jeopardizing American interests or principles? Most likely, it was a combination of these and other factors.

---

1. "Joint Statement by President George W. Bush and President Vladimir V. Putin on a New Relationship Between the United States and Russia," The White House, November 13, 2001, https://georgewbush-whitehouse.archives.gov/news/releases/2001/11/20011113-4 .html.

TRANSITION MEMORANDUM

S̶E̶C̶R̶E̶T̶

7744

NATIONAL SECURITY COUNCIL
WASHINGTON, D.C. 20504

Transition

January 5, 2009   NSC Declassification Review [E.O. 13526]
DECLASSIFY IN PART
by William C. Carpenter 3/23/2020

MEMORANDUM FOR THE RECORD

FROM: JANINE ELLISON, RUSSIA DIRECTORATE
          LESLIE HAYDEN, RUSSIA DIRECTORATE

SUBJECT: Managing Cooperation/Differences with Russia

THE SITUATION AS WE FOUND IT:

In early 2001, U.S.-Russia relations were in an uncertain period of transition as both nations continued to define national interests beyond the post-Cold War period. For the United States, this meant defining new priorities in the absence of a Soviet or Russian threat. For Russia, this meant defining a new national identity and reasserting an international role against a backdrop of internal and external challenges.

Russia's internal political transition at the time presented a complicated picture. In late December 1999, democratically-elected President Boris Yeltsin resigned amid failed policies, economic chaos, and corruption scandals. Yeltsin handed power over to his little-known Prime Minister, former KGB officer Vladimir Putin, who later won election in 2000 in a contest that was generally recognized as free and fair. In the face of strong Western criticism, Putin had (while still Prime Minister) re-engaged in a brutal military conflict in Chechnya in response to terrorist bombings in Moscow in late 1999 that left several hundred dead. Russia's oil-dependent economy (with oil at $19 per barrel) had just started to see signs of recovery following the ruble devaluation and financial crisis of 1998. Most Russians were disillusioned by the political and economic reforms encouraged by the West during the 1990s and remained wary of U.S. intentions. Russian attitudes toward the United States were hardened by ongoing resentment over the May 1999 NATO air strikes in Kosovo; a perceived lack of support for Russia's fight against terrorism in Russia's troubled North Caucasus; and mistrust of U.S. plans to build a National Missile Defense system.

S̶E̶C̶R̶E̶T̶
Reason: 1.4(b) (d)
Declassify on: 1/5/19

Re-Classified by: Ellen J. L. Knight
Reason: 1.4(b) and (d)
Declassify on: 1/5/2034

In the United States, frustrated expectations about Russia's democratic transition under Yeltsin and uncertainty about Putin left many in doubt about how the United States should deal with Russia. Russia's military and economic cooperation with Iran and revelations of successful Russian espionage in the United States, which culminated in the February 2001 arrest of Robert Hanssen and subsequent tit-for-tat diplomatic expulsions, exacerbated bilateral tensions. Yet it remained apparent that America's security was threatened less by Russia's strength than by Russian's weaknesses and internal vulnerabilities. Furthermore, both states faced shared threats by rogue states seeking to acquire nuclear weapons and by the spread of global terrorism.

THIS ADMINISTRATION'S POLICY:

President Bush recognized the need to enlist Russian cooperation in areas critical to U.S. national security. He made an effort to shift the paradigm of U.S.-Russia relations from one marked by strategic rivalry and "dependency" on western economic support, to one of strategic cooperation in a wide range of important areas where the United States and Russia had shared interests. These included promoting global and regional security, cooperating on counterproliferation and nuclear security, combating terrorism, expanding economic relations, science and health cooperation, and strengthening the ties between our societies. President Bush also engaged Russia's leadership on policy differences such as Kosovo, NATO enlargement, missile defense, and growing restrictions in Russia on media freedom and other democratic institutions, which appeared to be aimed at limiting if not eliminating political competition. When agreement could not be achieved, the President sought to manage differences. The President was realistic about the chances for success and was mindful of President Putin's authoritarian approach to democracy at home and zero-sum attitude on certain issues of importance to the United States. Despite these challenges, President Bush strove to expand areas of cooperation with Russia and move beyond the legacy of Cold War attitudes and instincts.

As part of this effort, President Bush cultivated and maintained a good personal relationship with President Putin, which allowed for continued engagement, even at the most difficult times. From their first meeting in Ljubljana, Slovenia in 2001, the President stressed to Putin the importance of frankness, honesty, and personal contact between leaders. He sought Putin's views on mutual challenges, such as the threat posed by rogue states, but also on issues that troubled the Russian leadership, such as the U.S. withdrawal from the Anti-Ballistic Missile (ABM) Treaty. The President believed a relationship built on trust was necessary, not only to talk frankly with Putin about cooperation, but also to address concerns about Putin's authoritarian approach to democracy. The President stressed to Putin that by allowing political competition and building democratic institutions, the Russian President had the opportunity to lead a dynamic, new, and free Russia, integrated into the democratic societies and free market economies of the West.

In order to face the new threats of the 21st Century, the President believed the United States needed to move beyond the Cold War-era concept of deterrence by the threat of retaliation toward a new concept of deterrence that relied on missile defenses as well as offensive systems. The President also recognized that the threats from terrorists and rogue states against both the United States and Russia were greater than the threats either posed to the other. To this end, the President invited Russia to join the United States in building a regional missile defense architecture that would defend Russia, Europe, and the United States against the emerging missile threats from the Middle East. This new cooperative approach on missile defense was combined with a joint commitment to make deep reductions in strategic nuclear forces. In order to do this, it was necessary to leave behind the constraints of the 30-year-old ABM Treaty and, at the same time, achieve a credible nuclear deterrent with the lowest possible number of nuclear weapons consistent with our national security needs. Such a cooperative relationship was intended to be reassuring rather than threatening and was premised on openness and mutual confidence.

In this spirit, President Bush consulted closely with President Putin, stressing that he wanted a transparent missile defense system Russia could live with. Although the President stipulated that the United States could pursue missile defense unilaterally, he emphasized his preference for reaching a deal on missile defense transparency and confidence building measures (TCBMs) that would assuage Russian concerns that proposed U.S. missile defense sites in Europe posed no threat to Russia. **See the Transition Memorandum on Missile Defense for a detailed account of this aspect of the United States-Russia relationship.**

The President also recognized that there was no greater challenge to the U.S.-Russia partnership than our two countries' interaction in the former Soviet space. The President viewed Russia's respect for the sovereignty of the Eurasian states as a key indicator of its approach to the world. The President charged high-level administration officials to work with their, Russian counterparts to work out some "rules of the road" for U.S.-Russia interaction in the region. The President's goal was to identify areas for cooperation or parallel action as a way of breaking down the zero-sum mindset afflicting the Russian bureaucracy and to advance the development of viable, sovereign, and democratizing states in the region. Recognizing that both Russia and the United States had legitimate and strategic interests throughout the former Soviet Union, the U.S. proposed a set of mutually acceptable principles based on transparency, communication, and cooperation to govern our two countries' actions in Russia's near abroad.

In the wake of Russia's invasion of Georgia, President Bush pursued a firm, measured response to Russia's actions. In concert with European allies, the United States worked to deny Russia success in Georgia; to ensure that Russia felt the strategic costs of its actions; and to reassure our Central European, Eastern European, and Central Asian allies. As part of this effort, the United States adopted a "no business as usual" approach to relations with Russia to demonstrate that Russia's isolation from the world was a consequence of its irresponsible behavior in Georgia. This policy underscored that Russia could not aspire to be integrated into 21st century institutions while at the same time undermining the very principles embodied by those institutions. Recognizing that Russia's hard-line approach would remain dominant for some time, this approach also sought to keep the door open to signs that Russia may be ready to change its course.

WHAT HAS BEEN ACCOMPLISHED:

President Bush's determination to achieve successful strategic cooperation with concrete results led to an initial period of intensified high-level engagement, including early visits to Moscow in the summer of 2001 by the National Security Advisor and the Secretaries of the Treasury and Commerce. During Putin's first visit to the White House in November 2001, the United States and Russia issued a historic joint statement on the New Relationship between the United States and Russia. Noting that our countries had overcome the legacy of the Cold War, the United States and Russia pledged to embark on a new relationship founded on a commitment to the values of democracy, the free market, and the Rule of Law. Not only was Putin the first world leader to reach out to President Bush following the September 11 terrorist attacks, but he was also broadly receptive to President Bush's initiatives, demonstrating early support for the War on Terror and U.S. operations in Afghanistan. Putin also responded to our early expressions of concern about the impact of various measures on Russia's democratic process, softening some proposed political "reforms."

As the relationship progressed, concerns that bureaucratic resistance might limit what could be accomplished led to the introduction of the "Presidential Checklist" system at President Bush's September 2003 Camp David meeting with Putin. The system identified priority bilateral initiatives and called for regular status reports by respective government agencies to both Presidents. To build greater confidence and transparency in the relationship (and to avoid surprises), President Bush also supported deliberate efforts to open key channels of communication. The White House-Kremlin Strategic Dialogue Group, initiated in the spring of 2003, was designed to address sensitive issues quietly and focused on developing a core set of principles for the U.S.-Russia partnership. Similarly, the Consultative Group for Strategic Security, established in May 2002, and the Foreign and Defense Ministers "2 + 2" forum, launched in October 2007, provided channels to engage on priority security issues and sensitive concerns, including missile defense.

While the President's strategy of personal diplomacy met with early success, disagreements with Putin following the Iraq War made this strategy more difficult. Emboldened by rising oil prices and Russia's rapidly growing economy, Putin quickly aligned himself with French and German leaders to oppose U.S. "unilateralism" and establish a "multi-polar" world. In return,

French and German leaders acquiesced to Putin's growing authoritarian approach at home and his reassertion of Russian   erests in neighboring countries.

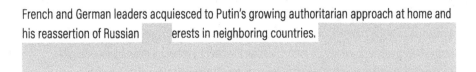

Other frictions included Putin's February 2007 "Wehrkunde" speech in Munich which attacked the United States for undermining global stability; Russian rejection of a solution in Kosovo, which enjoyed broad international support; and Russia's strong objections to NATO expansion and U.S. missile defense deployments in Central Europe. Nevertheless, U.S.-Russia relations in this period (2003—August 2008) were also characterized by important cooperation on various strategic issues (e.g., Iran, North Korea, counterterrorism, and nuclear issues).

Promoting Security. The President's strategy of a cooperative approach to missile defense combined with strategic offensive reductions was discussed in detail at his early meetings with Putin in Ljubljana in June 2001 and Genoa in July 2001, where agreement was reached to begin intensive consultations on offensive and defensive systems. Following further consultation at their October 2001 meeting at the APEC Summit in Shanghai, President Bush informed Putin in November 2001 that the United States intended to substantially reduce U.S. operationally deployed strategic nuclear warheads to a level between 1,700–2,200 over the next decade. Russia committed to implement similar reductions and our countries issued a joint statement at Crawford and later in the conclusion of the historic Moscow Treaty in May 2002.

In 2006, Secretary Rice arid Russian Foreign Minister Sergey Lavrov agreed that the 1994 Strategic Arms Reduction Treaty (START) should not be extended beyond its expiration in December 2009. Subsequent to this exchange, the United States and Russia sought to reach agreement on a post-START arrangement to supersede START. At the March 28, 2008, 2 + 2 Ministerial in Moscow, the United States concurred with Russia that START should be replaced with a legally binding agreement; this was reiterated in the Sochi Strategic Framework Declaration on April 6, 2008. To date, no concurrence has been reached on the substance of an agreement; U.S. and Russian views remain far apart. The Bush administration favors a Moscow Treaty-based approach, with its emphasis on operationally deployed strategic nuclear warheads, in conjunction with some agreed transparency and confidence building measures drawn from our START experience. Russia, however, prefers an approach more similar to the START Treaty, including limitations on delivery vehicles (ICBMS, SLBMs and heavy bombers) as well as an intrusive verification regime and preservation of the complex, outmoded counting rules. A U.S. draft text of a legally binding post-START treaty was conveyed to the Russian President's Foreign Policy Advisor, Sergey Prikhodko, in a November 4, 2008 letter from National Security Advisor Steve Hadley.

President Bush also made extensive efforts with President Putin to engage Russia on missile defense cooperation. During 2001, the President worked to ensure that despite Russian opposition to our withdrawal from the 1972 ABM Treaty, Russia would not take drastic action. At their October 2001 meeting in Shanghai, President Bush informed President Putin that he intended to withdraw the United States from the ABM Treaty, offering to delay the move until an agreement on a new framework was reached. President Putin kept his promise when President Bush announced the U.S. intention to withdraw from the ABM Treaty on December 13, 2001. Seizing on President Putin's offer at Kennebunkport in July 2007 of Russian radar sites at Qabala (Azerbaijan) and Armavir (southern Russia), the President built a cooperative proposal incorporating the Russian sites into a joint regional missile defense architecture in which Russia, Europe, and the United States would participate as equal partners. During their statement made at Kennebunkport, Putin said he believed such cooperation would raise the quality of U.S.-Russia cooperation to a new level and would lead to a gradual development of a strategic partnership in the area of security. In April 2008, at a press conference following his meeting with President Bush at Sochi, President Putin commented, that "in principle, adequate measures of confidence-building and transparency can be found." The Administration's efforts to engage Russia on missile defense also had the added benefit of assuaging some European concerns about U.S. intentions. Shortly after Russia's actions in Georgia in August 2008, the United States concluded an agreement with Poland for the basing of missile defense interceptors in Poland. (An agreement for stationing a missile defense radar in the Czech Republic was concluded earlier.)

Though Russia has yet to agree, the Administration has engaged in an unprecedented exchange of technical information and high-level dialogues on TCBMs for the planned U.S. missile defense sites in Central Europe to assuage Russia's concerns that these sites pose a threat to Russia. A final TCBM proposal was conveyed to Russian Foreign Policy Advisor Prikhodko in the November 2008 Hadley letter. The proposal offered to allow Russian liaison officers, accredited to their local Embassies, to work at U.S. missile defense sites in Poland and the Czech Republic to conduct monitoring activities, subject to host country approval and the principle of reciprocity. Despite this offer, however, Russia maintained its opposition to the sites. During his November 5 State of the Nation address, Medvedev announced specific countermeasures to U.S. missile defense sites in Central Europe, including placing Iskander surface-to-air missile systems and electronic jamming equipment in Kaliningrad to "neutralize" the threats posed by a U.S. missile defense system.

Political-Military Cooperation. During their September 2003 meeting at Camp David, Presidents Bush and Putin directed their respective militaries to establish a bilateral multi-year work plan to enhance military interoperability and allow for the conduct of future joint missions. This led to an intense schedule of high-level military engagement, U.S.-Russian military exercises and training programs focused on improving joint operations in counterterrorism and regional stabilization and on accelerating nuclear security and accountability efforts. In addition, the establishment of the NATO-Russia Council (NRC) in May 2002 created a forum for engaging Russia in strategic areas, including military cooperation. The NRC created several working groups to develop cooperation on issues including terrorism, proliferation, peacekeeping, theater missile defense, airspace management, and civil emergencies. Russia became a supporter of NATO's antiterrorism operation in the Mediterranean and Operation Active Endeavor (OAE) and has partnered with NATO on conducting four joint Theater Missile Defense exercises from March 2004 to January 2008. United States-Russia bilateral military cooperation, as well as NATO-Russia military exercises and Russia's participation in OAE, was suspended in August 2008, following Russia's invasion of Georgia.

Counterproliferation and Nuclear Security. From the outset, President Bush identified counterproliferation cooperation as one of his highest priorities with Russia. One of President Bush's most important initiatives was his agreement with Putin at Bratislava in February 2005 to cooperate on enhancing nuclear security and combating nuclear terrorism. The "Bratislava Initiatives" included commitments to share best practices and to accelerate cooperation on security upgrades of nuclear facilities in Russia, to include completing upgrades at the agreed-upon sites by 2008, a goal that will be achieved in December 2008. The two Presidents also agreed at Bratislava to continue joint efforts to develop low-enriched uranium fuel for use in U.S. and Russian-designed research reactors in third countries, cooperate in the area of emergency response and management, and develop strategies to enhance security culture.

In May 2004, Russia became the 15th country to endorse the Proliferation Security Initiative, which is aimed at preventing the spread of weapons of mass destruction, their delivery systems, and related materials. In July 2007, President Bush and President Putin issued a Joint Declaration on Nuclear Energy and Nonproliferation to promote the expansion of nuclear energy without spreading sensitive fuel cycle technologies. Under the Joint Declaration the United States and Russia engaged with a broad range of other countries with nuclear expertise, as well as with the nuclear industry, to provide incentives to "proliferation responsible" countries to forego indigenous enrichment and reprocessing, which could lead to diversions and clandestine weapons programs. Such incentives included the provision of assured fuel supplies and waste management services. In September 2007, Russia joined 15 other countries to form the Global Nuclear Energy Partnership (GNEP). The GNEP aims to promote the use of nuclear power while reducing the risk of proliferation by developing and by deploying next generation nuclear reactor and reprocessing capability that does not involve separating out plutonium, which could then fall into terrorist hands. Finally, in May 2008, President Bush signed a 123 Agreement for Cooperation in Peaceful Use of Nuclear Energy with Russia. Although President Bush later withdrew his determination in support of this agreement as a result of Russia's actions in Georgia, the underlying basis for the agreement remains sound and is a testament to the vast potential for U.S.-Russia civil nuclear cooperation.

International Terrorism. Putin's call to President Bush on September 11 made counterterrorism cooperation an early focus of engagement. This was underscored in the October 2001 Joint Statement on Counterterrorism, which called for broad cooperation, including through a bilateral Counterterrorism Working Group (CTWG). A CTWG Core Group, established to make inroads on sensitive issues, agreed in 2006 to expand information exchanges on Iranian terrorist threats and support for terrorist groups, narrow differences on terrorist designations, and strengthen public outreach on U.S.-Russia counterterrorism cooperation. Russia also faced its own terrorist attacks. The attack on the Dubrovka theater in 2002 and the Beslan hostage crises in 2004, exposed both Russian vulnerabilities and poor response capabilities. Nevertheless, the July 2006 launch of the Global Initiative to Combat Nuclear Terrorism (GICNT); Russian support for United Nations Security Council Resolutions (UNSCRs) 1617 (to strengthen sanctions on the Taliban, al-Qaida, and associates) and 1624 (to prevent incitement to terrorism and terrorist safe haven); and, counterterrorism cooperation through the NATO-Russia Council demonstrate a growing partnership in this area. The GICNT has shown particular promise by garnering support from more than 75 nations since it was launched by President Bush and President Putin on July 15, 2006 in St. Petersburg.

Regional Cooperation. In many respects, Russia has been a constructive partner in pursuing the goal of greater security in the Middle East and Asia, including through its participation in the Quartet Process on Middle East peace and through the Six-Party process to press for denuclearization of the Korean Peninsula. President Bush also recognized Putin's proposal for Russia to provide and take back nuclear fuel for Iran's Bushehr nuclear reactor as a constructive proposal to eliminate the need for Iran to acquire sensitive nuclear enrichment or fuel reprocessing technology. Russia shares our concerns about Iran acquiring nuclear weapons and has joined the United States and others in urging Iran to comply with the requirements of the IAEA Board of Governors and the UNSCRs 1737, 1747, and 1803. To date, Russia has by and large refused to utilize bilateral sanctions or otherwise impose consequences beyond the resolutions for Iran's refusal to heed these demands.

Significant differences with Russia occurred over our opposition to Russian arms sales to states hostile to the United States, including Iran and Syria. The State Department has regularly demarched the Russian Government on U.S. concerns about Russian arms sales; this was also a topic of discussion in the Strategic Dialogue Group. In December 2006 and August 2008, pursuant to the Iran, North Korea, and Syria Non-Proliferation Act (INKSNA), the United States imposed sanctions on

Russian state arms exporter Rosoboronexport for the transfer of conventional weaponry to Iran, including the TOR-M1 surface-to-air missile system.

Particular attention has also been paid to Russia's contract to transfer an SA-20 air defense system to Iran. In December 2006, President Putin informed President Bush of an existing Russian contract with Iran to provide the SA-20, noting that Russian support for UNSCRs 1737 and 1747 came with the understanding that preexisting contracts with Iran would remain in force. Putin told President Bush that Russia did not intend to fulfill this contract until 2009 or later and would condition delivery on Iran's behavior on nuclear issues. President Bush received further assurances from Putin that Russia was not implementing its SA-20 contract with Iran in Sochi in April 2008. President Medvedev renewed Russia's assurances at the July 2008 Hokkaido G-8 meeting. While seeming to respect these assurances regarding the SA-20, Russia currently does appear to be prepared to ship an earlier variant of the same weapon—the SA-10. Continued Russian arms sales to Iran, in particular, risk provoking regional instability, threatening Coalition forces in the region, and sending a mixed message to Iran at a time when firm resolve is needed to urge Iran to cease its enrichment activities.

Despite the Administration's efforts to break down zero-sum thinking on United States-Russia interaction in the former Soviet space, Russia remained wary of U.S. intentions and was cautious about engaging in joint or parallel actions in these regions. Russia perceived U.S. efforts to promote democracy in former Soviet countries, in particular in the aftermath of the so-called "color revolutions" in Georgia and Ukraine, as a smokescreen for advancing U.S. strategic interests at Russia's expense. The Kremlin's reassertions of "privileged interests" and "spheres of influence" along its periphery have further complicated Russia's relations with its neighbors and created major challenges for U.S. interests in the region. Russia has stepped up its campaign to undermine our presence throughout the former Soviet space, including in Central Asia. Russia has demonstrated increasing willingness to use energy as a means of pressuring countries along Russia's periphery, most notably Georgia, Ukraine, and the Baltics, but also close partners such as Belarus. Russia's aggressive approach on Georgia in August 2008 seemed designed to topple President Saakashvili, humiliate Georgia, and derail NATO enlargement. It also appeared aimed to exact delayed revenge for the West's recognition of Kosovo, which Russia strongly opposed, and for the perceived dismissal of Russian concerns.

Economic Relations. President Bush has consistently sought to promote U.S. commercial interests in Russia. Recognizing the potential of U.S.-Russia trade and investment relations and their importance to the broader relationship, Presidents Bush and Putin agreed at their first meeting in Ljubljana in June 2001 to make economic cooperation a priority area for engagement and created a new Russian-American Business Dialogue at their meeting in Genoa in July 2001. United States-Russia trade and investment relations have expanded over the past 8 years with U.S. exports to Russia increasing by over 20 percent each year over the last 3 years. According to the Commerce Department, U.S. companies, including their overseas subsidiaries, own direct investment of over $16 billion in Russia. Russian-owned direct investments in the United States are worth approximately $5.6 billion.

Despite some progress, there have also been setbacks. In 2002, the United States and Russia were engaged in a major dispute over poultry that had blocked American exporters from Russian markets for over 6 months. While the dispute was eventually resolved and American poultry exports resumed, Russian protectionist measures based on spurious health concerns continue to threaten to reduce American meat exports. After Russia's invasion of Georgia, Prime Minister Putin announced Russia's intention to block market access to 19 U.S. poultry plants and to reopen bilateral market access agreements, which he claimed hurt domestic Russian agriculture producers.

A series of anti-free market/Western investment actions by the Russian Government also called into question Russia's support for property rights, effective market access, and transparent, stable and effective regulatory frameworks. This was most evident in the Russian Government's centralized control over the oil and gas sector via support of state-owned pipeline (Transneft) and gas (Gazprom) monopolies and various opaque pricing schemes. Putin's drive to reassert state influence over the energy sector was further exemplified by the government's dubious attack on and nontransparent dismantling of the privately-owned YUKOS oil company to the benefit of state-owned oil company Rosneft. The Kremlin also stepped up efforts to squeeze foreign investment, especially in Russia's "strategic sectors," by limiting such investment to a minority stake or by pressuring western firms to surrender altogether investments to Russian partners. Among the most prominent of such cases was the 2006 involuntary sale to Gazprom of Royal Dutch Shell's interest in the Sakhalin II project due to regulatory harassment and excessive fines. In 2008, increasing state-supported pressure on BP's flagship investment in Russia, TNK-BP, including by taking the CEO to court on labor charges and denying visas to foreign employees, resulted in a deal that diluted BPs influence over the joint-venture and could lead to its takeover by state-owned companies.

Progress on Russia's accession to the World Trade Organization (WTO) has also advanced in fits and starts, despite the high priority President Bush placed on providing U.S. leadership to advance Russia's WTO accession, including through high-level coordination in the Strategic Dialogue Group. Conclusion and signature of a bilateral market access agreement in Hanoi in November 2006 helped to advance this goal. Intensive work in 2007 and early 2008 toward advancing multilateral talks was slowed by Russian Government changes in May, which transferred authority over trade issues to a new ministry, and the announcement of protectionist measures to ban the use of frozen meat in food processing. Other challenges include the need for Russia to complete and implement remaining legislation and to complete bilateral agreements with Ukraine and Georgia. Both countries froze their bilateral talks with Russia in spring 2008 as a result of Russian Presidential Instructions authorizing direct Russian ministry government contact with Georgia's separatist regimes. The United States decided to stop its proactive leadership role in assisting Russia with its accession efforts in August 2008 as a result of Russia's invasion of Georgia, though the United States continues to participate in routine work related to the accession process.

People-to-People. President Bush believed that expanding people-to-people and humanitarian ties between the United States and Russia was vital to dismantling barriers of mistrust. He underscored this commitment in a May 2002 joint statement with Putin, which called for strengthening contacts through trade and economic relationships, academic and cultural exchanges, and cooperation on the environment and the fight against infectious diseases. With over $1 billion in U.S. assistance budgeted for democracy and governance, economic growth, and health and humanitarian assistance programs in Russia from 2001 to 2007, the United States sponsored some 125,000 Russian Government officials, military officers, scholars, business leaders, and civil society leaders to participate in international exchanges and training activities in the United States. Through the Bratislava Initiatives on HIV/AIDS, the United States and Russia worked together to train medical and laboratory specialists in third countries and share best practices for HIV/AIDS treatment and prevention.

Democracy. United States-Russia differences over democracy and human rights issues became an increasingly contentious point in the United States-Russia dialogue during the Bush administration. Since the democratic elections of 2000, the Kremlin has restricted political participation, eliminated gubernatorial elections, eliminated or gained control of opposition political parties, manipulated election outcomes, and imposed onerous bureaucratic restrictions to constrain the activities of nongovernmental organizations (NGOs). Increased Kremlin control over media outlets as well as pressure on independent journalists, including through so-called anti-extremism laws, has left few critical voices, creating a culture of self-censorship for fear of government reprisal. It is estimated that at least 19 journalists have been murdered in Russia as a result of their professional activities, including American citizens Paul Klebnikov and Anna Politkovskaya; out of these cases, only one has resulted in a criminal conviction. Throughout this administration, U.S. assistance to Russia's civil society has played a vital role in sustaining indigenous NGOs in an increasingly restrictive environment. President Bush showed his support for Russian human rights activists, independent journalists, and dissidents by hosting meetings at the White House and other high-profile events. United States assistance supported the revision and implementation of Russia's Criminal Procedure Code, which now largely complies with the European Convention on Human Rights and provides for trial by jury.

FUTURE CHALLENGES:

Managing Differences. Russia's August 2008 invasion of Georgia and its recognition of the "independence" of South Ossetia and Abkhazia raised fundamental questions about Russia's broader intentions in the region, its long-term trajectory, and put at risk the prospects for achieving the kind of strategic partnership the United States has been trying to build with Russia for over 7 years. Russia's determination to assert its "Great Power" status belies worrisome insecurities that are inherent to Russia's institutional weaknesses, including an excessively corrupt bureaucracy; over-centralized institutions unwilling or unable to enforce the rule of law; underdeveloped civil society; and, Medvedev's own weak position vis-à-vis Putin. Looking ahead, these weaknesses will continue to drive decision-making that is at times at odds with our own foreign policy interests. Balancing a firm and measured response to Russian aggressiveness with continued Russian cooperation on strategic areas of U.S. national security interest, such as nonproliferation and counterterrorism, will remain a challenge for years to come.

Defending Russia's Neighbors. After years of retreat against what it perceives as strategic advances by the West in the wake of the "color" revolutions, Russia is now trying to reassert its influence with tactics of intimidation and direct meddling and interference in the sovereign affairs of its neighbors. As demonstrated by its actions in Georgia, Russia has proven its readiness to defend by force its perceived interests in these regions. Russia's intense opposition to NATO enlargement to Georgia and, in particular, to Ukraine will continue to undermine these countries' ability to maintain a western path. The next administration will be confronted with the challenge of how to reverse Russia's advance into Georgia, stop further Russian provocations, and restore Georgia's territorial integrity. Furthermore, Russia attempts to challenge the territorial integrity of Ukraine, particularly in Crimea, which is 59 percent ethnically Russian and is home to the Russian Navy's Black Sea Fleet, must be prevented. Russia covert action and propaganda activities to heighten ethnic tensions in Crimea and maintain instability in the region will likely continue.

Maintaining Unity With Europe. Russia will continue to attempt to exploit divisions within the European Union (EU), within NATO, and between the United States and the EU to its advantage. While Russia's invasion of Georgia raised alarm bells among some European countries with regard to Russia's intentions and its trajectory, major European powers appear ready largely to put the August conflict behind them and return to "business as usual" with Russia regardless of whether or not Russia has complied with all of its ceasefire obligations in Georgia. Russia will seek to use covert actions and sophisticated propaganda to ensure that European governments are tempted to lay the blame for any future tensions on Russia's "upstart" neighbors. Furthermore Russia will exploit Europe's dependence on Russian energy and its lowest-common-denominator policymaking to mitigate any European response to Russian aggressiveness. Russia will use political/economic levers to drive wedges between the United States and Europe on security and regional issues, including Russian ideas for a new "European security architecture." Sending a unified and firm message, together with European allies, will be paramount.

Promoting Energy Security. The consolidation of major oil and gas assets, now largely in the hands of state-owned entities Gazprom and Rosneft, the growing involvement and influence of organized crime elements within these entities, the state's monopoly control (through Gazprom and Transneft) over pipeline infrastructure, and Europe's growing dependency on Russian energy all present a mix of serious challenges to U.S. and European energy security interests. Russia's readiness to cut off gas supplies to its neighbors underline its willingness to leverage energy supplies to achieve political ends. Russia will continue to focus on keeping Europe dependent on Russian energy by undermining efforts to bring alternative supplies of energy, especially gas, to European markets. We must continue to urge Europe to diversify its energy supplies by actively engaging in the development of a Southern Corridor for Caspian gas. We must also encourage Europe to insulate eastern EU members from Russian use of energy as a weapon by connecting them to western European electricity and gas grids. In order to avoid Russian monopolization of European energy supply, refining, and transit, the EU should be encouraged to apply competition policy to Gazprom.

Democracy and Rule of Law. The shrinking of democratic and civic space, weak institutions, rampant official corruption, and limits placed on media freedoms remain a dark legacy of the Putin era. While President Medvedev has made rule of law and anti-corruption reform initiatives his early priorities, it is questionable whether he has the will or ability to follow through on these goals. Our own capacity to support advocates of democracy in Russia—and their ability to secure popular support in the near term—is severely limited by the identification of democracy with the chaos and corruption of the Yeltsin era. Nevertheless, while near-term prospects for improving Moscow's record on these issues are in doubt, a Russian Government accountable to a broad popular constituency rather than the Moscow bureaucratic elite will prove the difference between a Russia integrated into 21st century international institutions and a belligerent, authoritarian Russia threatening peace and stability in Europe and Asia. There are significant costs to Russia in either choosing its own authoritarian past, or continuing to leave the choice open. We therefore must consistently seek opportunities to engage with and influence Russians both inside and outside of government on democracy, human rights, and rule of law issues.

Attachments

Tab 1   Chronology for Managing Cooperation/Differences with Russia

Tab 2   Memorandum of Conversation of Restricted Meeting with President Putin of Russia
            (June 16, 2001)

Tab 3   Joint Statement by President Bush and Russian President Putin on Bilateral Trade and
            Investment Relations (July 22, 2001)

Tab 4   Letter to Russian President Putin (October 4, 2001)

Tab 5   Memorandum of Conversation of Meeting with President Putin of Russia (October 21, 2001)

Tab 6   Joint Statement by President Bush and President Putin (October 21, 2001)

Tab 7   Joint Statement on New U.S.-Russia Relationship (November 14, 2001)

POSTSCRIPT

THOMAS GRAHAM

The Bush Administration Approach

The Bush administration effort to build a more constructive, post–Cold War relationship with Russia produced mixed results. An initial period of intense high-level engagement led to important accomplishments, especially in counterterrorism. After 9/11, Russia promptly pledged to cooperate in the war on terrorism and provided significant intelligence and logistical support in the initial phases of the war in Afghanistan that led to the quick overthrow of the Taliban regime and eliminated al Qaeda's safe haven.

In the first year and a half of the administration, the intense engagement also advanced US goals in the realm of nuclear strategy. It contributed to a relatively muted Russian response to the US exit from the Anti-Ballistic Missile (ABM) Treaty, which allowed the United States to deploy its rudimentary ballistic missile defense capability in Alaska and California. The two nations defied skeptics and reached agreement on the Moscow Strategic Arms Reduction Treaty, reducing deployed strategic nuclear warhead levels by close to two-thirds, from some 6,000 to between 1,700 and 2,200 per side.

Over the succeeding years, the two nations partnered to enhance nuclear security and combat nuclear terrorism. They enhanced the security of Russia's nuclear weapons and infrastructure. Within a year of its launch, Russia endorsed the US-designed Proliferation Security Initiative and later the two countries jointly organized a global effort to combat nuclear terrorism. They also collaborated to promote nuclear energy while checking the spread of sensitive fuel cycle technologies (like reprocessing and enrichment).

Nonproliferation was a central element of the two country's cooperation on the North Korean and the Iranian nuclear programs (in the Six-Party process and the P5 + 1 process, respectively). They were especially successful regarding Iran, working jointly to pass three UN Security Council resolutions to pressure it to end its enrichment activities. That cooperation also reduced the risk of war in the Middle East, enhanced regional security, and reinforced broader US-Russian cooperation on Middle East peace (in the Quartet process).

At the same time, bilateral military engagement led to more ambitious exercises and training programs focused on joint operations in counterterrorism and regional stabilization. That military cooperation was broadened with the creation of the NATO-Russia Council and the establishment of NATO-Russia working groups to deal with counterterrorism, nonproliferation, peacekeeping, theater missile defense, airspace management, and civil emergencies.

The initial progress began to sour, however, starting early in 2003 when Putin joined French President Chirac and German Chancellor Schroeder in opposing the US intervention in Iraq. The real turning point came with the so-called color revolutions in the former Soviet space. These popular uprisings (particularly in Georgia and Ukraine) fed Russian suspicions that the United States sought to exploit Russian strategic weakness by promoting democracy in Eurasia. At this same time, Russia vigorously protested US plans to deploy limited theater ballistic missile defenses in Poland and the Czech Republic. Russian resentment burst out in public when Putin castigated the United States for undermining global stability at the 2007 Munich Security Conference.

US-Russia relations collapsed after Russia's invasion of Georgia in August of 2008. Fearing that Russia might next move against Ukraine and then the Baltic States, the Bush administration sought to thwart Russian success and to impose strategic costs. That meant ending "business as usual" and suspending most of the cooperative efforts it had developed with Russia. Relations with Russia at the end of the Bush administration were in worse shape than they had been at the beginning.

What Has Happened Since the End of the Bush Administration?
President Obama's administration traced a trajectory similar to Bush's in its relations with Russia. At the outset, Obama "reset" relations, including by scaling back Bush administration plans to deploy limited theater ballistic missile defenses in Europe. The Obama administration focused on a few priority tasks—nuclear security, counterterrorism, nonproliferation, and economic ties, embedded in a larger framework of cooperation under the Bilateral Presidential Commission overseen by the two foreign ministers. Like Bush, Obama established a good working relationship with his counterpart, the new Russian President Dmitry Medvedev (though Putin still retained considerable power as prime minister).

At first, this yielded some important progress. Building on the work of the Bush administration, the Obama team concluded the New START agreement, producing modest additional strategic nuclear reductions; deepened counterterrorism cooperation, organizing the Northern Distribution Network across Russia to supply US and coalition forces in Afghanistan; and partnered to pressure Iran to curtail its nuclear program. The Obama administration also facilitated Russia's entry into the World Trade Organization. In deference to Kremlin sensitivities, Obama abandoned Bush's Freedom Agenda and downgraded relations with former Soviet states, especially Georgia and Ukraine.

Nevertheless, by the end of Obama's first term, tensions resurfaced, first over the Arab Spring and then over domestic developments inside Russia. Although Medvedev refrained from vetoing UN Security Council authorization of NATO's humanitarian intervention in Libya in 2011, his decision irked many senior Russian officials, including Putin. Russian outrage erupted as the NATO campaign morphed into a regime change operation. After this experience, Putin became implacably opposed to any US-backed regime change—whether by popular uprising or US military intervention. At the same time, Putin felt unconstrained in his own efforts to undermine the governments of Georgia and Ukraine. Putin's decision in September 2011 to reclaim the presidency—which the Obama administration had opposed—along with the rigged parliamentary elections that December, put Russian authoritarianism squarely back on the bilateral agenda.

Deteriorating relations culminated in near-total collapse over developments in the former Soviet space—this time in Ukraine. In 2014, Russia countered a popular movement that had ousted the corrupt, Russian-backed Ukrainian president by illegally annexing Crimea and stoking a separatist rebellion in eastern Ukraine. This was exactly what the Bush administration had tried to deter by its shutdown of relations with Russia after its invasion of Georgia in 2008. Relations spiraled further downward with Russia's military intervention in Syria in 2015, Putin's increasing repression of Russian dissidents, and Kremlin interference in the 2016 US presidential elections. As with Bush, relations between the two countries were in worse shape at the end of the Obama administration than they had been at the beginning.

Although President Donald Trump extolled the value of "getting along with Russia" and praised Putin, suspicions about Trump's ties to Russia and a broad anti-Russian consensus in Congress and the media hindered his outreach to Putin. Trump's efforts to cultivate favor with Putin backfired in Helsinki in 2018 when Trump rejected the US intelligence community's assessment that Russia had interfered in the US presidential election in Trump's favor.

Despite Trump's rhetoric, his administration's policy for the most part picked up where Obama had left off, often under mounting pressure from Congress. The president himself issued a national security strategy that identified Russia together with China as the leading strategic threats to the United States. His administration toughened sanctions, withdrew from arms control agreements, and reduced the Russian diplomatic presence in the United States. The cumulative impact of these measures was diluted, however, by the administration's failure to articulate a coherent Russian policy and presidential actions that undermined America's alliances in Europe and East Asia. Meanwhile, the administration did little to address the burgeoning Russia-China strategic alignment. Despite his aspirations, Trump too left relations in much worse shape than he had found them.

In retrospect, the events in Ukraine in 2014 marked the end of the grand strategy toward Russia that had animated the Clinton, Bush, and Obama administrations—the integration of Russia into the Euro-Atlantic community as a free-market democracy, to turn the Cold War enemy into a strategic partner. Each administration was beguiled by the examples of Germany and Japan, bitter foes transformed into reliable allies under American guidance after the Second World War. Inspired by this vision, each pursued a similar set of policies, albeit with diminishing confidence and enthusiasm from administration to administration.

The three administrations traced remarkably similar paths from initial hopes to bitter disappointment. Their greatest successes came in the same area: nuclear security. Their gravest challenges arose out of regional conflicts, in the Balkans for Clinton; the former Soviet space for Bush; and the Middle East and then the former Soviet space for Obama. Each administration initially tempered its reservations about Russia's domestic developments despite deepening authoritarianism, only to end with dashed hopes. The United States only abandoned the effort to integrate Russia into the West when Putin attacked Ukraine in 2014. Thereafter, the Obama administration pivoted to trying to contain Russia. The Trump administration, despite the president's rhetoric and uncertain policies, reinforced that approach by regarding Russia as a great power competitor.

How Did the Bush Administration Do?

In his memoir, President Bush laments that "given what I'd hoped Putin and I could accomplish in moving past the Cold War, Russia stands out as a disappointment in the freedom agenda."[2] To what extent was the disappointment inevitable? To what extent was it the outcome of ill-designed US policy or of Russian choices or a combination of both? There is no simple answer.

---

2. George W. Bush, *Decision Points* (New York: Crown, 2010), 435.

The essentially competitive, often confrontational, character of US-Russian relations since the United States emerged as a great power at the end of the nineteenth century suggests a certain inevitability. Historically grounded debates over the principles of world order and fundamental political values, as well as clashing geopolitical imperatives, have long bedeviled relations. Nevertheless, lingering faith that democracy had triumphed in the grand twentieth-century ideological struggles against fascism and communism, confidence in unrivaled American power, and Moscow's strategic weakness led American policymakers to overestimate their ability to shape Russia's conduct or to counter its malign impulses.

These attitudes drove Bush administration policy at a pivotal moment in Russia's post–Cold War evolution. In the 2000s, Russia was slowly restoring its power after the chaos of the first post-Soviet decade. It could choose to redefine its priorities and use that power to partner with the United States on common challenges or, alternatively, to defend traditional Russian interests against perceived American encroachment—or something in between. US policy could influence that choice.

Genuine strategic partnership was perhaps never in the cards. But an enduring, more constructive relationship was. It depended heavily on the choices that Putin would make. But it also depended on US and European diplomatic skill in shaping the context in which he would choose. Did the United States and the Europeans miss something fundamental in the Russian situation and psyche at the time? Did they misread the situation and fail to craft an offer of cooperative relations that adequately accounted for Russian interests and perspectives? Or was Russia under Putin determined to go its own authoritarian way?

Conceptually, the administration was right to combine the offer of partnership with hedges against Russia's reversion to an aggressive, anti-American posture. Russia's future was uncertain. The challenge was to hedge in a way that did not unnecessarily repel Russia. That required great tact, as Russian pride made its leaders quick to see slights and hostility even where none were intended. The Bush team at times failed to strike the right balance.

NATO enlargement, a key hedge considering subsequent developments, provides an apt illustration. While displeased, Russia swallowed with little acrimony NATO's admission of seven Central European states in 2004. The new NATO-Russia Council and continuing hopes for beneficial relations with the United States eased Russian concerns. So too did French and German objections to the US intervention in Iraq, which highlighted tensions within NATO. By contrast, with relations strained in 2008, the intense administration push for granting Membership Action Plans to Ukraine and Georgia, two countries perceived by Russia as vital to its security, precipitated vehement Russian opposition. That effort did not justify the Russian action in US eyes, but it nonetheless formed the backdrop to Russia's war against Georgia in 2008, which caught an ill-prepared United States by surprise.

In other instances, the administration valued other goals over cooperation with Russia. With regard to Chechnya, for example, the administration argued that Chechen rebels had legitimate grievances, urging Moscow to moderate its brutal military response in favor of negotiations—even as the rebels openly collaborated with acknowledged terrorist forces. After a devastating terrorist attack in the North Caucasus in 2004, Putin concluded—wrongly in the US view—that the US counterterrorism campaign was just a smokescreen to cover American geopolitical advance in Eurasia at Russia's expense. Similarly, US support for the protesters who ousted the Russian-backed president in the Orange Revolution in Ukraine in 2004 led Putin to characterize US democracy promotion—again wrongly in the US view—as a tool aimed at regime change in Russia itself. In response to both these events, Russia tightened the screws on US-funded democracy promotion programs and independent civil society organizations in Russia, as it has continued to do to the present day.

Would different approaches to NATO, Chechnya, Ukraine, and other matters have paved the way to more durable cooperation, or simply delayed inevitable confrontation? Should the United States, by far the dominant party, have been willing to run greater risks to test Russia's commitment to cooperation? The questions remain open.

For example, up until its last days, the Bush administration made numerous and repeated attempts at very senior levels—including at the level of the two presidents—to engage the Russians in working jointly on ballistic missile defense. Those efforts in the end came to naught in part because the administration resisted Russian proposals that would have compromised the effectiveness of the US system or its acceptability to US allies—and in part from Russian disinterest in cooperation. Would greater US flexibility have made a difference?

Also, in the NATO-Russia Council, the United States was reluctant to allow allies to represent national positions to Russia, insisting that the allies agree in advance on a common NATO approach. That position was intended as a hedge against Russian efforts to divide NATO and was strongly supported by US NATO allies—particularly the newest members from Central and Eastern Europe. Should the United States have taken greater risk here, dropped the unanimity rule, and let Russia further into the NATO tent? A positive Russian response might have strengthened NATO-Russia cooperation, while any loss of NATO solidarity could with effort probably have been recovered if Russia acted in bad faith.

At the same time, the administration failed to anticipate the Russian-Chinese strategic alignment that now poses a growing challenge. With attention focused on trying to integrate Russia into the Euro-Atlantic community, while trying to turn China into a "responsible stakeholder," the administration failed to identify the possibility of their strategic collaboration—or to appreciate how Russia's hardening posture toward the West could lead the Kremlin to look eastward for a counterbalance. But such foresight would have required the administration to foresee the possibility that in the next decade someone like Xi Jinping would emerge as China's leader and pursue more aggressive behavior—and that Russia would overcome its historic suspicions about China while accepting junior partner status.

What Are the Lessons Learned?

Russia did not lie at the heart of the Bush administration's foreign policy, as it had for previous American presidents. Nor arguably should it have, given its political and economic disarray in 2001. At that juncture, the United States was threatened more by Russia's weakness than by its strength, as the first Bush National Security Strategy noted. That view captured the moment, but it overlooked Putin's authoritarian tendencies, determination to restore his country as a great power, and his ability to mobilize Russia's vast resources for that purpose.

This experience yields three main lessons:

- *Russia wills to be a great power.* Being a great power lies at the core of Russian national identity and purpose. That insight bears major implications for US policy on Russia. To begin, the most promising areas for cooperation are those where the two countries can work as equals, such as nuclear security, as was true for both the Bush and Obama administrations.
- *Russia covets the former Soviet space.* It will be tenacious in the defense of its interests in this region, which remains critical in its eyes to its great power status. Russia's brutal war against Ukraine provides a graphic illustration of how far Moscow is prepared to go to defend its interests, as it

understands them. This does not mean that the United States should shrink from advancing its own interests there—or that Russia's neighbors should accept coercion, invasion, or absorption by what they view as a corrupt, authoritarian neighbor. But the United States needs to anticipate and be prepared to meet fierce Russian resistance to American initiatives that threaten what it sees as its vital interests, as well as Russian aggression against former Soviet states that actively seek to escape its orbit.

- *Shared interests are the sole basis for cooperation.* Since Russia embeds in great power status enduring antidemocratic values, only areas of shared interests can provide a foundation for admittedly limited US-Russian cooperation amid continuing competition. This situation will not change unless the United States or Russia changes in fundamental ways. That of course is not impossible, but it is a poor wager, at least in the short run. As was true during the Cold War, managing the inevitable competition responsibly to minimize the risk of a direct military confrontation, which could escalate to a nuclear cataclysm, while keeping the door open to cooperation where interests align, thus becomes the primary task of US policy on Russia. As always, the challenge is to do so in ways consistent with our values and principles.

Contributors:
Eric Edelman
Jamie Fly
Daniel Fried

CHAPTER 18

China

PAUL HAENLE | MICHAEL GREEN | FARYAR SHIRZAD

As the Bush administration entered office in 2001, it faced many of the same questions regarding US policy toward China and US–East Asian alliances that continue to challenge policymakers in Washington today. How should the US grapple with a resurgent China? How does China factor into the United States' broader Asia policy? The two Transition Memoranda that follow anticipated many of the strategies that would be necessary to manage China's future emergence.

When the Bush administration entered the White House, China's GDP accounted for close to 3.6 percent of global economic output. At the end of the Bush administration, it had nearly doubled to 7.2 percent, and by 2018 China's share of global GDP more than doubled again to reach 16.3 percent. Some economists now expect China to overtake the United States as the largest economy in the world in the coming decade.

China's rapid economic development coincided with the growth and modernization of its military capabilities. In 2001, the ground, air, and naval forces of the People's Liberation Army (PLA) were sizable, but largely obsolete. Today, the PLA has the world's largest, and increasingly advanced, navy, land-based conventional missile arsenal, and long-range surface-to-air defense systems. China's technological capacity, including its dual-use capabilities, has become more advanced in nearly every respect.

During its time in office, the Bush administration not only dealt with a very different China but also with a very different set of Chinese leaders. President Jiang Zemin and Premier Zhu Rongji were outspoken advocates for market-oriented reform, and they pursued a low-profile approach to foreign affairs. Support for that approach has waned over the past two decades, especially since the rise of Xi Jinping who, since taking power in 2012, has centralized power and reinvigorated the role of the Chinese Communist Party (CCP) in the state, military, and economy. Despite initial hopes that China's economic development might go hand-in-hand with greater political openness, by the time the Bush administration left office in 2008, there was already growing concern over China's future political, economic, and security direction.

As outlined in the Transition Memoranda below, the core of the Bush administration's strategy for dealing with China's rise was to build a security and trade architecture with regional allies and partners that would reinforce the role of the United States as a Pacific power, encourage China to play a responsible role in East Asia, and hedge against the emergence of a more aggressive China.

SECRET

4611

NATIONAL SECURITY COUNCIL

Transition

WASHINGTON, D.C. 20504

November 10, 2008

MEMORANDUM FOR THE RECORD

FROM: DENNIS WILDER, EAST ASIAN AFFAIRS DIRECTORATE

SUBJECT: China Policy

THE SITUATION AS WE FOUND IT:

At the start of this Administration, we assessed that our policy in Asia was focused on an emerging China. There was widespread agreement that our alliances with traditional partners in Japan, South Korea, Thailand, the Philippines, and Australia had drifted with the end of the Cold War and because of concerns over Beijing's reaction to any reinvigoration of our security partnerships.

China, for its part, was deeply suspicious that the new Administration, due to the demise of the Soviet Union, would treat China as its main adversary and strategic threat. Bilateral relations remained bruised from the accidental bombing of the Chinese embassy in Belgrade in May 1999— which most Chinese were convinced was intentional. Moreover, the EP-3 crisis early in the Bush Administration only served to heighten concerns on both sides that it would be difficult to forge a stable and constructive relationship. Within the United States, China policy was politically controversial with many in Congress still upset about the granting of Permanent Normal Trade Relations (PNTR) to China and about evidence of successful Chinese espionage against our nuclear weapons secrets.

President Bush engaged Beijing based on the recognition of China's twin priorities of territorial integrity and economic growth. China's rapid emergence as a major political and economic player on the world stage offered both considerable opportunities to explore new avenues of bilateral

NSC Declassification Review [E.O.13526]
DECLASSIFY IN PART
by William C. Carpenter 3/23/2020

SECRET
Reason: 1.4(b) (d)
Declassify on: 11/10/18

Re-Classified by: Ellen J. L. Knight
Reason: 1.4(b), (c), and (d)
Declassify on: 11/10/2033

cooperation while also presenting potentially troublesome challenges to the international system and the established order in Asia. China's rapid emergence as a global economic power, for example, presented tremendous new opportunities for U.S. exporters while also presenting numerous challenges on issues ranging from trade and investment to commodity markets and the environment. But the inextricable interdependence of China's growth and that of the global economy requires a policy of engagement. In fact, the overriding importance of economic growth to China's leaders presents the best means of influencing its emergence as a global power and encouraging its integration into the international system.

THIS ADMINISTRATION'S POLICY:

President Bush's dedication to building constructive, cooperative, consistent, and candid relations with the Chinese leadership, while at the same time reinvigorating our military alliances in Asia, has paid substantial dividends and has laid the foundations for productive relations with the region in the 21st Century.

- The President reframed the relationship with China during the 2000 Presidential campaign, presenting it as more of a "strategic competitor" than a "strategic partner," which put China on notice that his Administration was going to recalibrate the U.S. approach to China and the region.

- The President's early statements of his willingness to defend Taiwan if attacked and his offer of a robust arms sales package in April 2001 signaled to Beijing that his Administration was going to continue the American commitment to Taiwan democracy and the people of Taiwan.

- The President's decision to revitalize the military alliances with our key partners in Asia (Japan, South Korea, Thailand, the Philippines, and Australia) sent a powerful message to the Chinese that his Administration would have a balanced policy in the region.

- The President's handling of the EP-3 crisis in April 2001 demonstrated to the Chinese leadership that this Administration would be both tough in defending U.S. national security and capable of compromise to avoid prolonged hostilities.

- Taken together, these initiatives created the political space the President needed to refine the U.S.-China relationship by requiring the Chinese leadership to review the relationship and consider anew how best to respond to what would become a strategic dialogue.

Ironically, the tragic events of September 11, 2001 had a salutary effect on China's view of the United States. President Jiang Zemin reportedly watched the attacks on the World Trade Center live on CNN and immediately told his advisors that the common fight against terrorism could cement his relations with President Bush in the same way that Deng Xiaoping's common cause with his U.S. counterparts against the Soviet Union improved relations in the 1980s. The President's decision to visit Shanghai for the APEC leaders meeting just days after 9/11 deeply impressed Chinese leaders because they understood what profound pressures he was under to respond to the al-Qaida challenge.

During the President's first meeting with President Jiang in Shanghai, President Bush set the tone of the relationship by making clear that, even though there would be disagreements, he would deal with China as a friend, not an enemy. The President welcomed China's entry into the World Trade Organization and appointed a former college classmate and personal friend as Ambassador to China. At the same time, President Bush was clear with the Chinese leaders that North Korea's leader, Kim Chong-Il, was going to be a major problem that China and the United States would need to address together. The President also laid down a marker with Jiang that he was compelled by his moral values to speak frankly to him about human rights and particularly religious freedom.

President Jiang saw clearly the President's resolve in responding to the attacks of 9/11. China had come to see the United States as "casualty averse" but—as he moved forward with Operation Enduring Freedom—the President dispelled any doubts that he was ready to respond forcefully to threats to national security.

Within this context, the President embarked on a strategy that encourages China to play a constructive and peaceful role in the world and in international institutions, to act as a partner in addressing common security challenges, to pursue peaceful economic growth and political liberalization, and to emerge as a responsible stakeholder in the international system. We engage China with and through our strong allies in the region, not in an effort to encircle China or turn the region against it, but as part of an effort to foster good relations with China and to encourage responsible action by China. Working with our regional allies, we also resist efforts to exclude the United States from Asian institutions as both the United States and China are Asia-Pacific nations.

The President's strategy also recognizes that China's strategic future remains uncertain and thus it is prudent to engage in contingency planning. The President's goal is to build good relations with China through bilateral and multilateral engagement and encourage its emergence as a responsible actor fully supportive of, and integrated into, the regional and international political and economic system. However, cognizant of China's growing military power and concerns among some that China's leaders may in the future choose the course of military adventurism, the President has sought to transform our military capabilities to meet the challenges of a modernizing Chinese military and to strengthen our military alliances so that China's leaders will not be tempted to take the wrong path in charting their relationship with the region.

WHAT HAS BEEN ACCOMPLISHED:

Taiwan. The President has placed the Taiwan issue in a more stable and positive context, allowing the United States to better manage cross-Strait tensions and to set the stage for improved relations between Beijing and Taipei. Prior to the President's historic public assertion to Chinese Premier Wen in December 2003 that we oppose any "unilateral changes to the status quo by either side," it looked as if the United States and China were on a collision course over Taiwan. Beijing believed that the United States secretly supported President Chen's desires for an independent Taiwan. But the President's declaration of December 2003 and his steadfast reassurances to Beijing dramatically eased China's concerns and bought time for China's political leadership. Soon after consolidating power in 2005, President Hu Jintao began to subtly, but markedly, alter China's Taiwan strategy—from Jiang's emphasis on a 2008 timeline for being prepared to take military action against Taiwan so as to force early reunification, to a policy of long-term patience and action only if Taiwan attempted to declare independence.

The results of Taiwan's presidential elections in March 2008 have provided the two sides with a fresh opportunity to reach out and engage one another in peacefully resolving their differences. In the few months since the inauguration of Taiwan's new President in May 2008, leaders from the two sides have met and cross-Strait tension has diminished. After a nine-year hiatus, leaders in Beijing and Taipei have met through their organizations responsible for cross-Strait exchanges— China's Association for Relations Across the Taiwan Strait (ARATS) and Taiwan's Straits Exchange Foundation (SEF)—and reached agreements on establishing regular cross-Strait charter flights and allowing PRC tourists to visit Taiwan. Taiwan has also liberalized economic exchanges, including currency conversion.

North Korea. Another success has been the President's ability to convince China's top leaders of U.S. sincerity on a North Korean peace agreement. When the President met dent Jiang in Crawford in October 2002, President Bush reassured Jiang in that meeting and subsequent conversations that the United States sought a diplomatic solution, but also persuaded the Chinese leader that North Korea was not an American problem to be solved by bilateral negotiations between Washington and Pyongyang, but instead was a Northeast Asian problem that the United States was ready to help China and the other key players in the region resolve. As a consequence, Jiang was willing to state unequivocally that China agreed with the United States that North Korea must be denuclearized. This was the turning point in Chinese views on North Korea that led to its agreement to host the Six-Party Talks and the subsequent agreement to the September 19, 2005 Joint Statement where, for the first time, North Korea committed to give up its nuclear weapons ambitions.

The President's April 20, 2006, lunch conversation with President Hu at the White House was another pivotal moment that had a demonstrable effect on the new Chinese leader's thinking. Chinese President Hu—as a result of that conversation—likely came to a personal conclusion that the North Koreans bore the lion's share of blame for blocking implementation of the 2005 Joint Statement. Following North Korea's threat in the Fall of 2006 that it would conduct a nuclear test, President Bush called President Hu to stress that a test would defy U.N. Security Council Resolution 1695 (passed unanimously after the North's missile launches in July 2006), and would severely undermine, if not end, efforts to implement the 2005 Joint Statement of the Six-Party Talks. President Bush made clear to President Hu that China needed to use all of its leverage to prevent a North Korean nuclear test, and should that fail, then the United States would expect China to cooperate fully with the United States in a tough U.N. Security Council resolution with Chapter VII sanctions. North Korea's subsequent detonation of a nuclear device on October 9, 2006 solidified Hu's view that he had to distance China from the North and place real pressure on Kim Chong-Il to end his provocations. It resulted in Hu's support in the passage a Chapter VII resolution, the most far-reaching international punitive action against North Korea since the Korean War.

China's closing of banking opportunities for the North also appears to have been a major factor in Kim's willingness to return to the Six-Party Talks in December 2006. Since then, Beijing has worked hard to see that the terms of the September 2005 Joint Statement and subsequent agreements have been honored by the North Koreans, resulting in the disablement of the Yongbyon nuclear facilities under U.S. monitoring and the submission by North Korea of a nuclear declaration on June 26, 2008. Now we face the hard work of putting in place a rigorous verification regime that includes unimpeded access to all sites, materials, personnel, and additional documentation, related to all aspects of the North's nuclear programs including uranium enrichment and proliferation activities. North Korea may be tempted to stall on verification, as well as during negotiations over Phase III, in hopes of slowing the speed of its denuclearization and maximizing the benefits it will receive from the Five Parties. We will continue to press China to play a central role in convincing North Korea to maintain forward progress on denuclearization.

Senior Dialogue. Establishment of the Senior Dialogue in 2005 and the challenge to Chinese leaders to become a responsible international stakeholder have been surprisingly effective strategies to engage China on global political issues. Through this dialogue—and the President's strong declarations to Chinese leaders—China has taken a more prominent role in United Nations peacekeeping operations, while following a somewhat more cautious approach in relations with problematic regimes in Latin America, in particular. In April 2006,

There remains much

more work to be done in this dialogue, however, as China's foreign policy remains mercantilist ▨▨▨▨▨ in much of the developing world, especially in Africa.

Getting Economic Relations Right. China has embraced the Strategic Economic Dialogue (SED) initiated by the President and chaired by Treasury Secretary Paulson with surprising fervor. The SED has set a higher tone for economic discussions, and exhibited to Americans our determination to improve the imbalances in U.S.-China economic ties. As a result of these talks, china's leaders have come to recognize the value of exchange rate adjustment, in particular, and have significantly accelerated the pace of the renminbi's appreciation. Between July 2005, when the Chinese Government first pegged the renminbi to the U.S. dollar, and mid-June 2008, the renminbi appreciated against the dollar by 20 percent on a nominal basis and 23 percent on a real basis. Seventy percent of that appreciation has occurred since the SED began, and half of it has occurred over the past year alone. China clearly has much further to go, but the progress to date is an example of how strategic dialogue can yield results.

But it is not entirely clear that China views the SED as more than a method to stem Congressional angst and stave off protectionist legislation. As a new group of Chinese economic policymakers joins the dialogue this year, we have pressed for opportunities to make the outcomes more penetrating in areas such as concluding a Bilateral Investment Treaty. At the same time, we have kept our focus on the long-range goal of helping China become a consumer-driven rather export-dependent economy, as this is the only effective fix to the imbalances in China's global trade.

Darfur. United States engagement and international pressure have led China to engage with the international community to stabilize Darfur. In 2007, China supported U.N. Security Council Resolution 1769, authorizing the hybrid United Nations/African Union Operation in Darfur (UNAMID); pressed Sudanese President Bashir to accept that plan; and agreed to deploy more than 300 engineers to UNAMID to construct the bases for the hybrid peacekeeping force. This marks a major evolution from China's traditional insistence on "non-interference" and its active protection of Khartoum's interests.

Engaging the Chinese Military. China is rapidly modernizing its military and, by 2010, will have mobile Intercontinental Ballistic Missiles (ICBMs) and at least five nuclear ballistic missile submarines on station in the western Pacific with missiles capable of striking the United States. ▨▨▨▨▨▨▨▨▨▨▨▨▨▨▨▨▨▨▨▨▨▨▨▨▨▨▨▨▨▨▨▨▨▨▨▨▨▨▨ President Bush, in April 2006, encouraged President Hu to expand our military-to-military contacts so that we not only engaged in senior-level meetings, but also began a serious dialogue on our respective nuclear strategies and doctrine. Since that time, there have been several important steps forward in bilateral military interactions:

- In June 2006, Chinese military officers were invited to observe a 3-carrier U.S. exercise off Guam.

- In November 2007, Secretary Gates visited China and concluded an agreement to create the first military hotline between the Pentagon and the Chinese Military Commission; that hotline became operational in April 2008.

- In April 2008, China sent representatives of the strategic missile forces to Washington for the first bilateral dialogue on nuclear strategy and policy. Working-level meetings with STRATCOM will begin by the end of the year.

China's Energy Future. Chinese leaders were caught by surprise when, in 2005, we proposed the Asia-Pacific Partnership on Clean Development and Climate. They are actively participating in the seven-country sector-based initiative with Australia, China, India, Japan, Republic of Korea, the United States, and, since 2007, Canada and have shown a high interest in clean coal technologies, in particular. They are also increasingly seeing the value in exchanging ideas and technology to reduce dependence on hydrocarbon fuel sources. The key challenge ahead is to convince China to play a leading role in cutting greenhouse gas emissions, rather than hide behind its developing country status. This is the challenge we pursued in the Major Economies Meetings process which resulted in a leaders declaration at the July 2008 G-8 meeting in Japan in which China joined all Major Economies leaders in acknowledging a "leadership role" in combating climate change, moving beyond the view that only developed countries need to "take the lead."

FUTURE CHALLENGES:

Despite the President's successes with China, there remains among the American people a great deal of suspicion if not apprehension about an emerging China. Protectionist voices speak loudly about the loss of manufacturing jobs to Chinese workers as China's trade surplus sets record highs. And the debate over whether China will be a strategic adversary 15 or 20 years from now will continue. Adversarial views on the U.S. side can feed those on the Chinese side who are equally certain that we will never allow China its "rightful" place in the world. An enduring challenge for U.S. policymakers will be dealing with public suspicion about China's rise and the cost and benefits of cooperative engagement.

Any optimistic policy outlook is predicated on a stable China. However, concerns about domestic stability are sufficiently serious to warrant our consideration of a sudden Chinese domestic crisis. China's Communist Party leaders have a historic predisposition to repress personal and political freedoms that denies the Chinese people the outlets to raise their grievances and denies the Chinese Government needed feedback on how to govern successfully. President Hu's concept of a "harmonious society" offers some hope that he will address the societal ills that have come with the rapid expansion of crony capitalism and official corruption. An enduring challenge for U.S. policymakers will be the balance between offering support to those in China pressing for fundamental liberties while retaining open and candid channels of communication with the Chinese leaders on these issues. This was a large part of the President's calculation in early 2007 that he would give China face by attending the 2008 Olympics in Beijing while also telling Hu that he was going to be the first American President to meet publicly with the Dalai Lama.

Ensuring Peace in Asia. Notwithstanding our strong economic ties with China, the underlying struggle for primacy in East Asia remains. As China rises, many Asian nations fear that China will seek to dominate them politically and economically. The President's strategy of engaging China while strengthening alliances has proven successful. A challenge for future policymakers will be to maintain this delicate balance. For example, by continuing a leadership role in the Asia-Pacific Cooperation (APEC) forum and supporting the pursuit of a Free Trade Area of the Asia-Pacific, future policymakers can send a strong signal of our commitment to remaining a major Asia-Pacific player and bolster like-minded countries.

Denuclearizing the Korean Peninsula. We have achieved concrete progress through the Six-Party framework, but there remain considerable challenges for future policymakers in achieving a nuclear-free Korean peninsula and an enduring peace in northeast Asia. The Chinese still cling to the notion that coping with an unpredictable Kim is better than any alternative. An enduring challenge for future policymakers will be to convince Beijing that its key goal is not preventing North Korean provocations, but rather getting the North to fundamentally alter its course, and, if this is not successful, to recognize when they should withdraw their support for the current leader of North Korea. Given North Korean leader Kim Chong-Il's tenuous health, future policymakers may wish to consider exploring with the Chinese contingency planning in the event of a North Korean collapse.

Managing Taiwan's Transition. The United States is building a productive relationship with Taiwan's new president and continues to ensure Taiwan's security. Beijing has developed trust in President Bush's cross-Strait policies, but we have yet to convince it to end the military buildup opposite Taiwan and enter into a productive dialogue with Taiwan's elected officials. The easing of cross-Strait tensions since Taiwan's new President took office has offered the leaders in Beijing and Taipei a new opportunity to engage one another in resolving their differences. We have witnessed some progress already in the few months since President Ma took office with the two sides concluding important agreements on establishing regular cross-Strait charter flights and allowing PRC tourists to travel to Taiwan. While these developments are encouraging, there has been little movement on more difficult security and political questions. In this regard, future U.S.

policymakers will face the challenge of convincing Beijing to show greater flexibility toward Taiwan's role in international organizations so as to further global interests and create goodwill in Taiwan. United States policymakers will also be faced with the challenge of finding a way to convince Beijing that the Chinese military build-up opposite Taiwan is destabilizing and that reducing forces in and around the Taiwan Strait will promote even more cross-Strait progress.

Channeling China's International Rise. A major challenge for future U.S. policymakers will be to ensure that China's rise does not disrupt the international order. China is an attractive model to those who want to maintain authoritarian regimes while achieving high rates of economic growth. The success of its state-led economic system challenges private rule-of-law based approaches to global trade and investment liberalization. China offers economic aid and military assistance while asking little in return, except for access to natural resources. In this manner, China undermines the Freedom Agenda and provides comfort to some of the world's most oppressive regimes. United States policymakers will need to be vigilant about China's global actions and continue to confront China's actions when they threaten to undermine democracy and provide comfort to brutal regimes.

Personal Bonds Still Key. We assess that much of the success in this Administration has come because of the extensive personal engagement President Bush has had with China's top leaders. President Bush's decision to attend the 2008 Summer Olympics in Beijing despite some international criticism has created a reserve of goodwill with the Chinese leadership and the Chinese people. President Hu recently revamped the Politburo Standing Committee, bringing up two new, fifth-generation leaders. A key challenge for future policymakers will be to cultivate good connections to this new generation and to look for ways to bring them to the United States for visits to deepen and broaden the personal ties.

Attachments

Tab 1   Chronology for China Policy
Tab 2   President's Letter to Chinese President Jiang Zemin (July 2001)
Tab 3   Press Briefing Material on APEC Meeting (October 2001)
Tab 4   Memorandum of Conversation of the President's Meeting with Chinese President Jiang Zemin in Shanghai (November 2001)
Tab 5   Memorandum of Conversation of the President's Meeting with Chinese President Jiang Zemin in Crawford (October 2002)
Tab 6   Six-Party Chairman's Statement on the Second Round of the Talks (February 2004)
Tab 7   Joint Statement on the Fourth Round of the Six-Party Talks (September 2005)
Tab 8   President's Speech in Kyoto Japan on Asian Democracy (November 2005)
Tab 9   Welcoming Remarks for Chinese President Hu Jintao on the White House Lawn (April 2006)

SECRET

4782
Transition

NATIONAL SECURITY COUNCIL
WASHINGTON, D.C. 20504

November 19, 2008

MEMORANDUM FOR THE RECORD

FROM: DENNIS WILDER, EAST ASIA DIRECTORATE

SUBJECT: East Asian Alliances and Architecture

THE SITUATION AS WE FOUND IT:

At the beginning of this decade, U.S. alliances in East Asia suffered from post-Cold War neglect, allowing China and North Korea to take advantage of these weaknesses. Nowhere was this more evident than in U.S.-Japan relations where trade frictions, disagreements over U.S. troops and bases in Okinawa, and differing approaches in dealing with the North Korean threat—particularly missile defense—had left the alliance in a fragile state. Emblematic of this decline in U.S. relations with our strongest Asian ally were accusations from Japan that the United States was implement-ing a "Japan passing" policy in Asia with relations with China as our priority. While the Japanese strains were the most pressing, relations throughout the region were equally tenuous.

- In Seoul, the Sunshine policy and inflated hopes for a North-South détente gave rise to a growing debate over the rationale for the presence of U.S. troops on the peninsula.
- In Southeast Asia, the United States had yet to recognize Indonesia as a strategically-important, moderate Muslim country that requires sustained, balanced, and steady engagement. Moreover, Malaysia's Prime Minister Mahathir had promoted an Asian values vision that the United States had not effectively rebutted.
- Relations with Australia were damaged by agricultural trade friction, most visibly following the July 1999 announcement of a 9-percent tariff on Australian lamb imports days before then-Prime Minister Howard's visit to Washington. And interactions with New Zealand were minimal due to the fallout from Wellington's 1985 ban on nuclear-powered and nuclear-armed ships.

As President Bush took office, several important Asian states, including Thailand, Indonesia, South Korea, and Singapore, were still recovering from the 1997-98 Asian financial crisis. Resentment of

SECRET
Reason: 1.4(b) (d)
Declassify on: 11/19/18

NSC Declassification Review [EO 13526]
DECLASSIFY IN FULL
by William C. Carpenter on 3/23/2020

Western economic power lingered because of a perception that U.S. firms had acted in a predatory manner by taking advantage of the crisis to grab up Asian assets at distress-sale prices. In addition, Asian economic, political, linguistic, and religious diversity hindered efforts for the region to act as a coherent entity.

THIS ADMINISTRATION'S POLICY:

President Bush came into office determined to restore our alliances in Asia while building a solid relationship with an emerging China. President Bush, for example, endorsed a strategy of placing the U.S.-Japan relationship in Asia more on par with the U.S.-British relationship in Europe, while working with the Japanese Government to transform the U.S. force posture so as to ease the tensions with the Japanese populace. His new approach to Japan was evident from the first meeting with Prime Minister Koizumi at Camp David on June 30, 2001. During that visit, the two leaders quickly bonded over their common values and vision for the relationship—as well as on a personal level over their love of baseball. The two leaders established the Economic Partnership for Growth to help promote economic reform in Japan to stimulate growth and expand trade and investment. After the 9/11 attacks in the United States, Koizumi quickly sent ships and, ultimately, troops to help in the War on Terror in Afghanistan and Iraq. This was the first Japanese combat deployment since World War II and was a huge change from Japan's hesitant role in the Persian Gulf War. The relationship, which continued to improve over the 5 years Koizumi was in office, was extraordinary and culminated in an historic visit to the Memphis, Tennessee, home of Elvis Presley. Clearly, the relationship is a far cry from that of only 15 years earlier when a book called "The Coming War with Japan" stirred up headlines in both nations.

To transform our Asian partnerships, the President has focused on repairing and upgrading security alliances; building deeper economic relationships; emphasizing American "soft power" of ideas, education, and values; and seeking to develop multilateral approaches to the promotion of shared peace and prosperity. In addition, President Bush has encouraged our East Asian friends and allies to engage a transforming China to help bring it into the international system and to reduce the possibility that future Chinese leaders will use China's growing economic and military power to coerce its neighbors and threaten regional peace and stability. The President has been clear that nations need not choose between the United States or China. Rather he has sought to design a regional architecture in which our strong alliances and partnerships with like-minded democracies can comfortably coexist with institutions in which China has an increasing stake.

With all this in mind, the President has pursued the following set of inter-related and mutually-reinforcing strategies:

- Revitalizing bilateral alliances and developing new partnerships via careful and steady cultivation of military, economic, and political relations.

- Encouraging the building of a <u>regional security architecture</u> that embraces China while reducing the risk that it will adopt a destabilizing role.
- Supporting <u>robust U.S. participation in existing multilateral institutions</u> that contribute to the security architecture, such as the Asia Pacific Economic Cooperation or the ASEAN Regional Forum, to demonstrate U.S. commitment to the region, while being careful not to join organizations whose lack of focus and absence of key states limited their potential.
- <u>Vigorously pursuing regional economic integration</u> through active U.S. engagement in the "free trade agreement (FTA) game" on bilateral and multilateral levels.
- Championing <u>ad-hoc multilateral coalitions</u> to maximize U.S. comparative advantages—including military capacity, scientific and technological advancement, and higher education—when addressing regional challenges such as the 2004 Asian Tsunami and Cyclone Nargis that hit Burma in early 2008.

WHAT HAS BEEN ACCOMPLISHED:

Bilateral Alliances and Partnerships. In Japan and South Korea, our military realignment and relocation efforts are improving our capabilities to deter future security threats, while reducing the U.S. military footprint and its impact on local communities. By making our force presence more relevant to the new security environment and more acceptable to the local communities, we are creating space for our long-term presence. In Japan, we are relocating U.S. air bases from urbanized to rural areas; preparing to move over 8,000 Marines from Okinawa to Guam; co-locating U.S. and Japanese command and control capabilities; and deploying U.S. missile defense capabilities. We also reached agreement with Tokyo to home base a nuclear-powered aircraft carrier in Japan for the first time and to jointly develop ballistic missile defenses—overcoming longstanding Japanese public resistance. On the Korean peninsula, we are relocating United States Forces Korea from Yongsan garrison in downtown Seoul to a less urban area, consolidating our military into two hubs south of the Han River, and preparing to transfer war fighting operational control to the Republic of Korea in 2012. At the same time, President Bush has succeeded in affirming our enduring commitment to these key allies. As a result, in contrast to trends in some parts of the world, polling data shows South Koreans and Japanese continue to view the U.S. presence in a favorable light.

President Bush has also worked to transform these alliances by broadening their regional focus into a global outlook. As noted, Japan deployed ground troops to be part of Operation ENDURING FREEDOM in Iraq—the first such deployment to a war zone since the demise of Imperial Japan. The President has also had good success in convincing his counterparts in Australia, New Zealand, South Korea, and Mongolia to deploy troops in significant numbers to join coalition efforts in Iraq and Afghanistan. Moreover, Indonesian and Singaporean military personnel have deployed in noncombat roles to Lebanon and Afghanistan.

The President has also strengthened bilateral relationships throughout Southeast Asia. Since 9/11, he expanded counterterrorism cooperation with Malaysia, Indonesia, Thailand, Singapore, and the Philippines.

Philippines. The United States has moved our "transactional" relationship with the Philippines to a "transformational" level by helping the Philippines fundamentally change its defense institutions through the Philippine Defense Reform Program to enable the Philippines to better handle its own and regional defense. The United States also advised, trained, and equipped the Armed Forces of the Philippines (AFP), helping to enable the AFP to counter successfully the terrorist Abu Sayyaf Group.

Indonesia. The President transformed our relations with Indonesia. The administration moved decisively to meet Indonesian needs by quickly forming a core group including Japan, Australia, Thailand, and Singapore to aid the Indonesian people in the aftermath of the devastating 2004 Asian tsunami. Seizing on the good-will generated by our significant response to the Asian Tsunami in late 2004, the United States also convinced Congress it was strategically important to remove legislative constraints on the bilateral relationship put in place in response to past human rights abuses committed by the Indonesian military. We now engage in military training and exercises, conduct frequent, high-level policy dialogues; and cooperate on counterterrorism, pandemic prevention, and peacekeeping. The President's actions transformed views of the United States in the world's most populous Muslim nation and contributed to the signing of a peace accord between the government and insurgent groups in the tsunami-devastated breakaway province of Aceh.

Singapore. At the same time, President Bush signed a groundbreaking. Strategic Framework Agreement (SFA) with Singapore in 2005, the most expansive security cooperation agreement ever signed by the Singapore Government. Singapore's strategic location and first-rate facilities offer U.S. forces an efficient, secure, and reliable transit and logistic hub at the heart of one of the most active shipping lanes on the planet. This security cooperation added to a strong trade relationship with Singapore, which was expanded even further with the implementation of the U.S.-Singapore Free Trade Agreement in 2004.

Vietnam. With Vietnam, President Bush has put relations on a more positive track by providing major funding to combat HIV/AIDs and giving Vietnam another major power to partner with in its struggle against Chinese economic domination. With full U.S. support, Vietnam joined the World Trade Organization in 2006 and the United States has become Vietnam's top export market with two-way trade now topping $12 billion annually. During the visit of Prime Minister Dung in June 2008, the two sides agreed that it was time to negotiate a bilateral investment treaty.

Australia. With Australia, President Bush formed a strong personal bond with Prime Minister Howard and strengthened our alliance, symbolized most recently by the signing of a landmark Defense Trade Treaty when the President visited Australia for the APEC Summit in September 2007.

The United States and Australia also concluded a Free Trade Agreement in 2004. Close relations have been sustained with Prime Minister Howard's successor as evidenced by the visit to Washington by Prime Minister Rudd early in 2008.

New Zealand. With New Zealand, President Bush and Prime Minister Helen Clark agreed to amiably disagree over Wellington's antinuclear foreign policy, while working to develop several areas of mutually-beneficial cooperation within multinational frameworks, including intelligence-sharing, counterterrorism, and free trade. For example, in September 2008, USTR Schwab announced that the United States would join with New Zealand, Brunei, Singapore, and Chile to begin work on a robust Transpacific Free Trade Agreement.

Regional Security Architecture. East Asia's regional security architecture is underdeveloped but, in the creation of the Six-Party framework, the President has laid the foundation for new habits of cooperation in North East Asia. President Bush's vision is to transform the Six-Party framework into a regional security architecture. Progress on the nuclear issue will determine what form such an entity will take. More broadly, we have broached informal discussions with some partners on the possibility of launching an "Asian-G-8" security consultative mechanism that would add Australia, India, and perhaps Indonesia to the Northeast Asian framework for discussions of confidence-building measures, military transparency, and security planning.

Multilateral Participation. Geographical distance and our unique global responsibilities have made it impossible for top U.S. officials to participate in the growing alphabet soup of institutions and groupings in East Asia. Rather than committing half-heartedly to the full array of organizations, we have focused on those Organizations that are most effective, to which we know we can devote sustained energy, and which can insure a U.S. role in the region. The President's vigorous participation in the Asia-Pacific Economic Cooperation (APEC) forum, whose Leaders Meeting he has attended every year, has ensured that this trans-Pacific organization has continued to overshadow the ASEAN-organized East Asia Summit, which excludes the United States. At the same time, the President has enhanced our direct outreach to ASEAN, forming the ASEAN Enhanced Partnership in 2005—a comprehensive, action-oriented approach to security, economic, and developmental cooperation with the region—launching a Trade and Investment Framework Agreement (TIFA) with ASEAN in 2006, and appointing a U.S. Ambassador to ASEAN in 2008.

Regional Economic Integration. The President's personal advocacy has advanced the vision of an eventual Free Trade Area of the Asia Pacific (FTAAP) based on high U.S. standards for liberalization, using APEC as the primary vehicle through which to promote an FTAAP. An eventual FTAAP could conceivably engender a seismic shift in global trade policy, leveraging the relative optimism and ambition of the Asia-Pacific region to push the rest of the world into action. Simultaneously, we have pursued other multilateral regional economic integration options, such as accession to an expanded version of the P-4 grouping (New Zealand, Chile, Singapore, and Brunei). On the bilateral level, the President has signed high-quality bilateral FTAs with Australia, Singapore, and Korea that have kept us at the center of regional trade policy and forestalled Chinese attempts to pressure regional economies.

Ad-hoc Multilateralism. Cases of the President's successful employment of ad-hoc multilateralism include:

- Formation of the tsunami core group, which coordinated regional aid efforts to countries devastated by the December 2004 Indian Ocean tsunami.
- Use of the Proliferation Security Initiative to stop shipments of weapons of mass destruction, their delivery systems, and related materials.
- Establishment of the Global Peace Operations Initiative, through which the United States helps to train and equip standing peacekeeping forces.
- Creation of the Asia-Pacific Democracy Partnership to promote democratic values in the region.
- Launching of the Asia-Pacific Partnership on Clean Development and Climate, which has created public-private partnerships to expand markets for investment and trade in cleaner, more efficient energy technologies.

FUTURE CHALLENGES:

Complete Alliance Transformation and Defense Reform. We are in the midst of our alliance transformation processes with Japan and the Republic of Korea (ROK). Key remaining steps include executing the transfer of wartime operational control to the ROK by 2012 and completing the relocation and consolidation of U.S. forces from Okinawa to Guam by 2014. These steps are important—not only to ensure that progress achieved to date does not unravel, but to make certain our alliances with Japan and the ROK are adequately postured to deal with the challenges of the future. Future policy makers may also wish to work on revitalization of the trilateral security dialogue with Japan and Korea now that the leaders in both nations are more like-minded. Meanwhile, future policy makers will want to ensure that the Philippines remains committed to its Defense Reform Program. In Singapore, a command and control center is being built under the auspices of the SFA, and there are additional areas, such as maritime security and humanitarian disaster assistance, for cooperation that future U.S. policy makers may wish to pursue.

Create a Pan-Asia-Pacific Security Architecture. Despite progress in establishing the basis for a new sub-regional framework in Northeast Asia, work remains for future U.S. policy makers in building a broader regional security architecture. This would almost certainly consist of a collection of major powers, including the United States, China, Japan, South Korea, Australia,

India, Russia, and Indonesia, and would likely stress military transparency, confidence-building measures, and security planning. There are obvious pros and cons of bringing India into the East Asia security community, but doing so is consistent with our vision of India as a global strategic partner for the United States. At the same time, situating China among states it sees as co-equals would: send a strong signal that we do not intend to contain China; allow for serious discussion of regional security issues; and make clear that China's growing profile and influence also entail greater responsibility. There may be some urgency for future U.S. policy makers in considering this concept because, as China's power grows, it may see less reason to join such a grouping.

Vigorously Pursue Regional Economic Integration. President Bush agreed that the United States would host APEC in 2011. This creates a crucial opportunity for U.S. policy makers to force the issue of launching active talks on a Free Trade Area of the Asia-Pacific (FTAAP), regardless of whether the approach is country-by-country, chapter-by-chapter, or as a single undertaking. At the same time, U.S. policy makers may wish to give priority to completing free trade agreement talks with Thailand, Malaysia, and the P-4 (Brunei, Singapore, New Zealand, and Chile), thereby ensuring that the United States is the hub around whose standards FTAAP is negotiated. As China is likely to block any FTAAP approaches that include Taiwan, future US policy makers may wish to consider launching talks on a separate bilateral quasi-FTA with Taiwan in 2009 or 2010 to compensate.

Solidify Relations with ASEAN. The ASEAN grouping greatly desires a more constant relationship with the United States that features regular, face-to-face ASEAN meetings with the President. A key question for future U.S. policy makers is how to work with ASEAN to do this without legitimizing the Burmese junta. We currently do this by increasing the Enhanced Partnership budget specifically dedicated to cooperation with ASEAN as a group and pushing ASEAN to work with us to enliven the ASEAN Regional Forum. However, if the Burmese regime is able to achieve a higher level of international acquiescence through its 2010 sham elections, U.S. policy makers will find mounting challenges to keeping pressure on the regime.

Attachments
Tab 1   Chronology for East Asian Alliances and Architecture
Tab 2   President Signed U.S.-Singapore Free Trade Agreement (May 6, 2003)
Tab 3   Remarks to the Philippine Congress on Defense Reform Program (October 18, 2003)
Tab 4   Radio Address Announcement of Tsunami Core Group (January 1, 2005)
Tab 5   U.S.-Singapore Strategic Framework Agreement (July 12, 2005)
Tab 6   Memorandum of Conversation with Prime Minister Junichiro Koizumi (November 16, 2005)
Tab 7   Joint Vision Statement on the ASEAN-U.S. Enhanced Partnership (November 17, 2005)

POSTSCRIPT

PAUL HAENLE, MICHAEL GREEN, FARYAR SHIRZAD

Few national security issues have evolved as dramatically since 2008 as has US-East Asia policy. While in 2008 it was still possible to be guardedly optimistic about US-Chinese relations, in a little over a decade that optimism had been replaced with a bipartisan consensus that China's rise to power posed a grave geopolitical challenge not just to America's relations in this crucial part of the world, but across the globe. The Bush administration did not solve the challenges posed by China's rise. In hindsight, however, the administration's efforts to revitalize security partnerships and establish new trade agreements formed a regional framework that subsequent administrations could build upon to meet the challenge of rising Chinese power.

The Bush Administration Approach

In dealing with a rising China, the Bush administration sought to encourage China to play a responsible role in Asia while building an architecture of alliances, partnerships, and institutions that would reinforce an open and rules-based order in the region. The administration recognized that China's growing military and economic power had the potential to destabilize the region and harm the interests of the United States and its allies.

The Bush administration's operating assumption was that China offered both opportunities and challenges. President Bush made this clear during the 2000 presidential campaign, as per the Transition Memorandum, when he said China was more of a "strategic competitor" than a "strategic partner." For this reason, the administration pursued a strategy of engagement backed by balancing and hedging. While the administration engaged directly with Chinese leadership to encourage their participation in the rules-based international order, it also strengthened the alliances and partnerships the president believed would shape China's choices but also be necessary should future leaders in China choose a different path—as now appears to be the case under Xi Jinping.

Many in China, the United States, and the international community had sound reasons to expect that Beijing would continue along a path of economic reform and political liberalization. The administration pursued policies to encourage China's evolution toward further openness. However, these policies were not predicated on the expectation that democracy would take hold in China anytime soon. The goal of the strategy was to integrate China into the regional and international political and economic architecture so that it would play a "responsible," "supportive," and "constructive" role—rather than seek to overturn that architecture. Strategic dialogue mechanisms were used to press for political and economic changes in China, but engagement was not premised on any assumption about the inevitably of liberalization. The administration maintained steady encouragement and pressure for reform but at the same time expressed openly its concerns about China's human rights record and mercantilist trade policies.

The Bush administration's simultaneous engagement with both Asian allies and with China laid the groundwork for a regional security and economic architecture that promoted US interests and values regardless of decisions by Chinese leaders on its future trajectory.

What Has Happened Since the End of the Bush Administration?

The global landscape has shifted dramatically since the Bush administration left office, as have Beijing's views of itself, the United States, and the world. In the eyes of senior Chinese leaders, the 2008 global financial crisis damaged the credibility of the US economic model and weakened Washington's ability to effectively build a regional architecture conducive to US interests. Populism that spread across Western democratic nations, including the United States and in Europe, has sown further doubt in Beijing about the primacy and efficacy of Western-style democracy and the rules-based international order. These doubts, reinforced even more recently following the January 6 attack on the US Capitol, seem to have eliminated any Chinese desire to converge with the US democratic system, increased China's confidence in its own system, and convinced it that the long-term trends—or the "correlation of forces"—are in China's favor. Despite slowing economic growth, aging demographics, and hardening international views of China, the Chinese Communist Party still believes that it will emerge as the world's strongest economic, diplomatic, and military power in the twenty-first century.

Crises in the international financial system and Western democracy coincided with surging Chinese ambition and nationalism. The most striking change has been the rise of its current leader, Xi Jinping. Xi has centralized CCP control in a way not seen since the era of Mao Zedong, reasserting the role of the CCP in every element of Chinese society. On the domestic front, China's grip on public discourse has tightened and violations of human rights in Xinjiang, Hong Kong, and

Tibet have worsened. Abroad China has ramped up assertive actions on its periphery and expanded its influence in international institutions. As the United States and its allies and partners have pushed back against Chinese assertiveness, Beijing has leaned further into its strategic partnership with Russia. Xi has abandoned China's "keep a low profile and bide your time" international strategy in favor of a more aggressive foreign policy with the stated goal of leading the reform of the global governance system in ways that further China's interests.

As Beijing's posture evolved, so too did subsequent US presidential administrations. Initially, the Obama administration maintained a considerable degree of policy continuity with the Bush administration. Obama expanded on the Bush administration's economic and security building blocks in the region and made a particular focus of Southeast Asia. As US commitments in the Middle East declined, the Obama administration's Pivot to Asia strategy enhanced Bush-era efforts to strengthen regional partnerships and shore up key alliances. The main economic component of this strategy, the Trans-Pacific Partnership (TPP), advanced Bush administration efforts to develop the rules and standards on trade as part of a trans-Pacific trading pact. The redeployment of military assets to the Asia-Pacific carried on efforts to strengthen key security partnerships in the region. Where it was deemed in US interests, the Obama administration also sought to emphasize more cooperative aspects of the US relationship with China, most successfully on the issue of climate change that culminated in the Paris Accords. As Beijing simultaneously pursued policies that undermined US interests, however, US policymakers began to reevaluate the efficacy of a US policy predicated on engagement. This became especially apparent toward the end of the Obama administration following China's failure to adhere to cybersecurity agreements and commitments not to militarize islands in the South China Sea.

Frustrations that emerged in the Obama administration carried into the Trump administration, which largely rejected the policies of its predecessors. The Trump administration frequently criticized the US policy of engagement and instead implemented a set of much more confrontational polices targeting areas where it believed Chinese behavior undermined US interests. Simultaneously, the administration abandoned key regional multilateral efforts that the Bush and Obama administrations had developed as building blocks for a regional architecture to incentivize China to integrate with the region and to hedge in the event it did not. President Trump withdrew from the TPP, which was designed to create a regional trade regime that would rally US allies and partners while encouraging

China to accept Western standards and practices. The administration preferred to deal with China and other countries in the region on a bilateral basis, failing to recognize the value of US alliances and partnerships in strengthening US leverage.

The Trump administration broke important new ground by emphasizing China's role as a strategic competitor and increasing defense spending and operations. However, these moves were undercut by excessive demands for burden sharing that alienated US allies, threats to withdraw US troops from South Korea, unilateralist trade policies, and a near total retreat from the region's multilateral diplomacy—especially in Southeast Asia.

How Did the Bush Administration Do?

The Bush administration strategy anticipated the possibility of China's evolution in a more menacing direction but was not premised on the inevitability of such an evolution. The subsequent shift to a more adversarial relationship raises the question of whether the Bush approach should have focused more on an adverse trajectory of development in China's posture toward the world. Although China has grown more aggressive since the Bush administration left office, the Asia-Pacific as a whole has remained stable and avoided major conflict. The same security and economic partnerships that formed the basis of the Bush administration's Asia policy continue to undergird America's footprint in the region today.

In hindsight, working with allies and partners in Asia was critical at a time when US defense efforts were focused on national security issues in the Middle East. The administration revitalized military alliances with key regional partners to, in the words of the Transition Memo, "engage China with and through our strong allies . . . and to encourage responsible action by China." This effort included transforming US security, economic, and political relations with Japan, South Korea, Australia, New Zealand, and the Philippines and forming an enhanced security, economic, and development partnership with ASEAN.

Efforts to revitalize security alliances did not come without difficulty. In the first year of the administration, a US Navy submarine collided with and sank a Japanese civilian training ship in the Pacific and, in the second year, a US Army vehicle struck and killed two South Korean schoolgirls. The incident in South Korea sparked large candlelight protests in downtown Seoul and poll numbers on American favorability temporarily sank to their lowest level in history. By the time the Bush administration left office in 2009, however, polls showed that public support for the United States in Asia was higher than when the administration had entered office. The administration's efforts to strengthen US commitments in Asia reduced the risk that China could play a destabilizing role in the region.

Efforts to engage directly with the Chinese political leadership and military to enhance understanding and reduce the risk of military confrontation or conflict also bore fruit. The administration inaugurated the first-ever bilateral dialogue on nuclear strategy and policy (with follow-up working-level meetings planned with STRATCOM) and established, in the words of the Transition Memo, "the first military hotline between the Pentagon and the Chinese Military Commission." At the same time, President Bush envisioned transforming initiatives like the Six-Party Framework into a lasting regional security architecture—an effort that proved elusive.

With respect to Taiwan, the administration adopted a policy of opposing "any unilateral changes to the status quo by either side [Taiwan or China]," providing robust arms sales packages to Taiwan, and making clear the administration's willingness "to defend Taiwan if attacked." The administration simultaneously encouraged improved relations between Taiwan and China and made clear that the Bush administration would not support a Taiwanese declaration of independence. While conflict between China and Taiwan—and between China and the United States over Taiwan—was avoided, China did not stop its military buildup, enter into effective dialogue with Taiwan's officials, or ease its hardline position on Taiwan's role in international organizations. As a result, cross-strait relations remain to this day one of the world's most dangerous flashpoints.

In the economic realm, the Bush administration successfully built a web of interlocking multilateral and bilateral trade agreements such as high-quality free-trade agreements with Australia, Singapore, and South Korea. The administration also launched the Trade and Investment Framework Agreement (TIFA) with ASEAN in 2006 and acceded to an expanded version of the "P-4 grouping" (the original Trans-Pacific Strategic Economic Partnership Agreement including New Zealand, Chile, Singapore, and Brunei), which later evolved into the 11-nation Trans-Pacific Partnership. Each of these trade and investment agreements served as building blocks for a future high-standards trade liberalization Free Trade Area of the Asia-Pacific (FTAAP) to be pursued through the Asia-Pacific Economic Cooperation (APEC) forum. These trade agreements had the potential to cement the United States as a rule-setter in the Asia-Pacific and gain leverage in trade negotiations with China. The Trump administration's later withdrawal from the TPP reflected in part the failure of prior administrations, including Bush's, to build public support for multilateral trade agreements and demonstrate their value to American interests.

At the same time as the administration built a regional trade architecture, it dealt directly with the Chinese leadership to encourage a transition from an investment and export-dependent economy to one driven by consumption. China's push to integrate into the global economy provided leverage for the Bush administration to encourage market reforms in China. Although the administration did not negotiate China's accession to the World Trade Organization (WTO), the administration was responsible for ensuring that China remained compliant with the agreement. Over the course of two terms, the Bush administration worked aggressively through bilateral means to address China's unfair trade practices and settled or won seven WTO disputes. In hindsight, the administration overestimated the extent to which the multilateral trading system in its current form could discipline the worst excesses of China's state-led economy. More needed to be done to reform the WTO and enable the institution to manage distortions from state-owned enterprises, intellectual property theft, state subsidies, and indigenous innovation policies.

Finally, the administration pressed Chinese leaders for greater engagement on issues of common concern. On clean energy and climate, the administration created the Asia-Pacific Partnership on Clean Development and Climate and the Major Economies Meetings process. These initiatives helped move the needle on climate issues, producing a July 2008 G-8 statement in which China joined other major economies in acknowledging a leadership role in combating climate change. In dealing with North Korea, Washington and Beijing cooperated in the United Nations Security Council on sanctions against Pyongyang and worked together to produce the September 19, 2005 Joint Statement wherein North Korea committed to give up its pursuit of nuclear weapons. On pandemics and disease control, the two sides established the Chinese Center of Disease Control. The administration also encouraged China's greater participation in UN peacekeeping operations, where Beijing is currently the largest contributor of peacekeeping forces and has played a constructive role in crises like Darfur.

What Are the Lessons Learned?
Even today, facing a very different geopolitical landscape, the key components of the Bush administration's China policy as well as the economic and security partnerships it championed continue to form the basis of America's strategy to

sustain peace and prosperity in Asia. Nevertheless, with the benefit of hindsight and given current realities, future US policy in East Asia should look different from the one pursued during the Bush presidency. An essential element will be to convince China that America and its allies and partners are prepared to compete and win where they must—and that China is wrong about the "correlation of forces" running in its direction.

- *While future administrations will blend adversarial, competitive, and cooperative approaches, as was the case under the Bush administration, the adversarial and competitive aspects are likely to be more pronounced.* This fact will make it even more difficult for future administrations to sustain the cooperative elements of the US relationship with China. Future policy must ensure that the United States is able to deter conflict in and around the Indo-Pacific, compete effectively in key economic and security domains, and cooperate or coordinate with China when it is in the interest of the United States. This will not be an easy balancing act. But Bush policy suggests that it is possible to both maintain stable relations with China, while also hedging and balancing against Chinese assertiveness. The best approach will be to lead with competition, be open to opportunities for cooperation or coordination, and avoid linkage between Chinese assistance on global challenges and concessions on US interests.

- *Future policy must give greater attention to technological competitiveness and supply chain resilience than was the case in earlier periods.* Critical twenty-first-century technologies (such as artificial intelligence, autonomy, quantum computing, cyber, and bioengineering) have emerged as a central aspect of US-China competition. Positioning the United States to compete successfully in these technologies, through domestic investments, market incentives, and other efforts to address American infrastructure, education, training, and economic deficiencies, will be an important element of US policy. The United States will need to do more to insulate critical technologies from predatory practices, while at the same time minimizing rent seeking in the domestic market. Future administrations should support private-sector innovation and clearly identify which market transactions in high-tech industries pose genuine threats to national security and which do not. Greater effort will have to be made to safeguard critical supply chains from overdependence on China in key areas. This will be complicated by Taiwan's central position as supplier of critical technology components (like semiconductors), its vulnerability to Chinese pressure, and the resulting tensions in the US-China relationship.

- *Future administrations will have to do more bilaterally and multilaterally to manage the distortions caused by China's state-led economic model.* Trump administration policy (including withdrawal from the TPP negotiations, attack on the WTO, and the initiation of trade disputes with some of America's closest allies), plus the widespread disaffection with free trade among both Democrats and now Republicans, will make it very difficult for the United States to initiate a significant trade agenda. To garner public support for an effective international economic and trade policy, future policymakers will need to highlight the benefits of international business and trade in terms of US jobs and exports. At the same time, more should be done to invest in infrastructure and human capital to enable American workers to remain globally competitive. Finally, the United States should do more to coordinate with allies and partners on investing in new technologies and on setting new rules and standards, especially for the digital economy. If the United States is unable to devise a long-term international economic and trade strategy, it will forfeit a substantial element of any successful effort to strengthen America's position in the Asia-Pacific and to better compete with China.

- *Much more needs to be done to enhance the military capability of the United States and its friends and allies in the Asia-Pacific.* This will build upon what was done in the Bush and Obama administrations but also expand beyond it, given China's considerable military modernization efforts. The United States should devote more resources to developing new technologies, enhancing deterrence capabilities, and streamlining the interoperability of the US military and that of its allies and partners. As US-China competition intensifies, it will be critical for the United States to continue to demonstrate its full commitment to the security interests of US allies and partners.

- *Finally, much more will have to be done to counter the ideological challenge presented by China.* The "China Policy" Transition Memorandum was rather prescient in describing China's unique ideological appeal. It argues that China serves as a model for authoritarian regimes looking to achieve high rates of economic growth while maintaining their grip on power. The relatively unconditional nature of Chinese economic aid and military assistance is often a boon to oppressive regimes the world over. In this area the United States should play to its strengths by advocating for the inherent benefits of its values and market-driven model, and work to provide high-standards trade and investment alternatives to countries in the region. Despite recent headwinds, many of the most successful states in Asia continue to have strong preferences for democratic norms. The United States should empower like-minded allies and partners to promote a plurilateral agenda in support of these democratic norms, both in Asia and around the world.

Contributors:
Ryan Featherstone
Nathaniel Sher
Lucas Tcheyan

CHAPTER 19

India

MARK WEBBER

Perhaps the most significant accomplishment of the Bush administration from a geopolitical perspective was its establishment of a strategic relationship between the United States and India. While increasing attention was being given to the rise of China, President Bush was also focused on the emergence of India as a global player. With its democratic values and increasing free-market reforms, President Bush saw India as a natural partner for the United States in addressing global challenges. Using civil nuclear cooperation as the keystone for change, he transformed the substance of the relationship and how both countries saw that relationship. India and the United States, with support from both their peoples, had started down the road of strategic partnership.

With the highly competitive if not adversarial character of the US-China relationship today, and its increasing framing as an ideological struggle between authoritarian state capitalism and free-market democracy, the transformation of US-India relations was in hindsight prescient and reset the table for the great power competition to come. The weight added by India to that of the United States and America's existing allies and partners, particularly in Asia, offers the potential for creating a balance of power that can not only help constrain China's hegemonic ambitions but also tip the scales toward freedom over autocracy.

TRANSITION MEMORANDUM

SECRET

NATIONAL SECURITY COUNCIL
WASHINGTON, D.C. 20504

6559

Transition

NSC Declassification Review [E.O. 13526]
DECLASSIFY IN PART
by William C. Carpenter 3/23/2020

November 17, 2008

MEMORANDUM FOR THE RECORD

FROM: MARK WEBBER, SOUTH AND CENTRAL ASIAN AFFAIRS
          JORGAN ANDREWS, SOUTH AND CENTRAL ASIAN AFFAIRS
          ANISH GOEL, SOUTH AND CENTRAL ASIAN AFFAIRS
          TRISH MAHONEY, SOUTH AND CENTRAL ASIAN AFFAIRS

SUBJECT: India

THE SITUATION AS WE FOUND IT:

The Clinton Administration, recognizing the importance of India as an emerging global power and its potential as a counterweight to China, had begun exploring ways to improve bilateral relations and develop the potential to align our respective national interests in the post-Cold War era. India's 1998 nuclear test, however, forced the imposition of sanctions under the Glenn amendment, limiting our cooperation and rekindling Indian stereotypes of the United States as paternalistic and dictatorial toward lesser developed nations. In addition to exacerbating Indian sensitivities, the sanctions did not persuade India to sign the Comprehensive Test Ban Treaty or the Nuclear Non-Proliferation Treaty, reduce its development of weapons systems, or end the production of fissile material.

To India, U.S. sanctions were part of an effort to keep India out of the great power "club" and deny India its rightful place on the world stage. For India, the true test of "transformed" relations with the United States would be our willingness to welcome India into the "club"—and maybe even sponsor its membership.

Our Cold War closeness to Pakistan was another source of Indian unease. Increased tension between the United States and Pakistan following the 1999 Kargil conflict may have reassured India that the United States held a balanced view toward the regional conflict, but it also reinforced the

SECRET
Reason: 1.4(b) (d)
Declassify on: 11/17/18

Re-Classified by: Ellen J. L. Knight
Reason: 1.4(d)
Declassify on: 11 /17/2033

Indian habit of filtering its own relationship with the United States through a Pakistan optic. Without the stabilizing hand of the United States, India feared a more troublesome Pakistan.

Despite sanctions, expanding bilateral private sector ties after India's 1991 economic reforms set the stage for increased government-to-government cooperation and provided enormous potential to boost bilateral trade and investment.

The Clinton Administration's efforts with India culminated in President Clinton's visit to India in May 2000 and the reciprocal visit of Prime Minister Vajpayee to Washington in September 2000.

THIS ADMINISTRATION'S POLICY:

Even before his election, President Bush had set as a strategic priority the strengthening of United States ties to India. In a speech at the Reagan Library in November 1999, then-candidate Bush said "This coming century will see democratic India's arrival as a force in the world, a vast population.... India is now debating its future and its strategic path and the United States must pay it more attention." India was emerging as a global player - diplomatically, economically, and geostrategically. And the President wanted this emerging player to be a strategic partner of the United States. The bases of this strategic partnership were the common values we shared and our commitment to democracy. Early in its tenure, this Administration conveyed its intention to transform relations with India, including, if desired by both parties, playing a helpful but quiet role with respect to Kashmir.

The Indians welcomed the President's May 1, 2001, speech on the new international strategic framework for nonproliferation, including missile defense and nuclear reductions, as the promise of a new era. With the President's waiver of Glenn amendment sanctions in September 2001, the path toward broader, multi-dimensional, long-term cooperation was open, and two months later, the President and Prime Minister Vajpayee met in Washington and agreed to work together on transforming the relationship. In addition to more conventional areas of bilateral cooperation like education, agriculture, military-to-military relations, counterterrorism, and trade, the two nations would expand ties in more sensitive areas, generally reserved for our closest allies, like civil space, civil nuclear energy, missile defense, and high technology cooperation. Progress in these more sensitive areas would occur along a "glide path" of gradual, reciprocal steps (an initiative known as the "Next Steps in Strategic Partnership" or NSSP) to ensure parity in actions taken by both governments and steps by India that would help allay our proliferation concerns. Both governments formally endorsed and announced the NSSP in January 2004.

The centerpiece of our transformed relations and its most ambitious and controversial element, the U.S.-India Civil Nuclear Cooperation Initiative (CNCI), sought to convert India from a nuclear outlier to an internationally recognized member of the nonproliferation community responsible for implementing and complying with global nonproliferation standards. Facilitating India's inclusion in this community would bring more than half of India's nuclear reactors under International Atomic Energy Agency (IAEA) safeguards, help meet India's rapidly expanding energy demand in an environmentally friendly manner, and be a tangible expression to the Indian Government and the Indian people of the President's desire to have India as a strategic partner of the United States.

In sum, our Strategic Partnership aimed to:

- Bring India into the nuclear non-proliferation mainstream;
- Mitigate tensions with Pakistan;
- Encourage India's role as a stabilizing influence and democratic model in the region;
- Foster the economic reforms that, together with our improved political relations, would make India a more productive partner in multilateral fora, including the United Nations and World Trade Organization (WTO);
- Encourage India's emergence as a responsible global power.

WHAT HAS BEEN ACCOMPLISHED:

The United States and India have made meaningful progress toward realizing the shared vision of President Bush and Prime Minister Singh, articulated in the July 2005 Joint Statement marking Prime Minister Singh's visit to Washington, D.C., "to transform the relationship between their countries and establish a global partnership."

Singh's visit coincided with the completion of the NSSP initiative. Through the NSSP, the United States agreed to remove export license restrictions on specified high-tech exports to India, thereby giving India greater access to the U.S. market and fostering increased high-tech trade. In return, India provided greater transparency of its market, and strengthened its own export controls through tighter regulation and new legislation governing the export of sensitive technology.

Building on that success, during the President's March 2006 visit to India, the two leaders mapped out an ambitious agenda of cooperation, including in the area of civil nuclear energy trade, defense cooperation and trade, bilateral trade and investment, economic reform, civil space, health, democracy, education, science and technology, agriculture, regional issues, and Indo-Pak relations.

1. Civil Nuclear Initiative

While completion of the civil nuclear initiative was not intended to be the measure of success of the overall relationship, it has remained the most high-profile component of the Strategic Partnership. Following the formal announcement of the civil nuclear initiative during Prime Minister Singh's July 2005 visit to the White House, the Administration moved quickly to explain the plan and its benefits to the Congress, the business community, academia and policy think tanks, and among members of the Nuclear Suppliers Group (NSG).

Concurrently, the Administration worked with the Indian Government to create a credible, defensible, and transparent separation plan that would address non-proliferation concerns raised by Members of Congress and NSG participating governments. That separation plan identifies and separates India's civil and military nuclear programs and places the civil sector under permanent international safeguards. The details of the plan were announced during the President's March 2006 visit to New Delhi.

With the foundation for establishing bilateral cooperation in place, the Administration built broad bipartisan support for the initiative in Congress, culminating in December 2006 in the passage of the Henry J. Hyde U.S.-India Peaceful Atomic Energy Cooperation Act of 2006 (known as the "Hyde Act") by wide margins in both Houses. In July 2007, the two governments concluded negotiations on a bilateral agreement for peaceful nuclear cooperation (also known as a "123" agreement) to govern civil nuclear trade between the two countries.

Under the Hyde Act, the United States and India had to complete several additional steps before the 123 Agreement could be sent to Congress for approval. Most importantly, India had to conclude a safeguards agreement with the International Atomic Energy Agency (IAEA) and the United States had to obtain an exception for India to NSG guidelines on civil nuclear trade.

In October 2007, the ruling United Progressive Alliance (UPA) faced strong opposition to the initiative from coalition partners on the left, who claimed closer ties with the United States would undermine Indian sovereignty, thereby stalling progress on the initiative. In July 2008, the UPA survived a no-confidence vote in Parliament, paving the way for the CNCI to continue to move forward.

On August 1, 2008, the IAEA approved the Indian Safeguards Agreement by consensus. On September 6, 2008, after convening two extraordinary plenaries, the NSG approved by consensus an exception for India to its guidelines requiring full-scope safeguards as a condition of supply of nuclear material and technology. This decision will enable India to trade in nuclear fuel, equipment, and technology with other countries and effectively ended India's 34-year isolation from the international civil nuclear market. Following this decision, India completed its nonproliferation commitments, and the Administration submitted the 123 Agreement to Congress on September 10, 2008. On October 1, 2008, Congress passed legislation approving the 123 agreement and the President signed the legislation on October 8, 2008. The 123 agreement was subsequently signed on October 10, 2008, by Secretary Rice and Indian Foreign Minister Pranab Mukherjee. Formalities to bring the initiative into force are expected to be completed by the end of 2008, although private contract negotiations for U.S. nuclear exports are likely to continue into 2009 and beyond.

2. Defense Cooperation and Trade

Defense cooperation and trade between the United States and India proved to be one of the most significant areas of growth. In 2005, the United States and India signed a defense cooperation framework agreement that sketched out areas for enhanced cooperation, including regional stability, counterterrorism, and counterproliferation. The April 2007 transfer to India of the USS TRENTON, an amphibious assault warship, under the Excess Defense Articles program was followed by the first visit of a U.S. nuclear-powered aircraft carrier (USS NIMITZ) to an Indian port in July 2007 and India's unprecedented hosting of 20,000 sailors in a five-nation naval exercise (including Australia, Japan, and Singapore) in September 2007. Each branch of the U.S. Armed Forces has regular exercises with its Indian counterpart. After decades of being frozen out of India's lucrative defense market, Lockheed Martin and Boeing are now leading contenders in what will be India's biggest defense sale (fighter aircraft potentially worth $10 billion) since independence.

By contrast, the bilateral missile defense dialogue has sputtered because of only sporadic Indian interest and has evolved minimally beyond joint tabletop exercises. In addition, several foundational defense agreements, such as the Communications Interoperability and Security Memorandum of Agreement (CISMOA), the Logistic Support Agreement (LSA), and End Use Monitoring (EUM), remain incomplete, delayed by Indian inaction.

3. Bilateral Trade and Investment

Insightful recommendations from the U.S.-India CEO Forum have helped forge a way ahead toward increased bilateral trade and investment. By the end of 2007, bilateral trade had more than tripled since 2000, jumping from approximately $13 billion to over $41 billion. The two nations revitalized the flagging bilateral Economic Dialogue and will soon begin formal negotiations of a bilateral investment treaty.

4. Economic Reform

Despite the progress in the bilateral trade relationship, key Indian economic reforms have flagged. After a promising early start, momentum for India's economic reform slowed to a near halt by 2006, abetted by the Indian Government's preoccupation with the prospect of early elections. For example, India has made little to no progress on tariff reductions, continues to retain non-tariff barriers on agricultural imports, has moved slowly on financial sector reforms, and maintains caps on foreign direct investment into many industries. In addition, India's political sensitivity to the concerns of small-holdings and subsistence farmers has caused it to be inflexible in the Doha Round and an obstacle to progress. Indian intransigence was in large part responsible for the failure to achieve a breakthrough on modalities during the July 2008 WTO negotiations in Geneva.

5. Civil Space Cooperation

In the area of civil space cooperation, the completion of the NSSP opened the door to joint coordination and research in a number of areas, including earth observation, weather forecasting, and space exploration. However, the use of Indian space launch vehicles for satellite launches remains restricted due to unresolved disagreements about a potential Commercial Space Launch Agreement (CSLA) that would accompany an already-negotiated Technology Safeguards Agreement (TSA). Both the TSA and the CSLA are intended to provide the necessary safeguards that would enable the United States to support the launch of U.S. satellites and satellite components on Indian vehicles. In an effort to jump-start stalled negotiations on the CSLA, in February 2008, the Administration offered a compromise solution, if India agreed to open a dialogue with the United States on market access issues related to the services provided by orbiting satellites, so-called satellite services. India, however, continues to express reservations with the way forward, in part to protect its domestic space industry from foreign competition. The way ahead in this area remains unclear.

6. Health Cooperation

Cooperation with India on public health is also an important element of the bilateral relationship, reinforced by India's hosting of the International Partnership on Avian and Pandemic Influenza conference in late 2007 and our assistance to the West Bengal state government in the wake of its avian influenza outbreak in early 2008.

7. Democracy Promotion

The President and Prime Minister Singh ensured that democracy was included as part of the bilateral cooperation agenda. Subsequently, India has begun to assume a helpful leadership role as the world's largest democracy, and even to take steps publicly with the United States regarding the benefits of democracy. In 2005, Prime Minister Singh co-hosted with the President the launching of the U.N. Democracy Fund, and India has indicated its willingness to participate in the inaugural meeting of the Asia Pacific Democracy Partnership.

8. Education Cooperation

India and the United States signed an agreement in spring 2008 doubling the number of Fulbright scholars between the two nations. But efforts to expand university-to-university ties have stalled, limiting our ability to increase educational cooperation.

9. Science and Technology Cooperation

Cooperation with India on science and technology has increased, due in large part to the India-U.S. Science and Technology Framework Agreement, signed in October 2005. This Agreement enabled joint research and collaborations to commence without concerns over intellectual property rights that had hampered previous cooperation. These intellectual property rights concerns were resolved through updated Indian legislation modernizing its intellectual property regimes and through the negotiation of the Framework Agreement itself.

10. Agricultural Cooperation

In March 2006, the President and Prime Minister Singh announced the Agricultural Knowledge Initiative (AKI), a $100 million initiative designed to help ease India's concerns over growing food insecurity and assist India with the modernization of its agricultural sector. The AKI is now completing its last year of implementation, having exhausted its funds, which included $27 million in U.S. assistance. While the AKI has raised greater awareness in the both governments on agricultural issues and resulted in promising research and developments, commercialization and distribution of new methods and technologies has proven difficult, often mired in Indian bureaucracy and a fundamental disagreement over the nature of agricultural cooperation. The United States has encouraged public-private partnerships, increased investment in infrastructure, and market access; India has tended to seek pure research and technology exchanges that seem to offer little practical benefit for improving productivity, investment, or a "second Green Revolution."

11. Regional Issues

After decades of trying to keep the United States out of what it viewed as its backyard, India now consults with us closely and frequently on regional developments, and in cases where our respective interests align (e.g., Afghanistan, Nepal, Sri Lanka) we have worked together beneficially. Where our interests do not align (e.g., Iran, Burma), there have been differences in strategic approach. Indian behavior at multilateral fora like the U.N. and the WTO often more closely resembles its old NAM and G-77 approach than its more recent transition to a Strategic Partner.

12. Indo-Pak Relations

Although the United States has signaled repeatedly its willingness to be quietly helpful on Kashmir, India has resisted U.S. involvement as a mediator in this highly sensitive issue. The United States continues to urge both parties to show flexibility,   India recognizes the usefulness of U.S. influence in discouraging Pakistani support for cross-border extremism and expects us to exercise it. Attacks in India traced to Pakistan-based terrorists also indirectly affect our relations with India, and Indian leeriness of our ties to Pakistan may have hindered our closer cooperation on counterterrorism with New Delhi. Steps toward a final resolution of bilateral tensions under the leadership of Prime Minister Singh and President Musharraf, while substantial, fell far short of a breakthrough, and Pakistan's domestic political turmoil in 2007 and 2008 stalled further progress. India is unlikely to pursue bold initiatives on Kashmir until it is assured Pakistan has strong, stable, and reliable leadership.

The United States and India are steadily building closer relations, bolstered by common interests like regional stability, democratic values, increased trade and investment, and people-to-people linkages. The President has transformed the U.S.-India relationship and has established a robust strategic partnership. This has been supported by the burgeoning Indian-American community, the 84,000 Indian students at U.S. universities—the largest foreign contingent—and the 25 percent jump in Indian demand for tourist visas to the United States over the past year. The question is not whether bilateral relations will continue to improve, but rather how fast they will improve.

FUTURE CHALLENGES:

While the United States and India continue to make progress on bilateral fronts that are high-profile, like civil nuclear cooperation and defense cooperation agreements, we have also expanded our engagement in equally valuable areas like health, education, science, and agriculture to build bilateral trust. Indian interest in sharing in U.S. research and technology provides a useful vehicle to broaden cooperation in those fields. In response to Indian concerns about its future food security, the United States is pursuing ways to build upon the Agricultural Knowledge Initiative (AKI), including through private sector participation, following its 3-year commitment and scope.

At the same time, the United States continues prodding India to demonstrate the leadership, both internationally and regionally, it believes has earned it a seat on the U.N. Security Council. Making amends in trade policy for its poor behavior in WTO Doha round negotiations, cooperating with us on an international approach toward climate change, and working with us on Burma and Iran are benchmarks along India's path toward becoming a global power. Resolution of its long-standing dispute with Pakistan over Kashmir would show that India has evolved beyond allowing regional rivalries to define and limit it.

The change in U.S.-India relations over the past eight years has been remarkable. The Strategic Partnership envisioned by the President and Prime Minister Singh has been a major success in building ties between the world's oldest and largest democracies. The bilateral relationship, fueled by private sector ties, will continue to improve in the next decade.

However, satisfactory progress on many of our more ambitious initiatives, such as defense cooperation agreements—and even on some hypothetically less controversial areas, such as the AKI—has proven elusive for a variety of reasons, including India's inability to shed fully old Cold War dichotomies and accept the political risks entailed in being the world power it wants to become.

As India continues its evolution from regional heavyweight to global leader, the zero-sum dynamic that still influences some Indian thinking about foreign policy will fade, and the mutual benefits of deeper strategic engagement with the United States will emerge more clearly.

Attachments

POSTSCRIPT

MARK WEBBER

At the time the Transition Memorandum on India was completed on November 17, 2008, the US-India relationship was at a historical high point. The successful completion of the civil nuclear cooperation initiative earlier that year had provided a clear signal of the US commitment to transforming the long-term bilateral relationship. Moving into the transition, the Bush administration considered the burgeoning relationship with India to be a major foreign policy success. The incoming Obama administration would be able to build on the strong foundation laid over the previous eight years to work together on issues of common interest and move beyond the historically transactional, and often contentious, relationship. The path to a more positive US-India relationship seemed assured.

Then, on November 26, only nine days after the Transition Memorandum was finalized, Pakistan-based extremists attacked Mumbai. India considered the Mumbai attacks to be the latest in a series of terrorist actions that threatened to plunge the India-Pakistan relationship into confrontation and conflict once again. The administration pivoted quickly into crisis management mode.

By January of 2009, the situation had stabilized, in large part through the personal efforts of President Bush and Secretary of State Rice working with Indian and Pakistani leadership to defuse tensions. Ultimately, the US-India bilateral relationship would grow stronger in the aftermath of the Mumbai attacks, but the state of affairs inherited by the Obama administration had changed from that described in the Transition Memorandum. The Mumbai attacks would mark the beginning of a tumultuous time in regional affairs when hopes of facilitating the resolution of long-standing India-Pakistan issues would fade.

The Bush Administration Approach

President Bush's approach to India was focused on achieving a transformation in bilateral relations that recognized India as a strong, stable democracy with shared values, and sought a more productive relationship with India as a strategic partner not only in Asia but globally. India was emerging as a diplomatic, economic, and geostrategic global player and, as the Transition Memorandum says, Bush "wanted this emerging player to be a strategic partner of the United States." By this measure, the Bush administration policy was an unmitigated success. While the United States and India continue to have disagreements, the relationship today is based on this vision and the potential for cooperation in areas of mutual interest.

With India's economic restructuring in the 1990s and movement away from Russia, President Clinton had begun efforts late in his administration to improve relations, but these efforts were derailed by mandatory Glenn Amendment sanctions put in place in response to India's 1998 nuclear tests. As the Transition Memorandum points out, this not only limited US cooperation with India but "rekindled Indian stereotypes of the United States as paternalistic and dictatorial toward lesser developed nations." President Bush believed that action needed to happen quickly if the relationship was to be transformed. Months before the terrorist attacks on September 11, 2001, the Bush administration had already begun to evaluate lifting the sanctions to lay the foundation for improved relations. And in the early days of the War on Terror, cooperation with India on Afghanistan helped to build trust and reinforce mutual security interests.

It quickly became clear, however, that a higher level of strategic cooperation was necessary. The Next Steps in Strategic Partnership (NSSP), as outlined in the Transition Memorandum, was essentially the first structured attempt to do just that. The president and senior administration officials dismissed less ambitious policy proposals and agreed to expand ties in more sensitive areas in which the United States only collaborates with its closest allies: civil space, civil nuclear energy, missile defense, and high technology. The price of this cooperation would be concrete steps by India to improve its export controls and counterproliferation policies. Once finalized, the NSSP was completed in a fraction of the expected timeframe. Without the NSSP, there could be no civil nuclear deal. The approach was simple: big bets now would pay dividends in the decades to come.

From the NSSP, the two nations proceeded to the civil nuclear deal. Without addressing the long-standing issues associated with the complex array of nonproliferation restrictions on India, there was no room for cooperation elsewhere. The deal brought India's civilian nuclear capability under international nuclear safeguards and Indian policy into compliance with global nonproliferation standards. But more important, it was, as the Transition Memorandum stated: "[A] tangible expression to the Indian [g]overnment and the Indian people of the President's desire to have India as a strategic partner of the United States."

What Has Happened Since the End of the Bush Administration?

In the first months of the Obama administration, South Asia policy pivoted toward fulfilling the key campaign promise to wind down the war in Afghanistan and implement a new "Af-Pak" strategy. The Afghanistan-Pakistan linkage at the center of the Obama administration's regional approach resulted in the unintended perception that India was a secondary priority. Indeed, the creation of new Af-Pak offices in the National Security Council, State Department, and more broadly in the US bureaucracy purposefully took the portfolio out of the traditional South Asia policy framework. During the Bush administration, coordinating Afghanistan policy with broader South Asia policy had been a challenge because Afghanistan was separated and combined with Iraq to support war-fighting efforts. With the new Obama administration's Af-Pak structure, the hole at the center of the regional doughnut became even larger. While the US policy restructuring may have helped coordinate US counterterrorism strategy, it alienated India and strained the bilateral relationship. India perceived that it was important to the United States only as it pertained to Af-Pak, particularly as the United States attempted to link resolution in Afghanistan to progress in Kashmir. This Kashmir linkage assumed incorrectly that India would make concessions to achieve what India viewed as a conditional precedent: Pakistan ceasing its continued harboring of extremists within its borders.

However, the characterization that India was a secondary priority is not really accurate. President Obama welcomed Indian Prime Minister Manmohan Singh to the White House for a state dinner in 2009—the first of the new administration—in a strong show of support for the relationship. President Obama would go on to visit India in November 2010 and again in January 2015, after the election of new Prime Minister Narendra Modi in May 2014. The trend of reciprocal visits during each presidential term would continue into the Trump administration, with President Trump hosting Prime Minister Modi in Washington in 2019 and travelling to India in February 2020. These visits were visible symbols of the importance the United States and India—and both major political parties in the two democracies—have placed on improving economic, national security, humanitarian, and democratic cooperation.

As US relations with Pakistan deteriorated after 2011, both the Obama and Trump administrations would move farther away from Pakistan and embrace a broad-based bilateral agenda with India focused on strengthening the strategic partnership that had been established during the Bush administration.

The cabinet-level dialogue by both the US Departments of State and Defense and Indian Ministries of External Affairs and Defense—the so-called 2 + 2 Dialogue—is a good example of how senior engagement became more regular and structured.

Notable policy successes have occurred over the past dozen years: the inclusion of India in the international nonproliferation framework; the completion of defense cooperation foundational agreements and marked increase in joint military exercises; reduction in caps on foreign investment; and expanded civil space cooperation. There have also been a number of disappointments and challenges that have slowed the pace of bilateral cooperation: the failure to fully realize the commercial potential of the civil nuclear deal; limited progress on trade issues; unrealized potential in defense trade; lack of cooperation on global security challenges (e.g., Iran); and the inability to resolve long-standing disputes over visas and social security contributions. New challenges have also emerged regarding the protection of human rights and religious freedoms, Russian defense cooperation, and the rise of China in the Indo-Pacific theater.

Yet, the response to these challenges is indicative of a normalized bilateral relationship founded on common principles and a joint desire to strengthen the partnership. For nearly two decades, the United States and India have been committed to steady and incremental improvement. The pace of these improvements may have been slower than the Bush administration had hoped, but there is little doubt that the US commitment to building and strengthening the US-India strategic partnership remains a key US foreign policy priority.

How Did the Bush Administration Do?
In his 2010 memoir *Decision Points*, President Bush wrote: "I believe India . . . has the potential to be one of America's closest partners. The nuclear agreement was a historic step because it signaled the country's new role on the world stage."[1] The civil nuclear deal would become the most substantive achievement of the Bush administration's India policy and visible symbol of the US commitment to the strategic partnership. Some supporters of the initiative viewed these policy changes as necessary to right perceived historical wrongs—decisions made decades before that excluded India from its rightful place among global democratic

---

1. George W. Bush, *Decision Points* (New York: Crown, 2010), 214.

powers. Others were skeptical of the prospect for the initiative's success, arguing that India did not deserve special treatment given its pursuit of nuclear weapons in the face of international nonproliferation norms. The Bush administration focused instead on the future: How would the United States and India be able to work with each other if they continued to be saddled by policies that prevented any inroads for cooperation? In mid-2008, sustained personal engagement by President Bush and Prime Minister Singh and their senior advisers cemented the civil nuclear deal.

The civil nuclear agreement highlighted another strength of the Bush administration's approach: working closely with Congress. No deal would have been possible without congressional support to change US law, thereby enabling nuclear cooperation. Like the civil nuclear deal itself, the legislation was an important symbol of US commitment to the relationship and a reminder that the most successful US foreign policy successes come when the president and Congress are united in purpose. The Bush administration also undertook a comprehensive campaign with the multilateral nonproliferation community to gain consensus for these changes. A coordinated effort with the International Atomic Energy Agency, Nuclear Suppliers Group, and targeted outreach with key allies and partners established the international support—and overcame opposition from countries initially opposed to India's new status—necessary to complete the deal.

Transformational change that heralded a new area of cooperation ultimately failed to produce some of the benefits that were promised. In the years to follow, the civil nuclear deal itself would prove to be a commercial disappointment as the Indian Parliament passed implementing legislation inconsistent with international standards, potentially locking US companies out of the commercial market. Yet, the goal of the nuclear deal was never just to promote US civil nuclear sales. The goal had always been to lay a foundation on which to build a strategic partnership. The policy successes that were realized by subsequent presidential administrations have been a product of that effort. President Bush's recognition that the time had come for revolutionary action and transformative change for the long-term benefit of both nations was indeed the historic step that put the US-India relationship on a new path of partnership.

The agenda set forth by President Bush and Prime Minister Singh in 2006—cooperation in civil nuclear, defense, trade and investment, economic reform, space, health, democracy, education, science and technology, agriculture, regional stability, and India-Pakistan relations—continues to dominate the bilateral policy agenda today. Several examples of how this cooperation has progressed—or not progressed—are worth highlighting:

Counterterrorism: One of the best examples of the transformative relationship that emerged from the new strategic partnership is bilateral cooperation on counterterrorism. The behind-the-scenes coordination here is often ignored, but it has been extremely beneficial for regional stability in South Asia and throughout the Indo-Pacific theater.

Defense: The Bush administration's focus on strengthening Indian defense cooperation helped to expand India's participation in joint military exercises and regional security frameworks, such as the US-Australia-India-Japan Consultations, known as "The Quad." And although it would take over a decade and two additional presidential administrations to complete the myriad of defense cooperative agreements that have enabled greater bilateral security cooperation and defense trade, negotiations begun during the Bush administration laid the foundation for progress in this area.

Nonproliferation: The effort to welcome India into the global nonproliferation community resulted in the Obama administration advocating for India to become a member of other multilateral nonproliferation regimes, including the Missile Technology Control Regime. This helped facilitate additional high-technology cooperation, including modifications to US export control policy during both the Obama and Trump administrations that offered new opportunities in defense and civil space cooperation and reciprocal efforts by India to protect sensitive technology.

Trade: The Bush administration had hoped that the United States and India would move swiftly to resolve long-standing trade policy and market access issues. Trade dialogues have continued with limited success, including some market access expansion, opening of foreign direct investment, and continuation of US trade preferences. Yet, twelve years later, there has been only minimal progress on high-profile "deliverables," such as a Bilateral Investment Treaty or a limited Free Trade Agreement. Indian domestic economic reforms have similarly been slow to materialize. Undoubtedly, global economic shocks have played a part in this slow progress, but many of the same barriers that constrained bilateral trade in 2008 remain in place today.

Global Engagement: In 2008, it seemed certain that India would continue to expand its global leadership aspirations. The Transition Memorandum assumed: "As India continues its evolution from regional heavyweight to global leader, the zero-sum dynamic that still influences some Indian thinking . . . will fade and the benefits of deeper strategic engagement with the United States will emerge more clearly." But India's emergence as a global power remains a work-in-progress. Today, it is unclear if India is prepared to take the steps necessary to embrace a global role commensurate with its aspirations. Like economic reforms, India's path has undoubtedly been affected by global challenges beyond its control, including the 2009 recession and COVID-19 pandemic. The Bush administration was correct that India would leave behind its nonaligned policies of the past and break out from a strictly regional role; it just assumed that moving toward a more global role would happen more quickly.

China: For decades, India has considered China as the point of comparison for its modernization, measuring the success of its economic growth and standing in the international community in relation to its northern neighbor. Analysis of regional relations has tended to focus on whether border disputes would reemerge, which, unfortunately, they have—with tragic results for both sides. However, the China question for both India and the United States is bigger than economic cooperation or border disputes. The Bush administration had emphasized that it wanted a strategic relationship with India for its own sake, in recognition of India's emergence on the global stage. To frame the strategic relationship explicitly as intended to balance China would have made it less likely for India to embrace it. But the Bush administration recognized early on that India could effectively help counterbalance China, although the Transition Memorandum did not fully appreciate how China would push India and the United States closer together. The response of the United States and its democratic partners in the Asia-Pacific to growing Chinese power will dominate the global national security and trade agenda for the next decade. And the ability of the United States and India to work together to address the China issue will be crucial to defining the bilateral relationship in the years to come.

What Are the Lessons Learned?

- *Patience and persistence are required.* Progress in strengthening the US-India strategic partnership since 2008 has been substantial, but the pace at which dialogue proceeds and issues are resolved remains slow. This is a troubling aspect of a relationship that offers so much promise for both nations. Unfortunately, the United States and India will continue to have different expectations for the pace of change.

- *The rise of China provides a strong impetus to increase bilateral cooperation.* But it will be important not to view the relationship with India only through the lens of competition with China. India must see that the United States values the bilateral relationship in its own right. Beyond the China issue, India's foreign policy posture will also remain a function of economic performance and domestic societal tensions.
- *The state of democracy and minority rights in both countries needs to be on the table.* The United States should not shy away from addressing the growing intolerance for minorities and opposition within India. At the same time, it must acknowledge and be prepared to address its own issues in this respect. Both countries can do more to highlight that the quality and character of democracy and the treatment of one's minority citizens is as important as the democratic institutions themselves.
- *Don't forget Pakistan.* Regional tensions will be enduring flashpoints and progress on India-Pakistan relations is as elusive as ever. This is not to say the United States should refrain from efforts to facilitate productive exchanges; a successful US foreign policy in South Asia would be advanced greatly by a normalized India-Pakistan relationship.
- *Build trusted relationships.* The greatest advancements in US-India relations over the past two decades have resulted from close ties between senior officials. Continued progress will require a strong relationship between the president and prime minister and recognition by both governments that the partnership between the two countries endures political transitions. In addition, both countries must emphasize and develop regular and institutionalized communication, consultations, and cooperation that extends beyond the two leaders and into the bureaucracies and institutions on both sides. A cooperative relationship—and a normalized foreign policy—is not reliant on historic initiatives to maintain momentum but depends rather on consistent interaction, with both nations committed to advancing mutual interests. Perhaps the most important lesson is the need to sustain a level of focus on India at all levels of government commensurate with its importance to global national security and economic priorities.

Contributors:
Ashley Tellis
Anish Goel

PART 6

Developing World and Regional Security Challenges

INTRODUCTION

STEPHEN J. HADLEY

As noted in the introduction to part 1, President Bush had an abiding faith in the human spirit. He sought to empower people to make the key decisions affecting their lives by freeing them from political oppression and the tyrannies of violence, ignorance, and disease. He believed that the then-current approaches to the challenges facing the developing world were generally ineffective in achieving this goal. His administration championed new approaches.

Subpart 1 of this part 6, "Transforming Development," deals with the administration's approach to economic development. Chapter 20 outlines what the administration called its "Smart Development" strategy. That strategy rejected the donor-recipient relationship that was at the heart of the traditional approach. It sought instead to partner with and empower those governments of developing countries that were willing to take responsibility for their own futures and to rule justly in the interest of their people. It sought to hold all participants in the development process accountable for achieving measurable results that would produce concrete benefits for the people affected. It sought to mobilize the full spectrum of development resources including not only government assistance but also trade, private investment (from both domestic and foreign sources), contributions from charitable foundations, support from faith-based organizations, and public-private partnerships. It sought to encourage a set of principles that it believed were the source of sustainable economic growth and enhanced social welfare: economic freedom, political liberty, respect for human rights, and the rule of law.

This new approach to development became, for the Bush administration, a key pillar of its national security strategy. Pursuant to this new approach, the administration pursued numerous programs and initiatives addressing the full range of challenges facing developing countries. But President Bush saw a particular opportunity to help free millions of people living in fragile states from the tyrannies of endemic disease and of violent conflict.

The administration's signature efforts against disease are described in subpart 2 of this part 6, "Combating Endemic Diseases." As there noted, the Bush administration increased US efforts—and initiated major international campaigns—to address HIV/AIDS, malaria, and a range of neglected tropical diseases. Here too, the administration adopted an innovative approach based on many of the same principles as its approach to "smart development." In addition, the administration undertook a major program at home and with international partners to prepare for potential disease pandemics. In this it was somewhat ahead of its time. Taken together, these efforts were unprecedented in focus, scale, and impact.

The administration's major development and health initiatives were implemented widely throughout the developing world but had their greatest impact in Africa. President Bush's extensive engagement with African leaders was key in the design of the central tenets of these initiatives. A precondition for their successful implementation, however, was ending the regional conflicts in Africa. As described in subpart 3, "Resolving Long-Standing Conflicts," the Bush administration undertook a series of major diplomatic initiatives to help end six of these conflicts, which had killed millions of Africans and ravaged numerous fragile African economies. The administration also sought an end to the Israeli-Palestinian conflict as part of a comprehensive Arab-Israeli peace in the Middle East. In retrospect, the administration's diplomatic initiatives to achieve an Israeli-Palestinian peace represented the high watermark of such efforts.

PART 6

Subpart 1

Transforming Development

INTRODUCTION

STEPHEN J. HADLEY

The Bush administration championed a different approach to economic development in the developing world. To help overcome resistance from those invested in established approaches, the administration expanded and increased funding to many existing programs even while it innovated new ones. The result was a surprising degree of acceptance of these new innovations by the established development community. The administration also enlisted active congressional support for its approach and encouraged, with some considerable success, other governments and relevant international organizations to adopt similar approaches. Perhaps this broad support accounts for the fact that several of the key initiatives have survived the transition to new presidential administrations even of the opposite party.

CHAPTER 20

A New Strategy

JOHN SIMON | JENDAYI FRAZER | BOBBY PITTMAN

The end of the Cold War and the globalization of trade and investment led to increased political freedom and economic opportunity for many countries around the world. But the development of many others continued to be held back by poverty, disease, educational deficiencies, humanitarian crises, civil conflict, corrupt and undemocratic governments, mounting debt burdens, and local business climates hostile to trade and private investment. President Bush and his administration attempted to address each of these challenges, elevating development as an essential pillar of national security strategy and a top policy priority. The goal, as articulated in the 2006 National Security Strategy, was "to help create a world of democratic well-governed states that can meet the needs of their citizens and conduct themselves responsibly in the international system."

President Bush laid out the objectives of the Bush administration's approach to development in his Inter-American Development Bank speech of March 2002 and secured international support for them in the Monterrey Consensus agreed at the UN Financing for Development Conference later that month. They were:

1. Empower developing countries to take responsibility for their own development;

2. Mobilize the full spectrum of resource flows to support development, including trade, investment, and domestic resources as well as foreign aid;
3. Ensure foreign aid provided to developing countries is held accountable for measurable results; and
4. Create a new relationship between developing and developed countries based on mutual partnership and accountability as opposed to the prevailing donor-recipient dynamic.

To achieve these objectives, President Bush launched multiple new development initiatives and institutions. These included: the Millennium Challenge Corporation (MCC); the President's Emergency Plan for AIDS Relief (PEPFAR); the President's Malaria Initiative (PMI); the Neglected Tropical Diseases Initiative (NTDs); initiatives with the World Health Organization (WHO) to counter avian and pandemic influenzas; the Multilateral Debt Relief Initiative (MDRI); regional trade and investment initiatives like the expansion of the Africa Growth and Opportunity Act (AGOA II and AGOA III); education initiatives like the President's Africa Education Initiative; efforts to address food insecurity like the President's Initiative to End Hunger in Africa; and steps to help end Africa's six major wars.

The presumption that sound policy, increasing freedom and democracy, and economic development interact in a self-reinforcing virtuous cycle underlaid all of these efforts. Progress in one aspect accelerates advances in the others. President Bush desired an end result of countries having full control of their development strategies subject to democratic accountability, with an ever-growing focus on leveraging private capital and their own domestic resources to finance growth and social needs.

TRANSITION MEMORANDUM

Release

NATIONAL SECURITY COUNCIL
WASHINGTON, D.C. 20504

January 14, 2009

MEMORANDUM FOR THE RECORD

FROM: CHRISTOPHER BROUGHTON RELIEF, STABILIZATION, AND
           DEVELOPMENT DIRECTORATE

SUBJECT: Smart Development

THE SITUATION AS WE FOUND IT:

The end of the Cold War led to the opening of previously closed societies, thereby bringing political freedom to millions of people. Concurrently, the globalization of trade and investment led to increased economic opportunity for countries around the world. Despite the progress that these changes brought to some countries, the development of many others continued to be hindered by persistent and widespread poverty; disease; civil conflict; weak, corrupt, and undemocratic governments; poor business climates; humanitarian crises; and mounting debt burdens.

Failed states such as Afghanistan continued to pose a direct threat to U.S. national security because of their potential to be used as a base of operations for terrorists and international criminal networks, to foment regional instability, and to trigger humanitarian crises. Development assistance was having only limited impact on the problems plaguing weak states, and assistance tools available in 2001 were inadequate for addressing the changing and increasingly complex development dynamics of the new millennium.

In addition, major donors and international development institutions did not insist on account-ability for foreign assistance and continued to measure success only by the metric of aid delivered, rather than results achieved. Assistance did too little to promote liberty, democracy, and good governance. United States Government foreign assistance was uncoordinated, burdened by congressional directives, and lacking strategic focus. Foreign assistance appro-priations had been declining for 15 years.

THIS ADMINISTRATION'S POLICY:

President Bush's development policy was first articulated in a March 2002 speech at the Inter-American Development Bank, where the President stated, "today I call for a new compact for global development, defined by new accountability for both rich and poor nations alike. Greater contributions from developed nations must be linked to greater responsibility from developing nations." One week later, at the United Nations Conference on Financing for Development at Monterrey, Mexico, the President presented world leaders with a new model of development. The President remarked, "for decades, the success of development aid was measured in dollars spent, not results achieved. Developed nations have a duty not only to share our wealth, but also to encourage sources that produce wealth: economic freedom; political liberty; the rule of law; and human rights."

While development assistance played an important role in the Cold War and has been an important moral and economic imperative for the United States since the Marshall Plan, this Administration elevated the importance of development by establishing it as a pillar of the national security strategy of the United States. The President's 2002 National Security Strategy described development as "one of the top priorities of U.S. policy." The strategy set a goal to double the size of the world's poorest economies within a decade, while recognizing that "sustained growth and poverty reduction is impossible without instituting the right policies. Where governments have implemented real policy changes, we will provide significant new levels of assistance."

The President undertook efforts to reform U.S. development assistance given its importance to national security, the promotion of liberty, and the alleviation of human suffering. The President created the Millennium Challenge Corporation (MCC), an agency charged with executing a new model of development assistance that would provide aid only to countries that rule justly, invest in their people, and provide economic freedom.

The President also created a new office within the Department of State, the Office of the Director of U.S. Foreign Assistance, to better coordinate the assistance of USAID and the State Department, and align that assistance more closely with U.S. foreign policy objectives. By 2006, the goal of U.S. assistance was formally aligned with the goal of U.S. statecraft, as articulated in the 2006 National Security Strategy: "to help create a world of democratic, well-governed states that can meet the needs of their citizens and conduct themselves responsibly in the international system." The President insisted on accountability and results not only for assistance given by the United States, but also for other donors, developing countries, and multilateral development banks.

The President took decisive action to confront HIV/AIDS by establishing the Office of the Global AIDS Coordinator to administer the President's Emergency Plan for AIDS Relief (PEPFAR), the largest bilateral assistance program in history targeting a single disease. The President also created other health, education, economic, and regional initiatives to improve the allocation and effectiveness of U.S. development assistance.

The President's development policy emphasized the expansion of trade, the mobilization of private capital, and the creation of opportunities for greater private sector-led growth. As the President stated in Monterrey, "the work of development is much broader than development aid. The vast majority of financing for development comes not primarily from aid, but from trade and domestic capital and foreign investment." To maximize the impact of official development assistance, the Administration made a concerted effort to work closely with businesses, foundations, and faith-based organizations.

The Administration also reformed U.S. assistance to make it a more effective tool to prevent and respond to conflict. The Administration employed development assistance as an integral element of its counterinsurgency and state-building efforts in Afghanistan and Iraq, and peace-building work in the West Bank and Gaza, Haiti, Kosovo, and elsewhere. The President created the Office of the Coordinator for Reconstruction and Stabilization in the Department of State to better coordinate civilian efforts with the military and create a standing civilian capacity to conduct large-scale stability operations.

These policies, when combined with the Administration's increase in foreign assistance funding, the largest increase since the Marshall Plan, have arguably led to the most significant changes to U.S. assistance since the passage of the Foreign Assistance Act in 1961.

WHAT HAS BEEN ACCOMPLISHED:

At Monterrey, the President announced a 50 percent increase in U.S. core development assistance by 2006. The President not only met this commitment early, but by 2007 U.S. official development assistance was $21.8 billion, more than double the 2000 level. Of the 2007 total, $3.7 billion was allocated to Iraq and $1.6 billion to Afghanistan.

The Millennium Challenge Account. The President also stated in Monterrey that "we must tie greater aid to political and legal and economic reforms," as "when nations respect their people, open markets, invest in better health and education, every dollar of aid, every dollar of trade revenue and domestic capital is used more effectively." In order to support countries that govern justly, invest in their people, and encourage economic freedom, the President announced the creation of a Millennium Challenge Account (MCA) at Monterrey. With MCA, the President created a new model of development assistance that rewards governments on the basis of policy performance with direct funding to execute programs selected by the countries themselves. Subsequently, a new public corporation, the Millennium Challenge Corporation (MCC), was formed to administer the MCA. Through September 2008, the MCC has committed over $6.3 billion in assistance in 5-year compacts with the following 18 countries, grouped by region, that met rigorous, objective, and transparent eligibility criteria:

El Salvador	Benin	Armenia	Mongolia
Honduras	Burkina Faso	Georgia	Vanuatu
Nicaragua	Cape Verde		
	Ghana		
	Lesotho		
	Madagascar		
	Mali		
	Morocco		
	Mozambique		
	Namibia		
	Tanzania		

Consistent with its mandate, the MCC has also demonstrated its willingness on behalf of the United States Government to suspend funding if governments change behavior or otherwise do not meet benchmarks for political and economic reforms. For example, in December 2008, the MCC Board voted to suspend assistance for new activities under the $175 million compact in Nicaragua, based on actions taken by the Nicaraguan Government that are inconsistent with MCC's criteria. While the MCC will review the Government of Nicaragua's response to these concerns and determine subsequent actions based on the review, the suspension is indicative of U.S. commitment to the rigor of this development approach.

MCA countries are currently executing programs selected through national consultations across a wide range of sectors, including transportation, agriculture, and small business development, with the goal of alleviating poverty and promoting economic growth. The MCC, in partnership with USAID, has also executed $400 million in threshold programs to assist governments to improve specific policies in order to qualify for MCA funding. Threshold programs are currently being implemented in the following 15 countries, grouped by region.

Guyana	Kenya	Jordan	Albania	Kyrgyz Republic
Paraguay	Niger		Moldova	Indonesia
Peru	Sao Tome and Principe		Ukraine	Philippines
	Uganda			
	Zambia			

Examples of reform in countries selected for MCA compacts and threshold programs include more robust prosecution of corruption cases in Tanzania; increased immunization rates in Indonesia; improvements in tax administration in Albania; and reductions in the number of days to register property sales and open a business in Zambia. These and other examples demonstrate the results that are attributable to the approach to development embodied in the MCA.

Further, the MCA has played a key role in the President's Freedom Agenda by providing a significant financial incentive for governments to expand political freedom, guarantee civil liberties, and justly administer the law. The President also demonstrated his commitment to freedom by more than doubling foreign assistance funding for democracy, governance and human rights programs since 2001. To institutionalize the Freedom Agenda, the President signed National Security Presidential Directive/NSPD-58 in July 2008. NSPD-58 codifies the policies and practices put in place by this Administration to promote freedom and sets a benchmark for future administrations. For more information, see Memorandum for the Record on the Freedom Agenda.

Debt. While promoting political liberty, democracy, and good governance, the President also worked with other donors to help alleviate the burden of debt for poor countries. The President, along with then British Prime Minister Tony Blair, led efforts at the 2005 Gleneagles G-8 Summit to create the Multilateral Debt Relief Initiative, which, combined with the Highly Indebted Poor Countries Initiative, will relieve the world's poorest countries of up to $128 billion in debt. The Administration also pressed the World Bank to provide increased levels of assistance through grants rather than loans in order to further relieve poor countries from increasing their debt burdens.

Trade, Investment, and Public-Private Partnerships. While increasing assistance, promoting good governance, and reducing debt burdens, the President also worked actively to open trade and investment opportunities for developing countries. The United States spearheaded efforts during the World Trade Organization Doha trade round to increase global trade in agriculture, manufacturing, and services. The President also supported regional trade and investment initiatives, such as the Africa Growth and Opportunity Act (AGOA) to spur trade, investment, and economic growth in Africa. Following the enactment of AGOA, exports from Sub-Saharan Africa to the United States have reached $50 billion, more than six times the level in 2001. While a portion of this increase is attributable to higher oil prices, AGOA has afforded African entrepreneurs new economic opportunities and unprecedented access to the U.S. market. Growing private sector opportunity in Sub-Saharan Africa has accelerated GDP growth, which averaged 7 percent in 2007.

U.S. private capital flows to Sub-Saharan Africa exceed U.S. development assistance to the region. United States foreign direct investment in Sub-Saharan Africa grew from $6.9 billion in 2000 to $9.9 billion in 2007. Over the same period, official development assistance grew from $2 billion to $5.6 billion. Beyond Africa, the economies of developing countries also have been significantly bolstered by the 14 trade and investment treaties the Administration has concluded since 2000.

The cumulative total of net private investment, private grants, and personal remittances from the United States to developing countries was $159 billion in 2007, more than seven times the amount of U.S. official development assistance.

In the 1970s, official development assistance accounted for 70 percent of all resource flows to developing countries, while the private sector contributed only 30 percent. By 2008, 85 percent of all resource flows to developing countries were from the private sector and 15 percent were from official development assistance. In recognition of the rising importance of private sector resource flows, the Administration took steps to partner with the private sector, foundations, faith-based groups, and other organizations to maximize the impact of official development assistance. As a result of these efforts, the Administration has leveraged a combined total of $9 billion in public and private resources through 680 partnerships with over 1,700 partners. For every dollar of U.S. assistance, the private sector has contributed three dollars. Public-private partnerships have not only raised new resources for development, but also introduced new technologies, encouraged market creation, and harnessed new sources of expertise for development.

Global Public Health. Despite the opportunities that the globalization of trade and investment have afforded, infectious diseases continue to afflict the world's poorest people, with entire countries put at great risk by the rapid spread of HIV/AIDS. The President responded to this threat by creating the PEPFAR, the largest bilateral assistance program in history devoted to a single disease. Nearly $19 billion in budget authority has been provided for the program to date. The program has funded life-saving treatment for approximately 1.73 million people, provided medicine to prevent 194,000 infant infections, and supported more than 33 million testing or counseling sessions for men, women, and children. The President also responded multilaterally to this threat by setting out the principles and vision of—and becoming the largest donor to—the Global Fund to Fight HIV/AIDS, Tuberculosis and Malaria, whose programs compliment PEPFAR. For additional details, see Memorandum for the Record on PEPFAR.

The President also took action to prevent and treat malaria, a leading killer of children under the age of 5 and a vector for HIV/AIDS. Through the President's Malaria Initiative (PMI), the President committed $1.2 billion over 5 years to the objective of halving malaria mortality in the 15 African countries with a high burden of infection. The program has reached over 25 million people to date. For additional details, see Memorandum for the Record on the PMI.

Beginning in 2005, the President took steps to counter the international threat of avian and pandemic influenza. Working with the World Health Organization in an international public-private partnership, the Administration helped to organize early warning systems, stockpile vaccines, and develop plans to respond to a global outbreak of pandemic influenza. In 2008, the President launched an expanded initiative to combat neglected tropical diseases such as river blindness and hookworm, and secured a pledge of support from the G-8 to combat the diseases. By October 2008, the initiative has reached 14 million people and is expected to reach 300 million people in 30 countries by 2013. See Memorandum for the Record on neglected tropical diseases for additional details.

Education. The President extended his commitment to build human capital and create prosperous societies by investing in new education initiatives. For example, the President's Africa Education Initiative has led to the improvement of schools for over 13 million children, the training of nearly a quarter million teachers, and the distribution of nearly 1.9 million textbooks.

Food Security. The President led efforts to take rapid action to address rising global food prices in 2008. With $1.8 billion in new funding, and a combined total of over $5.5 billion in assistance over fiscal years 2008 and 2009, the Administration is joining the private sector, universities, multilateral organizations, and other governments to respond to immediate food security needs while addressing the long-term causes of hunger. This funding builds upon the President's Initiative to End Hunger in Africa and ongoing humanitarian assistance programs.

Development and Conflict. The Administration made further reforms to the architecture of U.S. foreign assistance to systematically address conflict and the problem of failed states such as Afghanistan and Somalia. To build lasting capability for the United States Government to respond to conflict, the President created the Office of the Coordinator for Reconstruction and Stabilization in the Department of State. The Office is creating active, standby, and reserve corps of skilled and trained civilian personnel to respond rapidly to conflict. The Office also has engaged with the military to establish civil-military doctrine, joint plans, training and exercises. This innovation in foreign assistance provides the personnel, doctrine, and organization needed to work effectively in failed states, and diminish the threat they pose to the United States. See Presidential Memorandum on Reconstruction and Stabilization Operations for additional details.

Development assistance has proven vital as a tool in the wars in Afghanistan and Iraq. The Administration has used development assistance—particularly assistance directed toward the creation of jobs, stimulation of economic growth, and strengthening of weak polities—as a tool in the counterinsurgency campaigns in Afghanistan and Iraq. See Presidential Memoranda on Afghanistan and Iraq for additional details.

The Department of Defense has expanded its range of activities by allocating targeted assistance to stabilize communities in the wake of combat operations, and to help build the capacity of partner countries to defend their borders and bolster regional stability. Development assistance has also proven vital as a soft power tool in the West Bank and Gaza, Sudan, Haiti, and Pakistan, where it has been used to mitigate simmering conflicts and address the underlying economic and political sources of instability.

Foreign Assistance Reform. As foreign assistance was employed as an instrument of national power, it became increasingly important to strategically align it with U.S. foreign policy. In order to achieve this objective, the Administration created the Office of the Director of Foreign Assistance within the Department of State. The Office has played a key role of foreign assistance reform by bringing authority for all State Department and USAID funding under the authority of one official, the Director of U.S. Foreign Assistance. The office evaluates program performance to increase aid effectiveness, and has created a taxonomy of foreign assistance funding and a database that more closely ties funding to foreign policy objectives. Information on foreign assistance programs is now readily accessible for policymakers, with clearly defined and standardized objectives and measures of success.

International Support. The Administration has worked to build support abroad for an approach to international development that is country-led and results-based, rewards good performers, and recognizes the need to leverage all sources of financing. The 2002 Monterrey Consensus on Financing for Development enshrines these principles, as do G-8 leaders' declarations from the summits in Gleneagles (2005), Heiligendamm (2007), and Toyako (2008). For example, at Heiligendamm, G-8 leaders agreed "to actively assist countries which make efforts to govern justly, invest in their people, favor open and democratic debate on priorities and policies and create an environment of economic opportunity." The G-8 reiterated at Toyako that their work on development would be grounded in this set of core principles of development policy. However, a number of G-8 and other donors continue to focus much of their assistance through direct budget support, often with few explicit ties to measurable results or accountability provisions.

FUTURE CHALLENGES:

The Administration's restructuring of U.S. development assistance has led to achievements in health, democracy and good governance, economic growth, education, and the promotion of peace and stability. Challenges remain, however. A number of steps could be taken to further improve the performance of development assistance programs:

- The coherence and coordination of development assistance with U.S. trade, investment, diplomacy, military, and public diplomacy policies could be further improved. Civil-military cooperation and engagement could also be further strengthened.
- The programs of the 20 United States Government departments and agencies providing development aid could be further integrated and coordinated through joint planning, budgeting, and evaluation.
- Disbursements by the MCC have been slow, at $496 million out of approximately $7.5 billion in appropriations to date. Congressional support has waned as a result.

- Overlapping assistance responsibilities for assistance programs implemented by different agencies could be better clarified; examples include:
  - Economic growth (USAID; the Departments of Treasury Agriculture, and Commerce; Overseas Private Investment Corporation; Export-Import Bank; U.S. Trade and Development Agency; and MCC);
  - Health (USAID, State, Health and Human Services);
  - Democracy and governance (State and USAID);
  - Rule of law (Justice, State, and USAID);
  - Policing (State and USAID); and
  - Other donors, including in the G-8, need continued pressure to move to a more results-based approach.

Attachments

POSTSCRIPT

JOHN SIMON, JENDAYI FRAZER, BOBBY PITTMAN

The Bush administration embraced a radical departure from the traditional approach to development. Its initiatives were designed to support country-led efforts; catalyze additional resources from trade and private and domestic investment; engage the full range of public, private, and international actors; and achieve specific output metrics. The underlying principle was to partner with governments in developing countries that showed a commitment to rule justly, to respect human rights and the rule of law, to invest in their people, and to promote economic freedom. Only in this way could American development efforts be truly effective.

The Bush Administration Approach
President Bush believed that the United States had an obligation not just to provide development assistance but to produce sustainable results offering concrete benefits to the citizens of developing countries—including empowering them with ownership over their futures.

For example, the MCC, which sought to double the economies of the poorest countries within a decade, could only spend money pursuant to "compacts" negotiated with partner countries that included key performance indicators. PEPFAR committed to its two-seven-ten targets at the outset—providing antiretroviral (ARV) treatment to two million people, preventing seven million new infections, and caring for ten million of those infected. PMI had the goal to reduce malaria-related mortality by 50 percent across fifteen high-burden countries in sub-Saharan Africa. MDRI sought to relieve highly indebted countries from the perpetual burden of debt to the World Bank and IMF (the so-called lend and forgive cycle) and the micromanagement it entailed, allowing these countries to access financing in the private markets based on their own development strategy.

Measured against the metrics established for each Bush administration development initiative, the programs have been almost universally successful. For example, both PEPFAR and PMI achieved their goals on time and then increased their targets for the future, resulting in more than twenty-five million lives saved to date.[1] As a result of MDRI, developing countries stabilized their debt levels such that debt restructurings at the Paris Club declined from 196 in the fifteen years prior to 2005 to only twenty-eight in the fifteen years since (not including those since March due to COVID).[2] Despite the Global Finance Crisis of 2008/9, Least Developed Country economies were nearly double their 2003 level in 2013 on a purchasing power parity (PPP) basis.[3]

The 2008 global financial crisis posed an early and critical test for the Bush administration's approach to development. It could have wreaked havoc on developing economies as commodity prices cratered. Yet while poor economies bent, they did not break. As scholar Ethan Kapstein wrote in 2009 in *Africa's Capitalist Revolution*: "While the tired industrialized nations of the West are nationalizing their banks and engaging in various forms of protectionism, Africa remains open for business—promoting trade, foreign direct investment, and domestic entrepreneurship."[4] Low-income countries saw their economic growth fall from above 8 percent in 2007 to 5.5 percent by 2009, and then recover close to 7 percent in 2010.[5]

What Has Happened Since the End of the Bush Administration?

In a remarkable yet underappreciated bipartisan validation, the Obama and Trump administrations both embraced the major initiatives of the Bush Administration—MCC, PEPFAR, PMI, MDRI—as the primary engines of their development policies. The Obama administration's Feed the Future initiative—a multiagency effort led by USAID focused on ending global hunger—built on the tenets of country ownership, accountability, and private sector leverage embodied in the Bush approach. The Build Act that created the Development Finance Cor-

---

1. *The United States President's Emergency Plan for AIDS Relief, 2019 Annual Report to Congress,* https://www.state.gov/wp-content/uploads/2019/09/PEPFAR2019ARC.pdf; *U.S. President's Malaria Initiative, Fourteenth Annual Report to Congress,* April 2020, https://d1u4sg1s9ptc4z.cloudfront.net/uploads/2021/11/2020-pmi-fourteenth-annual-report.pdf.

2. See Paris Club data, https://clubdeparis.org/en/communications/press-release/the-paris-club-releases-comprehensive-data-on-its-claims-as-of-31-4.

3. See World Bank data, https://databank.worldbank.org/source/world-development-indicators.

4. Ethan Kapstein, "Africa's Capitalist Revolution," *Foreign Affairs,* July/August 2009, https://www.foreignaffairs.com/articles/africa/2009-07-01/africas-capitalist-revolution.

5. World Bank data, https://databank.worldbank.org/source/world-development-indicators.

poration during the Trump administration emphasized the mobilization of investment capital alongside development aid. President Trump's USAID administrator, Mark Green, articulated the concept of the "Journey to Self-Reliance"—an approach based on "USAID working with host country governments . . . to achieve locally-sustained results, helping countries mobilize public and private revenues, strengthening local capacities, and accelerating enterprise-driven development"—as the guiding principle for Trump-era development policies, harkening back to the partnership model espoused by the MCC.

Though affirming the Bush principles, the Trump administration also attempted to dramatically reduce aid spending. Yet the bipartisan resistance to this effort on Capitol Hill successfully preserved aid levels and demonstrated the strong support the Bush administration programs had engendered. While neither President Obama nor Trump has been able to come close to replicating the 12 percent annual increases in development budgets during the eight years of the Bush administration, Congress has continued to augment development resources based on clear measures of success that have been achieved.

The years since the Bush administration have reinforced the value of country-led, accountable, and private-sector-oriented development, not least because China has been slowly chipping away at these pillars and because the twin global trends of authoritarianism and protectionism have stalled development progress in recent years. Freedom House found that 2020 was the fifteenth consecutive year of decline in global freedom, and economic growth in poor countries fell from an annual rate over ten years of 7.6 percent in 2008 (enough to double an economy in ten years) to 5.5 percent in 2019.

Perhaps the greatest challenge for the development model espoused by the Bush administration has been the dramatic increase in the People's Republic of China's (PRC) development activity, which was formalized in Beijing's launch of its massive ($1 trillion) Belt and Road Initiative (BRI) in 2013. PRC development assistance is a double-edged sword. Given its size, BRI can finance large-scale infrastructure projects beyond the wherewithal of developing countries and other donors. China also brings valuable expertise in constructing complex projects in difficult environments. However, the Chinese approach undermines the emphasis on sound governance policies so essential to the success of the Bush initiatives, particularly in the realm of transparency and fighting corruption. Furthermore, by providing the vast majority of BRI resources as debt, PRC lending threatens the hard-won debt sustainability achieved through MDRI.

China's undermining of good governance and transparency is just one element in recent policy and governance setbacks that have hindered progress since the end of the Bush administration. In general, the trend toward authoritarianism across the globe—in rich and poor countries alike—has inhibited development progress as poor countries have less institutional and economic resilience to maintain the virtuous cycle of economic and political freedoms so necessary to development.[6]

Another global trend inhibiting development is the pullback from international trade. This hits poor countries particularly hard, given their less diversified economies and desperate need to export to generate foreign exchange. A particularly galling example is US imports under the Africa Growth and Opportunity Act, which hit a high of $65 billion in 2008 but plummeted to just $8 billion in 2019.[7]

Higher debt burdens, political unrest, and global protectionism have all set the predicate for the most pressing developmental challenge—the COVID-19 pandemic. The crisis has been particularly devastating in Latin America, where the disease as well as the economic lockdowns required to contain it have pushed many countries into severe economic and political distress. India has also suffered severely. Africa had initially been spared massive case counts and deaths, but still suffered from the economic isolation imposed by travel bans and trade declines and now is facing a more virulent resurgence. As a result, many African countries are facing crippling "debt cliffs" in the next few years. Without the investments in health systems, scientific progress against endemic diseases, and economic reforms initiated in the 2000s, state failure would be a threat across the developing world.

How Did the Bush Administration Do?

Bush administration development policies met their specific performance metrics and even overcame unexpected challenges, but on their own, they have not been able to counteract global and regional trends that undermine their underpinnings. While the Bush administration could not have anticipated all of these trends, it knew well that development progress is fragile. The major rationale of the MCC

---

6. Freedom House, *Freedom in the World 2020*, https://freedomhouse.org/sites/default /files/2020-02/FIW_2020_REPORT_BOOKLET_Final.pdf.

7. See Trade Law Center, AGAO.info, https://agoa.info/data/trade.html.

was to accelerate institutional development within countries so as to equip them to withstand the inevitable disruptions that plague the developing world. In many instances, this worked. Despite razor-thin margins in the past few election cycles, Ghana has maintained peaceful transfers of power—an essential pillar of democratic governance. Mongolia has tripled its GDP while making dramatic progress on education, child mortality, and democracy as it fends off interference from its two powerful authoritarian neighbors, China and Russia. Georgia rebounded from a Russian invasion in 2008 to successfully graduate from the MCC. The concept of the "Journey to Self-Reliance" would have been impossible to envision without the foundation laid by Bush administration initiatives.

Yet in other places development progress did not advance quickly enough to create the necessary buffers against exogenous events. El Salvador and Honduras have not been able to withstand the destructive forces of criminal gangs; Nicaragua has slipped back into authoritarian rule; Mali could not overcome the wave of extremism passing over the Sahel; corruption and violence have stunted growth in Mozambique and Madagascar; political unrest due to authoritarianism in Sri Lanka ousted the President in July 2022.

Of course, it would be the height of arrogance to presume any country's development policies—even a country as powerful as the United States—could protect the seedlings of development against all malevolent forces. But that was the whole point of the Bush approach: to encourage countries to take control of their own development so that in the first instance they could respond to these challenges—and then seek reinforcement from wealthy nations and the development community. In addition, such countries would have the confidence and wherewithal to set the terms of their engagement with actors who might otherwise undermine sound development principles, like China.

The problem is that too often the old donor-recipient relationship prevails. In some instances, this is due to the fact that many international organizations or bilateral donors—despite acceding to the Monterrey Consensus—still view development assistance through this traditional prism. This is a problem that requires continued diplomatic pressure at all levels. During the Bush administration, these issues were raised not just by ambassadors, but by cabinet secretaries and the president himself, particularly at the G-8 Summits. Since then, the G-8 has largely withered, both literally, by shrinking back to the G-7 upon Russia's expulsion, and metaphorically, by inaction and ineffectiveness (there was no G-7 meeting in 2020 when the United States held the presidency).

In other cases, it is because the US government's own programs do not speak with one voice on this issue. One glaring example were the pronouncements on foreign aid from the Trump White House, which (contrary to its own USAID administrator) viewed aid in the context of a short-term tit-for-tat transaction completely counter to the long-term capacity building inherent in the Bush administration approach.

The view of the Trump White House highlights the most important challenge to the Bush administration development approach that many policymakers did not anticipate—the withdrawal of the United States from global engagement. President Bush himself warned often during his second term against the emerging trends of "protectionism, isolationism, and nativism" in public attitudes. Prior to the Bush administration, foreign aid was often a partisan issue, with Republicans using it as a political cudgel against Democrats. With MCC, PEPFAR, and PMI, President Bush fundamentally changed that dynamic. One of the Senate's fiercest critics of foreign aid, Senator Jesse Helms, became an ardent supporter of the president's HIV/AIDS programs as one of his last acts in Congress. During the remainder of the Bush administration, bipartisan support for not only foreign aid, but overall engagement with the developing world, was the norm, one that seemed to be permanent.

But even before the Trump administration, that consensus began to fray, and not only with regard to aid budgets. President Bush advanced three free-trade deals with developing countries—Jordan, Morocco, and the Central American Free Trade Agreement (CAFTA), which encompassed six countries. There have been none since. Instead, we have withdrawn or undermined organizations like the WHO or WTO that play a critical role in building the capacities needed for development. Central to the Bush administration approach is patience, engagement, and partnership with our development partners. Maintaining its successes must start with a recommitment of the American people, as well as its policymakers, to these principles.

What Are the Lessons Learned?

US development policy faces several critical challenges: the fragility of its results in the face of countervailing trends; the lack of a coordinated approach among multiple actors; and the falling support at home for engagement abroad, especially in an era of rising populism. The experience of the past two decades offers six lessons learned to address these challenges.

- *Recognize the limits of US soft power.* In terms of addressing development fragility, the United States cannot impose from outside or will institutions into existence that need to grow organically within a country. What it can do is provide support to help these institutions grow (or in a small way make up for their absence). MCC and PEPFAR did this when they created and strengthened their local in-country counterparts, some of which now have assumed significant development responsibility.
- *Engage regional organizations like the African Union (AU) or Organization of American States (OAS).* There are 137 developing countries; the United States can hardly be expected to engage intensively with each one, but it can build institutions at the regional level that can buttress weak institutions in individual countries. This requires significantly more engagement with and funding to these organizations than the United States has historically provided.
- *Work with development partners—both bilateral and multilateral—to leverage their combined resources and voices to build the new dynamic of partnership.* The Monterrey Consensus was tremendously effective in this regard, and it was followed by the Paris Declaration on Aid Effectiveness and the Accra Agenda for Action. All three of these documents laid out a shared vision for development largely consistent with the Bush administration approach. Grounding US policies in these and similar multilateral frameworks is a force multiplier for US efforts, if the United States commits to following them itself and engaging diplomatically when others do not.
- *Coopt major players, particularly China, working at odds with the US approach.* A unique challenge is posed when a major nation operates outside agreed frameworks. Such is the case with China. The United States can wring its hands about China's negative influence on development, or it can seek to use China's resources and engagement to US advantage by bringing China closer to the US approach. While the United States cannot disregard China's history of undermining or negatively influencing multilateral organizations in which it is a member, it might consider, in particular instances, inviting China inside global development institutions from which it is now excluded, like the Paris Club and the Development Assistance Committee of the OECD (the main standard-setting body for international development). The United States might also consider China's long-standing desire for a greater voice in the International Financial In-

stitutions, like the IMF and World Bank, and joining the Asian Infrastructure Investment Bank (AIIB). This runs counter to much of today's strategy of confronting China in other areas. And, based on China's record, it is right to be skeptical as to whether China will not try to turn its participation in these institutions toward its own narrow economic and diplomatic advantage. But as the experience with the AIIB demonstrated, leaving China on the outside of existing international organizations can lead it to try to create its own competitor institutions.

- *More aggressively enlist the private sector in development.* Global and local investors and corporations can be critical partners to help curtail negative trends. Kenya provides a good example—following the violent aftermath of the 2007 election, the Kenyan private sector engaged in long-term peacebuilding efforts that helped keep the peace in the 2013 and 2017 elections.

- *Reconnect US development policy and programs with values that Americans hold dear such as generosity, empowerment, accountability, sovereignty, and freedom.* We need to show results by setting clear metrics for success and monitoring them rigorously. Doing so can help assure American taxpayers that their resources are being well stewarded and making a positive impact. Few programs have enjoyed the bipartisan support of PEPFAR, and that is because few programs have as impressive a record of demonstrated results. The American people cannot be expected to support development efforts at face value—and it is to the American people that the case needs to be made, not just their elected representatives in Washington. Perhaps the most important lesson of the last twelve years is that the support of the American people cannot be taken for granted.

PART 6

Subpart 2

Combating Endemic Diseases

INTRODUCTION

STEPHEN J. HADLEY

As was the case with its strategy for economic development, the Bush administration took an innovative approach to endemic diseases. The President's Emergency Plan for AIDS Relief (PEPFAR), the President's Malaria Initiative (PMI), and the Neglected Tropical Diseases (NTDs) initiative to a great extent reflected a common vision for helping to free the people of the developing world from the scourge of these diseases. At the core of this vision were: (1) promoting recipient country ownership through partnership rather than paternalism; (2) focusing on accountability and results rather than dollars spent; (3) promoting good governance to maximize impact; (4) pushing for local involvement and local control; and (5) shifting from a government-to-government paradigm to one involving private partners as well.

A key to success was strong and sustained presidential leadership and novel organizational strategies to drive change across the US government and to overcome bureaucratic resistance and inertia. Equally important was President Bush's insistence that these three health initiatives not be the work of one US president or a single political party. He made the case that these initiatives not only served America's narrow national security interests but also were in its broader "enlightened" self-interest—and represented the best tradition of American global leadership. Strong but inclusive leadership from the top, an inspirational vision, and bipartisan legislative action helped ensure robust support for these initiatives across various presidential administrations and shifts in congressional majorities.

Taken together, these three initiatives helped to galvanize an international response to seemingly intractable health crises that have plagued humanity for decades, centuries, and, in the case of malaria, millennia. Subsequent administrations picked up, developed, and, for the most part, improved upon them. The early culture of innovation helped create an adaptability to evolving data; unintended consequences; and changed local, national, regional, and global circumstances—an essential factor for achieving lasting impact.

The approach reflected in these three initiatives represented a seismic shift: from Washington-managed programs to recipient-country efforts conducted at the national and local level and including government, community- and faith-based organizations, and the private sector. Local ownership was critical since the most impactful innovations often come from those closest to the problem. And local ownership is key to turning an emergency response into a sustainable long-term solution, with local actors taking responsibility for managing their own problems.

Pandemic preparedness is included in this subpart 2. The Homeland Security Council (HSC) had the lead on pandemic preparedness, so the NSC prepared no Transition Memorandum on this subject. But because of the prominence that this issue has gained as a result of COVID-19, and because of its close relationship to other Bush administration health initiatives, those involved in the issue during the Bush administration were asked to prepare an essay describing the pandemic preparedness effort. They were led by Rajeev Venkayya, who was special assistant to the president and senior director for biodefense in the Bush administration HSC.

The positive results from these health programs and initiatives provide a strong argument that the US government can be most effective when it sets out a bold vision; establishes transparent, accountable, and flexible administrative structures; provides catalytic resources and support; and then involves and relies on local governments, the private sector, civil society, and community groups for implementation and execution. This is the formula for real and sustainable change.

CHAPTER 21

HIV/AIDS

MARK DYBUL | DANA DeRUITER

In 2000, life-saving antiretroviral therapy (ART) was widely available in high-income countries, converting HIV from a death sentence to a manageable chronic disease. However, Africa, home to two-thirds of infections in the world, was being devastated by the disease. In the hardest hit countries, nearly 40 percent of the adult population was infected. Only a few thousand people who could afford life-saving treatment were receiving it.

Release

3183

NATIONAL SECURITY COUNCIL
WASHINGTON, D.C. 20504

Transition

January 14, 2009

MEMORANDUM FOR THE RECORD

FROM: DANA DERUITER, RELIEF, STABILIZATION, AND
DEVELOPMENT DIRECTORATE

SUBJECT: President's Emergency Plan for AIDS Relief

THE SITUATION AS WE FOUND IT:

Before 2003, HIV/AIDS in resource-limited settings was a death sentence. While many people—mostly in sub-Saharan Africa—were beginning to learn their status and subsequently prepare for the worst, only 50,000 people living with HIV in sub-Saharan Africa were receiving antiretroviral treatment.

U.S. assistance to fight global HIV/AIDS at the time was scattered among various U.S. agencies, and U.S. efforts and resources were not coordinated at the country level. While in many countries there were many U.S. agencies on the ground—USAID, CDC, DOD, Peace Corps, and others—there was little discussion and planning among them. Consequently, departments and agencies funded many different programs and had independent relationships with ministries of health. This resulted in generally uncoordinated strategies and programs that were contradictory in some cases.

This approach was not suited to a multifaceted disease such as HIV/AIDS. Given the devastation HIV/AIDS wreaks on health, social structures, economies, and overall development, it was neither effective nor a good use of resources to employ such a scatter-shot approach. More resources were needed, and they needed to be coordinated to best match the strengths of each U.S. agency involved.

THIS ADMINISTRATION'S POLICY:

Several high-level meetings led to a coordinated United States Government approach that would later be known as the President's Emergency Plan for AIDS Relief (PEPFAR). In March 2001, President Bush established a Cabinet-level Council on HIV/AIDS, co-chaired by the Secretaries of State and HHS. The Council was to serve as an "international focal point" for HIV/AIDS issues. It was to be supported by an interagency Policy Coordination Committee (PCC) and the White House

Office of National AIDS Policy (ONAP), which at the time had a broad mandate to "facilitate domestic and international policy efforts on HIV/AIDS."

President Bush played a central role in the development of the U.S. response to the global epidemic. Convinced early on of the severity of the problem, he was willing to explore the emerging concept of a multilateral "global fund" to finance the response. In May 2001, in a Rose Garden ceremony attended by U.N. Secretary General Kofi Annan and President Obasanjo of Nigeria, the President made the first public financial pledge of $200 million in support of the to-be-formed Global Fund and outlined a vision for its core principles, effectively launching the Fund. In July 2001, at the G-8 Summit in Genoa, Italy, G-8 leaders formally launched the Global Fund to Fight AIDS, Tuberculosis, and Malaria.

National Security Council staff worked through G-8 channels to influence the design and structure of the Fund and to promote financial accountability, scientific review of proposals, and an independent governance structure. The result was a stronger model for the Fund, but one that was new, untested, and not yet able to move fast enough to adequately address the needs of the epidemic.

With the President committed to doing more to fight HIV/AIDS, the United States launched a program that would tackle the prevention of mother-to-child transmission (PMTCT). National Security Advisor Condoleezza Rice proposed this initiative in May 2002, and in June, the President launched it in a Rose Garden ceremony. Even with this additional direct contribution, the President did not abandon his support for the idea of the Global Fund, emphasizing in his speech: "We've committed $500 million to the Global Fund to Fight AIDS and other infectious diseases, and we stand ready to commit more as this fund demonstrates its success."

While the PMTCT initiative was an important first step, the epidemic demanded more. President Bush gave Josh Bolten, then the Deputy Chief of Staff, and Gary Edson, then Deputy Assistant to the President and Deputy National Security Advisor for International Economic Affairs, the freedom to "think big"—particularly relative to the possibility for anti-retroviral treatment.

Shortly after the Rose Garden announcement of the PMTCT initiative, Bolten and Edson met with key high-level United States Government staff to discuss the President's interest in a bold initiative that could turn the tide in fighting HIV/AIDS.

Three months later, staff at the National Institutes of Health responded with an expansive initiative based on an emerging "network" model, then being pioneered in Uganda and elsewhere to integrate prevention, treatment, and care.

After a series of meetings with outside experts, including Dr. Peter Mugenyi from Uganda, who was later invited to the 2003 State of the Union Address, White House staff became convinced of the feasibility of such a scaled-up model and took the proposal to the President.

This initial proposal called for roughly one-third of the approximately $15 billion in proposed funding to be applied to the Global Fund. The direct funding was to be spread out among countries that exhibited a mix of mature and emerging epidemics.

The President did not approve this proposal.

To move forward with the proposed initiative at such dramatic funding levels, the President insisted on accountability to the American people and measurable results. The way to achieve them was through a bilateral approach. The President wanted to complement multilateral action, and to demonstrate to the taxpayers and partner countries that the United States was serious about results.

Further, the President noted that funding in the proposal was spread too thin, and should be concentrated on highly endemic countries. He wanted to make sure that assistance was targeted to those who needed it the most and to those nations willing to partner with us.

White House staff went back to the technical experts and returned to the President with the proposal for PEPFAR.

President Bush announced PEPFAR during his 2003 State of the Union Address. The initiative represents the largest commitment by a single country toward a specific disease. With $15 billion over 5 years to fight HIV/AIDS in key endemic countries around the world, and ambitious goals to accompany this financial commitment, PEPFAR became the multifaceted approach the United States needed.

PEPFAR also became another example of the change in paradigm of U.S. development that the President established in 2002 with the creation of the Millennium Challenge Account (MCA). The former "donor-recipient" model was again replaced with one of "partnership." Principles such as country ownership, accountability (for both donors and partners), good governance, and an emphasis on results (measurable outputs, not just inputs) are tenets upon which MCA, PEPFAR, and subsequent U.S. development programs are all based.

The partnership principle, which includes support for partner countries as they take ownership and responsibility for their own HIV/AIDS plans, has become entrenched in United States Government assistance. Host country governments are just one of many actors necessary to make this model work. Civil society groups, local communities, and other donor governments are other important partners. Faith-based groups quickly emerged as necessary and effective participants. They play a key role in the delivery of prevention messages, care, and treatment, because they are willing to operate in difficult areas where other groups will not. Faith and community-based organizations also have credibility on personal and behavioral issues that allow them to be especially helpful.

On May 27, 2003, President Bush signed P.L. 108–25, the United States Leadership Against Global HIV/AIDS, Tuberculosis, and Malaria Act of 2003. This legislation included a provision from

Congress mandating that the U.S. contribution to the Global Fund may not exceed 33 percent of the Global Fund's cash on hand, which has proven to be a valuable tool in eliciting funding for the Global Fund from other donors.

The 33 percent ceiling on the United States contribution was interpreted by some advocacy groups as a guarantee that the U.S. would give one dollar for every two from the rest of the world. However, the 33 percent was never intended to be a "match" in this sense. With the cap, the United States did not commit to maintain one-third of the contributions of the Fund, but that it would not ever give more than one-third of all funds.

President Bush nominated Randall L. Tobias as the first U.S. Global AIDS Coordinator. Tobias' office, S/GAC, reported to the Secretary of State and was given the task of coordinating all U.S. assistance and activities for global HIV/AIDS.

The mandate for this new level of coordination required concerted efforts from the agencies. Several levels of leadership were required to emphasize the new interagency nature of HIV/AIDS program planning. U.S. Ambassadors needed to provide leadership to what used to be fairly free-roaming teams. Agency leaders in Washington and Atlanta became key players in the ongoing effort to coordinate a single United States Government response. S/GAC set up several new interagency meeting structures and teams to direct these efforts.

Fifteen countries, chosen because they had a high burden of HIV/AIDS, and a relatively higher capacity to carry out such a new program (thanks both to host country capacity and in-country U.S. government presence) were designated "focus" countries in which to begin this ground-breaking effort: Botswana, Cote d'Ivoire, Ethiopia, Guyana, Haiti, Kenya, Mozambique, Namibia, Nigeria, Rwanda, South Africa, Tanzania, Uganda, Vietnam, and Zambia. Following the development and release of a 5-year global HIV/AIDS strategy, the Coordinator's office obligated the first PEPFAR funds to the field in early 2004.

After Senate confirmation in August 2006, Ambassador Mark Dybul took office as the second U.S. Global AIDS Coordinator.

In addition to the substantial resources committed to bilateral programs, the United States was the first and remains the largest contributor to the Global Fund to Fight AIDS, Tuberculosis, and Malaria (GFATM), contributing $3.3 billion to date. United States Government representatives sit on its Board and on various committees, and provide support for the development of Global Fund proposals and technical assistance to the Global Fund grants on the ground that have run into implementation bottlenecks.

WHAT HAS BEEN ACCOMPLISHED:

In just four years, PEPFAR is well on its way to meeting its goals. It remains a demonstration of the Administration's approach to measuring success in lives saved and services provided—not just dollars transferred. The United States has fulfilled the President's commitment to support treatment for two million people. As of the end of September 2008, PEPFAR has supported life-saving treatment for more than 2.1 million people around the world, including more than 2 million people in Sub-Saharan Africa.

Nearly 9.7 million people affected by HIV/AIDS in the focus countries had received care, including nearly 4 million orphans and vulnerable children. Globally, the United States is supporting care for more than 10.1 million people. Nearly 240,000 babies have been born HIV-free through programs to prevent mother-to-child transmission.

In addition to life-saving treatment, behavior change efforts employed by PEPFAR and its partners are also important. A critical one is the evidence-based and balanced "A-B-C" ("abstinence, be faithful, and condoms") prevention approach, a concept developed in Africa. Achieved results would not have been possible without the heavy involvement of NGOs, faith-based groups, and host country government partnerships.

PEPFAR's bilateral results have taken place alongside a Global Fund that is now supported by many countries, including the United States, and reinforced with specific U.S. legislative funding requirements designed to ensure transparency, audits, and accountability. To date, the Global Fund reports they have committed $11.3 billion globally to fight the three diseases, and reports support for anti-retroviral treatment of approximately 1.45 million people as of the end of 2007.

Support for specific diseases has also meant stronger health systems in the countries in which we work. In 2007 alone, PEPFAR committed more than $638 million to health system strengthening, in support of more than 55,000 health service outlets. A recent study from Rwanda showed that the addition of basic HIV services to primary health centers contributed to an increase in the use of other health services, including antenatal and pediatric care. Health workers trained by PEPFAR to deliver anti-retroviral treatment, counsel or test patients, and/or deliver prevention messages, serve multiple roles in their communities.

Procedurally, the United States Government coordination efforts continue, and the interagency "flavor" remains a hallmark of the implementation. S/GAC has managed to oversee the execution of a significant amount of resources while harnessing technical leadership from the various agencies and tracking and reporting results. Though there were growing pains, it is clear that such a successful outcome is due in part to the direct connection of S/GAC to Secretary Rice and her authorities over foreign assistance.

Due in part to PEPFAR's ability to demonstrate results, PEPFAR has enjoyed bipartisan political support. In May 2007, President Bush asked Congress to double our commitment with an additional 30 billion dollars over the next five years. At the 2007 G-8 Summit in Heiligendamm, Germany, G-8 Leaders committed to match U.S. efforts, agreeing to collectively spend $60 billion over the coming years.

Just as with PEPFAR I, reauthorization comes with a set of ambitious goals and measures success by the number of lives saved—not with the number of dollars spent. To that end, a reauthorized PEPFAR will support treatment for at least 3 million people, prevent 12 million new infections, and provide care and support for 12 million people, including 5 million orphans and vulnerable children. As the President had successfully challenged the rest of the G-8 at the 2007 Heiligendamm Summit to commit to match the U.S. targets, the President returned to the G-8 at the Hokkaido Summit in 2008 calling for accountability and pressing other countries to demonstrate progress toward the 2007 commitment.

On July 30, 2008, President Bush signed H.R. 5501, the Tom Lantos and Henry J. Hyde United States Global Leadership Against HIV/AIDS, Tuberculosis and Malaria Reauthorization Act of 2008. This bill solidified another five years of U.S. support for the global fight against HIV/AIDS and reauthorized up to $39 billion for HIV/AIDS programs and $9 billion for TB and malaria.

FUTURE CHALLENGES:

PEPFAR's efforts have changed the lives of millions. We have met our commitments, challenged other donors, and demonstrated accountability to both our partners and our taxpayers. PEPFAR's presence on the world scene has supported a shift in the global conversation on HIV/AIDS, modifying it from one of despair to one of hope. We've put our partners beside us in the effort, modeling the partnership ethic that has come to characterize the U.S. approach to development. As we press on to the second phase, the new Administration may face the following challenges:

- Budget constraints: PEPFAR's ability to demonstrate results prompted full funding of the initial $15 billion authorization. With the support of Congress, the United States Government through PEPFAR provided $18.8 billion over the past five years, including support to the Global Fund. In order to meet the ambitious goals set out for the next phase, it will be important not only that PEPFAR enjoy the same full funding status as with PEPFAR I, but also that PEPFAR continue to realize increased efficiencies in what may be a daunting budget scenario. PEPFAR should keep the focus on results.
- Connecting the dots: PEPFAR programs are and should be increasingly linked to other development programs to meet the needs of people affected by HIV/AIDS and address other critical but related needs such as nutrition and education. While PEPFAR should remain focused on HIV

treatment, care, and prevention and not replace other development efforts, these linkages will allow the United States to respond effectively to a range of interrelated development challenges and maximize the comparative advantages of different U.S. programs. It can be difficult at times to overcome the bureaucratic hurdles necessary to accomplish this goal, but closely linked to budget concerns and the need for increased efficiency, it makes good sense to utilize a multi-program approach where possible.

- Holding others to account: G-8 and other pledges for HIV/AIDS—particularly those that matched the PEPFAR reauthorization goals for prevention, care, and treatment—are not insignificant. It will be important that we continue to hold ourselves and other donors to account for meeting these and other commitments, even in the midst of financial crises and other challenges.

Attachments

Tab 1   Chronology for PEPFAR
Tab 2   Memorandum for the President from Secretaries Powell and Thompson, "Creating a Leadership Structure for HIV/AIDS" (March 27, 2001)
Tab 3   Memorandum for the President from Margaret Lamontagne and Condoleezza Rice, "White House Office of National AIDS Policy" (April 7, 2001)
Tab 4   Information Memorandum from Condoleezza Rice, "International HIV/AIDS Initiative" (May 29, 2002)
Tab 5   Executive Summary of Report by Mark Dybul, "Comprehensive, results-based, global initiative for the prevention, care, and treatment of HIV, TB, and Malaria" (August 2002)
Tab 6   Presentation: Scope of the Global HIV/AIDS Problem and Proposed U.S. Response (2002)
Tab 7   Proposal for a Comprehensive, Results-Based Global Initiative for the Prevention, Care and Treatment of HIV, TB and Malaria (2002)
Tab 8   State of the Union Address (January 28, 2003)
Tab 9   Fact Sheet: The President's Emergency Plan for AIDS Relief (January 29, 2003)
Tab 10   Speech of PEPFAR (January 31, 2003)
Tab 11   Remarks on the Signing of H.R. 1298, U.S. Leadership Against HIV/AIDS, Tuberculosis and Malaria Act of 2003 (May 27, 2003)
Tab 12   World AIDS Day Fact Sheets (2003–2007)
Tab 13   Announcement of Five-Year, $30 Billion HIV/AIDS Plan (May 30, 2007)
Tab 14   Remarks on the Signing of H.R. 5501, the Tom Lantos and Henry J. Hyde United States Leadership Against HIV/AIDS, Tuberculosis and Malaria Reauthorization Act of 2008 (July 30, 2008)

POSTSCRIPT

MARK DYBUL, DANA DeRUITER

The Bush Administration Approach

President Bush was determined to fundamentally change the course of the HIV pandemic by investing boldly in the hardest hit countries. In the 2003 State of the Union Address he announced the President's Emergency Plan for AIDS Relief (PEP-FAR). As the Transition Memorandum notes, the initiative represented "the largest commitment by a single country toward a specific disease" and promised $15 billion over five years to fight HIV/AIDS in key countries where the disease was endemic.

In just five years, the program harnessed the heft of the United States and the global community to fight HIV in an unprecedented way. On the back of overwhelming bipartisan support, by World AIDS Day 2008, the United States had supported life-saving treatment for two million people, care for ten million including orphans and vulnerable children, and produced a substantial reduction in new infections—meeting the Bush administration's goals on time and on budget. That year the program was renewed for another five years when President Bush signed the Tom Lantos and Henry J. Hyde United States Global Leadership Against HIV/AIDS, Tuberculosis and Malaria Reauthorization Act of 2008. That act reauthorized up to $39 billion for HIV/AIDS programs and $9 billion for tuberculosis and malaria.

PEPFAR—as intended—has galvanized global action beyond its original goals. The program, the largest international health initiative in history for a single disease, initially aimed to spur global action to provide a total of $45 billion over five years, the amount international consensus estimated would be needed to treat those in need and to control the pandemic. Instead, by 2008, with a strong push from President Bush, the G7 that year committed to provide $65 billion to the effort.

PEPFAR did more than address the pain of people and countries being ravaged by the disease. It transformed the way that the United States approached development. The traditional (and patronizing) donor-recipient model was replaced by one of partnership. This partnership approach was comprehensive, involving not only host governments but also NGOs, faith-based groups, civil society, local community-based organizations, and other donors. As the Transition Memorandum also notes, "[p]rinciples such as country ownership, accountability (for both donors and partners), good governance, and an emphasis on results (measurable outputs, not just inputs)" became the hallmarks of Bush administration development efforts generally. The administration also emphasized the need for unity of effort, requiring extraordinary coordination across US government agencies. For PEPFAR, this unity of effort was achieved by establishing a US Global AIDS Coordinator.

PEPFAR also focused on strengthening the health systems in the countries in which it operated. In 2007 alone, it committed to this effort more than $638 million in support of 55,000 health service outlets. These capacity-building investments then became available to provide a variety of health services and for the management and treatment of other diseases.

What Has Happened Since the End of the Bush Administration?

The Obama administration embraced the ambitious vision and efforts behind PEPFAR. Secretary Clinton, for instance, called for an AIDS-free generation. The administration strongly supported PEPFAR, built on bipartisan support in Congress, and sought to institutionalize the program in the broader context of healthcare and development.

To help ensure long-term sustainability of the program, the Obama administration expanded Partnership Compacts, begun in the final years of the Bush administration, which aligned US funding with national plans and formalized commitments to increase local in-country financing over time. In doing so, it advanced the transition of PEPFAR from an emergency response to a durable strategy linked to stronger local systems for healthcare.

The Obama administration also significantly expanded the Bush administration's efforts to "connect the dots" of a whole-of-person HIV effort by linking PEPFAR to other US government, multilateral, and host country programs. For example, building on a pilot project that the Bush administration started in Zambia in 2006, Secretary Clinton joined with the George W. Bush Institute and other partners to launch Pink Ribbon Red Ribbon, a public-private partnership to combat high rates of cervical cancer in young women in Africa that are directly related to HIV.

More broadly, the Obama administration enhanced the focus on global engagement, including increased funding for the Global Fund, instituting successful efforts to enhance its impact, and hosting the fourth replenishment of the fund at the White House in 2017. The Obama administration also broadened the purview of the PEPFAR coordinator by "dual hatting" the coordinator as the Special

Representative for Global Health Diplomacy, thereby recognizing the coordinator's key role in diplomacy, international advocacy, and execution for the program. Moreover, it institutionalized PEPFAR by shifting the primary point of contact from the White House to the secretary of state. While President Obama and the NSC remained engaged, Secretaries of State Clinton and then Kerry assumed leading roles. By the end of the Obama administration, PEPFAR was supporting antiviral treatment for 11.5 million people and care for 6.2 million orphans and vulnerable children.

In large part thanks to strong bipartisan support in Congress, PEPFAR continued throughout the Trump administration despite administration efforts to reduce funding. The administration submitted budgets each year that would have reduced funding for PEPFAR by approximately $1 billion and for the Global Fund by approximately $350 million. On a strong bipartisan basis, Congress rejected those efforts.

By contrast, the Trump administration launched innovative programs with nongovernmental partners to address holistically startling rates of infection in adolescent girls and young women, a group highly vulnerable to HIV. Financing and direct engagement in the management of Pink Ribbon Red Ribbon was enhanced. In December 2020, the administration reported support for ART for 17.2 million people and care for 6.7 million orphans and vulnerable children.

Despite this continued support, the PEPFAR program suffered from reduced attention to HIV overall by the White House and State Department, and from the more confrontational approach the Trump administration took toward countries, international organizations, and partners.

How Did the Bush Administration Do?

There are good reasons why PEPFAR is often lauded as one of the greatest foreign policy achievements of the Bush administration. From the beginning, President Bush insisted that PEPFAR should not be the effort of one president or political party but a long-standing and bipartisan commitment of the American people. His administration's emphasis on bipartisanship has been essential to the program's resilience in the face of many challenges. The focus on results, accountability, and transparency has been transformational for PEPFAR, the US government, host countries, the Global Fund, and beyond.

Prior to PEPFAR, there was not a clear and consistent way to set targets and regularly track and report results and use of funds in US development programs.

Where rudimentary efforts did exist, they were different across various departments and agencies. Establishing one centralized data system with reporting every six months on key indicators, by country, provided the credibility that led to increases in funding by as much as $1 billon in a year. It provided nearly real-time information that could be used to identify gaps and better direct resources to improve impact, thereby leading to greater credibility and funding, in a virtuous cycle. PEPFAR's focus on results and reporting has also driven greater accountability and transparency at the Global Fund. Moreover, PEPFAR's focus on data and accountability has created a ripple effect throughout US development programs, beginning with the President's Malaria Initiative. It is now expected that all US development programs regularly collect and report key data and that every new initiative will have clear targets.

PEPFAR's focus on data also drove the development of the in-country capacity (laboratory, data, epidemiological, and the like) that is required for accurate reporting and the health system improvements needed to achieve the results being reported. Supporting health professionals in collecting and interpreting data provided them with the capacity to manage HIV and other programs. Many of the systems developed for HIV have formed the backbone of broader improvements in health and have played a role in the response to other emergent threats, like Ebola and COVID-19.

Building capacity for data and analysis was only one of several capacity-building endeavors that was both key to the success of the program and that increased country ownership. Also important were the efforts to build capacity to enable the successful transition of large grants from USAID and the CDC to local governmental and nongovernmental organizations. This transition was to occur within a three-to-five-year period as a condition of renewal. While the CDC has successfully transitioned large programs (now approximately 60 percent of its funds go to local partners), USAID's response has been uneven (resulting in only 30 percent of its funds going to local partners).

Country ownership was further encouraged by the establishment of Partnership Compacts, begun in 2007, between the US government and host governments on the role of PEPFAR in national strategies and on future funding commitments. As noted, the Obama administration further developed Partnership Compacts and placed even greater emphasis on strengthening health systems.

Despite the many successes of the PEPFAR program, looking back, in addition to program implementation challenges sometimes faced in-country, the Bush administration confronted three more systematic challenges: the unintended consequences of an emphasis on data and results, a slower-than-needed shift to funding local partners, and culture wars.

- *Data emphasis.* In some countries, antiviral treatment received more weight than other equally important PEPFAR priorities like prevention because ART was lifesaving in an emergency and easy to measure. These qualities also led resources from other important health issues to be reprogrammed to ART. The Obama administration's focus on broader health issues helped rebalance the scales toward more prevention and greater alignment with national strategies as the emergency transitioned to a sustainable response.
- *Local organizations.* Despite its successes, PEPFAR struggled to expedite the transition to the point where its funds were going directly to local organizations. This is due, in part, to actions by the Trump administration. Although the goal of local control was established by the Bush administration, the Trump administration sought to transition it without building the necessary local capacity. In so doing it generated considerable resistance from US government agencies and implementers, including from the national governments with which PEPFAR sought to align during the Bush and Obama administrations. In retrospect, the Bush administration could have initiated the shift to local partners earlier and been more creative and forceful in ensuring that the strategy was fully embraced and implemented long before the Trump administration took office.
- *Culture wars.* The Bush administration should have also better anticipated and prepared for the culture wars that were perhaps inevitable when dealing with a disease that is spread by sex and that accelerated among marginalized and vulnerable communities, such as young women, gay men, sex workers, and people who use intravenous drugs. The first PEPFAR authorization included language, adopted by party-line votes in the House, requiring a formulaic resource allocation for abstinence programs and agreement by grantees to oppose the legalization of sex work. These issues played out not only in Washington, DC, but in Africa as well, where some constitutions forbid sex work and homosexuality and where gender-based discrimination, abuse, and violence are a major issue. While some of the legislative issues were resolved in the subsequent appropriations process and later in the PEPFAR reauthorization, the early divisiveness, which

narrowed the base of support for the program, has persisted, although it has substantially waned.

What Are the Lessons Learned?

The programmatic success and political durability of PEPFAR was far from inevitable. The preponderance of public health experts, including in the US government, did not believe ART was feasible in Africa or other lower-income countries. The politics and intergovernmental turf wars were intense. There were, however, several factors critical to the program's success, which could be relevant to future transformational initiatives.

- *Bold and accountable.* PEPFAR demonstrated that a bold international initiative can save and lift up many millions of lives while transforming the US government, host countries, and international organizations. That transformation laid the foundation for other health system gains, including those that have contributed to responding to the COVID-19 pandemic.

  A focus on targets, data, and results was essential to ensure maximal impact and, thereby, to secure sustainable support across successive US administrations. PEPFAR contributed significantly to a seismic shift in development programs from a focus on money spent to results achieved. It helped build capacity in the collection and analysis of data that will be essential for future pandemic preparedness, detection, and response. However, great care should be taken to see that the focus on data is not myopic and does not lead to the starvation of worthy but less quantifiable initiatives.

- *Leadership.* For any major new initiative, especially one that requires coordination across the government, the importance of presidential leadership, from conception to implementation, cannot be overstated. It was also essential that the PEPFAR coordinator had control over resources to ensure a government-wide approach. Once established politically and administratively, the primary focus could then safely shift to cabinet-level leadership.

- *Coalitions.* A focus on bipartisanship, driven by the president from the beginning, was essential in sustaining support. Then, even in the face of a later administration's attempts to cut the program significantly, the initiative could survive. Having a broad coalition of health-related implementers and advocates, the private sector, and community and faith-based organizations was important to ongoing support, particularly as congressional membership changed. Coalitions are difficult to maintain as policies and programs shift, but they are essential for sustainability.

- *Country ownership.* A key impetus for PEPFAR was President Bush's visceral rejection of paternalistic impulses that are systemic in development programs. National scale to achieve transformational results and sustainability can only be achieved through country ownership by government, community—and faith-based organizations, the private sector, and many others, depending on the local ecosystem. This requires a belief in, and respect for, countries, communities, and people. It also requires an intentional and continual effort to transfer implementation and financing to local organizations, and that, in turn, requires significant investments in local capacity building.

- *International engagement.* The United States cannot and should not stand alone. It should enlist the international community as well. But engagement with international organizations requires leadership and being a trusted partner. Even where there are significant policy differences, respect and partnership is possible. However, trust can be rapidly lost if US leadership falters and/or US representatives do not engage with the highest levels of character and integrity.

- *Humility.* No country, initiative, organization, or person has all the answers or a corner on compassion. Knowledge and circumstances evolve. Any new, large initiative must establish structures, systems, and a culture that welcomes change while retaining core principles. PEPFAR has evolved over the years and across administrations, in some positive and negative directions. The key for the coming years is to embrace learning lessons from the past with humility, to proceed from sound first principles, and to be willing to learn and adapt.

Contributors:
Gary Edson
Jendayi Frazer
Daniel Price
Faryar Shirzad
Kristen Silverberg
John Simon
Tim Zeimer

CHAPTER 22

Malaria

MICHAEL MILLER | TIM ZIEMER

At the time of the launch of the President's Malaria Initiative (PMI) in 2005, nearly one million people were estimated to be dying from the disease each year, the victims being overwhelmingly African children under five years of age. Malaria is one of the greatest killers of human history, yet it is preventable and treatable with relatively inexpensive and widely available interventions—a fact that only compounded the tragedy.

The PMI has been sustained as a presidential initiative by each successive president since President Bush. It is the engine of the ongoing global effort that in just over a decade has cut the number of deaths from malaria by more than half, surpassing the original, ambitious goal of a 50 percent reduction. This global success led by the PMI is unprecedented, but the tenacity of malaria means the success is fragile.

6883

Release

NATIONAL SECURITY COUNCIL

WASHINGTON, D.C. 20504

REDO

Transition

January 14, 2009

MEMORANDUM FOR THE RECORD

FROM: DANA DERUITER
          RELIEF, STABILIZATION, AND DEVELOPMENT
          DIRECTORATE

SUBJECT: The President's Malaria Initiative

THE SITUATION AS WE FOUND IT:

Each year more than one million people die of malaria, most of them in sub-Saharan Africa. Although a treatable and preventable disease, malaria is a leading cause of death in African children.

Malaria eradication efforts during the 1950s and 1960s succeeded in eliminating or controlling the disease in some areas in the world, but the problem persists in Africa. The Sub-Saharan climate provides ideal conditions for malaria transmission; and poverty and political instability can create obstacles to a country's ability to control malaria successfully.

USAID had the lead for the United States Government on the U.S. global efforts to combat malaria. However, before the President's Malaria Initiative (PMI), funding for malaria activities was sprinkled across many countries. There were no treatment or prevention targets and program funding was not based on measurable results.

In response to these concerns, USAID began working to restructure the malaria program, focusing on reforms that would produce measurable results.

THIS ADMINISTRATION'S POLICY:

In early 2005, the United Kingdom, which held the G-8 Presidency for 2005, made Africa a priority on the agenda for the Summit in Gleneagles, Scotland. Building on the President's Emergency Plan for AIDS Relief (PEPFAR) and the Millennium Challenge Account, the Administration developed initiatives to further achieve our objectives and highlight our commitment to Africa.

Newly proposed initiatives included education, malaria, and women's justice and empowerment. The largest share of funding would be focused on malaria because it was both rapidly achievable and measurable.

The proposal for the PMI was presented to the President in an informal meeting in June 2005. Given the redesigned malaria program's emphasis on both compassion and results, the President decided to move forward.

On June 30, 2005, the President announced the PMI in a speech one week before the G-8 Summit in Gleneagles.

PMI was announced as a five-year, $1.2 billion initiative to cut malaria mortality by 50 percent in 15 African countries with a high burden of malaria. Like PEPFAR, this was an ambitious but achievable goal. USAID led implementation, and the PMI began in three focus countries: Angola, Tanzania, and Uganda.

PMI's interventions take a four-pronged approach, using proven and cost-effective prevention and treatment measures. These measures include use of insecticide-treated mosquito nets; indoor residual spraying of insecticides; preventive treatment for pregnant women; and use of artemisinin-based combination therapies for those who have malaria.

The initiative was launched in advance of the Gleneagles Summit as a way to challenge other G-8 members to follow suit. With U.S. encouragement, the G-8 agreed in Gleneagles "to scale up action against malaria to reach 85 percent of the vulnerable populations with the key interventions that will save 600,000 children's lives a year by 2015."

WHAT HAS BEEN ACCOMPLISHED:

In November 2005, the first funds were appropriated for PMI and implementation began. By June 2006, Mrs. Bush announced the addition of four additional PMI focus countries—Malawi, Mozambique, Rwanda, and Senegal—as well as the creation of the position of Malaria Coordinator to manage the program. Admiral Timothy Ziemer took the post in 2006. At the White House Summit on Malaria in December 2006, the President announced the final eight PMI focus countries: Ghana, Madagascar, Mali, Zambia, Kenya, Liberia, Ethiopia, and Benin.

In two years of implementation, PMI has reached an estimated 25 million people in sub-Saharan Africa with its comprehensive measures to fight malaria. In Zanzibar, Tanzania, after the distribution of insecticide-treated nets and indoor spraying, the percentage of infants with malaria went from approximately 20 percent in 2005 to less than 1 percent in 2007.

In addition, the President's sponsorship of this initiative has helped raise malaria awareness domestically. In collaboration with its private sector and NGO partners, the international challenge of malaria has become well known. The President and Mrs. Bush taped messages that appeared on "American Idol," a popular television program.

Another strength of the Initiative is its engagement with the private sector. In partnership with Malaria No More and other groups, PMI distributed free, long-lasting, insecticide-treated nets through national campaigns in Uganda. In Zambia, PMI and PEPFAR joined with the Global Business Coalition to distribute more than 500,000 nets through home-based care programs serving people affected by HIV/AIDS. More than 6.5 million nets have been distributed through public-private partnerships like these. In December 2006, Mrs. Bush announced the Malaria Communities Program to support small NGOs and FBOs involved in malaria-related activities in the PMI focus countries. Five grants were awarded to NGOs and local organizations in 2007. To date, PMI has supported more than 70 nonprofit organizations, of which more than 20 are faith-based.

In 2007, two years after the President's PMI announcement, the United States gained further G-8 agreement in Heiligendamm, Germany, to match PMI's efforts in 15 additional countries through adoption of measurable targets. G-8 countries together committed, "using existing and additional funds, to individually and collectively work to enable the 30 highest malaria prevalence countries in Africa reach at least 85 percent coverage of the most vulnerable groups with effective prevention and treatment measures and achieve a 50 percent reduction in malaria related deaths."

At their summit in Hokkaido Toyako, Japan in July 2008, the G-8 added a commitment to provide 100 million bed nets by 2010. The G-8 also released a report on the implementation of commitments on health, including malaria.

In late July, President Bush signed H.R. 5501, the Tom Lantos and Henry J. Hyde United States Global Leadership Against HIV/AIDS, Tuberculosis and Malaria Reauthorization Act of 2008, authorizing up to $5 billion over 5 years for the President's Malaria Initiative.

FUTURE CHALLENGES:

PMI is in its third year of operation, and is on track toward its overall goal of reducing malaria-related deaths by half in the 15 focus countries selected by the United States. While saving lives through prevention and treatment interventions is a top priority, PMI is also working to program its resources in ways that build national health systems and help strengthen overall capacity of host country government malaria control programs.

In the current financial climate, it may be difficult to persuade other donors to keep the promises they have made for malaria, or to convince other nations to make pledges.

Attachments

POSTSCRIPT

MICHAEL MILLER, TIM ZIEMER

The Bush Administration Approach

As President Bush embraced Africa as a special focus early in his first term, it became clear that any strategic goal with respect to the continent would be complicated, if not unattainable, without addressing malaria. The disease cost the continent $12 billion annually, as estimated by the World Bank, and at the time was estimated to take one million or more lives each year. The profound human and economic losses across the continent were a moral affront to President Bush—one that he felt the United States had an obligation to address. Moreover, he rejected previous approaches by donors and international institutions characterized by lofty promises without requisite commitment and action. The challenge was fundamentally one of leadership and accountability, and he set out to provide both.

The PMI sought to address two fundamental deficits of the weak global malaria control effort. The first was simply a lack of support for continuous diagnosis and treatment—a perpetual requirement for a disease whose transmission is constant via the ubiquitous vector of the mosquito. For those who succumb, typically death comes within just a few days following infection, which means that uninterrupted, ready access to diagnostics and treatments in some of the most challenging environments in the world was required. Growing resistance of the parasite to treatments and of mosquitoes to insecticides, along with growing human populations, meant the global malaria burden and death toll were on the rise.

The second deficit was global leadership—among donors, international institutions, and the affected countries themselves. Malaria, particularly in sub-Saharan Africa where the burden is greatest, had become tolerated and expected; it was in effect viewed as something that a future technological innovation might defeat, but current interventions and efforts would not. With requisite resources and leadership, President Bush judged that defeating malaria was possible, and that the United States must lead by example.

The PMI was made possible by dramatic, internal changes in how USAID's malaria program operated. Prior to the PMI, USAID's global malaria program had grown to $90 million, but as funding increased it had not evolved in its approach, with little emphasis on scaling up life-saving interventions. Resources and effort were scattered across too many countries, with many country programs too limited or too poorly focused to have any meaningful effect. The effort could point to little real, measurable progress, and congressional critics charged that a substantial share of the funding went to US-based consultants, even as malaria deaths increased globally.

The congressional criticism provided an opportunity for USAID staff to seek the backing of agency leadership for rapid and decisive internal reforms. USAID eliminated too-small country-level programs, rededicating the resources to places where additional funding could help bring efforts to meaningful scale. USAID also updated policies that were outdated or ineffective. The result was more effective approaches to the use of free distribution of bed nets, the use of indoor spraying, and improved (but more expensive) drug treatments to control the disease. Specific requirements for dedication of resources for services and commodities to prevent or treat infection—interventions that save lives—became the foundation of country-level programs.

The reforms garnered the attention of the White House because they signaled the ability to combat malaria on a much greater scale, with greater effectiveness, and to institute accountability. The reforms provided a ready basis not only for rapid scale-up of the effort but also an effective foundation for true country-level partnerships and a global initiative.

The PMI approach was distinctive from earlier efforts in important ways, combining presidential leadership (and that of the First Lady) with a "business model" that sought to establish partnerships with African leaders and institutions, to hold agencies and implementers accountable for demonstrable results, and to leverage the efforts of the United States to obtain greater commitments from other donors and actors. This ambitious approach to fighting malaria effectively married President Bush's interest in Africa with his focus on effective, accountable governance.

What Has Happened Since the End of the Bush Administration?
Presidents Obama, Trump, and Biden continued the PMI with the robust support of Congress. PMI and the reforms that paved the way created a "results constituency" in Congress and with the public—a virtuous cycle of achieving measurable outcomes and receiving generous funding. Since its launch, Congress has consistently supported PMI on a bipartisan basis with continued investments, increasing across administrations, with an annual budget of around $66 million in the first full year of implementation scaling very rapidly to an annual budget by year-five of over a half-billion dollars covering fifteen focus countries.

The rapid scale-up of the PMI continued without pause across the transition from President Bush to President Obama, and from President Obama to President Trump, reaching a current level of twenty-four focus countries and an annual congressional funding level approaching $800 million. The funding continuity of the PMI is also attributable to leadership continuity. There have only been three PMI coordinators across its entire history, serving continuously under four presidents drawn from both parties.

The rapid growth of the PMI in the early years was a vote of confidence in the leadership and strategy, even before results could be clearly demonstrated. It also reflected buy-in by Congress to the original vision of malaria as a beatable enemy where American leadership would be decisive. But the value of the investments and the virtuous cycle between results and funding is reflected in lives saved. In year one of the PMI implementation (2006), current estimates for global deaths from malaria were 716,000 annually. By the end of year five of implementation (2010), deaths had been cut dramatically, to an estimated 594,000, and down to 409,000 by the end of 2019. Results specific to the PMI are even more dramatic, with a 60 percent decline in malaria deaths in the PMI focus countries. The PMI itself estimates that, since its launch, the global effort it has led has prevented 1.5 billion malaria infections and averted 7,600,000 malaria deaths. By the simplest and most important measure, the PMI was and continues to be a historic success. A fourth president now sustains the program's presidential designation and pursues President Bush's original vision.

But the success is fragile and the rapid scale-up and early gains are increasingly hard to duplicate. Global malaria control efforts and the PMI's scale and funding have leveled off and the gains against mortality have slowed. The explanation for this plateauing is not just resources but the fact that the second half of the battle is significantly more difficult than the first, with the targeted populations being more difficult to reach and more expensive to support on a sustained basis. Malaria transmission is not defeated once, and the war moves on to the next battlefield. Rather, sustaining progress requires fighting and winning the same battle year after year, holding that ground while at the same time expanding the fronts of engagement in the face of an ever-growing human population. The insidious effect of resistance to treatments and to preventive insecticides are scientific fronts where success is never assured. Even a small slip in levels of commitment could invite backsliding, and the compounding of the challenge and true effects of the SARS-CoV-2 pandemic are still not fully known.

How Did the Bush Administration Do?

The success of the PMI in meeting and exceeding its goals was in no small part due to its decisionmaking and implementation architecture, where responsibility for meeting ambitious targets is coupled with necessary authority to do so, providing a clear line of accountability with results measured in actual human lives rather than process, buildings, and money spent.

The PMI success also stemmed from a different vision for multilateralism and an impatient approach to the crisis. The PMI was a direct challenge to other donors and affected countries to ramp up their commitments and efforts in order to help reach the Roll Back Malaria goal of cutting malaria deaths in half globally by 2010—a goal to which they had already signed up, but for which specific commitments and efforts were few.

President Bush did what others had not done, committing the United States to carry a sizable portion of the global responsibility while challenging others to do the same. The challenge was a decisive departure from the typical approach to shared responsibility by the international community. And it was successful, rallying other countries and institutions to devote their own resources to complement those of the United States, both directly and through the Global Fund. President Bush used the PMI to gain commitments to specific, ambitious targets by other donors at the G-8 Summits in 2005, 2007, and again in 2008.

The PMI's offer of partnership with the United States helped boost leadership at the country level in sub-Saharan Africa, where poverty, ineffective public health institutions, and profound discouragement had taken their devastating toll. The PMI sought to build meaningful, lasting partnerships with African leaders and institutions: working together to identify strategies and resources, and then holding each other mutually accountable for meeting the agreed-upon goals. The PMI looked to the African nations themselves to mobilize resources from the Global Fund and their own economies to complement the funding provided by the US initiative.

Ultimately, the PMI's success in meeting its targets depended on funding and commitment by other countries. This reliance on cooperation was intentional and was clearly communicated to partners as the basis for shared commitment and shared responsibility. The approach reflected the new model for development President Bush proposed in his speech at the Inter-American Development Bank in March 2002 and embodied in the Monterrey Consensus later that month. It was consistent with other Bush administration initiatives like the MCC and

PEPFAR, fostering mutual respect and initiating a significant global shift away from a tired donor-recipient model of development that had too little to show for decades of investments of effort and resources.

By the end of the Bush administration, through its new business model, the PMI had filled the deficit in global leadership. The PMI rejected the approach of creating a top-down, unfunded mandate for the world to achieve, instead taking on concrete responsibilities and making specific commitments as the foundation for a partnership between the United States, other donors, and affected countries.

The structure of the PMI and concrete methods for assessing its success helped ensure ongoing support for the initiative across multiple Congresses and administrations. This continuity has been important for ensuring the sustained commitment required to control and ultimately eradicate the disease. The PMI mobilized resources and gained congressional support for continued, growing investments by building on successful reforms of USAID's global malaria programs and then adding a level of discipline and effectiveness necessary to merit significant annual funding.

What Are the Lessons Learned?

The PMI's success demonstrated first and foremost that malaria could be defeated—a goal that had all but disappeared in recent decades. But the PMI's success also offers many specific lessons about development assistance that reach far beyond malaria and even beyond the battle against infectious diseases:

- *Visionary leadership is critical for tackling seemingly intractable problems.* American leadership was instrumental in soliciting strategies, commitments, and ultimately a level of effort that was lacking in previous decades. Presidential leadership is unique in its ability to create the necessary momentum and marshal the critical commitments and resources needed to initiate change on a global scale.
- *Clarity of goals and outcomes drives and sustains success.* The ability of the PMI to directly connect specific inputs (in terms of dollars) with specific outcomes (in terms of lives saved) helped the program win support from successive administrations and Congresses. The clear objectives and the necessary pairing of authority with responsibility for achieving outcomes changed not only the US government's approach to development but reached well beyond to other governments and international institutions.

- *Building true, accountable partnerships is essential for success.* The PMI's partnership with African countries most affected by malaria was and still is critical to its success. Mutual commitments and mutual accountability for results was a different business model, but also a long-overdue shift away from the paternalism that Africans felt characterized so much of donor-funded development.
- *The United States can leverage its own commitments to win the support and partnership of others.* The commitment of the United States was significant and meaningful, but it was only a portion of the total financial and know-how commitment required to tackle malaria on a global scale. Nevertheless, the size of the US commitment and the personal engagement of the president and other senior US officials helped stimulate additional global commitments and resources—and these have been sustained.

Contributors:
Dana DeRuiter
Mark Dybul
Gary Edson
Jendayi Frazer
Daniel Price
Faryar Shirzad
Kristen Silverberg
John Simon

CHAPTER 23

Neglected Tropical Diseases

DANA DeRUITER | MARK DYBUL

Globally, Neglected Tropical Diseases (NTDs) affect more than one billion people, predominantly those living in poor populations, causing relatively low death rates but high rates of illness. They can result in severe disability, poor mental and physical development, and contribute to childhood malnutrition and school absences, all of which can negatively affect economic development as well as individual health outcomes. The Bush administration's increased attention to those NTDs that were treatable and beatable was part of a bold and focused global health agenda that also included the creation of the President's Emergency Plan for AIDS Relief (PEPFAR) and the President's Malaria Initiative (PMI). The leadership and funding of the Bush administration toward elimination of these relatively ignored diseases were a critical ingredient for the increased global attention to them and another example of how and where the United States can amplify its own efforts by participating as part of the global system.

As of 2019, the program that started in five countries had expanded to thirty-two, and the US government has provided more than 2.8 billion treatments to more than 1.4 billion people. This support has contributed to at least ten countries' ability to eliminate at least one disease, and today, thanks to support from the US government, more than 280 million people no longer require treatment for Lymphatic Filariasis (elephantiasis); more than 114 million no longer need treatment for trachoma (eye infection); and more than six million no longer need treatment for onchocerciasis (river blindness).

TRANSITION MEMORANDUM

Release

NATIONAL SECURITY COUNCIL

WASHINGTON, D.C. 20504

December 22, 2008

MEMORANDUM FOR THE RECORD

FROM: DANA DERUITER, RELIEF, STABILIZATION, AND
               DEVELOPMENT DIRECTORATE

SUBJECT: Neglected Tropical Diseases

THE SITUATION AS WE FOUND IT:

More than one billion people—mostly in the developing world—suffer from one or more neglected tropical diseases (NTDs). These diseases disproportionately impact poor and rural populations, which lack access to safe water, sanitation, and essential medicines. These diseases cause sickness and disability, contribute to childhood malnutrition, compromise children's mental and physical development, and can result in blindness and severe disfigurement.

Seven of these NTDs—lymphatic filariasis (elephantiasis); schistosomiasis (snail fever); trachoma (eye infection); onchocerciasis (river blindness); and soil-transmitted helminthes (hookworm, roundworm, whipworm)—can be controlled through targeted mass drug administration. Research has shown that when treatment is provided to at-risk populations annually over 3–5 successive years, NTDs may be controlled or eliminated to a prevalence rate at which they no longer pose a threat to public health.

While there had been widespread public support for interventions to fight HIV/AIDS and malaria, funding for NTDs had not received the same high-profile status. As a result, diseases that were treatable and beatable were simply not being addressed, even though the costs to treat them were relatively low and the impact on developing societies potentially significant.

THIS ADMINISTRATION'S POLICY:

Improving the health of populations contributes to their economic growth and prosperity.

In September 2006, USAID initiated a $100 million Neglected Tropical Diseases Control Project, with the goal of delivering treatment to 40 million people over 5 years, focusing initially in five countries in Africa—Burkina Faso, Ghana, Mali, Niger, and Uganda. The program leveraged donated and discounted drugs from GlaxoSmithKline, Merck, and Pfizer to target the seven major neglected tropical diseases that can be controlled through mass drug administration. This project represented one of the first large-scale efforts to integrate existing NTD-specific treatment programs to expand care to millions of the world's poorest people. No longer would there be one program to treat schistosomiasis, and another to treat onchocerciasis: rather, this program would focus on integrated control of the seven major NTDs so that they could be treated collectively and inexpensively. USAID's program was an important first step in combating these diseases, but a relatively small commitment compared to the enormity of the need.

The USAID program became fully operational in early 2007. By late 2007 and early 2008, discussion began on potential initiatives for a planned trip by the President to Africa in February 2008 and for the July 2008 G-8 Summit in Japan. Given the early success of USAID's NTD control program, the Administration consulted with health experts, including at the National Institutes of Health, to determine the possibility of impacting a greater number of lives affected by NTDs for relatively low cost. Based on these consultations, an expanded NTD initiative was developed that could be announced on the Africa trip. This would then serve as a "challenge" to the rest of the G-8 to match U.S. efforts.

President Bush announced an enhanced U.S. initiative to combat neglected tropical diseases in February 2008 in Ghana. The Initiative expands the current program to make available a total of $350 million over 5 years to provide integrated treatment to more than 300 million people in Africa, Asia, and Latin America. The program will continue to utilize the drugs donated by pharmaceutical companies, and USAID also will work closely with Ministries of Health in each country and key international partners such as the World Health Organization (WHO) who are leading efforts in NTD control.

Countries in Africa, Asia, and Latin America will be eligible to participate in the expanded program based on the presence of overlapping NTD disease burdens (more than one NTD in the same country and region), funding gaps in delivery of NTD treatment, feasibility of implementation, and political commitment. The program aims to enhance efficiency of drug delivery by leveraging existing initiatives such as the Basic Education Initiative, the President's Malaria Initiative (PMI), and the President's Emergency Plan for AIDS Relief (PEPFAR)—three programs with established delivery systems and networks.

Finally, president Bush challenged other donors—including G-8 partners, foundations, and others—to provide an additional $650 million so that a $1 billion total commitment would allow us collectively to treat 75 percent of the people affected by NTDs in affected populations in Africa, Asia, and Latin America. With sustained treatment for a period of 3–5 years, this would enable an 80–90 percent reduction of the current burden, with elimination of some of the diseases.

WHAT HAS BEEN ACCOMPLISHED:

USAID's current NTD Control Project has been operational since 2007, and in the first year reached 14 million people in the five initial African countries. The new Initiative will expand the work to a total of 30 countries by 2013 and will reach more than 300 million people.

Since the President's February 2008 announcement of the NTD initiative, NTDs have gained increased international attention. For example, in her opening speech at the World Health Assembly in May 2008, Dr. Margaret Chan, Director General of the World Health Organization (WHO), thanked the United States for its financial commitment to NTDs. She asserted that "with a comparatively modest, time-limited financial push, many of these [neglected tropical] diseases can be controlled by 2015."

After sustained advocacy, the Administration secured support for the G-8 commitment it sought to combat NTDs. At the Toyako Summit in July 2008, G-8 leaders agreed to support the control or elimination of certain major neglected tropical diseases. Leaders set a target of working to reach "at least 75 percent of the people affected by certain major neglected tropical diseases in the most affected countries in Africa, Asia, and Latin America, bearing in mind the WHO Plan." The Summit declaration noted that, "with sustained action for 3–5 years, this would enable a very significant reduction of the current burden with the elimination of some of these diseases." The inclusion of a specific target was a critical element, consistent with the President's desire to stress the need for enhanced accountability within the G-8 for follow-through on commitments.

No G-8 countries made a specific financial commitment for NTDs at the Summit. However, the United Kingdom announced a £50 million commitment to NTDs on September 22, 2008. Secretary Douglas Alexander noted that the U.K. contribution built upon President Bush's $350 million announcement and the call to the G-8.

FUTURE CHALLENGES:

In the face of many competing global health issues, a new Administration may face challenges in holding other G-8 nations to account for following through on their commitment for NTDs. A new Administration should consider the low-cost/high-impact results of treating NTDs, not only for the immediate health benefits to the individual, but also for the positive economic and educational effects on the community.

Attachments
Tab 1   Chronology for Neglected Tropical Diseases
Tab 2   USAID Announcement of Award of Neglected Tropical Diseases Control Project to RTI
               International (September 2006)

POSTSCRIPT

DANA DeRUITER, MARK DYBUL

The Bush Administration Approach
While relatively smaller in size than the efforts of the Bush administration to tackle AIDS and malaria in the developing world, the NTD program bore some of the same hallmarks that have come to define these other programs:

1. *Focused investments.* The NTD program focused on approaches that had the highest potential to achieve global control and elimination goals: mapping the disease burden, initiating large-scale treatment programs, and measuring impact of the work.
2. *Focused on results.* Success of the program was measured not by how many dollars were spent, but by the number of people treated, and ultimately the movement toward the elimination of the disease in various countries. Further, these individual diseases have been tackled in an integrated way, working with countries to deliver the treatments at schools and community centers, enabling them to reach more people and treat multiple diseases at the same time.
3. *Leveraging private-sector partnerships.* The NTD program partnered with the pharmaceutical industry leveraging $26 in donated medicines (valued at $19 billion to date) for every $1 invested by the US government. These partnerships, and others with governments, philanthropic donors, and multilateral institutions, increased the US government's ability to contribute to the overall effort.
4. *Strong partnerships with a range of partners at national, regional, and global levels.* In addition to the critical partnerships with Ministries of Health and Education in the countries where the program was active, the United States structured the program to play an important role globally in support of WHO goals for NTD control and elimination with respect to twenty neglected diseases. In May 2008, Dr. Margaret Chan, then–director general of the WHO, recognized the United States for its additional financial commitment to NTDs in her address to the sixty-first World Health Assembly.

As with the Bush administration's other signature global health efforts, from the very beginning this was not a "go it alone" proposition. The United States both increased its own bilateral efforts while challenging other donors to do the same through the G-8 and other international venues. It both set its own targets but worked to ensure that they contributed to the WHO's global goals, while continuing to lend significant time and technical expertise at the country level to ensure the success of the collective effort.

What Has Happened Since the End of the Bush Administration?

Since the end of the Bush administration, the United States has continued its contributions toward the WHO-defined agenda, working to help accelerate progress toward the WHO 2020 NTD goals and the Sustainable Development Agenda, as well as the updated global NTD roadmap for 2021–2030.

The Obama administration embraced the NTD work and program as part of its own global health effort, including the global leadership piece, by reaffirming its commitment to the global goals embodied in the 2012 London Declaration with a broad range of partners committed to eliminating NTDs. Bipartisan congressional support, including through appropriations, has remained strong, despite lower proposed funding for NTDs and other global health programs during the Trump administration.

Today the US government remains one of the largest funders of NTD programs and an important partner in the global effort, which includes significant attention and funding from actors such as the United Kingdom, the Bill & Melinda Gates Foundation, The Carter Center, and several pharmaceutical companies.

How Did the Bush Administration Do?

The NTDs initiative was highly successful in bringing treatment to hundreds of millions of people suffering from debilitating diseases for which there are known, cost-effective treatments. Presidential leadership and the commitment of senior officials allowed a program that was started relatively late in President Bush's tenure to be expanded and solidified by 2008, the last year of the administration. The initiative drove strong relationships with, and increased focus from, pharma, the WHO, and the United Kingdom, along with other donors. Today's global results and collective achievements show this to have been a strong strategy. In setting further ambitious goals for 2030, the WHO reports significant progress since the implementation of the first NTD roadmap, including elimination of at least one disease in forty countries, territories, and areas.

In retrospect, however, it is possible to point to some areas where the initiative could have produced even more significant results. While the United States has been able to draw attention to these diseases, and the opportunity to address them at low cost to the international community, NTD control and elimination has not received the prominence required to attract larger commitments from other countries, such as those in the (now) G-7. Had the administration had more time in office or begun the initiative earlier, it is likely it would have also pressed for accountability for previous commitments and for additional resources for NTDs within the (then) G-8 context as part of its effort to lead while bringing others along. Finally, the impact of the program to tackle NTDs might have been even more consequential had the Bush administration been able to hit the ground running at its inception, which it was unable to do given the understaffing at USAID at the time it was launched.

What Are the Lessons Learned?

US investments in global health during the Bush administration, while not perfect, were bold and impactful and a boon to health outcomes across the globe. The lessons flowing from the NTDs initiative are very similar to those identified from other Bush administration health initiatives.

- *Strong White House leadership.* The success of the NTDs initiative can be attributed to strong leadership from the White House to develop, with bipartisan support from Congress, a program that identified specific needs, solutions, and intended results that then provided the basis for clear accountability to the American taxpayers.
- *Targeted goals.* US government global health programs are arguably at their best when they are focused around a set of targeted goals (in this case, designed to tackle the seven diseases that can be controlled by mass drug administration).
- *Challenge other donors.* The United States can effectively use its own very tangible commitments to challenge other donors and nudge them toward more actionable contributions. Announcements of bilateral US commitments were usually followed by a challenge to the global community or a significant contribution to a multilateral entity so that the United States could amplify its own efforts and results in tandem with others.

- *Bipartisan congressional support.* Bipartisan support from Congress, further bolstered by continued demonstration of results, has helped ensure key programs remain funded, even in the face of subsequent administrations that may have other funding priorities.
- *Steward and leverage US government funding.* US government funding is not infinite, and funding increases for individual disease initiatives at the levels seen during the Bush years are challenging to replicate today, particularly as the world grapples with the COVID pandemic response and recovery. US government funding itself cannot be and should not be the answer to sustainable progress, given other development imperatives and changing global health needs that require more integrated programs and broader systemic support.
- *Maintain US global leadership.* US global health leadership is likely to reflect the larger trends in American global leadership. Apart from funding, the US commitment to global health followed the broader pattern of US international retrenchment over the past few years, culminating at one point in the beginnings of US withdrawal from the WHO during the height of the coronavirus pandemic.
- *The need for new thinking.* Future US policy should consider a return to the principles embodied in the signature global health initiatives of the Bush administration—country ownership, targets and results, partnerships—and determine, within that framework, an appropriate role for US leadership in meeting current health challenges, which are far broader than specific diseases and demand new ideas and fresh thinking to strengthen systems that can better address these complex needs.

Contributors:
Gary Edson
Faryar Shirzad
Jendayi Frazer
Kristen Silverberg
Michael Miller
John Simon
Daniel Price
Tim Zeimer

CHAPTER 24

Pandemic Preparedness

Biodefense and Pandemic Planning

RAJEEV VENKAYYA

In the wake of 9/11 and the anthrax attacks in October 2001, the Bush administration established the Biodefense Directorate in the Homeland Security Council (HSC) staff at the White House. Over the course of the administration, an unprecedented range of biodefense initiatives was undertaken—at first to prepare the nation for a deliberate biologic attack, but then pivoting to the broader responsibility of preparing for and responding to naturally occurring biological outbreaks and pandemics.

From the outset, it was understood that many of the biodefense preparations would have civilian applications against biological accidents, emerging infectious diseases, and pandemics. But in response to the incipient pandemic threat posed by the avian influenza strain (H5N1) in 2003, the SARS outbreak, and his own reading about the 1918 influenza pandemic, President Bush realized much more needed to be done by way of pandemic preparation. What began as largely a biodefense effort expanded substantially to become a pandemic planning effort.

THE BUSH ADMINISTRATION APPROACH

The newfound appreciation for the terrorist threat that followed the 9/11 attacks, along with the expansion of, and easy access to, tools to manipulate biological materials, led to a historic set of programs and policies to protect the United States against deliberate biological attacks—both attacks on humans, with agents such as smallpox, anthrax and botulinum toxin, and attacks on the food and agriculture system, with a range of agents.

Biodefense
Central to these efforts were two foundational presidential directives:

- *HSPD 10/NSPD 33:* Biodefense for the Twenty-first Century. This joint HSC/NSC policy outlined the essential pillars of the nation's biodefense program and provided specific directives to further strengthen the significant measures put in place earlier in the administration:
  - *Threat awareness,* included biological weapons-related intelligence, vulnerability assessments, and anticipation of future threats.
  - *Prevention and protection,* included interdiction and critical infrastructure protection.
  - *Surveillance and detection,* included attack warning and attribution.
  - *Response and recovery,* included response planning, mass casualty care, risk communication, medical countermeasures, and decontamination.
- *HSPD 9:* Defense of US Agriculture and Food. This document established a national policy to defend the agriculture and food system against terrorist attacks, major disasters, and other emergencies.

These presidential directives outlined the strategy and policy for the United States to counter deliberate biological threats. They were accompanied by a broad range of programs targeting national, state, and local preparedness and response:

- *BioWatch (2003).* BioWatch monitored the air in over thirty metropolitan areas for biological agents likely to be used in a bioterrorism attack. If a detection occurred, public health and other local and state officials would use the information to coordinate emergency response, including prompt medical care and other actions to protect public health and safety. This combination of early warning and rapid response could reduce illness and death from a bioterrorism attack.

- *Cities Readiness Initiative (2004).* The Centers for Disease Control and Prevention (CDC)'s Cities Readiness Initiative (CRI) was a federally funded program designed to enhance preparedness in the nation's largest population centers, where nearly 60 percent of the population resided, in order to effectively respond to large public health emergencies needing life-saving medicines and medical supplies. State and large metropolitan public health departments used CRI funding to develop, test, and maintain plans to quickly receive medical countermeasures from the Strategic National Stockpile and distribute them to local communities.

- *Project BioShield (2004).* Project BioShield accelerated the research, development, purchase, and availability of effective medical countermeasures against biological, chemical, radiological, and nuclear agents.
  - *Funding of needed countermeasures:* Project BioShield authorized $5.6 billion in funding over ten years for the advanced development and purchase of priority medical countermeasures.
  - *Facilitating research and development:* Project BioShield granted the National Institutes of Health/National Institute of Allergy and Infectious Diseases authorities to expedite and simplify the solicitation, review, and award of grants and contracts for the development of critical medical countermeasures.
  - *Facilitating the use of medical countermeasures in an emergency:* Project BioShield established the Emergency Use Authorization (EUA) to provide access to the best available medical countermeasures following a Declaration of Emergency by the Secretary of Health and Human Services. The EUA authority has since been used throughout COVID-19 to make vaccines, drugs, and diagnostics available for the US response.

- *National Science Advisory Board for Biosecurity (NSABB) (2005).* The NSABB was established as a federal advisory committee to address issues related to biosecurity and dual-use research at the request of the United States government. The NSABB was set up to have twenty-five voting members with a broad range of expertise including molecular biology, microbiology, infectious diseases, biosafety, public health, veterinary medicine, plant health, national security, biodefense, law enforcement, scientific publishing, and other related fields.

- *Subsequent Presidential Directives.* The Bush administration issued two additional Homeland Security Presidential Directives (HSPDs) to further enhance the nation's preparedness for deliberate and naturally occurring biological threats.
  - *HSPD 18:* Medical Countermeasures Against Weapons of Mass Destruction. Outlined a two-tiered approach for development and acquisition of medical countermeasures, balancing the immediate need to provide a capability to mitigate the catastrophic effects of known chemical, biological, radiological, and nuclear (CBRN) threats with long-term requirements to develop more flexible spectrum countermeasures to address future threats. These threats included a novel biological agent that was highly communicable and without known countermeasure at the time of its discovery.[1]
  - *HSPD 21:* Public Health and Medical Preparedness. Addressed preparedness for catastrophic "all-hazard" health events by:
    - Establishing a biosurveillance capability for early warning and ongoing situational awareness;
    - Fostering medical countermeasure stockpiling and distribution;
    - Developing a "disaster medical capability that can satisfy the needs of the population during a catastrophic health event"; and
    - Promoting community public health and medical preparedness and enhancing community resilience.
- *Congressional action.* Two important pieces of legislation were signed into law during the Bush administration, each of which would have a significant and enduring impact on preparedness for biological events.
  - *Public Readiness and Emergency Preparedness (PREP) Act (2005).* This act authorized the Secretary of Health and Human Services (HHS) to issue a PREP Act declaration to provide immunity from liability (except for willful misconduct) for claims of loss caused, arising out of, relating to, or resulting from administration or use of countermeasures to diseases, threats, and conditions, such immunity to extend to

---

1. Administration of George W. Bush, "*Directive on Medical Countermeasures against Weapons of Mass Destruction.*" Homeland Security Presidential Directive HSPD–18, January 31, 2007, https://www.hsdl.org/?view&did=456436.

entities and individuals involved in the development, manufacture, testing, distribution, administration, and use of such countermeasures.

- *Pandemic and All-Hazards Preparedness Act (PAHPA) (2006).* This act amended the Public Health Service Act to establish within the HHS a new Assistant Secretary for Preparedness and Response (ASPR); provide new authorities for a number of programs, including the advanced development and acquisition of medical countermeasures through the Biomedical Advanced Research and Development Authority (BARDA); establish a quadrennial National Health Security Strategy; and include a number of provisions to strengthen public health preparedness and medical surge capabilities.

The first four initiatives described above (BioWatch, Cities Readiness Initiative, Project BioShield and the National Science Advisory Board for Biosecurity) remain active and funded at the time of this report.

Pivoting to Pandemic Preparedness

In 2003, a highly pathogenic avian influenza strain (H5N1) was found in poultry in Hong Kong, with a demonstrated ability to infect humans and with mortality over 50 percent. This led to a large culling of bird populations by the then–minister of health in Hong Kong, Margaret Chan (who later became director-general of the World Health Organization). When the virus spread to other countries in the region, the specter of crossover to humans and evolution of efficient human-to-human transmission led to a rising concern of an influenza pandemic. National and regional responses were undertaken in Asia, and the United States formed the International Partnership for Avian and Pandemic Influenza (IPAPI) to help coordinate the international response across the animal and human health sectors.

In the United States, awareness and concern about biological threats continued to increase following the SARS outbreak in 2003 and as ongoing biodefense assessments highlighted the gaps in preparedness for deliberate biological attacks with agents such as anthrax, smallpox, and botulinum toxin. In this context, President Bush became acutely concerned about the impact of an influenza pandemic upon reading John Barry's book *The Great Influenza* about the 1918 pandemic. It was apparent to him and his advisers that the United States and the world were woefully unprepared for such a catastrophic health threat, the impact of which would extend well beyond the health sector to all of society.

Over the summer of 2005, the Department of Health and Human Services had been working on a pandemic plan that focused on health preparedness. In parallel, the State Department was advancing international cooperation efforts. Preparation of an emergency budget supplemental was initiated, with a principal focus on domestic preparedness, but also with resources for the international effort through IPAPI.

Surveying these efforts against the magnitude of the threat, President Bush decided that more needed to be done. In October 2005, he requested his Homeland Security Adviser, Frances Fragos Townsend, to lead the development of a national strategy to tackle pandemic influenza, taking an all-of-society approach. This responsibility was directed to the Biodefense Directorate of the HSC staff.

The National Strategy for Pandemic Influenza   In early November 2005, President Bush released the twelve-page National Strategy for Pandemic Influenza and an emergency budget supplemental request of $7.1 billion to fund domestic and international preparedness. Immediately after this, the HSC Biodefense staff assembled a team of seven individuals from across the US government (HHS, USDA, DHS, VA, State, and DoD) to develop a comprehensive implementation plan for the strategy.

The Implementation Plan for the National Strategy for Pandemic Influenza was issued in May 2006, identifying over 300 actions for federal departments and agencies, each with specific deliverables, accountabilities, and timelines as appropriate. Its comprehensive content is well captured by the headings of the various sections of the plan:

- US Government Planning for a Pandemic
- Federal Government Response to a Pandemic
- International Efforts
- Transportation and Borders
- Protecting Human Health
- Protecting Animal Health
- Law Enforcement, Public Safety and Security
- Institutions: Protecting Personnel and Ensuring Continuity of Operations

The Implementation Plan was fully coordinated with various relevant departments and agencies through the policy coordination process led by the HSC and was then approved at the cabinet level. Following the creation of the Implementation Plan, a team comprised of senior personnel from fourteen departments and agencies was assembled to oversee its execution. The HSC convened meetings of this group on a weekly basis to report out on progress and barriers, and to identify issues that needed to be addressed through the policy process. Examples of such issues included border policies, vaccine prioritization, and community mitigation guidance. Given the magnitude of the threat, and in the spirit of transparency and accountability, the HSC tracked the progress of implementation and issued annual reports at the level of each individual action. This process occurred for three years following issuance of the plan in May 2006.

Community Mitigation Strategy   One of the most significant outcomes of the administration's pandemic planning was the community mitigation strategy. Based on prior experience and contemporary technology, it was clear that vaccines would not be available for six months or more after the start of a pandemic, through the first and possibly second wave (based on the 1918 experience).

In considering strategies to protect communities prior to the arrival of vaccines, the HSC team became aware of disease modeling that suggested a combination of partially effective measures such as school closures, reduction of social contact, and keeping ill persons at home, could have a synergistic effect on the accumulation of infections, illness, and deaths in a pandemic. The team commissioned three groups in the MIDAS consortium of the National Institutes of Health (NIH) to model the impact of early implementation of a predetermined combination of public health measures. Those groups uniformly showed that, when implemented early, and even with only modest compliance, the peak of the case curve (representing maximal burden on the health system) could be delayed and reduced in magnitude, ultimately reducing the total cases in a community.

Given the potential of this strategy to substantially reduce illness, suffering, and death prior to the availability of vaccines, the HSC and CDC led an interagency team to translate this concept of pandemic mitigation into a concrete strategy. It was ultimately issued by the CDC in 2007 as the Community Strategy for Pandemic Influenza Mitigation. This document was updated in 2017 and its principles were applied during COVID-19 as the "flattening the curve" strategy.

What Has Happened Since the End of the Bush Administration?

The Obama administration eliminated the Biodefense Directorate after taking office in 2009 but did leverage the Bush administration's work to respond effectively to the H1N1 influenza pandemic when it emerged just four months into the new administration. Several HSC staff members who were actively involved in the pandemic preparedness effort during the Bush administration were still working at the White House when H1N1 began, and President Obama immediately supplemented this team with additional alumni of the Directorate. Thus there was considerable continuity on pandemic preparedness between the two administrations, at least in the early days of the Obama administration.

Five years later, early in 2014, came the outbreak of Ebola in West Africa, which principally affected Guinea, Liberia, and Sierra Leone. By the summer of 2014 the region was experiencing high rates of transmission, with as many as 1,000 new cases every week. The Obama administration made an emergency funding request in November 2014 for $6.2 billion. In December, Congress appropriated $5.4 billion in emergency Ebola funding, most of which was to be directed to international activities. The outbreak was declared over in 2016 but only after there had been over 28,000 cases and 11,000 deaths.[2]

The Obama administration played a key role in establishing the Global Health Security Agenda (GHSA), a multilateral initiative to strengthen countries' preparedness for outbreaks of infectious diseases, as a complement to the International Health Regulations. Since its creation, sixty-seven countries have joined the GHSA, along with several multilateral institutions. GHSA was initially launched for a five-year period that was renewed through 2024.

Following the Ebola response and creation of GHSA, the Obama administration established a Directorate for Global Health Security and Biodefense to coordinate policies related to infectious disease preparedness and response, and to lead implementation of the GHSA.

The Directorate for Global Health Security and Biodefense was eliminated early in the Trump administration, with the personnel and responsibilities transferred to the Trump administration's Directorate for Counterproliferation and

---

2. Jennifer Kates, Josh Michaud, Adam Wexler, and Allison Valentin, "The U.S. Response to Ebola: Status of the FY2015 Emergency Ebola Appropriation," Kaiser Family Foundation (website), December 11, 2015, https://www.kff.org/global-health-policy/issue-brief /the-u-s-response-to-ebola-status-of-the-fy2015-emergency-ebola-appropriation/.

Biodefense within the NSC staff, reportedly with a principal focus on deliberate threats. It is not clear whether any roles related to biodefense or pandemic preparedness were eliminated.

COVID-19 was first recognized in January 2020. The administration's actions during the pandemic are well described in public sources and will not be recounted in detail here. But there are a number of conclusions regarding pandemic preparedness that can be drawn from that effort.

- Bush administration experts had been skeptical as to the utility of border closures as a tool for responding to a pandemic. Their use by many nations in the face of COVID-19 showed that they could buy time for a nation to prepare and adopt mitigation measures. In the case of COVID-19 in the United States, what little time bought was not effectively used.
- The United States did not have an early, coordinated, or effective response to the COVID-19 pandemic, due in large part to dysfunction within the executive branch. The response could have been better if the Trump administration had taken advantage of the pandemic preparedness work that had been done during the Bush administration.
- Social media fueled the politicization of mitigation measures, the spread of misinformation, the decline in confidence in institutions and experts, and the balkanization of the response. This is a problem that has largely arisen since the Bush administration and for which no good solution has yet emerged.
- Basic capabilities such as diagnostic testing and surveillance were not available for most of the first year of the pandemic and continued to be a major limitation through 2021.

How Did the Bush Administration Do?

The pandemic planning undertaken in the Bush administration was prescient in many ways. Not only did it anticipate the potential cross-societal impact of a pandemic, but it also pioneered an all-of-government approach to preparedness in advance of the crisis. Many of these lessons were understood at the time and confirmed with the emergence of COVID-19.

What Are the Lessons Learned?
- *There is no substitute for advance planning and exercising.* The cross-government connectivity of the pandemic planning effort brings nonhealth

entities into public health preparedness. This benefits responses to other public health threats as well as pandemic planning. Of equal importance are regular exercises to test and evaluate the plan.

- *Pandemics require an "all-hands-on-deck" response.* Pandemics affect entire societies and require not just an all-of-government approach but an all-of-society approach.
- *It takes time to gather the necessary evidence.* It is difficult to understand the epidemiology of a novel virus in real time, given the limitations of surveillance and reporting mechanisms. Efforts must be made to collect high-quality, timely information to inform decisions, and precautionary approaches are warranted while this information is being gathered.
- *Decisions must still be made with the best available facts.* Public health authorities have difficulty making firm recommendations in the absence of a robust, rigorous evidence base. Regardless, time-sensitive decisions must be made with the best available facts, with the best interests of public health and national security in mind, and with public candor about the limitations about what is known and not known at the time.
- *Medical countermeasures may not be available in the first wave of a pandemic.* Nonpharmaceutical interventions are essential to mitigate spread and burden on the health system. And they are most effective when defined and exercised prior to the pandemic, and implemented in an early, coordinated fashion.
- *Economic impacts must be managed.* Many of the negative consequences of mitigation strategies, particularly the economic impacts, can be blunted through smart policies. Prior planning is required here as well.

Contributors:
Richard Hatchett
Carter Mecher
Kenneth Bernard
Robert Kadlec

PART 6

Subpart 3

Resolving Long-Standing Conflicts

INTRODUCTION

STEPHEN J. HADLEY

The Transition Memoranda in this subpart 3 of part 6 address Bush administration efforts to resolve long-standing armed conflicts in Africa and to reach a peace agreement between the Israelis and the Palestinians as part of a broader Middle East peace. Previous Transition Memoranda have discussed other Bush administration conflict resolution efforts, including in Latin America, in the Western Balkans of Europe, and elsewhere in the Middle East. Taken together, these efforts produced a somewhat checkered record of accomplishment. And each situation was different. As noted in the introduction to part 3, success in such efforts requires careful planning, sound strategies, adequate resources, and sustained engagement. It requires a strong and committed local partner. And it requires an American president willing to invest their own time, effort, and political capital.

CHAPTER 25

Africa

JENDAYI FRAZER | BOBBY PITTMAN | JOHN SIMON

There were six major conflicts across Africa when President Bush entered office in 2001. However, there were positive trends as well, exemplified by many African states establishing, strengthening, and growing their regional organizations, as more democratic leaders and infrastructure emerged and gained momentum. The Bush administration sought to leverage and partner with these growing movements for peace, stability, and democracy. From the outset, the Bush approach involved intensive presidential and cabinet-level diplomatic engagement. The administration also created, supported, and resourced new institutions to advance US diplomacy and peace efforts.

By the end of the administration, the wars in Liberia, Sierra Leone, Burundi, Angola, Sudan North-South, and the civil and regional war in the Democratic Republic of the Congo had ended. The conflict in Darfur and insecurity in Eastern Congo continued, but with infrastructure in place to support their resolution. A civil war was averted after Kenya's violent 2007 elections.

TRANSITION MEMORANDUM

~~SECRET~~ WITH
SECRET/NOFORN
ATTACHMENTS

NATIONAL SECURITY COUNCIL
WASHINGTON, D.C. 20504

6927
Transition

January 16, 2009

MEMORANDUM FOR THE RECORD

FROM: BOBBY PITTMAN, AFRICAN AFFAIRS

SUBJECT: Africa Conflict Resolution Policy

THE SITUATION AS WE FOUND IT:

Protracted Conflicts. When the Administration assumed office in 2001, there were six major conflicts in Sub-Saharan Africa (Angola, Democratic Republic of the Congo, Burundi, Sierra Leone, Liberia, and Sudan North-South). Some of these conflicts, such as the Sudan conflict, had lasted several decades. The overall impact in terms of lives lost and economic destruction was catastrophic. The Sudan North-South conflict killed an estimated 2 million people, and over 5 million died as a result of the Congo war. Despite efforts by previous administrations to secure lasting peace, these conflicts continued unabated.

U.S. Conflict Strategy. Africa conflict strategy during the previous administration largely focused on addressing humanitarian needs and capitalizing on targets of opportunity. The previous administration was constrained by limited budgetary resources and attention by senior policymakers. Bilateral aid to Africa declined from roughly $1.2 billion in 1992 to $635 million in 1996. Aid levels did not return to pre-1992 levels until 2001. Even then, a significant percentage of African aid was focused on humanitarian issues. This did not allow for adequate support to African policymakers to improve peacekeeping capacity and address underlying development, social, and political issues. This approach limited their ability to wield regional diplomatic influence and address conflict.

Limited Regional Peacekeeping Capacity. In 2001, most subregional organizations in Africa did not possess the capacity to plan, deploy, and manage sizable peacekeeping missions. The main exception was the Economic Community of West African States (ECOWAS), anchored by the

~~SECRET~~ WITH SECRET/NOFORN ATTACHMENTS
Reason: 1.4(b)(d)
Declassify on: 1/16/29

NSC Declassification Review [E.O. 13526]
DECLASSIFY IN PART
by William C. Carpenter 3/23/2020

Nigerian military. Several individual countries, such as South Africa, possessed sufficient capacity to deploy peacekeepers as well.

U.S. Peacekeeping Training. The Clinton administration began large-scale peacekeeping training assistance in 1997, when it launched the African Crisis Response Initiative (ACRI). The ACRI's annual budget was roughly $20 million. Between 1997 and 2000, this program trained nearly 6,000 peacekeepers from 7 African countries. Four countries (Benin, Ghana, Mali, and Senegal) sent peacekeepers to the United Nations (U.N.) or regional missions. However, the United States did not provide significant airlift support to help African militaries deploy peacekeepers, limiting the ACRI's effectiveness in alleviating the shortage of peacekeeping capacity for subregional and U.N. missions.

THE ADMINISTRATION'S POLICY:

This Administration has been guided by the following overarching principles:

- Facilitate peace by working with and within the region, including through regional leads (rather than imposing peace arrangements from outside);
- Build regional capacities to make and sustain peace; and
- Work through multilateral channels, such as the U.N., and the World Bank, to ensure that peacekeeping and reconstruction have broad international support and financial backing.

WHAT HAS BEEN ACCOMPLISHED:

Following the principles outlined above, the United States, in close coordination with other actors, has helped resolve all major conflicts that existed when it took office (Angola, Burundi, Democratic Republic of the Congo, Liberia, Sierra Leone, and Sudan North-South). In nearly every instance, the African Union or sub-regional organizations played a leading role in mediating peace talks and providing peacekeepers. The United States played a supporting or facilitating role as needed.

Sudan North-South. In his first month in office, the President ordered a comprehensive policy review on Sudan that would put in place the policies and structures that would fundamentally alter our relations with Sudan, help end Africa's longest running civil war, and posture the United States for responding to the unforeseen crisis in Darfur. In May of 2001, the President named Andrew Natsios as Special Humanitarian Coordinator for Sudan and by September had named Senator John Danforth as his Special Envoy for Sudan, creating at the same time a dedicated Office of Sudan Programs inside the State Department to support our diplomatic efforts. Under the direction of the Special Envoy and the President, the United States ended its diplomatic isolation of the

Khartoum regime. We took steps to expand our efforts to cooperate on countering terrorism inside Sudan, tried to convince Khartoum to end its regional destabilization efforts, and pressured the North on a just peace with the South.

The United States supported these latter efforts through the sub-regional organization, the Intergovernmental Authority on Development (IGAD), which led the mediation between the Sudanese Government and the Sudan People's Liberation Movement (SPLM) leadership. Throughout the years of negotiations, the President conducted targeted interventions, as needed, in support of former Kenyan President Moi's efforts in Naivasha, Kenya. The President dispatched a team of diplomats to support the peace talks. In October 2002, the President signed into law the Sudan Peace Act which solidified U.S. support for the multilateral peace effort already underway and included sanctions options for compelling Khartoum to continue negotiations in good faith. In December 2003, the President called President Bashir and SPLM leader John Garang to press for their continued discussions over wealth-sharing. The President made similar calls on two other occasions in 2004, both times when it looked like the peace process was close to collapse, as in March when the President pushed for a final agreement on the status of Abyei, or in November when he pushed for the parties to sign onto the final peace agreement.

These collective efforts led to the historic Comprehensive Peace Agreement (CPA) that was signed in January 2005. The Agreement established the Government of National Unity, wealth-sharing arrangements, provisions for national elections before July 2009, and protocols for moving Sudanese and SPLM troops away from the border. The U.N. and the World Bank have supported this agreement through a robust peacekeeping presence and large reconstruction efforts in Southern Sudan. To date, the United States has supported implementation with more than $2 billion in humanitarian, development, and security sector reform assistance to the South.

Six months after signing the peace agreement, SPLA leader John Garang died in a helicopter crash, calling implementation of the entire agreement into question. Immediately afterward, in August 2005, the President again called President Bashir and Garang's widow, Rebecca, to urge their continued commitment to the CPA. By November, Garang's replacement, Salva Kiir, was in Washington for meetings with Vice President Cheney and Secretary Rice, as a signal of clear U.S. support to the South. That same month, the United States opened it first consulate in Juba, capital of Southern Sudan. By May of 2006, the President once again called President Bashir to press for his continued implementation of the CPA and by July of that year, Salva Kiir was received in the Oval Office for the first of three meetings with the President over the next 2 years as a demonstration of U.S. support to the peace process. Throughout this era, the President was served by a succession of Special Envoys and senior officials, including John Danforth, Robert Zoellick, Andrew Natsios, and Richard Williamson, all of whom traveled frequently to the region and reported back to the President at regular intervals with reports of progress and roadblocks on the path to sustained peace.

Liberia. The Administration worked with the international community for several years to remove Charles Taylor from power and end Liberia's destructive civil war. In 2003, the United Nations Security Council, with support from the United States, adopted a resolution to extend the existing diamond ban, arms embargo, and travel ban to include a 10-month ban on the export of Liberian timber products. This severely crippled Charles Taylor's ability to supply and arm his forces. At the same time, the United States supported peace talks led by the Economic Community of West African States (ECOWAS). On June 26, 2003, prior to departing for his first trip to Africa, President Bush gave a speech at the Corporate Council on Africa, calling on Charles Taylor to step down. The need for Taylor to step down remained a central discussion point with African leaders during the trip to Africa. Upon returning from the trip, President Bush met with United Nations Secretary General Kofi Annan in the Oval Office and reiterated the United States position on Liberia. In early August, President Bush insisted that Taylor must leave Liberia before U.S. Marines deployed to assist in humanitarian relief efforts. Taylor stepped down on August 11, 2003 and went into exile in Nigeria. Three days later, 200 U.S. Marines accompanied an ECOWAS peacekeeping force to secure the port in Monrovia, restore delivery of humanitarian assistance, and establish order in the capital. A U.N. peacekeeping force followed this mission.

The United States also played a lead role in the effort to pass UNSCR 1635 which authorized the United Nations Mission in Liberia to arrest Charles Taylor and transfer him to the Special Court for Sierra Leone (SCSL). In March 2006, Taylor was arrested and eventually taken into custody by the SCSL. The arrest was coordinated by the United Nations and the United States, working closely with President Sirleaf of Liberia, President Obasanjo of Nigeria, and President Kabbah of Sierra Leone. The United States pushed for Taylor to be imprisoned at International Criminal Court facilities in the interest of regional security. Taylor was transferred to The Hague in June 2006, where the SCSL is trying him for crimes against humanity.

Since 2003, the United States has provided $750 million in bilateral assistance to rebuild the Liberian national army, build government capacity, and help deliver services to the Liberian people. In October 2005, President Bush sent a Presidential Delegation to observe Liberia's elections. In January 2006, First Lady Laura Bush and Secretary of State Condoleezza Rice headed the Presidential Delegation that was sent to participate in President Ellen Johnson Sirleaf's historic inauguration. Since her inauguration, President Bush has met with President Sirleaf four times in the Oval Office to discuss key issues such as security sector reform, debt relief, education and health programming, and governance reforms. President Bush and First Lady Laura Bush also traveled to Liberia in February 2008.

The United States has committed $423 million in bilateral debt relief for Liberia. The United States also led the negotiations that resulted in the international financial institutions committing $1.5 billion in debt relief to the new government and over $440 million in additional financing.

Democratic Republic of the Congo (DRC). The United States worked closely with South Africa and the international community to end the destructive and destabilizing civil war that lasted between 1998 and 2002. At one point, there were at least seven foreign national armies on Congolese soil involved in the fighting. The United States, through high-level engagement and pressure, supported South Africa's mediation effort leading to the Sun City Agreement in April 2002. The Agreement outlined a framework that led to a unified and multiparty government and democratic elections. In September 2002, President Bush worked closely with South African President Mbeki to broker the withdrawal of Rwandan troops from the DRC. The United States launched the Tripartite Joint Commission in 2004—with the DRC, Rwanda, and Uganda—to prevent renewed conflict and address issues in Central Africa. In 2006, the United States, working closely with bilateral and multilateral partners, supported the DRC's first free and fair elections in over 40 years. Following the landmark election, the United States has supported the elected governments' efforts to address remaining internal security challenges. In October 2007, President Bush hosted President Kabila at the White House to discuss bringing peace to eastern DRC and economic development across the country. Since then, the United States facilitated two agreements that outline a framework for demobilizing remaining armed groups in eastern Congo, including the Forces for Democratic Liberation of Rwanda (FDLR). The United States provided $2.3 billion in bilateral debt relief to the DRC; the international financial institutions will ultimately provide over $7 billion in debt relief.

Angola. The United States supported U.N. sanctions against the National Union for the Total Independence of Angola (UNITA) and also worked with the Government of Angola and regional leaders to encourage Angola's democratic transition and recovery from civil war. UNITA's leader was killed on February 22, 2002. Four days after his death, President Bush held a pull-aside with Angolan President dos Santos and urged him to reach out to UNITA leaders to come to a peaceful resolution of Angola's 26-year long civil war. President dos Santos also met with Vice President Cheney and Secretary of State Powell and promised to pursue political negotiations with UNITA rather than a military victory. A formal cease-fire was signed on April 4, 2002. From 2002–2004, senior Administration officials engaged with the Angolan Government to encourage consolidation of the peace process. In May 2004, President Bush received President dos Santos in the Oval Office and dos Santos promised to hold elections in 2006. In June 2005, President Bush announced that Angola was selected as a pilot country for the President's Malaria Initiative.

Burundi. The United States supported the efforts of the United Nations, the African Union, and regional leaders to help bring an end to Burundi's civil war. In 2002, President Bush wrote on a National Security Council briefing paper on Burundi that he wanted to prevent genocide on his watch. This led to a series of focused planning efforts to prevent a worsening of Burundi's civil conflict. From 2002–2003, the U.S. implemented a diplomatic strategy designed to urge the deployment of a regional peacekeeping force to Burundi. In September 2003, President Bush met with South African President Mbeki at the U.N. General Assembly and offered financial support for an African Union force in Burundi. The African Union Mission to Burundi began in 2003 and eventually transitioned to the United Nations Operation in Burundi. From 2004–2005, U.S. diplomats continued to work with Burundi's political leaders to keep the transition on track leading to Burundi's national elections which brought Pierre Nkurunziza to power. In September 2005, Burundi joined the Tripartite Process, a U.S.-facilitated mechanism designed to address instability in the Great Lakes region. The process became known as the Tripartite Plus Process. In December 2007, Secretary Rice hosted a meeting with the heads of state from the Tripartite Plus Process countries in Ethiopia where the leaders recommitted to continue efforts to bring peace to and address instability in the Great Lakes.

Sierra Leone: Prior to the war being declared over, the United States pushed for United Nations sanctions and a U.N. Mission in Sierra Leone. From FY 2003—FY 2007, the United States provided $48 million to the Special Court for Sierra Leone which was a special tribunal designed to deal with the perpetrators most responsible for the atrocities against civilians. The United States also supported Sierra Leone's Truth and Reconciliation Commission (TRC) which created an independent, objective, and impartial record of abuses committed during the conflict. In 2007, the United States provided nearly $4 million in assistance for elections and governance programs. In September, 2007 Sierra Leone held successful elections and Ernest Koroma was sworn-in as President.

Peacekeeping Operations Support. The Administration expanded the existing African Crisis Response Initiative after assuming office in terms of the number of countries, troops trained, and the type of assistance. In 2004, this initiative expanded to become the Africa Contingency Operations Training Assistance (ACOTA) program. ACOTA focuses on training African trainers and programs tailored to individual country needs. Furthermore, the Administration convinced the G8 to adopt the same approach and commit to training and equipping 75,000 troops by 2010, with a focus on Africa. To date, the Administration has provided training and nonlethal equipment to over 55,000 peacekeepers from 18 African countries. The Administration also increased assistance for equipment and unit deployment, which significantly enhanced regional capacity to field peacekeeping missions. The countries whose troops have been trained under this program have sent peacekeeping contingents to Sudan, Sierra Leone, DRC, Guinea-Bissau, Central African Republic, Ethiopia-Eritrea border area, Cote d'Ivoire, Liberia, Burundi, Somalia, Kosovo, Beirut, and Haiti. In FY07, ACOTA funding (including supplemental funds) totaled $50 million. The FY08 enacted budget is $44 million. Global training operations also have provided peacekeeping capacity that may be deployed to operations in Africa.

FUTURE CHALLENGES:

Sudan/Darfur. At the outset of the Administration, the situation in Darfur was quiet, even though the seeds of marginalization and unrest were present. Violence spiked very quickly in 2003, resulting in the death of roughly 200,000 people and the displacement of an additional two million. The central tenet of the Administration's policy has been the deployment of a sizable and capable international peacekeeping force, which has been painfully slow to deploy. The African Union Mission in Sudan (AMIS) force that began deploying in 2004 transitioned to a U.N. blue-helmeted operation on January 1, 2008, but given logistical constraints, bureau-cratic impediments, lack of troop-contributing country capacity, and Sudanese intransigence, the deployment of the bulk of the force has been severely delayed. Our goal of having the entire force deployed by the end of 2008 has gone unmet. Speeding up the deployment of peacekeepers must remain our essential priority, but it must be coupled with promoting a political dialogue between rebel combatants and the Sudanese Government, promoting a more efficient and effective U.N. mediation process, and putting pressure on potential spoilers to refrain from undermining the peace process. We are currently diplomatically engaged in all of these efforts.

In the final days of the Administration we will begin a new program of non-reimbursable airlift operations in support of the U.N. deployment. However, as the United Nations dithers in trying to deploy a new set of troop contributors in the Spring of 2009, more U.S. air support may be necessary if our desire for rapid deployment is maintained. This effort to deploy as many peacekeepers as quickly as possible takes on even greater importance in the context of a potential International Criminal Court (ICC) indictment of Sudanese President Bashir, which many U.N. officials and outside observers believe could once again drive home Sudanese fears of regime change and turn the government from mildly cooperative to openly hostile to any U.N. presence. This potential to quickly erode our modest gains to date cannot be overstated. The U.N., despite its Chapter VII mandate, is still very much an uninvited guest in Sudan In this context, we are challenged by a group of European allies who, through their support of the ICC, believe that justice must be carried out to preserve the legitimacy of the ICC's mandate irrespective of the potential consequences to the peace process on the ground. Thus far, we have maintained silence over our potential support for an Article XVI resolution that would delay any potential ICC action for up to twelve months. Moreover, to the extent that actions by the ICC can be delayed we likely increase the time we have to achieve real progress on the ground. [See also the Darfur Transition Memo]

Sudan North-South. The Comprehensive Peace Agreement has proven to be a durable accord, but it is not immune from potentially unraveling. Though progress has been made, important deadlines and benchmarks have not yet been met, which could derail the agreement. The most important benchmark is the conduct of national elections throughout Sudan sometime in mid- to late 2009. Key elements of the Abyei Protocol also have still not been implemented; primary among them is the border demarcation between North and South, through the country's most important oil fields. The methods by which the border is drawn, oil revenue is finally divided, and compensation for preexisting oil infrastructure is agreed upon remain outstanding and are contentious issues which could ultimately derail adherence to the Agreement. Lastly, and perhaps most importantly, the 2011 referendum on Southern succession, as required under the terms of the CPA, looms large in the conscious of all Sudanese. Much like the CPA itself, the conduct and outcome of the referendum will be precedent setting. The U.S. commitment to implementation of all aspects of the CPA will remain crucial to its survival and for Sudan avoiding a return to war. Parallel to that effort must be a renewed U.S. commitment to strengthening the South's capacity to govern itself politically and financially, and defend itself militarily. These efforts should be viewed in the context of helping to make the Government of Southern Sudan an equal partner to Khartoum within the Government of National Unity, with the understanding that it also bolsters its chances for survival as an independent state depending on the outcome of the 2011 referendum.

Eastern Congo. While there are frameworks in place for the demobilization of remaining armed groups in eastern Congo, implementation remains slow. In October 2008, tensions rose between Congo and Rwanda with Rwanda claiming that the Congolese military continues to work directly with the Democratic Forces for the Liberation of Rwanda (FDLR) and the Congo claiming that Rwanda is supporting Laurent Nkunda and his rebel forces. Nkunda continues to express his disdain for the Kabila government and his recent attempts to take more territory in eastern DRC have worsened the already precarious humanitarian situation. We should continue to support the U.N. Special Envoy, former Nigerian President Obasanjo, in his efforts to facilitate a dialogue between the Government of the Congo and Laurent Nkunda's National Congress for the Defense of the People. We must also continue to push for resolution of the FDLR issue and the maintenance of a robust U.N. peacekeeping force.

Lord's Resistance Army (LRA). Efforts to deal once and for all with Joseph Kony and his roughly 1,000 LRA fighters began anew in December 2008 through an historic military and diplomatic collaboration between Uganda, Congo, and Southern Sudan. After Kony failed for a fifth time to sign the Final Peace Agreement with the Government of Uganda in late November, Kampala began to operationalize a combat action that had been nearly one year in the planning.

Perhaps of even greater value, however, has been the United States political and diplomatic support for this mission, based on our shared belief that Kony was using the peace process to regroup and rearm and that he represented a real and growing threat to four nations in the region. Key to the operation were several interventions by the President, National Security Advisor Hadley, Secretary Rice, and Assistant Secretary Frazer with Presidents Kabila and Museveni _____ to ensure proper diplomatic support and coordination. As of late December, Joseph Kony has not yet been brought to justice and is believed to be alive and on the run. However, all LRA base camps and crops have been destroyed and the group has deeply splintered. Short of killing or capturing Joseph Kony, our shared regional objective of eroding the strength of the LRA and degrading its ability to foment violence and instability is being achieved. Concerted diplomatic support to the operation will remain crucial going forward, especially if Kony is not killed or captured, requiring Ugandan forces to perhaps extend their time inside of Congo. Also, in the hoped for event that LRA leadership is decapitated and the hundreds of thousands of people currently displaced from their homes feel able to return, the United States should continue to play a lead role in assisting in rebuilding of so many communities devastated by Kony's wrath.

Attachments

Tab 1   Chronology for Sudan North/South

Tab 2   Chronology for Liberia

Tab 3   Chronology for Democratic Republic of Congo

Tab 4   Chronology for Angola

Tab 5   Chronology for Burundi

Tab 6   Chronology for Sierra Leone

Tab 7   Summary of Conclusions for the Principals Committee Meeting on Sudan, March 27, 2001

Tab 8   Report to the President of the United States on the Outlook for Peace in Sudan, April 26, 2002

Tab 9   Memorandum of Telephone Conversation between the President and Chairman Garang, March 22, 2003

Tab 10   Discussion Paper from Principals Committee Meeting on Sudan, July 1, 2003

POSTSCRIPT

JENDAYI FRAZER, BOBBY PITTMAN, JOHN SIMON

The Bush administration's strategy to facilitate sustainable peace in Africa required:

- Focusing on strategic African partners and prioritizing the conflicts for resolution;
- Supporting Africa's reforming states, the African Union, and subregional organizations; and
- Leveraging US power with coalitions of willing countries and multilateral institutions.[1]

The Bush Administration Approach

The first strategic choice entailed identifying partners with the diplomatic and military capabilities in each subregion to help end Africa's major wars. Nigeria, Kenya, Ethiopia, and South Africa were clear choices given their negotiating and peacekeeping experience, relative stability, and subregional political and economic leadership. The administration also partnered with the African Union, the subregional organizations, especially the Economic Community of West African States (ECOWAS) and the Inter-Governmental Authority on Drought and Disaster (IGAD), and the region's capable reforming states such as Senegal, Ghana, Mali, and later Rwanda and Uganda. These organizations and countries formed diplomatic coalitions for peacemaking. In 2006 the administration appointed an ambassador and staff to the African Union, becoming the first non-African country with a dedicated diplomatic mission to the African Union (USAU).

Second, came prioritizing conflicts with the greatest casualties, and most damaging to regional stability. Sudan North-South, Democratic Republic of the Congo (DRC), Sierra Leone, and Liberia stood at the top of the agenda. As the strategy unfolded, new opportunities and new threats emerged, requiring attention, including in Angola, Burundi, Darfur, and Kenya. The death of UNITA's Jonas Savimbi in February 2002 created space to end an almost three-decades-long

---

1. President George W. Bush, "The National Security Strategy of the United States of America," The White House, September 2002, https://georgewbush-whitehouse.archives.gov/nsc/nss/2002/.

civil war in Angola. President Bush decided in 2002 that the threat of a possible genocide in Burundi required preemptive diplomatic action. The Darfur conflict, starting in 2003, descended into genocide, and also threatened the administration's Sudan North-South peace efforts. The failure of Kenya's leaders and institutions to resolve its disputed 2007 election led to widespread ethnic conflict that threatened civil war, which led the United States to play a key leadership role in mobilizing international diplomatic efforts to end the crisis.

Third, supporting capable forces was key to protecting civilians and implementing peace agreements. Working through the UN Security Council, the Bush administration pushed for more robust missions, with better trained peacekeepers, and the necessary mandates and rules of engagement for peace enforcement. The administration launched several security assistance initiatives to train and equip peacekeepers through the Africa Contingency Operations Training Assistance Initiative (ACOTA), which was incorporated into the Global Peace Operations Initiative (GPOI) in 2004. To support African nations facing the growing threat of terrorism, the administration supported counterterrorism training and cooperation with the East Africa Counterterrorism Initiative, which in 2009 became the Partnership for Regional East Africa Counterterrorism (PREACT); and the Pan-Sahel Initiative that transitioned to the Trans-Sahara Counterterrorism Partnership (TSCTP) in 2005. The administration also provided intelligence assets, armored personnel carriers, and airlift for deploying African peacekeepers to improve their operational capability. A new combatant command, US Africa Command (AFRICOM), was created in 2007 with responsibility for all US Department of Defense operations, exercises, and security cooperation on the African continent.

Underlying the Bush administration approach was the recognition that ownership rested with Africa, especially the countries in conflict, and their neighbors impacted by war. Behind African leadership, the United States could play supporting roles as a reliable partner, back needed institutions and initiatives, and project hard and soft power.

What Has Happened Since the End of the Bush Administration?

Stressor events such as economic crises, ethnic and religious divisions and marginalization, and especially national elections that raise country-wide tensions, can push Africa's fragile democracies and postconflict societies into war. Power transferring from one political party to another through free and fair elections is an important milestone in the consolidation of peace. The withdrawal of peace-keepers is also a key test for the stability of postconflict societies.

By these indicators, Liberia, Sierra Leone, and Angola have achieved relative stability following decades of civil war. Liberia and Sierra Leone have held three postwar presidential and parliamentary elections, and power has shifted peacefully from ruling to opposition presidential candidates. The UN peacekeepers first deployed to Sierra Leone in 1999 left in December 2005, and those deployed to Liberia in 2003 withdrew in February 2018. Both countries also weathered the Ebola pandemic from 2014 to 2016 with significant assistance from the Obama administration. Angola's civil war ended with UNITA's transition from insurgent force to opposition political party in 2003. Power finally changed hands when President dos Santos stepped down after thirty-eight years, and the ruling-party candidate Joao Lourenco was elected in August 2017. Angola has achieved stability but not yet a full democratic transition since the governing party continues to dominate Angolan politics.

The Sudan North-South Comprehensive Peace Agreement held, although overcoming the many delays required active engagement by the Bush and Obama administrations. The Obama team successfully shepherded the January 2011 referendum for South Sudan's independence, but then turned its attention elsewhere, and without key diplomats in place, failed to engage to prevent the Republic of South Sudan's descent into civil war from 2013 to 2016.[2] Fighting started over lingering ethnic tensions and a dispute within the ruling party between the president and vice president over who would run for president. The Obama and Trump administrations sent senior-level diplomatic missions to Juba and the region, and imposed asset freezes and travel bans on individuals on both sides to resolve the crisis. A 2018 power-sharing agreement was signed but has not yet led to nationwide peace. UN peacekeepers deployed in July 2011 remain in-country today.

The Darfur conflict was declared over by the Government of Sudan in February 2010; however, conflict still lingers with one rebel group still active. War-related deaths significantly declined in Darfur over the years since the deployment of the African Union Mission (AMIS) in 2004 and its rehatting as an

---

2. Jon Temin, *From Independence to Civil War: Atrocity Prevention and US Policy Toward South Sudan*, US Holocaust Memorial Museum, July 2018, 13–15, https://www.ushmm.org/m/pdfs/Jon_Temin_South_Sudan_Report_July_2018.pdf.

AU-UN mission (UNAMID) in July 2017. UNAMID's mission ended in December 2020 with a phased drawdown concluded on June 30, 2021.

The Democratic Republic of the Congo held three general elections in 2006, 2011, and 2018; each more flawed than the last. Power transferred to an opposition candidate in 2018 after President Kabila failed in his efforts to change the constitution to allow him a third term in office and following significant domestic and international pressure. The Congo's armed forces still struggle to secure the DRC's large territory against local militias, especially in eastern Congo. The intercommunal conflicts have not resulted in a return to civil war, but UN peacekeepers first deployed in 1999 remain in the DRC, reflecting that country-wide stability remains elusive.[3]

In Burundi, international action helped prevent genocide, and because the country was on a sufficient path to stabilization, UN peacekeepers withdrew in December 2006. After two successful elections in August 2005 and June 2010, in April 2015 the country descended into five years of low-intensity conflict when President Nkurunziza held on to power for an unconstitutional third term in office. In May 2020 the ruling party candidate Evariste Ndayishimiye won the presidency, opening a new window for peace diplomacy.

Over the last fifteen years, Kenya's institutions have proven more capable of mediating conflict than in its 2007 election, which was marked not only by violence but also by the failure of its institutions to adjudicate the dispute between President Kibaki and opposition candidate Raila Odinga. In 2007, the head of the electoral commission admitted not knowing who won the contest, and the opposition took to the streets rather than petition a court they considered illegitimate and under the control of the executive. A power-sharing agreement, mediated by Kofi Annan, and backed by the African Union and the international community, prevented both candidates from imposing themselves as leader of the country. Under the agreement Kibaki remained president and Odinga became prime minister.

---

3. The first mission, the United Nations Organization Mission (MONUC), was mandated in July 1999 to support the end of the regional war in DRC that involved Angola, Namibia, Rwanda, Uganda, and Zimbabwe. It was renamed the United Nations Organization Stabilization Mission in the DRC (MONUSCO) in July 2010 with the mandate to protect civilians, humanitarian workers, and assist the government with its stabilization and peace consolidation efforts. MONUC United Nations Organization Mission to the Democratic Republic of the Congo, "MONUC Background," https://peacekeeping.un.org/mission/past/monuc/background.shtml.

Since then, Kenya has changed its laws and amended its constitution to strengthen its institutions, which have gained greater legitimacy. The 2013 election saw Uhuru Kenyatta win a very narrow victory declared by the electoral commission. Raila Odinga contested the results through Kenya's Supreme Court rather than calling for street demonstrations that could lead to violence. The next general election in August 2017 was a rare case where an African high court ruled against the incumbent and accepted Odinga's claims that the electronic vote tally was hacked. The court annulled the results and ordered fresh presidential elections. Kenyatta accepted the legitimacy of the court to rule but questioned the judgment. He went on to win the rerun election in October 2017 that Odinga boycotted, arguing that the electoral commission must be reformed before the contest because he was widely believed to have run out of campaign funds.

Kenya's civil society remains an important force pushing for nonviolent and credible elections since the success of its "Save Our Beloved Country" campaign to stop ethnic violence in 2007. Postelection violence in 2017 resulted in a reported fifty deaths compared to 1,000 in 2007. Tensions are building in advance of its upcoming election in August 2022, but Kenya's institutions are stronger today, if not fully consolidated, in the face of ethnic-based political mobilization by politicians hoping to govern all Kenyans.

The most significant change in Africa's conflict landscape is the spread of terrorism from the Horn of Africa across the Sahel and into West Africa and northern Mozambique. At the end of the Bush administration the main terror threats were al Qaeda and Al-Shabaab operating in Somalia and the Algerian-origin Salafist Group for Preaching and Combat (GSPC), rebranded al Qaeda in the Islamic Maghreb (AQIM) in 2006, which operates across the Sahel. The terror threat spread exponentially with the collapse of the Libyan state following NATO's intervention against Muammar Gaddafi in 2011. Fighters and arms spilling out of Libya became the spark for a more lethal conflict environment that resulted in a coup in democratic Mali in March 2012. Today there is a growing number of African terror groups linked to global terror networks, including both al Qaeda and the Islamic State of Iraq and the Levant (ISIL). In Africa, the jihadist threat to regional stability and international order is most active in the Lake Chad Basin, the Sahel, Libya, Somalia, and now Mozambique.

China's rising influence constitutes the major geostrategic shift in Africa, especially as America's engagement waned precipitously during the Trump administration. China's expanding trade and infrastructure investments in Africa paved the way for its growing political influence and security footprint, which threaten to undermine US interests, access, and operations. Chinese peacekeepers are deployed in nine operations across Africa. Except for the United States, China contributes more than any other permanent members of the UN Security Council to peace operations. In 2017 China acquired military basing rights near the US Naval Expeditionary base in Djibouti. China's growing dominance in Africa's telecommunication infrastructure poses a counterintelligence threat to the United States and African countries.[4] China is also acquiring African broadcasting stations and offering young Africans scholarships to China as part of its ideological contest for hearts and minds. African countries that make up more than a quarter of UN member states now regularly vote in line with China's political agenda.[5]

How Did the Bush Administration Do?

- *Diplomatic engagement*: A key differentiator for the success of the Bush administration was that President Bush expended his personal capital to resolve Africa's six civil and regional conflicts. President Bush, National Security Advisers Condoleezza Rice and Stephen Hadley, and Secretary of State Colin Powell's high-level engagement signaled the priority the administration placed on African conflict resolution. Their intensive diplomatic efforts allowed the United States to keep African mediators at the forefront by coordinating with the many Western peace envoys and preventing African combatants from "forum shopping" in hopes of more favorable terms. With new actors, including Saudi Arabia, United Arab Emirates, Qatar, Russia, and Turkey, increasingly involved in African conflicts, this role will be ever more important and yet far more difficult.
- *Conflict resolution*: There has been considerable continuity in the approach to resolving conflicts, and the institutions and security assistance initiatives, of the Bush, Obama, and Trump administrations. To varying de-

---

4. Judd Devermont, "Implications of China's Presence and Investment in Africa," Statement before the Senate Armed Services Committee, Subcommittee on Emerging Threats and Capabilities, December 12, 2018.

5. Yun Sun, "The Strategic Implications of Chinese Investments in Africa," Testimony before the Subcommittee on Emerging Threats and Capabilities of the Senate Armed Services Committee, December 12, 2018.

grees, all forged regional coalitions, built regional capabilities, and leveraged multilateral institutions to cut off assistance to warring parties; negotiate peace agreements; stand up capable peace-enforcement contingents to protect lives; and support implementation of cease-fire and peace agreements. Presidents Bush and Obama adopted holistic approaches to conflict prevention and resolution that recognized democracy, development, and peace are inextricably linked. Both administrations worked through multilateral channels, such as the UN and the World Bank, and regional organizations like the AU and ECOWAS, to ensure that peacekeeping and reconstruction had broad international support, financial backing, and local leadership. The Trump administration, by contrast, was more unilateral in its approach and avoided the kind of personal presidential engagement exhibited by his two predecessors.

- *Countering terrorism*: The Bush administration used a combination of diplomatic engagement, regional capacity building and cooperative security initiatives (such as TSCTP and EACTI), and occasional drone strikes against high-value targets, especially in Somalia, to defeat and deter the transnational threats operating mainly in Somalia and the Sahel. The Obama and Trump administrations also supported the creation and training of African multinational coalitions supported by NATO countries and US combat forces—specifically, the G-5 Sahel Joint Force made up of Burkina Faso, Chad, Niger, Mali, and Mauritania, and the Lake Basin Multinational Task Force (MNTJF) made up of Benin, Cameroon, Chad, Niger, and Nigeria. Both Presidents Obama and Trump went beyond intelligence, logistics, and air support to deploy more US fighters in theaters supporting regional joint counterinsurgency operations in the Sahel[6] and East Africa.[7] While these

---

6. The US Air Force built a new facility (Air Base 201) in 2020 to host unmanned aerial surveillance flights in Agadez, Niger, and to support US Special Forces that accompany partner countries on CT missions. Judd Devermont and Marielle Harris, "Rethinking Crisis Responses in the Sahel," CSIS Briefs, December 2020, 1–12. Washington, D.C.: Center for Strategic and International Studies, https://www.csis.org/analysis/rethinking-crisis-responses-sahel.

7. The Obama administration deployed US Special Forces in Kismayo and Camp Bale Dogle in Lower Shabelle Somalia to undertake intelligence, drone strikes, special operations, and military assistance programs in support of the multinational African Union Mission in Somalia (AMISOM) established during the Bush administration. Ty McCormick, "US Operates Drones From Secret Bases in Somalia," *Foreign Policy*,

military operations have succeeded in reducing the extremists' military capability and scope of operations, they have also led to fragmentation, with new groups forming, and have failed to create the conditions for sustained stability.

- *Balancing China*: China was not a major competitor undermining US influence in Africa during the Bush administration. Under Hu Jintao, China's interests in Africa were mainly mercantilist. Africa was a source of natural resources and provided markets for Chinese exports. While China exported weapons to rogue regimes in Sudan and Zimbabwe, it had no real military footprint in Africa and showed no signs of becoming a serious competitor. At the time, Washington did not view China's increasing investment in African infrastructure as a threat to American interests. This changed in 2013 with Xi Jinping's rise to power; his more ambitious global aspirations transformed China into a clear strategic competitor to the United States. China's Belt and Road initiative, the primary vehicle for its investment in Africa's ports, rails, roads, and energy sectors, has commercial, security, and strategic consequences for US foreign policy. China's rapid advancement stands in contrast to US global retrenchment under Trump's America First approach. The Trump administration largely ended the high-level engagement with African leaders on development challenges and strategic US private-sector investments. In contrast, President Xi Jinping and his foreign minister have made over nineteen trips to sub-Saharan African countries since January 2017.[8] The triennial Summit-level Forum for China-Africa Cooperation (FOCAC) meetings are attended by nearly all African heads of state. High-level reengagement between the United States and Africa is needed to counter China's increasing regional influence.

What Are the Lessons Learned?

The overarching guiding principles of the Bush administration's Africa conflict resolution policy remain relevant and offer six key lessons learned. The last two lessons have become even more important with hindsight.

July 2, 2015, https://foreignpolicy.com/2015/07/02/exclusive-u-s-operates-drones-from -secret-bases-in-somalia-special-operations-jsoc-black-hawk-down/.

8. Devermont, "Implications of China's Presence and Investment in Africa."

- *Facilitate peace by working with and within the region as a partner.* Early and consistent engagement by the US president and US senior officials with African leaders and officials is essential to advance and protect US interests in Africa. While President Bush personally engaged from the first days of his administration, President Obama turned more attention to Africa conflict resolution during his second term, including hosting the very successful US Africa Leader's Summit in August 2014 in Washington, DC. President Trump showed little interest in Africa and never visited the region in four years. This presidential neglect degraded US regional influence. The lessons are:
  - No region can be considered peripheral to US national security, especially with China seeking to replace US global primacy, and extremist threats at home and abroad;
  - Regaining the US diplomatic edge requires US presidents to build personal relations with African leaders at the outset of their terms, especially with key partner countries; and
  - Consider reviving the US Africa Leader's Summit as an annual or biennial event.
- *Build regional capacities to make and sustain peace.* While Africa has many skilled diplomats and peace negotiators, more needs to be done to build African peacekeeping capabilities and capacity for rapid deployment to prevent and to end future conflicts. The Bush administration supported rapid deployment of African Union peacekeeping missions in Burundi, Liberia, Somalia, and Darfur that were eventually rehatted, as the slower, but better resourced, UN peacekeeping missions mobilized. The lessons are:
  - Support partner coordination of training assistance programs to the African Union and subregional organizations to build institutional and interoperable peace-enforcement capabilities;
  - Utilize the Regional Arrangements Chapter VIII of the UN Charter to establish a sustainable financing mechanism for AU peacekeeping missions, for under Chapter VIII the Security Council can authorize the AU, as a regional organization, to undertake the task of maintaining international peace and security using the AU's Standby Force peacekeepers made up of military, police, and civilian contingents;

- ° A holistic approach combining development, governance, and counter-insurgency efforts is the best way over time to defeat terrorists, since battlefield victories are ephemeral; and
- ° Monitor congressional efforts to give authorities directly to AFRICOM to provide security assistance, as they risk undermining the State Department's diplomatic lead in US conflict resolution.
- *Work through multilateral channels to ensure peacekeeping and reconstruction have broad international support and financial backing.* Diplomatic engagement to prevent conflicts is far more effective than trying to end wars once they start. Until African countries make more progress consolidating democratic governance and building state capabilities, conflicts will break out. Somalia from the 1990s and Libya post-2013 show the consequences of failed states in Africa for US interests, including spawning terrorist safe havens. Liberia and Sierra Leone provide models where intensive diplomatic engagement, security assistance, and financial investment worked. The Bush administration rebuilt Liberia's army and heavily invested with the UN and World Bank in the country's reconstruction, and the United Kingdom did the same in neighboring Sierra Leone. In contrast, no lead country invested sufficient diplomatic capital in the DRC to reform its army and support its postconflict development and stability. As a result, twenty-two years later, UN peacekeepers remain in the DRC, while the average peacekeeping operation for the six conflicts prioritized by the Bush administration was twelve years. The lessons are:
  - ° Adopting a long-term view, and working multilaterally with the UN, World Bank, and other international organizations, are required for successful peace consolidation;
  - ° Maintaining the largely bipartisan US Africa policy allows successive administrations to continue peace efforts, building on the initiatives of prior administrations; and
  - ° The United States has multiple initiatives for addressing the development and social issues that underpin peaceful and stable countries, the foremost being African Growth and Opportunity Act (AGOA), the President's Emergency Plan for AIDS Relief (PEPFAR), the Millennium Challenge Account (MCC), Prosper Africa, and the US International Development Finance Corporation.

- *Adequate resourcing for these strategies is key.* There is a history of Africa policy not being backed by proper and adequate resourcing. The cross-cutting experience of the Bush administration demonstrated that with sufficient resources, these strategies can be successful. The administration grew the budgetary resources going to Africa significantly and across all dimensions. Moreover, President Bush spent his time in meetings with African leaders and in discussing strategy with key administration personnel. High-level administration officials spent a significant amount of time on Africa policy issues, and there were high-level efforts to recruit the best and the brightest to key Africa policy posts. The lessons are:
  - Ensure that bold policy initiatives are backed with proper and adequate budget resourcing;
  - Senior administration officials, including the president, must give adequate time to the efforts supporting the design and execution of these policy initiatives; and
  - Key Africa policy positions should be held by experienced Africa experts and not be traded off for internal bureaucratic personnel priorities.
- *Shore up efforts to promote democratic consolidation.* The Bush administration encouraged free elections as a route to enduring and sustainable democracies. However, a succession of leaders who gained power democratically then undermined democracy by overriding term limits or manipulating subsequent elections. In addition, contestation over elections is one of the key triggers leading to conflict and war in Africa. Elections remain the only legitimate avenue to power normatively; however, democratic space and election fairness are increasingly challenged. The lessons are:
  - Significantly scale up programs working with African parliaments (that can and have stopped presidents from abolishing term limits), with African courts (that are the main adjudicators of election disputes), and with regional organizations (like the AU and regional economic communities that monitor the legitimacy of elections) while maintaining programs engaging civil society prodemocracy advocates;
  - Strengthen and expand educational and cultural exchanges with African youth who are the strongest champions for democracy in Africa, including expanding the Young African Leaders Initiative (YALI); and

- Use quiet diplomacy and frank conversations—built on a foundation of strong prior engagement by the US president—which are often more effective than loud public statements.
- *Recognize that these strategies are challenged by China's emerging global aspirations.* During the Bush administration, China's narrow mercantilism made it easier for the United States to be a key influencer and partner of choice for Africa. Moreover, there was no active opposition by any leading global powers to the US push for democratic ideals and institutions. Now, China's elevated and broadened engagement is a direct challenge to democratic ideals and institutions across Africa. The lessons are:
  - It is especially important to engage and resource African institutions as those relationships will be challenged by China's ideology and resources;
  - The United States needs to enhance its support for democratic transitions and institutions given the alternative Chinese approach, bolstered by Chinese technology companies acting at the behest of the state;
  - Building long-term partnerships in the region will face competition from Chinese diplomacy and resources; and
  - The United States can best answer the China challenge in Africa by building a robust US Africa policy and engagement strategy rather than asking Africans to choose between two rival global powers.

CHAPTER 26

Middle East Peace

MICHAEL SINGH

Few of those working on Middle East policy during the George W. Bush administration would have suspected that his presidency would represent the high-water mark of Israeli-Palestinian peace diplomacy. Yet in hindsight this was indeed the case.

While subsequent administrations have continued to pursue a resolution to the Israeli-Palestinian conflict, little progress has been made. Contact between Israeli and Palestinian officials has gradually but inexorably diminished since the end of the Bush administration. The Israeli 2005 withdrawal from Gaza and certain settlements in the northern West Bank remain the last instance of territorial transfer from Israeli to Palestinian control; the Bush administration's 2007 Annapolis Conference proved to be the last major international meeting on the Israeli-Palestinian conflict; and former Israeli Prime Minister Ehud Olmert's 2008 peace offer to Palestinian Authority President Mahmoud Abbas—which Abbas refused to pursue—remains the most expansive such Israeli offer to date.

TRANSITION MEMORANDUM

~~CONFIDENTIAL~~

3998
Transition

NATIONAL SECURITY COUNCIL
WASHINGTON, D.C. 20504

December 22, 2008

MEMORANDUM FOR THE RECORD

FROM: MICHAEL PASCUAL
        NEAR EAST AND NORTH AFRICAN AFFAIRS DIRECTORATE

SUBJECT: Middle East Peace Process

THE SITUATION AS WE FOUND IT:

In early 2001, the Israeli/Palestinian conflict was descending rapidly into the second intifada. Camp David II and subsequent negotiations had collapsed, and the Palestinian leadership remained compromised by terror and rampant corruption, wrecking the incipient trust that had been built between Israelis and Palestinians over the preceding years and alienating the Palestinian people themselves from their leaders. While some progress was made at Camp David II in defining and even narrowing differences between the parties, the ultimate outcome served as a reminder that peacemaking could not come through negotiation alone, but required work on the ground to prepare populations for compromise. Camp David II also underscored the limits of any peacemaking effort which lacked the support of the international community, and especially of the Arab States.

In sum, the momentum toward a peaceful settlement and Palestinian statehood had ended. Israel had not yet developed a political consensus on the need to withdraw from the West Bank and Gaza. The Palestinian leadership at that time used terror as a tool, and was not developing the institutions that would be needed for a peaceful and democratic Palestinian state. Large portions of the Palestinian population remained unreconciled even to the existence of Israel.

THIS ADMINISTRATION'S POLICY:

Our overarching goal has been to end the conflict and realize the President's vision of two democratic states, Israel and Palestine, living side-by-side in peace and security. This Administra-

~~CONFIDENTIAL~~
Reason: 1.4(b)(d)
Declassify on: 12/22/18

NSC Declassification Review [EO 13526]
DECLASSIFY IN FULL
by William C. Carpenter on 3/23/2020

tion continued and deepened the United States' longstanding and firm support for Israel's security as a Jewish state, while making two vital changes to U.S. policy. First, President Bush, in his remarks to the United Nations General Assembly on November 10, 2001, and then in a major policy speech on the Middle East in the Rose Garden on June 24, 2002, became the first President of the United States to call for a Palestinian state as a matter of firm policy. Second, while past administrations had focused heavily on the outward characteristics of a Palestinian state—for example its borders—this Administration shifted the focus to the character of that future state. On this ground the President refused to deal with the then-current Palestinian leadership and called for new leadership uncompromised by corruption and terror. And on this ground the President committed the United States to help Palestinians to build the security, political, and economic institutions of a democratic Palestinian state even before borders had been defined.

To help prepare the ground for progress on Middle East peace, the President's approach contained several other elements:

- The President identified terrorism as the primary obstacle to peace in the Middle East, the factor that was preventing the Palestinians from achieving a homeland for their people by making it politically impossible for Israelis to make the compromises necessary to establish a Palestinian state.
- The President sought to discredit and delegitimize terror, insisting that violence against innocents cannot be justified by any cause and that a Palestinian state would never be born of terror.
- The President supported the Israeli Government's right to defend its people from attack, which gave the Israelis confidence that they would not be forced into negotiations by terror tactics.

WHAT HAS BEEN ACCOMPLISHED:

Working to End the Intifada. On April 30, 2001, in the midst of the second intifada, the Mitchell Committee issued its report, which presented a sequenced plan to halt the violence, rebuild trust and confidence between the parties, and resume negotiations. Although the Mitchell Committee had been established by the Clinton administration in the wake of the collapse of the Camp David II negotiations, President Bush embraced its recommendations and worked with both sides to sign it. The intifada raged on, however, and it became clear that the first step of the Mitchell plan—a complete cessation of violence—was becoming increasingly difficult to achieve. To that end, the President sent CIA Director George Tenet to the region in June 2001 to negotiate a cease-fire. Israel and the Palestinian Authority (PA) signed the cease-fire plan on June 13, 2001. The cease-fire did not hold amid continued Palestinian terror attacks, including a restaurant bombing that killed 7 and wounded 130 people in August, and the assassination of an Israeli cabinet member in October 2001. In November 2001, the President appointed General Anthony Zinni, USMC (Ret.) as Special Envoy to Israel and the Palestinian

Authority. Zinni's mission was also to work on a cease-fire. He presented his three-phased plan in March 2002; it was accepted by the Israelis but not the Palestinians.

At the same time, in February 2002, Crown Prince Abdallah of Saudi Arabia presented a historic proposal that offered the establishment of normal relations between Arab states and Israel in return for a comprehensive peace agreement based on the 1967 borders. The plan was endorsed unanimously by the Arab League in Beirut in March 2002 after which, in April 2002, the President met with Crown Prince Abdallah in Crawford, Texas to discuss the peace initiative and the President's vision for Middle East peace.

The Roadmap. Having called for the creation of an independent Palestinian state in his June 24, 2002 Rose Garden speech, the question for the President and the United States Government remained how to get there. In the months following the President's Rose Garden speech, the Quartet, established in April 2002, when Spanish Prime Minister Jose Maria Aznar invited the United States, the European Union, the United Nations, and Russia, to Madrid to discuss the growing violence of the intifada, created a performance-based, step-by-step plan to realize the President's vision, which became known as the Roadmap.

As the two-state strategy became widely accepted, key Arab leaders came together on June 3, 2003 in Sharm el-Sheikh, Egypt to show their commitment, in the midst of an intifada, to this goal and to the Roadmap. Heads of State from Jordan, Saudi Arabia, Egypt, Bahrain, and the PA came together with President Bush to call for an end to the violence in a historic show of regional support.

The following day, June 4, 2003, at a summit in Aqaba, Jordan, the President launched direct discussions with the Government of Israel and the PA on implementing the Roadmap. Israel's then-Prime Minister Ariel Sharon called for an end to Israeli rule over Palestinians and for a Palestinian state, and then-Prime Minister Mahmoud Abbas pledged "a complete end to violence and terrorism." They accepted the Roadmap that laid out a practical sequence of performance-based benchmarks leading to an independent Palestinian state. That same month, the United States appointed John Wolf to establish a Roadmap monitoring mission in Jerusalem.

On September 6, 2003, Abbas resigned in frustration over Yasir Arafat's interference in his efforts to meet his Aqaba pledge. We continued to work with the parties and our regional partners toward the President's two-state vision of peace even in the absence of credible Palestinian leadership.

Gaza Disengagement. Having suffered tremendous losses from the violence of the intifada, beginning in 2002, the Israeli Government devised a defensive plan to build a separation barrier (not a political border) to protect Israeli citizens from terrorist infiltration and attack. The President obtained a commitment from the Israelis that the barrier would not be a political border and would not prejudge the outcome of any final status issues, and then supported the plan. The separation barrier resulted in an immediate drop in terrorist incidents in Israel, with no terrorist attacks in Israel proper originating from the West Bank since 2005.

Buoyed by the President's support, in the spring of 2004 Prime Minister Sharon decided to disengage from Gaza and parts of the northern West Bank even though it required the wrenching decision by the "Father" of the Israeli settlement movement to remove settlements and settlers. The President was one of the few international leaders to provide prompt and full support. Sharon presented his plan to President Bush on April 14, 2004. The President's strong commitment to Israel's security helped Sharon conceive and implement a seismic shift in Israeli politics, abandoning the dream of "Greater Israel," and leading to a national consensus on a policy of territorial compromise and withdrawal. In a letter to Sharon, President Bush adopted a new U.S. policy by stating that it "seemed clear" that in the ultimate settlement, Palestinian refugees would return to Palestine and not Israel. He also called it "unrealistic" in light of "new realities on the ground, including already existing major Israeli populations centers" to expect a full and complete return to the 1949 Armistice lines. The President restated our understandings with the Government of Israel that the separation barrier is a security barrier "rather than a political barrier, should be temporary rather than permanent," and "not prejudice any final status issues."

New Palestinian Leadership. In November 2004, Arafat died. On January 9, 2005, Prime Minister Abbas was elected as President of the Palestinian Authority on a platform of peace, which created new opportunities to help the Palestinian people build the institutions of statehood and develop their economy. We increased our foreign assistance to the PA, urging other governments to do so as well, and established the United States Security Coordinator (USSC) to help the Palestinians train and equip their security forces.

By autumn 2005, Israel had withdrawn all IDF soldiers and nearly 8,000 settlers from the Gaza settlements, and had conducted a partial withdrawal from the northern end of the West Bank. With the help of the United States, Israeli and Palestinian leaders began negotiating practical arrangements to gain the benefits of that withdrawal and improve conditions in the rest of the Palestinian territories. The result was the Agreement on Movement and Access in November 2005, aimed at improving the daily lives of average Palestinians by giving them the freedom to move, to trade, and to live more normal lives.

In January 2006, Sharon suffered a massive stroke that incapacitated one of the key leaders driving the movement toward peace. He was succeeded by Deputy Prime Minister Ehud Olmert. That same month, the peace process suffered another setback when Hamas narrowly won Palestinian elections with 44.45 percent of the vote, putting Hamas in control of the Palestinian Legislative Council and the Prime Minister's Office. President Abbas had believed, and had forcefully argued to U.S. officials, that Hamas, as the main opposition to the Fatah party, had to be included in the election for it to be seen as legitimate. President Bush supported Palestinian elections believing that "free elections cannot wait for perfect conditions" and that "elections strengthen the forces of freedom and encourage citizens to take control of their own destiny." In a speech to the American Legion a month after the Palestinian vote, the President stated that "the idea that lasting stability can be achieved by denying people a voice in the future control of their destiny is wrong" and that the democratic ability to choose leaders is the only way to defeat radical extremism. Despite United States Government urgings, Fatah had been unable to undertake reforms that would have permitted it to assert itself as a new, moderate political force. In the aftermath of the vote, many Fatah leaders concluded that the vote was not so much "pro-Hamas" as "anti-Fatah," and now knew they had to reform their party—though over time Fatah's reform efforts have proved to be very disappointing.

In June 2007, Hamas led a coup against President Abbas' government in Gaza and seized control of the area. President Abbas responded by expelling Hamas from the Palestinian Government and declaring a state of emergency. He named Salam Fayyad as the new Prime Minister. The new Palestinian leadership was quickly recognized by the United States, the European Union, and Israel. The Palestinian territories were now effectively divided, with Hamas in control of Gaza and the PA in control of the West Bank. But the Hamas leadership was now isolated by the international community, and the legitimate Palestinian Government now had two leaders who opposed terror and understood that it is the enemy of the Palestinian people and their hopes for a Palestinian state.

Annapolis and Paris Conferences. In a speech on July 16, 2007, the President announced that the advent of new Palestinian leadership committed to fighting terror and to a peaceful resolution of the conflict created the conditions necessary for reinvigorated peace efforts. He said that the United States had lifted financial restrictions that had been placed on the Palestinian Authority after Hamas took power, and announced new measures to support Palestinian businesses and help reform the Palestinian security services. The President called for a conference in the fall of 2007 to include Palestinians, Israelis, and regional neighbors who support the creation of a Palestinian state.

In November 2007, the Annapolis Conference was convened. Through concerted Presidential diplomacy, Arab leaders were persuaded to be part of the process from its inception, in contrast to prior unsuccessful efforts at a negotiated peace. The Annapolis Conference, and the Paris Conference that followed a few weeks later, signaled broad international support for a peaceful resolution of the conflict. Participation by the Arab States was a significant step forward. The Annapolis conference elicited international and regional political support for bilateral negotiations, Palestinian institution-building, fulfillment of Roadmap obligations, and greater Arab outreach to Israel, in recognition of the Arab Peace Initiative and the absolute necessity of Arab support of any final peace agreement.

The Paris conference marshaled financial support for Palestinian institutions, and its success was due in large part to the international community's respect for Prime Minister Fayyad. Since 2002, Fayyad, first as Finance Minister, then as Prime Minister, had made great strides in combating corruption, through the creation of a single treasury account, centralization of the payroll, and culling of civil service rosters.

Security, Political, and Economic Reform. In the period following both conferences, the Administration increased its programs to build capacity in the Palestinian security sector, named an envoy to work on a final status "security concept" (General Jones), and stood up a Roadmap monitoring mission to monitor and judge the fulfillment of Roadmap commitments (General Fraser). The USSC (General Dayton) continued to assist Palestinian security forces as they began to resume security responsibility in areas of the West Bank such as Nablus and later Jenin, and began training programs in Jordan for Palestinian police and Presidential Guards to make them more capable in the fight against crime, violence, and terror. The Quartet's envoy, former British Prime Minister Tony Blair, worked with Israelis and Palestinians to promote economic growth in the West Bank and to build the institutions of a future Palestinian state.

New Structure for Peace Negotiations. Palestinian and Israeli negotiators met throughout 2008, with the support and encouragement of Secretary Rice. The key advance in this area was that both parties agreed that bilateral peace negotiations would occur in parallel with the implementation of both sides' Roadmap obligations, rather than only after those obligations had been fulfilled. Progress on each would encourage progress on—and give credibility to—the other in the eyes of both Israelis and Palestinians. The parties, with United States support, set up four parallel tracks (bilateral negotiations, Roadmap implementation, Palestinian institution-building, and Arab outreach to Israel) that are meant to be mutually-reinforcing and designed to ensure that none of these sectors lags the other and scuttles the process. Negotiations were slowed later in 2008 by a political crisis in Israel that eventually led to the resignation of Prime Minister Olmert.

Assurances. Over the course of the Administration, we have provided a number of public statements and assurances (quoted below) regarding core issues as well as the fulfillment of Roadmap obligations. The bulk of the assurances were made in the exchange of letters between President Bush and Prime Minister Sharon on April 14, 2004. In parallel, and recognizing the importance of Arab support for the PA, we consulted with Saudi Arabia and other leading Arab nations frequently to maintain political and financial support for the PA. The United States remained the largest donor to Palestinians, directly to the PA, through United Nations Relief and Works Agency, and through other channels.

Borders/Territory.

- In light of new realities on the ground, including already existing major population centers, it is unrealistic to expect that the outcome of final status negotiations will be a full and complete return to the armistice lines of 1949. It is realistic to expect that any final status agreement will only be achieved on the basis of mutually agreed changes that reflect these realities. (April 14, 2004 letter)
- A Palestinian state must be viable and contiguous and negotiations must lead to a territorial settlement, with mutually agreed borders reflecting previous lines and current realities, and mutually agreed adjustments. (July 16, 2007 Speech by the President)
- While territory is an issue for both parties to decide, any peace agreement between them will require mutually agreed adjustments to the armistice lines of 1949 to reflect current realities and to ensure that the Palestinian state is viable and contiguous. (January 10, 2008 Statement by the President)

Refugees.

- The United States is strongly committed to Israel's security and well-being as a Jewish state. It seems clear that an agreed, just, fair, and realistic framework for a solution to the Palestinian refugee issue as part of any final status agreement will need to be found through the establishment of a Palestinian state, and the settling of Palestinian refugees there, rather than in Israel. (April 14, 2004 letter)
- The agreement must establish Palestine as a homeland for the Palestinian people, just as Israel is a homeland for the Jewish people. (January 10, 2008 Statement by the President)
- We need to look to the establishment of a Palestinian state and new international mechanisms, including compensation, to resolve the refugee issue. (January 10, 2008 Statement by the President)

Security.

- Security is fundamental. No agreement and no Palestinian state will be born of terror. America is steadfastly committed to Israel's security. (January 10, 2008)

Roadmap.

- The Roadmap is the route to the vision of two states living side by side in peace and security. (April 14, 2004 letter)
- The Palestinian obligation to stop terror extends to Gaza. (Pre-Annapolis conference assurance)
- Implementation of any agreement is subject to implementation of the roadmap. (January 10, 2008 Statement by the President)

As the President prepared to leave office, no agreement had yet been reached on final status. However, there has been progress. Because of the President's leadership, the Israeli security situation has been vastly improved, giving Israelis the confidence they need to negotiate; the Palestinian people have new leaders who reject terror and seek peace with Israel; Palestinian leaders have made progress toward building the governing and security institutions of a future state; Israel has withdrawn from Gaza; both Israeli and Palestinian leaders have accepted the principle of territorial compromise; both sides have agreed to a Roadmap for the eventual creation of a Palestinian state; Arab leaders are actively supporting the peace process; and the United States, Israel, and the Palestinians have all agreed on a common goal: an independent, democratic, viable Palestinian state that lives side by side with Israeli in peace and security.

FUTURE CHALLENGES:

The challenges for the next administration are mutually reinforcing; progress on each of the below matters is required for the eventual achievement of peace and stability.

Final Status Agreement. The Roadmap monitoring mission would be needed after this Administration to operate in parallel to the implementation of a final status agreement, as the parties slowly fulfill their obligations, build confidence, and establish the necessary building blocks for peace.

Security-Sector Reform. Estimates for security sector reform that will provide capable security forces sufficient to fight terrorism and enforce law and order in an independent Palestinian state vary widely, but the investment will be significant and long term. The next administration may want to continue the programs of the USSC as well as work to implement final status "security concepts" agreed to by the parties.

Internal Palestinian Political Reform. After losing parliamentary elections to Hamas and after the coup in Gaza, Fatah still remains the largest political movement able to contend with Hamas for public support. At the same time, the movement is led by an upper echelon of older, often corrupt leaders who lack popular legitimacy and support and who are primarily concerned with maintaining control rather than undertaking serious reform. United States Government technical assistance provided to Fatah assists with the reform process. This support focuses on improving Fatah's ability to communicate with members and mobilize them in advance of future elections. However, technical assistance is only part of the answer. Fatah's leadership needs to decide on a path of meaningful reform and developing new leaders, which the "Old Guard" continues to resist.

Hamas/Gaza. The Israeli and PA policy of isolation has been effective in containing Hamas but not in weakening its grip on power. The growing political, economic, and social gaps between Gaza and the West Bank will need to be bridged for peace to take hold. Hamas control of Gaza, combined with Syrian and Iranian support for Hamas and other terrorist groups, are today perhaps the greatest threats to a resolution of the conflict. Israel will not make the difficult concessions a peace treaty requires if Gaza and Hamas remain a threat to its security. On the other hand, the definition of a Palestinian state will allow the PA and Fatah to present a clear choice to the people of Gaza: peace, a Palestinian state, and the end of terror versus continuation of the deprivation and violence of Gaza under Hamas.

Implementation of Arab Peace Initiative. The Arab League reaffirmed the Saudi peace proposal in Riyadh in March 2007, and it was within this context that the goal of greater Arab outreach to Israel was included as one of the four "pillars" of Annapolis in November 2007. In the aftermath of the Annapolis Conference, however, Arab contacts with Israel actually decreased. Steps toward the normalization of relations between Israel and Arab States would advance the cause of peace by giving Israelis confidence in a better future and more incentives to take risks for peace.

Attachments

POSTSCRIPT

MICHAEL SINGH

President Bush regarded both Israeli security and Palestinian freedom and dignity as important in their own right and to the advancement of American interests. Bush and his senior officials devoted much energy and effort to promoting both. Yet unlike their predecessors—and strongly influenced by the attacks of September 11, 2001, and their aftermath—they did not regard the Israeli-Palestinian conflict as the issue on which all others in the Middle East hinged. Instead, they viewed the absence of freedom and prosperity and the prevalence of extremism as the region's foremost challenges. That the United States was able to maintain good relations with both Israelis and Palestinians and advance relations between them despite this shift—or, arguably, in large part because of it—offers clues to how American policymakers should address the Israeli-Palestinian conflict in the years to come.

The Bush Administration Approach

American involvement in the Israeli-Palestinian peace process has been a story of both continuity and change. As is the case with so many foreign policy issues, successive administrations carried on key elements of their predecessors' policies—often more than they liked to admit. What changes they made reflected both shifts in national security strategy, priorities, and philosophy from one president to the next and changing realities on the ground.

This was certainly the case with President Bush's policy toward the Israeli-Palestinian conflict. On one hand, there was considerable continuity between his approach and President Clinton's—the emphasis on bilateral, US-mediated negotiations on the so-called core issues; stark opposition to Palestinian "rejectionists" and support for the Palestinian Authority (PA); and a close strategic partnership with Israel on broader regional threats. Even President Bush's historic pledge of support for Palestinian statehood built on the "Clinton Parameters" for a peace agreement, which were publicized at the end of the Clinton administration but never constituted official US policy.

Yet the Bush administration also differed from its predecessors in important ways, reflecting the failure of previous diplomatic efforts to yield durable progress, and, most prominently, the outbreak of the second intifada in 2001— which saw Israel subjected to an onslaught of terrorism just as the United States found itself attacked by al Qaeda. The major elements of the Bush administration approach included the following:

— President Bush offered full-throated support for Israel's security and Israel's right to defend itself against terrorist attack. This position was criticized by many at the time. But Bush's commitment to Israeli security—and strong criticism of Palestinian violence during the intifada—helped earn Prime Minister Sharon's trust. This reassurance arguably made it easier for Sharon to make the difficult decisions he faced.

— Perhaps that the most difficult of these decisions was that Israel had to "divide the land" with the Palestinians even though it meant giving up territory that included Israeli settlements. This decision transformed the context for seeking an Israeli-Palestinian peace. The result was the Israeli withdrawal from Gaza, and from settlements in the northern part of the West Bank, and ultimately Israeli-Palestinian peace negotiations.

— Bush also emphasized terrorism as the principal obstacle to peace and insisted that those who advocated terror and sought to wield it as leverage— most prominently longtime PLO Chairman Yasser Arafat—could not be involved in any political process. To the dismay of many at the time, Bush called for new Palestinian leadership uncompromised by terror or corruption and committed to peace and a democratic future for the Palestinian people. This ultimately led to Mahmoud Abbas' selection as the post-Arafat leader of the Palestinians.

— The diplomatic stalemate he inherited led President Bush to rethink the approach to peace and to a Palestinian state. He broadened Washington's focus from Palestinians' territorial demands to the need for institutional development and state-building, which he viewed to be more important to the long-term success of a Palestinian state than the mapping of its borders. The Bush administration partnered with numerous local Palestinian leaders and organizations, as well as then–Palestinian Authority (PA) Prime Minister Salam Fayyad, to this end. The focus on institutions led to bottom-up developments, such as youth centers and tourism development, and top-down efforts including elections and government reform.

— President Bush broadened the focus of US interaction with Palestinian security forces from intelligence to security. He transferred responsibility for

Palestinian security coordination from the intelligence community to the Defense Department, leading to the Palestinian Authority Security Forces' transformation into a body able both to provide security for Palestinians and to coordinate effectively with Israel. This development contributed to a reduction in terrorism and an increase in quiet on the West Bank.

— Finally, President Bush declared as a matter of US policy certain realities that most people on both sides tacitly acknowledged but could not admit publicly—including, in the 2004 Bush-Sharon letters, that there would be no return to the 1949 armistice lines and that Palestinian refugees would return to a future Palestinian state rather than to Israel. While controversial at the time, these steps helped slow Israeli settlement expansion and kick-start negotiations.

What Has Happened Since the End of the Bush Administration?

Elements of both continuity and change also characterized the approaches to the Israeli-Palestinian conflict adopted by the Obama and Trump administrations. For all of its tensions with the government of Israel, the Obama administration maintained the Bush administration's strong commitment to Israel's security and built upon it in important ways. For example, it supported what would eventually become the Iron Dome antirocket system, a critical element of Israel's security architecture. President Obama also preserved key elements of President Bush's approach to the peace process. For example, he continued efforts to professionalize the Palestinian security services and facilitate their security coordination with Israel. And he continued an initiative designed to assess how a peace agreement could advance Israel's security, led under President Bush by former NATO commander Jim Jones—who would go on to become President Obama's first national security adviser—and under President Obama by General John Allen.

Yet the Obama administration also departed from President Bush's policies in important ways. President Obama entered office highly critical of key elements of the Bush administration's foreign policy—especially the Iraq War and elements of the Global War on Terror, such as the operation of the detention facility at Guantanamo Bay, Cuba. He was determined to repair what he saw as frayed relations with Muslim-majority states and with allies in Europe and elsewhere. But as Dennis Ross, President Obama's first-term Middle East adviser has written, "The Obama administration's national security priorities almost guaranteed that Israel would be a problem."[1] President Obama sought to create distance between the United States and Israel (going so far as to avoid traveling there until March 2017 in his second term) and made the demand for a freeze on Israeli settlement activity the centerpiece of his approach to the Israeli-Palestinian conflict. President Obama's approach not only exacerbated tensions with Israel—despite his otherwise strong support for the US-Israel security partnership—but failed to produce flexibility on the part of the Palestinians or the Arab states. This was due not just to US policy but to changes within the region itself.

When President Obama entered office, Israel was undergoing a seismic political shift—the Israeli electorate was moving to the right, the Israeli left was correspondingly in decline, and Israeli politics overall was becoming increasingly atomized, with an increasing number of small parties accumulating outsized influence. As for the Palestinians, it is clearer in hindsight that Hamas' takeover of Gaza in 2006 had a chilling effect on peace diplomacy. It not only created the problem of how to incorporate the Gaza Strip into any peace plans but made President Abbas less willing to take political risks and increasingly suspicious of those he regarded as domestic rivals. These included not just Hamas and its ilk, but also technocrats such as Salam Fayyad, who had served as a bridge between the PA and the West and, as noted earlier, was responsible for much of the PA's success in attracting aid and promoting reform.

At the same time, Palestinian terrorism was being supplanted by Iranian regional disruption as Israel's foremost security preoccupation. A similar shift was happening among US-allied Arab states as well, albeit for different reasons. While Israel worried about Iran's nuclear program and its support for anti-Israel terrorists such as Lebanon's Hezbollah, Arab states such as Saudi Arabia saw Iran as emboldened by the chaos in Iraq and increasingly intent on sowing instability in their countries. At the same time, the Arab uprisings of 2011, and the resurgence of political Islam in places like Tunisia and Egypt, likely resulted in increased wariness throughout the region of the risks in creating a Palestinian state—especially one where Hamas, a Muslim Brotherhood affiliate, would enjoy strong support. While key US officials still viewed the Israeli-Palestinian conflict as central to the region's stability, US partners in the region no longer did. The days when Saudi leaders

---

1. Dennis Ross, *Doomed to Succeed: The US-Israel Relationship from Truman to Obama* (New York: Farrar, Strauss, and Giroux, 2015), 346.

would tie relations between Riyadh and Washington to the US position on the Palestinians—as then-Crown Prince Abdullah did in 2002—were over.

While these factors had led most analysts to conclude by 2016 that the time was not ripe for an accord between the Israelis and Palestinians, the Trump administration nevertheless entered office determined to pursue one, which it termed "the deal of the century." The Trump administration returned to many of the principles and approaches of the Bush administration, emphasizing, for example, the economic empowerment of Palestinians and the importance of acknowledging realities on the ground as a means of accelerating movement toward a resolution of the Israeli-Palestinian conflict. And just as surely as the Obama administration sought to establish "daylight" between the United States and Israel, the Trump administration moved in the opposite direction, slamming that gap shut.

At the same time, however, the Trump administration made little headway with the Palestinian Authority, which eventually severed contact with the United States over America's recognition of Jerusalem as the capital of Israel. While there were many factors contributing to this estrangement—including the Trump administration's unqualified support for Israel, its explicit use of aid to the Palestinians as leverage, and President Abbas' deepening intransigence—the result was that President Trump, like President Obama, was unable to spur meaningful Israeli-Palestinian negotiations, settling instead for issuing his own peace plan.

While President Trump's efforts to craft the "deal of the century" came to naught, he enjoyed far more success crafting deals of another sort between Israel and US-allied Arab states. The regional factors that stymied President Obama's efforts at spurring Israeli-Palestinian peace—Israel's increasing preoccupation with Iran and diminishing emphasis in the Arab world on the Israeli-Palestinian conflict—had since the beginning of the twenty-first century gradually brought Israel and the conservative Arab states closer together. This was true not just of Egypt and Jordan—which had previously recognized Israel and worked closely with it to combat transnational Islamist groups as well as Iranian proxies—but of the Gulf Arab states, which theretofore had refused to grant Israel diplomatic recognition. Motivated by the convergence of their threat perceptions, their common alarm at the stated intention of successive US presidents to scale back the American commitment to the region, and the shift in the center of gravity in the Arab world from the Levant to the Gulf, the UAE was ready to bring its tacit cooperation with Israel into the open and others were ready to follow. The result was the Abraham Accords normalizing relations between these Arab states and Israel.

How Did the Bush Administration Do?

The swings in US policy toward the Israeli-Palestinian conflict during the first two decades of the twenty-first century have been driven by how different administrations have answered three key questions. The first of these is what role the United States should play. Conventional wisdom says the United States should be an honest broker. Many would view an honest broker as being equidistant between the two parties to the conflict, at least with respect to the issues in dispute. This was the approach of the Obama administration—it viewed President Bush as being too close to Israel, which it believed undermined the US position with the Palestinians and indeed with Muslim-majority states in general. But the Obama administration discovered what the Bush administration had already learned—that efforts to demonstrate US distance from Israel yielded not flexibility or reasonableness from Israel's critics but demands for more.

What is actually required of an effective honest broker is not equidistance but rather closeness to both sides. Any number of states could claim neutrality in the Israeli-Palestinian conflict, and many could claim an affection for one side or another; what distinguishes the United States, however, is its deep and longstanding commitment to both Israel and to the Palestinians, represented by a rich array of diplomatic, economic, and security assistance across administrations. The United States is most effective when each party trusts it—and knows that the other side trusts it as well. When the United States deliberately moves away from one side or another—as both the Obama and Trump administrations did, albeit in opposite directions—its utility as a peace negotiator diminishes for both. On this score, President Bush did well. While he was widely and correctly regarded as deeply pro-Israel and refused to deal with PLO chairman Yasser Arafat, he developed genuinely close relations with Arafat's successor, President Abbas, which was key to moving negotiations forward.

The second key question is whether peace should be built from the top down or the bottom up, as it were. That is to say, will stability and prosperity on the ground be products of a peace agreement, or will they be causes of one? The Bush administration initially came down firmly in favor of the latter view. It forcefully argued that Israeli security was nonnegotiable, that no Palestinian state would be born of terror, and that the character and institutions of any Palestinian state mattered just as much as its borders. Indeed, President Bush's most lasting achievements on the Israeli-Palestinian issue came not at the negotiating table but on the ground. The United States helped Israel fend off the threat of Hezbollah, Hamas, and the second intifada. Together with the Palestinian Authority, President Bush made great strides in promoting economic reform and institution building for Palestinians. And perhaps most importantly, the Bush administration led an effort to professionalize the Palestinian security services, which tangibly improved the lives of both Israelis and Palestinians and was carried forward by the Obama administration and, for a time, the Trump administration.

Despite this focus on building peace rather than simply negotiating it, the Bush administration eventually concluded that in fact top-down and bottom-up approaches had to proceed in parallel. For example, making negotiations contingent on the security situation and the absence of terrorist attacks (or "calm," as Prime Minister Sharon used to call it) risked inadvertently allowing terrorists to hold the political process hostage. Yet to proceed with negotiations heedless of the need for calm was untenable politically within Israel and risked absolving the Palestinian leadership of any responsibility for addressing extremism within its own ranks. On the Palestinian side, proceeding to negotiations without tangible gains on the ground would lose needed Palestinian domestic support. Yet economic and security progress, if not buttressed by a viable negotiation, risked being swallowed up by conflict and derailed by political pressure not to "beautify" the Israeli occupation. Likewise, building institutions without also building political accountability inevitably brought setbacks, whether Hamas' victory in the 2005 elections, the decline in the professionalism of the Palestinian Authority Security Forces, or the endemic corruption that has come to characterize the Palestinian Authority. Managing the balance between top down and bottom up, between pushing for political progress and insisting on reform and accountability, was difficult and often controversial.

The third key question is the relationship of the Israeli-Palestinian conflict to other issues in the region. Is resolution of the conflict the key to unlocking progress on other issues; is the reverse true; or is the conflict simply independent of and not linked to the region's other conflicts and problems? President Bush rejected the notion of linkage, viewing the key fault line in the region and the driver of these other issues as not being tensions between Arabs and Israelis (as many Western officials once held) but tensions between moderates and extremists, for lack of better terms.

On this question, the intervening years have largely validated President Bush's view. While by no means resolved—new conflicts on Israel's frontiers with Gaza and Lebanon could break out at any time, and even stability in the West Bank is not assured—the Israeli-Palestinian conflict can no longer be said to pose a fundamental threat to stability in the region. And US relations in the Arab world, and indeed relations between Israel and the Arab states, have improved markedly despite the lack of progress in resolving the Israeli-Palestinian conflict. This success, however, is tempered by the fact that the opposite has also proved true—that while the lack of Israeli-Palestinian progress has not hampered US or Israeli relations in the region, neither have advances in those relations yet contributed to a solution to that conflict, which continues to threaten long-term American interests and Israeli security.

What Are the Lessons Learned?

- *An alternative to the two-state solution has yet to emerge.* The Biden administration entered office with a challenge and an opportunity, both of which preceding administrations had a hand in shaping. The challenge is that the two-state solution—which under President Bush became US policy and gained wide international acceptance—seems further from being realized today than it was in 2008. However, no clear alternative has yet emerged—a single, binational state raises serious problems for both Israel and Palestinians, as do other options, such as Palestinian confederation with Egypt and Jordan or the "statehood-minus" suggested by Prime Minister Netanyahu. On the other hand, there is an opportunity here, because, while the Israeli-Palestinian conflict has not been solved, it has been shrunk—transformed from an intractable challenge threatening the stability of the Middle East to a perhaps no less intractable but certainly less threatening one.

- *There is a new opportunity for greater cooperation and stability in the Middle East.* Israel's relations with Arab states have experienced a revolution, one that opens new possibilities for regional cooperation and stability. Until recently, it had almost universally been assumed that an Israeli-Palestinian settlement would both precede and enable a broader reconciliation between Israel and its Arab neighbors. The Abraham Accords have begun to turn that logic on its head. The opportunity for future US administrations is to encourage the deepening and broadening of Arab-Israeli relations as a key to a more stable, cooperative, and less extremist Middle East. As it does so, future US administrations will inherit one of the clearest bipartisan, long-term foreign policy successes the United States can claim, though one that is not always clearly recognized—the development of Israel as one of the United States' closest and most capable allies, and of the US-Israel relationship as an indispensable strategic asset.

- *Achieving a Palestinian-Israeli peace will require new approaches.* The emerging Arab-Israeli reconciliation can, in turn, put pressure on the Palestinians to reach a settlement with Israel. It can also serve to facilitate contacts toward that end. It is no coincidence that prior to the Abraham Accords, Jordan and Egypt were both the only Arab states to recognize Israel and those playing the most constructive role in managing the Israeli-Palestinian conflict. Normalization between Israel and the UAE and Bahrain raises the prospect that the latter two states may likewise become more active in leveraging their diplomatic and other resources to further Israeli-Palestinian peace. The exact terms of such a settlement are less and less clear, given developments on the ground and in the region. Also unclear is whether it will be reflected in a formal peace agreement or in a set of de facto understandings that mature over time into a de facto peace. In either event, new and creative thinking will be required on all sides.

Contributor:
Elliott Abrams

PART 7

Emerging Challenges

INTRODUCTION

STEPHEN J. HADLEY

A number of issues have gained great public prominence since the end of the Bush administration. Three of particular note are cybersecurity, climate change, and authoritarian populism. Only the latter was the subject of an NSC Transition Memorandum, and it is found in chapter 29 of this part 7. Although it covers authoritarian populism only as it arose in Latin America, it offers lessons of potentially broader applicability to a problem that has metastasized into a global phenomenon.

For the other two issues, the Homeland Security Council and the Council for Environmental Quality, respectively, had the lead rather than the NSC. Hence there is no NSC Transition Memorandum on either of these topics. But because the NSC was intimately involved in both issues, and because these issues have become so central to today's national security debate, essays have been prepared on each one for inclusion in this book. They describe the Bush administration approach, what the administration thought it accomplished, what has occurred since, and how the administration's approach stands up in hindsight. The leads for the preparation of these essays were former Bush administration Homeland Security Adviser Kenneth L. Wainstein, in the case of cybersecurity (essay found in chapter 27 of this part 7), and former chair of the Bush administration Council on Environmental Quality, James L. Connaughton, for climate change (essay found in chapter 28 of this part 7).

CHAPTER 27

Cyber

Cyber Preparedness

**KENNETH L. WAINSTEIN | KEITH AUSBROOK |
NEILL SCIARRONE**

The eight years of President George W. Bush's administration coincided with the nation's full entry into the digital age and its dawning realization of both the opportunity and the threat presented by the digital environment. From its first days, the administration devoted energy and resources to the effort to diagnose the threat—in both its criminal and national security dimensions, to develop policies to defend against the threat, and to build a governmental infrastructure to implement those policies in coordination with private-sector actors that controlled much of the internet. Throughout all of these efforts, the Bush administration's focus was on ensuring coordinated cyber awareness, response, and recovery activities; increasing the security of federal networks and systems; and reducing the nation's overall cyber vulnerabilities.

The Bush Administration Approach

The Nature of the Threat

At the start of the Bush administration, the primary cyber concern related to the threat of digital-borne attacks against critical infrastructure. The Clinton administration had focused on this threat with its 1998 issuance of Presidential Decision Directive 63 (PDD 63), which discussed the imperative of defending the nation's infrastructure against cyber wrongdoers. The Y2K issue then galvanized public attention and mobilized public and private efforts around that threat, illustrating our growing dependence on digital infrastructure and the real-world impact that cyber vulnerabilities could have on critical infrastructure.

That concern was heightened in 2003 when the Northeast blackout demonstrated how a cyber incident could bring critical infrastructure and a region's economy to its knees. This widespread power outage—which at the time was the world's second most widespread blackout in history—affected parts of the Northeastern and Midwestern United States and the Canadian province of Ontario and was initially feared to be an act of terrorism. Although it was ultimately determined to have resulted from a software bug that disrupted load redistribution, the ensuing investigation and response provided a dry run for what the FBI and other law enforcement agencies would face in the event that terrorists launched attacks against our power grid and the energy-critical infrastructure.[1]

During this same period, the nation experienced a series of crippling attacks directed against computer systems and enterprise networks, notably the "ILOVEYOU" virus and Nimda. The latter was a malicious file that infected computers and servers running certain versions of Windows software and came just days after the 9/11 terrorist attacks on New York and the Pentagon, raising concern that it was launched by or coordinated with al Qaeda. Although this theory proved unfounded, the incident led to the first widespread discussion of the potential use of a cyberattack by a foreign adversary or terrorist group.

---

1. "FBI Concerned About Threat of Terror-Induced Blackouts," CNN, September 5, 2003, http://www.cnn.com/2003/ALLPOLITICS/09/04/blackout.hearing/index.html; see also Sandy Smith, "The Great Blackout of 2003," EHS Today (website), August 12, 2003, https://www.ehstoday.com/emergency-management/article/21918569/the-great -blackout-of-2003.

Initial Executive Branch Approach

The Bush administration had inherited a nascent cyber policy operation run by Richard "Dick" Clarke, whom President Clinton had appointed the National Coordinator for Security, Infrastructure Protection, and Counter-terrorism. President Bush retained Clarke on the NSC staff and appointed him as the Special Adviser to the President on Cybersecurity. Clarke then created the President's Cybersecurity Board, which focused on raising awareness about the cybersecurity threat within government and industry. Clarke at one point chided American corporations for devoting a paltry 0.0025 percent of their revenue to IT security, warning them that "[i]f you spend more on coffee than on IT security, then you will be hacked. What's more, you deserve to be hacked."[2]

On October 8, 2001, President Bush established the Office of Homeland Security within the White House, and as one of its first responsibilities directed it to produce the first homeland security strategy. That document, the National Strategy for Homeland Security, was released in July 2002. Coming before the passage of the Homeland Security Act on November 25, 2002, and prior to the official opening of the Department of Homeland Security (DHS) on March 1, 2003, it was the first attempt to outline the policy goals for critical infrastructure protection, including cybersecurity.

That strategy was soon followed by two supporting strategies—the National Strategy to Secure Cyberspace, and the National Strategy for the Physical Protection of Critical Infrastructures and Key Assets—both drafted in large part by members of Clarke's Cybersecurity Board team with support from staff of the Office of Homeland Security and released on February 14, 2003.

This strategy identified three primary objectives: "(1) Prevent cyberattacks against America's critical infrastructures; (2) Reduce national vulnerability to cyberattacks; and (3) Minimize damage and recovery time from cyberattacks that do occur." To meet these objectives, the National Strategy outlined five national priorities:

- Creation of a National Cyberspace Security Response System, focusing on improving the government's response to cyberspace security incidents and reducing the potential damage from such events;

---

2. Comments at the RSA Conference 2002.

- Development of a National Cyberspace Security Threat and Vulnerability Reduction Program;
- Creation of a National Cyberspace Security Awareness and Training Program;
- Securing federal cyberspace and encouraging state and local governments to consider establishing information technology security programs; and
- Establishment of a system of National Security and International Cyberspace Security Cooperation to enhance the protection of national security assets and improve the international management of the cyber threat.

In furtherance of these priorities, the National Strategy laid out a series of concrete recommendations, including calling for a single center to help detect, monitor, and analyze attacks; encouraging companies to regularly review their technology security plans and individuals to add firewalls and antivirus software to their systems; and urging the expansion of cybersecurity research and improved government-industry cooperation.

Legislative Action

In parallel with this executive branch policymaking process was a legislative effort to address the growing cyber threat. The Homeland Security Act of 2002, which included the Critical Infrastructure Information Act of 2002 and the Cyber Security Enhancement Act of 2002, led to a series of improvements in the cybersecurity posture of the government. They ranged from the establishment of NET Guard (a national technology group of volunteers to assist local communities with responding to and recovering from cyberattacks) to the enhancement of criminal sentences for cybercrimes and the required disclosure of cyber incidents.

An important innovation in this legislation was the definition of a category of information relating to the protection of critical infrastructure—Critical Infrastructure Information[3]—and the mandated sharing of that information among

---

3. "Critical Infrastructure Information" was defined as the following:

"[I]nformation not customarily in the public domain and related to the security of critical infrastructure or protected systems . . . [concerning]
A) actual, potential, or threatened interference with, attack on, compromise of, or incapacitation of critical infrastructure or protected systems by either physical or computer-based attack or other similar conduct (including the misuse of or

the relevant actors in government and private industry. With this definition, the law acknowledged that cyber was a primary medium of potential attack against our critical infrastructure and mandated the sharing of all critical infrastructure information (including that relating to the cyber threat) between and among federal, state, tribal, and private-sector entities.

Finally, the Homeland Security Act substantially reorganized the federal government to better meet the cyber threat. A number of existing offices and agencies with a cyber mission from across the federal government were transferred into DHS with the hope of creating one larger cybersecurity capability. The transferred entities included:

- The National Infrastructure Protection Center of the Federal Bureau of Investigation (other than the Computer Investigations and Operations Section);
- The National Communications System of the Department of Defense;
- The Critical Infrastructure Assurance Office of the Department of Commerce;
- The National Infrastructure Simulation and Analysis Center of the Department of Energy and the energy security and assurance program and activities of the Department;
- The Federal Computer Incident Response Center of the General Services Administration.

Although the legislation successfully consolidated these entities on the organizational chart, the new organization faced a number of challenges. In many instances, for example, the entities transferred without the resources or staff to operate them, requiring DHS to staff and rebuild the offices virtually from

---

unauthorized access to all types of communications and data transmission systems) that violates federal, state, or local law, harms interstate commerce of the United States, or threatens public health or safety;

(B) the ability of any critical infrastructure or protected system to resist such interference, compromise, or incapacitation, including any planned or past assessment, projection, or estimate of the vulnerability of critical infrastructure or a protected system, including security testing, risk evaluation thereto, risk management planning, or risk audit; or

(C) any planned or past operational problem or solution regarding critical infrastructure or protected systems, including repair, recovery, reconstruction, insurance, or continuity, to the extent it is related to such interference, compromise, or incapacitation."

scratch. Also, in transferring these new authorities to DHS, Congress failed to remove the corresponding authorities from the transferring agencies or to clarify the allocation of cyber authorities and responsibilities across the federal government. This resulted in a framework of conflicting and overlapping authorities that generated operational confusion and interagency rivalry that still hinders our federal cybersecurity efforts today.

The Comprehensive National Cybersecurity Initiative

Starting in 2003, the US government discovered a series of coordinated intrusions or attacks by hackers from the Chinese People's Liberation Army that accessed sensitive information in both US government and defense contractor systems, including those at Lockheed Martin, Sandia National Laboratories, Redstone Arsenal, and NASA. These intrusions—coined the Titan Rain attacks[4]—highlighted the need to focus on the threats against our government and other critical networks. In May of 2007, Director of National Intelligence Mike McConnell convened a cyber study group to make recommendations specifically addressing the cyber threat to Intelligence Community and Department of Defense (DOD) entities.

In the course of the study group's briefings to the president, it quickly became apparent that the problem extended beyond just the Intelligence and Defense agencies, and that it needed to be raised to a higher level of White House involvement and wider interagency coordination. The president tasked the National Security Council (NSC) and Homeland Security Council (HSC) to work jointly on this issue with Homeland Security Adviser Frances (Fran) Townsend in the lead.

To address this issue in a sustained way, the HSC created a new Cybersecurity Directorate with a staff largely comprised of employees detailed from the various departments and agencies with roles, responsibilities, and expertise in cybersecurity. HSC also established the Communications Security and Cyber Policy Coordinating Committee (CSC PCC) comprised of assistant secretary-level officials from all of the relevant departments and agencies to coordinate the interagency process that would oversee both the development of cyber defense policy initiatives and their ultimate implementation.

---

4. "Titan Rain," Council on Foreign Relations, August 2005, https://www.cfr.org/cyber
-operations/titan-rain; Nathan Thornburgh, "The Invasion of the Chinese Cyberspies
(And the Man Who Tried to Stop Them)," *Time*, September 5, 2005, https://courses.cs
.washington.edu/courses/csep590/05au/readings/titan.rain.htm.

President Bush tasked this PCC with creating a plan that could provide "an enduring and comprehensive approach to cybersecurity that anticipates future cyber threats and technologies and involves applying all elements of national power and influence to secure our national interests in cyberspace."[5] The overall goals were to:

- Establish a frontline of defense, i.e., stop the bleeding by reducing current vulnerabilities and preventing future intrusions;
- Position the federal government to keep ahead of our adversaries—including nation-state actors, cybercriminals, and rogue lone-wolf operators—by using all available means (including intelligence efforts and strengthening our supply chain) to defend against the full spectrum of cyber threat; and
- Understand and prepare for future needs by enhancing research, development, and education as well as investing in leap-ahead technology.

Acknowledging the continued existence of conflicting and overlapping authorities among the federal cybersecurity actors, the president also directed that the PCC "ensure ongoing coordination of the US government policies, strategies, and initiatives related to cybersecurity."[6]

Given how prior attempts at development of government-wide cybersecurity policy had all too often become mired in interagency debates over ownership of the different policy and operational areas and responsibilities, the discussion of who should be responsible for oversight and implementation of each action was divorced from the discussion of what action needed to be taken. The objective was to produce an agreed-upon list of actions to the president and cabinet, secure presidential approval to pursue those actions, and then have the Deputies' Committee consider agency ownership (or shared ownership with at most one other agency) of each action. The resulting plan was a list of policy tasks, studies, reports, and initiatives that were primarily assigned to four agencies—DHS, DOD, ODNI, and Office of

---

5. National Security Presidential Directive/NSPD-54, Homeland Security Presidential Directive/HSPD-23, The White House, January 8, 2008, https://fas.org/irp/offdocs/nspd/nspd-54.pdf.

6. National Security Presidential Directive/NSPD-54, Homeland Security Presidential Directive/HSPD-23, The White House, January 8, 2008, https://fas.org/irp/offdocs/nspd/nspd-54.pdf.

Science and Technology Policy (OSTP) (with several tasks being assigned to OMB, DOJ, and the NSC). This slate of actions became known as the Comprehensive National Cybersecurity Initiative (CNCI) that was described and included in National Security Presidential Directive 54/Homeland Security Presidential Directive 23 (NSPD-54/HSPD-23) released on January 8, 2008. In summary, the CNCI consisted of the following initiatives (with agency leads shown in parentheses):

1. *Trusted Internet Connections (TIC) (OMB/ DHS).* This initiative primarily sought to consolidate and reduce the number of external internet access points across the federal government systems.

2. *Deployment of an Intrusion Detection System (IDS) across the Federal Government (DHS).* This initiative was to deploy passive, signature-based sensors across the civilian systems of the executive branch that could scan the contents of internet packets to determine if they were malicious and provide intrusion alerts in real time. This enterprise-wide IDS was based on a new technology called Einstein 2 that would be implemented by DHS.

3. *Deployment of an Intrusion Prevention System with Countermeasures (DHS/DOD).* Known as Einstein 3, this initiative supplemented the automated detection capability of Einstein 2 with countermeasures to actively prevent the detected breaches across the US government networks.

4. *R&D Coordination (OSTP).* This initiative sought better coordination of research and development efforts with a focus on coordinating both classified and unclassified R&D for cybersecurity. The goal was to prioritize, harmonize, and fill gaps in federal cybersecurity R&D efforts.

5. *Connecting the Cyber Centers (ODNI).* This initiative focused on improving cyber situational awareness across the federal government by connecting and integrating the operations of the existing cyber operational centers. It also established the National Cybersecurity Center within DHS, which colocated representatives of the government's different cybersecurity centers and focused on coordinating and integrating information from these centers.

6. *Cyber Counterintelligence Plan (ODNI/Department of Justice).* This initiative directed the development and implementation of a government-wide counterintelligence (CI) plan to detect, deter, and mitigate foreign-sponsored cyber intelligence threats to government and private-sector IT systems and networks.

7. *Security of Classified Networks (DOD/ODNI).* This initiative called for the increased security of the government's classified networks.
8. *Expand Cyber Education (DHS/DOD).* This initiative expanded efforts in cyber education, including a comprehensive federal cyber education and training program. Emphasis was placed on developing offensive and defensive skill and capabilities.
9. *Leap-Ahead Technology (OSTP).* This initiative directed OSTP to define and develop enduring leap-ahead technology, strategies, and programs by: investing in high-risk, high-reward research and development, and working with both private-sector and international partners. The goal was to be thinking five to ten years ahead and preparing for the serious cybersecurity threats of the future.
10. *Deterrence Strategies and Programs (NSC).* This initiative sought to define and develop enduring strategies and programs that reduce vulnerabilities and deter interference and attacks in cyberspace. It tasked policymakers to think beyond traditional approaches and consider long-term measures, such as ramped-up warning capabilities, meaningful engagement with the private sector and worldwide allies, and the development of a slate of responses to attacks from both state and nonstate actors.
11. *Global Supply Chain Risk Management (DHS/DOD).* This initiative directed the development of a multipronged approach to protect the global supply chain and to address the risks posed by globalization and the malign efforts directed against the supply chain.
12. *Public and Private Partnerships "Project 12" (DHS).* This initiative directed DHS to define new mechanisms for the federal government and private industry to work together to protect the nation's critical infrastructure and key resources. DHS and their private-sector companions were tasked with setting forth a series of milestones to reach the goal of expanding CNCI activities to the private sector.

The CNCI Policy Directive made significant progress in providing clarity as to the federal government participants. It defined the roles of DHS and its cybersecurity division response organization, the US Computer Emergency Readiness Team (US CERT), in cyber response, awareness, and federal systems security; delineated the entities responsible for protecting the ".gov" or US government networks; and established the Joint Interagency Cyber Task Force to serve as the focal point for monitoring and coordinating projects.

This Policy Directive, for the first time, also defined new terms for the cybersecurity environment—including the definitions of a Computer Network Attack (CNA), a Computer Network Exploitation (CNE), and Computer Network Defense (CND)—which was an important step in defining and establishing policy norms in cyber warfare.

Other Cyber Policy Efforts

Although the CNCI was the most prominent area of cyber policy activity, the Bush administration undertook other notable initiatives in the cyber arena. The NSC and HSC policy councils addressed the terrorist use of the internet, the growing criminal use of digital infrastructure for illicit and often international criminal activity, the use of cyber means to perpetrate financial crimes, and issues surrounding internet freedom and the role of the Internet Corporation for Assigned Names and Numbers (ICANN), a global nonprofit organization responsible for coordinating the maintenance of and procedures for naming and assigning internet space.

In addition to these policy efforts, the president signed the Electronic Government Act of 2002 into law on December 17, 2002, creating the Office of Electronic Government and Information Technology in the Office of Management and Budget (OMB), or "E-Gov office" as it became known. This law also created a federal Chief Information Officer (CIO) Council that was chaired by the administrator of the E-Gov office.

That administrator was tasked with implementing IT systems and policies throughout the federal government, advising the OMB director on the performance of IT investments, overseeing the development of enterprise architectures within and across agencies, directing the activities of the CIO Council, and overseeing the use of the E-Government Fund to support interagency partnerships and innovation. The placement of the Administrator of the E-Gov office within OMB, which controls department and agency budgets, allowed for a carrot-and-stick approach to ensure government-wide compliance with its programs and allowed the administrator to provide strong support for the adoption of the CNCI initiatives.

Finally, the Bush administration also addressed the cyber threat as it played out on the trade front and in electoral campaigns. Several cases were brought to the Committee on Foreign Investment in the US (CFUIS) involving a foreign company's purchase of a US cyber company with a national security nexus. The Bush administration also was the first to deal with cyber interference in our national elections by foreign governments of the type that affected the 2016 presidential election. In 2008, the administration learned that Chinese operators had hacked into the campaigns of the two presidential candidates, John McCain and Barack Obama, and provided a defensive briefing to each campaign to warn them about the hacking activity.[7]

What Has Happened Since the End of the Bush Administration?

When the Obama administration came into office, it largely adopted and built upon the Bush administration efforts in developing its cyber program. Several of the key personnel who participated in the Bush administration CSC PCC meetings and were responsible for overseeing and implementing the CNCI policies in their respective departments and agencies moved into key roles in overseeing cyber policy in the Obama administration. Some of these same staff would move to additional roles in cybersecurity policy in the Trump administration, and several have roles in the Biden administration today.

Within three months of his inauguration, President Obama ordered a review of cybersecurity related plans, programs, and activities throughout the federal government, resulting in the issuance of "The Cyberspace Policy Review." That report largely reaffirmed the CNCI, while significantly expanding its activities and reach.

President Obama took a number of steps to enhance our cyber defenses. In June of 2009, he established the US Cyber Command as a subunified military command merging components that had previously performed offensive and defensive cyber missions. Although originally focused on the protection of military and DOD related networks, its mission evolved to also address threats to critical infrastructure, terrorist use of the internet, and cyber efforts by foreign adversaries to influence and interfere with our elections and democratic processes.

Expanding on this, in October 2012, the Obama administration released a classified Presidential Policy Directive 20 (PPD-20) providing a framework for undertaking cyber operations against a cyber threat. This policy wrestled with

---

7. Michael Isikoff, "Chinese Hacked Obama, McCain Campaigns, Took Internal Documents, Officials Say," NBC News, June 7, 2013, https://www.hsgac.senate.gov/media /majority-media/lieberman-and-collins-step-up-scrutiny-of-cyber-security-initiative.

the situational proportionality and appropriateness of such actions and with the distinction between an offensive and a defensive action in the rapidly evolving world of cyber war and cyberterrorism. While it held that an offensive response could be appropriate in certain circumstances, it directed that government use the least aggressive action necessary to mitigate any threat and explained that network defense and law enforcement should be the first line of defense.

This policy was followed by Presidential Policy Directive 41 (PDD-41), United States Cyber Incident Coordination, that established principles for cyber incident response and differentiated between "significant cyber incidents and steady-state incidents" through a new cyber incident severity schema. This directive acknowledged that some amount of cyber intrusion would continue despite our best efforts and emphasized that cybersecurity requires an allocation of effort and resources based on an ongoing assessment of existing cyber risk. In line with this reorientation, the National Institute of Standards and Technology stood up a commission devoted to risk assessment in 2016 and subsequently issued a risk assessment framework that was widely adopted by the private sector and is still used today.

In addition to these policy initiatives, the Obama administration also dealt with several momentous cyber incidents that had a lasting impact on our cyber program. In April 2015, the Office of Personnel Management (OPM), the agency that manages the government's civilian workforce and a large part of the US security clearance process, discovered that its systems had been hacked.[8]

In the aftermath of this attack, the Obama administration undertook an effort to seek out and punish those foreign states and actors that were perpetrating attacks, resulting in the imposition of sanctions against Russia and North Korea

---

8. As reported in the *Wall Street Journal* and *Washington Post,* government officials believe that the Chinese were responsible for the hack that included the access of detailed personal information on US military and intelligence personnel, putting the records of 4.2 million people at risk. This breach led to a congressional investigation and resignation of several OPM officials. Ellen Nakashima, "Chinese Breach Data of 4 Million Federal Workers," *Washington Post,* June 4, 2015, https://www.washingtonpost.com/world /national-security/chinese-hackers-breach-federal-governments-personnel-office/2015/06 /04/889c0e52-0af7-11e5-95fd-d580f1c5d44e_story.html; Damian Paletta, "Cybersecurity Firm Says it Found Spyware on Government Network in April," *Wall Street Journal,* June 15, 2015, https://www.wsj.com/articles/firm-tells-of-spyware-discovery-in -government-computers-1434369994.

and the indictment of government-linked hackers from China and Iran. This effort succeeded in securing an agreement from Chinese President Xi Jinping to halt purely commercial hacking, an agreement that the Chinese honored in a limited fashion.

The Obama administration also dealt with the leak of critical NSA information by Edward Snowden. This leak critically compromised the government's cyber defense capabilities, and the resulting exposure of certain NSA surveillance activities undermined the relationship between the NSA and private telecom providers that is elemental to a national cyber defense. Finally, the end of the Obama administration saw the Russian manipulation of public opinion and interference with the 2016 election that highlighted the vulnerability of our democratic institutions and processes to this cyber threat.

The Trump administration made progress in several areas of cybersecurity, but with a distinct shift of focus from response, risk assessment, and remediation to a more aggressive stance against cyber adversaries, including a confrontational posture against China and its cyber misconduct and the embrace of more forward-leaning military cyber operations. During his first year in office, President Trump released Executive Order 13800 modernizing federal IT infrastructure to increase security and announced that Cyber Command would be elevated to a unified combatant command and then took a series of steps to enhance the role of DOD in cyber defense. He rescinded the Obama-era PPD-20, which had limited the role of the DOD and designated DHS as the lead for cyber defense of civilian infrastructure, and gave DOD more authority in that area.

With White House blessing, DOD then released a 2018 Cyber Strategy introducing the principle of "defend forward," changing DOD's role in responding to cyber threats from responsive to a more active defensive posture and moving the responsibility for the cybersecurity of the "defense critical infrastructure" (i.e., defense industrial base companies) to DOD and away from DHS. Finally, the Trump administration highlighted the cyber threat from China, initiating the Clean Network Program that focused on protecting our networks from "authoritarian malign actors" and responding to state-sponsored cyber incidents with an increased tempo of public attribution and criminal indictments.

Congress has also contributed to the effort with significant pieces of legislation. For example, in the 2019 National Defense Authorization Act, Congress chartered the US Cyberspace Solarium Commission, whose resulting report was released in 2020, and in January of 2021 the FY '21 NDAA included twenty-seven provisions pulled directly from the cyber defense recommendations in the Commission's report.

How Did the Bush Administration Do?

The Bush administration's response to the emerging cyber threat—though necessarily nascent in many respects—provided strong and enduring building blocks for today's cyber security system. At the same time, it wrestled—sometimes successfully and sometimes unsuccessfully—with issues that present continuing challenges that still handicap the government's cyber defense efforts.

None of these continuing challenges has proven more vexing than the ongoing lack of clarity in the operational roles and responsibilities among the many federal agencies with cyber capabilities. While the Bush administration and each subsequent administration has sought to solve it, this bureaucratic problem continues to limit the effectiveness and efficiency of US cyber efforts.

This bureaucratic confusion within the executive branch is mirrored in the organization of Congress. Dozens of committees and subcommittees have some kind of cyber jurisdiction, all overlapping and largely uncoordinated. This situation weakens the quality of resulting oversight, creates confusion and unnecessary work for agencies who have to answer to multiple committees, and unnecessarily extends the time to get cyber legislation passed. Many authorities and expert groups have recommended that Congress streamline its cyber oversight, yet Congress failed to do so under the Bush administration and has failed to do so since.

Another enduring challenge is integrating and coordinating the efforts between the federal government and the private sector. Despite the early recognition of the importance of information sharing between government and industry and some improvement in that process in recent years, there are still significant problems. For instance, there is inadequate sharing around cyber vulnerabilities, especially zero-day vulnerabilities, and around the methodologies that would help private companies in their effort to diagnose and address threats to their systems.

Related to this problem is the ongoing challenge of balancing the private industry's desire for transparency from the government about looming threats with the government's legitimate interest in protecting the sources and methods that may have alerted the government to those threats. It will require stronger legislation and even stronger incentives to force the level of sharing that will permit more seamless defenses against cyber threats.

What Are the Lessons Learned?

In spite of the progress and efforts that have been made, the nation's record on cybersecurity has been mixed at best.

- *First, the cyber threat is simply a fundamentally difficult problem to address.* It presents unprecedented challenges that cannot be met with the policies and measures that the nation has used to meet the threats of the past. Because the medium of a cyber attack is ones and zeroes in amorphous cyber code, it is often difficult to identify the perpetrators or to derive the true purpose of an attack. As a result, the nation is often left without sufficient certainty about the identity of the perpetrator to allow it to deliver responses that will deter future attacks.
- *Second, the nation still does not have a fully developed slate of meaningful responses that are effective at persuading our foreign adversaries to desist from future government-sponsored attacks or to restrain nongovernmental cyber wrongdoers operating within their borders.* With no guarantee of any meaningful sanction or repercussion, nation-states like China and Russia will continue their current campaigns of official and unofficial malign cyber activity against the US economy and government.
- *Third, US government entities have yet to undertake a coordinated and comprehensive effort to develop and disseminate information about the solutions that will provide operational cybersecurity beyond baseline standards.* Absent clearer guidance about cybersecurity expectations and the technologies that meet those expectations, US systems will remain the cybersecurity patchwork they are today, and the country will remain a ripe target for easy cyber exploitation.
- *Finally, the United States has failed as a society to take on the financial burden that is required to achieve cybersecurity.* While corporate America has come a long way since Dick Clarke bemoaned the paltry amount of corporate revenue devoted to cybersecurity in 2002, it has yet to articulate the true return on investment in this area or to commit the resources necessary to defeat the cyber threat. With the increasing frequency of ransomware attacks and other intrusions affecting corporate bottom lines, as well as the

other attendant costs thereof (i.e., reputational damage, data compromise, costs of remediation, etc.), companies are starting to realize that cybersecurity investment should be seen as a requirement for sustained corporate viability and not just as an inconvenient cost center on the company books.

CONCLUSION

In sum, although the nation has developed a variety of cyber defenses over the years, the hard truth is that the cyber threat has outpaced the combined cybersecurity efforts of governmental and private-sector actors. Cyber adversaries now present a more potent—and in some ways more existential—threat to society than they did two decades ago. As a consequence, the need to redouble those combined efforts is even more urgent today than it was when the Bush administration began laying the foundation for the nation's cyber defense.

Contributor:
Elizabeth Tippett

CHAPTER 28

Climate Change

Climate Change and Clean Development

JAMES L. CONNAUGHTON

The adoption of the UN Framework Convention on Climate Change (UNFCCC) in 1992 and the development of the Kyoto Protocol in 1996 brought domestic and international calls for increasingly aggressive US action and international collaboration on climate change. Despite President Bush's firm commitment to the UN-FCCC's goal of stabilizing atmospheric greenhouse gas concentrations at a level that would prevent dangerous human interference with the climate, the subject was fraught with controversy, both internationally and domestically, throughout both terms of the Bush presidency.

The controversy stemmed in part from the president unsurprisingly acting on his opposition to US participation in the Kyoto Protocol, a position he took during the campaign because the Protocol required unrealistically deep emissions reductions with corresponding harm to US jobs and the economy. At the same time, it contained no corresponding commitments from China, India, and other major developing countries with substantial and rapidly growing greenhouse gas emissions. Another contributing factor to the controversy was President Bush's unexpected reversal of his campaign commitment calling for legislation establishing a cap-and-trade program to reduce power plant carbon dioxide emissions (modeled on the extremely successful Acid Rain Trading Program enacted as part of the 1990 Clean Air Act Amendments). He decided instead to proceed only with reductions of sulfur dioxide, nitrogen oxide, and mercury. The president announced these positions early in his new administration in a March 2001 letter to the Senate.[1]

Nonetheless, President Bush and his administration remained firmly committed to taking sensible action on climate change—at home and abroad—recognizing that climate change is a serious, long-term challenge that requires an effective, sustainable policy. The administration's approach was science-based, encouraged research leading to technological innovation, and took advantage of the power of markets to bring breakthrough technologies into widespread use. The administration's strategy staked out broader common ground for action politically and among stakeholders based on a wider and mutually reinforcing combination of interests. It sought not only to reduce greenhouse gas emissions, but also to improve energy security, cut air pollution harmful to human health and natural resources, and accelerate opportunities for substantially cleaner development abroad. Central to this approach was ensuring continued economic growth and prosperity for US citizens and for citizens throughout the world, so as to sustain and expand investment in the technologies and practices needed to achieve these objectives.[2]

The Bush Administration Approach

While not the conventional wisdom, the fact is that President Bush was committed to confronting the serious challenge of global climate change from the earliest days of his administration. He began by focusing on both climate change science and on the technologies needed to solve the problem.

In March of 2001, the president convened a cabinet-level working group, including the Departments of Treasury, State, Agriculture, Commerce, Energy,

---

1. "Text of a Letter from the President to Senators Hagel, Helms, Craig, and Roberts," The White House, March 13, 2001, https://georgewbush-whitehouse.archives.gov/news/releases/2001/03/20010314.html.

2. "President Announces Clear Skies & Global Climate Change Initiatives," The White House, February 14, 2002, https://georgewbush-whitehouse.archives.gov/news/releases/2002/02/20020214-5.html.

Transportation, Interior, and the Environmental Protection Agency, to conduct a comprehensive review of climate change science and policy. To help guide that review, the White House asked the National Academies of Sciences (NAS) to convene an expert panel of the National Research Council (NRC) to prepare an authoritative report on the state of climate change science. The members of the NRC panel included a number of the most accomplished and highly respected scientists from diverse scientific fields critical to an understanding of climate change, including Dr. James Hansen of NASA, Dr. Richard Lindzen of MIT, Dr. Ralph Cicerone of the University of California Irvine, and Thomas Karl of NOAA. The NRC provided its report, *Climate Change Science: An Analysis of Some Key Questions* ("NRC Report"), to the president and the public in June of 2001.

After ten weeks of consultation by the president's cabinet with outside scientists and policy experts, and following receipt of the NRC Report, on June 11, 2001, President Bush announced in a Rose Garden address that global climate change is "an issue that should be important to every nation in every part of our world."[3] Further, the president stated, "The issue of climate change respects no border. Its effects cannot be reined in by an army nor advanced by any ideology. Climate change, with its potential to impact every corner of the world, is an issue that must be addressed by the world." The president reaffirmed the long-standing obligations of the United States under the UNFCCC. And he said the United States would "work within the United Nations framework and elsewhere to develop with our friends and allies and nations throughout the world an effective and science-based response to the issue of global warming." Accompanying the president's June 2001 speech was a thirty-three-page policy book describing the Bush administration's initial approach for addressing climate change, highlighting in detail current domestic actions, an analysis of the Kyoto Protocol, scientific research priorities, ways to promote and advance technology, and efforts to address climate change on an international level.

During his speech, the president criticized the Kyoto Protocol, calling it a "fatally flawed" approach to effectively addressing climate change, principally because the treaty exempted some of the world's largest emitters of greenhouse gases from its requirements. At the time, the Energy Information Administration (EIA) projected that annual developing country emissions of carbon dioxide

---

3. "President Bush Discusses Global Climate Change," The White House, June 11, 2001, https://georgewbush-whitehouse.archives.gov/news/releases/2001/06/20010611-2.html.

would double between 1990 and 2010—an increase that represented over twice as many tons as the reductions the United States would be required to make under the Kyoto Protocol. (Such projections ultimately fell well short of reality, with China's emissions alone exceeding those of the United States in 2006, and all of the developed world in 2019.) Another major flaw was the severe burden the treaty would have imposed on the US economy. According to a scenario EIA analyzed during the prior administration, US implementation of the Kyoto Protocol could have reduced US GDP by as much as 4 percent.

President Bush's critique of Kyoto was neither new nor unique. In 1997 the US Senate had voted ninety-five to zero to approve the Byrd-Hagel resolution (including then-Senators Biden and Kerry). The resolution stated that the United States would not be a signatory to any international climate change treaty that exempted developing country parties (such as China, India, Brazil, South Africa, and Mexico) from the treaty's mandates or that would result in serious harm to the US economy. Because the Kyoto Protocol failed the Byrd-Hagel test, in its remaining three years, the Clinton administration never submitted the treaty to the Senate for ratification. As then Vice President Al Gore stated the day Kyoto was finalized: "As we said from the very beginning, we will not submit this agreement for ratification until key developing nations participate in this effort."[4]

Had the US ratified Kyoto, it is likely that not only would many energy-intensive US jobs have been lost to other countries that were exempt from the treaty, but the emissions associated with those jobs would have gone overseas too—undermining any claim to producing an actual reduction in global emissions. In fact, given the significantly more carbon-intensive energy mix in those countries, the shift in jobs would have caused a significant net increase in cumulative emissions, as evidenced by that actually transpiring from market forces leading to the surprisingly accelerated rise in Chinese manufacturing. Nevertheless, the president's well-founded opposition to the Kyoto Protocol triggered an avalanche of misinformation about his administration's climate policies, which continues to this day.

The rejection of Kyoto, however, represented the beginning, not the end, of the Bush administration's plan of action for dealing with global climate change.

---

4. "Clinton Hails Global Warming Pact," CNN All Politics, December 11, 1997, https://edition.cnn.com/ALLPOLITICS/1997/12/11/kyoto/.

As the president stated in his June 2001 speech, "America's unwillingness to embrace a flawed treaty should not be read by our friends and allies as any abdication of responsibility. To the contrary, my administration is committed to a leadership role on the issue of climate change. We recognize our responsibility and will meet it—at home, in our hemisphere, and in the world."[5]

The president based his climate policy on several principles. In addition to reaffirming US obligations under the Framework Convention (the UNFCCC), he called for policies that are "measured as we learn more from science and build on it; flexible to adjust to new information and take advantage of new technology; balanced to ensure continued economic growth and prosperity; based on market-based incentives to spur technological innovation; and based on global participation, including developing countries."[6] According to these principles, the president articulated an overarching philosophical framework to guide climate change policy formation. "The policy challenge is to act in a serious and sensible way, given the limits of our knowledge," he said. "While scientific uncertainties remain, we can begin now to address the factors that contribute to climate change."[7]

The president articulated his new policy on February 14, 2002 in a major address that reaffirmed the US commitment to the Framework Convention "and its central goal, to stabilize atmospheric greenhouse gas concentrations at a level that will prevent dangerous human interference with the climate."[8] To meet this objective, the president set a specific near-term goal "to reduce America's greenhouse gas emissions relative to the size of our economy," and called for cutting US greenhouse gas intensity by 18 percent by 2012. This goal was designed to "set America on a path to slow the growth of greenhouse gas emissions and, as science justifies, to stop and then reverse the growth of emissions."[9] This ambitious but achievable commitment represented a nearly 30 percent improvement in the projected rate of improvement in emissions intensity at the time (14 percent).

---

5. "President Bush Discusses Global Climate Change," June 11, 2001.

6. "President Bush Discusses Global Climate Change," June 11, 2001.

7. "President Bush Discusses Global Climate Change," June 11, 2001.

8. "President Announces Clear Skies & Global Climate Change Initiatives," February 14, 2002.

9. "President Announces Clear Skies & Global Climate Change Initiatives," February 14, 2002.

To achieve this goal, the president urged policymakers in his administration "to move forward on many fronts, looking at every sector of our economy. We will challenge American businesses to further reduce emissions... We will build on these successes with new agreements and greater reductions."[10]

His administration accordingly developed and implemented a government-wide portfolio of pragmatic and increasingly consequential policies and collaborations both domestically and internationally. Domestically, this included:

- *Enactment of broadly bipartisan legislation:*
  - Successive annual appropriations totaling tens of billions of dollars to advance climate change science and research and development of a broad portfolio of clean energy and other technologies.
  - Enactment of tax, loan programs, and other financial incentives to unleash tens of billions in new capital investment in cleaner, more efficient energy technology, commercial and industrial equipment, and facilities.
  - Farm Bill Reauthorization and successive annual appropriations totaling more than $50 billion to foster conservation and associated conservation of farmland and forests.
  - 2005 Energy Policy Act, which established a broad energy research and development program covering: (1) energy efficiency; (2) renewable energy; (3) oil and gas; (4) coal; (5) Indian energy; (6) nuclear matters and security; (7) vehicles and motor fuels, including ethanol; (8) hydrogen; (9) electricity; (10) energy tax incentives; (11) hydropower and geothermal energy; and (12) climate change technology.
  - 2007 Energy Independence and Security Act, which established the largest national program (then or since) of mandatory, market-based greenhouse abatement programs focused on vehicle fuel efficiency, renewable fuels, lighting efficiency, appliance and equipment efficiency, and government operations. These programs are projected to save US consumers over $2 trillion, reduce oil use by almost 3 million barrels a day in 2030, reduce total energy use by 8 percent in 2030, and cut cumulative CO_2 emissions by 17 billion metric tons. In addition, these

---

10. "President Announces Clear Skies & Global Climate Change Initiatives," February 14, 2002.

programs are driving correspondingly consequential reductions all around the world through the adoption of the advanced technologies developed to comply with the legislation.[11]

- *Establishing public-private partnerships and specific greenhouse abatement commitments* from every major greenhouse gas emitting commercial and industrial sector,[12] and launching the highly successful Climate Leaders and Climate VISION programs.
- *Removing technical, regulatory, permitting, and other governmental barriers* to deployment of clean energy and other technologies.[13]
- *Providing financial, technical, and policy support to the states* to implement incentives and mandates, such as renewable portfolio standards, that are practically tailored to their local circumstances.
- *Enhancing the voluntary climate reporting registry* under 1605(b) of the 1992 Energy Policy Act.

In parallel, President Bush and his administration applied a similar portfolio approach to broaden and deepen international engagement on climate change through a series of "confidence-building" bilateral, minilateral, multilateral, and fully international agreements and partnerships. These included:

- *The Methane to Markets Partnership*, launched in 2004, to advance cost-effective, near-term methane recovery and use as a clean energy source from coal beds, natural gas facilities, landfills, and agricultural waste management systems. The Partnership included eighteen countries: Argentina, Australia, Brazil, Canada, China, Colombia, Ecuador, Germany, India, Italy, Japan, Mexico, Nigeria, Republic of Korea, Russia, Ukraine, the United Kingdom, and the United States, and was subsequently joined by the European Commission. The Partnership embodied the multiplicity of interests approach

11. Lowell Ungar, "How a Bill Signed by Bush and Implemented by Obama Is Saving Consumers Billions," ACEEE (blog), October 29, 1995, https://www.aceee.org/blog/2015/10/how-bill-signed-bush-and-implemented.

12. "Clean Energy and Climate Change," The White House, July 13, 2001, https://georgewbush-whitehouse.archives.gov/ceq/clean-energy.html.

13. George W. Bush administration, "Executive Order 13212—Actions To Expedite Energy-Related Projects, May 18, 2001," https://www.govinfo.gov/content/pkg/WCPD-2001-05-21/pdf/WCPD-2001-05-21-Pg770.pdf.

to reducing global methane emissions—a much more potent greenhouse gas than carbon—to enhance economic growth, promote energy security, address climate change, improve mine safety, reduce waste, and improve local air quality and the environment.

- *The Asia Pacific Partnership on Clean Development and Climate,* launched in 2005, included China, India, South Korea, Australia, and Japan, accounting at the time for more than 50 percent of the global economy, energy use, and greenhouse gas emissions. This partnership took a regional and sector-based approach to developing, promoting, and sharing cleaner energy technologies to achieve results in the areas of energy efficiency, methane capture and use, rural/village energy systems, clean coal, civilian nuclear power, geothermal, liquefied natural gas, building and home construction, bioenergy, agriculture and forestry, hydropower, wind power, and solar power.
- *The G-8.* Climate change was among the top agenda items during each of the G-8 meetings President Bush attended (to the exclusion of discussion of other important global environmental imperatives such as water for the poor, food security, and overfishing). Most consequentially, during the 2007 G-8 Summit in Heiligendamm, Germany, President Bush and the other G-8 leaders declared that they would "consider seriously" the goal of "at least halving global emissions by 2050"[14] in the context of their agreement to launch new negotiations in the UNFCCC for a successor agreement to the Kyoto Protocol. Based on emissions profiles at the time, this figure assumed an 80 percent absolute reduction in emissions by developed countries and a 50 percent reduction of projected emissions by the major emitting developing countries, including China and India. Updated to take into account the unexpectedly substantial jump in greenhouse gas emissions in China, India, and other developing countries, the 2007 G-8 leaders' goal is essentially in line with the nonbinding objective later adopted by UN COP (the "Conference of the Parties," the decisionmaking body of the UNFCCC) in the 2015 Paris Agreement to achieve net-zero emissions in the second half of this century.

---

14. "Chair's Summary," G8 Summit, Heiligendamm, Germany, June 7, 2007, http://www .g-8.de/Content/EN/Artikel/__g8-summit/anlagen/chairs-summary,templateId =raw,property=publicationFile.pdf/chairs-summary.pdf.

- *International Partnerships,* including Gen IV Nuclear International Forum, Group on Global Earth Observations, Global Nuclear Energy Partnership, Renewable Energy and Energy Efficiency Partnership, International Partnership for the Hydrogen Economy, Carbon Sequestration Leadership Forum, Tropical Forest Conservation Partnership, and numerous others.
- *US-led Amendment to the Montreal Protocol on Ozone Depleting Substances (ODS),* in 2007, securing binding international agreement to accelerate the global phaseout of HCFCs (hydrochlorofluorocarbons), an ODS that is also one of the most potent and long-lasting greenhouse gases. This agreement is producing substantially more greenhouse gas emissions reductions than the Kyoto Protocol would have delivered if the participating countries had met their commitments, which most did not.
- *The Major Economies Meetings on Energy Security and Climate Change,* launched in 2007, brought together countries representing more than 80 percent of global greenhouse gas emissions: Australia, Brazil, Canada, China, the EU, France, Germany, Italy, India, Indonesia, Japan, Korea, Mexico, Russia, South Africa, the United Kingdom, and the United States. This process was expressly established to drive substantive progress and feedback into the UNFCCC Conference of Parties (UN COP) negotiations in Bali, Indonesia. As one analyst noted: "A reasonable deal within this group would be nearly five time more effective than the commitment period of the Kyoto Protocol, which only covered 15% of global emissions."[15]

All of this culminated in the UN COP agreement on the Bali Roadmap and Bali Plan of Action at the end of 2007, which launched negotiations on a successor treaty to the Kyoto Protocol. Building on the international collaborations described above, the Bush administration focused on securing a negotiating framework that could correct the flaws of the Kyoto Protocol in a way that could enable ultimate Senate ratification and US participation. The key elements of that approach included:

---

15. Timmons Roberts, "Beyond the Climate Impasse: How the Major Economies Forum Can Lead the Way," Up Front (blog), April 8, 2013, https://www.brookings.edu/blog/up-front/2013/04/08/beyond-the-climate-impasse-how-the-major-economies-forum-can-lead-the-way/.

- Binding, trade enforceable commitments from all major emitting countries, developed and developing.
- Nationally determined and enforceable strategies to achieve those commitments.
- Agreement on a common and accountable system of measurement, reporting, and verification of each nation's progress.

Inclusion of these elements was strongly resisted by the major developing countries, led by China, who attempted to closely align itself with the smaller (G-77) developing countries, arguing that such elements would be unduly burdensome and unfair. However, behind the closed doors of the negotiating room, representatives from the smaller developing countries objected to China's positioning and for the first time expressed their view that China and the other large developing country emitters were now just as much a part of the greenhouse gas emissions problem as developed countries and should be equally accountable to take action under any new treaty. When the very contentious discussion concluded, the parties did not accept the China-led effort to be free of any future binding obligations and allowed the elements raised by the United States to be included for consideration in a future treaty, leaving the resolution of such matters for another day. So, the outcome in Bali was critical in ensuring the expectation of meaningful commitment from China and the other major developing countries, laying the foundation for the 2009 Copenhagen Accord and the 2015 Paris Agreement.

Building on the prospect of a more effective international framework, US progress in reducing emissions, and the bipartisan success of the 2007 Energy Independence and Security Act with the newly Democrat-led Congress, President Bush announced in April 2008 a new national goal to stop the growth of US greenhouse gas emissions by 2025.[16] To help achieve this objective, he announced that he was ready to support legislation mandating reductions in power plant emissions, simplifying the complicated weave of incentives that had developed over time, and removing barriers to more rapid investment in and deployment of new emissions-reducing technologies. He then outlined nine principles underlying legislation that he could support. However, not long thereafter, congressional leadership decided to wait until after the election for a potentially "better deal" on new legislation under a Hillary Clinton, Barack Obama, or John McCain presidency.

---

16. "President Bush Discusses Global Climate Change," April 16, 2008.

What Happened Since the End of the Bush Administration?

Notwithstanding their apparently and at times wildly differing expressions of political rhetoric, legislative objectives, policy initiatives, and diplomatic positioning, the Obama and Trump (often with deep resistance) administrations largely followed through on the legislated and administrative portfolio of policies and partnerships advanced by the Bush administration. Each president presided over relatively modest progress in US greenhouse gas emissions reductions and drove numerous international initiatives to help other countries do likewise. While President Bush had announced a goal in 2008 to stop the growth of greenhouse gases by 2025 based on US Department of Energy projections then available, US greenhouse gas emissions actually peaked in 2005 and have come down about 15 percent since then. This outcome was the result not only of the governmental portfolio of policies and partnership such as the 2007 legislative mandate to improve lighting efficiency by 70 percent, but also market forces and innovations, such as the dramatic displacement of coal with lower-cost fracked gas for use in US electricity generation.

Immediately following his election in 2008, and with a large Democratic majority in the House and a filibuster-proof Democratic majority in the Senate, President Obama pressed for legislation to establish a national, economy-wide carbon cap-and-trade program, with the strong support of most of the US electricity sector. Although that measure passed the House on a purely partisan basis, it foundered in the Senate. Shortly after the legislation's demise, President Obama asked Congress in his State of the Union Address to enact a Clean Energy Standard (similar to cap and trade) focused only on power plant emissions. That too foundered in the Senate and was never taken up in the House. President Obama nevertheless successfully implemented all of the programs established by the 2007 Energy Independence and Security Act. Seven years into his administration, President Obama's Environmental Protection Agency finalized the Clean Power Plant regulation mandating power plant carbon dioxide emissions reductions, which was subsequently stayed by the courts. Nevertheless, the long pendency of the rule, the uncertain outcome of litigation challenging the rule, a separate rule sharply cutting coal power plant mercury emissions, and lower-cost competition from fracked natural gas led to escalating shutdowns of coal power plants and a de facto ban on investment in new coal power plants—an outcome far more dramatic than the original carbon dioxide emissions rule would have required.

On the international front, to help advance negotiations in the UN COP, President Obama continued President Bush's strategy of high-level multilateral engagement among the major emitting nations under the renamed "Major Economies Forum on Energy and Climate," with the same members as the Bush process. President Obama inexplicably discontinued the Asia Pacific Partnership and the substantial program of work that was still underway. In the run-up to the UN COP negotiations in Paris in 2015, President Obama emphasized bilateral engagement with China (a sound idea). He jointly announced with Chinese President Xi Jinping their respective post-2020 (purely voluntary) goals on climate change, with the United States seeking to achieve an economy-wide target of reducing emissions by 26–28 percent in 2025 and China to achieve the peaking of emissions around 2030 (a very weak outcome).[17]

The negotiating objectives of the Obama administration for the UN COP in Paris were similar to the ones pursued by both the Clinton and Bush administrations, with only limited success. The Paris Agreement achieved a breakthrough in securing specified emissions reductions commitments and plans to achieve them from China and the other major developing countries. These are embodied in what are called "nationally determined contributions," which are voluntary and subject to updating only after five years. None of these commitments are binding or enforceable in any way, and many of the national programs to achieve them are vague. The parties also did not settle on a common system of measurement, verification, and reporting—a linchpin of ensuring the desired outcomes of environmental and other treaties. This discussion has proceeded unresolved for nearly thirty years since the 1992 UNFCCC. Given the nonbinding character of the Paris Agreement and the claim that it did not require any new domestic implementing legislation, the Obama administration decided not to submit the document to the Senate for ratification and argued that it likewise did not run afoul of the 1995 Senate Resolution.

The next year, the Obama administration took a page out of the Bush administration playbook and led international agreement on the 2016 Kigali Amendment to the Montreal Protocol. The Kigali Amendment accelerated the phase down of hydrofluorocarbons (HFCs), which have a global warming po-

---

17. "U.S.-China Joint Announcement on Climate Change," The White House, press release, November 11, 2014, https://obamawhitehouse.archives.gov/the-press-office /2014/11/11/us-china-joint-announcement-climate-change.

tential thousands of times higher than CO2. Global implementation is projected to reduce the equivalent of seventy billion tons of carbon dioxide by 2050. Once again, China and other developed countries undertook binding, internationally measurable, and enforceable commitments to reduce a potent greenhouse gas under the Montreal Protocol, in sharp contrast to their refusal to do so under the Paris Agreement.

Notwithstanding his very strong campaign rhetoric and later declarations that climate change is a "hoax," his withdrawal of the United States from the Paris Agreement, and his budget proposals to slash funding for clean energy and other climate change programs, President Trump signed a series of bipartisan legislation and appropriations by both Republican and Democrat-led Congresses substantially increasing funding and strengthening programs for clean energy technologies, conservation-based carbon abatement, carbon capture and storage, and related international activities. President Trump was also a strong proponent of the natural gas fracking boom driving emissions reductions in electricity generation. And at the very end of his administration, President Trump signed the broadly bipartisan American Energy Act of 2020, which modernizes and refocuses the Department of Energy's research, development, and demonstration programs on the most pressing technology challenges—scaling up clean energy technologies such as advanced nuclear, long-duration energy storage, carbon capture, and enhanced geothermal.[18] Most consequentially, this legislation codified the 2016 Kigali Amendment to the Montreal Protocol into US law, despite four years of active opposition to the provision by the Trump administration and their refusal to send the Kigali Amendment to the Senate for requisite ratification. On the diplomatic front, the absence of any affirmative climate work is what most sets President Trump's administration apart from its predecessors. However, the actual emissions reduction outcomes of President Trump's one term in office should prove to be as substantial as his predecessors, whether he wanted it or not.

Confronting climate change was one of the central pillars of President Biden's campaign for president and, since taking office, he has initiated what is likely the furthest-reaching government-wide agenda of policy initiatives and

---

18. "The Energy Act of 2020: A Monumental Climate and Clean Energy Bill," Clearpath (blog), April 1, 2021, https://clearpath.org/our-take/the-energy-act-of-2020-a-monumental-climate-and-clean-energy-bill/.

staffing. President Biden has called for achieving net-zero emissions from US power plants by 2035 and net-zero economy-wide by 2050. President Biden has asked Congress to enact a market-based Clean Energy Standard to achieve the power plant goal and has proposed a wide range of policies to advance the economy-wide goal. While the 2035 power plant objective per se is likely to prove practically and therefore politically unachievable, a very broad range of US electricity companies, businesses, and major trade associations, such as the Business Roundtable, have publicly committed to at least an 80 percent reduction in emissions by 2050 (with many committing to net-zero) and called for predictable and durable national policies to achieve it.

In November 2021, Congress passed a major bipartisan infrastructure bill containing very substantial new funding and program authorizations focused on climate change. Subsequently, Congress has deliberated on a very broad, wholly partisan, and therefore controversial, reconciliation bill that contains climate mitigation measures and incentives with broad support, and other climate measures that do not currently muster even a majority of support and are likely to be stripped. The net outcome, however, should be an unprecedented level of funding for climate change.

How Did the Bush Administration Do?

Private-sector action combined with the comprehensive suite of mandates, incentives, and partnerships at the federal and state level contributed to meaningful progress in reducing the growth of US greenhouse gas emissions, even as the US population grew, and the economy continued to expand. While the United States was behind the curve through much of the 1990s, during the Bush presidency, the US outperformed most of the industrialized world in tackling emissions. By 2012, the United States had achieved the target of 18 percent improvement in greenhouse gas intensity set by President Bush ten years earlier, with US greenhouse gas emissions actually peaking in 2005 and declining thereafter.[19] The Bush administration program of action performed well beyond even the best case projections of progress at the time.

---

19. Timothy Herzog, Kevin A. Baumert, and Jonathan Pershing, *Target: Intensity—An Analysis of Greenhouse Gas Intensity Targets.* Washington, DC: World Resources Institute, April 2006, http://pdf.wri.org/target_intensity.pdf.

What Are the Lessons Learned?

Though global climate change is a very complex subject, the crux of the matter politically and diplomatically is the still unsettled consensus about how far, how fast, and at what cost greenhouse gas emissions must be reduced nationally and internationally. National legislatures and treaty negotiators routinely settle on such matters in the context of establishing binding and enforceable requirements to control other harmful environmental constituents such as air pollutants, water pollutants, and hazardous substances. Once a specifically quantified outcome is agreed, then the supporting suite of policies, partnerships, and market forces tend to readily fall into place. That is largely not yet the case for US domestic and international climate change policy.

Nonetheless, remarkably substantial common ground exists, and political support has grown across multiple US presidential administrations and Congresses on the portfolio of strategies and quantum of action needed to make continued progress confronting climate change. The challenge is that none of these strategies are presently scaled in scope and speed to meet the urgency for action on climate change that the science would presently say is required.

Presidents Bush, Obama, and Trump (however ironically) demonstrated that broadly bipartisan legislation and binding treaty arrangements are possible. Yet the most fundamental need for legislation establishing a national emissions reduction target and timeline remains elusive. As does a more focused target and timeline for power plant emissions reductions and a corresponding market-based mandate to achieve it. As does any prospect for the UNFCCC COP to establish a binding treaty regime on par with the highly effective and wholly successful modalities of the Montreal Protocol.

A renewed effort internationally and domestically is required to define more reasonably achievable targets on more reasonably achievable timelines, on a sector-by-sector basis, informed by technological feasibility, economic realities, and national circumstances, along with a credible process for adjusting targets as need be (either faster or slower) as changing circumstances may require. As noted, that is how the Montreal Protocol and correspondingly successful national market-based mandates already work. Such approaches can work again for climate change.

CHAPTER 29

Authoritarian Populism

THOMAS SHANNON | DANIEL W. FISK

President George W. Bush was animated by a deep faith in democracy, the power of individual liberty, and the community created by the solidarity of free peoples. In the Americas he sought to consolidate the region's democratic progress, energize it through the innovation and dynamism of market economies and trade, and extend the benefits of peace and prosperity throughout the Americas. He articulated this vision for the Americas in his first National Security Strategy. The United States would build "flexible coalitions with countries that share our priorities" to "promote a truly democratic hemisphere where our integration advances security, prosperity, opportunity, and hope."[1] Although the United States faced dramatic security challenges in the aftermath of the September 11 terrorist attacks, President Bush never lost his commitment to reshaping how the United States engaged with its neighbors and partners in the Americas.

In this regard, President Bush believed that the hemisphere had embarked on the next great phase of its political, economic, and social development. He understood that the democratization that the Americas had experienced through

---

1. George W. Bush, "The National Security Strategy of the United States of America, IV: Work with Others to Defuse Regional Conflicts," The White House, September 2002, https://georgewbush-whitehouse.archives.gov/nsc/nss/2002/nss4.html.

the 1980s and 1990s—the transition from military to civilian government, election of leaders, peaceful transition of power, and protection of individual rights—was only the first and necessary step toward a larger goal: for these democracies to generate the opportunities and provide the economic resources and security necessary for their peoples to have a voice in determining their own destinies. The nations of the Americas were attempting to use democratic governance to create truly democratic societies.

This was an audacious goal for a hemisphere largely defined by poverty, inequality, and social exclusion. The Bush administration sought through new political and economic initiatives to empower the people of the region while helping governments build sustainable democratic institutions that delivered for their peoples. But it did so in the face of a rising tide of authoritarian populism.

TRANSITION MEMORANDUM

~~CONFIDENTIAL~~ 4300

WITH SECRET **NATIONAL SECURITY COUNCIL** Transition

ATTACHMENTS WASHINGTON, D.C. 20504

NSC Declassification Review [E.O. 13526]

November 17, 2008 DECLASSIFY IN PART
by William C. Carpenter 3/23/2020

MEMORANDUM FOR THE RECORD

FROM: ROBERT A. KING, WESTERN HEMISPHERE AFFAIRS
DIRECTORATE

SUBJECT: Confronting Authoritarian Populism

THE SITUATION AS WE FOUND IT:

Democracy in Discredit and the Rise of Chavez. In 2000, democracy in Latin America was showing considerable signs of strain. Two decades of anemic economic growth punctuated by periodic economic crises, pervasive corruption, increasing threats to personal security, and continuing political instability had led to growing skepticism that the so-called "Washington Consensus" on democratic institutions and free market economics could address poverty or economic inequality. Latin Americans expressed increasingly deep disappointment with how democracy was performing, democratic institutions were held in low regard, and long-standing traditional political parties were falling into discredit.

As 2001 opened, populism did not yet pose a coordinated, region-wide threat, but there was already ample evidence that democratic institutions would come under increasing assault. In Peru, for example, Alberto Fujimori was forced from office in November 2000 only after years of repeatedly violating democratic and electoral norms. The overthrow of governments in Paraguay (1999) and Ecuador (2000) further demonstrated that democracy and the rule of law were by no means consolidated throughout region.

The 1998 election of populist former coup-maker Hugo Chavez in Venezuela had raised concerns that Venezuela's long-standing democracy would become subject to the instability and abuses that

~~CONFIDENTIAL~~ WITH
SECRET ATTACHMENTS Re-Classified by: Ellen J. L. Knight
Reason: 1.4 (b) (d) Reason: 1.4(d)
Declassify on: 11/17/18 Declassify on: 11/17/2033

were frequent elsewhere in the region. Even in 2001, however, the extent to which Chavez would over time become the champion of a broader regional revival of authoritarian populism and the principal threat to institutional democracy in the region was not yet fully apparent. Chavez was elected by promising to sweep Venezuela's moribund traditional parties from power and create a democracy that would more equitably distribute Venezuela's oil wealth. He has sought to redefine democracy in terms of outcome rather than process—his "participatory democracy" focuses on the benefits that government provides to its citizens, especially the disenfranchised, and downplays the importance of institutions and the legitimacy of political opposition. To this redefinition of democracy Chavez added a virulently anti-American strain of Latin American nationalism that characterized the influence of the United States as a fundamental threat to the well-being of all Latin Americans.

THIS ADMINISTRATION'S POLICY:

The Bush Administration policy is to support democratic governments and their ability to promote social justice and provide for the security of their citizens. Success against authoritarian populism is directly related to the success of democratic governments.

From its inception, the Administration actively promoted the strengthening of democratic institutions throughout the region, and worked to ensure the credibility and success of governments capable of serving as models of the benefits of democratic institutions and responsible governance. These policies also have sought to demonstrate that democracy and equitable economic growth and development, along with initiatives to enhance personal security, are not mutually exclusive. This has been a significant element of our cooperation with countries like Mexico, Peru, Colombia, and in Central America.

From the earliest months of the Administration, we sought to make clear, including with the President's first foreign trip being to Mexico and at the Summit of the Americas in Quebec, a willingness to work with Latin America governments in the region to consolidate democratic gains and improve economic conditions. The President also began early on his push for free trade to create jobs and force economic reforms. These priorities were later outlined in National Security Presidential Directive 32 (January 23, 2004), which reaffirmed our commitment to bolstering security, strengthening democratic institutions, promoting prosperity, and investing in people.

However, the consequences of "democratic disillusionment" and a perception that the United States only cared about trade, fighting drugs and terrorism, and closing our border created a sense in Latin America both of U.S. detachment from the everyday realities of the hemisphere and that the political and economic progress of the last two decades only benefited elites, not the average person.

In the first 4 years of the Bush Administration, Chavez's effort to export his self-styled "revolution" was not viewed as a significant threat, in part because Chavez's resources were limited and his own domestic political problems represented a distraction. Chavez's brand of populism became a significant threat to the evolution of democracy in the region only after his resounding victory in the August 2004 referendum, and because growing oil prices provided him with substantial resources to cultivate alliances and influence elections. He has inspired imitators in neighboring countries, and he has actively worked to support their election through his resources and his rhetoric. He has also strongly opposed U.S. interests and engagement with the region, directly undermining U.S. efforts to promote sustainable economic growth and development. Chavez-style challengers to the status quo emerged as serious contenders for the presidency in Honduras, Bolivia, Costa Rica, Peru, Mexico, Ecuador, and Nicaragua during the election cycle of November 2005 to December 2006. These elections produced populist leaders in Honduras, Bolivia, Ecuador, and Nicaragua. The period was capped by the overwhelming re-election of Chavez himself in December 2006.

Faced with a growing threat to democracy region-wide and the risk that Chavez would further exploit misperceptions about U.S. intentions in the region, the Bush Administration began reframing its Western Hemisphere strategy to demonstrate more effectively how U.S. policies improve the lives of peoples in the region. A new emphasis on social justice linked democracy and development and identified poverty and social exclusion as the major threats to democracy.

While the Administration's initial policy focus was not designed to counter populist demagogues directly, those policies did form the foundation for initiatives coming out of the new Western Hemisphere strategy to blunt the appeal of populist rhetoric and to engage democratically elected leaders who appeared predisposed to following the Chavez model. This strategy involved several distinct activities:

- First, we have proactively reached out to freely elected leaders with a clear message that we will not prejudge or base our relations with them on any ideological criteria, but rather on a shared commitment to democratic processes and individual rights. This was the President's message to Brazilian President Lula upon his election in 2002 and has been pursued with every elected leader since that time.
- Second, we have challenged undemocratic actions by populist governments, worked to strengthen international standards for democratic governance, and forced populists to move carefully to avoid international condemnation.
- Third, in countries ruled by populist authoritarians, the United States has ▉▉▉▉▉▉▉ ▉▉▉▉▉▉▉▉▉▉▉▉▉▉▉▉▉▉▉▉▉▉▉▉▉▉ while taking steps to limit the ability of populist leaders to effectively scapegoat the United States as the reason for their antidemocratic behavior.
- Finally, we developed a set of policy and public diplomacy initiatives that emphasized social justice and challenged the caricature of the United States and the Bush Administration as focused solely on "trade and terrorism."

We have undertaken a wide variety of initiatives to diminish the threat of authoritarian populism.

- To assist civil society confront authoritarian regimes, we have:
  - Supported Venezuelan civil society during the December 2007 referendum by training thousands of poll watchers; and
  - Supported non-governmental organizations working on "good government" and electoral transparency in Nicaragua since the November 2006 election of Daniel Ortega and his effort to close political space and limit independent civil society in that country.
- To strengthen democratic institutions that can deliver the benefits of democracy, we have:
  - Supported election observer missions and political party development in Guatemala, Bolivia, Honduras, Venezuela, Haiti, Nicaragua, and Paraguay;
  - Sustained and expanded Plan Colombia to strengthen state authority over most of Colombia and improve the everyday security situation for most Colombians; and
  - Developed, in cooperation with Mexico and the countries of Central America, and gained congressional approval of an initial $450 million in funding for the Merida Initiative to strengthen the ability of those countries to combat transnational criminal organizations and end the impunity from which these elements benefit.
- To challenge populism regionally, we have:
  - Secured approval of the Inter-American Democratic Charter, obligating governments to promote and defend democracy;
  - Completed free trade agreements with Chile, five Central American countries, and the Dominican Republic, Peru, Colombia, and Panama;
  - Strengthened North American competitiveness through the Security and Prosperity Partnership (SPP), especially bolstering economic development in Mexico;
  - Supported debt cancellation in the IMF, World Bank, and Inter-American Development Bank totaling more than $3.4 billion in relief for the poorest countries: Bolivia, Guyana, Haiti, Honduras, and Nicaragua;
  - Announced a $200 million program, under Treasury and State Department auspices, to encourage market-based bank lending to small- and medium-sized enterprises;
  - Promoted economic innovation through the Commerce Department's "Americas Competitiveness Forum" program, which brings together the Hemisphere's private sector, and the establishment of the Brazil-United States CEO Forum;
  - Supported, through the biofuels partnership with Brazil, the development of alternative and renewable energy sources to address the dependence of Central American and Caribbean countries on imported oil and other energy products; and
  - Worked to lower the costs of sending remittances to Latin America; remittances to the region amount to an estimated $45 billion annually from family and workers in the United States.

- To invest in people, we have:
  - Created the Millennium Challenge Account and signed Compacts with Honduras, Nicaragua, and El Salvador; approved Threshold Programs for Guyana, Paraguay, the Dominican Republic, and Peru; and determined Bolivia's eligibility for a Compact;
  - Supported the Inter-American Development Bank's effort to triple the amount of credit available to small businesses;
  - Helped 640,000 individuals receive antiretroviral therapy;
  - Launched the Partnership for Latin American Youth, a 3-year, $75 million effort to help disadvantaged youth learn English and develop technical skills to improve their ability to gain employment;
  - Provided, through the Overseas Private Investment Corporation, more than $380 million in guarantees to expand the availability of affordable housing for working families in Latin America;
  - Convened with the participation of the President, Mrs. Bush, and five Cabinet Secretaries, the first "White House Conference on the Americas" to showcase the efforts of nongovernmental organizations, faith-based groups, volunteer associations, and the private sector; and
  - Strengthened healthcare through a new Central American Healthcare Training Center in Panama, which allows Health and Human Services (HHS) to partner with Central American nations in training nurses, technicians, and community health care workers; the establishment of the Partnership for Breast Cancer Awareness and Research to increase research, training, and community outreach in Latin America; the 2007 deployment of the U.S. Navy medical ship "Comfort" on a 12-country, 4-month mission that provided more than 98,000 people with medical care; and the 2008 deployments of the USS Boxer and USS Kearsarge to 9 countries to provide medical care.

WHAT HAS BEEN ACCOMPLISHED:

While U.S. policies have been partly successful in containing authoritarian populism, the United States has faced two significant constraints to confronting these populist demagogues. First, these populists have all been democratically elected and are perceived as the products of their countries' long-standing political and economic inequities. This confers upon them a degree of legitimacy that it is difficult to gainsay, in spite of their repeated violations of democratic norms. Second, countries in the Western Hemisphere remain wary of criticizing each other's internal affairs, especially if they are perceived as doing so at the behest of the United States. Populists are able to manipulate these long-standing regional hypersensitivities regarding sovereignty and United States "interference" to undercut U.S. efforts to expose and contain them.

Despite these constraints, in most countries in the region, democratic government increasingly has become strengthened and institutionalized with our help. In much of the region, the political consensus in favor of moderate, responsible political and economic policies has held.

The Administration's policies of positive and comprehensive engagement with the leaders of the region and development of concrete actions to help these leaders has reinforced this situation, especially by pursuing policies that show that democracy and fighting poverty are not mutually exclusive.

The integration of historically far left parties into the democratic mainstream in many countries in the region has been critical in serving as an alternative to Chavez-style populism and a vital step in the further consolidation of democracy in Latin America. Brazil's President Lula and Uruguay's President Vazquez have demonstrated that it is possible to reconcile commitment to respecting democratic institutions and pursuing moderate, responsible economic policies with a greater attention to addressing poverty and economic inequality. The Administration has contributed to their credibility and success by working aggressively to build solid relations that transcended these leftist leaders' long-held suspicions about the United States.

As President of Brazil, Luiz Inacio Lula da Silva has overseen 6 years of moderate fiscal policies combined with a greater government attention to poverty alleviation. In the process, he has moved his formerly radical, obstructionist Worker's Party toward the political center and he has broadened the consensus in favor of responsible economic policy. From the earliest moments following Lula's election, the Bush Administration, starting with the President, demonstrated our willingness to work with him and his government. As a signal to nervous Brazilian and international markets, President Bush invited President-elect Lula to visit him in Washington in December 2002. This was the first in a series of frequent visits and consultations between the two Presidents that resulted in concrete cooperation in diverse areas. The United States and Brazil signed a biofuels cooperation agreement in March 2007 that highlighted Brazilian competitiveness in the alternative fuels industry and will boost regional cooperation to help economically vulnerable and energy-dependent Caribbean and Central American states with local biofuels production and consumption. The United States and Brazil have also increased law enforcement cooperation to help Brazil combat its burgeoning crime problem. In broader areas, the two countries are cooperating on anti-malaria programs in Africa. On a global scale, in recognition of and to reinforce Brazil's ability to serve as a bridge between developed and developing countries, the positive working relationship has also extended to the Doha Round of multilateral trade negotiations, an area where the United States and Brazil are usually at odds.

The 2004 Uruguayan presidential election of Tabare Vazquez, the leader of a coalition that included political parties deeply antipathetic towards the United States, threatened to undo the strong relations that the United States had enjoyed with Uruguay under President Batlle. By reaching out to President Vazquez and assuring him that the United States was prepared work with countries that respected democratic norms regardless of their ideology, the Administration gave Vazquez the leverage to overcome resistance within his own coalition. The initial result was a Bilateral Investment Treaty in 2005. The United States further showed a willingness to be flexible in how it approached deepening economic relations with Uruguay leading to the establishment of a Trade Investment Framework Agreement in 2007, and greater U.S. market access for Uruguayan products, including agricultural products that are important for Uruguay.

In other cases, such as those of Honduras and Nicaragua, the earlier actions of the Administration to pursue trade agreements and extend the benefits of development mechanisms like the Millennium Challenge Account has had a constraining effect on the worst tendencies of populist leaders. Mel Zelaya of Honduras and Daniel Ortega of Nicaragua both accept our bilateral assistance, continue to implement MCA Compacts, and sustain their countries membership in CAFTA, all while providing Chavez rhetorical support and participating in his Bolivarian Alternative to CAFTA, and in the case of Nicaragua, while Ortega is implementing political changes that seek to perpetuate himself in power.

In the 10 years since Chavez's election, other populist demagogues, some elected with Chavez's assistance, have adopted Chavez's methods for undermining democratic institutions, purportedly in the name of greater democracy. Populists such as Evo Morales in Bolivia (elected in 2006), Daniel Ortega in Nicaragua (reelected in 2006), and Rafael Correa in Ecuador (elected in 2006) have worked to disband institutions that limit their authority and to replace them with new constitutions and laws that limit, if not eliminate, the voice of their political opponents. Like Chavez, these populists dismiss opponents as illegitimate, oligarchs, and proxies of the United States. Like Chavez, they have rolled back the economic reforms of the 1980s and 1990s, nationalizing privatized companies and increasing state control over their economies. And like Chavez, they have rejected positive relations with the United States and opposed liberalized trade in the hemisphere.

Elsewhere, U.S. efforts to promote prosperity have succeeded in helping to check the spread of authoritarian populism and the Chavez model. Mexican voters rejected populism in 2006, and Mexico's institutions proved strong enough to withstand the internal backlash. Peruvians in 2006 rejected the presidential candidacy of a populist demagogue closely associated with Chavez and expressed a clear preference for sustainable growth and close relations with the United States.

FUTURE CHALLENGES:

Over the last 8 years, Latin America has made important strides in reducing poverty and, in most countries, in consolidating genuine democratic institutions. The conditions that make populism possible, such as grossly uneven distributions of wealth and exclusive, corrupt, and unresponsive political structures, continue to exist in much of the region. The amelioration of these conditions is a long-term project that requires the long-term commitment of U.S. attention and resources.

Despite the difficulties that populists are likely to face in the near term, at the end of the year, Presidents Chavez, Correa, Morales, and Ortega will still be in office and will still be working to increase their authority and marginalize their political opposition. Populist governments may come to power elsewhere in the near future, such as in El Salvador via 2009 presidential elections. In the short run, the U.S. focus should remain on forcing populist authoritarians to live up to international democratic standards for governance, on strengthening those standards, and on ensuring that democratic oppositions have the ability to compete with the populists.

Looking back, the success that Chavez allies enjoyed in the series of elections that took place throughout the region in 2005 and 2006 probably represents the high-water mark of his international influence. Although Venezuelans and Latin Americans have shown that they have become more wary of Chavez's promises, the United States must continue to expose the increasingly apparent economic flaws and undemocratic character of the Chavez model. As the Chavez model receives greater attention, its electoral appeal in other countries will be undermined, as happened during 2006 elections in Mexico and Peru. Even in Venezuela, voters stepped back from the populist agenda when they handed Chavez a critical defeat with the rejection of his December 2007 constitutional reforms to perpetuate his tenure. In a region with a preoccupation on "sovereignty" and "noninterference," Chavez's undemocratic actions and Venezuela's increasing poverty (despite its oil wealth) speak for themselves.

Attachments

Tab 1   Chronology for Confronting Authoritarian Populism, with compared copy
Tab 2   National Security Presidential Directive/NSPD-32 (January 23, 2004)
Tab 3   Next Steps on Venezuela (March 9, 2005)
Tab 4   Summary of Discussion for NSC Meeting (April 1, 2005)
Tab 5   Summary of Discussion for NSC Meeting (May 23, 2005)
Tab 6   Memorandum of Conversation with President of Brazil (November 6, 2005)
Tab 7   President Bush Discusses Democracy in the Western Hemisphere (November 6, 2005)
Tab 8   Summary of Discussion for the NSC Meeting and "The Democracy and Prosperity Partnership of the Americas" Notional Policy Initiative (March 27, 2006)
Tab 9   Memorandum of Conversation with President of Peru (October 10, 2006)
Tab 10   Summary of Conclusions of the Principals Committee Meeting (February 13, 2007)
Tab 11   President Bush Discusses Western Hemisphere Policy (March 5, 2007)
Tab 12   Scope Memorandum for Trip to Latin America (March 8–14, 2007)
Tab 13   Summary of Discussion for NSC Meeting (January 18, 2008)

POSTSCRIPT

THOMAS SHANNON, DANIEL W. FISK

The Bush Administration Approach

When President Bush first took office, as a former governor of a border state, he was most familiar with Latin America and had a firsthand appreciation for the region's relationship with the United States. He understood the deep disappointment that many in Latin America and the Caribbean felt toward their democratic institutions and political leaders, and the anger generated by their frustrated expectations when democracy and free markets failed to deliver the economic and social progress that so many had expected.

This assessment required the new administration to reframe US Western Hemisphere strategy. In National Security Presidential Directive 32, the administration defined its Americas strategy as based upon four pillars: bolstering security, strengthening democratic institutions, promoting prosperity, and investing in people. Underpinning this strategy was the belief that social justice linked democracy and development, and that the major threats to democracy in the hemisphere were poverty, inequality, and social exclusion.

This belief was reflected in three important multilateral documents: the Summit of the America's Declaration of Quebec City (2001), the Inter-American Democratic Charter (2001), and the Declaration on Security in the Americas (2003). All three defined democracy as being essential to political, economic, and social development, and identified the principal threat to democratic institutions as the social inequity that haunted much of the hemisphere. The vision reflected in the three documents was challenged by the emergence of populist leaders who in turn were the product of weak, ineffective, and corrupt democratic institutions and processes in many countries. The political energy coursing through these discredited democracies, like a deluge of water, had no place to go but over the banks. Populism had become the flood plains of failed democracy.

The Bush administration took four approaches to dealing with the populist challenge. First, sending clear messages that the United States would work with any elected leader who wanted to work with the United States, eliminating ideological criteria as the basis of engagement. Second, strengthening the standards and norms of democratic governance while challenging undemocratic actions of populist leaders. Third, limiting the ability of populist leaders to scapegoat the

United States for their failures. And finally, developing a set of policy and public diplomacy initiatives that emphasized social justice and challenged the caricature of the United States and the Bush administration as focused solely on trade and terrorism.

As to the first approach, the administration recognized that historically leftist political parties which nonetheless accepted democratic norms offered an alternative to Chavez-style populism. So somewhat surprisingly, given their very different backgrounds and politics, President Bush reached out to Lula da Silva in 2002 upon his election as Brazil's new president and formed a close personal relationship with this leader of the leftist Worker's Party. What resulted was intensive US-Brazilian cooperation on a range of issues including biofuels as an alternative to imported oil and gasoline, law enforcement as a way to help Brazil deal with an escalating crime rate, antimalaria programs in Africa, and the Doha Round of multilateral trade negotiations. President Bush took a similar approach to Tabare Vazquez upon his 2004 election as president of Uruguay at the head of a largely anti-American coalition of political parties. The result was a Bilateral Investment Treaty, a Trade Investment Framework Agreement, and greater access to the US market for Uruguayan products. Cooperation with these and other governments (such as in Mexico and Peru) showed the region that it was possible for democratic administrations pursuing responsible economic policies to nonetheless still address poverty and economic inequality.

Second, as to strengthening democratic governance in the face of populist challenges, the administration mounted a number of initiatives. For example, the administration obtained congressional approval and funding for the $450 million Merida Initiative to help Mexico and the countries of Central America combat transnational crime. The administration supported Plan Colombia to strengthen state authority and improve security for the Colombian people. It supported democratic political party development and election observer missions throughout the hemisphere. It completed free-trade agreements with Chile; five Central American countries; and the Dominican Republic, Peru, Colombia, and Panama. And it secured approval of the Inter-American Democratic Charter obligating governments in the region to promote democracy.

Third, as to the handling of populist leaders (and especially Hugo Chavez), the administration sought to strengthen electoral processes, civil society, and political opposition within their countries in an effort to deny them the legitimacy that comes from democratic election or referendum support. The administration also refused to engage them publicly or respond to their provocations, thereby frustrating their efforts to use the United States as a scapegoat or excuse for their own domestic political and economic failings.

Fourth, the Bush administration was also active in supporting social justice and economic progress for the hemisphere's poorest. Initiatives here included offering $3.4 billion in debt relief to the hemisphere's poorest countries, funding to encourage market-based bank lending to small- and medium-sized enterprises, and working to lower the costs for families and workers in the United States to send remittances back to their home countries. The Bush administration also created the Millennium Challenge Account and completed programs with at least seven countries in the region to improve infrastructure, enhance economic growth, and improve service delivery. And the administration funded efforts to expand affordable housing for working families and to provide healthcare research, training, and services.

What Has Happened Since the End of the Bush Administration?
The Obama administration, while employing a different rhetorical style, continued the Bush administration policy of positive engagement with those countries interested in working with the United States. Although challenged early by a constitutional crisis in Honduras following the coup against President Mel Zelaya, the Obama administration helped restore constitutional order and a democratically elected government while successfully resisting efforts by some in the region to impose an authoritarian populist on Honduras. The Obama administration worked to win Senate ratification of trade agreements negotiated during the Bush administration with Colombia and Panama. This created an unbroken string of trade agreements stretching along the hemisphere's Pacific Rim from Canada to Chile.

The Obama administration also became an observer to the Pacific Alliance, a regional integration initiative created by Chile, Colombia, Peru, and Mexico in 2011 that sought to further deepen trade and investment. The administration negotiated the Trans-Pacific Partnership (TPP), a trade agreement that linked free-trade partners in the Western Hemisphere with some of the most dynamic markets of Asia and the Pacific. This agreement built a trade and regulatory structure to shape the globalization of Latin America, while ensuring that democracies and open markets would have a place of privilege in cross-Pacific trade.

Unfortunately, the TPP did not reach its potential when the United States failed to join it. The Obama administration's late and indifferent push for congressional approval was followed by both Democratic nominee Hillary Clinton and Republican nominee Donald Trump opposing TPP during the 2016 presidential campaign. President Trump then withdrew the United States from TPP shortly after taking office in 2017. America's absence from the TPP hurt economic engagement with our Southern Hemisphere neighbors (as well as our Asian allies in the face of Chinese economic competition).

The Obama administration also normalized relations with Cuba. While this rapprochement with Havana failed to curb the communist regime's grip on power, repression of its own people, or support for the authoritarian regime in Venezuela, it did at least remove a long-term friction in regional relations and reduce the ability of some authoritarian populists to use Cuba to separate the United States from the rest of the hemisphere. In an effort to address migration from Central America, the Obama administration launched the Alliance for Prosperity with Honduras, Guatemala, and El Salvador. Working with the governments of these countries, the Inter-American Development Bank, and other multilateral development banks and institutions, the United States sought to accelerate economic and social development in these countries, address security issues, and enhance cooperation within Central America. Through such actions, the Obama administration continued the Bush administration's efforts to promote integration, trade, and development to enhance and strengthen democracy.

By the end of the Obama administration, the political tide showed some signs of turning in Latin America. Especially in South America, left-of-center governments were being replaced by right-of-center governments. Notwithstanding these hopeful trends, authoritarian populism has remained resilient in some parts of the western hemisphere. Following Hugo Chavez's death, the Nicolas Maduro regime continued its hold on power in Venezuela, even as its populist misrule has driven the once-wealthy country into extremes of destitution, penury, and oppression. Populists of other stripes have also taken power in Mexico, Brazil, and Peru and, in the case of Nicaragua, have consolidated power in the form of Daniel Ortega's growing tyranny.

Meanwhile, amid these competing regional trends of democratic capitalism and authoritarian populism, the Trump administration brought a different approach to regional relations. Its nationalist agenda focused on a smaller set of issues, such as migration, counterdrug cooperation, and correcting trade imbalances, and had little space for pursuing trade and investment agreements or the broader effort to promote regional integration, democracy, and development.

While its updated version of NAFTA, known as the US-Mexico-Canada Agreement (USMCA), was well received in Mexico and Canada, in other instances the Trump administration used trade to force agreements on migration and asylum. Its decision to end assistance through the Alliance for Prosperity, and its tougher stances on the authoritarian regimes in Cuba and Venezuela, also generated some resentments in the region—though other nations quietly supported the increased pressure on Maduro.

Ultimately the Trump administration's regional policies failed to achieve many of their goals and fueled much dissatisfaction in the region. The revival, by the Trump administration, of the Monroe Doctrine as an argument to dissuade extrahemispheric engagement in South America was roundly rejected by the region and seen as an unacceptable effort by the United States to assert influence over how the region would treat with the world.

In hindsight, it is apparent that the rise of authoritarian populist leaders in some countries in the Americas was part of an effort to use democratic processes and institutions to capture governments and then challenge and confront the United States and its partners in the hemisphere. It was a reaction to the broadening commitment to free trade and regional economic integration largely driven by the United States.

How Did the Bush Administration Do?

Looked at across two decades and now three presidencies, it is useful to ask what remains of the political and strategic vision that President Bush brought to hemispheric diplomacy. The pandemic has fractured much of the Americas, isolating individual countries, and driving each to seek its own salvation. The regional multilateral organizations that had played such a central role in President Bush's engagement have fallen afoul of the political partisanship that defines Washington, DC, and many capitals in the Americas, and are viewed increasingly not as fora of engagement and cooperation but of political posturing.

At the same time, regional integration and focus on trade and commerce as drivers of economic growth have opened the hemisphere to globalization. This has created new challenges. The hemisphere's rich agricultural production, its important mineral wealth, its growing middle class, and its significant infrastructure needs have made it an attractive trading and investment partner for Asian economies and raised the specter of China as a major competitor of the United States in the Americas.

The Bush administration approach would have helped to create a bulwark against such influence. Bush believed that democracy's value included the development that would follow, and that increasingly political legitimacy would be created not by democratic processes alone but by the accomplishments that democratic governments would produce. The administration saw the hemisphere as a strategic reserve of countries that shared a commitment to democratic values, common economic understandings, and a belief in the value of individual liberty and open societies—along with the institutions and diplomatic practice necessary to keep the peace and promote prosperity. A commitment to individual freedoms and open societies made the countries of the hemisphere natural partners for the United States. But for this vision to be realized, democracy would have to succeed in the hemisphere.

President Bush believed American power was potentially transformational for the hemisphere. He did not understand the United States as committed to the status quo or bound by tradition or interests to always take the side of stability, order, and established constituencies. In this regard, he saw the rise of authoritarian populists in some countries in the hemisphere as evidence of their peoples' desperation, but he was convinced that these democracies could be saved by engagement that was designed to meet the challenges facing each society. His administration's willingness to address issues of corruption, gender-driven violence, epidemics and chronic disease, ethnic and racial discrimination, migration, and remittances are examples of how he sought to unlock the energies and potential that existed throughout the hemisphere. He sought to identify the United States with the forces of innovation and change that were fundamentally reshaping the Americas and to knit the region together in closer harmony.

In the end, it must be said that Bush administration policies were only partially successful in achieving their objective and in containing authoritarian populism in the hemisphere. Other populists followed in Chavez's footsteps and seized power: Morales in Bolivia, Ortega in Nicaragua, and Correa in Ecuador. In addition to adopting undemocratic means to perpetuate their "democratic" election, they rolled back economic reforms, nationalized private companies, and increased state control of the economy. At the same time, however, voters rejected populist bids for power in Mexico and Peru, and the administration's efforts like those with Lula in Brazil and Vazquez in Uruguay were able to help those democracies avoid the populist trap.

President Bush had a coherent view of the hemisphere as a rich and diverse region that was united by a shared commitment to democracy, common economic understandings, and a belief in the sanctity of the individual and the fundamental freedoms that accrue to all. This helped shape his belief that the hemisphere inspired a solidarity among free peoples that lent a special quality and urgency to the institutions, organizations, and practices that defined the inter-American system. It was a vision he pursued with only partial success.

What Are the Lessons Learned?

- *Authoritarian populism is a symptom, not a cure.* While it recurs out of popular frustrations with inequality, corruption, and despair, it has never yet been able to develop an effective governing agenda.
- *Authoritarian populism will not be sustainable over the long term.* Contemporary concerns about democratic backsliding in the region often miss the dynamic nature of these societies and the insistent demand of voters for outcomes that directly affect their well-being. As more and more people are given political voice, governments will be increasingly measured and evaluated by their outcomes or accomplishments and not their origins. If populists do not deliver this social content of governance—and so far they have not done so—they will be at risk.
- *To be a successful alternative to authoritarian populism, democracy must deliver.* Democracy reflects the highest aspirations of the human spirit. But it also must deliver security, prosperity, and a better life—or people will be susceptible to alternative approaches. That is what the populists count on— that democracy will fail to meet the social and economic expectations of the people.
- *Democratic progress is precarious.* Democracy has a social content and cannot be understood only in institutional terms. It is about human development and opportunity, not just governance structures. Advances in democracy can be undermined or reversed by economic stagnation, corruption, and failure to build durable democratic institutions.
- *The United States must have an affirmative agenda for the hemisphere.* American power is most effective when it is used for more than mere transactional purposes. It needs to be married to a positive vision centered on democratic values. And that positive vision must be responsive to the needs and desires

of the people of the hemisphere—premised on mutual respect, not advantage, and partnership, not paternalism.

- *This affirmative agenda must include democratic institution building.* The region's populists have used democratic elections to take power and then proceeded to undermine alternative power centers (like the legislature and the judiciary), to remove constitutional barriers to continued rule, and to attack political opponents, the free press, and independent civil society—perpetuating their "democratic" rule with undemocratic means. The need is to strengthen democratic institutions, laws, and practices in advance to make it more difficult for authoritarian populists to subvert democracy should they initially gain power even by democratic means.

- *Being there matters.* President Bush engaged directly in the region. No president traveled more frequently to the region; no president participated in as many Summits of the Americas; no president attended as many North American Leaders fora; no president provided more foreign assistance to the region; and no president concluded more trade and investment agreements. Whatever their political or ideological differences, the leaders and the peoples of the Americas understood President Bush's commitment to deepening relationships within the hemisphere. In the Americas, President Bush was a constant gardener, and it was reflected in the quality of the relationships he forged.

PART 8

Commentary

INTRODUCTION

STEPHEN J. HADLEY

The book concludes with three stand-alone essays prepared by three independent scholars. These essays provide the scholars' respective initial assessments of the materials contained in this book. They also offer some initial conclusions not only about Bush foreign policy but about American foreign policy more generally over the last two decades.

Melvyn P. Leffler's essay in chapter 30 (entitled "An Illuminating Hand-Off") looks at the Bush record through the prism of the Freedom Agenda and evaluates that concept as an organizing principle of Bush foreign policy. It provides an interesting counterpoint to the concept of a "balance of power that favors freedom" discussed elsewhere in this book.

Hal Brands' essay in chapter 31 (entitled "Reassessing Bush's Legacy: What the Transition Memos Do (and Don't) Reveal") provides an initial overall assessment of the Bush foreign policy record—its achievements and its failures. It also tries to evaluate Bush foreign policy in light of the efforts of its three successor administrations in dealing with the same set of challenges.

Martha Joynt Kumar's essay in chapter 32 (entitled "Transferring Presidential Power in a Post-9/11 World") examines the transition from the Bush to the Obama administrations. It then compares it to subsequent presidential transitions and draws lessons learned to guide future presidents in their transition planning.

CHAPTER 30

An Illuminating Hand-Off

MELVYN P. LEFFLER

Steve Hadley and his former colleagues in the Bush administration have provided an invaluable collection of Transition Memoranda that illuminate the foreign policy of the George W. Bush administration in its many dimensions. More than that, they have written succinct introductions and interesting postscripts that place the memoranda in context, extrapolate lessons, and compare their own performance to those of their successors. As citizens we can be grateful for the serious, systematic effort to provide information to a successor administration on the issues they deemed most salient. As scholars we can now appreciate the full range of issues absorbing the attention of policymakers. As students and teachers we can benefit immensely from the lists of attachments to each memorandum that identify the speeches, memoranda, conversations, and policy directives that shaped attitudes and actions on each particular topic. We can hope that in due time all these documents might be declassified and made easily accessible.

There are several ways to assess the value of this volume. We can look at the memoranda collectively and reflect on what they illuminate about the totality of the Bush administration's foreign policies. We can address the documents individually and discuss how valuable each might have been to an incoming administration. We can aggregate them and use them to reexamine our thinking about the long-term evolution of American foreign relations and the country's role in the international arena. We can use the postscripts in particular to wrestle with the intrinsic difficulties of almost every foreign policy issue and to weigh the relative, qualitative performance of the Bush administration compared to its successors. In this short essay I will try to do a little of all these things.

I want to begin by emphasizing the great value of this collection for illuminating the history of the Bush administration's foreign policies. We can garner a sense of the overall challenges it faced through its own assessments of how it dealt with terrorism and proliferation challenges while grappling with the dilemmas of stabilization and reconstruction. We can read about familiar issues like Afghanistan and Iraq, but also learn about its relations with Pakistan, Libya, and India as well as its foreign aid and developmental practices and peacemaking efforts in Africa. These transition memos, moreover, capture the administration's efforts to deal with Russia while seeking to expand NATO and make Europe "whole and free." They illuminate the efforts to strengthen alliances in East Asia and find new partners in the Indo-Pacific region in order to coopt and contain a China that was growing richer, stronger, and more confident. They portray the efforts to nurture a settlement of the Palestinian-Israeli imbroglio in the midst of surging Islamic fundamentalism, rabid anti-Americanism in the Arab world, and a continuing global war against terrorism. One of the striking features of the memoranda and postscripts is the readiness to engage in self-criticism, to assess failures as well as successes, and to identify continuities and discontinuities with their successors. Yet one cannot help but note how often Hadley and his assistants judge themselves to have done a better job than their successors in the Obama and Trump administrations.

The memoranda do much more than summarize policy. They highlight the glue that connected all these efforts to one another—the so-called Freedom Agenda—and that will become the focus of my critique. Hadley, who served as deputy national security adviser in President George W. Bush's first administration and his principal national security adviser from 2005–2009, chose to underscore the significance of the Freedom Agenda by placing it at the forefront of the volume. This choice seems well founded given its centrality in the evolving thinking of President Bush himself. In the memorandum on this topic that Hadley passed on to the Obama administration, Michael G. Kozak wrote, "Promotion of freedom became the central element of our foreign policy and the priority policy objective of the United States."[1] In so writing Hadley and his aides underscored the president's words in his second inaugural address and highlighted the central theme of their own 2006 National Security Strategy statement, a theme that was incorporated into a formal national security policy directive in July 2008. NSPD-58 stated that "it is the policy of the United States to seek and support the growth of democratic movements and institutions in every nation and culture, with the ultimate goal of ending tyranny in the world."[2]

In the Transition Memorandum and postscript on the Freedom Agenda and in the one on Iraq, Hadley and his colleagues outlined the evolution of the president's thinking. He did not begin with a freedom agenda. It evolved from the experiences in Iraq and the challenges of waging a global war on terrorism. In the postscript to Brett McGurk's memorandum on Iraq, Meghan O'Sullivan stresses that "the critical emphasis placed on helping Iraqis build democratic institutions came more out of post-Saddam experience in Iraq than prewar rationales for the US invasion. Saddam Hussein was deposed because the Bush administration believed he represented a national security threat to the United States and its friends and allies." After the invasion, when "security virtually collapsed," the president and his advisers could have chosen "a Western-friendly autocrat" to carry out the policies desired by the United States. But Bush, emphasizes O'Sullivan, chose not to follow this route. He made a choice to nurture the development of democratic institutions and to encourage Iraqis "to build a democratic political system as the only way a traumatized nation could peacefully manage the competition for power and resources among Sunni, Shi'a, and Kurds, and the many other groups within Iraq." The effort, O'Sullivan admits, was flawed and costly. Yet the administration became increasingly committed to it.[3]

---

1. Michael G. Kozak, Memorandum for the Record, "Freedom Agenda," November 15, 2008.

2. George W. Bush, Inaugural Address, American Presidency Project, January 20, 2005, https://www.presidency.ucsb.edu/documents/inaugural-address-13; National Security Strategy Statement (NSSS), March 2006, https://georgewbush-whitehouse.archives.gov/nsc/nss/2006/; NSPD 58, July 17, 2008, https://irp.fas.org/offdocs/nspd/nspd-58.pdf. In their Preface to this volume, Condoleezza Rice and Stephen Hadley stress that the president wanted to pursue a "balance of power that favors freedom," but the Freedom Agenda evolved to dominate Bush's rhetoric and thinking.

3. Meghan O'Sullivan, postscript to Transition Memorandum on "Iraq."

According to Michael Gerson and Peter Wehner, who write the postscript to the Freedom Agenda, this was because President Bush came to believe that "advancing democracy and the institutions that sustain liberty were the only viable alternative to repression and radicalism" and constituted "the best path to sustainable economic growth and political stability." After 9/11, Michael Kozak explained in his November 2008 Transition Memorandum, "the President determined that the struggle with worldwide terrorism was ideological in nature and could not be won by military, law enforcement or traditional diplomatic means alone." The president recognized that "the dark ideology of the terrorists was attractive to a significant segment of the populations in the broader Middle East and elsewhere not because they favored the form of oppression the terrorists espoused, but because it offered the only alternative to the existing repressive regimes which robbed them of hope. The popular frustration with the status quo that the terrorists were harnessing was directed at us not because of our democratic values but because we had become identified with those repressive regimes." Consequently, the president resolved that oppressed peoples had to be offered "a positive alternative to the status quo, and that the only viable alternative was political freedom."[4]

This volume forces readers to take the Freedom Agenda seriously. It was not simply a rationalization for the failure to assess the Iraqi weapons of mass destruction (WMD) threat correctly. The Freedom Agenda emanated from the grueling experiences of waging a global War on Terror and grappling with the occupation of Iraq. The president read the 2002 United Nations report on human development in the Arab World, and noted the emphasis on three key deficits: freedom, women's empowerment, and education.[5] He also read the memoranda sent to him by Donald Rumsfeld, his defense secretary. Frustrated and exasperated by the global War on Terror, Rumsfeld wanted to repudiate its misleading nomenclature. "The important point," Rumsfeld wrote Bush, "is that what we face is an ideologically-based

---

4. Michael Gerson and Peter Wehner, postscript to "Freedom Agenda"; also see Kozak, "Freedom Agenda."

5. For the report, see UN Development Programme, Arab Human Development Report, 2002, http://hdr.undp.org/sites/default/files/rbas_ahdr2002_en.pdf. Eric Edelman, the vice president's foreign policy adviser, recounted Bush's interest in this report in an interview with the author of this essay, March 10, 2011; for Bush's interest, also see Condoleezza Rice, *No Higher Honor: A Memoir of My Years in Washington* (New York: Crown, 2011), 326–27.

challenge." To win the battle against Islamic extremism, the United States had to support reform, champion women's rights, and help moderate forces "institute representative systems that are respectful of all their people. . . ." This approach was "not do-goodism," Rumsfeld emphasized, it was "wise calculation" aiming to co-opt the middle classes against the extremists.[6] It accorded, moreover, with the president's strong religious convictions. Bush believed deeply that human freedom and individual dignity were divinely inspired; they were natural rights, and best nurtured in democratic polities.[7] Further, he imbibed the clichés of the democratic peace circulating through the academies of higher learning and popularized in countless books and articles. "Free governments," he wrote in his introduction to the National Security Strategy of 2006, "do not oppress their people or attack other free nations. Peace and international stability are reliably built on a foundation of freedom."[8]

The Transition Memoranda reveal how seriously the administration took the Freedom Agenda. Freedom and economic development, Bush believed, were intertwined and mutually reinforcing. If they could be nurtured simultaneously, they constituted a virtuous cycle. Failed states endangered US security and provided fertile territory for the growth of radicalism, religious fundamentalism, and terrorism. Consequently, Bush made development a pillar of his National Security Strategy. The excellent Transition Memorandum on "smart development" highlights how much importance the president assigned to this priority, how ambitious he was in terms of goals and the allocation of resources, and how innovative he was in trying to initiate new measures of accountability. He launched major new initiatives to fight HIV/AIDS, malaria, and other infectious

---

6. Donald Rumsfeld to Bush, June 18, 2004, The Rumsfeld Archive, https://www.rumsfeld.com/endnotes/chapter-50/.

7. "Freedom is the design of our Maker," Bush declared in a famous speech in Prague in June 2007, "and the longing of every soul." "Remarks to the Democracy and Security Conference," June 6, 2007, https://www.presidency.ucsb.edu/documents/remarks-the-democracy-and-security-conference-prague; for Bush's religious convictions, see George W. Bush, *A Charge to Keep* (New York: William Morrow, 1999), 1–13, 132–39; Gary Scott Smith, *Faith and the Presidency: From George Washington to George W. Bush* (New York: Oxford University Press, 2006), 365–414; David Aikman, *A Man of Faith: The Spiritual Journey of George W. Bush* (Nashville, TN: W Publishing Group, 2004).

8. Bush's introduction to NSS, March 16, 2006; for academic debates about the "democratic peace," see, for example, the articles by Christopher Layne, David E. Spero, and John W. Owen in *International Security* 19, no. 2 (Fall 1994): 5–125.

diseases. He created new institutions like the Millennium Challenge Corporation. He provided "significant financial incentive for governments to expand political freedom, guarantee civil liberties, and justly administer the law." Over the years of his two administrations he more than doubled foreign assistance for democracy, governance, and human rights programs. In return, he required reforms like "robust prosecution of corruption cases in Tanzania, increased immunization rates in Indonesia, and administrative tax reform in Albania." He also worked with other donor nations to alleviate the debt burdens of poor countries and negotiated free-trade agreements with several of them to boost their exports to America. Following the passage of the Africa Growth and Opportunity Act, imports from sub-Saharan Africa reached $50 billion, six times greater than in 2001.[9]

The Transition Memorandum on stabilization and reconstruction operations nicely complements the one on "smart development" and illustrates how the administration's bias against nation-building evaporated as it realized that it had to build infrastructure and nurture civil society in failed states lest they become havens for terrorists. Acknowledging how ill prepared it was to carry out its missions in Afghanistan and Iraq, the administration focused more attention and more resources on reorganizing governmental processes and mitigating bureaucratic conflicts. Between 2001 and 2008 it increased funding for development and diplomacy by 50 percent and asked Congress for 1,400 new positions in the State Department and US Agency for International Development. It reassigned primary responsibility for reconstruction and stabilization from the Defense Department to the State Department, created a new office to recruit and train an "expeditionary civilian corps" to conduct stability operations, and provided additional funding to support these tasks. America's security, it believed, was inextricably linked to economic development and political freedom abroad. It had learned.[10]

The Freedom Agenda shaped the administration's approach to Europe where it yearned to expand NATO and make Europe "whole and free and at peace." Citing the importance of President Bush's speech in Warsaw in June 2001, the

---

9. Christopher Broughton, Memorandum for the Record, "Smart Development," January 14, 2009.

10. Christopher Broughton, Memorandum for the Record, "Reconstruction and Stabilization Efforts," January 16, 2009.

Transition Memorandum underscored that the administration believed that "all of Europe's new democracies, from the Baltic to the Black Sea and all that lie between, should have the same chance for security and freedom—and the same chance to join the institutions of Europe—as Europe's old democracies have." The administration wanted to eradicate Cold War thinking, eliminate the demarcation lines between East and West, support the enlargement of the European Union, encourage the admission of Turkey, and back the development "of stable, democratic states in the western Balkans, including Kosovo, with viable prospects for full integration into Europe." Bush wanted to create "a sense of inevitability about the ultimate expansion of NATO and the EU to all the democracies of Central and Eastern Europe and the Western Balkans."[11]

The administration expected Russia to accept the new strategic realities that would allow the consummation of a Europe whole and free and at peace. The Transition Memos on Europe, Russia, and missile defense emphasize that the administration wanted to reach out and cooperate with Russia. President Bush "made an effort to shift the paradigm of U.S.-Russia relations from one marked by strategic rivalry and 'dependency' on western economic support to one of strategic cooperation on a wide range of important areas where the United States and Russia had shared interests," for example, counterproliferation and counterterrorism, nuclear security, cuts in strategic warheads, Iran, and North Korea. Where acrimony was expected, for example, over NATO expansion, missile defense, and Kosovo, the president wanted to "manage differences."[12]

But the administration's approach was infused with a sense of hubris and power, with a recognition "that America's security was threatened less by Russia's strength than by Russia's weaknesses and internal vulnerabilities." Accordingly, the administration asserted that "both Russia and the United States had legitimate and strategic interests throughout the former Soviet Union." It expected Russia to defer to the incorporation of former Soviet republics into NATO, accept the renunciation of the antiballistic missile treaty and the stationing of missile

11. Judy Ansley, Damon Wilson, and Adam Sterling, Memorandum for the Record, "Europe Whole, Free and at Peace," January 9, 2009; also Judy Ansley, Damon Wilson, Betram Braun, and Katherine Helgerson, Memorandum for the Record, "Western Balkans," November 17, 2008.

12. Janine Ellison and Leslie Hayden, Memorandum for the Record, "Managing Cooperation/Differences with Russia," January 5, 2009; also see Jamie Fly, Memorandum for the Record, "Missile Defense," January 16, 2009.

defenses in Poland and the Czech Republic, and acquiesce to the color revolutions in Georgia and Ukraine. "The president viewed Russia's respect for the sovereignty of the Eurasian states as key indicator of its approach to the world."[13]

The Transition Memorandum noted that Putin grew increasingly upset by US initiatives and by the political dynamics inside the former Soviet space. "Russia perceived U.S. efforts to promote democracy in former Soviet countries, in particular in the aftermath of the so-called 'color revolutions' in Georgia and Ukraine, as a smokescreen for advancing U.S. strategic interests at Russia's expense." Putin remonstrated against "the intense administration push" for granting NATO Membership-Action-Plans to Ukraine and Georgia. He occupied parts of Georgia, employed his energy supplies as a lever to pressure America's allies in NATO, tightened his government's control over trade and investment, and restricted the actions of NGOs supporting civil society initiatives inside Russia. The outgoing Bush administration recognized that Russia had "stepped up its campaign to undermine our presence throughout the former Soviet space. . . ." Its determination to assert its great power status rankled Bush administration officials and, in their view, revealed "worrisome insecurities that are inherent to Russia's institutional weaknesses. . . ." The challenge for the next administration would be to "balance a firm and measured response to Russian aggressiveness with continued Russian cooperation in strategic areas of U.S. national security interests."[14]

In other words, Russian weakness, as well as the superiority of American values, undercut Russia's right to assert its great power interests, control its periphery, or shape the political dynamics in the former Soviet space. Nonetheless, the Bush administration wanted to elicit cooperation in areas that mattered to Washington. Success was not deemed likely until the Russian government allowed itself to be accountable "to a broad popular constituency," a development that would confirm Russia's "integration" into twenty-first-century international institutions.[15]

In writing the introduction and postscript to the Transition Memorandum on Russia, Thomas Graham emphasizes that the administration's policies failed—that relations were worse with Russia at the end of 2008 than they had been in

---

13. Ellison and Hayden, "Managing Cooperation/Differences with Russia."

14. Ellison and Hayden, "Managing Cooperation/Differences with Russia"; see also Thomas Graham, Postscript to "Managing Cooperation/Differences with Russia."

15. Ellison and Hayden, "Managing Cooperation/Differences with Russia."

2001. The popular uprisings in Georgia and Ukraine, he acknowledges, "fed Russian suspicions that the United States sought to exploit Russian strategic weakness by promoting democracy in Eurasia." Whether alternative approaches might have produced different outcomes is unknowable, but he notes "that the Bush team at times failed to strike the right balance" between its aspirations to contain and coopt Russia largely because it assigned higher priorities "to other goals over cooperation with Russia." Hubris and power were determinative, Graham writes: "lingering faith that democracy had triumphed in the . . . ideological struggles against fascism and communism, confidence in unrivaled American power, and Moscow's strategic weakness led American policymakers to overestimate their ability to shape Russia's conduct or to counter its malign impulses."[16]

The Transition Memos illuminate greater success dealing with China, India, and Asia than with Europe and Russia. In this part of the globe the Freedom Agenda reinforced great power considerations. From the outset of the administration, President Bush assigned great importance to recalibrating America's relationship with India. He wanted to form a strategic partnership with India. "The bases of this strategic partnership were the common values we shared and our commitment to democracy." He lifted sanctions against India for its nuclear testing in 1998 and labored to expand trade in high-technology goods and to cooperate more closely on counterterrorism, civil nuclear energy, and missile defense. The "centerpiece" of the transformed relationship was the US-India Civil Nuclear Cooperation initiative. The eventual agreement brought half of India's nuclear reactors under International Atomic Energy Agency safeguards and converted India "from a nuclear outlier to an internationally recognized member of the nonproliferation community. . . ." It set the stage for peaceful nuclear cooperation, for Indian trade in nuclear fuel and technology, and for increased US military sales and joint military exercises. Although the Transition Memorandum on India indicated that Indian economic reforms lagged, tariffs remained too high, and bilateral defense agreements remained incomplete, the author of the postscript—Mark Webber—judges the strategic partnership to be "perhaps the most significant accomplishment of the Bush administration from a geopolitical perspective."[17]

---

16. Graham, "Postscript" to "Managing Cooperation/Differences with Russia."
17. Mark Webber, Jorgan Andrews, Anish Goel, and Trish Mahoney, Memorandum for the Record, "India," November 17, 2008; also see the introduction and postscript by Mark Webber.

Although Bush was attracted to India by its democratic values, his administration clearly perceived it as a strategic partner in the future contest with China for supremacy in Asia. In their introduction to the Transition Memorandum on China, Paul Haenle, Michael Green, and Faryar Shirzad succinctly explain that "the core of the Bush administration's strategy for dealing with China's rise was to build a security and trade architecture with regional allies and partners that would reinforce the role of the United States as a Pacific power, encourage China to play a responsible role in East Asia, and hedge against the emergence of a more aggressive China." Although the president labeled China a "strategic competitor" during the 2000 campaign for the presidency, stated his willingness to defend Taiwan, and offered a "robust" arms package to Taipei, he chose to "deal with China as a friend, not an enemy." Recognizing that China's economic aspirations provided the United States with leverage, he encouraged China "to play a constructive and peaceful role in the world and in international institutions, to act as a partner addressing common security challenges, to pursue peaceful economic growth and political liberalization, and to emerge as a responsible stakeholder in the international system." Yet he also sought to revamp and strengthen alliances with Japan, South Korea, and Australia as a hedge against potential Chinese misconduct. In the Transition Memorandum, Dennis Wilder explained that "we engage China with and through our strong allies in the region, not in an effort to encircle China or turn the region against it, but as part of an effort to foster good relations with China and to encourage responsible action by China." Bush worked hard to enlist China in his nonproliferation efforts regarding North Korea and welcomed Chinese collaboration in UN peacekeeping operations.[18]

In his insightful memorandum on China, Dennis Wilder concluded that the major challenge facing Bush's successors was to ensure "that China's rise does not disrupt the international order" based on free markets and free people. "China," Wilder stressed, "is an attractive model to those who want to maintain authoritarian regimes while achieving high rates of economic growth. The success of its state-led economic system challenges private rule-of-law based approaches to global trade and investment liberalization." China offered economic and military

---

18. Dennis Wilder, Memorandum for the Record, "China Policy," November 10, 2008; Dennis Wilder, Memorandum for the Record, "East Asian Alliances and Architecture," November 19, 2008; see also Paul Haenli, Michael Green, and Faryar Shirzad, introduction to "China Policy and East Asian Alliances and Architecture."

aid to many governments with few conditions except access to their natural resources. "In this manner, China undermines the Freedom Agenda and provides comfort to some of the world's most oppressive regimes. United States policymakers will need to be vigilant about China's global actions. . . . when they threaten to undermine democracy and provide comfort to brutal regimes."[19]

In its own way the Freedom Agenda also shaped the administration's approach to the Middle East and especially to peacemaking between Israel and the Palestinians. In his postscript to the Transition Memorandum, Michael Singh explains that, in the aftermath of 9/11, the administration "did not regard the Israeli-Palestinian conflict as the issue on which all others in the Middle East hinged. Instead, they viewed the absence of freedom and prosperity and the prevalence of extremism as the region's foremost challenges."[20] In the Transition Memorandum itself, Michael Pascual stressed the singular importance of President Bush's readiness to support the creation of a Palestinian state. But rather than focusing on borders and territory, Bush "shifted the focus to the character of that future state." He refused to deal with Yasar Arafat, the longtime Palestinian leader, who Bush regarded as a former terrorist in sheepskin. Instead, the Transition Memorandum stressed that the administration placed its emphasis on helping Palestinians "build the security, political and economic institutions of a democratic Palestinian state even before borders had been defined." Much as the administration was scorned for its repudiation of Arafat and its full-throttled embrace of Israeli Prime Minister Ariel Sharon, the Bush team felt that it made progress cajoling the withdrawal of Israeli troops from Gaza and supporting the holding of elections in Palestinian territories, even though they led to a narrow Hamas victory. When Hamas then seized control of Gaza and President Abbas expelled Hamas from the Palestinian Government in the West Bank and declared a state of emergency, the president not only defended his support of elections—insisting that "the democratic ability to choose leaders is the only way to defeat radical extremism"—but also threw his support behind a new effort to negotiate a peace agreement with Arafat's successors in the West Bank.[21]

---

19. Wilder, "China Policy."

20. Michael Singh, postscript to Transition Memorandum on "Middle East Peace Process."

21. Michael Pascual, Memorandum for the Record, "Middle East Peace Process," December 22, 2008.

Bush believed that the Israeli government had "a right to defend its people from attack." By embracing Israel, by assuring its leaders that he regarded their fight against the intifada much as he regarded his own worldwide struggle against terror, he hoped to elicit concessions, slow the expansion of settlements, garner the help of other Arab nations, and set the framework for a peace settlement that the administration focused on in 2007–2008. Although no agreement was reached, the Transition Memorandum underscored the progress that had been made, especially in strengthening Palestinian institutions and the Palestinian economy and establishing some fundamental axioms for a final agreement. Further progress depended on the Palestinian determination to reform Fatah, their largest political movement, and to create viable democratic institutions. It was led by a "corrupt" echelon of older leaders "who lack popular legitimacy and support and who are primarily concerned with maintaining control rather than undertaking serious reform."[22]

Complicating peacemaking in the Middle East was the support Iran gave to Hamas and other terrorist organizations. The Transition Memorandum on Iran starkly stated, "Iran has established itself as the primary sponsor, trainer, and financier of extremist forces in the Middle East." It posed itself as an ideological and strategic "challenge" to the United States. "The regime oppresses the people of Iran, undermines stability by providing lethal assistance to militant groups in Iraq and Afghanistan, supports terrorism globally, backs Hamas actions to frustrate Israeli/Palestinian peace efforts, uses extremists and terrorists to threaten and intimidate the region's emerging democracies and moderate governments, openly threatens Israel, and finally seeks weapons of mass destruction and their means of delivery ... that will one day allow it to develop a nuclear weapon—which exacerbates all these threats." Tehran, the memorandum continued, wanted to dominate the region and "spread its radical ideology throughout the world, including vulnerable parts of Africa and Latin America."[23]

In an excellent postscript to the Transition Memorandum, Michael Singh explains that that the administration did not seek regime change; it sought "a strategic shift in Tehran's policies." It aimed to present Iranian leaders with a strategic choice—"continue pursuing their destabilizing policies and prolong their

---

22. Pascual, "Middle East Peace Process."
23. Kelly Magsamen, Memorandum for the Record, "Our Approach to Iran," January 16, 2009.

international isolation; or drop those destabilizing policies and reap the benefits of economic and diplomatic engagement with the world." Toward these ends, the administration embraced partners, engaged in multilateral diplomacy, and applied more rigorous sanctions. Acknowledging that its efforts had failed—it "had not yet prompted a strategic shift"—the Transition Memorandum clarified for a new administration why Iran constituted such a confounding problem.[24]

Iran's nuclear ambitions and support of terrorism highlighted why the administration put such a premium on its own counterproliferation and counterterrorism initiatives. In several illuminating Transition Memoranda on these issues, Hadley's subordinates outlined what the administration had been doing, where it had experienced success and failure, and what remained to be done. Counterproliferation constituted an overriding priority of the administration from its first days in office—even before the attacks on 9/11. Rogue regimes yearned to acquire weapons of mass destruction in order "to intimidate their neighbors, and to keep the United States and other responsible nations from helping allies and friends in strategic parts of the world." Should this happen, Bush's national security experts, like their predecessors, feared that the United States might self-deter—might decide not to take action in a crisis lest it trigger the use of such weapons by the rogue adversary. The Transition Memorandum explained that weapons of mass destruction in the hands of tyrants "created the prospect that the United States could be susceptible to coercion or blackmail by the world's most dangerous regimes."[25]

The attacks on 9/11, of course, magnified this perception of threat. Juan Zarate and Michael Allen began their Transition Memorandum on "WMD Terrorism" noting that "September 11, 2001 provided graphic evidence of what terrorists were willing to do to inflict damage on the United States and our interests." Thereafter, "we had to assume—with some confidence—that a catastrophic attack involving WMD was within the reach and capability of al Qaeda or associated terrorist groups." This threat was magnified "by the increased willingness of rogue states with ties to terrorist groups to engage in proliferation of WMD and associated materials." The Transition Memos nicely outlined the initiatives

---

24. Magsamen, "Our Approach to Iran"; see also Michael Singh, postscript to "Our Approach to Iran."

25. Michael Allen, Renee Pan, Charles Lutes, Joyce Connery, and Jamie Fly, Memorandum for the Record, "Counterproliferation Policy," January 16, 2009.

"to proactively interdict the movement of WMD materials, expertise, and technologies to WMD-seeking states and terrorist groups"; to convince WMD-seeking states to abandon their quest to acquire such weapons; to persuade supplier states not to deal with rogue regimes and terrorist groups; and to defend against their use and manage the consequences should they be used.[26] Broadly speaking, the Bush administration felt that it had experienced considerable success, for example, dealing with Libya and the nuclear proliferation network of the Pakistani scientist, A. Q. Khan. It also felt that it had made progress establishing new international norms, improving intelligence, developing missile defenses, applying financial pressure, preparing for biological attacks, and instituting bureaucratic reforms and organizational changes within the US government.[27] Nonetheless, in its memoranda on Iran and North Korea it did not hide its faltering efforts. Indeed, these memoranda outlined just how difficult and complicated were the problems.[28]

In passing off their knowledge to the incoming Obama administration, Bush's national security team stated clearly that "the most effective current measure that we could take to address the challenge of WMD Terrorism would be to eliminate the safe haven that the al-Qaida senior leadership currently enjoys in the Federally Administered Tribal Areas (FATA) of Pakistan.[29] Yet the Transition Memorandum on Pakistan beautifully illuminated why it was so difficult to address this issue. In the immediate aftermath of 9/11, Secretary of State Colin Powell and President Bush himself talked to Pakistani President Musharraf, labored to enlist his cooperation in the global war on terrorism, and proceeded to lift sanctions and offer military and economic aid. Musharraf wanted to cooperate yet was constrained by his own conflicting priorities, the weakness of his regime, the country's economic woes, and the long-standing linkages of

26. Juan Zarate and Michael Allen, Memorandum for the Record, "Weapons of Mass Destruction (WMD) and Terrorism," November 10, 2008; also see Allen, Pan, Lutes, Connery, and Fly, "Counterproliferation."

27. Zarate and Allen, "Weapons of Mass Destruction (WMD) and Terrorism"; Allen, Pan, Lutes, Connery, and Fly, "Counterproliferation"; see also Renee Pan and Jamie Fly, Memorandum for the Record, "U.S. Efforts to Turn Libya and Dismantle the A. Q. Khan Nuclear Proliferation Network," January 14, 2009.

28. In addition to the citations in notes 23–27 above, also see Dennis Wilder and Michael Allen, Memorandum for the Record, "North Korea and Six Party Talks," January 14, 2009.

29. Zarate and Allen, "WMD Terrorism," memo, 7.

the Pakistani intelligence service with the Taliban regime in Afghanistan. Progress was made but it was far from satisfactory.[30] In an informative postscript to the Transition Memorandum, Mark Webber candidly acknowledges that "the Bush administration was unable to achieve the strategic shift sought from Pakistan." It did prevent a regional war between India and Pakistan, forestalled an economic collapse, and sustained pressure on extremist groups, but it did not get Pakistan to reconfigure "its fundamental national security posture, stem cross-border attacks into Afghanistan, or to eradicate the extremist safe havens within its own borders." To achieve success, Pakistan required economic growth, political stability, and internal security. How such goals could be achieved presented daunting challenges that the Freedom Agenda alone could not solve. Webber notes: "The Bush administration's approach to democratization in Pakistan was tempered by the need for Pakistan's support in Afghanistan.... Relations with Pakistan will remain tumultuous, no matter the US strategy."[31]

The Transition Memoranda on counterterrorism, counterproliferation, the Middle East peace process, and Pakistan, among others, illustrate why the Freedom Agenda, as sweeping as it was, could not constitute an effective framework for the conduct of US foreign policy. Allegedly, nothing was more important than the pursuit of freedom, but other priorities constantly assumed greater salience. Efforts to stop the proliferation of weapons and thwart the actions of terrorist groups impelled uncomfortable compromises and unsettling accommodations with authoritarian states, like Putin's Russia, and even with rogue regimes, like Qadhafi's Libya.[32] Seeking peace in the Middle East meant turning one's attention away from the promotion of freedom and the protection of human rights in Egypt and tolerating, even supporting, the authoritarian practices of President Hosni Mubarak.[33] Waging counterinsurgency warfare required military bases and the cooperation of repressive regimes in places like Uzbekistan and Kyrgyzstan.[34]

---

30. Mark Webber, Jorgan Andrews, Anish Goel, and Patricia Mahoney, Memorandum for the Record, "Pakistan," January 16, 2009.

31. Webber, postscript to Transition Memorandum on "Pakistan."

32. James Fly, Memorandum for the Record, "Missile Defense," January 16, 2009; Pan and Fly, "Libya and A. Q. Khan."

33. Jason Brownlee, *Democracy Prevention: The Politics of the U.S.-Egyptian Alliance* (New York: Cambridge University Press, 2012).

34. Matthew Crosston, *Fostering Fundamentalism: Terrorism, Democracy and American Engagement in Central Asia* (Hants, England: Ashgate Publishing, 2006); Rosemary

Most of all, the global War on Terror encouraged the administration to adopt practices that blatantly transgressed the Freedom Agenda. There are no Transition Memoranda on extraterritorial rendition, secret prisons, torture, and human rights. In the Iraq memorandum, there is no mention of Abu Ghraib and the torturous practices that went on there. Throughout these memoranda, there is a striking absence of self-recognition and self-reflection on how the administration's own transgressions of human rights undercut and often made a mockery of its self-proclaimed Freedom Agenda.[35] This is sad because there is no doubt that administration officials sincerely believed in that agenda. President Bush was convinced that America was a benighted nation seeking to bring justice and liberty to the rest of the world.[36] Yet the belief that America was imperiled catalyzed actions that tarnished America's reputation and beleaguered its conduct of foreign policy. Asserting the right to take preemptive action and employing its power to intervene anywhere it deemed threatened belied assertions that Washington respected the sovereign rights of other nations.[37]

President Bush ardently and idealistically called upon Americans to treat their Muslim neighbors respectfully and lovingly, but secret prisons, black sites, waterboarding, and pictures of naked Iraqi detainees being humiliated by white Christian women soldiers ruined America's reputation in much of the Muslim world and beyond. A March 2008 poll of Arab public opinion in six nations

---

Foot, "Collateral Damage: Human Rights Consequences of Counterterrorist Action in the Asia-Pacific, *International Affairs* 81, no. 2 (March 2005): 411–25; Alexander Cooley, "U.S. Bases and Democratization in Central Asia," *Orbis* (Winter 2008): 65–90.

35. See Senate Select Committee on Intelligence, *The Senate Intelligence Committee Report on Torture: Committee Study of the Central Intelligence Agency's Detention and Interrogation Program* (Brooklyn: Melville House, 2014); also see, for example, Jane Mayer, *Dark Side: The Inside Story of How the War on Terror Turned Into a War on American Ideals* (New York: Doubleday, 2008).

36. See, for example, his speech to the National Endowment for Democracy, November 6, 2003, https://georgewbush-whitehouse.archives.gov/news/releases/2003/11/20031106 -2.html; his second inaugural address, cited in note 2 above; and his speech in Prague, cited in note 7 above.

37. For increasingly unfavorable views of the United States, see Pew Research Center, "America's Image in the World: Findings from the Pew Global Attitudes Project," March 14, 2007, https://www.pewresearch.org/global/2007/03/14/americas-image-in -the-world-findings-from-the-pew-global-attitudes-project/; see also APSA, Task Force Report, Jeffrey W. Legro and Peter J. Katzenstein, "U.S. Standing in the World: Causes, Consequences, and the Future" (Washington, DC: American Political Science Association, 2009), 5.

(Egypt, Jordan, Lebanon, Morocco, Saudi Arabia, and the UAE) conducted by the University of Maryland in conjunction with Zogby International found that 64 percent of the respondents had a very unfavorable view of the United States and 19 percent had a somewhat unfavorable view. In 2007, according to public opinion surveys, only 9 percent of Turks, 21 percent of Egyptians, 20 percent of Jordanians, 29 percent of Indonesians, and 13 percent of the Palestinians in occupied territories had favorable views of the United States.[38]

Administration officials, then and now, appear unwilling to grapple with the gap between their self-proclaimed intentions and the external perceptions of their actions. More worrisome, they minimize the fact that freedom in the world was declining, not growing, when they left office. Freedom House reported that the year 2007 was "marked by a notable setback for global freedom." For the first time in fifteen years, freedom declined in two consecutive years. Thirty-eight countries showed downturns in freedom; only ten displayed a positive trajectory. In the Middle East, declines were apparent in Egypt, Syria, Lebanon, and the Palestinian Authority. The trajectory did not improve in 2008.[39] In writing his Transition Memorandum on the Freedom Agenda in 2008, Michael Kozak disregarded the worrisome new trend. He concluded his memorandum stressing that "this Administration has significantly advanced the cause of freedom, the strategy for realizing it, and the capacity of the United States, both bilaterally and multilaterally, to support those struggling for freedom worldwide." In their postscript to Kozak's memorandum, Michael Gerson and Peter Wehner do not deny that freedom flagged. Rather than focusing on globalization, economic disarray, financial chaos, supply chains, employment patterns, income distribution within nations, and America's own tarnished image, they assign blame to Bush's successors: "The

---

38. For Bush's statements on Islam, see, for example, his remarks at the Islamic Center of Washington, DC, September 17, 2001, https://www.presidency.ucsb.edu/documents/remarks-the-islamic-center-washington; also "Backgrounder: The President's Quotes on Islam," The White House, https://georgewbush-whitehouse.archives.gov/infocus/ramadan/islam.html; for Arab public opinion, see Shibley Telhami, with Zogby International, "2008 Arab Public opinion Poll," https://www.brookings.edu/wp-content/uploads/2012/04/0414_middle_east_telhami.pdf; for additional polling data, see Legro and Katzenstein, "U.S. Standing in the World," 5.

39. Freedom House, *Freedom in the World 2008* (New York: Rowman and Littlefield, 2008), 3–11; for a balanced assessment of the trends during the Bush administrations, stressing the reversal of fortune after 2005, see Freedom House, *Freedom in the World 2009* (New York: Rowman and Littlefield, 2009), 3–12.

inescapable fact is this: Presidents Obama and Trump both generally neglected and even disdained supporting freedom and democracy."[40]

The focus on the Freedom Agenda perhaps accounts for the failure of the administration to pass on Transition Memoranda on issues like climate change, pandemics, and cyber preparedness. Looking back, it is clear that these were looming issues of critical importance. To his credit, Hadley recognized this fact and asked several of his colleagues to write memoranda for this volume capturing what the administration did on these issues and how it performed in comparison to its successors. The memoranda helpfully summarize the most important initiatives undertaken by the administration. With regard to "biodefense and pandemic planning," Rajeev Venkayya praises the administration's "prescience." It designed a series of directives and organizational practices to protect the nation's population and food supply; it allocated $7.1 billion in 2005 for domestic and international pandemic preparedness; and it developed an Implementation Plan in May 2006. Venkayya assigns agency to the president himself who read John Barry's book about the 1918 Spanish flu epidemic and realized the nation was woefully unprepared.[41] In their memorandum on cyber preparedness, Kenneth Wainstein, Keith Ausbrook, and Neill Sciarrone focus on organizational initiatives. They outline the many steps the administration took to begin grappling with the challenges foreseen, yet they acknowledge that progress was not commensurate with the scope of the problem. Like the memorandum on biodefense and pandemics, the cyber memorandum stresses considerable continuity with the Obama administration.[42] More provocative are the claims of James L. Connaughton in his analysis of the administration's performance regarding climate change and global warming. He argues that the Bush administration "developed and implemented a government-wide portfolio of pragmatic and increasingly consequential policies and collaborations both domestically and internationally." The Obama and Trump administrations, he insists, continued these policies. Whether they were commensurate with the gravity of the issue is left unaddressed. Connaughton seems satisfied with the "overarching philosophical framework" that guided climate change policy in the

---

40. Kozak, Memorandum for the Record, "Freedom Agenda," November 15, 2008; Gerson and Wehner, postscript to "Freedom Agenda."
41. Rajeev Venkayya, "Biodefense and Pandemic Planning."
42. Kenneth Wainstein, Keith Ausbrook, and Neill Sciarrone, "Cyber Preparedness."

Bush administration: "to act in a serious and sensible way, given the limits of our knowledge."[43] The unacknowledged complacency of such a vacuous statement disappoints.

In many of the postscripts, even when admitting considerable continuity between administrations, Hadley's colleagues cast their successors in a less favorable light. In Iraq, Meghan O'Sullivan writes, "Obama inherited a stable, if fragile, situation." After initially proceeding carefully and seeking to build on the tenuous accomplishments of the Surge, Obama mistakenly decided to support Prime Minister Nouri al-Maliki's continuation in office, then downgraded Iraq's importance, and attached unnecessary conditions to the maintenance of a small number of US troops. Maliki refused these conditions, forcing the withdrawal of American forces and leading to the debacle that then ensued when ISIS came close to overrunning the country.[44] In Afghanistan, write Paul Miller, Doug Lute, and O'Sullivan, Obama did no better than Bush despite his belief that Afghanistan was the good war. After initially surging troops and augmenting resources, Obama reversed course in 2010 and "moved decidedly away from a fully-resourced counterinsurgency or state-building strategy." US funding for reconstruction declined every year after 2010 and US troops began to leave after 2011, providing opportunities for Taliban advances.[45] Whereas Bush had learned that success in Afghanistan and Iraq required more resources for stabilization and reconstruction, Obama and Trump, writes Richard Hooker, "increasingly abandoned" these efforts "in favor of narrowing US objectives to counterterrorism, reducing the American role more generally, and bringing US troops home."[46]

The negative comparisons continue. In his postscript to the memorandum on India, Mark Webber argues that Obama's focus on the Afghanistan-Pakistan linkage "resulted in the unintended perception that India was a secondary priority." This approach "alienated India and strained the bilateral relationship."[47] With regard to Russia, Damon Wilson, Judy Ansley, and Daniel Fried claim that Obama tried a "reset" but made no more progress than had Bush. Obama's efforts

---

43. James L. Connaughton, "Climate Change and Clean Development."
44. O'Sullivan, postscript to "Iraq" memorandum.
45. Miller, Lute, and O'Sullivan, postscript to "Afghanistan" memorandum.
46. Richard Hooker, postscript to memorandum on "Stabilization and Reconstruction Operations."
47. Webber, postscript to "India" memorandum.

to improve relations with Russia, his "deference to European capitals on European issues," and his focus on Asia and the Middle East diminished "attention to a Europe whole, free, and at peace."[48] Most starkly and interestingly, Michael Singh asserts in his introduction to the Middle East memorandum that notwithstanding the image of Bush's indifference to the Palestinian-Israeli struggle, his administration may well represent the "high-watermark of Israeli-Palestinian peace diplomacy."[49]

These invidious comparisons to their successors sometimes detract from the thoughtful, serious effort to engage in self-criticism. In her postscript to the Transition Memorandum on Iraq, for example, Meghan O'Sullivan succinctly delineates the shortcomings of the Bush administration's policies between 2003 and 2006: "relying on planning assumptions that turned out to be wrong; a reluctance or inability to match resources to goals at the outset; competing visions and varying levels of commitment and capability among US departments and agencies; an inability to forge a common program with the region and the international community; and difficulty maintaining the reservoir of US popular support that is so essential for long, grinding campaigns." The Surge, she had emphasized in her 2008 Transition Memorandum, made a difference, but even then she anticipated future setbacks and acknowledged "there is no magic formula in Iraq." Wrestling with the right lessons to extrapolate, she emphasizes, "significant efforts to rebuild countries should only be undertaken when truly vital interests are at stake."[50]

This advice strikes at the heart of the Freedom Agenda as a framework for the conduct of US national security policy. The Freedom Agenda reified ideological conflict, the struggle with religious extremism, and the global War on Terror. It did little to identify vital interests. The goal—ending tyranny—exceeded capabilities. Grand strategy, admittedly a vague concept, is about linking means and ends, tactics with objectives. Creating a policy aimed at supporting "the growth of democratic movements and institutions in every nation and culture," establishes a goal that was (and remains) unachievable. It served to create cynicism abroad and frustration at home. Arabs and Muslims did not believe that this was

---

48. Damon Wilson, Judy Arsley, and Daniel Fried, "Postscript" to memorandum on "Europe Whole, Free, and at Peace and Western Balkans." Fried, it should be noted, served in the Obama as well as the Bush administrations.

49. Singh, introduction to memorandum on "Middle East Peace."

50. O'Sullivan, "Iraq"; also O'Sullivan, postscript to "Iraq" memorandum.

our goal, and Americans did not deem democracy promotion to be especially important.[51] Designing such a goal and reaffirming it, however inspiring, reflects a lack of self-knowledge, a poor understanding of how nations perceive their vital interests, and of learning. Receiving Transition Memos trumpeting a Freedom Agenda when the economy was plummeting and American resources were dwindling must have perplexed the incoming administration.

The authors of these Transition Memoranda and of the postscripts were and remain hard-working, diligent, and intelligent public servants. How, then, can one account for a national security strategy that reflected so little regard for the linkage of means and ends? I suspect that fear, hubris, and power shaped the Freedom Agenda. Fear of another attack, even worse than the one on 9/11; a belief that free people and free markets were values appropriate for all countries and human beings; and a confidence that the United States had the power to shape the world in its own image.[52]

Most Americans shared these feelings, so the criticism offered here is not intended in any personal or partisan way. Fear prevailed. But one looks in vain in these memos for a careful assessment of threat. The memorandum on "WMD Terrorism" asserts that "a catastrophic attack against U.S. targets, or on the Homeland itself [was] a realistic possibility," but was it? Did policymakers "have to assume—with some confidence—that a catastrophic attack involving WMD was within the reach and capability of al Qaeda or associated terrorist groups"? Al Qaeda quested for such weapons, but was it within its reach? Was there evidence that it was within its reach? Was there reason to assume that rogue states would hand off such weapons to terrorist groups? No matter how sincerely felt, readers need to address whether these judgments were correct, and whether they should have catalyzed actions that far exceeded capabilities.[53] At the same

---

51. For Arab views of US motives, see the public opinion poll cited in note 37 above; for scant American support for democracy promotion, see the 2008 poll conducted by the Chicago Council of Foreign Relations, cited in Legro and Katzenstein, APSA, "U.S. Standing in the World," 2.

52. These are key themes in the administration's two national security strategy statements in 2002 and 2006. See https://georgewbush-whitehouse.archives.gov/nsc/nss /2002/; https://georgewbush-whitehouse.archives.gov/nsc/nss/2006/intro.html.

53. For the assertions, see Zarate and Allen, "WMD Terrorism;" for doubts about these matters, see, for example, US Senate, Select Committee on Intelligence, *Report of the U.S. Intelligence Community's Prewar Intelligence Assessments on Iraq* (Washington,

time, critics of the administration need to acknowledge two great achievements of the Bush administration: Osama bin Laden's power was emasculated and no subsequent attack on the homeland occurred that was similar to, or greater than, 9/11.[54]

Nonetheless, the goals set by the administration overtaxed American resources and skill. Policymakers assumed they had more power than they actually possessed. Meghan O'Sullivan acknowledges that the administration did not allocate the funds or prepare the personnel to meet the challenges it encountered in Iraq.[55] Likewise, in Afghanistan, the authors of the postscript write that at the end of 2008 "almost every meaningful metric [suggested] the situation was getting worse."[56] In both these countries—Iraq and Afghanistan—writes Richard Hooker in the postscript to the memorandum on stabilization and reconstruction, the administration's ambitious goals were not realized because of inadequate funding, bureaucratic conflicts, mistaken priorities, partisan divisions, and the intractable indigenous difficulties.[57] Regarding Pakistan, Iran, Russia, and the Middle East, the memoranda and postscripts indicate that the United States lacked the power to achieve the objectives the administration set for itself. Bush administration officials possessed laudable goals but they overestimated their ability to achieve them. They had far less power than they required. They needed more resources than Congress and the American people were willing to allocate. Their goals exceeded their means, notwithstanding the reso-

---

DC Government Publishing Office, 2004), especially 342–49; John E. Mueller, *Overblown: How Politicians and the Terrorism Industry Inflate National Security Threats and Why We Believe Them* (New York: Free Press, 2006); Patrick Porter, "Long Wars and Long Telegrams: Containing al-Qaeda," *International Affairs* 85, (2009): 285–305; Paul R. Pillar, *Intelligence and U.S. Foreign Policy: Iraq, 9/11 and Misguided Reform* (New York: Columbia University Press, 2011), 13–68; Peter L. Bergen, *The Longest War: The Enduring Conflict Between America and Al-Qaeda* (New York: Free Press, 2011), 86–173; Robert Draper, *To Start A War: How the Bush Administration Took America Into Iraq* (New York: Penguin Press, 2020).

54. Nelly Lahoud, *The Bin Laden Papers* (New Haven: Yale University Press, 2022), 286–87; Daniel Byman, "The Good Enough Doctrine," *Foreign Affairs* (September/October 2021); Elliot Ackerman, "Winning Ugly: What the War on Terror Cost America," *Foreign Affairs* (September/October 2021).

55. O'Sullivan, postscript to "Iraq" memorandum.

56. Miller, Lute, and O'Sullivan, postscript to memorandum on "Afghanistan."

57. Hooker, postscript to memorandum on "Stabilization and Reconstruction Operations."

nance of their ideals: "liberty and justice are right and true for all peoples everywhere."[58]

Although the Freedom Agenda was not a viable strategy, these memoranda and postscripts illustrate how hard and intractable were the problems facing the Bush administration after 2001. As one might expect, they illuminate the tireless efforts to redress the unanticipated setbacks in Iraq and Afghanistan. But they do much more than that. They demonstrate how relentlessly and thoughtfully Bush administration officials labored to counter the spread of weapons of mass destruction; allay disease, misery, and distress globally; and promote development and trade. Far from unilateralist, they valued alliances. They sought partners to settle territorial disputes and end civil wars in Africa, stop the trade in fissile materials and dangerous technologies, mitigate conflict in the Middle East, thwart the nuclear ambitions of Iran and North Korea, and, most of all, contain the rise of China. Far from disdaining NATO, they labored to heal the wounds caused by the invasion of Iraq and struggled to expand the alliance as the core of their European policy and the vehicle for making Europe whole, free, and at peace. They bequeathed problems to their successors, but also solutions that could be built on.

While these memoranda and postscripts beautifully illustrate how difficult it is for officials in Washington to assess mortal threats and reconcile interests and values, they should also impel readers to interrogate the Freedom Agenda and question whether it was or remains the appropriate vision to undergird the nation's foreign policies. Should the United States be seeking to end tyranny and nurture democracy everywhere, or should it be engaged in a more realistic assessment of mortal threats, vital interests, achievable goals, and available resources? No matter how we assess the triumphs or failures of the Bush administration—or its successors—we will not find a precise formula for resolving the ongoing American struggle to deal with a dangerous world. But we need to keep trying with a keener sense of our vital interests and our capabilities, and an appreciation of how US power can produce harm as well as good.

---

58. Quotation from the National Security Strategy Statement, 2006, 2.

CHAPTER 31

Reassessing Bush's Legacy

What the Transition Memoranda
Do (and Don't) Reveal

HAL BRANDS

Presidential transitions are fraught moments. For a superpower, foreign policy never stops. There are constantly strategies to be devised, initiatives to be pursued, crises to be managed. Yet transitions create discontinuity in America's approach to the world, even as the world itself keeps moving.

Key policies may lose momentum as an incoming team pauses to review its inheritance. The US government loses institutional memory as one team of officials cycles out; miscommunication happens amid harried handovers of power. Indeed, major problems in US foreign policy—from the Bay of Pigs invasion to the inadequate response to terrorism before 9/11—are often rooted, at least partially, in the disruption that transitions inevitably cause.[1]

The difficulty of managing transitions is also a product of the US political system. America's massive national security bureaucracy is overseen by political appointees who rotate out when a given administration ends. The crucial benefit

---

1. Kurt Campbell and James Steinberg, *Difficult Transitions: Foreign Policy Problems at the Outset of Presidential Power* (Washington, DC: Brookings Institution, 2008).

of this system is that it makes government more responsive to fresh ideas and presidential direction. The downside is that it increases the churn that accompanies a handover of power.

In hindsight, the transition between George W. Bush and Barack Obama stands out for several reasons. It occurred amid two ongoing wars, as well as the worst global economic crisis in decades. It was, remarkably, the only "normal" transition that America has experienced in this century. (The Clinton-Bush transition was delayed by a contested election outcome; the Obama-Trump transition was marred by chaos within the incoming team; the Trump-Biden transition was disrupted by the outgoing president's effort to subvert democracy.) Against this backdrop, the Bush-Obama transition is noteworthy for its professionalism and for the care that the outgoing team took to ensure that its successors were well prepared to face oncoming challenges—care that is reflected in the Transition Memoranda that constitute the basis of this volume.

Indeed, the Bush-Obama transition is also unusual because we have early access to some relevant documentation. It typically takes twenty to thirty years for classified materials to be released. The Transition Memoranda and other files made available through this project is only a sliver of the material that will be needed to evaluate the transition, let alone the larger record of Bush's foreign policy. But the documentation allows us to begin exploring what the critical issues in that transition were. More important, it offers a chance to see how the Bush administration assessed its legacy in real time, and to reevaluate that legacy today.

Debates about the foreign policy that Bush handed over to Obama were already underway in January 2009. When Bush left office, his approval ratings were as low as those of any president since World War II, thanks partly to controversies over Iraq, Afghanistan, and the War on Terror. In 2008, an overwhelming majority—98.2 percent—of historians considered Bush's presidency a failure, and a clear majority—61 percent—classified it as the worst in American history.[2] Bush, by contrast, argued that his record would look better over time, much as another unpopular president, Harry Truman, later came to be regarded as one of America's great foreign policy presidents.[3] Truman was not the only leader to benefit from such a reassessment: the historical treatment of

---

2. "HNN Poll: 61% of Historians Rate the Bush Presidency Worst," *History News Network*, November 6, 2008.

3. George W. Bush, *Decision Points* (New York: Crown, 2010), 174–75.

other presidents, such as Eisenhower and Reagan, became more favorable as new records emerged and partisan rancor faded.

A fully considered assessment of Bush's presidency will not be possible for many years. But the memoranda reproduced in this book, along with the accompanying postscripts, can allow historians to think more carefully about what Bush bequeathed to Obama—and what that tells us about his foreign policy record.[4]

If transitions are often fraught, so are Transition Memoranda. Those documents represent a sort of midpoint between real-time archival documentation and the retrospective history such documentation ultimately informs. Transition Memoranda are written by knowledgeable insiders who have access to the critical debates and documentation through which US policy is shaped. Yet these memoranda are themselves retrospective documents, which necessarily condense and package history for the incoming administration. They are written to be useful references for—and to shape the thinking of—an arriving team that will be severely pressed for time as a new presidency unfolds, not to serve as comprehensive postmortems. They are typically weighted toward summarizing key lines of effort, noting achievements, and identifying challenges ahead.[5]

This is particularly evident regarding the most controversial aspects of Bush's presidency—the wars in Afghanistan and especially Iraq. Readers expecting long,

---

4. In a piece of this length, it is difficult to do more than offer initial observations on the range of issues that made up the Bush foreign policy legacy. For longer assessments by the same author, which show a certain evolution over time, see Hal Brands, *What Good is Grand Strategy? Power and Purpose in American Statecraft from Harry S. Truman to George W. Bush* (Ithaca: Cornell University Press, 2014); Hal Brands and Peter Feaver, "The Case for Bush Revisionism: Reevaluating the Legacy of America's 43rd President," *Journal of Strategic Studies* 41 (2017).

5. The Bush Transition Memoranda are not as complete as the gold standard for internal histories of an administration. This would be the administrative histories and NSC histories that the Lyndon Johnson administration compiled before leaving office in 1969, which combined extensive, contemporaneous documentation of decisionmaking as well as substantial narratives (sometimes running hundreds of pages) produced by the relevant officials and organizations. In this essay, I have only cited the Bush Transition Memoranda and accompanying postscripts when quoting directly from them, although the entire essay is influenced by the material in the collection.

detailed reviews of the decision to invade Iraq, what went so badly wrong after that, or the course of the Afghan war during its crucial early years will be disappointed. The relevant memoranda simply cover progress and challenges since the administration's most recent policy reviews, which occurred, in both cases, in 2006. In fairness, the accompanying postscripts seek to place the memoranda in perspective, and Bush administration officials have been forthcoming about the successes and failures of these interventions in other forums. And there were, in Afghanistan and Iraq, successes and failures alike. In Afghanistan, the administration should receive a great deal of credit for devising a plan that initially succeeded beyond all expectations—an innovative, agile approach that used airpower, special operations forces, CIA paramilitary assets, and other capabilities to rout al Qaeda and the Taliban in record time. The trouble came later, when key elements of the al Qaeda leadership slipped away in December 2001, and especially when America found itself stuck between the need to stabilize the country—the better to prevent a Taliban and al Qaeda resurgence—and a reluctance to invest large amounts of money and manpower on such unpromising terrain. The administration's chief failure, arguably, was that it did not so much reconcile these imperatives as elide the gap between them. As Paul Miller, Douglas Lute, and Meghan O'Sullivan write in this volume, "Initially, from 2001–2006, the Bush administration pursued a more limited, counterterrorism-centric approach while espousing ambitious state-building goals at the same time."[6]

The resulting mismatch, combined with the policies of a fickle and hedging Pakistan, and exacerbated by the intense resource demands of the Iraq War from late 2002 onward, created space for a Taliban-led insurgency that was causing, by the end of Bush's presidency, an accelerating erosion of security.[7] Bush left a deteriorating situation for his successor, albeit one rooted in the same fundamental dilemma that frustrated every post-9/11 administration: the fact that securing America's critical aims in Afghanistan seemed to require producing some degree of lasting stability, but achieving that lasting stability seemed to require a commitment of resources beyond what the country—under any president—was willing to bear. Indeed, in view of the twenty-year history of America's failed war in

---

6. See Miller, Lute, and O'Sullivan, "Afghanistan," in this volume.

7. See Seth Jones, *In the Graveyard of Empires: America's War in Afghanistan* (New York: Norton, 2010).

Afghanistan, Bush may simply have been the first president to learn that there was no easy way of squaring this circle.[8]

Regarding Iraq, the Transition Memoranda are largely silent on the invasion itself and the course of the subsequent stabilization mission that was failing catastrophically by late 2006. Multiple memoranda do touch indirectly on the strategic consequences of that failure—cascading instability in the Middle East, deep divisions in key international relationships, a loss of leverage in promoting Bush's own Freedom Agenda, eroded American credibility on the international stage, weakness across critical issues ranging from North Korea to Iran, and damage that outlasted the eventual righting of the situation in Iraq in 2007–08.[9]

My own view is that objective historians may eventually be more sympathetic to the initial decision to invade, in light of several factors that are now well established: (1) that the containment policy of the 1990s was collapsing and Saddam Hussein was gaining greater freedom of action over time; (2) that non-military options for addressing the threat (whether "smart sanctions" or covert action) seemed unavailing; (3) that after 9/11 any administration would have taken a harder line toward a dictator who combined extensive support for terrorism, known WMD aspirations, and a history of aggression; and (4) that the WMD-related intelligence failures were the result of analytical blunders rather than deliberate politicization. It is still possible, of course, to understand all of those factors and conclude—as I have argued elsewhere—that the invasion was nonetheless, on balance, a mistake.[10]

I believe there will also be greater appreciation of some of the dilemmas the administration faced in Iraq after April 2003—the fact, for instance, that the alternative to a strict de-Baathification policy that helped provoke a Sunni upris-

---

8. On the course of the war, see Carter Malkasian, *The American War in Afghanistan: A History* (New York: Oxford University Press, 2021); on this particular dynamic, see Hal Brands, "The Afghanistan Papers Reveal a Tragedy, Not a Crime," *Bloomberg Opinion*, December 17, 2019.

9. See David Sanger, *The Inheritance: The World Obama Confronts and the Challenges to American Power* (New York: Crown, 2009).

10. See Frank Harvey, *Explaining the Iraq War: Counterfactual Theory, Logic and Evidence* (New York: Cambridge University Press, 2013); Hal Brands and Peter Feaver, "Lessons from the Iraq War," *National Review*, June 20, 2019.

ing was a weak one that might have provoked a Shia uprising. Here, though, the president's consistent failure, through late 2006, to adjust course, to resolve crippling dysfunction, or even to fully acknowledge how badly things were going should continue to be judged quite harshly, not least because it was the collapse of Iraqi stability that unleashed so many of the wider strategic consequences that persisted for years thereafter—indeed, in many cases those consequences could not be undone even when Iraq was temporarily stabilized a few years later.

Where this volume does promote a reassessment of Bush's legacy in Iraq is by providing greater perspective on the period from late 2006 through the end of 2008. Rather than accept the conventional critique of the war circa 2006—that it had failed and withdrawal was the only sensible option—the administration conducted a searching policy review that led to the commitment of additional troops, the implementation of a new counterinsurgency strategy, and other policy changes that collectively constituted the Surge.

That Surge was very much Bush's doing: it was chosen over the objections of some of his top military and civilian advisers. As careful scholarship has established, it allowed the United States to capitalize on the ongoing Anbar Awakening, leading to dramatic reductions in violence and moves toward political reconciliation.[11] The war, it now appears, was on a trajectory toward success, or at least an acceptable outcome, when Bush left office.

Yet a Transition Memorandum authored by Brett McGurk also warned, presciently, that this progress was fragile and reversible.[12] It would indeed be reversed, partially if not wholly because the Obama administration subsequently disengaged from Iraq's politics and prematurely ended the US military presence there.[13] The resulting collapse precipitated another US military intervention, one that also created—albeit to a lesser degree—distraction and weakness across an array of issues. If nothing else, viewing the Iraq War against the longer arc of

---

11. Stephen Biddle, Jeffrey Friedman, and Jacob Shapiro, "Testing the Surge: Why Did Violence Decline in Iraq in 2007?" *International Security* 37 (2012). On the background, see the essays in Jeffrey Engel, Timothy Sayle, Hal Brands, and William Inboden, eds., *The Last Card: Inside George W. Bush's Decision to Surge in Iraq* (Ithaca: Cornell University Press, 2019).

12. See the McGurk Transition Memorandum in O'Sullivan, "Iraq," in this volume.

13. Rick Brennan, "Withdrawal Symptoms: The Bungling of the Iraq Exit," *Foreign Affairs* (November/December 2014).

history reminds us that the eventual outcome was not written in stone from the moment the United States invaded—and that not all of its failures and disappointments can be laid at Bush's feet.

———

The Bush administration always viewed the wars in Iraq and Afghanistan as part of a larger struggle to keep America safe from catastrophic terrorism. The Transition Memoranda make this abundantly clear: a far larger number of them pertain to the global War on Terror than to any other issue. A second theme to emerge from this volume is just how expansive—and, in many ways, effective—that larger approach to counterterrorism was. "After the nightmare of September 11, America went seven and a half years without another successful terrorist attack on our soil," Bush would write in his memoirs. "If I had to summarize my most meaningful accomplishment as president in one sentence, that would be it."[14]

This is not a universally shared assessment. There remain intense debates about the morality and efficacy of particular US policies, such as enhanced interrogation and domestic surveillance. It is certainly fair to argue—and some of the Transition Memoranda obliquely acknowledge—that the Bush administration should have shown far greater urgency regarding terrorism before 9/11, even if it is far from clear that such a posture would have thwarted the attacks. On the whole, though, the administration outperformed most post-9/11 expectations.

To understand that conclusion, it helps to recall just how terrifying the initial post-9/11 period was. Roughly 85 percent of Americans, and the vast majority of US national security officials and members of Congress, believed that further attacks were likely. In October 2001, Secretary of Defense Donald Rumsfeld warned that "more people are going to be killed if we don't produce some results fast." In the nearly two years that followed, the president received, from the CIA, an average of 400 specific threats per month.[15]

As this collection reminds us, the administration's response was broad and multifaceted. In the near term, military action in Afghanistan deprived al Qaeda

———

14. Bush, *Decision Points*, 180.
15. Bush, *Decision Points*, 151–53, 157–58; Rumsfeld to Myers and Pace, October 10, 201, Rumsfeld Papers; "Source: '100-percent Chance' of Another Attack: Lawmakers Caution There's No Specific Threat," CNN.com, October 5, 2001; Jack Goldsmith, *The Terror Presidency: Law and Judgment inside the Bush Administration* (New York: Norton, 2007), 187.

of safe haven and led to the killing or capture of the most of the group's membership and leadership. Aggressive intelligence and law enforcement measures, coordinated with Pakistan and other countries, led to the arrest of hundreds of operatives.[16]

The administration was simultaneously developing a longer-term counterterrorism program, featuring targeted financial sanctions, law enforcement and intelligence partnerships with dozens of countries, the creation of new bureaucratic entities from the National Counterterrorism Center to the Office of the Director of National Intelligence and the Department of Homeland Security, the approval of new intelligence and covert action authorities, enhanced (but mostly nonintrusive) domestic security measures, and many other initiatives. It was no exaggeration, as one administration official concluded, that America had deployed a "whole new set of tools and approaches for advancing our Nation's security."[17]

Bush's counterterrorism campaign was closely linked to his signature Freedom Agenda. Contrary to the common caricature, the Freedom Agenda was not a messianic program to democratize the world at the point of a gun. It was an intellectually serious, if hugely ambitious, effort to address the political causes of key security threats. The Freedom Agenda resulted in a push to recalibrate key relationships across the Middle East and other regions, as well as the creation of incentives for the State Department and other entities to strengthen their commitment to advancing human rights and democracy. It notched important, if sometimes transitory, achievements in countries such as Georgia, Ukraine, and Lebanon; the Arab Spring later validated one of its central insights by showing that the absence of democracy was indeed a cause of radicalism and instability in the Muslim world. Yet the Freedom Agenda also proved very difficult to execute amid the competing demands of near-term counterterrorism cooperation with repressive states, the regional instability that the Iraq War created, and the fact that democratic elections—in Palestine, for instance—sometimes produced undesired and undemocratic results.

Bush's broader counterterrorism agenda also had ups and downs, and it is still hard, in certain areas, to fully assess its outcomes. Some administration

---

16. Lawrence Wright, "The Rebellion Within: An Al Qaeda Mastermind Questions Terrorism," *New Yorker*, June 2, 2008; Daniel Byman, "'Are We Winning the War on Terrorism?" Brookings Institution, Middle East Memo, May 23, 2003.

17. See especially chapters 2 and 3 in this volume.

officials and outside observers have argued that enhanced interrogation yielded critical intelligence and forestalled lethal attacks; other academic observers have argued that the program—whatever intelligence it may have produced—backfired strategically by drawing additional jihadists to the fight.[18] The Iraq War was massively counterproductive from a counterterrorism perspective, because it reenergized a battered jihadist movement and unleashed sectarian forces that polarized the Middle East.

Partly as a result, the United States struggled under Bush—as it struggled under every post-9/11 president—to win the "war of ideas" by delegitimizing radical voices in the Islamic world. "Some 20 years after the attacks of September 11, 2001," one former official acknowledges, "America still has not 'won' the ideological battle originally outlined against Al Qaeda."[19] By the end of Bush's presidency, the homeland threat was reemerging, as al Qaeda regrouped in the tribal areas of Pakistan and affiliates in Yemen and elsewhere grew stronger. Bush had always said that the global War on Terror would be a generational struggle, and America certainly had not won it when he left office. He had, however, established a framework for managing it—one that was certainly imperfect but nonetheless proved fairly enduring.

More than twenty years after 9/11, a growing body of evidence suggests that many of the measures Bush put in place after 9/11 did, individually and cumulatively, contribute to spoiling future attacks, making America a harder target, and keeping the country safer than many experts would have thought possible.[20] In fact, even as Barack Obama tried to distance himself from certain aspects of

---

18. See Michael Morell with Bill Harlow, *The Great War of Our Time: The CIA's Fight against Terrorism—From al Qa'ida to ISIS* (New York: Twelve, 2015); Jose Rodriguez and Bill Harlow, *Hard Measures: How Aggressive CIA Actions after 9/11 Saved American Lives* (New York: Simon & Schuster, 2012); Ali Soufan, *The Black Banners: Inside the Hunt for Al Qaeda* (New York: Penguin Books, 2011); Senate Select Committee on Intelligence, "Committee Study of the Central Intelligence Agency's Detention and Interrogation Program," April 2014; Robert Jervis, "The Torture Blame Game: The Botched Senate Report on the CIA's Misdeeds," *Foreign Affairs* (May/June 2015); and Pape's detailed analysis in "Forum on the Senate Select Committee on Intelligence (SSCI) Report and the United States' Post-9/11 Policy on Torture," *International Security Studies Forum*, February 16, 2015.

19. See Farah Pandith, "The War of Ideas," in this volume.

20. This evidence is summarized in Hal Brands and Michael O'Hanlon, "The War on Terror Has Not Yet Failed: A Net Assessment After 20 Years," *Survival* 63 (2021); also Brands and Feaver, "Case for Bush Revisionism."

Bush's counterterrorism program—namely, enhanced interrogation and extended military detention—he quietly embraced much of his predecessor's program. His administration relied on preventive military strikes against terrorist groups; aggressively used drones and special operations forces to take the fight to the enemy; refined and employed many post-9/11 financial tools; retained and improved the Bush-era bureaucratic framework for counterterrorism; and extensively utilized Bush-era legal, policy, and intelligence authorities regarding the use of force and other aspects of the counterterrorism campaign.

As Jack Goldsmith later wrote, "Barack Obama campaigned against the Bush approach to counterterrorism and came to office promising to repudiate it and to restore the rule of law. . . . But in perhaps the most remarkable surprise of his presidency, Obama continued almost all of his predecessor's counterterrorism policies."[21] When it came to laying the foundations of a long struggle against violent extremism, Bush succeeded more than he failed.

———

Among the virtues of the Transition Memoranda is that they offer a panoramic view of the administration's foreign policy. There was, after all, a world beyond Iraq, Afghanistan, and the grim imperatives of counterterrorism. The wider the perspective one takes, the more obvious the need for a balanced assessment of Bush's record becomes.

A partial list of achievements, highlighted in the relevant Transition Memoranda and attested to by other sources, would include the following:

- In South Asia, the administration twice helped avert wars between nuclear-armed regional powers, following deadly attacks in India by Pakistan-based terrorists.[22] Bush also presided over a major breakthrough in US-India relations, which started a slow but crucial process of strategic alignment that has only become more important with time.
- In the Asia-Pacific region, Bush kept US-China relations on a relatively stable footing, defusing the EP-3 crisis in April 2001 and later dissuading an

21. Jack Goldsmith, *Power and Constraint: The Accountable Presidency after 9/11* (New York: Norton, 2012), x.
22. Condoleezza Rice, *No Higher Honor: A Memoir of My Years in Washington* (New York: Crown, 2012), 436–42; Ashley Tellis, "The Merits of Dehyphenation: Explaining U.S. Success in Engaging India and Pakistan," *The Washington Quarterly* 31 (2008).

independence-minded Taiwanese leadership from unilaterally altering the status quo. Although 9/11 spoiled plans for an "Asia pivot," and although the balance of power shifted unfavorably vis-à-vis China, the administration nonetheless invested (quietly) in alliances and partnerships, modestly enhanced American military forces in the region, and laid the initial groundwork for key multilateral groupings—such as the Quad—that have since taken on greater importance.[23]

- In Latin America, Bush expanded and intensified Plan Colombia. In doing so, he helped that country make a near-miraculous transition from a failing state into a close strategic partner and security exporter, while also facilitating the eventual conclusion of a peace deal that ended a decades-long civil war. And although the administration initially struggled in dealing with Hugo Chavez's radical government in Venezuela, Bush eventually adopted a prudent policy of mostly ignoring Chavez while cultivating relationships with a range of leaders—including left-of-center presidents in Brazil, Uruguay, and Chile—as sources of stability in the region.
- In the realm of nonproliferation, the administration helped roll up the notorious A. Q. Khan network. It used coercive diplomacy (amplified by the initially successful invasion of Iraq) to induce Qaddafi's Libya to surrender most of its WMD stockpiles and become a partner in the global War on Terror.[24] And contrary to Bush's reputation as an unrepentant unilateralist, the administration fashioned a creative multilateral institution—the Proliferation Security Initiative—to impede the flow of WMD components and technologies.
- In the realm of arms control, the administration managed the tensions created by its withdrawal from the Anti-Ballistic Missile Treaty and negotiated the Moscow Treaty, which codified further reductions in the US and Russian strategic nuclear arsenals.

---

23. Michael Green, "The Iraq War and Asia: Assessing the Legacy," *The Washington Quarterly* 31 (2008); Nina Silove, "The Pivot before the Pivot: U.S. Strategy to Preserve the Power Balance in Asia," *International Security* 40 (2016).

24. See, for instance, Andrew Winner, "The Proliferation Security Initiative: The New Face of Interdiction," *The Washington Quarterly* 28 (2005); Bruce Jentleson and Christopher Whytock, "Who 'Won' Libya? The Force-Diplomacy Debate and Its Implications for Theory and Policy," *International Security* 30 (2005/06).

- In Europe, the administration presided over a second expansion of NATO, which served as a sound hedge against potential Russian revanchism, while also smoothing the relationship between that alliance and the European Union.
- In the realm of foreign assistance, Bush overhauled the provision of American development aid, pushing—through the Millennium Challenge Corporation and other initiatives—public-private partnerships and accountability provisions that continue to be emphasized today. Regarding trade, the administration negotiated (and succeeded in having ratified) a number of free-trade agreements, most notably the CAFTA-DR pact.
- In Africa, one of Bush's signature programs—the President's Emergency Plan for Aids Relief—helped change the public health trajectory of a continent, by providing "life-saving treatment for ... more than 2 million people."[25] To a degree that is far less appreciated, Bush also personally invested in diplomacy that addressed and helped resolve brutal conflicts in places such as Liberia and Sierra Leone.

To be clear, in some of these areas (e.g., Colombia, NATO expansion, Libya) Bush was building on a constructive inheritance from Clinton, as is often the case with foreign policy success. And there were, no doubt, a substantial list of failures:

- The administration failed to blunt Iran's regional influence or meaningfully impede its nuclear program, even as it did eventually devise a formula—sanctions plus the promise of engagement—that the Obama administration would adapt and exploit. In dealing with Iran, moreover, the mishandled occupation of Iraq was a strategic millstone for Washington. "If the Bush administration's careful coalition-building and restraint on the nuclear front hemmed Iran in," writes one administration official, "the international disunity and regional tumult that followed the initial US success in Iraq and Afghanistan produced the opposite."[26]

---

25. See Dana Deruiter's Transition Memorandum, in Mark Dybul and Dana Deruiter, "HIV/AIDS," in this volume.
26. Michael Singh, "Iran," in this volume.

- After withdrawing from the Agreed Framework (an admittedly problematic agreement), Bush largely failed to constrain North Korea's advancing missile and nuclear programs. As discussed below, he left his successor a situation that was far worse than the one he inherited.
- Early in his presidency, Bush had criticized the Clinton administration for making an ill-fated push for Middle East peace that failed and led to violence. Yet while Bush left some constructive legacies in this area—supporting Israeli withdrawal from Gaza and rejecting the argument that the Israeli-Palestinian conflict was the root of all the region's problems—he ultimately did not do much better than Clinton. In fact, Bush left office in early 2009 with another ambitious peace initiative having failed and a brief, intense war in Gaza just having concluded.
- If the expansion of NATO in 2004 was sound, the later, unsuccessful push to get Ukraine and Georgia into the alliance in 2008 was a diplomatic fiasco. It divided NATO, gave Tbilisi a false sense of American support, and—by US officials' own later admission—"likely encouraged Putin to invade Georgia just four months later."[27]
- The Bush administration made important strides in strengthening US alliances and partnerships in the Asia-Pacific, but also promoted unrealistic ambitions in declaring that China could become a "responsible stakeholder" in an American-led order.[28]

Reasonable analysts can disagree about the merits and demerits of these specific cases, and about whether the failures outweigh the successes or vice versa. What emerges from a more comprehensive review of Bush's policies, though, is a picture of an administration that often operated in ways contrary to the most common caricatures of the president, one that got a number of important things right, and one whose overall record was thus far more complex than many initial assessments allowed.

---

27. Damon Wilson, Judy Ansley, and Daniel Fried, "Europe," in this volume.
28. Robert Zoellick, "Whither China? From Membership to Responsibility," Remarks to National Committee on U.S.-China Relations, September 21, 2005, https://2001-2009 .state.gov/s/d/former/zoellick/rem/53682.htm.

The question of policy failures highlights an additional way of looking at the Bush record, one that is suggested less by the Transition Memoranda themselves than by the perspective that is now available more than a decade after they were written. There were plenty of areas in which the Bush administration struggled, and some in which it surely failed to meet the standards it set for itself. In several of these areas, however, other recent presidents didn't fare markedly better.

Consider again the issue of Russia. The Bush administration could rightly claim to have strengthened the Western position with the expansion of NATO, yet its failure to establish a sustainable relationship with Moscow—or deter aggression in Russia's "near abroad"—was painfully evident by the end of 2008. In this context, the president's infamous comment about looking into Putin's eyes and getting a sense of his soul did not age particularly well.

The fact is, though, that every post–Cold War president has started by trying to reset relations with Moscow in one way or another—and every post–Cold War president has failed to make that reset last. In 2014, the Obama administration found itself in a predicament similar to Bush's quandary in August 2008, when an effort to pull Ukraine toward the West was one of the factors that triggered a Russian invasion of that country. Every US administration since the Cold War has sought to engage Russia while simultaneously supporting countries in Central and Eastern Europe that wish to align with the West; every US administration has eventually found that these objectives are in tension—as shown, most recently, by Russia's invasion of Ukraine in 2022. The problem, one suspects, is not so much the ineptitude of any single leader as the fact that Washington and Moscow have been competing for influence in the old Soviet periphery, and that Russia has become more assertive in that contest as it has become more deeply authoritarian and has gradually recovered from its extreme post–Cold War weakness.[29]

Or consider the case of North Korea. It is beyond dispute that the Bush administration fared poorly in dealing with North Korea, handing off to Obama a problem that had gotten dramatically worse since 2001. The administration withdrew from the Clinton-era Agreed Framework in response to indications that North Korea was still vigorously pursuing, and perhaps already had, a nuclear weapon. Bush declared that "the United States of America will not permit

---

29. See Robert Kagan, *The Return of History and the End of Dreams* (New York: Knopf, 2008).

the world's most dangerous regimes to threaten us with the world's most destructive weapons."[30]

For a moment, in mid-2003, it appeared as though a then-successful invasion of Iraq might provide the coercive leverage necessary for that policy to succeed. But that leverage collapsed along with US policy in Iraq, which left the administration reliant on insufficient expedients such as economic sanctions and appeals for Chinese support. "The Bush administration's strategy," one Transition Memorandum acknowledges, "may have had misplaced expectations of China as a partner in dealing with North Korea."[31] Pyongyang crossed red line after red line, testing nuclear weapons in late 2006 and—despite Bush's stern warning—transferring nuclear reactor technology to Syria, which the Israelis eventually had to destroy. It was not an impressive record.

But then again, America compiled a bipartisan record of failure on North Korea after the end of the Cold War. Clinton navigated a dangerous crisis in 1993–94, but never put a lid on Pyongyang's nuclear or missile ambitions. Obama tried sanctions and "strategic patience," only to admit at the close of his presidency—following a flurry of missile and nuclear tests—that the problem had again gotten significantly worse.[32] Donald Trump then tried "maximum pressure" before pivoting to maximum engagement: neither one worked. The Biden administration has now committed to seeking compete and irreversible denuclearization, virtually ensuring that it, too, will fail to achieve its objective.

The root of the problem in North Korea is not the policy of one president or another, although analysts can debate which administration failed least. The root of the problem is that a despotic regime is determined to have nuclear weapons no matter the cost, and there is no way of stopping that regime absent a bloody, potentially catastrophic war that president after president has declined—rightly—to wage. Some problems just do not have good solutions. The course of US policy toward North Korea over the past thirty years, not just under the Bush administration, is a testament to this fact.

---

30. "President Bush's State of the Union Address," *Washington Post*, January 29, 2002.
31. Victor Cha, Michael Allen, J. D. Crouch, Michael Green, and Paul Haenle, "North Korea," in this volume.
32. Gerald Seib, Jay Solomon, and Carol Lee, "Barack Obama Warns Donald Trump on North Korea Threat," *Wall Street Journal*, November 22, 2016.

The postscripts that accompany the Transition Memoranda do not simply end the story in January 2009; they bring us up to date by explaining how US policy has evolved in the years since. Framing the Bush presidency against the longer history of the post–Cold War era illustrates a final theme of this collection—just how dramatically the strategic setting has changed since 2001.

Twenty years ago, the threat of catastrophic terrorism within the United States loomed very large; there was significant debate on *how* to wage a global War on Terror, but not *whether* to do so. There was still considerable optimism about the future trajectories of both China and Russia; it was possible to argue, as the Bush administration did in its 2002 National Security Strategy, that "today, the world's great powers find ourselves on the same side—united by common dangers of terrorist violence and chaos."[33] The freedom tide was still rising, with color revolutions in Ukraine, Georgia, and other countries; the number of democracies in the world reached an all-time high in 2005, around the time of Bush's second inaugural address. One of the great debates in international politics was whether the United States had *too much* power and influence for the good of the global system.

It is a different world today. The United States is involved in persistent, dangerous rivalries with Russia and China, as both countries challenge the international system and try to reorder—sometimes violently—the regions around them. The threat of great-power war seems all too real, given the conflict in Ukraine; analysts debate whether we are entering a "new Cold War."[34] Meanwhile, the world is experiencing a democratic recession that began in 2006 and has continued since then. Fears of terrorism have faded significantly enough that the Biden administration could take the risk of accepting defeat in Afghanistan and trying to "demilitarize" the campaign against violent extremism. Today, the question is not whether America is too strong and assertive; it is whether America is strong and assertive enough to defend a world order under strain.

Against this backdrop—and as some essays in this volume acknowledge—aspects of Bush's record look worse than they did at the time. The administration

---

33. George W. Bush, "The National Security Strategy of the United States of America," The White House, September 2002, https://georgewbush-whitehouse.archives.gov/nsc/nss/2002/.

34. See Richard Fontaine and Ely Ratner, "The U.S.-China Confrontation is another Cold War. It's something new," *Washington Post*, July 20, 2020; Hal Brands and John Lewis Gaddis, "A New Cold War: America, China, and the Echoes of History," *Foreign Affairs*, (November/December 2021).

was too sanguine about the prospects for, and consequences of, near-term democratization in the Middle East. It was slow to recognize, as were many American observers, the depth of Chinese and Russian hostility to the existing order—and the strength of those countries' desire to revise it to their liking. Most broadly, the human and material costs of the Iraq War, and the damage it did to the American psyche, probably retarded the country's reaction to a range of other, more severe, threats in subsequent years. As a result of 9/11, Iraq, and Afghanistan, Rice later wrote, America was simply "out of steam and out of ammunition."[35]

In other areas, however, a longer view makes the administration's record look better. Bush's efforts to solidify alliances and partnerships in Asia takes on greater significance in light of the US-China competition; the breakthrough in relations with India in 2005– 2006 looms larger with every passing year. Expanding NATO in Eastern Europe and the Baltic annoyed Putin but pushed the dividing line of the US-Russia competition that reemerged in 2007– 2008 considerably farther to the east. The Bush administration paid considerable attention to transnational issues, such as pandemics, that have since emerged as potentially existential threats. And to the extent that the terrorist threat has receded in significance for many Americans in recent years, it is partially because the United States—starting with the Bush administration—developed such a formidable suite of intelligence, diplomatic, law enforcement, financial, and military tools for keeping that threat at bay.

Part of the value of this collection is that it reminds us that the Bush administration was part of a larger era of post–Cold War foreign policy. That era, like the Bush presidency, was not the utter and complete disaster that many analysts would have us believe.[36] It saw the United States pursue, under several presidents, various versions of the strategy that Bush himself pursued—trying to deepen favorable global changes that the end of the Cold War had made possible, while warding off threats to that progress.

During this period, the United States racked up major achievements—delaying the return of vicious great-power rivalry for a generation, extending the democratic

---

35. Rice, *No Higher Honor*, 568.

36. For a polemic, see Stephen Walt, *The Hell of Good Intentions: America's Foreign Policy Elite and the Decline of U.S. Primacy* (New York: Macmillan, 2018); for balance, see Christopher Griffin, "Strategies of Dominance," in the forthcoming third edition of *Makers of Modern Strategy*. For the author's assessment, see Hal Brands, *American Grand Strategy in the Age of Trump* (Washington, DC: Brookings Institution, 2018).

"zone of peace" into new areas such as Eastern Europe, promoting an upsurge of global prosperity, preventing unchecked nuclear proliferation, halting brutal conflicts, and stopping the wholesale destabilization of areas such as the Persian Gulf and the Balkans. There were also plenty of failures and disappointments—interventions that Americans might wish, in retrospect, that they had undertaken (e.g., Rwanda) and those that they might wish to have avoided (e.g., Iraq and Libya); a bipartisan propensity for failed resets with Russia; an engagement policy toward China that lasted at least a decade too long—although no one has yet made a credible, historically informed argument that those failures were significantly worse than those in any comparable period of US diplomacy.

This era was always likely to end in a return to a more competitive environment, simply because the unprecedented imbalance of power that the end of the Cold War produced could not last forever. Its history shows that foreign policy is hard, that successes are sometimes less obvious than failures, that those failures typically result not from the mendacity or malignity of policymakers but from the inherent difficulty of the task, and that perspectives on key events do change over time—all of which points might inform a considered reckoning with the Bush administration's legacy, as well.

CHAPTER 32

Transferring Presidential Power
in a Post-9/11 World

MARTHA JOYNT KUMAR

"We face economic challenges that will not pause to let a new President settle in. This will also be America's first wartime Presidential transition in four decades. We're in a struggle against violent extremists determined to attack us, and they would like nothing more than to exploit this period of change to harm the American people."

President George W. Bush, remarks to
White House Staff, November 6, 2008

The 2008–2009 presidential transition took place in the midst of consequential domestic and international financial and security-related crises. In this unsettled environment, President Bush and his leadership team took particular care to establish a smooth transition and in doing so, set new standards for when an administration begins planning for a transition, what information the incumbent provides to his successor, and how they do so. The Transition Memoranda featured in this book were an important part of that effort and worthy of close scrutiny. While their existence has been known since 2009, the memoranda were classified and would normally not be available to scholars and the public for decades. It is highly unusual to have access to information like this so soon after the end of an administration. Yet, as important as they were and are, they were just part of the larger transition effort that was praised at the time and looks better in hindsight after the tumultuous transitions of 2016 and 2020.

Many of the voluntary actions the Bush administration took later became law in two pieces of legislation, the Pre-Election Transition Act of 2010 and the Edward "Ted" Kaufman and Michael Leavitt Presidential Transitions Improvements Act of 2015 [PL 111-283 and PL 114-136]. For their part, President-elect Obama and his team worked with members of the outgoing administration and benefited from the information they provided and the actions they took. With the outgoing and incoming presidential staff working together, the Bush transition was the most successful in modern times. The actions the Bush team took set new standards that Congress later adopted as law and influenced the formal and informal ways succeeding presidents shaped their transitions. It also established the critical role in the twenty-first century of the national security transition, a vital part of the overall presidential transition that is mostly conducted in secret.

"Months before the 2008 election, I had decided to make it a priority to conduct a thorough, organized transition," President George W. Bush reflected in his memoir, *Decision Points*. Rather than approach the transition as a matter of solely following the letter of the law, President Bush directed his administrative team to focus on what was needed to make the transition "the best." He tasked White House Chief of Staff Bolten to lead the transition. Bolten recalls his conversation with President Bush:

> . . . about a year before the end of the administration. And he and I . . . had a conversation probably in late '07, in which he said that he wanted to make sure that his transition was the best; that he recognized that regardless of who won the election, we were still going to be in a situation where the country was under threat. And he basically said go all out to make sure that the transition is as effective as it possibly can be, especially in the national security area.[1]

The combination of the early directions that the president gave and the discretion he provided for Bolten and for National Security Adviser Stephen Hadley

---

1. Joshua Bolten, interview by Martha Joynt Kumar, June 25, 2009.

provided the impetus and the freedom to innovate and adapt to the unique conditions faced in 2008. Above all, it meant that both Bolten and Hadley started the transition process much earlier than previously had been the case, with Bolten holding an early meeting with representatives of the presumptive major party presidential candidates and Hadley collecting the organizational, policy, and personnel information a new national security team would need well before the parties had chosen their nominees.

PRACTICES ESTABLISHED BY PRESIDENT GEORGE W. BUSH AND HIS LEADERSHIP TEAM: LAW, TACIT UNDERSTANDINGS, AND DISCRETION

Both Bolten and Hadley began their preparations in late 2007 and relied on three elements to create a smooth passage to power for a new team. They are: transition law; tacit understandings between the outgoing and incoming teams; and the discretion that laws allow for a White House and administration transition. The Presidential Transition Act of 1963 and its amendments provide the basic contours of the resources provided to an incoming team and the rules governing their distribution. By 2008, the law and its amendments called for office space, technical information support for computers and other devices after the election, as well as limitations on funding and public reporting requirements. The Bush initiatives moved up the timeline from postelection to months beforehand.

The Law: Current Law Reflects Bush Team Practices

The Bush administration interpreted the 1963 President Transition Act in a broad way. Instead of simply meeting the minimum requirements of the law, President Bush wanted to meet the transition needs of a post-9/11 world. Several practices the president and his administration adopted are memorialized in the 2010 and 2015 transition laws as well as provided for in the 2004 Intelligence Reform and Terrorism Prevention Act:

- Instituted preelection planning with the two major party candidates. In the summer of 2008, Bolten brought representatives of the presumptive presidential candidates into the White House to develop an agreed-upon memorandum of understanding that would govern their transition relationship with the federal government.

- Established through executive order a White House Transition Council with broad White House and administration membership and an Agency Transition Directors Council composed of career officials representing departments and agencies. The 2015 law now requires a president to create both councils by six months prior to a presidential election.

- Organized and operated a tabletop exercise on a national security issue, which later was mandated in the 2015 law. All administrations since then have held one or more, with a variety of exercises featuring natural disasters, terrorism attacks, and a pandemic.

- Established procedures for early preelection security clearances for transition staff. Following up on a recommendation from the 9/11 commission and the 2004 act, Bolten worked with the candidate representatives and the Department of Justice to allow both candidates to submit. Preelection, the names to Justice that could be cleared for working in the transition.

- Initiated terrorism assessment. The 2004 act called for the intelligence community to create a terrorism threat assessment to be given postelection to the president-elect. [PL 108-458]

Tacit Understandings Between Presidents: Continuity in the Presidency

An important element in the 2008 transition was the tacit understanding by both President Bush and President-elect Obama that continuity in the presidency was critical to the successful transfer of power, particularly in a post-9/11 world and even when there was a change of party. The two leaders began early preparations and then, postelection, worked together to handle issues, such as avoiding the possible collapse of American automobile companies. Transition law did not detail how to manage crises, which allowed the Bush and Obama teams to work on the auto bailout as they saw fit within their general goal of a stable and peaceful transition.

Discretion: Memoranda; One-on-One Conversations and Briefings; a Functioning Staff

Discretion provided the flexibility that allowed the Bush transition to start early and work on preparing to hand over responsibility for the national security issues the president and his staff considered central to the transition. Just as President

Bush provided Bolten with the discretion to work toward Bush's stated goal of a smooth transition, Stephen Hadley exercised discretion in defining how they reached Bush's goal in the national security area. Over the course of close to a year prior to the inauguration, Hadley developed a three-pronged information process. The memoranda featured in this book and their supporting documents, as well as contingency plans; second, briefings and one-on-one staff meetings between the incoming and outgoing staff members. The briefings included operational issues related to military and intelligence activities as well as myriad policy issues across the full spectrum of geopolitical concerns. The third prong was maintaining a functioning staff system prior to the arrival of the new team. All three prongs aimed to avoid any needless interruptions in the national security area so that the Obama team could, if need be, meet the demands of an unfolding crisis even during the earliest minutes of Obama's tenure.

Forty Memoranda and Accompanying Appendices for an Incoming Team   The NSC leadership staff and the senior directors worked together deciding what categories of information they would assemble for the memoranda. The template called for information in four areas. "The first section will be what we found, then what our strategy was, then what we think we accomplished, and finally, what was left to do, what was going to hit the new team early on," Hadley explained.[2]

Equally important were the documents accompanying the memoranda. Most of the memos included a combination of publicly released documents such as presidential speeches, joint statements by President Bush and a foreign leader, and highly classified materials that the incoming team would be seeing for the first time. The classified appended documents, for example, included "Summary of Conclusions" for NSC and NSC Principals meetings. The most sensitive of the documents were collections of "Memoranda of Conversations" ("memcons") of in-person meetings President Bush had with a foreign leader and phone call transcripts ("telcons") the president had, along with those that his top foreign policy officials might have had. In order to access such conversations, however, the few people who were designated as authorized to read them had to request permission. Hadley said to the incoming team: "If you decide you need any of these [memcons and telcons], call us, and we'll get you a copy."[3]

---

2. Stephen Hadley, interview by Martha Joynt Kumar, June 10, 2009.
3. Stephen Hadley, interview by Martha Joynt Kumar, June 10, 2009.

An incoming Obama NSC official commented on the memoranda and on relations with the outgoing NSC team: "The spirit in which they were produced was extremely positive. I can't think of a better way . . . [to get] the facts of life when it comes to a transition . . . Hadley made it very clear to us from the beginning, and his whole staff—and this emanated down . . . everyone was super-cooperative, committed to making it the best transition possible."[4]

On the other hand, the policy work important to the incumbent Republican administration had less impact on the incoming Democratic team. During the campaign, President Obama spoke of foreign policy as well as domestic issues. That meant the incoming team was "already well along from the campaign . . . in thinking through . . . what the U.S. should or shouldn't be doing on a particular issue."[5]

The memoranda had a value beyond the first days of an administration. Not only were they useful at the moment but "sometimes learning occurs over time. It's not just part of the transition . . . Even today [late in Obama's first term] we may look back and say, how did our predecessors deal with a certain set of problems, to help inform us going forward?"[6] For the outgoing administration the memoranda are important legacy documents for historians and others interested in the actions of a president and his team.

Follow-on Briefings and One-on-One Conversations   For some of the incoming Obama officials at the NSC leadership level, the memoranda and associated material were a starting point in discussions they had with the person who held the post they now occupied. One person discussed how he used the materials. "Early on was process, how does the deputies committee work? How does the principals committee work?"[7] An area that was particularly important for members of the incoming team was intelligence. Many were last in the NSC during the Clinton years well before the major intelligence reforms brought about by the 9/11 attack.

> . . . the government was dramatically different in 2008 than in 2000 when many of us had left. . . . The Homeland Security Council did not exist. . . .

---

4. Background interview, 2011.
5. Background interview, 2011.
6. Background interview, 2011.
7. Background interview, 2011.

when we had all been in government under the Clinton administration. . . . the more process-type things were really important because—we had no reason to know any of this stuff before. So we were . . . being introduced to it for the first time.[8]

Conversations about the rationale behind organizational decisions proved helpful as well. In looking at the organization of the NSC, meeting one-on-one led to conversations about why certain directorates included the countries or subjects they had in 2008. "We recognize this seems weird when you look at it from an organization chart perspective," a Bush staff member explained. "But here's the reason why we did it, and here's why we think it works. . . . So that a lot of it was this kind of back-and-forth conversation which I found was very useful . . . because you could have more give and take. . . . You got a better understanding of where they were coming from."[9]

Meetings between incoming and outgoing officials enhanced the usefulness of the memoranda. Some of those meetings involved several officials in a formal setting on an issue deemed by the Bush team as critical, such as the subject briefings on Iran, Iraq, and Afghanistan. Informal sessions where incoming and outgoing officials spoke about their work included meetings in the workplace as well as in more informal settings. Secretary of State Condoleezza Rice hosted a dinner for Hillary Clinton, the incoming secretary. Rice's guests included officials from both the incoming and outgoing foreign policy and national security teams.

Organizational Continuity: Leaving a Functioning Staff in Place with Relevant Organizational Information   Given the stakes, continuity on the staff level is especially important—arguably more important for the National Security Council than most of the other White House functions. At the same time, every incoming president will want to move quickly to put his or her new stamp on national security policy and will have a senior team of handpicked advisers ready to do so on day one. Accordingly, Hadley worked with Obama NSC Adviser General James Jones to ensure that President Obama would have the benefits

---

8. Background interview, 2011.
9. Background interview, 2011.

of both change and continuity in staffing the NSC. To support change, Hadley asked for the resignation of the NSC senior directors prior to January 20 with the intention that the incoming Obama team was free to bring in their appointees. To support continuity, Hadley asked the more junior detailees from the intelligence community and the Defense and State Departments to stay on and identified one of them from each directorate to serve as acting senior director so that Obama would have a functioning staff ready to work at the time he took office on January 20, 2009. In one important case, Obama kept on a senior staff member, Lieutenant General Douglas Lute, who served as deputy national security adviser responsible for Iraq and Afghanistan. He was the most senior national security staffer who worked through the Bush administration and straight into the Obama administration, continuing on for several years in that post to ensure a smooth transition in the running of the wars.

Steve Hadley arranged for other information to be provided to the senior national security team advising Obama:

- *National Security Council records.* The Presidential Records Act provides the records of an administration, including those of the NSC, be given to the National Archives for processing for the incumbent president's library. In the past, sometimes incoming administrations have arrived to discover the safes empty with no paper trail as to what was happening and why. Hadley got permission from the NSC Records office to let those remaining in leadership roles in the NSC to copy relevant documents so that the incoming team would have the information they needed for a quick start.
- *Organization charts and list of NSC staff.* Additionally, Hadley and his team "offered to review them [the lists] with the incoming national security adviser and deputy to help them decide which ones they wanted to retain for their staff."[10]
- *Files of pending actions.* Steve Hadley created a file of pending actions where they would seek the guidance of Obama's team as to "whether they wanted us to: (1) go ahead and take the action we proposed to take; or (2) take no action and hold the matter for the new NSA/DNSA [national

---

10. Stephen Hadley, message to Martha Joynt Kumar, November 13, 2021.

security adviser and deputy national security adviser] to handle once they came into office. Where there was a question I and the new NSA/DNSA would consult with our respective principals, (i.e., the outgoing and incoming presidents)."[11]

- *Tabletop exercise.* In early January, led by Josh Bolten, the transition team worked through with the Obama appointees the preparations required for handling a national security crisis.

THE 2016 AND 2020 TRANSITIONS: PREELECTION PREPARATIONS AND POSTELECTION TENSIONS AND PROBLEMS

In the period since the 2008 transition, there were change-of-party presidential transitions in 2016 and 2020. While both met with problems, there was a commitment of transition staff to use the 2008 model as a guide. The laws memorializing the Bush to Obama practices ameliorated some of the difficulties experienced by both incoming and outgoing presidents and their staffs.

Pre- and Postelection in 2016

The 2016 presidential transition preparations started off well in the preelection phase. Following the election, however, the transition changed course abruptly. At the outset, President Obama stated he wanted to follow the precedents of the 2008 transition. "President Barack Obama told cabinet officers that he appreciated the cooperative attitude and helpfulness of his predecessor, George W. Bush" commented John Helgerson, who has been involved in and written about the CIA process of briefing candidates and presidents on intelligence matters.[12] "Obama stressed that he wanted to do everything Bush had done, and more, to facilitate the transition to his successor." To that end, Obama created the White House Transition Coordinating Council and named Chief of Staff Denis McDonough

---

11. Stephen Hadley, message to Martha Joynt Kumar, November 13, 2021.

12. John L. Helgerson, *Getting to Know the President: 1952–2016* (Washington, DC: Central Intelligence Agency, Center for the Study of Intelligence, 2021), 231, https://www.cia.gov/static/242fbcb4c50958e6d49fa7a3c2718a05/Getting-to-Know-the-President-Fourth-Edition-2021-web.pdf.

to lead the transition. The General Services Administration began its preparations on schedule with a team in place headed by Federal Transition Coordinator Mary Gibert, and work was underway in the spring by the Agency Transition Directors Council with its representatives from the fifteen departments and five large agencies. All of these preparations were underway by early May. Following the conclusion of the two party-nominating conventions, both candidates had transition teams in place headed by experienced officials and with support teams. In August, McDonough met with representatives of the candidates soon after Donald Trump and Hillary Clinton were nominated by their parties.

These early preparations were summarily dismissed following the election. Before election day, the Trump preelection transition operation was headed by former Governor Chris Christie and run day-to-day by Christie's former chief of staff and member of the New Jersey Senate, Rich Bagger. Shortly after the election results were announced, President-elect Trump replaced Christie with Vice President Mike Pence and Trump family members. From that point on, the Trump team struggled to assemble an administration.

The new transition team consisted of an ad hoc group in New York made up primarily of campaign staff and family members. For their transition, they drew on those who had worked with the campaign, few of whom had government experience. Trump's background as a businessman with no government or military experience—and Trump's failure to unify the party after securing the nomination—made it difficult for him to field a team ready to govern when they came into office.

A week after the 2016 election, President-elect Trump announced his appointment of Michael Flynn to be his national security adviser, who then assembled his team and took part in transition briefings. Less than a month after the inauguration, however, Flynn was fired for misleading Vice President Pence about Flynn's contacts with Russian Ambassador Sergey Kislyak. In addition to Flynn, there were several commissioned staff members who were fired or left voluntarily during Trump's first six months in office.

A significant part of the transition problems in the Trump postelection national security operation came about because of his mistrust of the intelligence community. Trump smarted over charges that Russia was involved on his behalf in the 2016 election, charges that were supported by an intelligence community report that concluded the "United States had a very complete picture of who had hacked the DNC computers, as well as when and how they had done it."[13] In early January the intelligence community leaders met with Trump and explained their findings. At the end of the meeting, FBI Director James Comey told Trump about the dossier that was circulating with derogatory personal information about him. When the contents of the dossier leaked to news organizations, Trump was furious and blamed the intelligence community for releasing the information. Trump's rocky relationship with the intelligence community was a significant factor in the post-election phase of his transition and remained during his presidency. His security appointments reflected concern. The Director of the Office of National Intelligence, Dan Coats, for example, was not named as a member of the National Security Council while Trump's political strategist, Steve Bannon, was.

The NSC Transition in 2020: Stress Testing the 2008 Model
How durable is the 2008 NSC transition model? Has the paradigm mixture of document preparation supplemented by meetings of principals and middle-level staff proved successful? The 2020 transition provides a good example of a certain amount of durable cooperation between outgoing and incoming staff even when the political environment is a tumultuous one. While postelection some Trump White House staff members and department secretaries continued to speak of a second term even though Trump had lost, Robert O'Brien focused on preparing the NSC staff to hand over responsibility for national security to the incoming Biden team. Shortly after the election, he commented on the American tradition of peaceful transitions. "And the great thing in the United States of America, we've passed the baton and had peaceful, successful transitions even in the most contentious periods." He also said in that forum that the "Biden transition team is going to have very professional folks who are coming in to take these positions, many of whom have been here before and spent a lot of time in the White House in the prior administration."[14]

As contentious as the times continued to be with President Trump not conceding his election loss, an insurrection at the Capitol, and key department and agencies resisting the kinds of cooperation that existed in 2008—most notably in

---

13. Helgerson, *Getting to Know the President*, 249.
14. Robert O'Brien. Soufan Center Global Security Forum, November 12, 2020, https://www.youtube.com/watch?v=7ehZIA_CBrE [transition remarks at 34:36].

the Department of Defense, where a newly appointed team of acting officials took over after Trump fired Secretary Mark Esper after losing the election—O'Brien insisted in postelection interviews that he stayed his course and tried to work toward a peaceful transition. O'Brien commented that he used "the influence I had and the ability I had to . . . make sure there was an excellent transition . . . in the NSC itself and not beyond that. And so that's what I focused on, and my team focused on, was making sure that the NSC transition was proper."[15] In determining what was "proper," in the fall O'Brien spoke with Hadley. "Early on before the election, I went and spoke with Stephen Hadley because I think Stephen . . . [established] the gold standard when he ran the transition from Bush to Obama."[16] With an early start, O'Brien described the preparations he and his NSC prepared for an incoming team: "We had 30 transition binders that we put together for the different directorates . . . We had strategic documents and strategic intelligence reports pertaining to each regional and functional directorate. Every directorate had a binder with our key documents . . . strategy documents . . . for whatever we were working on and also the key intelligence reports relating to that directorate."[17]

They hosted "over 50 meetings with the Biden transition team, which was incredible under the circumstances. The Biden transition team met with every senior director of all of our directorates."[18] Additionally, O'Brien recounted, Biden team members had approximately 200 written questions relating to the operation of the office, which O'Brien's team answered.

As a sign of goodwill and of unity in approaching our allies, O'Brien made calls to foreign officials. "I made over 25 calls to foreign governments, primarily to national security advisers but in some cases, the foreign minister if there wasn't an equivalent to me . . . letting them know that Jake was coming in for me," O'Brien said. "And asking them to extend him every courtesy and take his calls immediately. A number of them had . . . messages to pass on to the Biden folks. So I passed those messages to Jake."[19]

In view of the extraordinary chaos of the transition, it is noteworthy that incoming national security adviser Jake Sullivan made a point of publicly praising

---

15. Robert O'Brien, interview by Martha Joynt Kumar, September 20, 2021.

16. Robert O'Brien, interview by Martha Joynt Kumar, September 20, 2021.

17. Robert O'Brien, interview by Martha Joynt Kumar, September 20, 2021.

18. Robert O'Brien, interview by Martha Joynt Kumar, September 20, 2021.

19. Robert O'Brien, interview by Martha Joynt Kumar, September 20, 2021.

O'Brien for his efforts. In a late January conversation moderated by Condoleezza Rice with Jake Sullivan and Robert O'Brien, Sullivan remarked about the work of O'Brien and the NSC staff. "Robert, thank you just for everything that you did, to help pave the way for me to come into this [seat], for our team to get onboard, and for us to get up and running at a moment when we face considerable challenges around the world of great power competitors, and of course, a range of transnational threats as well," Sullivan remarked.[20]

RECENT DEVELOPMENTS IN TRANSITION PRACTICES

"Unconventional Challenges"

With problems in three out of the four presidential transitions of the twenty-first century, candidates will likely put a premium on preparing for the unknown. This is precisely what President Biden's team said they did. In addition to the conventional issues Biden could face as president, the Biden team developed protocols for what they termed "unconventional challenges," which were built on the assumption they would face multiple crises as well as face a lack of cooperation from the Trump administration. They had a group of five longtime aides who developed seventy protocols, later reduced to a broad dozen with subsets. Jeff Peck, a key figure in the group who tracked the implementation of their mitigating strategies for each, commented about their process. "The first step is to identify the challenges. The second step is to categorize them ... thematically. The third step is then making sure you're tracking all of the developments on the ones you've identified and ... new ones as they emerge," he commented.[21] Once they had their list and a short explanation of each, they noted who was accountable for each, their progress, who they were coordinating with, and then timeframes. In assessing the value of identifying "unconventional challenges" and then developing mitigating strategies, Peck commented: "I think of it more as avoiding the hazards and then ... the opportunities are [you] really have to expand your

---

20. Condoleezza Rice, "Passing the Baton," event at US Institute for Peace, January 29, 2021, 15:47, https://www.usip.org/events/passing-baton-2021-securing-americas-future -together.

21. Jeffrey Peck, interview with Martha Joynt Kumar, September 7, 2021.

thinking, which allows you to plan better for post-inauguration day and find the most talented possible people."[22]

There is no clean slate when a president-elect comes into office. Former Chief of Staff Mack McLarty, for example, spoke of the "carryover" issues President Clinton met when he came into office. They had the developing issues of assistance to Somalia and to Haiti, but also Bosnia, an issue that proved difficult for both George H. W. Bush and Bill Clinton. Bosnia was an issue "that just took an enormous amount of time and effort . . . there just wasn't an easy solution. And we really struggled with it, as Bush had."[23]

A Focus on Non-Senate Confirmed Appointments
The Biden team had an emphasis on presidential appointees that did not require Senate confirmation. Biden came into office with 206 staff members selected for White House positions. That included Jake Sullivan's leadership team as well as senior directors of almost all of the existing directorates. The role of the National Security Council staff has become especially critical with the Senate's slow confirmation process for those below the cabinet secretary level. At the end of October 2021, of the 170 positions in the national security leadership level cited by the Partnership for Public Service, eight months into the administration, only 26 percent of his nominees had been confirmed. At the same time in 2001, 57 percent were Senate confirmed.[24] Such vacancy pressures on the departments and their secretaries means a heightened importance for the NSC staff at least in the first year of an administration.

Virtual Transition Preparations
The Biden policy and agency review teams worked on a virtual basis. Salman Ahmed, who headed the intelligence, foreign policy, and defense teams, spoke about the benefits of meeting virtually. Except for some postelection sessions held in secure locations around the country, team members did not meet in person.

---

22. Jeffrey Peck, interview with Martha Joynt Kumar, September 7, 2021.

23. Thomas McLarty, interview with Martha Joynt Kumar, August 22, 2021.

24. Elizabeth Williamson, "Top National Security Posts Sit Empty, Mired in Senate 'Purgatory,'" *New York Times*, September 12, 2021.

So, it's much, much more conducive to having people spread out around the country. It's cheaper if you don't have to physically fly people in for things, which you don't have money for in any event, so a lot of this has to be out of your pocket. . . . So it's cost effective. It's more conducive to inclusion of people around the country. It's much more conducive to secrecy. You don't want the names of people who are engaged in all this to leak.[25]

With its savings and the ability to bring in team members from all parts of the country, the virtual model is likely to be replicated in future transitions, although it is not known whether this approach introduced communications vulnerabilities.

TWENTY-FIRST-CENTURY TRANSITION LESSONS

Unlike earlier ones, presidential transitions in the twenty-first century regularly experienced difficulties. With the Florida election recount underway, President George W. Bush had only thirty-seven days for his transition instead of the normal approximately seventy-five days. As we have seen, his handoff of power in 2008 was a fairly ideal one. In 2016, however, the Trump transition lost momentum when President-elect Trump fired Chris Christie, former New Jersey governor and Trump transition director along with his senior leadership team. The 2020 transition with its delayed GSA ascertainment of a winner, a president who cast doubt with his constituents on the validity of President Biden's victory, and the insurrection at the Capitol, all presented the greatest danger to the peaceful transfer of power we have experienced in at least a century. With such an unsteady record, transition preparations need to be taken seriously early in a presidential election year, especially the national security component. Through recent transition experiences, we have learned several lessons:

1. **A Well-Ordered Transition Brings Together Law and Precedent.** The basic assurance we have for an effective transfer of power is the cache of transition laws beginning with the 1963 one. Even though discretion is also critical in the development of a well-ordered transition, the law sets a baseline that provides

---

25. Salman Ahmed, interview with Martha Joynt Kumar. March 28, 2021.

some minimum guarantees, for instance, making clear what resources there are and what the basic requirements are for an administration leaving office. With the 2015 law, the president must prepare for a transition even if he is running for re-election, as was the case in 2020. In the past, after four years, presidents made few preparations to leave. Instead, they focused on planning for a second term. Under the 2015 act, the Trump administration did not have the choice in 2020. That law required they create the two councils as well as file reports to Congress on transition preparations. Chris Liddell, who managed the Trump transition out of office stressed that his actions were guided by the law and by precedent. "What I tried to do was use precedent as my friend," Liddell said. "In particular, in the pre-election period, but then in the post-election period as well."[26]

2. **Presidents Set the Tone.** Presidents set the tone and chart the course for what kind of transition they want. They drive the system. It is presidents who let their administration officials know how they want the transition to operate. Presidents-elect are also important in signaling to their team what their level of cooperation should be. In George W. Bush's case, his early actions and then words provided the impetus for career and political staff to work toward a smooth transfer of power. While postelection President Trump would not concede his loss, the NSC and White House transition operations sought to follow the law. Although they did so in different ways, each of the twenty-first-century presidents—Bush, Obama, and Trump—took great interest in shaping their transitions out of office.

3. **NSC Staff Professionalism.** As detrimental to a smooth transition as the postelection phase of the 2020 transition was, the NSC transition benefited from having an experienced, committed career and political staff with a commitment to the national security mission. Alone among White House political staff offices, the NSC has a seventy-thirty split of agency detailees to political appointees that results in a substantial number of people working in the office on a rotating basis who come from defense, intelligence, and State Department staff.[27]

Career staff joined the NSC political leadership in taking seriously the preparation of materials for the incoming Biden team. Deputy National Security Adviser Matthew Pottinger commented:

26. Christopher Liddell, interview with Martha Joynt Kumar, August 21, 2021.
27. James Jones, interview with Martha Joynt Kumar, November 11, 2001.

[T]here's a professionalism there. In part it's continuity; in part tradition; part trust based on the types of material we have exposure to. And then it's just the fact that the stakes are so damn high. You can't . . . afford to . . . [play] political games. . . . we're handing over at a time when we're facing a constitutional crisis at home, and the prospect of cyber warfare by several governments designed to undermine our elections and their credibility.[28]

4. **Importance of Teams.** Teams are critical to a successful national security process. John Negroponte observed that a successful team "depends on the president, and it depends on . . . the three top individuals in his or her national security apparatus, and that is . . . the national security adviser, the secretary of defense, and the secretary of state. And normally, if those three people get along reasonably well, they usually have pretty smooth sailing in terms of the decision-making process. . . . when it was Hadley, Rice, and Gates, they got along so well they formed a company together. . . ."[29]

In Democratic administrations as well, there is an emphasis on building teams. Former Chief of Staff Mack McLarty spoke of the importance of the same mixture of three top positions in the Clinton administration. "[National Security Advisor] Sandy Berger, because he had been deputy [NSA] and because of his natural managerial skills, really worked effectively when he was national security adviser with not only the President . . . But also with the cabinet officers, Bill Cohen [Defense], Madeleine Albright [State]. And there was really a camaraderie, very collegial working [relationship]."[30]

5. **National Security Council: Reflecting Current Issues and Pressures.** Incoming White House staff talk about reducing the numbers of NSC staff, but with little success. There is a shifting environment with more actors on the international stage, nonstate actors, and the fast communications that characterize contemporary foreign relations. Steve Hadley spoke of the conversation he and his team had with outgoing National Security Adviser Sandy Berger.

Why does it [staff numbers] creep back? When we cut it back and showed Sandy Berger our new org chart, Sandy said a couple things. He said,

---

28. Matthew Pottinger, interview with Martha Joynt Kumar, September 8, 2021.
29. John Negroponte, interview with Martha Joynt Kumar, September 5, 2020.
30. Thomas McLarty, interview with Martha Joynt Kumar. August 22, 2021.

"One, you don't understand how much time you're going to spend dealing with the issue of terrorism. And you got to make sure that you're staffed for that." Secondly, he said, "You've cut back congressional relations. You've cut back communications. You don't understand in the new technology world in which we are moving with the 24/7 news cycle and all of the social media, you're going to be overwhelmed on the communication side, just managing the communications."[31]

In 1990 under National Security Adviser Brent Scowcroft, the NSC had ten geographical and subject directorates and thirteen commissioned officers. In the post-9/11 configurations, there have been as many as twenty-two offices and directorates and twenty-six commissioned officers. Some of the expansion has come in the form of a homeland security adviser with a supporting staff integrated into the NSC staff.[32] No directorates have been eliminated though some of their geographical divisions have been reconfigured.

The directorates that have been added in the past twenty years provide a window into changes in the world political scene since the Scowcroft era: Homeland Security; Counterterrorism; Border and Transportation Security; Cybersecurity; Democracy and Human Rights; International Energy and Environment; Resilience (global health and preparedness). Internal operations grew as well with Strategic Planning, Legal, and Communications all as separate and expanded offices.

All of these operations are responding to a post–Cold War world. The current national security environment is one where the president is at the center and people want a presidential response, not one from the State or Defense Departments. The demands on the office mean that an incoming staff needs the kinds of analytical information, documents, and one-on-one contact with staff of the order incoming staff received in 2008.

6. **A Lack of Rules Can Come at a Cost: Tension Between Teams.** Tensions sometimes develop between the two teams in a setting where there are few rules detailing exactly what information outgoing presidents and their NSC teams must provide to those coming into office. Whether it is general briefings or one-on-one

---

31. Stephen Hadley, interview by Martha Joynt Kumar, September 15, 2021.
32. Information obtained from Leadership Connect (formerly *The Federal Yellow Book*), https://www.leadershipconnect.io.

sessions, the presidents themselves guide the information-distribution process and they will develop their own practices. For his part, President Bush did not want his staff to brief President-elect Obama on a select number of issues. Rather, he wanted to do it himself. Moreover, President Bush did not want Obama team members to receive security briefings unless they were coming into the administration. President-elect Obama, though, wanted to decide briefing attendees based on whom he wanted in the sessions and how he preferred to do business.[33]

An additional area of discretion and possible tension is the basic one of whether to consult with the incoming team on pending decisions and whether to involve them in final outcomes. The 2008 transition provided a window on differing views consulting the incoming team on current decisions under review. Because the Bush team chafed at being largely excluded from policy deliberations late in the Clinton administration, they took pains to invite the Obama team to consult on pending actions. When President Bush came into office, Joshua Bolten, the incoming deputy chief of staff for policy, spoke with John Podesta, Clinton's final chief of staff and the director of the outgoing transition. Bolten recounted a conversation with John Podesta during a transition meeting where aides from both staffs gathered. As the policy person among the Bush group in the meeting, he was concerned with what actions President Clinton might take at the end of the administration. Bolten recounted that he said to Podesta:

> You know, we would really like that you not move forward on this agreement pending the arrival of the new president. And Podesta said, "Yeah, no" . . . That was my lesson in one president at a time. And Podesta was right. The incoming team has no right to make any request of the outgoing president to not do what the president has full power to do while the president has full power, until noon on January 20.[34]

However, nothing prevents the outgoing team from initiating such consultations, which is what the Bush team sought to do in 2008.

---

33. Stephen Hadley, message to Martha Joynt Kumar, November 13, 2021.

34. Joshua Bolten, interview with Martha Joynt Kumar, "National Security Transition: Session 4," LBJ Library and Museum, September 23, 2016, https://whitehousetransition project.org/experts-news/events/national-security-transition/.

PRACTICES SUCCESSFULLY EXERCISED BY
RECENT ADMINISTRATIONS

Outgoing Transition Officials:

1. *President guides the transition out of office.* It is important for the success of a transition for presidents to state their support for a smooth transition. Presidents can use the May deadline requirement for creating the two transitions councils to telegraph to officials their obligation to effectively prepare. The more deeply involved the presidents are, the more seriously officials will undertake the transition mission.

2. *Laws and precedents guide a successful transition.* Transition laws have developed in response to the situations presidents experienced and the resources they found they needed. So too have precedents from earlier years.

3. *Provide memoranda and documents on policies and actions.* The 2008 NSC memoranda served the purpose of preparing incoming staff on the course of particular policies during an administration as well as the actions officials took. For the outgoing team, the memoranda serve as legacy documents. Internal strategy documents can be important as well, but they might not have the same comprehensive historical summary as a well-crafted Transition Memorandum that explains why the strategy took the form it did. Attached documents of presidential and foreign leader statements, presidential conversations with foreign leaders, and other key background material provide critical context for understanding the policies.

4. *Make organizational preparations: Budgets, charts and staff lists.* Practical information is important as incoming presidents and their team decide how to structure the NSC. In making organizational decisions, charts reflecting the structure of the office over several presidencies is instructive. Charts that identify staff members are very helpful when an incoming staff member wants to talk to a previous holder of the office.

5. *Present contingency plans for possible situations and crises.* Contingency plans have both direct and indirect benefits. First, they provide thinking on what issues could become crises and identify the alternative ways of handling the situations. Second, crisis planning provides a new team of a way to segue from campaigning to governing.

6. *Track candidate issue statements and positions.* By keeping track of the positions candidates have taken, the outgoing staff will be better prepared to highlight what the incoming team will want to know and prepare for his or her priorities once elected.

Candidate National Security Teams:
7. *Virtual transition.* Notwithstanding the obvious risks of collection by outside intelligence services, a virtual transition can bring people together in a cost-effective way and allows a team to bring in people who would ordinarily not be able to participate because of travel restrictions or other demands from pre-administration work commitments.
8. *Unconventional challenges.* It is useful to have a team during the campaign that is not connected to day-to-day operations give thought during the campaign to identify unanticipated events and develop possible responses. This is a useful exercise as it involves identifying a broad range of problems and identifying specialists who could be called on.

Incoming Transition Team:
9. *Decisionmaking process comes first.* It is important to work out with presidents what role they want the NSC staff to play and what the kinds of coordination the staff should arrange with counterparts at State, Defense, and the intelligence community.
10. *Tabletop exercises.* In addition to the one the outgoing administration hosts, a tabletop exercise is helpful to the new team in working through the decisionmaking process with the incoming president. In 2008, President-elect Obama hosted one with his team.
11. *Homeland Security and Directorate decisions.* Should the NSC include a homeland security component or should it be a separate office with its own reporting stream? Do new world dynamics call for additional directorates?
12. *Hold over one or more key officials.* It is helpful to keep some key officials who work on issues that remain salient over several administrations, especially ones involving ongoing military operations. This was done with Doug Lute, who served from Bush to Obama and, more recently, with Brett McGurk, who served in positions in the Obama, Trump, and now Biden NSC staff.

13. *Internal White House coordination with NSC.* In recent years, there has been an official who serves in the White House Counsel's office as well as the NSC. There have been similar dual-hatted arrangements in the economic and intelligence directorates. Additional policy experts from the National Economic Council and the Domestic Policy Council staffs can be brought in from time to time as well.

14. *Create an NSC advisers sounding board.* It is important to have a group of former national security advisers who can talk freely to the new adviser, either individually or in groups.

APPENDIX A

Complete List of Bush Administration National Security Council Transition Memoranda

- Afghanistan
- Africa Conflict Resolution Policy
- China Policy
- Colombia
- Combating Terrorist Financing and Using Financial Tools to Isolate Rogue Actors
- Confronting Authoritarian Populism
- Counterproliferation Policy
- Darfur*
- Defense Transformation and Global Defense Posture Realignment*
- Detaining and Prosecuting Combatants in the War on Terror*
- Dismantling al-Qaida
- East Asian Alliances and Architecture
- Eurasia Energy*
- Europe Whole, Free, and at Peace
- Freedom Agenda
- India
- Institutionalizing the War on Terror
- The Horn of Africa*
- Intelligence Reform and New Ways to Do Intelligence*
- Iraq

- Lebanon
- Managing Cooperation/Differences with Russia
- Middle East Peace Process
- Missile Defense
- National Space Policy*
- NATO Transformation*
- Neglected Tropical Diseases
- North Korea and Six-Party Talks
- Nuclear Posture Review*
- Our Approach to Iran
- Pakistan
- President's Emergency Plan for AIDS Relief
- Reconstruction and Stabilization Operations
- Smart Development
- The President's Malaria Initiative
- Turkey/PKK*
- U.S. Efforts to Turn Libya and Dismantle the A.Q. Khan Nuclear Proliferation Network
- War of Ideas
- Weapons of Mass Destruction (WMD) Terrorism
- Western Balkans

---

* Not included in this book but planned to be available in the SMU digital archive.

APPENDIX B

Description of Digital Archive
To Be Maintained at SMU

The Center for Presidential History at SMU, directed by Dr. Jeffrey Engel, intends to establish within its Collective Memory Project an online archive that will be an invaluable companion to this volume. The plan is for this archive to host digital copies of the thirty declassified Transition Memoranda contained in this book, plus up to ten others that have been or may be declassified but do not appear in this volume. In addition, each Transition Memorandum had attached to it the presidential speeches, records of presidential meetings and phone calls, notes of NSC and Principal and Deputies Committee meetings, relevant policy documents, and other materials that document the policy described in the Transition Memorandum. Digital copies of this voluminous and rich set of documents, containing both unclassified and declassified materials, will also appear in the SMU online archive.

The SMU digital archive can be accessed as follows:

https://www.smu.edu/Dedman/Research/Institutes-and-Centers/Center-for -Presidential-History/CMP

A shorter version is www.smu.edu/cph

The Center for Presidential History at SMU has played a similar role in a number of other such projects including, most recently, online electronic hosting of the transcripts and video of the twenty-eight interviews that were the foundation for the book *The Last Card: Inside George W. Bush's Decision to Surge in Iraq* (Cornell University Press 2019). It served the same function for a bipartisan, indeed non-partisan, oral history of the 2004 presidential election as recalled by participants and commentators alike.

CONTRIBUTING AUTHORS

George W. Bush served as the forty-third President of the United States from 2001 to 2009. He had previously served as Governor of Texas. He and his wife, Laura, live in Dallas, where they founded the George W. Bush Presidential Center at SMU. He is the author of four #1 bestsellers.

Condoleezza Rice served as the sixty-sixth U.S. Secretary of State and as National Security Advisor to President George W. Bush. She is currently the Director of the Hoover Institution at Stanford University and is a founding principal of Rice, Hadley, Gates & Manuel, LLC, an international strategic consulting firm.

Stephen J. Hadley served for four years as the Assistant to the President for National Security Affairs from 2005 to 2009. From 2001 to 2005, Mr. Hadley was the Assistant to the President and Deputy National Security Advisor, serving under then National Security Advisor Condoleezza Rice.

Peter D. Feaver served as Special Advisor for Strategic Planning and Institutional Reform on the National Security Council Staff at the White House from 2005 to 2007. He is currently a Professor of Political Science and Public Policy at Duke University.

William C. Inboden served as Senior Director for Strategic Planning on the National Security Council and also on the State Department's Policy Planning Staff. He is currently the Executive Director of the Clements Center for National Security and associate professor at the LBJ Policy School, both at the University of Texas Austin.

Meghan L. O'Sullivan was Special Assistant to President George W. Bush and Deputy National Security Advisor for Iraq and Afghanistan from 2004 to 2007. She is currently the Jeane Kirkpatrick Professor of the Practice of International Affairs and the Director of the Geopolitics of Energy Project at Harvard University's Kennedy School.

Hal Brands is the Henry Kissinger Distinguished Professor of Global Affairs at Johns Hopkins University, a senior fellow at the American Enterprise Institute, and a Bloomberg Opinion columnist.

Martha Joynt Kumar is an emeritus professor of political science at Towson University. Her book, *Before the Oath: How George W. Bush and Barack Obama Managed a Transfer of Power*, details that transition. Kumar is the director of the White House Transition Project, a nonpartisan, nonprofit group of presidency scholars who prepare information on White House offices, operations, and transitions.

Melvyn P. Leffler is Professor Emeritus of American History at The University of Virginia. He is the author of prize-winning books on the Cold War. His new book, *Confronting Saddam Hussein: George W. Bush and the Invasion of Iraq*, will be published by Oxford University Press in March 2023.

POSTSCRIPT AUTHORS
Titles Held during the Bush 43 Administration

Michael Allen   NSC Special Assistant to the President and Senior Director for Counterproliferation Strategies

Judy Ansley   NSC Assistant to the President and Deputy National Security Adviser

Keith Ausbrook   HSC Special Assistant to the President for Homeland Security and Counterterrorism and Executive Secretary, Homeland Security Council

Victor Cha   NSC Director for Japan, Korea, Australia and Oceanic Affairs; U.S. Deputy Delegation Head for the Six-Party Talks

James L. Connaughton   Chairman, White House Council on Environmental Quality

J.D. Crouch   NSC Assistant to the President and Deputy National Security Adviser

Dana DeRuiter   NSC Director for Global Health, International Economic Affairs

Mark Dybul   US Global AIDS Coordinator

Daniel W. Fisk   NSC Special Assistant to the President and Senior Director for Western Hemisphere Affairs

Jendayi Frazer   NSC Special Assistant to the President and Senior Director for African Affairs; U.S. Ambassador to South Africa; Assistant Secretary of State for African Affairs

Daniel Fried   NSC Senior Director for European and Eurasian Affairs; Assistant Secretary of State for Europe and Eurasia

Michael Gerson	Assistant to the President for Policy and Strategic Planning
Thomas Graham	NSC Special Assistant to the President and Senior Director for Russia
Michael Green	NSC Special Assistant to the President for National Security Affairs and Senior Director for Asian Affairs
Paul Haenle	NSC Director for China, Taiwan and Mongolian Affairs
Richard Hooker	NSC Director for Iraq
Douglas Lute	NSC Assistant to the President and Deputy National Security Adviser for Iraq and Afghanistan
Michele L. Malvesti	NSC Senior Director for Combating Terrorism Strategy
Michael Miller	NSC Director for Africa; Deputy Assistant Administrator for Global Health, USAID
Paul D. Miller	NSC Director for Afghanistan
Meghan L. O'Sullivan	NSC Special Assistant to the President and Deputy National Security Adviser for Iraq and Afghanistan
Farah Pandith	NSC Director for Middle East Regional Initiatives
Bobby Pittman	NSC Special Assistant to the President and Senior Director for African Affairs
Nicholas Rasmussen	NSC Senior Director for Combating Terrorism
Neill Sciarrone	HSC Special Assistant to the President and Senior Director, Cybersecurity and Information Sharing Policy
Thomas Shannon	NSC Senior Director for Western Hemisphere Affairs; Assistant Secretary of State for Western Hemisphere Affairs
Faryar Shirzad	NSC Deputy Assistant to the President and Deputy National Security Adviser for International Economic Affairs
John Simon	NSC Special Assistant to the President and Senior Director for Relief, Stabilization, and Development
Michael Singh	NSC Senior Director for Near Eastern and North African Affairs
William Tobey	NSC Director of Counterproliferation; Deputy Administrator for Defense Nuclear Nonproliferation, National Nuclear Security Administration
Rajeev Venkayya	HSC Special Assistant to the President and Senior Director for Biodefense
Kenneth L. Wainstein	Assistant to the President for Homeland Security and Counterterrorism ("Homeland Security Adviser")
Mark Webber	NSC Special Assistant to the President and Senior Director for South and Central Asian Affairs

Peter Wehner	Deputy Assistant to the President and Director of the Office of Strategic Initiatives
Damon Wilson	NSC Special Assistant to the President and Senior Director for European Affairs
Tim Ziemer	Coordinator, President's Malaria Initiative

INDEX

Abbas, Mahmoud, 561, 564, 565–66, 573, 575–77, 645
Abdallah II, King of Jordan, 564
Abkhazia and South Ossetia, 358, 366, 383, 403
ABM. *See* Anti-Ballistic Missile Treaty
Abraham Accords, 111, 579–80
Abyei Protocol (Sudan), 545
Accelerating Success Initiative (2003), 221
Accra Agenda for Action, 485
ACI. *See* Andean Counter-Drug Initiative
ACOTA. *See* Africa Contingency Operations Training Assistance
ACP. *See* American Charities for Palestine
Active Response Corps, 222
Adriatic Charter/Adriatic Three, 361
Aegis Ballistic Missile Defense, 333, 334
Afghanistan, 115; Afghanistan National Development Strategy, 117; al-Qaida operations in, 37–38, 127–28; Bush administration accomplishments, 117–21, 660–62, 664–65; Bush administration approach, 124–26; Bush administration assessment, 129–32; Bush administration policy, 22, 116–17, 129–32; democratic elections in, 10; development assistance as vital tool, 475; future challenges, 44,

121–23; human development in, 125–26; impact of Bonn Agreement on, 116; Independent Directorate for Local Governance, 118–19; Lessons Learned, 132–34; Obama and Trump administration approaches, 126–28, 130, 134, 226, 227, 653–54; Operation Enduring Freedom, 41; Postscript, 124–34; Provincial Reconstruction Teams in, 125, 221, 226, 228–29; Reconstruction Opportunity Zones, 121, 145; support from East Asian allies, 429, 430; Transition Memorandum text, 116–23; trends since end of Bush administration, 126–29; U.S. displaced AQ safe haven from, 59; U.S. goals exceeded means, 656–57; U.S.-led coalition objectives, 13, 16, 38–39, 111; U.S. reconstruction and stabilization operations in, 219, 221; U.S. withdrawal of troops from, 61, 112, 127–28, 129, 134, 152, 176. *See also* Taliban
Afghanistan National Army (ANA), 119–20
Afghan National Security Forces (ANSF), 119–20, 125
Afghan Uniformed Police (AUP), 120

Africa: Bush administration policy, 474–75; China's telecommunications dominance in, 554; diplomacy, 549, 554; East Africa Counter Terrorism Initiative, 75, 81; Ebola outbreak, 532; lack of ART, 489; long-standing conflicts when Bush took office, 537; new state actors involved in conflicts, 554; NTD control project began in, 518–19; OFAC sanctions on AQ in East, 51. *See also* President's Emergency Plan for AIDS Relief; President's Malaria Initiative; *specific countries*

Africa Conflict Resolution Policy: accomplishments, 539–43, 669; administration approach, 549–56; administration assessment, 554–56; administration policy, 539; future challenges, 544–48; Lessons Learned, 556–60; Postscript, 549–60; Transition Memorandum text, 538–48; trends since end of Bush administration, 550–54

Africa Contingency Operations Training Assistance (ACOTA), 543, 550

Africa Growth and Opportunity Act (AGOA) (2000), 473, 482, 640

African Union (AU): peacekeeping missions, 557; power-sharing agreement in Kenya, 552; U.S. support for, 549

African Union Mission (AMIS)/AU-UN mission (UNAMID): to Burundi, 543; to Sudan, 544, 551–52

AFRICOM. *See* U.S. Africa Command

AGOA. *See* Africa Growth and Opportunity Act

Agreed Framework (U.S.-North Korea) (1994), 304–05, 306–07

Agricultural cooperation, India-U.S., 452, 453

Ahmadinejad, Mahmoud, 287, 296

Ahtisaari, Martti/Ahtisaari Plan, 174–75, 377, 379

Airborne Laser and Kinetic Energy Interceptors, 334

Al-Abadi, Haider, 175

Al-Assad, Bashar, 203, 210, 213, 214, 259

Al-Baghdadi, Abu Bakr, 61

Albania: Adriatic Charter/Adriatic Three, 361

Al-Bashir, Omar, 111, 423, 540, 544

Alexander, Douglas, 519

Algeria: overthrow of Bouteflika, 111; U.S. maintained political focus on AQ-affiliated groups in, 40

Al-Haramain, 51–52

Al-Kadhimi, Mustafa, 176

Allen, John, 232

Alliance for Progress, 11

Alliance for Prosperity, 627–28

Al-Maliki, Nouri, 160, 161, 162, 163, 173–75, 177, 653

Al-Qaida in Iraq (AQI): emergence of, 171; reduced capabilities of, 61, 163, 167, 173, 174; and sectarian violence, 159; Sons of Iraq against, 161, 168, 172, 173, 174, 175; U.S. counterterrorism initiatives, 41, 44

Al-Qaida/Qaeda (AQ), 420; adaptation since Bush administration, 62; in Afghanistan, 661, 664–65; in Africa, 553; decline in support for among Muslims, 93, 100; elimination of safe havens in Pakistan, 648; Iran policy, 290; WMD capabilities of, 247–48, 274–75, 655–56. *See also* Dismantling al-Qaida; Taliban; Terrorism; War of Ideas

Al-Rimi, Qasim, 61

Al-Sadr, Muqtada, 163, 172

Al-Shabaab, 553

Al-Wuyashi, Nasir, 61

Al-Zarqawi, Abu Musab, 59, 171, 174

Al-Zawahiri, Ayman, 37, 40, 43, 274–75, 290

"America First," 102, 260, 382, 556

America.gov, 92

American Charities for Palestine (ACP), 92–93

American Energy Act (2020), 611

Americas. *See* Central America; Latin America; Western Hemisphere

Americas Competitiveness Forum, 619

AmSouth, 52

ANA. *See* Afghanistan National Army

Andean Counter-Drug Initiative (ACI), 187

Andean Trade Preference Act (ATPA), 188

Andean Trade Preference and Drug Eradication Act (2002), 188

Angola: new threats emerged, 549; resolving long-standing conflicts, 537, 538, 542, 549–50, 551

Annan, Kofi, 202, 491
Annapolis Conference (2007), 561, 566, 570
ANSF. *See* Afghan National Security Forces
Anthrax letter attacks, 31
Anti-Ballistic Missile Treaty (ABM) (1972), 234, 237, 239, 329, 330, 331, 333, 340, 394–95, 398, 408, 668
Anti-money laundering policies, U.S., 49–50, 52, 59
Antiviral therapy (ART), 489, 494
APEC. *See* Asia-Pacific Economic Cooperation
Approval ratings, of presidents, 659–60, 673–74
AQI. *See* Al-Qaida in Iraq
A. Q. Khan. *See* Khan, Abdul Qadeer; U.S. Efforts to Turn Libya and Dismantle the A.Q. Khan Nuclear Proliferation Network
Arab Bank, New York, 52
Arab leaders: focus on Iran and Iraq, 575; relations with Israel, 564, 567, 576, 579–80
Arab League: Doha Agreement (2008), 202, 212, 215; Neighbor Process with Iraq, 161; reaffirmed Saudi Middle East peace proposal, 570
Arab Spring (2011): anticipated by Bush, 28; in Libya, 277–78; Obama's minimal involvement in conflict, 25, 175; source of radicalism, 665; uprisings of, 110
Arafat, Yasir, 564, 565, 573, 577, 645
Armenia, 383. *See also* Nagorno-Karabakh (Azerbaijan and Armenia)
Armitage, Richard, 203, 330
Aronson, Bernard, 194
ART. *See* Antiviral therapy
ASEAN. *See* Association of Southeast Asian Nations
Asian financial crisis (1997–98), 428
Asia-Pacific alliances, 670, 674
Asia-Pacific Democracy Partnership, 15, 22, 433
Asia-Pacific Economic Cooperation (APEC), 425, 432–33, 440; launched Asia-Pacific Democracy Partnership (2007), 15, 22; multilateral efforts to combat terror, 76, 81

Asia-Pacific Partnership on Clean Development and Climate, 433, 441, 606
Association of Southeast Asian Nations (ASEAN), 432–35, 440
ATPA. *See* Andean Trade Preference Act
AUC. *See* United Self-Defense Forces of Colombia
AUP. *See* Afghan Uniformed Police
Australia: agricultural trade friction with U.S., 428; Defense Trade Treaty and Free Trade Agreement, 431–32; as member of Asia-Pacific Democracy Partnership, 15; as member of "Quad," 354; missile defense cooperation with U.S., 336
Authoritarian governments: China as attractive model, 426, 443–44; compromises and accommodations with, 649–50; development theory approach, 11; global trends toward, 481; instability of, 8; populism as symptom, not cure, 630; reduced cooperation in War on Terror and Middle East Peace Process as threats, 16; U.S. supported reforms on, 12; and WMD proliferation, 264, 266
Authoritarian populism. *See* Confronting Authoritarian Populism
Aviation and Transportation Security Act (2001), 71, 80
Axis of Evil, 210, 286, 295–96, 322
Azerbaijan. *See* Nagorno-Karabakh (Azerbaijan and Armenia)
Aznar, Jose Maria, 564

Bagger, Rich, 685
Bahrain: Abraham Accords, 111
Bali Roadmap and Bali Plan of Action (2007), 607–08
Ballistic Missile Defense Agreement (2007), 335
Ballistic missiles: in counterproliferation policy, 239; in Libya, 269–70, 272, 276; in nuclear states, 234. *See also* Missile Defense
Banco Delta Asia, 306, 308
Banking systems, and isolated rogue entities, 60
Bank Saderat, 289
Bank Sepah, 288

China (cont.)
Africa, 554; threats to international order, 436–38, 485–86, 553–54, 556–57, 559–60; undermining of good governance and transparency, 482; U.S. concerned about threats to international order, 349–54, 429; and World Trade Organization, 441. *See also* Belt and Road Initiative (China)

China Policy: accomplishments, 421–24, 430–33; administration approach, 436–37; administration assessment, 439–41; administration policy, 262, 418–20, 429–30; future challenges, 424–27, 433–35; Lessons Learned, 441–44; Postscript, 436–44; Transition Memorandum text, 418–27; trends since end of Bush administration, 437–39

Chirac, Jacques: broke with U.S. over Iraq (2003), 170; co-authored UNSC Resolution 1559, 201; vision of Europe as counterweight to U.S. influence, 365

Christianity, and extremist ideologies, 103

Christie, Chris, 685

CIA. *See* Central Intelligence Agency

Cicerone, Ralph, 601

Cities Readiness Initiative (2004) (CDC), 527

Civilian Reserve Corps, 223–24, 226, 230

Civil space cooperation, India-U.S., 450–51

Clarke, Richard "Dick," 585, 597

Clean Development, 604. *See also* Climate Change and Clean Development

Clean Energy Standard, 612

Clean Network Program, 595

Climate change: Asia-Pacific Partnership on Clean Development and Climate, 433, 441; China's energy future, 424, 438; Connaughton analysis, 652–53

Climate Change and Clean Development, 599–600, 613; administration approach, 600–08; administration assessment, 612; economic impact of agreements, 602–04; international engagement/partnerships, 605–08; Lessons Learned, 613; trends since end of Bush administration, 609–12

Climate Change Science: An Analysis of Some Key Questions (NRC Report), 600–01

Climate Leaders and Climate VISION programs, 605

Clinton, Hillary, 23, 278, 682

Clinton, William J. "Bill": administration focus on cybersecurity, 583–84; approach to Israeli-Palestinian peace, 572; building on foreign policy efforts of, 669–71; Clinton-Bush transition, 689, 690; democracy promotion in National Security Strategy, 11; end of grand strategy that animated three administrations, 411; Iran policy, 285; Libya policy, 265; major intelligence reforms after presidency, 681–82; negotiated 1993 North Korean missile crisis, 672; nuclear planning, 327n4; Plan Colombia, 22, 184, 186

Clinton-Bush transition, 689, 690

CNCI. *See* U.S.-India Civil Nuclear Cooperation Initiative

CNCI Policy Directive. *See* Comprehensive National Cybersecurity Initiative

Coalitions: of health-related implementers and advocates, 502–03; for peacemaking, 549

Coalition Support Funds (CSF), 142

Coats, Dan, 686

Cocaine. *See* Colombia

Cold War: democracy promotion during, 10–11; framing Bush presidency against longer history of, 673–75; ideological battle against communism, 88, 96; national security responding to post-Cold War world, 693

Colombia, 183–84; Bush administration accomplishments, 188–89, 195; Bush administration approach, 192–93; Bush administration assessment, 195; Bush administration policy, 186–88; future challenges, 189–90; Lessons Learned, 196–97; Postscript, 192–97; refugees from Venezuela, 197; Transition Memorandum text, 185–91; trends since end of Bush administration, 193–95; youth antiterrorism networks against FARC, 93. *See also* Plan Colombia

Colombian National Police, 185

Combating Terrorist Financing and Using Financial Tools to Isolate Rogue Actors:

accomplishments, 50–55; administration approach, 58–61; administration policy, 49–50, 63–65; future challenges, 55; Lessons Learned, 65–66; Postscript, 58–66; Transition Memorandum text, 48–57; trends since end of Bush administration, 61–63

Comey, James, 686

Commander's Emergency Response Program (CERP), 161

Community of Democracies, 15, 21

Community Strategy for Pandemic Influenza Mitigation (2007), 531

Composite Dialogue with India (2004), 144, 146

Comprehensive National Cybersecurity Initiative (CNCI), 588–92

Comprehensive Peace Agreement (CPA). *See* Sudan Comprehensive Peace Agreement

Conference of the Parties (COP), 606–07, 613. *See also* U.N. Framework Convention on Climate Change

Conflicts: continuity in U.S. approach to Africa, 554–55; frozen, 366; prioritizing those with greatest casualties, 549–50; resolving long-standing, 464, 535. *See also* Africa; *specific countries*

Confronting Authoritarian Populism: accomplishments, 620–22; administration approach, 614–16; administration assessment, 628–30; administration policy, 617–20; future challenges, 622–23; Lessons Learned, 630–31; Postscript, 624–31; supporting democracy in the Americas, 614–15, 668; Transition Memorandum text, 616–23; trends since end of Bush administration, 626–28. *See also* Latin America

Congo, Democratic Party of (DRC): civil and regional wars ended, 537; conflicts in neighboring states, 545–46; efforts to end civil war, 542, 549; elections, 10, 552; resolving long-standing conflicts, 537, 538, 542, 545–46, 549, 552, 558

Connaughton, James L., 581, 652–53

Conspiracy theories as domestic threat, in U.S., 103

Consultative Group for Strategic Security, 396

Container Security Initiative (DHS), 71, 244, 251, 258–59

Continuity, organizational: budgets, charts and staff lists, 695; leaving functional and informed staff in place, 682–83, 696; preparation of materials for new administration, 691–92

Continuity of policy, between administrations, 572–76, 679; climate change and clean development, 613; Europe, 382; foreign policy, 390, 438; health initiatives, 511, 513, 530, 532, 581

Cooperation, shared interests as basis for, 415

Copenhagen Accord (2009), 608

Correa, Rafael, 622–23, 629

Correlation of forces, 437, 442

Corruption: makes populism possible, 622–23, 624; problem in Balkans, 380

Council for Environmental Quality (CEQ), 581

Countering Iranian Influence strategy, 292

Countering Violent Islamic Extremism (CVIE). *See* National Implementation Plan (NIP) (2008)

Counternarcotics Strategy (2007): in Afghanistan, 120

Counterproliferation Policy, 235–36; accomplishments, 240–44, 261–62; administration approach, 255–58; administration policy, 239; future challenges, 244–45; Lessons Learned, 263–64; Postscript, 255–64; Transition Memorandum text, 237–46; trends since end of Bush administration, 258–61

Counterradicalization efforts, 42

Counterterrorism (CT), U.S.: bilateral cooperation with India, 460; legal framework, 674; organizations, 400, 550, 555–56. *See also* Combating Terrorist Financing and Using Financial Tools to Isolate Rogue Actors; Dismantling al-Qaida; Institutionalizing the War on Terror; Terrorism; War on Terror

Counterterrorism Campaign Plan, 146

Counterterrorism Working Group (CTWG) (G-8), 400

East Asian Alliances (cont.)
administration assessment, 439–41; administration policy, 429–30; Bush administration accomplishments, 430–33; future challenges, 433–35; Lessons Learned, 441–44; Postscript, 436–44; security threat deterrence, 430, 432, 433–34, 437, 439–40, 443; struggle for primacy, 425; Transition Memorandum text, 428–35; trends since end of Bush administration, 437–39; U.S. multilateral participation, 432–33

Ebola, 532

Economic Community of West African States (ECOWAS), 541, 549, 668

Economic relations: China, 423; East Asia, 434; India's economic reforms, 447, 448, 450. *See also* Trade and investment

ECOWAS. *See* Economic Community of West African States

Ecuador, 622–23, 629

Edson, Gary, 491

Education cooperation, 451, 475

Edward "Ted" Kaufman and Michael Leavitt Presidential Transition Improvement Act (2015), 677, 679, 691

Egmont Group of Financial Intelligence Units (Egmont Group), 53

E-gov office, 592

Egypt: held first contested presidential election, 10, 16; imprisoned opposition presidential candidate, 10; maintained political focus on AQ-affiliated groups in, 40; U.S. supported approved NGOs, 12; U.S. supported disabled vote in fraudulent elections, 12; U.S. supported Mubarak, 14, 16

Einstein 2 and Einstein 3 technology, 590

Eisenhower, Dwight D., 96, 198, 660

Elections: Afghanistan, 10; Africa, 10, 540–43, 545, 550–53, 559; Asia, 421, 434, 450; cyber interference, 592–93, 594, 595; Europe, 55, 364, 371, 373, 384, 389; Kenya, 486, 537, 550, 552–53; Latin America, 618, 623, 631; Middle East, 10, 13, 16, 28, 112, 171, 173, 565–66, 569, 573, 578; Russia, 403, 410; Russian interference, 344, 363, 410, 685–86

Electric power outage, in U.S. (2003), 584

Electronic Government Act (2002), 592

ELN. *See* National Liberation Army

El Salvador, 11, 483, 623

Emergency Use Authorization (EUA), 527

Endemic diseases, 464; accountability in combating, 487–88, 491–92, 512. *See also* Neglected Tropical Diseases; Pandemic preparedness; President's Emergency Plan for AIDS Relief; President's Malaria Initiative

Endless wars, use of term, 181

Energy: China's energy future, 424, 438; development in Latin America and Caribbean, 619; Russian government's centralized control, 402, 404–05. *See also* Climate change

Energy, U.S. Department of (DOE): Megaports Initiative, 244, 251, 258, 263

Energy Independence and Security Act (2007), 604–05, 608, 609

Energy Policy Act (1992), 605

Energy Policy Act (2005), 604

EP-3 crisis, 418, 419, 667

Erdogan, Recept Tayyip: Bush meeting with, 362; initial support for EU accession, 356, 384–85; Trump's relationship with, 26

Esper, Mark, 687

Europe, 355–56; EU-3 agreement with Iran, 260, 287, 295; maintaining unity with U.S. vs. Russia, 404; missile defense systems, 335, 337–38. *See also* Western Balkans; *specific countries*

Europe, Whole Free and at Peace, 355–56; accomplishments, 361–65, 375–77; administration approach, 381–85; administration policy, 358–61; Bush administration assessment, 386–88; future challenges, 365–68; Lessons Learned, 389–90; Postscript, 381–90; Transition Memorandum text, 357–68; trends since end of Bush administration, 381–85

European Neighborhood Policy, 359

European Security and Defense Policy (ESDP), 366

European Union (EU): accelerating EU integration in Balkans, 377; approach to democracy promotion with repressive regimes, 18; enlargement into Central and Eastern Europe, 361–62, 365–67, 386; EU Rule of Law Mission, 377; negotiations with Central and East European countries, 357–58; Operation Concordia, 372; and Russian exploitation of divisions within NATO, 386–87, 404; U.S. support for expansion, 356, 357, 359, 360, 370, 375–76, 641; WMD discussions with Iran, 288

Export control system, 243, 255, 263, 269

Export-Import Bank Act (1945), 272n1

Failed states, 218–20, 469, 475, 558, 639–40

FARC. *See* Rebel Armed Forces of Colombia

Far-right conspiracy theories, in U.S., 103

Fatah al-Islam, 205, 211

Fatah party, 565–66, 569–70, 646

FATF. *See* Financial Action Task Force

Fayyad, Salam, 22, 566–67, 573, 575

Federal Bureau of Investigation (FBI): Domestic Violent Extremists (DVEs) threat, 84–85; Guidelines for Domestic FBI Operations, 73; Joint Terrorism Task Forces, 73, 81; Render Safe mission, 252; WMD Directorate, 250, 255

Feed the Future initiative, 480

Feltman, Jeff, 211

Financial Action Task Force (FATF), 48, 53, 243

Financial sanctions. *See* Combating Terrorist Financing and Using Financial Tools to Isolate Rogue Actors

FISA Amendments Act (2008), 70, 76

Flynn, Michael, 685

FMF. *See* Foreign Military Financing

FMS. *See* Foreign Military Sales

Food security cooperation, 145, 475

Foreign affairs bureaucracy, and democracy promotion, 18

Foreign assistance: reform, 476. *See also* Development assistance

Foreign Military Financing (FMF), 142, 211

Foreign Military Sales (FMS), 160

Foreign Narcotics Kingpin Designation Act (1999), 187

Foreign policy: impact of transitions on, 658–59; need for congressional support, 459

Foreign Terrorist Asset Tracking Center, 52

"Forever wars" rhetoric, 133

Forum for China-Africa Cooperation (FOCAC), 556

France: Arab Spring interventions, 277–78; broke with U.S. over Iraq (2003), 170; co-authored UNSC Resolution 1559, 201; co-authored UNSC Resolution 1701, 202; EU-3 agreement with Iran, 260, 287, 295; Lebanon policy, 211; missile defense cooperation, 336, 338; opposed Iraq War, 396, 409, 412–13

Frazer, Jendayi, 546

Freedom, global decline since 2006, 23, 651

Freedom Agenda: abandoned by Obama, 409–10; accomplishments, 16–17, 112; administration approach, 20–23; administration assessment, 26–29, 411–12; administration policy, 13–15, 26–29, 110, 210, 234; compromised by association with Iraq War, 355–56, 650–52; democracy promotion, 10–30; development theory approach, 11–12; future challenges, 17–18; Lessons Learned, 29–30; National Security Presidential Directive/NSPD-58 (2008), 473; policy shaped by 9/11 attacks, 13–15, 31–34, 38–41, 170, 638–40; Postscript, 20–29; premise of, 7–8; Putin's actions against, 386–88; support for foreign democratic dissidents and activists, 11–13, 14, 15, 18; Transition Memorandum text, 9–19; trends since end of Bush administration, 23–26, 212. *See also* "Illuminating Hand-Off, An" (Leffler)

Freedom House: on long democratic recession, 23; on Obama's approach to democracy promotion, 23–24; percentage of "not free" countries (2005), 10; on ratings for Middle East (2006), 27–28; setback for global freedom (2007), 651

Freedom Support Act (FSA), 359

Freezing of assets. *See* Combating Terrorist Financing and Using Financial Tools to Isolate Rogue Actors

G-5 Sahel Joint Force, 555
G-8. *See* Group of 8
Gaddafi, Muammar. *See* Qaddafi, Muammar
Gang issues, in Central America, 483
Garang, John, 540
Garang, Rebecca, 540
Gates, Robert M., 162, 223, 253, 278–79, 336–37, 342, 343
Gaza: Hamas in, 566, 569, 570, 575, 645; Israeli disengagement, 564, 565, 569, 573; Palestinian obligation to stop terror, 568
GBI. *See* Ground-Based Interceptors
GCC+3, 161, 166
Geiges, Daniel, 271
Genocide: Burundi and Darfur, 549–50; preventing in Burundi, 542–43
Georgia, Republic of: color revolution (Rose), 17–18, 22, 356, 363–64, 401; democratic elections in, 10; NATO membership question, 351–52, 366, 382–85, 413; recovery from Russian invasion, 483; Russian invasion (2008), 363, 395–96, 398, 403–04; Russian ministry contact with separatist regimes, 402
Germany: commitment to dismantling Khan network, 271; EU-3 agreement with Iran, 260, 287, 295; missile defense cooperation, 336, 338; opposed Iraq War, 396, 409, 412–13; and U.S.-led coalition in Afghanistan, 125
Gerson, Michael, 651–52
Ghana, 483
Gibert, Mary, 685
Gillani, Yousaf Raza, 140, 143
Glenn Amendment, sanctions after India's 1998 nuclear tests, 446, 447, 456
Global Coalition to Defeat ISIS, 175
Global Community Engagement and Resilience Fund, 102
Global Counterterrorism Forum, 102
Global Fragility Act (2020), 227–28
Global Fund to Fight HIV/AIDS, Tuberculosis and Malaria, 474, 491–97, 498–500, 501, 507, 512
Global Health Security Agenda (GHSA), 532
Global Initiative to Combat Nuclear Terrorism, 144, 244, 245, 250, 256, 262, 281

Global Nuclear Energy Partnership (GNEP), 243, 399–400
Global Partnership Against the Spread of Weapons and Materials of Mass Destruction (G-8), 242, 258
Global Peace Operations Initiative (GPOI), 433, 550
Global Strategic Engagement Center (GSEC), 92, 100, 102
Global Supply Chain Risk Management, 591
Global Threat Reduction Initiative (GTRI), 242, 250, 257, 258, 262–63
GNEP. *See* Global Nuclear Energy Partnership
Godane, Ahmed Abdi, 61
GOP. *See* Pakistan, Government of
Gourdault-Montagne, Maurice, 201
Gradualism, drawbacks of, 17
Graham, Thomas, 642–43
Great Influenza, The (Barry), 529, 652
Great power competition, 135; and Biden administration policy, 228; and Bush administration policy, 349–54; and Middle East region, 179; and WMD proliferation, 264. *See also* China; Europe, Whole Free and at Peace; India; Russian Federation; Western Balkans
Green, Mark, 481, 483–84
Green Revolution, in Iran (2009), 24
Ground-Based Interceptors (GBIs), 334, 342, 343, 345
Ground-Based Midcourse Defense, 333, 334
Group of 8 (G-8): Counterterrorism Action Group, 53; Gleneagles Summit (2005), 473, 505–06; Global Partnership Against the Spread of Weapons and Materials of Mass Destruction, 242, 258, 262–63; Heiligendamm (2007), 606; multilateral efforts to combat terror, 76, 81; Neighbor Process with Iraq, 161; and Nuclear Suppliers Group, 242; Partnership for Progress and a Common Future and Broader Middle East and North Africa, 15; pledge for bed nets, 507; reconstruction and stabilization operations, 224; summits on development policy and priorities, 476; Tokayo Summit (2008), 94, 519; withered into G-7 with no meeting in 2020, 483

GSD. *See* Gulf Security Dialogue

GSEC. *See* Global Strategic Engagement Center

GTRI. *See* Global Threat Reduction Initiative

Guinea: Ebola outbreak, 532

Gülen, Fetullah, 384

Gulf Cooperation Council, 161

Gulf Security Dialogue (GSD), 162

Hadley, Stephen J., 201, 202, 204, 253, 330, 337, 546, 554, 677–83, 687, 692–93

Haiti: Bush's efforts to secure elections in, 11

Hamadeh, Marwan, 207

Hamas: in control of Gaza, 566, 569, 645; elected in Palestinian territories, 10, 28, 565, 578, 645; Iran alliance with, 285, 289, 570; as Muslim Brotherhood affiliate, 575; OFAC sanctions on, 51; Syria alliance with, 210

Hamdan, Salim, 71–72

Hansen, James, 601

Hariri, Rafiq, 199, 201, 204, 207, 211

Hariri, Saad, 201

HCFCs (hydrochlorofluorocarbons), phaseout, 607

Health and Human Services, U.S. Department of: Project BioShield, 251

Health cooperation: endemic diseases, 474–75; India-U.S., 451

Health initiatives: bipartisan support, 484, 486, 495, 497–99, 502, 510–11, 513; bipartisan support for NTD programs, 518, 522, 524; funding capacity building for health service outlets, 498; in Latin America, 620

Hedayah, 102

Helgerson, John, 684

Hezbollah. *See* Hizballah

High-value targets, in War on Terror, 41. *See also specific individuals*

HIV/AIDS. *See* Global Fund to Fight HIV/AIDS, Tuberculosis and Malaria; President's Emergency Plan for AIDS Relief

Hizballah: control of western Beirut, 215; Iran alliance with, 206–07, 210, 214, 215, 284, 289; and LAF, 205, 211–12; OFAC

sanctions on, 51, 213, 215; Syria alliance with, 201, 206–07, 210, 214, 215; undermined Siniora Lebanese government, 202–03, 211; waged terror attacks on Israel, 200; won seats in parliament (2018), 214

Hollen, Van, 121

Holy Land Foundation for Relief and Development, 51

Homegrown Violent Extremist (HVE), U.S., 62–63

Homeland Security, U.S. Department of (DHS): BioWatch (bioaerosol monitoring system), 251, 526–27; consolidation of entities under, 80; Container Security Initiative, 71, 244, 251, 258–59; Domestic Nuclear Detection Office, 250, 255; mergers and establishment of, 71, 72; National Technical Nuclear Forensics Center, 250; Office of Homeland Security, 585; overlapping entities and lack of resources, 587–90, 592, 596, 597–98; sought international cooperation to isolate AQ, 39–40

Homeland Security Act (2002), 71, 586–88

Homeland Security Council (HSC): community mitigation strategy, 531; establishment of, 72; interagency planning, 74, 81; as NSC directorate, 696; Obama enlisted members from Bush administration, 532; Policy Coordinating Committee for Strategic Communications, 100; Presidential Directives (HSPDs), 526, 528; staff integration with NSC staff, 82. *See also* Biodefense Directorate

Honduras, 483, 622, 626

H1N1 avian influenza, 525, 529, 532

Hooker, Richard, 653, 656

HSC. *See* Homeland Security Council

Hu Jintao, 308–11, 320, 323, 556

Human rights: Bush's efforts on, 14, 15, 18, 21, 313, 321–22, 323; Carter's priority of, 11; Obama's efforts on, 25; U.S. transgressions in Iraq War, 650

Human Rights Defenders Fund, 14, 21

Humility, in development assistance, 503

HUMINT collection, 77

Hussein, Saddam, 28, 112, 170, 180, 241, 637

HVE. *See* Homegrown Violent Extremist

program in Pakistan, 145; economic reform in Lebanon (2006), 205; International Compact with Iraq (2007), 162, 166; Stand-By Agreement, 166; working multilaterally with, 558

International Security Assistance Forces (ISAF) (NATO), 119, 127, 128, 292

Internet communications: access points reduction for trusted connections, 590; of AQ and affiliates, 39, 44; "ILOVEYOU" computer virus, 574; Nimda malicious file, 574; social media, politicization of mitigation measures, 533; and War of Ideas, 103–04, 106. *See also* Cyber Preparedness

Internet Corporation for Assigned Names and Numbers (ICANN), 586

Interventions and stabilization, 109–13, 217. *See also* Afghanistan; Colombia; Iraq; Lebanon; Pakistan, Government of; Reconstruction and Stabilization Operations

Intrusion detection systems (IDS), 590

Iran: alliance with Hizballah, 206–07, 214, 215; ballistic missile development, 338; became Israel's main security preoccupation, 575; Bush administration policy, 162, 240–41, 260; Bush cooperation with Europe, 388; as customer of Khan WMD network, 271, 273; Green Revolution (2009), 24; held AQ members in detention as bargaining chips, 44; Joint Comprehensive Plan of Action (2015), 260, 298; Ministry of Defense and Armed Forces Logistics, 291; Ministry of Intelligence and Security, 290; nuclear agreements under Obama, 213; nuclear energy and security, 350, 400–01, 408, 669; P5 + 1 multilateral efforts with, 240–41, 260, 288–89, 296, 297, 300; pursuit of nuclear weapons, 233–34, 262, 278, 283, 285, 287, 295–96; as signatory to Paris Agreement, 287; as state sponsor of terrorism, 54, 289–90; supported Assad regime (2011), 213; support for foreign democratic dissidents and activists, 646–48; Tehran Agreement (2003), 287; Trump administration policy, 214, 260,

298–99, 301; undermined Iraq-U.S. agreements, 166. *See also* Our Approach to Iran

Iran, North Korea, and Syria Non-Proliferation Act (INKSNA), 400–01

Iranian Islamic Revolutionary Guard Corps (IRGC), 200, 213, 289, 291

Iraq: accomplishments of Bush administration, 163–66; Af-Pak structure combined with, 457; Bush administration approach, 171–73; Bush administration assessment, 177–78; Bush administration policy, 159–63, 177–78, 241; Coalition Provisional Authority, 171, 221; Council of Representatives, 165; democratic elections in, 10, 28, 112, 171, 173; development assistance as vital tool, 475; Executive Council, 165; future challenges, 17, 44, 166–68; International Compact with Iraq (2007), 162, 166; Iraq Reconstruction Management Office, 221; Kurdistan Regional Government, 162–63, 176; Lessons Learned, 178–82; as member of GCC+3, 161, 166; Operation Iraqi Freedom, 41; Postscript, 170–82; Provincial Reconstruction Teams in, 160–61, 165, 221, 226, 228–29; regime change via elections, 13, 16; Transitional Administrative Law, 171; Transition Memorandum text, 158–69; trends since end of Bush administration, 173–77; U.S. hopes for China collapsed with policy in, 672; U.S. reconstruction and stabilization operations in, 219, 221; U.S. supported creation of democratic governance, 22. *See also* Al-Qaida in Iraq

Iraqi National Police, 159, 164

Iraqi Security Forces (ISF), 159, 161, 164, 167, 174, 175

Iraqiya Party, 173

Iraq War: Freedom Agenda compromised by, 355–56, 360, 362, 365, 388, 637–38, 662; growth of Islamic State, 384; insufficient funds and personnel, 656; Obama's policies embraced by Europeans, 381; opposed by Russia, France and Germany, 396, 409, 412; "Reassessing Bush's Legacy" (Brands), 660–64;

Mowatt-Larssen, Rolf, 274–75
Mozambique, 483
Mubarak, Hosni, 14, 16, 649
Mugenyi, Peter, 491
Mukherjee, Pranab, 449
Multilateral Debt Relief Initiative (MDRI), 468, 473, 479–81
Multilateralism: in approach to Africa, 558; in counterterrorism, 76, 81, 119, 124; efforts abandoned by Trump, 438–39, 628; U.S. alliances in East Asia, 432–33. *See also* P5+1
Multi-National Forces-Iraq (MNF-I), 160, 162
Mumbai terrorist attacks (2008), 135, 143, 144, 146, 151, 153, 455
Munich Security Conference (2007), Putin's "Wehrkunde" speech, 341–42, 397, 409
Musharraf, Pervez, 120–21, 138, 139–40, 143–44, 153, 274–75, 452
Muslim Americans: anti-Muslim backlash, post 9/11, 105–06; outreach partnership programs, 91, 100; U.S. efforts to undermine idea that "West is at war with Islam," 94–95, 101
Muslims. *See* Islam; War of Ideas

Nagorno-Karabakh (Azerbaijan and Armenia), 358, 366
NAPCTF. *See* National Action Plan to Combat Terrorist Financing
National Action Plan to Combat Foreign Fighters (2006), 74, 83
National Action Plan to Combat Terrorist Financing (NAPCTF) (2007), 50, 74, 83
National Congress for the Defense of the People (DRC), 545
National Council of Resistance of Iran (NCRI), 287
National Counterproliferation Center (NCPC), 249, 255
National Counterterrorism Center (NCTC), 70, 72, 74, 77, 80, 92, 249, 252
National Cybersecurity Center, 590
National Cyberspace Security Awareness and Training Program, 586
National Cyberspace Security Response system, 585

National Cyberspace Security Threat and Vulnerability Reduction Program, 586
National Defense Authorization Act (1961), 223
National Defense Authorization Act (2019), 595–96
National Endowment for Democracy: and Bush's November 2003 speech, 14; establishment of, 12; funding for, 14
National Exercise Program, 252
National Homeland Security Strategy (2007), 91, 100
National Implementation Plan (NIP) (2008): as blueprint for WOT, 50, 84; Countering Violent Islamic Extremism, 89–91, 100, 101; establishment of, 74
National Institutes of Health (NIH): MIDAS consortium, 531; network model for combating HIV/AIDS, 491–92; research into medical countermeasures for WMDs, 251
National Liberation Army (ELN): designated as foreign terrorist organization by U.S., 185; reduced capabilities of, 190
National Missile Defense Act (1999), 329–30
National Money Laundering Strategies, 50
National Response Framework, 252, 256
National Science Advisory Board for Biosecurity (NSABB) (2005), 527
National security: development as essential pillar, 487–88, 639; discretion in presidential transitions, 679–80; transition mostly conducted in secret, 677
National Security and International Cyberspace Security Cooperation system, 586
National Security Council (NSC): advisors sounding board, 697; Deterrence Strategies and Programs, 591; interagency planning, 74, 696; meetings between incoming and outgoing officials, 681–82; National Security Policy Directive 58 (2008), 18; Policy Coordinating Committee for Strategic Communications, 100; records and organization charts for new administration, 683; Senate's slow confirmation process, 689; staffing of,

691–93. *See also* NSC Transition Memoranda

National Security Presidential Directive 32 (January 2004), 617, 624

National Security Presidential Directive/ NSPD-44 (2005), 222–24, 226

National Security Presidential Directive/ NSPD-58 (July 2008), 18, 473

National Security Strategy: (2002), 18, 332, 673; (2006), 21, 159–61, 223; (2007) New Way Forward (surge in Iraq), 160, 172, 177–78, 180, 221, 653–54, 663; consideration of means and ends, 655; counterterrorism programs, 665

National Security Strategy (NSPD-58) (2006), 637, 639; development as essential pillar, 467–68, 470, 572

National Security Summit, 260

National Strategy for Countering Domestic Terrorism: 2018, 261; 2021, 102

National Strategy for Homeland Security (2002), 585–86

National Strategy for Pandemic Influenza, 530–31

National Strategy to Combat Terrorism (2003/2006), 83; dismantling of AQ, 39; initial goals of, 69; NSPD-17 National Strategy to Combat WMD, 239; NSPD-23 National Policy on Ballistic Missile Defense, 332–35; NSPD-46/HSPD-15 update, 69–70, 84, 89, 99–100; NSPD-55/ NSPD-56, export controls, 243

National Strategy to Combat Terrorist Financing (NSCTF) (2006), 50

National Strategy to Combat Terrorist Travel (2006), 74, 83

National Strategy to Combat Weapons of Mass Destruction, 239, 244, 255

National Union for the Total Independence of Angola (UNITA), 542, 549, 551

Nation building: in Afghanistan, 131; in Colombia, 196–97; in Iraq, 179–80. *See also* Reconstruction and Stabilization Operations

NATO (North Atlantic Treaty Organization): accelerating integration in Balkans, 377, 382; Arab Spring interventions, 278; Bucharest Summit (2008), 118,

119; Comprehensive Strategic Political-Military Plan, 119; international missile defense cooperation, 336, 338; Libya intervention in 2011, 410; Membership Action Plans, 357, 363–66, 378, 382, 388; multilateral efforts to combat terror, 76, 81, 119, 124; patrolling Serbia-Kosovo border, 371; Putin's dismay at proposed second expansion, 412–13, 641–42, 669–70, 674; role expanded under Bush, 386; Russian exploitation of divisions within NATO and EU, 386–87, 404; Strategic Vision Statement for Afghanistan, 119; Trump policy, 260; U.S. alliance on Theater Missile Defense capabilities, 335; U.S. support for expansion, 351–52, 359, 361, 376, 412–13, 641, 669, 670, 674; withdrawal of troops from Afghanistan (2021), 129. *See also* International Security Assistance Forces

NATO-Russia Council, 399, 400, 409, 412–13

NCPC. *See* National Counterproliferation Center

NCRI. *See* National Council of Resistance of Iran

NCTC. *See* National Counterterrorism Center

Ndayishimiye, Evariste, 552

Neglected Tropical Diseases, 474–75, 487–88, 515–16; administration accomplishments, 519; administration approach, 521–22; administration assessment, 522–23; administration policy, 517–18; donor funding to leverage U.S. contributions, 522, 523; future challenges, 519–20; Lessons Learned, 523–24; Postscript, 521–24; Transition Memorandum text, 517–20; trends since end of Bush administration, 522

Neglected Tropical Diseases Control Project, 517–19

Negotiations on a Security Agreement (U.S.-Iraq), 163, 164, 165, 166, 167, 174, 178

Neo-Nazism, in U.S., 103

NET Guard, 586

Netherlands: missile defense cooperation with U.S., 336

equally important, 680–81; early access to some relevant documentation, 659, 660–64, 676–77, 695; failure to pass on TMs on some issues, 652; on some important issues not passed on, 652

NSSP. *See* Next Steps in Strategic Partnership

NTDs. *See* Neglected Tropical Diseases

Nuclear energy and security: advancement of U.S. goals with Russia, 399–400, 408; India, 447–50, 455–56, 458–59, 643, 667; Iran, 350, 400–01, 408, 641, 669; North Korea, 400, 408, 425, 671–72

Nuclear Nonproliferation Prevention Act (NNPA) (1994), 272n1

Nuclear Nonproliferation Treaty (NPT), 238, 241, 242, 307, 310

Nuclear Protective Action Guides, 252

Nuclear Security Summit, 258

Nuclear Suppliers Group (NSG), 242, 258, 263–64

Nuclear terrorism. *See* Weapons of Mass Destruction (WMD) Terrorism

Nuclear weapons, 234. *See also specific nuclear states*

OAS. *See* Organization of American States

Obama, Barack H.: Afghanistan policy, 126–28, 130, 134, 226, 227; Africa policy, 551, 554–55, 557; approach to health assistance, 498–99, 500–01, 510–11, 522, 532; Bush-Obama transition, 658–60, 677–78, 679, 681–84, 690, 694; China and East Asia policy, 438, 672; climate change and clean development policy, 609–11, 613; continued counterterrorism framework, 33, 61, 82–83; continued Plan Colombia, 193–94; cybersecurity policy, 593–95; on dealing with probabilities, 279n30; democracy promotion as low priority for, 23–25, 28–29, 213; development assistance, 480; Europe policy, 381–85; on failure in Libya as worst mistake, 25; focus in War of Ideas, 101, 104; focus on Pakistan-based insurgents, 150–51, 153; Homegrown Violent Extremists threat, 62–63; India policy, 457–58; Iran policy, 260, 297–98, 301;

Iraq policy, 173–75, 178, 227; Latin America policy, 626–27; Lebanon policy, 212–13; Middle East policy, 574–75, 653, 663–64, 666–67; minimal involvement in Arab Spring uprisings, 25, 175, 278; missile defense, 343–44; North Korea policy, 317, 318, 321, 323; Obama-Trump transition, 684–86; Peace Colombia, 194; Presidential Policy Guidance standards, 83; Russia policy, 297, 409–11, 671, 673–75; Syria policy, 25, 259, 384; Turkey policy, 384–85, 388; WMD proliferation initiatives, 258, 260, 263, 279, 280–81, 282

Obama-Trump transition, 684–86

Obasanjo, Olusegun, 491, 541

O'Brien, Robert, 686–88

Odierno, Raymond T., 161

Odinga, Raila, 552–53

OECD. *See* Organization of Economic Cooperation and Development

OFAC. *See* Office of Foreign Assets Control

Office of Foreign Assets Control (OFAC), 51–52. *See also* Foreign Terrorist Asset Tracking Center

Office of Personnel Management (OPM), 594

Office of Science and Technology Policy (OSTP), 589–90

Office of the Coordinator for Reconstruction and Stabilization, 471

Office of the Director of National Intelligence (DNI), 70, 72, 77, 80, 252; WMD Terrorism Steering Group, 249

OIC. *See* Organization for Islamic Cooperation

Olmert, Ehud, 561, 565

Onchocerciasis (river blindness), 516, 517

One-on-one conversations and briefings, 680

OPCW. *See* Organization for the Prohibition of Chemical Weapons

Operation Concordia, 372

Operation Enduring Freedom, 41, 119, 230, 430

Operation Iraqi Freedom, 41, 230

Organization for Security and Cooperation (OSCE), 366, 372

Organization for the Prohibition of Chemical Weapons (OPCW), 259, 270, 272, 276

Organization of American States (OAS), 11
Organization of Economic Cooperation and
Development (OECD), 195
Organization of Islamic Cooperation (OIC),
105
Organization of the Islamic Conference:
Charter revision to combat terrorism,
94, 100
Ortega, Daniel, 619, 622–23, 627, 629
OSCE. *See* Organization for Security and
Cooperation
O'Sullivan, Meghan, 637, 653, 654, 656
Our Approach to Iran, 283; accomplish-
ments, 299–300; administration
approach, 286–92, 295–96; administra-
tion policy, 285–86; future challenges,
292–93; Lessons Learned, 300–02;
Postscript, 295–302; Transition Memo-
randum text, 284–94; trends since end of
Bush administration, 297–99
Overmilitarization of foreign policy
concept, 131–32, 181–82, 212

PAC-3. *See* Patriot Advanced Capability-3
Pacific Alliance, 626
Pakistan, Government of (GOP): al-Qaida
in, 40, 648–49; Bush administration
accomplishments, 139–45; Bush
administration approach, 149–50; Bush
administration assessment, 152–54; Bush
administration policy, 39, 41, 59, 61,
138–39, 152–54; counterterrorism
cooperation, 665; declaration of state of
emergency (2007), 140; deteriorating
relations with U.S., 457; extremist attacks
on India, 455, 667; future challenges,
121–23, 146–47; future challenges in
tribal areas, 43; governance challenges in
FATA and NWFP, 39, 41, 43, 59, 61,
141–42, 145, 146, 252; Lessons Learned,
154–56; level of cooperation combating
terrorism, 130–31, 135–36, 140–41, 149,
150–51; Postscript, 149–56; and A.Q.
Khan, 271, 280–81; Reconstruction
Opportunity Zones, 121, 145; tensions
with India, 137–38, 143, 153, 446–47,
452–53, 457, 459, 462; Transition
Memorandum text, 137–48; trends since

end of Bush administration, 150–52;
U.S-Pakistan Strategic Partnership, 139
Pakistani Army, 142
Pakistan People's Party Parliamentarians
(PPPP), 140
Pakistan Science Foundation, 271
Palestinian conflict with Israel. *See* Middle
East Peace Process
Palestinian Islamic Jihad, 210, 289
Palestinian territories: delegitimization of
terror as strategy, 563; election favoring
Hamas, 10, 28; top-down and bottom-up
approaches necessary, 578; two-state
strategy, 564, 579, 645
Pan Am 103 bombing (1988), 277
Panama: Bush's efforts to secure elections
in, 11; free trade agreement with U.S., 625
Pandemic and All-Hazards Preparedness
Act (PAHPA) (2006), 488, 529
Pandemic preparedness: administration
approach, 525, 529–31; administration
assessment, 533, 674; community
mitigation strategy, 531; Homeland
Security Council had lead, 488; Lessons
Learned, 533–34; trends since end of
Bush administration, 532–33. *See also*
Biodefense; Biodefense and pandemic
planning; COVID-19 pandemic;
Influenza pandemic
Pan-Sahel Initiative/Trans-Saharan
Counterterrorism Partnership (TSCTP),
75, 81, 550, 555
Paris Agreement (2015), 287, 608, 610
Paris Club, 166
Paris Conference, 566–67
Paris Declaration on Aid Effectiveness, 485
Partnership for Latin American Youth, 620
Partnership for Progress and a Common
Future and Broader Middle East and
North Africa (BMENA) (G-8), 15
Partnership for Regional East Africa
Counterterrorism (PREACT), 550
Partnership principle, 492; identifying
partners to help end Africa's wars, 549; in
PMI, 510, 512–14; as replacement for
donor-recipient model, 468, 492, 497
Partnerships for Public Service, 689
Pascual, Michael, 645

President's Emergency Plan for AIDS Relief (PEPFAR): accomplishments, 474, 479–80, 484–85, 494–95, 669; accountability, 494–96, 499–500, 502, 509–10; administration approach, 497–98; administration assessment, 499–502; administration policy, 490–94; common vision to free people from disease, 487–88; focus countries for first PEPFAR funds, 493; future challenges, 495–96; largest bilateral assistance program targeting single disease, 470, 474, 492; Lessons Learned, 502–03; linking to other development programs, 495–96; Postscript, 497–503; Transition Memorandum text, 490–96; trends since end of Bush administration, 498–99

President's Initiative to End Hunger in Africa, 475

President's Malaria Initiative (PMI): accomplishments, 474, 479–80, 484–85, 506–07; accountability, 510, 513–14; administration approach, 509–10; administration assessment, 512–13; administration policy, 505–06; four-pronged approach, 506; future challenges, 507–08; launch in 2005, 504; Lessons Learned, 513–14; Postscript, 509–14; Transition Memorandum text, 505–08; trends since end of Bush administration, 510–11

Private sector engagement: challenges with internet policy, 583–84, 596–98; in counterterrorism, 48, 49, 50, 52, 60, 76, 77–78, 85; in development assistance, 471, 475, 479–81, 486, 487–88, 556; PEPFAR, 487–88, 498, 502–03; PMI, 507; in War of Ideas, 95–96, 101. See also Public-private partnerships

Project BioShield (2004), 251, 527

Proliferation Security Initiative (PSI) (2003), 253; Bush administration accomplishments, 262, 281, 433; country members, 321; disruption of Khan network, 268; establishment of, 241, 250, 256, 306; expansion by Obama administration, 258; future challenges, 244–45; Russian endorsement of, 399, 408

Protectionism: concern in Russia's WTO accession, 402; concern in U.S.-China relations, 423, 424; global trends toward, 481

Provincial Reconstruction Teams (PRTs): in Afghanistan, 125, 221, 226, 228–29; in Iraq, 160–61, 165, 221, 226, 228–29

PSI. See Proliferation Security Initiative

Public Health and Medical Preparedness (HSPD 21), 528

Public-private partnerships: for greenhouse abatement, 605; health initiatives, 498, 507, 521; investments vs. official development assistance, 473–74; NTD control project integrated programs, 521; Pink Ribbon Red Ribbon, 498–99; Project 12, 591. See also Private sector engagement

Public Readiness and Emergency Preparedness (PREP) Act (2005), 528–29

Puddington, Arch, 27

Putin, Vladimir: broke with U.S. over Iraq (2003), 170; Bush's relationship with, 391–92, 396, 401; growing authoritarianism, 386–88, 394, 396–97, 403; missile defense talks, 330–31, 336, 341, 344; Munich Security Conference speech (2007), 341–42, 397, 409; NATO expansion considered as threat, 351–52, 356, 381–82, 642–43; reclaiming of presidency, 410; Trump's relationship with, 25, 383, 384, 410

Qaddafi, Muammar, 259, 268–69, 276–77, 278–79, 298, 553, 668

Qaddafi, Saif, 282

Qadhafi, Muammar. See Qaddafi, Muammar

QAnon, 102

QF. See Quds Force

Qods Force. See Quds Force

"Quad" regional security network, 354, 460, 668

Quartet process (Middle East), 400, 564, 567

Quds Force (QF), 162, 289, 291

Racially or Ethnically Motivated Violent Extremist (RMVE), 63

Radiation detection reporting protocols, 251
Radio Free Europe, 88
Reagan, Ronald: approval ratings of, 660; democracy promotion, 11, 12; missile defense, 345; rhetoric of, 27
REAL ID Act (2005), 71
"Realist" thought, on democracy promotion, 17, 28–29
"Reassessing Bush's Legacy" (Brands), 3, 633; Bush-Obama transition, 658–60; counterterrorism agenda, 664–67; framing presidency against post-Cold War era, 673–75; Iraq War, 660–64; successes and failures, 667–72
Rebel Armed Forces of Colombia (FARC): designated as Significant Foreign Narcotics Traffickers by U.S., 187; reduced capabilities of, 188, 190, 193; revenue from drug trade, 183, 185–86; Santos-led peace agreement with (2016), 194; youth antiterrorism networks against, 93
Reconstruction and Stabilization Operations: accomplishments, 221–24; administration approach, 226–27; administration assessment, 228–31; administration policy, 219–20; future challenges, 224; Lessons Learned, 231–32; Postscript, 226–32; Transition Memorandum text, 218–25; trends since end of Bush administration, 227–28
Reconstruction Opportunity Zones (ROZ): in Afghanistan, 121, 145; in Pakistan, 121, 145
Refugees: al-Qaida affiliates in Palestinian camps, 205, 207; Palestinian, 568, 574; from Venezuela, 197
Remittances, reduced costs to send, 619, 626
Rice, Condoleezza, 14, 34, 201, 202, 204, 212, 286, 288, 296, 297, 311, 335, 336–37, 397, 491, 541, 546, 554, 682, 688
Riggs Bank, 52
RMVE. See Racially or Ethnically Motivated Violent Extremist
Roadmap, for independent Palestinian state, 564, 566–69
Roosevelt, Franklin D.: Four Freedoms, 10
ROZ. See Reconstruction Opportunity Zones

Rule of law. See Democracy; Democracy promotion
Rumsfeld, Donald H., 333, 638–39, 664
Russian-American Business Dialogue, 401–02
Russian Federation: arms sales to states hostile to U.S., 400–01; Bush administration policy, 297, 330–31, 641–43; Bushehr nuclear power plan deal, 288; centralized control of energy sources, 402, 404–05; continued challenges to U.S. and Freedom Agenda, 389–90; contractions of freedom in, 10; Criminal Procedure Code updated, 403; Declaration on Nuclear Energy and Nonproliferation, 243; election interference claims, 344, 363, 410, 685–86; expanded promotion of authoritarianism after U.S. Capitol attack (2021), 26; focused on internal extremist threats, 45–46; greatest successes in nuclear security, 411; intervention in Western elections (2016), 344; invasions and annexations of neighbors, 344, 363–64, 381–82, 395–96, 398, 403–04, 410, 414–15, 671; journalists murdered in, 403; military intervention in Syria, 410; missile defense talks, 330–31, 336, 341–42, 344; North Korea and Six-Party Talks, 307, 309–11, 316, 321; Obama's efforts, 654; opposed Iraq War, 396, 409, 412; policy failures of Bush and Obama administrations, 671, 673–75; removed from full participant status in Community of Democracies, 15; supported Assad regime (2011), 213, 259; support for democracy not aimed at, 360–61; threat to veto any plan not accepted by Serbia, 374–75; U.S. concerned about threats to international order, 349–54; use of chemical weapons-grade poisons against individuals, 261, 344. See also Managing Cooperation/Differences with Russia; Moscow Strategic Arms Reduction Treaty (2002) (U.S.-Russia); Putin, Vladimir
Rwanda: HIV services increased health service usage, 494; withdrawal of troops from DRC, 542

Saakashvili, Mikheil, 363, 401

Safe havens, for terrorists, 39, 43, 59, 61–62, 146

Safe Port Act (2006), 71, 259, 263

Sahel: terrorist threats, 483, 550, 553, 555

Salafist Group for Preaching and Combat (GSPC)/AQ in the Islamic Magreb (AQIM), 51, 553

Samper, Ernesto, 183

Santos, Juan Manuel, 194

Sarkozy, Nicolas, 336

SARS outbreak (2003), 525, 529

Saudi Arabia: Bush administration assessment, 106; destroyed AQ presence in, after Riyadh attacks, 42, 51–52; U.S. maintained political focus on AQ-affiliated groups in, 40

Savimbi, Jonas, 549

Schistosomiasis (snail fever), 517

Schroeder, Gerhard, 170, 365

Science and technology cooperation, India-U.S., 451

Scowcroft, Brent, 693

Second Line of Defense program, 251

Secure Freight Initiative, 144

Security and Prosperity Partnership (SPP), 619

Security assistance initiatives launched by U.S.: Africa, 550, 555, 558; United States Security Coordinator, 565, 567, 569

Security clearances for transition staff, 679

Security Development Plan, 146

Security of Classified Networks, 591

Security threats. See North Korea and Six-Party Talks; Nuclear energy and security; Weapons of Mass Destruction (WMD) Terrorism

Senior Dialog with China, 422–23

September 11, 2001 terrorist attacks: administration's approach to Middle East, 645; attacks not repeated on American soil, 664; bilateral relations strengthened since, 431; biodefense and pandemic planning in response, 525–26; Bush strategy shaped by, 13–15, 31–34, 38–41, 170, 210, 638; China's reaction, 420; counterproliferation as priority prior

to, 647–48; cyber intrusions after, 584; impact of, 31; Japan's reaction, 429; Russia's reaction, 408; U.S. identified with repressive regimes, 638. See also War on Terror

Sequentialism, drawbacks of, 17

Serbia: Albanian insurgency, 370–71, 372–73, 376–77; Clinton's democracy promotion in, 11; overthrow of Milosevic regime, 369; setting on pro-western path, 377; U.S. policy toward, 373–75, 382. See also Kosovo

SFA. See Strategic Framework Agreement

Shalgham, Abdel Rahman, 269

Sharif, Nawaz, 151

Sharif, Shehbaz, 151

Sharon, Ariel, 564–65, 567, 573, 578, 645

Shevardnadze, Eduard, 363

Sierra Leone: democratic elections in, 10; Ebola outbreak, 532; prioritized conflict, 549; resolving long-standing conflicts, 537, 538, 539, 541, 543, 549, 551, 558, 669; Truth and Reconciliation Commission, 543. See also Special Court for Sierra Leone

Singapore: Strategic Framework Agreement, 431, 433; U.S. targeted financial sanctions on, 54

Singh, Manmohan, 448, 451–53, 457, 459

Singh, Michael, 645, 646–47

Siniora, Fouad, 201–03, 204, 205

Sirleaf, Ellen Johnson, 541

Six Plus Two group on Afghanistan, 285

Sleiman, Michel, 202

Smart Development, 463–64, 467–68, 639–40; accomplishments, 471–76; administration approach, 479–80; administration assessment, 482–84; administration policy, 469–71; future challenges, 476–78; Lessons Learned, 484–86; Postscript, 479–86; Transition Memorandum text, 469–78; trends since end of Bush administration, 480–82

Snowden, Edward, 595

Sochi Strategic Framework Declaration (2008), 397

Social justice: as link between democracy and development, 624, 626

Society for Worldwide Inter-Bank Financial Telecommunication (SWIFT), 53
SOI. *See* Sons of Iraq
Solana, Javier, 288, 289
Somalia: U.S. maintained political focus on AQ-affiliated groups in, 40
Sons of Iraq (SOI), 161, 165, 168, 172, 173, 174, 175
South Africa: commitment to dismantling Khan network, 271; as new generation democracy, 18
South Asia: ungoverned regions attractive to AQ and affiliates, 61, 154
Southern Methodist University: Center for Presidential History, 701–02; Digital Archive, 4, 33, 701
South Korea: debate over presence of U.S. troops, 428; deterring security threats, 430; as member of Asia-Pacific Democracy Partnership, 15; North Korea and Six-Party Talks, 307, 309–10, 316, 321; security dialogue, 433; U.S. Army vehicle accident, 439
South Sudan: referendum on succession, 545. *See also* Sudan North-South conflict
Spain: missile defense cooperation with U.S., 336
Special Court for Sierra Leone (SCSL), 541, 543
Special Envoy on Human Rights in North Korea, 313
Special Envoy to the Organization of the Islamic Conference (OIC), 92, 100
Special Inspectors General for Iraq and Afghanistan Reconstruction, 231
Special Representative for Afghanistan Reconciliation, 128
Special Tribunal for Lebanon (STL) (UNSC), 204–05, 211, 212, 214
Sri Lanka: authoritarian governments, 483
Standard Missile-3 (SM-3) interceptors, 343, 345
START agreements. *See* Strategic Arms Reduction Treaty
State, U.S. Department of, 92; Access Micro-scholarship Program, 93; Advisory Board on Strategic Engagement, 96; Bureau for Conflict and

Stabilization Operations, 227; Counter-terrorism Communications Center, 92, 100; designated state sponsors of terrorism, 291; Foreign Assistance Bureau, 15; National Security Presidential Directive/NSPD-44 (2005), 222–24, 226; Near-Term Anti-Al-Qaida Communication Action Plan, 92; Office of the Coordinator for Reconstruction and Stabilization, 221–22, 224, 226, 229–30; Office of WMD Terrorism, 250, 255; plans to revise training and promotion systems, 18; reconstruction and stabilization operations, 219, 220, 226–27, 228–30; Regional Strategic Initiatives, 75; role in legal/policies of counterterrorism, 34, 51, 161; role in War of Ideas, 91–93, 95, 100; Under Secretary for Public Diplomacy, 95, 100; sought international cooperation to isolate AQ, 39–40; staffing funding, 220; *United States Strategy to Prevent Conflict and Promote Stability*, 227; on U.S.-Iran interactions, 285. *See also* Global Strategic Engagement Center
State/Global AIDS Coordinator (S/GAC), 493, 494
State Sponsors of Terrorism List, 312, 323–24
Status of Forces Agreement. *See* Negotiations on a Security Agreement (U.S.-Iraq)
Stent, Angela, 342
Strategic Arms Reduction Treaty (START agreements), 331, 381, 397–98, 409
Strategic Economic Dialogue (SED) with China, 423
Strategic Framework Agreement (SFA) (U.S.-Iraq), 163, 164–65, 166, 167, 172
Strategic National Stockpile, 527
Sub-Saharan Africa, 423; accelerated GDP growth, 473; resolving long-standing conflicts, 537, 538. *See also specific countries*
Sudan: Abraham Accords, 111; overthrow of al-Bashir, 111; Sudan Peace Act, 540; U.S. targeted financial sanctions on, 54. *See also* Sudan North-South conflict
Sudan Comprehensive Peace Agreement, 222

Sudan/Darfur, 544–45; China's participation in peacekeeping operations, 423, 441; genocide, 549–50; resolving long-standing conflicts, 537, 539, 549–50, 551–52, 557

Sudan North-South conflict: resolving long-standing conflicts, 537, 538, 539–40, 545, 549–50, 551–52

Sudan People's Liberation Movement (SPLM), 540

Sullivan, Jake, 687–88, 689

Summit of the Americas, Declaration of Quebec City (2001), 624

Sunni Awakening, 172

Supply-chain resilience, 442–43

Surge (Iraq War). See Iraq War

SWIFT. See Society for Worldwide Inter-Bank Financial Telecommunication

Syria: alliance with Hizballah, 206–07, 210, 214, 215; AQI fighters travel through to Iraq, 44; arms sales to states hostile to U.S., 400; Bush administration policy, 162, 203–04, 206, 241; chemical weapons, 259, 261; decline in foreign fighter flow into Iraq, 166; Obama administration policy, 25, 260, 384; Russian military intervention, 410; withdrawal from occupation of Lebanon, 198–99, 200, 201, 204

Syria Accountability and Lebanese Sovereignty Restoration Act (2008), 211

Tabletop exercises, on national security issues, 679, 684, 696

Taepo Dong-2 ballistic missiles, 309

Tahir, B.S.A., 271

Taiwan, 419, 421, 425–26, 440, 443–44

Tajikistan: color revolution in, 22

Taliban: future challenges, 112; governance of Afghanistan after U.S. withdrawal, 61, 129–30; Iran alliance with, 291, 292; OFAC sanctions on, 51; protection of al-Qaida, 37; removal from power in Afghanistan, 41, 124, 661; resurgence of (2015), 128; revenue from drug trade, 121; Trump administration peace talks with (2020), 128–29, 152; U.S. efforts to deny AQ safe haven in ungoverned areas of, 39

Tang Jiaxuan, 308, 309

Tanzania: U.S. cruise missile strikes on AQ targets for embassy bombing (1998), 37

Taylor, Charles, 541

Teams and transitions, 692, 693–94

Technological competitiveness, 442–43

Technology company engagement: Bush administration accomplishments, 85; recommendations for, 107; to stem spread of extremism, 106

Telecommunications: China's growing dominance in Africa, 554. See also Society for Worldwide Inter-Bank Financial Telecommunication

Tenet, George, 274–75, 563

Terminal High Altitude Area Defense (THAAD), 332, 333, 334

Terrorism: association with cybersecurity, 584, 592; Bush considered as primary obstacle to peace in Middle East, 562–70, 577–78; consensus definition of, 77, 84; countering in Africa, 553, 555–56, 557; intifada in Israel (2001), 572–74; Iranian supplanting Palestinian, 575; threat assessments for president-elect, 679; U.S. identified with repressive regimes, 638; U.S.-Russia agreements on international, 400, 408. See also Institutionalizing the War on Terror; War on Terror

Terrorist Screening Center (TSC), 72

Terrorist suspect detention, U.S. prosecution under laws of war, 33, 41

THAAD. See Terminal High Altitude Area Defense

Thailand: U.S. targeted financial sanctions on, 54

Theater Missile Defense (TMD) (NATO), 335

Thessaloniki Agenda for the Western Balkans, 361

3-plus-1 (Argentina, Paraguay, and Brazil), 81

Three-pronged information process, 680

Threshold programs. See Millennium Challenge Corporation (MCC)/Millennium Challenge Account (MCA)

Titan Rain Attacks, 588

Tobias, Randall L., 493

Townsend, Frances Fragos, 530, 588

738   Index

TPP. *See* Trans-Pacific Partnership

Trachoma (eye infection), 516, 517

Trade and investment: agreements in Western Hemisphere, 625–28, 669; with Colombia, 188, 190; India-U.S. bilateral investment, 450, 460; no free trade deals since Bush advanced, 484; with Pakistan, 139. *See also* Drug trade; Trans-Pacific Partnership; World Trade Organization

Trade and Investment Framework Agreement (TIFA), 440

Trading with the Enemy Act (TWEA) (1917), 310, 311, 323–24

Transatlantic relations: new issues, 386. *See also* Europe

"Transferring Presidential Power in a Post-9/11 World" (Kumar), 3–4, 633; Bush-Obama transition, 676–78; Lessons Learned, 690–94; practices established by Bush and leadership team, 678–84; practices successfully exercised by recent administrations, 694–97; recent developments in transition practices, 688–94

Transition Directors Council, 679

Transition Memoranda. *See* NSC Transition Memoranda; *specific Memoranda by title*

Transnistria, 366

Trans-Pacific Partnership (TPP), 438–39, 440–41, 626–27

Transportation Security Administration, U.S. (TSA), 71, 80

Trans-Saharan Counterterrorism Partnership (TSCTP). *See* Pan-Sahel Initiative/ Trans-Sahara Counterterrorism Partnership

Treasury, U.S. Department of: North Korean banking activities, 306; Office of Intelligence and Analysis, 52; Office of Terrorism and Financial Intelligence, 53, 73, 81; on risks of doing business with Iran, 289; role in legal/policies of counterterrorism, 51, 52, 260; sought international cooperation to isolate AQ, 39–40; Terrorist Financing Tracking Program, 53. *See also* Office of Foreign Assets Control

Tripartite Joint Commission (DRC, Rwanda, Uganda), 542, 543

Tropical diseases. *See* Neglected Tropical Diseases

Truman, Harry S., 96, 659–60

Trump, Donald J.: Afghanistan policy, 128–29, 226, 227, 653–54; Africa policy, 551, 554–57; approach to health assistance, 499, 501, 510–11, 532–33; brokered talks with Taliban, 128–29, 152; China and East Asia policy, 438–39, 595–96, 672; climate change and clean development policy, 611, 613; continued counterterrorism framework, 33, 61, 82–83; continued Plan Colombia, 195; continued WMD-T, 260–61; Domestic Violent Extremists (DVEs) threat, 63, 102; eroded democratic norms in U.S., 26, 84; Europe policy, 382, 383–84; focus in War of Ideas, 102, 104; India policy, 457–58; Iran policy, 214, 260, 298–99, 301; Iraq policy, 176, 226, 227; Lebanon policy, 214; Middle East policy, 576, 653; missile defense, 345; nationalist agenda approach to Latin America, 627–28; neglected Freedom Agenda, 25–26, 28–29; North Korea policy, 260, 317–20, 321, 322, 323; Obama-Trump transition, 684–86; relationships with authoritarian leaders, 25–26, 318–19, 383, 385, 410; Russia policy, 410–11; Stabilization Assistance Review (2018), 227; Syria policy, 259; Trump-Biden transition, 686–88, 689, 690, 691; Turkey policy, 384–85, 388; view of foreign aid, 480–81, 483–84; widening of transatlantic discord, 385; withdrawal from WHO, 524; WMD proliferation initiatives, 258, 279–80, 281

Trump-Biden transition, 686–88, 689, 690, 691

Truth and Reconciliation Commission (TRC), Sierra Leone, 543

TSC. *See* Terrorist Screening Center

Tuberculosis. *See* Global Fund to Fight HIV/ AIDS, Tuberculosis and Malaria

Turbowicz, Yoram, 202

Wisser, Gerhard, 271
WMD attribution process, 252
WMD Commission, 70
WMD proliferation, 647–48, 655, 668.
· *See also* Weapons of Mass Destruction
(WMD) Terrorism
WOI. *See* War of Ideas
Wolfowitz, Paul, 330
World Bank: approved Afghanistan
National Development Strategy (2008),
117–18; China seeking to play larger role,
352; International Compact with Iraq
(ICI) (2007), 162, 166; pressed for debt
relief assistance, 473, 479; support for
Liberia reconstruction, 558; support for
Sudan's CPA, 540; working multilaterally
with, 558
World Health Organization (WHO): NTD
program support, 521–22; Trump's
withdrawal from, 524
World Trade Center attack (1993), 68
World Trade Organization (WTO): Bush
supported regional trade and investment
initiatives, 473; ensuring China's
compliance, 441; Indian inflexibility in
Doha Round, 450, 453; Iranian applica-

tion to, 287; Iraq application to, 166;
Russia's accession, 402–03, 410
WOT. *See* War on Terror
WTO. *See* World Trade Organization

Xi Jinping, 320; commercial hacking
agreement, 595; consolidation of control,
353, 417, 437–38; emergence as more
aggressive Chinese leader, 414, 556;
Trump's relationship with, 25; voluntary
goals on climate change, 610

Yanukovych, Viktor, 383, 387–88
Yemen: al-Qaida operations in, 37–38;
maintained political focus on AQ-
affiliated groups in, 40; presidential
elections in, 10
Young African Leaders Initiative (YALI), 559
Yushchenko, Viktor, 363

Zardari, Asif Ali, 121, 140, 143, 151
Zelaya, Mel, 622, 626
Zelensky, Volodymyr, 29
Zhu Rongji, 417
Zinni, Anthony, 563–64
Zubaydah, Abu, 37, 41